## DATE DUE

| | | |
|---|---|---|
| MAY 0 5 1999 | | |
| Oct 23 2001 | | |
| AUG 18 2002 | | |
| | | |
| | | |
| | | |
| | | |
| | | |
| | | |
| | | |
| | | |
| | | |
| | | |
| | | |
| | | |
| | | |
| | | |
| GAYLORD | | PRINTED IN U.S.A. |

CARTOGRAPHY BY PHILIP'S. COPYRIGHT REED INTERNATIONAL BOOKS LTD

OXFORD

# DESK
# REFERENCE
# ATLAS

# DESK
# REFERENCE
# ATLAS

# Contents

Cartography by Philip's

Text
Keith Lye

Executive Editor
Caroline Rayner

Executive Art Editor
Alison Myer

Editor
Kara Turner

Production
Claudette Morris

Picture Research
Claire Gouldstone

Picture Acknowledgements
Robert Harding Picture Library /Photri 1
Image Bank /Lionel Brown 10
Rex Features /Sipa 6, 24
Still Pictures 26, /Anne Piantanida 8, /
Chris Caldicott 16, /Mark Edwards 18, 20, /
Hartmut Schwarzbach 14, 22, /Luke White 4
Tony Stone Images /Kevin Kelley 2, /Art Wolfe 12

George Philip Limited,
an imprint of Reed Books,
Michelin House, 81 Fulham Road, London SW3 6RB,
and Auckland, Melbourne, Singapore and Toronto

Cartography by Philip's

Published in North America by
Oxford University Press, Inc.,
198 Madison Avenue, New York, N.Y. 10016, U.S.A.

Oxford is a registered trademark of Oxford University Press

Library of Congress Cataloging-in-Publication Data

George Philip Limited.
  Desk reference atlas/ [cartography by Philip's].
   p. cm.
  At head of title: Oxford.
  Includes index.
  Summary: Includes information on the solar system,
   volcanoes, earthquakes, climate, weather, oceans,
   the environment, population, trade, energy,
   agriculture, tourism, international organizations,
   and world flags.
  ISBN 0–19–521263–0
  1. Children's atlases. [1. Atlases.]. 1. Oxford
   University Press. II. Title.
G1021.G43284 1996 <G&M>
912—dc20                        96–17697
                                 CIP
                                 MAP AC

ISBN 0–19–521263–0

Printing (last digit): 9 8 7 6 5 4 3 2 1

Printed and bound in China

## World Statistics

vi–ix      Countries

x–xi       Cities

xii–xv     Physical

xvi        Climate

## The Earth in Focus

2–3        The Universe & Solar System

4–5        The Changing Earth

6–7        Earthquakes & Volcanoes

8–9        Water & Ice

10–11      Weather & Climate

12–13      Landscape & Vegetation

14–15      Population

16–17      Languages & Religions

18–19      Agriculture & Industry

20–21      Trade & Commerce

22–23      Transport & Travel

24–27      International Organizations

28–29      Regions in the News

30–32      World Flags

# World Maps

| | | | |
|---|---|---|---|
| 1 | General Reference | 52–53 | Northeast Africa |
| 2–3 | Northern Hemisphere | 54–55 | Northwest Africa |
| 4–5 | Southern Hemisphere | 56–57 | Central Africa |
| 6–7 | Europe | 58–59 | Southern Africa |
| 8–9 | Scandinavia | 60–61 | Australia |
| 10–11 | British Isles | 62–63 | Southeast Australia |
| 12–13 | France | 64–65 | New Zealand, Central & Southwest Pacific |
| 14–15 | Germany & Benelux | | |
| 16–17 | Central Europe | 66–67 | North America |
| 18–19 | Spain & Portugal | 68–69 | Eastern Canada |
| 20–21 | Italy & the Adriatic | 70–71 | Western Canada |
| 22–23 | Greece & the Balkans | 72–73 | Northeast USA |
| 24–25 | Eastern Europe | 74–75 | Southeast USA |
| 26–27 | Asia | 76–77 | North central USA |
| 28–29 | Western Russia & Central Asia | 78–79 | Southern USA |
| 30–31 | Eastern Siberia | 80–81 | Northwest USA |
| 32–33 | Japan | 82–83 | Southwest USA |
| 34–35 | China | 84–85 | Mexico |
| 36–37 | Southeast Asia | 86–87 | Caribbean & Central America |
| 38–39 | Philippines & Eastern Indonesia | | |
| 40–41 | Eastern India, Bangladesh & Burma | 88–89 | South America |
| | | 90–91 | South America – Northwest |
| 42–43 | Western India & Pakistan | 92–93 | South America – Northeast |
| 44–45 | Iran, the Gulf & Afghanistan | 94–95 | South America – South |
| 46–47 | The Middle East & Turkey | 96 | Antarctica |
| 48–49 | Arabia & the Horn of Africa | | |
| 50–51 | Africa | 97–160 | **Index to World Maps** |

# World Statistics – Countries

Listed below are all the countries of the world; the more important territories are also included. If a territory is not completely independent, then the country it is associated with is named. The area figures give the total area of land, inland water and ice. Annual income is the GNP per capita. The figures are the latest available, usually 1995.

| Country/Territory | Area (1,000 sq km) | Area (1,000 sq mi) | Population (1,000s) | Capital City | Annual Income US$ |
|---|---|---|---|---|---|
| Afghanistan | 652 | 252 | 19,509 | Kabul | 220 |
| Albania | 28.8 | 11.1 | 3,458 | Tirana | 340 |
| Algeria | 2,382 | 920 | 25,012 | Algiers | 1,650 |
| Andorra | 0.45 | 0.17 | 65 | Andorra la Vella | 14,000 |
| Angola | 1,247 | 481 | 10,020 | Luanda | 600 |
| Argentina | 2,767 | 1,068 | 34,663 | Buenos Aires | 7,290 |
| Armenia | 29.8 | 11.5 | 3,603 | Yerevan | 660 |
| Australia | 7,687 | 2,968 | 18,107 | Canberra | 17,510 |
| Austria | 83.9 | 32.4 | 8,004 | Vienna | 23,120 |
| Azerbaijan | 86.6 | 33.4 | 7,559 | Baku | 730 |
| Azores (Port.) | 2.2 | 0.87 | 238 | Ponta Delgada | na |
| Bahamas | 13.9 | 5.4 | 277 | Nassau | 11,500 |
| Bahrain | 0.68 | 0.26 | 558 | Manama | 7,870 |
| Bangladesh | 144 | 56 | 118,342 | Dhaka | 220 |
| Barbados | 0.43 | 0.17 | 263 | Bridgetown | 6,240 |
| Belarus | 207.6 | 80.1 | 10,500 | Minsk | 2,930 |
| Belgium | 30.5 | 11.8 | 10,140 | Brussels | 21,210 |
| Belize | 23 | 8.9 | 216 | Belmopan | 2,440 |
| Benin | 113 | 43 | 5,381 | Porto-Novo | 420 |
| Bhutan | 47 | 18.1 | 1,639 | Thimphu | 170 |
| Bolivia | 1,099 | 424 | 7,900 | La Paz/Sucre | 770 |
| Bosnia-Herzegovina | 51 | 20 | 3,800 | Sarajevo | 2,500 |
| Botswana | 582 | 225 | 1,481 | Gaborone | 2,590 |
| Brazil | 8,512 | 3,286 | 161,416 | Brasília | 3,020 |
| Brunei | 5.8 | 2.2 | 284 | Bandar Seri Begawan | 9,000 |
| Bulgaria | 111 | 43 | 8,771 | Sofia | 1,160 |
| Burkina Faso | 274 | 106 | 10,326 | Ouagadougou | 300 |
| Burma (= Myanmar) | 677 | 261 | 46,580 | Rangoon | 950 |
| Burundi | 27.8 | 10.7 | 6,412 | Bujumbura | 180 |
| Cambodia | 181 | 70 | 10,452 | Phnom Penh | 600 |
| Cameroon | 475 | 184 | 13,232 | Yaoundé | 770 |
| Canada | 9,976 | 3,852 | 29,972 | Ottawa | 20,670 |
| Canary Is. (Spain) | 7.3 | 2.8 | 1,494 | Las Palmas/Santa Cruz | na |
| Cape Verde Is. | 4 | 1.6 | 386 | Praia | 870 |
| Central African Republic | 623 | 241 | 3,294 | Bangui | 390 |
| Chad | 1,284 | 496 | 6,314 | Ndjaména | 200 |
| Chile | 757 | 292 | 14,271 | Santiago | 3,070 |
| China | 9,597 | 3,705 | 1,226,944 | Beijing | 490 |
| Colombia | 1,139 | 440 | 34,948 | Bogotá | 1,400 |
| Comoros | 2.2 | 0.86 | 654 | Moroni | 520 |
| Congo | 342 | 132 | 2,593 | Brazzaville | 920 |
| Costa Rica | 51.1 | 19.7 | 3,436 | San José | 2,160 |
| Croatia | 56.5 | 21.8 | 4,900 | Zagreb | 4,500 |
| Cuba | 111 | 43 | 11,050 | Havana | 1,250 |
| Cyprus | 9.3 | 3.6 | 742 | Nicosia | 10,380 |

| Country/Territory | Area (1,000 sq km) | Area (1,000 sq mi) | Population (1,000s) | Capital City | Annual Income US$ |
|---|---|---|---|---|---|
| Czech Republic | 78.9 | 30.4 | 10,500 | Prague | 2,730 |
| Denmark | 43.1 | 16.6 | 5,229 | Copenhagen | 26,510 |
| Djibouti | 23.2 | 9 | 603 | Djibouti | 780 |
| Dominica | 0.75 | 0.29 | 89 | Roseau | 2,680 |
| Dominican Republic | 48.7 | 18.8 | 7,818 | Santo Domingo | 1,080 |
| Ecuador | 284 | 109 | 11,384 | Quito | 1,170 |
| Egypt | 1,001 | 387 | 64,100 | Cairo | 660 |
| El Salvador | 21 | 8.1 | 5,743 | San Salvador | 1,320 |
| Equatorial Guinea | 28.1 | 10.8 | 400 | Malabo | 360 |
| Eritrea | 94 | 36 | 3,850 | Asmara | 500 |
| Estonia | 44.7 | 17.3 | 1,531 | Tallinn | 3,040 |
| Ethiopia | 1,128 | 436 | 51,600 | Addis Ababa | 100 |
| Fiji | 18.3 | 7.1 | 773 | Suva | 2,140 |
| Finland | 338 | 131 | 5,125 | Helsinki | 18,970 |
| France | 552 | 213 | 58,286 | Paris | 22,360 |
| French Guiana (Fr.) | 90 | 34.7 | 154 | Cayenne | 5,000 |
| French Polynesia (Fr.) | 4 | 1.5 | 217 | Papeete | 7,000 |
| Gabon | 268 | 103 | 1,316 | Libreville | 4,050 |
| Gambia, The | 11.3 | 4.4 | 1,144 | Banjul | 360 |
| Georgia | 69.7 | 26.9 | 5,448 | Tbilisi | 560 |
| Germany | 357 | 138 | 82,000 | Berlin/Bonn | 23,560 |
| Ghana | 239 | 92 | 17,462 | Accra | 430 |
| Greece | 132 | 51 | 10,510 | Athens | 7,390 |
| Grenada | 0.34 | 0.13 | 94 | St George's | 2,410 |
| Guadeloupe (Fr.) | 1.7 | 0.66 | 443 | Basse-Terre | 9,000 |
| Guam (US) | 0.55 | 0.21 | 155 | Agana | 6,000 |
| Guatemala | 109 | 42 | 10,624 | Guatemala City | 1,110 |
| Guinea | 246 | 95 | 6,702 | Conakry | 510 |
| Guinea-Bissau | 36.1 | 13.9 | 1,073 | Bissau | 220 |
| Guyana | 215 | 83 | 832 | Georgetown | 350 |
| Haiti | 27.8 | 10.7 | 7,180 | Port-au-Prince | 800 |
| Honduras | 112 | 43 | 5,940 | Tegucigalpa | 580 |
| Hong Kong (UK) | 1.1 | 0.40 | 6,000 | – | 17,860 |
| Hungary | 93 | 35.9 | 10,500 | Budapest | 3,330 |
| Iceland | 103 | 40 | 269 | Reykjavik | 23,620 |
| India | 3,288 | 1,269 | 942,989 | New Delhi | 290 |
| Indonesia | 1,905 | 735 | 198,644 | Jakarta | 730 |
| Iran | 1,648 | 636 | 68,884 | Tehran | 4,750 |
| Iraq | 438 | 169 | 20,184 | Baghdad | 2,000 |
| Ireland | 70.3 | 27.1 | 3,589 | Dublin | 12,580 |
| Israel | 27 | 10.3 | 5,696 | Jerusalem | 13,760 |
| Italy | 301 | 116 | 57,181 | Rome | 19,620 |
| Ivory Coast | 322 | 125 | 14,271 | Yamoussoukro | 630 |
| Jamaica | 11 | 4.2 | 2,700 | Kingston | 1,390 |
| Japan | 378 | 146 | 125,156 | Tokyo | 31,450 |
| Jordan | 89.2 | 34.4 | 5,547 | Amman | 1,190 |
| Kazakstan | 2,717 | 1,049 | 17,099 | Alma-Ata | 1,540 |
| Kenya | 580 | 224 | 28,240 | Nairobi | 270 |
| Korea, North | 121 | 47 | 23,931 | Pyongyang | 1,100 |
| Korea, South | 99 | 38.2 | 45,088 | Seoul | 7,670 |

| Country/Territory | Area (1,000 sq km) | Area (1,000 sq mi) | Population (1,000s) | Capital City | Annual Income US$ |
|---|---|---|---|---|---|
| Kuwait | 17.8 | 6.9 | 1,668 | Kuwait City | 23,350 |
| Kyrgyzstan | 198.5 | 76.6 | 4,738 | Bishkek | 830 |
| Laos | 237 | 91 | 4,906 | Vientiane | 290 |
| Latvia | 65 | 25 | 2,558 | Riga | 2,030 |
| Lebanon | 10.4 | 4 | 2,971 | Beirut | 1,750 |
| Lesotho | 30.4 | 11.7 | 2,064 | Maseru | 660 |
| Liberia | 111 | 43 | 3,092 | Monrovia | 800 |
| Libya | 1,760 | 679 | 5,410 | Tripoli | 6,500 |
| Lithuania | 65.2 | 25.2 | 3,735 | Vilnius | 1,310 |
| Luxembourg | 2.6 | 1 | 408 | Luxembourg | 35,850 |
| Macau (Port.) | 0.02 | 0.006 | 490 | Macau | 7,500 |
| Macedonia | 25.7 | 9.9 | 2,173 | Skopje | 730 |
| Madagascar | 587 | 227 | 15,206 | Antananarivo | 240 |
| Madeira (Port.) | 0.81 | 0.31 | 253 | Funchal | na |
| Malawi | 118 | 46 | 9,800 | Lilongwe | 220 |
| Malaysia | 330 | 127 | 20,174 | Kuala Lumpur | 3,160 |
| Maldives | 0.30 | 0.12 | 254 | Malé | 820 |
| Mali | 1,240 | 479 | 10,700 | Bamako | 300 |
| Malta | 0.32 | 0.12 | 367 | Valletta | 6,800 |
| Martinique (Fr.) | 1.1 | 0.42 | 384 | Fort-de-France | 3,500 |
| Mauritania | 1,025 | 396 | 2,268 | Nouakchott | 510 |
| Mauritius | 2.0 | 0.72 | 1,112 | Port Louis | 2,980 |
| Mexico | 1,958 | 756 | 93,342 | Mexico City | 3,750 |
| Micronesia, Fed. States of | 0.70 | 0.27 | 125 | Palikir | 1,560 |
| Moldova | 33.7 | 13 | 4,434 | Kishinev | 1,180 |
| Mongolia | 1,567 | 605 | 2,408 | Ulan Bator | 400 |
| Morocco | 447 | 172 | 26,857 | Rabat | 1,030 |
| Mozambique | 802 | 309 | 17,800 | Maputo | 80 |
| Namibia | 825 | 318 | 1,610 | Windhoek | 1,660 |
| Nepal | 141 | 54 | 21,953 | Katmandu | 160 |
| Netherlands | 41.5 | 16 | 15,495 | Amsterdam/The Hague | 20,710 |
| New Caledonia (Fr.) | 19 | 7.3 | 181 | Nouméa | 6,000 |
| New Zealand | 269 | 104 | 3,567 | Wellington | 12,900 |
| Nicaragua | 130 | 50 | 4,544 | Managua | 360 |
| Niger | 1,267 | 489 | 9,149 | Niamey | 270 |
| Nigeria | 924 | 357 | 88,515 | Abuja | 310 |
| Norway | 324 | 125 | 4,361 | Oslo | 26,340 |
| Oman | 212 | 82 | 2,252 | Muscat | 5,600 |
| Pakistan | 796 | 307 | 143,595 | Islamabad | 430 |
| Panama | 77.1 | 29.8 | 2,629 | Panama City | 2,580 |
| Papua New Guinea | 463 | 179 | 4,292 | Port Moresby | 1,120 |
| Paraguay | 407 | 157 | 4,979 | Asunción | 1,500 |
| Peru | 1,285 | 496 | 23,588 | Lima | 1,490 |
| Philippines | 300 | 116 | 67,167 | Manila | 830 |
| Poland | 313 | 121 | 38,587 | Warsaw | 2,270 |
| Portugal | 92.4 | 35.7 | 10,600 | Lisbon | 7,890 |
| Puerto Rico (US) | 9 | 3.5 | 3,689 | San Juan | 7,020 |
| Qatar | 11 | 4.2 | 594 | Doha | 15,140 |
| Réunion (Fr.) | 2.5 | 0.97 | 655 | Saint-Denis | 3,900 |
| Romania | 238 | 92 | 22,863 | Bucharest | 1,120 |

| Country/Territory | Area (1,000 sq km) | Area (1,000 sq mi) | Population (1,000s) | Capital City | Annual Income US$ |
|---|---|---|---|---|---|
| Russia | 17,075 | 6,592 | 148,385 | Moscow | 2,350 |
| Rwanda | 26.3 | 10.2 | 7,899 | Kigali | 200 |
| St Lucia | 0.62 | 0.24 | 147 | Castries | 3,040 |
| St Vincent & Grenadines | 0.39 | 0.15 | 111 | Kingstown | 1,730 |
| São Tomé & Príncipe | 0.96 | 0.37 | 133 | São Tomé | 330 |
| Saudi Arabia | 2,150 | 830 | 18,395 | Riyadh | 8,000 |
| Senegal | 197 | 76 | 8,308 | Dakar | 730 |
| Sierra Leone | 71.7 | 27.7 | 4,467 | Freetown | 140 |
| Singapore | 0.62 | 0.24 | 2,990 | Singapore | 19,310 |
| Slovak Republic | 49 | 18.9 | 5,400 | Bratislava | 1,900 |
| Slovenia | 20.3 | 7.8 | 2,000 | Ljubljana | 6,310 |
| Solomon Is. | 28.9 | 11.2 | 378 | Honiara | 750 |
| Somalia | 638 | 246 | 9,180 | Mogadishu | 500 |
| South Africa | 1,220 | 471 | 44,000 | Pretoria/Cape Town/ Bloemfontein | 2,900 |
| Spain | 505 | 195 | 39,664 | Madrid | 13,650 |
| Sri Lanka | 65.6 | 25.3 | 18,359 | Colombo | 600 |
| Sudan | 2,506 | 967 | 29,980 | Khartoum | 750 |
| Surinam | 163 | 63 | 421 | Paramaribo | 1,210 |
| Swaziland | 17.4 | 6.7 | 849 | Mbabane | 1,050 |
| Sweden | 450 | 174 | 8,893 | Stockholm | 24,830 |
| Switzerland | 41.3 | 15.9 | 7,2681 | Bern | 36,410 |
| Syria | 185 | 71 | 14,614 | Damascus | 5,700 |
| Taiwan | 36 | 13.9 | 21,100 | Taipei | 11,000 |
| Tajikistan | 143.1 | 55.2 | 6,102 | Dushanbe | 470 |
| Tanzania | 945 | 365 | 29,710 | Dodoma | 100 |
| Thailand | 513 | 198 | 58,432 | Bangkok | 2,040 |
| Togo | 56.8 | 21.9 | 4,140 | Lomé | 330 |
| Trinidad & Tobago | 5.1 | 2 | 1,295 | Port of Spain | 3,730 |
| Tunisia | 164 | 63 | 8,906 | Tunis | 1,780 |
| Turkey | 779 | 301 | 61,303 | Ankara | 2,120 |
| Turkmenistan | 488.1 | 188.5 | 4,100 | Ashkhabad | 1,400 |
| Uganda | 236 | 91 | 20,466 | Kampala | 190 |
| Ukraine | 603.7 | 233.1 | 52,027 | Kiev | 1,910 |
| United Arab Emirates | 83.6 | 32.3 | 2,800 | Abu Dhabi | 22,470 |
| United Kingdom | 243.3 | 94 | 58,306 | London | 17,970 |
| United States of America | 9,373 | 3,619 | 263,563 | Washington, DC | 24,750 |
| Uruguay | 177 | 68 | 3,186 | Montevideo | 3,910 |
| Uzbekistan | 447.4 | 172.7 | 22,833 | Tashkent | 960 |
| Vanuatu | 12.2 | 4.7 | 167 | Port-Vila | 1,230 |
| Venezuela | 912 | 352 | 21,800 | Caracas | 2,840 |
| Vietnam | 332 | 127 | 74,580 | Hanoi | 170 |
| Virgin Is. (US) | 0.34 | 0.13 | 105 | Charlotte Amalie | 12,000 |
| Western Sahara | 266 | 103 | 220 | El Aaiún | 300 |
| Western Samoa | 2.8 | 1.1 | 169 | Apia | 980 |
| Yemen | 528 | 204 | 14,609 | Sana | 800 |
| Yugoslavia | 102.3 | 39.5 | 10,881 | Belgrade | 1,000 |
| Zaïre | 2,345 | 905 | 44,504 | Kinshasa | 500 |
| Zambia | 753 | 291 | 9,500 | Lusaka | 370 |
| Zimbabwe | 391 | 151 | 11,453 | Harare | 540 |

# World Statistics – Cities

Listed below are all the cities with more than 600,000 inhabitants (only cities with more than 1 million inhabitants are included for China, Brazil and India). The figures are taken from the most recent census, and as far as possible are for the metropolitan area, e.g. greater New York, Mexico or London. The figures are in thousands.


|  | Population (1,000s) |
| --- | --- |
| **Afghanistan** | |
| Kābul | 1,424 |
| **Algeria** | |
| Algiers | 1,722 |
| Oran | 664 |
| **Angola** | |
| Luanda | 1,544 |
| **Argentina** | |
| Buenos Aires | 11,256 |
| Córdoba | 1,198 |
| La Plata | 640 |
| Mendoza | 775 |
| Rosario | 1,096 |
| San Miguel de Tucumán | 622 |
| **Armenia** | |
| Yerevan | 1,254 |
| **Australia** | |
| Adelaide | 1,070 |
| Brisbane | 777 |
| Melbourne | 3,081 |
| Perth | 1,193 |
| Sydney | 3,657 |
| **Austria** | |
| Vienna | 1,560 |
| **Azerbaijan** | |
| Baku | 1,149 |
| **Bangladesh** | |
| Chittagong | 2,041 |
| Dhaka | 6,105 |
| Khulna | 877 |
| **Belarus** | |
| Minsk | 1,613 |
| **Belgium** | |
| Brussels | 952 |
| **Bolivia** | |
| La Paz | 1,126 |
| Santa Cruz | 695 |
| **Brazil** | |
| Belém | 1,246 |
| Belo Horizonte | 2,049 |
| Brasília | 1,596 |
| Curitiba | 1,290 |
| Fortaleza | 1,758 |
| Manaus | 1,011 |
| Nova Iguaçu | 1,286 |
| Pôrto Alegre | 1,263 |
| Recife | 1,290 |
| Rio de Janeiro | 5,336 |
| Salvador | 2,056 |
| São Paulo | 9,480 |
| **Bulgaria** | |
| Sofia | 1,221 |
| **Burkina Faso** | |
| Ouagadougou | 634 |
| **Burma (Myanmar)** | |
| Rangoon | 2,513 |
| **Cambodia** | |
| Phnom Penh | 900 |
| **Cameroon** | |
| Douala | 884 |
| Yaoundé | 750 |
| **Canada** | |
| Calgary | 754 |


|  | Population (1,000s) |
| --- | --- |
| Edmonton | 840 |
| Hamilton | 600 |
| Montréal | 3,127 |
| Ottawa–Hull | 921 |
| Québec | 646 |
| Toronto | 3,893 |
| Vancouver | 1,603 |
| Winnipeg | 652 |
| **Chile** | |
| Santiago | 5,343 |
| **China** | |
| Anshan | 1,204 |
| Beijing | 6,690 |
| Changchun | 2,470 |
| Changsha | 1,510 |
| Chengdu | 2,760 |
| Chongqing | 3,870 |
| Dalian | 2,400 |
| Fushun | 1,202 |
| Fuzhou | 1,380 |
| Guangzhou | 3,750 |
| Guiyang | 1,080 |
| Hangzhou | 1,790 |
| Harbin | 3,120 |
| Hefei | 1,110 |
| Jilin | 1,037 |
| Jinan | 2,150 |
| Kunming | 1,500 |
| Lanzhou | 1,340 |
| Linhai | 1,012 |
| Macheng | 1,010 |
| Nanchang | 1,440 |
| Nanjing | 2,490 |
| Ningbo | 1,100 |
| Qingdao | 2,300 |
| Qiqihar | 1,070 |
| Shanghai | 8,930 |
| Shenyang | 4,050 |
| Shijiazhuang | 1,610 |
| Taiyuan | 1,720 |
| Tangshan | 1,044 |
| Tianjin | 5,000 |
| Ürümqi | 1,130 |
| Wuhan | 3,870 |
| Xi'an | 2,410 |
| Zhengzhou | 1,690 |
| Zibo | 2,400 |
| **Colombia** | |
| Barranquilla | 1,049 |
| Bogotá | 5,132 |
| Cali | 1,687 |
| Cartagena | 726 |
| Medellín | 1,608 |
| **Congo** | |
| Brazzaville | 938 |
| **Croatia** | |
| Zagreb | 931 |
| **Cuba** | |
| Havana | 2,119 |
| **Czech Republic** | |
| Prague | 1,216 |
| **Denmark** | |
| Copenhagen | 1,337 |


|  | Population (1,000s) |
| --- | --- |
| **Dominican Republic** | |
| Santo Domingo | 2,200 |
| **Ecuador** | |
| Guayaquil | 1,508 |
| Quito | 1,101 |
| **Egypt** | |
| Alexandria | 3,380 |
| Cairo | 6,800 |
| El Gîza | 2,144 |
| Shubra el Kheima | 834 |
| **El Salvador** | |
| San Salvador | 1,522 |
| **Ethiopia** | |
| Addis Ababa | 2,213 |
| **France** | |
| Bordeaux | 696 |
| Lille | 959 |
| Lyons | 1,262 |
| Marseilles | 1,087 |
| Paris | 9,319 |
| Toulouse | 650 |
| **Georgia** | |
| Tbilisi | 1,279 |
| **Germany** | |
| Berlin | 3,475 |
| Cologne | 693 |
| Dortmund | 602 |
| Essen | 622 |
| Frankfurt | 660 |
| Hamburg | 1,703 |
| Munich | 1,256 |
| **Ghana** | |
| Accra | 965 |
| **Greece** | |
| Athens | 3,097 |
| **Guatemala** | |
| Guatemala | 2,000 |
| **Guinea** | |
| Conakry | 810 |
| **Haiti** | |
| Port-au-Prince | 1,402 |
| **Honduras** | |
| Tegucigalpa | 679 |
| **Hong Kong** | |
| Hong Kong | 6,149 |
| **Hungary** | |
| Budapest | 2,009 |
| **India** | |
| Ahmadabad | 3,298 |
| Bangalore | 4,087 |
| Bhopal | 1,064 |
| Bombay (Mumbai) | 12,572 |
| Calcutta | 10,916 |
| Coimbatore | 1,136 |
| Delhi | 7,207 |
| Hyderabad | 4,280 |
| Indore | 1,104 |
| Jaipur | 1,514 |
| Kanpur | 2,111 |
| Lucknow | 1,642 |
| Ludhiana | 1,012 |
| Madras | 5,361 |
| Madurai | 1,094 |


|  | Population (1,000s) |
| --- | --- |
| Nagpur | 1,661 |
| Patna | 1,099 |
| Pune | 2,485 |
| Surat | 1,517 |
| Vadodara | 1,115 |
| Varanasi | 1,026 |
| Vishakhapatnam | 1,052 |
| **Indonesia** | |
| Bandung | 2,027 |
| Jakarta | 8,259 |
| Malang | 650 |
| Medan | 1,686 |
| Palembang | 1,084 |
| Semarang | 1,005 |
| Surabaya | 2,421 |
| Ujung Pandang | 913 |
| **Iran** | |
| Ahvaz | 725 |
| Bakhtaran | 624 |
| Esfahan | 1,127 |
| Mashhad | 1,759 |
| Qom | 681 |
| Shiraz | 965 |
| Tabriz | 1,089 |
| Tehran | 6,476 |
| **Iraq** | |
| Al Mawsil | 664 |
| Arbil | 770 |
| As Sulaymaniyah | 952 |
| Baghdad | 3,841 |
| Diyala | 961 |
| **Ireland** | |
| Dublin | 1,024 |
| **Italy** | |
| Genoa | 668 |
| Milan | 1,359 |
| Naples | 1,072 |
| Palermo | 697 |
| Rome | 2,723 |
| Turin | 953 |
| **Ivory Coast** | |
| Abidjan | 1,929 |
| **Jamaica** | |
| Kingston | 644 |
| **Japan** | |
| Chiba | 851 |
| Fukuoka | 1,269 |
| Hiroshima | 1,102 |
| Kawasaki | 1,200 |
| Kitakyushu | 1,020 |
| Kobe | 1,509 |
| Kumamoto | 640 |
| Kyoto | 1,452 |
| Nagoya | 2,159 |
| Okayama | 605 |
| Osaka | 2,589 |
| Sakai | 806 |
| Sapporo | 1,732 |
| Sendai | 951 |
| Tokyo | 11,927 |
| Yokohama | 3,288 |
| **Jordan** | |
| Amman | 1,272 |

| | Population (1,000s) |
|---|---|
| Az-Zarqa | 605 |
| **Kazakstan** | |
| Alma-Ata (Almaty) | 1,147 |
| Qaraghandy | 613 |
| **Kenya** | |
| Nairobi | 1,429 |
| **Korea, North** | |
| Chinnampo | 691 |
| Chongjin | 754 |
| Hamhung | 775 |
| Pyongyang | 2,639 |
| **Korea, South** | |
| Inchon | 1,818 |
| Kwangju | 1,145 |
| Puchon | 668 |
| Pusan | 3,798 |
| Seoul | 10,628 |
| Suwon | 645 |
| Taegu | 2,229 |
| Taejon | 1,062 |
| Ulsan | 683 |
| **Kyrgyzstan** | |
| Bishkek | 628 |
| **Latvia** | |
| Riga | 840 |
| **Lebanon** | |
| Beirut | 1,500 |
| **Libya** | |
| Tripoli | 990 |
| **Madagascar** | |
| Antananarivo | 1,053 |
| **Malaysia** | |
| Kuala Lumpur | 1,145 |
| **Mali** | |
| Bamako | 746 |
| **Mauritania** | |
| Nouakchott | 600 |
| **Mexico** | |
| Ciudad Juárez | 798 |
| Culiacán Rosales | 602 |
| Guadalajara | 2,847 |
| León | 872 |
| Mexicali | 602 |
| Mexico City | 15,048 |
| Monterrey | 2,522 |
| Puebla | 1,055 |
| Tijuana | 743 |
| **Moldova** | |
| Chişinău (Kishinev) | 667 |
| **Mongolia** | |
| Ulan Bator | 601 |
| **Morocco** | |
| Casablanca | 3,079 |
| Fès | 735 |
| Marrakesh | 665 |
| Oujda | 661 |
| Rabat–Salé | 1,344 |
| **Mozambique** | |
| Maputo | 1,070 |
| **Netherlands** | |
| Amsterdam | 1,091 |
| Rotterdam | 1,069 |
| The Hague | 694 |
| **New Zealand** | |
| Auckland | 896 |
| **Nicaragua** | |
| Managua | 974 |
| **Nigeria** | |
| Ibadan | 1,295 |

| | Population (1,000s) |
|---|---|
| Kano | 700 |
| Lagos | 1,347 |
| Ogbomosho | 661 |
| **Norway** | |
| Oslo | 714 |
| **Pakistan** | |
| Faisalabad | 1,104 |
| Gujranwala | 659 |
| Hyderabad | 752 |
| Karachi | 5,181 |
| Lahore | 2,953 |
| Multan | 722 |
| Rawalpindi | 795 |
| **Paraguay** | |
| Asunción | 945 |
| **Peru** | |
| Arequipa | 620 |
| Lima–Callao | 6,601 |
| **Philippines** | |
| Caloocan | 629 |
| Cebu | 641 |
| Davao | 868 |
| Manila | 6,720 |
| Quezon City | 1,667 |
| **Poland** | |
| Kraków | 751 |
| Lodz | 847 |
| Warsaw | 1,655 |
| Wroclaw | 643 |
| **Portugal** | |
| Lisbon | 2,561 |
| Oporto | 1,174 |
| **Puerto Rico** | |
| San Juan | 1,816 |
| **Romania** | |
| Bucharest | 2,067 |
| **Russia** | |
| Barnaul | 665 |
| Chelyabinsk | 1,170 |
| Irkutsk | 644 |
| Izhevsk | 651 |
| Kazan | 1,107 |
| Khabarovsk | 626 |
| Krasnodar | 751 |
| Krasnoyarsk | 925 |
| Moscow | 8,957 |
| Nizhniy Novgorod | 1,451 |
| Novokuznetsk | 614 |
| Novosibirsk | 1,472 |
| Omsk | 1,193 |
| Perm | 1,108 |
| Rostov | 1,027 |
| St Petersburg | 5,004 |
| Samara | 1,271 |
| Saratov | 916 |
| Simbirsk | 638 |
| Togliatti | 677 |
| Ufa | 1,100 |
| Vladivostok | 675 |
| Volgograd | 1,031 |
| Voronezh | 958 |
| Yaroslavl | 637 |
| Yekaterinburg | 1,413 |
| **Saudi Arabia** | |
| Jedda | 1,400 |
| Mecca | 618 |
| Riyadh | 2,000 |
| **Senegal** | |
| Dakar | 1,730 |

| | Population (1,000s) |
|---|---|
| **Singapore** | |
| Singapore | 2,874 |
| **Somalia** | |
| Mogadishu | 1,000 |
| **South Africa** | |
| Cape Town | 1,912 |
| Durban | 1,137 |
| East Rand | 1,379 |
| Johannesburg | 1,196 |
| Port Elizabeth | 853 |
| Pretoria | 1,080 |
| Vanderbijlpark–Ver. | 774 |
| West Rand | 870 |
| **Spain** | |
| Barcelona | 1,631 |
| Madrid | 3,041 |
| Sevilla | 714 |
| Valencia | 764 |
| Zaragoza | 607 |
| **Sri Lanka** | |
| Colombo | 1,863 |
| **Sweden** | |
| Göteburg | 783 |
| Stockholm | 1,539 |
| **Switzerland** | |
| Zürich | 840 |
| **Syria** | |
| Aleppo | 1,445 |
| Damascus | 1,451 |
| **Taiwan** | |
| Kaohsiung | 1,405 |
| T'aichung | 817 |
| T'ainan | 700 |
| T'aipei | 2,653 |
| **Tajikistan** | |
| Dushanbe | 602 |
| **Tanzania** | |
| Dar-es-Salaam | 1,361 |
| **Thailand** | |
| Bangkok | 5,876 |
| **Tunisia** | |
| Tunis | 1,395 |
| **Turkey** | |
| Adana | 916 |
| Ankara | 2,559 |
| Bursa | 835 |
| Gaziantep | 603 |
| Istanbul | 6,620 |
| Izmir | 1,757 |
| **Uganda** | |
| Kampala | 773 |
| **Ukraine** | |
| Dnipropetrovsk | 1,190 |
| Donetsk | 1,121 |
| Kharkiv | 1,622 |
| Kiev (Kyyiv) | 2,643 |
| Kryvyy Rih | 729 |
| Lviv | 807 |
| Odesa | 1,096 |
| Zaporizhye | 898 |
| **United Kingdom** | |
| Birmingham | 1,400 |
| Glasgow | 730 |
| Liverpool | 1,060 |
| London | 6,378 |
| Manchester | 1,669 |
| Newcastle | 617 |
| **United States** | |
| Atlanta | 3,143 |

| | Population (1,000s) |
|---|---|
| Baltimore | 2,434 |
| Boston | 5,439 |
| Buffalo | 1,194 |
| Charlotte | 1,212 |
| Chicago | 8,410 |
| Cincinnati | 1,865 |
| Cleveland | 2,890 |
| Columbus | 1,394 |
| Dallas | 4,215 |
| Denver | 2,089 |
| Detroit | 5,246 |
| Hartford | 1,156 |
| Houston | 3,962 |
| Indianapolis | 1,424 |
| Kansas City | 1,617 |
| Jacksonville | 661 |
| Los Angeles | 15,048 |
| Memphis | 610 |
| Miami | 3,309 |
| Milwaukee | 1,629 |
| Minneapolis–St Paul | 2,618 |
| New Orleans | 1,303 |
| New York | 19,670 |
| Norfolk | 1,497 |
| Oklahoma | 984 |
| Omaha | 656 |
| Philadelphia | 5,939 |
| Phoenix | 2,330 |
| Pittsburgh | 2,406 |
| Portland | 1,897 |
| St Louis | 2,519 |
| Sacramento | 1,563 |
| Salt Lake City | 1,128 |
| San Antonio | 1,379 |
| San Diego | 2,601 |
| San Francisco | 6,410 |
| San Jose | 801 |
| Seattle | 3,131 |
| Tampa | 2,107 |
| Washington, DC | 4,360 |
| **Uruguay** | |
| Montevideo | 1,384 |
| **Uzbekistan** | |
| Tashkent | 2,094 |
| **Venezuela** | |
| Barquisimeto | 745 |
| Caracas | 2,784 |
| Maracaibo | 1,364 |
| Maracay | 800 |
| Valencia | 1,032 |
| **Vietnam** | |
| Haiphong | 1,448 |
| Hanoi | 3,056 |
| Ho Chi Minh City | 3,924 |
| **Yugoslavia (Serbia and Montenegro)** | |
| Belgrade | 1,137 |
| **Zaïre** | |
| Kinshasa | 3,804 |
| Lubumbashi | 739 |
| Mbuji-Mayi | 613 |
| **Zambia** | |
| Lusaka | 982 |
| **Zimbabwe** | |
| Bulawayo | 622 |
| Harare | 1,189 |

# World Statistics – Physical

Under each subject heading, the statistics are listed by continent. The figures are in size order beginning with the largest, longest or deepest, and are rounded as appropriate. Both metric and imperial measurements are given. The lists are complete down to the > mark; below this mark they are selective.

## Land & Water

| | km² | miles² | % |
|---|---|---|---|
| The World | 509,450,000 | 196,672,000 | – |
| Land | 149,450,000 | 57,688,000 | 29.3 |
| Water | 360,000,000 | 138,984,000 | 70.7 |
| | | | |
| Asia | 44,500,000 | 17,177,000 | 29.8 |
| Africa | 30,302,000 | 11,697,000 | 20.3 |
| North America | 24,241,000 | 9,357,000 | 16.2 |
| South America | 17,793,000 | 6,868,000 | 11.9 |
| Antarctica | 14,100,000 | 5,443,000 | 9.4 |
| Europe | 9,957,000 | 3,843,000 | 6.7 |
| Australia & Oceania | 8,557,000 | 3,303,000 | 5.7 |
| | | | |
| Pacific Ocean | 179,679,000 | 69,356,000 | 49.9 |
| Atlantic Ocean | 92,373,000 | 35,657,000 | 25.7 |
| Indian Ocean | 73,917,000 | 28,532,000 | 20.5 |
| Arctic Ocean | 14,090,000 | 5,439,000 | 3.9 |

## Seas

| Pacific Ocean | km² | miles² |
|---|---|---|
| South China Sea | 2,974,600 | 1,148,500 |
| Bering Sea | 2,268,000 | 875,000 |
| Sea of Okhotsk | 1,528,000 | 590,000 |
| East China & Yellow | 1,249,000 | 482,000 |
| Sea of Japan | 1,008,000 | 389,000 |
| Gulf of California | 162,000 | 62,500 |
| Bass Strait | 75,000 | 29,000 |

| Atlantic Ocean | km² | miles² |
|---|---|---|
| Caribbean Sea | 2,766,000 | 1,068,000 |
| Mediterranean Sea | 2,516,000 | 971,000 |
| Gulf of Mexico | 1,543,000 | 596,000 |
| Hudson Bay | 1,232,000 | 476,000 |
| North Sea | 575,000 | 223,000 |
| Black Sea | 462,000 | 178,000 |
| Baltic Sea | 422,170 | 163,000 |
| Gulf of St Lawrence | 238,000 | 92,000 |

| Indian Ocean | km² | miles² |
|---|---|---|
| Red Sea | 438,000 | 169,000 |
| The Gulf | 239,000 | 92,000 |

## Mountains

| Europe | | m | ft |
|---|---|---|---|
| Mont Blanc | France/Italy | 4,807 | 15,771 |
| Monte Rosa | Italy/Switzerland | 4,634 | 15,203 |
| Dom | Switzerland | 4,545 | 14,911 |
| Liskamm | Switzerland | 4,527 | 14,852 |
| Weisshorn | Switzerland | 4,505 | 14,780 |
| Taschorn | Switzerland | 4,490 | 14,730 |
| Matterhorn/Cervino | Italy/Switzerland | 4,478 | 14,691 |
| Mont Maudit | France/Italy | 4,465 | 14,649 |
| Dent Blanche | Switzerland | 4,356 | 14,291 |
| Nedelhorn | Switzerland | 4,327 | 14,196 |
| > Grandes Jorasses | France/Italy | 4,208 | 13,806 |
| Jungfrau | Switzerland | 4,158 | 13,642 |
| Barre des Ecrins | France | 4,103 | 13,461 |
| Gran Paradiso | Italy | 4,061 | 13,323 |
| Piz Bernina | Italy/Switzerland | 4,049 | 13,284 |
| Eiger | Switzerland | 3,970 | 13,025 |

| Europe (cont.) | | m | ft |
|---|---|---|---|
| Monte Viso | Italy | 3,841 | 12,602 |
| Grossglockner | Austria | 3,797 | 12,457 |
| Wildspitze | Austria | 3,772 | 12,382 |
| Monte Disgrazia | Italy | 3,678 | 12,066 |
| Mulhacén | Spain | 3,478 | 11,411 |
| Pico de Aneto | Spain | 3,404 | 11,168 |
| Marmolada | Italy | 3,342 | 10,964 |
| Etna | Italy | 3,340 | 10,958 |
| Zugspitze | Germany | 2,962 | 9,718 |
| Musala | Bulgaria | 2,925 | 9,596 |
| Olympus | Greece | 2,917 | 9,570 |
| Triglav | Slovenia | 2,863 | 9,393 |
| Monte Cinto | France (Corsica) | 2,710 | 8,891 |
| Gerlachovka | Slovak Republic | 2,655 | 8,711 |
| Torre de Cerrado | Spain | 2,648 | 8,688 |
| Galdhöpiggen | Norway | 2,468 | 8,100 |
| Hvannadalshnúkur | Iceland | 2,119 | 6,952 |
| Kebnekaise | Sweden | 2,117 | 6,946 |
| Ben Nevis | UK | 1,343 | 4,406 |

| Asia | | m | ft |
|---|---|---|---|
| Everest | China/Nepal | 8,848 | 29,029 |
| K2 (Godwin Austen) | China/Kashmir | 8,611 | 28,251 |
| Kanchenjunga | India/Nepal | 8,598 | 28,208 |
| Lhotse | China/Nepal | 8,516 | 27,939 |
| Makalu | China/Nepal | 8,481 | 27,824 |
| Cho Oyu | China/Nepal | 8,201 | 26,906 |
| Dhaulagiri | Nepal | 8,172 | 26,811 |
| Manaslu | Nepal | 8,156 | 26,758 |
| Nanga Parbat | Kashmir | 8,126 | 26,660 |
| Annapurna | Nepal | 8,078 | 26,502 |
| Gasherbrum | China/Kashmir | 8,068 | 26,469 |
| Broad Peak | China/Kashmir | 8,051 | 26,414 |
| Xixabangma | China | 8,012 | 26,286 |
| Kangbachen | India/Nepal | 7,902 | 25,925 |
| Jannu | India/Nepal | 7,902 | 25,925 |
| Gayachung Kang | Nepal | 7,897 | 25,909 |
| Himalchuli | Nepal | 7,893 | 25,896 |
| Disteghil Sar | Kashmir | 7,885 | 25,869 |
| Nuptse | Nepal | 7,879 | 25,849 |
| Khunyang Chhish | Kashmir | 7,852 | 25,761 |
| Masherbrum | Kashmir | 7,821 | 25,659 |
| Nanda Devi | India | 7,817 | 25,646 |
| Rakaposhi | Kashmir | 7,788 | 25,551 |
| Batura | Kashmir | 7,785 | 25,541 |
| Namche Barwa | China | 7,756 | 25,446 |
| Kamet | India | 7,756 | 25,446 |
| Soltoro Kangri | Kashmir | 7,742 | 25,400 |
| Gurla Mandhata | China | 7,728 | 25,354 |
| Trivor | Pakistan | 7,720 | 25,328 |
| > Kongur Shan | China | 7,719 | 25,324 |
| Tirich Mir | Pakistan | 7,690 | 25,229 |
| K'ula Shan | Bhutan/China | 7,543 | 24,747 |
| Pik Kommunizma | Tajikistan | 7,495 | 24,590 |
| Elbrus | Russia | 5,642 | 18,510 |
| Demavend | Iran | 5,604 | 18,386 |
| Ararat | Turkey | 5,165 | 16,945 |
| Gunong Kinabalu | Malaysia (Borneo) | 4,101 | 13,455 |
| Yu Shan | Taiwan | 3,997 | 13,113 |
| Fuji-San | Japan | 3,776 | 12,388 |

| Africa | | m | ft |
|---|---|---|---|
| Kilimanjaro | Tanzania | 5,895 | 19,340 |
| Mt Kenya | Kenya | 5,199 | 17,057 |
| Ruwenzori (Margherita) | Uganda/Zaïre | 5,109 | 16,762 |
| Ras Dashan | Ethiopia | 4,620 | 15,157 |

| Africa (cont.) | | m | ft |
|---|---|---|---|
| Meru | Tanzania | 4,565 | 14,977 |
| Karisimbi | Rwanda/Zaire | 4,507 | 14,787 |
| Mt Elgon | Kenya/Uganda | 4,321 | 14,176 |
| Batu | Ethiopia | 4,307 | 14,130 |
| Guna | Ethiopia | 4,231 | 13,882 |
| Toubkal | Morocco | 4,165 | 13,665 |
| Irhil Mgoun | Morocco | 4,071 | 13,356 |
| Mt Cameroon | Cameroon | 4,070 | 13,353 |
| Amba Ferit | Ethiopia | 3,875 | 13,042 |
| Pico del Teide | Spain (Tenerife) | 3,718 | 12,198 |
| Thabana Ntlenyana | Lesotho | 3,482 | 11,424 |
| Emi Koussi | Chad | 3,415 | 11,204 |
| Mt aux Sources | Lesotho/South Africa | 3,282 | 10,768 |
| Mt Piton | Réunion | 3,069 | 10,069 |

| Oceania | | m | ft |
|---|---|---|---|
| Puncak Jaya | Indonesia | 5,029 | 16,499 |
| Puncak Trikora | Indonesia | 4,750 | 15,584 |
| Puncak Mandala | Indonesia | 4,702 | 15,427 |
| Mt Wilhelm | Papua New Guinea | 4,508 | 14,790 |
| Mauna Kea | USA (Hawaii) | 4,205 | 13,796 |
| Mauna Loa | USA (Hawaii) | 4,170 | 13,681 |
| Mt Cook | New Zealand | 3,753 | 12,313 |
| Mt Balbi | Solomon Is. | 2,439 | 8,002 |
| Orohena | Tahiti | 2,241 | 7,352 |
| Mt Kosciusko | Australia | 2,237 | 7,339 |

| North America | | m | ft |
|---|---|---|---|
| Mt McKinley (Denali) | USA (Alaska) | 6,194 | 20,321 |
| Mt Logan | Canada | 5,959 | 19,551 |
| Citlaltepetl | Mexico | 5,700 | 18,701 |
| Mt St Elias | USA/Canada | 5,489 | 18,008 |
| Popocatepetl | Mexico | 5,452 | 17,887 |
| Mt Foraker | USA (Alaska) | 5,304 | 17,401 |
| Ixtaccihuatl | Mexico | 5,286 | 17,342 |
| Lucania | Canada | 5,227 | 17,149 |
| Mt Steele | Canada | 5,073 | 16,644 |
| Mt Bona | USA (Alaska) | 5,005 | 16,420 |
| Mt Blackburn | USA (Alaska) | 4,996 | 16,391 |
| Mt Sanford | USA (Alaska) | 4,940 | 16,207 |
| Mt Wood | Canada | 4,848 | 15,905 |
| Nevado de Toluca | Mexico | 4,670 | 15,321 |
| Mt Fairweather | USA (Alaska) | 4,663 | 15,298 |
| Mt Hunter | USA (Alaska) | 4,442 | 15,573 |
| Mt Whitney | USA | 4,418 | 14,495 |
| Mt Elbert | USA | 4,399 | 14,432 |
| Mt Harvard | USA | 4,395 | 14,419 |
| Mt Rainier | USA | 4,392 | 14,409 |
| Blanca Peak | USA | 4,372 | 14,344 |
| Longs Peak | USA | 4,345 | 14,255 |
| Tajumulco | Guatemala | 4,220 | 13,845 |
| Grand Teton | USA | 4,197 | 13,770 |
| Mt Waddington | Canada | 3,994 | 13,104 |
| Mt Robson | Canada | 3,954 | 12,972 |
| Chirripó Grande | Costa Rica | 3,837 | 12,589 |
| Mt Assiniboine | Canada | 3,619 | 11,873 |
| Pico Duarte | Dominican Rep. | 3,175 | 10,417 |

| South America | | m | ft |
|---|---|---|---|
| Aconcagua | Argentina | 6,960 | 22,834 |
| Bonete | Argentina | 6,872 | 22,546 |
| Ojos del Salado | Argentina/Chile | 6,863 | 22,516 |
| Pissis | Argentina | 6,779 | 22,241 |
| Mercedario | Argentina/Chile | 6,770 | 22,211 |
| Huascaran | Peru | 6,768 | 22,204 |
| Llullaillaco | Argentina/Chile | 6,723 | 22,057 |
| Nudo de Cachi | Argentina | 6,720 | 22,047 |
| Yerupaja | Peru | 6,632 | 21,758 |
| N. de Tres Cruces | Argentina/Chile | 6,620 | 21,719 |
| Incahuasi | Argentina/Chile | 6,601 | 21,654 |
| Cerro Galan | Argentina | 6,600 | 21,654 |
| Tupungato | Argentina/Chile | 6,570 | 21,555 |

| South America (cont.) | | m | ft |
|---|---|---|---|
| Sajama | Bolivia | 6,542 | 21,463 |
| Illimani | Bolivia | 6,485 | 21,276 |
| Coropuna | Peru | 6,425 | 21,079 |
| Ausangate | Peru | 6,384 | 20,945 |
| Cerro del Toro | Argentina | 6,380 | 20,932 |
| Siula Grande | Peru | 6,356 | 20,853 |
| Chimborazo | Ecuador | 6,267 | 20,561 |
| Cotapaxi | Ecuador | 5,896 | 19,344 |
| Pico Colon | Colombia | 5,800 | 19,029 |
| Pico Bolivar | Venezuela | 5,007 | 16,427 |

| Antarctica | m | ft |
|---|---|---|
| Vinson Massif | 4,897 | 16,066 |
| Mt Kirkpatrick | 4,528 | 14,855 |
| Mt Markham | 4,349 | 14,268 |

## Ocean Depths

| Atlantic Ocean | m | ft |
|---|---|---|
| Mt Kirkpatrick | 4,528 | 14,855 |
| Puerto Rico (Milwaukee) Deep | 9,220 | 30,249 |
| Cayman Trench | 7,680 | 25,197 |
| Gulf of Mexico | 5,203 | 17,070 |
| Mediterranean Sea | 5,121 | 16,801 |
| Black Sea | 2,211 | 7,254 |
| North Sea | 660 | 2,165 |
| Baltic Sea | 463 | 1,519 |

| Indian Ocean | m | ft |
|---|---|---|
| Java Trench | 7,450 | 24,442 |
| Red Sea | 2,635 | 8,454 |
| Persian Gulf | 73 | 239 |

| Pacific Ocean | m | ft |
|---|---|---|
| Mariana Trench | 11,022 | 36,161 |
| Tonga Trench | 10,882 | 35,702 |
| Japan Trench | 10,554 | 34,626 |
| Kuril Trench | 10,542 | 34,587 |
| Mindanao Trench | 10,497 | 34,439 |
| Kermadec Trench | 10,047 | 32,962 |
| Peru–Chile Trench | 8,050 | 26,410 |
| Aleutian Trench | 7,822 | 25,662 |

| Antarctica | m | ft |
|---|---|---|
| Molloy Deep | 5,608 | 18,399 |

## Land Lows

| | | m | ft |
|---|---|---|---|
| Caspian Sea | Europe | −28 | −92 |
| Dead Sea | Asia | −403 | −1,322 |
| Lake Assal | Africa | −156 | −512 |
| Lake Eyre North | Oceania | −16 | −52 |
| Death Valley | North America | −86 | −282 |
| Valdés Peninsula | South America | −40 | −131 |

## Rivers

| Europe | | km | miles |
|---|---|---|---|
| Volga | Caspian Sea | 3,700 | 2,300 |
| Danube | Black Sea | 2,850 | 1,770 |
| Ural | Caspian Sea | 2,535 | 1,575 |
| Dnepr (Dnipro) | Volga | 2,285 | 1,420 |
| Kama | Volga | 2,030 | 1,260 |
| Don | Volga | 1,990 | 1,240 |
| Petchora | Arctic Ocean | 1,790 | 1,110 |
| Oka | Volga | 1,480 | 920 |

| Europe (cont.) | | km | miles |
|---|---|---|---|
| Belaya | Kama | 1,420 | 880 |
| Dnister (Dniester) | Black Sea | 1,400 | 870 |
| Vyatka | Kama | 1,370 | 850 |
| Rhine | North Sea | 1,320 | 820 |
| North Dvina | Arctic Ocean | 1,290 | 800 |
| Desna | Dnepr (Dnipro) | 1,190 | 740 |
| Elbe | North Sea | 1,145 | 710 |
| >Wisla | Baltic Sea | 1,090 | 675 |
| Loire | Atlantic Ocean | 1,020 | 635 |
| West Dvina | Baltic Sea | 1,019 | 633 |

| Asia | | km | miles |
|---|---|---|---|
| Yangtze | Pacific Ocean | 6,380 | 3,960 |
| Yenisey–Angara | Arctic Ocean | 5,550 | 3,445 |
| Huang He | Pacific Ocean | 5,464 | 3,395 |
| Ob–Irtysh | Arctic Ocean | 5,410 | 3,360 |
| Mekong | Pacific Ocean | 4,500 | 2,795 |
| Amur | Pacific Ocean | 4,400 | 2,730 |
| Lena | Arctic Ocean | 4,400 | 2,730 |
| Irtysh | Ob | 4,250 | 2,640 |
| Yenisey | Arctic Ocean | 4,090 | 2,540 |
| Ob | Arctic Ocean | 3,680 | 2,285 |
| Indus | Indian Ocean | 3,100 | 1,925 |
| Brahmaputra | Indian Ocean | 2,900 | 1,800 |
| Syrdarya | Aral Sea | 2,860 | 1,775 |
| Salween | Indian Ocean | 2,800 | 1,740 |
| Euphrates | Indian Ocean | 2,700 | 1,675 |
| Vilyuy | Lena | 2,650 | 1,645 |
| Kolyma | Arctic Ocean | 2,600 | 1,615 |
| Amudarya | Aral Sea | 2,540 | 1,575 |
| Ural | Caspian Sea | 2,535 | 1,575 |
| >Ganges | Indian Ocean | 2,510 | 1,560 |
| Si Kiang | Pacific Ocean | 2,100 | 1,305 |
| Irrawaddy | Indian Ocean | 2,010 | 1,250 |
| Tarim–Yarkand | Lop Nor | 2,000 | 1,240 |
| Tigris | Indian Ocean | 1,900 | 1,180 |
| Angara | Yenisey | 1,830 | 1,135 |
| Godavari | Indian Ocean | 1,470 | 915 |
| Sutlej | Indian Ocean | 1,450 | 900 |

| Africa | | km | miles |
|---|---|---|---|
| Nile | Mediterranean | 6,670 | 4,140 |
| Zaïre/Congo | Atlantic Ocean | 4,670 | 2,900 |
| Niger | Atlantic Ocean | 4,180 | 2,595 |
| Zambezi | Indian Ocean | 3,540 | 2,200 |
| Oubangi/Uele | Zaïre | 2,250 | 1,400 |
| Kasai | Zaïre | 1,950 | 1,210 |
| Shaballe | Indian Ocean | 1,930 | 1,200 |
| Orange | Atlantic Ocean | 1,860 | 1,155 |
| Cubango | Okavango Swamps | 1,800 | 1,120 |
| >Limpopo | Indian Ocean | 1,600 | 995 |
| Senegal | Atlantic Ocean | 1,600 | 995 |
| Volta | Atlantic Ocean | 1,500 | 930 |
| Benue | Niger | 1,350 | 840 |

| Australia | | km | miles |
|---|---|---|---|
| Murray–Darling | Indian Ocean | 3,750 | 2,330 |
| Darling | Murray | 3,070 | 1,905 |
| Murray | Indian Ocean | 2,575 | 1,600 |
| Murrumbidgee | Murray | 1,690 | 1,050 |

| North America | | km | miles |
|---|---|---|---|
| Mississippi–Missouri | Gulf of Mexico | 6,020 | 3,740 |
| Mackenzie | Arctic Ocean | 4,240 | 2,630 |
| Mississippi | Gulf of Mexico | 3,780 | 2,350 |
| Missouri | Mississippi | 3,780 | 2,350 |
| Yukon | Pacific Ocean | 3,185 | 1,980 |
| Rio Grande | Gulf of Mexico | 3,030 | 1,880 |
| Arkansas | Mississippi | 2,340 | 1,450 |
| Colorado | Pacific Ocean | 2,330 | 1,445 |
| Red | Mississippi | 2,040 | 1,270 |

| North America (cont.) | | km | miles |
|---|---|---|---|
| Columbia | Pacific Ocean | 1,950 | 1,210 |
| Saskatchewan | Lake Winnipeg | 1,940 | 1,205 |
| Snake | Columbia | 1,670 | 1,040 |
| Churchill | Hudson Bay | 1,600 | 990 |
| Ohio | Mississippi | 1,580 | 980 |
| Brazos | Gulf of Mexico | 1,400 | 870 |
| >St Lawrence | Atlantic Ocean | 1,170 | 730 |

| South America | | km | miles |
|---|---|---|---|
| Amazon | Atlantic Ocean | 6,450 | 4,010 |
| Paraná–Plate | Atlantic Ocean | 4,500 | 2,800 |
| Purus | Amazon | 3,350 | 2,080 |
| Madeira | Amazon | 3,200 | 1,990 |
| São Francisco | Atlantic Ocean | 2,900 | 1,800 |
| Paraná | Plate | 2,800 | 1,740 |
| Tocantins | Atlantic Ocean | 2,750 | 1,710 |
| Paraguay | Paraná | 2,550 | 1,580 |
| Orinoco | Atlantic Ocean | 2,500 | 1,550 |
| Pilcomayo | Paraná | 2,500 | 1,550 |
| Araguaia | Tocantins | 2,250 | 1,400 |
| Juruá | Amazon | 2,000 | 1,240 |
| Xingu | Amazon | 1,980 | 1,230 |
| Ucayali | Amazon | 1,900 | 1,180 |
| >Maranón | Amazon | 1,600 | 990 |
| Uruguay | Plate | 1,600 | 990 |
| Magdalena | Caribbean Sea | 1,540 | 960 |

# Lakes

| Europe | | km² | miles² |
|---|---|---|---|
| Lake Ladoga | Russia | 17,700 | 6,800 |
| Lake Onega | Russia | 9,700 | 3,700 |
| Saimaa system | Finland | 8,000 | 3,100 |
| Vänern | Sweden | 5,500 | 2,100 |
| Rybinskoye Reservoir | Russia | 4,700 | 1,800 |

| Asia | | km² | miles² |
|---|---|---|---|
| Caspian Sea | Asia | 371,800 | 143,550 |
| Aral Sea | Kazak./Uzbek. | 33,640 | 13,000 |
| Lake Baykal | Russia | 30,500 | 11,780 |
| Tonlé Sap | Cambodia | 20,000 | 7,700 |
| >Lake Balqash | Kazakstan | 18,500 | 7,100 |
| Lake Dongting | China | 12,000 | 4,600 |
| Lake Ysyk | Kyrgyzstan | 6,200 | 2,400 |
| Lake Orumiyeh | Iran | 5,900 | 2,300 |
| Lake Koko | China | 5,700 | 2,200 |
| Lake Poyang | China | 5,000 | 1,900 |
| Lake Khanka | China/Russia | 4,400 | 1,700 |
| Lake Van | Turkey | 3,500 | 1,400 |
| Lake Ubsa | China | 3,400 | 1,300 |

| Africa | | km² | miles² |
|---|---|---|---|
| Lake Victoria | East Africa | 68,000 | 26,000 |
| Lake Tanganyika | Central Africa | 33,000 | 13,000 |
| Lake Malawi/Nyasa | East Africa | 29,600 | 11,430 |
| Lake Chad | Central Africa | 25,000 | 9,700 |
| Lake Turkana | Ethiopia/Kenya | 8,500 | 3,300 |
| Lake Volta | Ghana | 8,500 | 3,300 |
| Lake Bangweulu | Zambia | 8,000 | 3,100 |
| Lake Rukwa | Tanzania | 7,000 | 2,700 |
| Lake Mai-Ndombe | Zaïre | 6,500 | 2,500 |
| >Lake Kariba | Zambia/Zimbabwe | 5,300 | 2,000 |
| Lake Mobutu | Uganda/Zaïre | 5,300 | 2,000 |
| Lake Nasser | Egypt/Sudan | 5,200 | 2,000 |
| Lake Mweru | Zambia/Zaïre | 4,900 | 1,900 |
| Lake Cabora Bassa | Mozambique | 4,500 | 1,700 |
| Lake Kyoga | Uganda | 4,400 | 1,700 |
| Lake Tana | Ethiopia | 3,630 | 1,400 |
| Lake Kivu | Rwanda/Zaïre | 2,650 | 1,000 |
| Lake Edward | Uganda/Zaïre | 2,200 | 850 |

| Australia | | km² | miles² |
|---|---|---|---|
| Lake Eyre | Australia | 8,900 | 3,400 |
| Lake Torrens | Australia | 5,800 | 2,200 |
| Lake Gairdner | Australia | 4,800 | 1,900 |

| North America | | km² | miles² |
|---|---|---|---|
| Lake Superior | Canada/USA | 82,350 | 31,800 |
| Lake Huron | Canada/USA | 59,600 | 23,010 |
| Lake Michigan | USA | 58,000 | 22,400 |
| Great Bear Lake | Canada | 31,800 | 12,280 |
| Great Slave Lake | Canada | 28,500 | 11,000 |
| Lake Erie | Canada/USA | 25,700 | 9,900 |
| Lake Winnipeg | Canada | 24,400 | 9,400 |
| Lake Ontario | Canada/USA | 19,500 | 7,500 |
| Lake Nicaragua | Nicaragua | 8,200 | 3,200 |
| Lake Athabasca | Canada | 8,100 | 3,100 |
| Smallwood Reservoir | Canada | 6,530 | 2,520 |
| Reindeer Lake | Canada | 6,400 | 2,500 |
| Lake Winnipegosis | Canada | 5,400 | 2,100 |
| Nettilling Lake | Canada | 5,500 | 2,100 |
| Lake Nipigon | Canada | 4,850 | 1,900 |
| Lake Manitoba | Canada | 4,700 | 1,800 |

| South America | | km² | miles² |
|---|---|---|---|
| Lake Titicaca | Bolivia/Peru | 8,300 | 3,200 |
| Lake Poopo | Peru | 2,800 | 1,100 |

# Islands

| Europe | | km² | miles² |
|---|---|---|---|
| Great Britain | UK | 229,880 | 88,700 |
| Iceland | Atlantic Ocean | 103,000 | 39,800 |
| Ireland | Ireland/UK | 84,400 | 32,600 |
| Novaya Zemlya (North) | Russia | 48,200 | 18,600 |
| West Spitzbergen | Norway | 39,000 | 15,100 |
| Novaya Zemlya (South) | Russia | 33,200 | 12,800 |
| Sicily | Italy | 25,500 | 9,800 |
| Sardinia | Italy | 24,000 | 9,300 |
| Northeast Spitzbergen | Norway | 15,000 | 5,600 |
| Corsica | France | 8,700 | 3,400 |
| Crete | Greece | 8,350 | 3,200 |
| Zealand | Denmark | 6,850 | 2,600 |

| Asia | | km² | miles² |
|---|---|---|---|
| Borneo | South-east Asia | 744,360 | 287,400 |
| Sumatra | Indonesia | 473,600 | 182,860 |
| Honshu | Japan | 230,500 | 88,980 |
| Celebes | Indonesia | 189,000 | 73,000 |
| Java | Indonesia | 126,700 | 48,900 |
| Luzon | Philippines | 104,700 | 40,400 |
| Mindanao | Philippines | 101,500 | 39,200 |
| Hokkaido | Japan | 78,400 | 30,300 |
| Sakhalin | Russia | 74,060 | 28,600 |
| Sri Lanka | Indian Ocean | 65,600 | 25,300 |
| Taiwan | Pacific Ocean | 36,000 | 13,900 |
| Kyushu | Japan | 35,700 | 13,800 |
| Hainan | China | 34,000 | 13,100 |
| Timor | Indonesia | 33,600 | 13,000 |
| Shikoku | Japan | 18,800 | 7,300 |
| Halmahera | Indonesia | 18,000 | 6,900 |
| Ceram | Indonesia | 17,150 | 6,600 |
| Sumbawa | Indonesia | 15,450 | 6,000 |
| Flores | Indonesia | 15,200 | 5,900 |
| Samar | Philippines | 13,100 | 5,100 |
| Negros | Philippines | 12,700 | 4,900 |
| Bangka | Indonesia | 12,000 | 4,600 |
| Palawan | Philippines | 12,000 | 4,600 |
| Panay | Philippines | 11,500 | 4,400 |
| Sumba | Indonesia | 11,100 | 4,300 |
| Mindoro | Philippines | 9,750 | 3,800 |
| Buru | Indonesia | 9,500 | 3,700 |

| Asia (cont.) | | km² | miles² |
|---|---|---|---|
| Bali | Indonesia | 5,600 | 2,200 |
| Cyprus | Mediterranean | 3,570 | 1,400 |

| Africa | | km² | miles² |
|---|---|---|---|
| Madagascar | Indian Ocean | 587,040 | 226,660 |
| Socotra | Indian Ocean | 3,600 | 1,400 |
| Réunion | Indian Ocean | 2,500 | 965 |
| Tenerife | Atlantic Ocean | 2,350 | 900 |
| Mauritius | Indian Ocean | 1,865 | 720 |

| Oceania | | km² | miles² |
|---|---|---|---|
| New Guinea | Indon./Papua NG | 821,030 | 317,000 |
| New Zealand (South) | New Zealand | 150,500 | 58,100 |
| New Zealand (North) | New Zealand | 114,700 | 44,300 |
| Tasmania | Australia | 67,800 | 26,200 |
| New Britain | Papua NG | 37,800 | 14,600 |
| New Caledonia | Pacific Ocean | 19,100 | 7,400 |
| Viti Levu | Fiji | 10,500 | 4,100 |
| Hawaii | Pacific Ocean | 10,450 | 4,000 |
| Bougainville | Papua NG | 9,600 | 3,700 |
| Guadalcanal | Solomon Is. | 6,500 | 2,500 |
| Vanua Levu | Fiji | 5,550 | 2,100 |
| New Ireland | Papua NG | 3,200 | 1,200 |

| North America | | km² | miles² |
|---|---|---|---|
| Greenland | Greenland | 2,175,600 | 839,800 |
| Baffin Is. | Canada | 508,000 | 196,100 |
| Victoria Is. | Canada | 212,200 | 81,900 |
| Ellesmere Is. | Canada | 212,000 | 81,800 |
| Cuba | Cuba | 110,860 | 42,800 |
| Newfoundland | Canada | 110,680 | 42,700 |
| Hispaniola | Atlantic Ocean | 76,200 | 29,400 |
| Banks Is. | Canada | 67,000 | 25,900 |
| Devon Is. | Canada | 54,500 | 21,000 |
| Melville Is. | Canada | 42,400 | 16,400 |
| Vancouver Is. | Canada | 32,150 | 12,400 |
| Somerset Is. | Canada | 24,300 | 9,400 |
| Jamaica | Caribbean Sea | 11,400 | 4,400 |
| Puerto Rico | Atlantic Ocean | 8,900 | 3,400 |
| Cape Breton Is. | Canada | 4,000 | 1,500 |

| South America | | km² | miles² |
|---|---|---|---|
| Tierra del Fuego | Argentina/Chile | 47,000 | 18,100 |
| Falkland Is. (East) | Atlantic Ocean | 6,800 | 2,600 |
| South Georgia | Atlantic Ocean | 4,200 | 1,600 |
| Galapagos (Isabela) | Pacific Ocean | 2,250 | 870 |

# World Statistics – Climate

For each city, the top row of figures shows total rainfall in inches whilst the bottom row shows the average temperature in ° Fahrenheit. The total annual rainfall and average annual temperature are given at the end of the rows.

| | Jan. | Feb. | Mar. | Apr. | May | June | July | Aug. | Sept. | Oct. | Nov. | Dec. | Total |
|---|---|---|---|---|---|---|---|---|---|---|---|---|---|
| **Europe** | | | | | | | | | | | | | |
| Berlin, Germany | 1.8 | 1.6 | 1.3 | 1.7 | 1.9 | 2.6 | 2.9 | 2.7 | 1.9 | 1.9 | 1.8 | 1.7 | 23.7 |
| Altitude 180 feet | 30 | 32 | 39 | 48 | 57 | 63 | 66 | 64 | 59 | 48 | 41 | 34 | 48 |
| London, UK | 2.1 | 1.6 | 1.5 | 1.5 | 1.8 | 1.8 | 2.2 | 2.3 | 1.9 | 2.2 | 2.5 | 1.9 | 23.3 |
| 16 ft | 39 | 41 | 45 | 48 | 54 | 61 | 64 | 63 | 59 | 52 | 46 | 41 | 52 |
| Málaga, Spain | 2.4 | 2.0 | 2.4 | 1.8 | 1.0 | 0.2 | 0 | 0.1 | 1.1 | 2.5 | 2.5 | 2.4 | 18.7 |
| 108 ft | 54 | 55 | 61 | 63 | 66 | 84 | 77 | 79 | 73 | 68 | 61 | 55 | 66 |
| Moscow, Russia | 1.5 | 1.5 | 1.4 | 1.5 | 2.1 | 2.3 | 3.5 | 2.8 | 2.3 | 1.8 | 1.9 | 2.1 | 24.6 |
| 512 ft | 9 | 14 | 25 | 43 | 55 | 61 | 64 | 63 | 54 | 43 | 30 | 19 | 39 |
| Paris, France | 2.2 | 1.8 | 1.4 | 1.7 | 2.2 | 2.1 | 2.3 | 2.5 | 2.2 | 2.0 | 2.0 | 2.0 | 24.4 |
| 246 ft | 37 | 39 | 46 | 52 | 59 | 64 | 68 | 66 | 63 | 54 | 45 | 39 | 53 |
| Rome, Italy | 2.8 | 2.4 | 2.2 | 2.0 | 1.8 | 1.5 | 0.6 | 0.8 | 2.5 | 3.9 | 5.1 | 3.7 | 29.3 |
| 56 ft | 46 | 48 | 52 | 57 | 64 | 72 | 77 | 77 | 72 | 63 | 55 | 50 | 61 |
| **Asia** | | | | | | | | | | | | | |
| Bangkok, Thailand | 0.3 | 0.8 | 1.4 | 2.3 | 7.8 | 6.3 | 6.3 | 6.9 | 12.0 | 8.1 | 2.6 | 0.2 | 55 |
| 7 ft | 79 | 82 | 84 | 86 | 84 | 84 | 82 | 82 | 82 | 82 | 79 | 77 | 82 |
| Bombay, India | 0.1 | 0.1 | 0.1 | <0.1 | 0.7 | 19.1 | 24.3 | 13.4 | 10.4 | 2.5 | 0.5 | 0.1 | 71.4 |
| 36 ft | 75 | 75 | 79 | 82 | 86 | 84 | 81 | 81 | 81 | 82 | 81 | 79 | 80 |
| Ho Chi Minh, Vietnam | 0.6 | 0.1 | 0.5 | 1.7 | 8.7 | 13.0 | 12.4 | 10.6 | 13.2 | 10.6 | 4.5 | 2.2 | 78.1 |
| 30 ft | 79 | 81 | 84 | 86 | 84 | 82 | 82 | 82 | 81 | 81 | 81 | 79 | 82 |
| Hong Kong | 1.3 | 1.8 | 2.9 | 5.4 | 11.5 | 15.5 | 15.0 | 14.2 | 10.1 | 4.5 | 1.7 | 1.2 | 85.2 |
| 108 ft | 61 | 59 | 64 | 72 | 79 | 82 | 82 | 82 | 81 | 77 | 70 | 64 | 73 |
| Tokyo, Japan | 1.9 | 2.9 | 4.2 | 5.3 | 5.8 | 6.5 | 5.6 | 6.0 | 9.2 | 8.2 | 3.8 | 2.2 | 61.6 |
| 20 ft | 37 | 39 | 45 | 55 | 63 | 70 | 77 | 79 | 73 | 63 | 52 | 43 | 58 |
| **Africa** | | | | | | | | | | | | | |
| Cairo, Egypt | 0.2 | 0.2 | 0.2 | 0.1 | 0.1 | <0.1 | 0 | 0 | <0.1 | <0.1 | 0.1 | 0.2 | 1.1 |
| 1380 ft | 55 | 59 | 64 | 70 | 77 | 82 | 82 | 82 | 79 | 75 | 68 | 59 | 71 |
| Cape Town, South Africa | 0.6 | 0.3 | 0.7 | 1.9 | 3.1 | 3.3 | 3.5 | 2.6 | 1.7 | 1.2 | 0.7 | 0.4 | 20 |
| 56 ft | 70 | 70 | 68 | 63 | 57 | 55 | 54 | 55 | 57 | 61 | 64 | 66 | 62 |
| Lagos, Nigeria | 1.1 | 1.8 | 4.0 | 5.9 | 10.6 | 18.1 | 11.0 | 2.5 | 5.5 | 8.1 | 2.7 | 1.0 | 72.4 |
| 10 ft | 81 | 82 | 84 | 82 | 82 | 79 | 79 | 77 | 79 | 79 | 82 | 82 | 81 |
| Nairobi, Kenya | 1.5 | 2.5 | 4.9 | 8.3 | 6.2 | 1.8 | 0.6 | 0.9 | 1.2 | 2.1 | 4.3 | 3.3 | 37.8 |
| 5,970 ft | 66 | 66 | 66 | 66 | 64 | 61 | 61 | 61 | 64 | 66 | 64 | 64 | 64 |
| **Australia, New Zealand & Antarctica** | | | | | | | | | | | | | |
| Christchurch, New Zealand | 2.2 | 1.7 | 1.9 | 1.9 | 2.6 | 2.6 | 2.7 | 1.9 | 1.8 | 1.7 | 1.9 | 2.2 | 25.1 |
| 33 ft | 61 | 61 | 57 | 54 | 48 | 43 | 43 | 45 | 48 | 54 | 57 | 61 | 53 |
| Darwin, Australia | 15.2 | 12.3 | 10.0 | 3.8 | 0.6 | 0.1 | <0.1 | 0.1 | 0.5 | 2 | 4.7 | 9.4 | 58.7 |
| 98 ft | 84 | 84 | 84 | 84 | 82 | 79 | 77 | 79 | 82 | 84 | 86 | 84 | 83 |
| Mawson, Antarctica | 0.4 | 1.2 | 0.8 | 0.4 | 1.7 | 7.1 | 0.2 | 1.6 | 0.1 | 0.8 | 0 | 0 | 14.3 |
| 46 ft | 32 | 23 | 14 | 7 | 5 | 3 | 0 | 0 | -1 | 9 | 23 | 30 | 12 |
| Sydney, Australia | 3.5 | 4.0 | 5.0 | 5.3 | 5.0 | 4.6 | 4.6 | 3.0 | 2.9 | 2.8 | 2.9 | 2.9 | 46.5 |
| 138 ft | 72 | 72 | 70 | 64 | 59 | 55 | 54 | 55 | 59 | 64 | 66 | 70 | 63 |
| **North America** | | | | | | | | | | | | | |
| Anchorage, Alaska, USA | 0.8 | 0.7 | 0.6 | 0.4 | 0.5 | 0.7 | 1.6 | 2.6 | 2.6 | 2.2 | 1.0 | 0.9 | 14.6 |
| 131 ft | 12 | 18 | 23 | 36 | 45 | 54 | 57 | 55 | 48 | 36 | 23 | 12 | 35 |
| Kingston, Jamaica | 0.9 | 0.6 | 0.9 | 1.2 | 4.0 | 3.5 | 1.5 | 3.6 | 3.9 | 7.1 | 2.9 | 1.4 | 31.5 |
| 112 ft | 77 | 77 | 77 | 79 | 79 | 82 | 82 | 82 | 81 | 81 | 79 | 79 | 80 |
| Los Angeles, USA | 3.1 | 3.0 | 2.8 | 1.0 | 0.4 | 0.1 | <0.1 | <0.1 | 0.2 | 0.6 | 1.2 | 2.6 | 15 |
| 312 ft | 55 | 57 | 57 | 61 | 63 | 66 | 70 | 72 | 70 | 64 | 61 | 57 | 63 |
| Mexico City, Mexico | 0.5 | 0.2 | 0.4 | 0.8 | 2.1 | 4.7 | 6.7 | 6.0 | 5.1 | 2.0 | 0.7 | 0.3 | 29.5 |
| 7,574 ft | 12 | 13 | 16 | 18 | 19 | 19 | 17 | 18 | 18 | 16 | 14 | 13 | 16 |
| New York, N. Y., USA | 3.7 | 3.8 | 3.6 | 3.2 | 3.2 | 3.3 | 4.2 | 4.3 | 3.4 | 3.5 | 3.0 | 3.6 | 42.8 |
| 315 ft | 30 | 30 | 37 | 50 | 61 | 68 | 73 | 73 | 70 | 59 | 45 | 36 | 53 |
| Vancouver, Canada | 6.1 | 4.5 | 4.0 | 2.4 | 2.0 | 1.8 | 1.3 | 1.6 | 2.6 | 4.5 | 5.9 | 7.2 | 43.8 |
| 46 ft | 37 | 41 | 43 | 48 | 54 | 59 | 63 | 63 | 57 | 50 | 43 | 39 | 50 |
| **South America** | | | | | | | | | | | | | |
| Antofagasta, Chile | 0 | 0 | 0 | <0.1 | <0.1 | 0.1 | 0.2 | 0.1 | <0.1 | 0.1 | <0.1 | 0 | 0.6 |
| 308 ft | 70 | 70 | 68 | 64 | 61 | 59 | 57 | 57 | 59 | 61 | 64 | 66 | 63 |
| Buenos Aires, Argentina | 3.1 | 2.8 | 4.3 | 3.5 | 3.0 | 2.4 | 2.2 | 2.4 | 3.1 | 3.4 | 3.3 | 3.9 | 37.4 |
| 89 ft | 73 | 73 | 70 | 63 | 55 | 48 | 50 | 52 | 55 | 59 | 66 | 72 | 61 |
| Lima, Peru | 0.1 | <0.1 | <0.1 | <0.1 | 0.2 | 0.2 | 0.3 | 0.3 | 0.3 | 0.1 | 0.1 | <0.1 | 1.7 |
| 394 ft | 73 | 75 | 75 | 72 | 66 | 63 | 63 | 61 | 63 | 64 | 66 | 70 | 68 |
| Rio de Janeiro, Brazil | 4.9 | 4.8 | 5.1 | 4.2 | 3.1 | 2.1 | 1.6 | 1.7 | 2.6 | 3.1 | 4.1 | 5.4 | 42.8 |
| 200 ft | 79 | 77 | 75 | 72 | 70 | 70 | 70 | 70 | 70 | 72 | 73 | 77 | 74 |

# The Earth in Focus

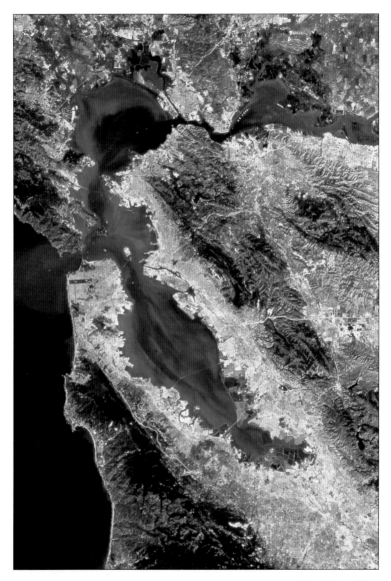

> Landsat image of the
San Francisco Bay area.
The narrow entrance to
the bay (crossed by the
Golden Gate Bridge)
provides an excellent
natural harbor. The
San Andreas Fault runs
parallel to the coastline.

# The Universe & Solar System

Between 10 and 20 billion (or 10,000 to 20,000 million) years ago, the Universe was created in a huge explosion known as the 'Big Bang'. In the first $10^{-24}$ of a second the Universe expanded rapidly and the basic forces of nature, radiation and subatomic particles, came into being. The Universe has been expanding ever since. Traces of the original 'fireball' of radiation can still be detected, and most scientists accept the Big Bang theory of the origin of the Universe.

> The Lagoon Nebula is a huge cloud of dust and gas. Hot stars inside the nebula make the gas glow red.

## The Nearest Stars ▾

The 20 nearest stars, excluding the Sun, with their distance from Earth in light years.*

| | |
|---|---|
| Proxima Centauri | 4.25 |
| Alpha Centauri A | 4.3 |
| Alpha Centauri B | 4.3 |
| Barnard's Star | 6.0 |
| Wolf 359 | 7.8 |
| Lalande 21185 | 8.3 |
| Sirius A | 8.7 |
| Sirius B | 8.7 |
| UV Ceti A | 8.7 |
| UV Ceti B | 8.7 |
| Ross 154 | 9.4 |
| Ross 248 | 10.3 |
| Epsilon Eridani | 10.7 |
| Ross 128 | 10.9 |
| 61 Cygni A | 11.1 |
| 61 Cygni B | 11.1 |
| Epsilon Indi | 11.2 |
| Groombridge 34 A | 11.2 |
| Groombridge 34 B | 11.2 |
| L789-6 | 11.2 |

* A light year equals approximately 9,500 billion km [5,900 billion miles].

## GALAXIES

Almost a million years passed before the Universe cooled sufficiently for atoms to form. When a billion years had passed, the atoms had begun to form proto-galaxies, which are masses of gas separated by empty space. Stars began to form within the protogalaxies, as particles were drawn together, producing the high temperatures necessary to bring about nuclear fusion. The formation of the first stars brought about the evolution of the protogalaxies into galaxies proper, each containing billions of stars.

Our Sun is a medium-sized star. It is

Mercury · Venus ○ Earth ◑ Mars ○ Jupiter

## PLANETARY DATA

| | Mean distance from Sun (million miles) | Mass (Earth = 1) | Period of orbit (Earth years) | Period of rotation (Earth days) | Equatorial diameter (miles) | Escape velocity (miles/sec) | Number of known satellites |
|---|---|---|---|---|---|---|---|
| **Sun** | – | 332,946 | – | 25.38 | 865,000 | 383.7 | – |
| **Mercury** | 36.2 | 0.06 | 0.241 | 58.67 | 3,031 | 2.65 | 0 |
| **Venus** | 66.9 | 0.8 | 0.615 | 243.0 | 7,521 | 6.44 | 0 |
| **Earth** | 93.0 | 1.0 | 1.00 | 0.99 | 7,926 | 6.95 | 1 |
| **Mars** | 141.2 | 0.1 | 1.88 | 1.02 | 4,217 | 3.13 | 2 |
| **Jupiter** | 483.4 | 317.8 | 11.86 | 0.41 | 88,730 | 37.0 | 16 |
| **Saturn** | 886.8 | 95.2 | 29.46 | 0.42 | 74,500 | 22.1 | 20 |
| **Uranus** | 1,784.8 | 14.5 | 84.01 | 0.45 | 31,763 | 13.2 | 15 |
| **Neptune** | 2,797.8 | 17.2 | 164.79 | 0.67 | 30,775 | 14.5 | 8 |
| **Pluto** | 3,662.5 | 0.002 | 248.54 | 6.38 | 1,450 | 0.68 | 1 |

one of the billions of stars that make up the Milky Way galaxy, which is one of the millions of galaxies in the Universe.

**THE SOLAR SYSTEM**

The Solar System lies toward the edge of the Milky Way galaxy. It consists of the Sun and other bodies, including planets (together with their moons), asteroids, meteoroids, comets, dust and gas, which revolve around it.

The Earth moves through space in three distinct ways. First, with the rest of the Solar System, it moves around the center of the Milky Way galaxy in an orbit that takes 200 million years.

As the Earth revolves around the Sun once every year, its axis is tilted by about 23.5 degrees. As a result, first the northern and then the southern hemisphere lean toward the Sun at different times of the year, causing the seasons experienced in the mid latitudes.

The Earth also rotates on its axis every 24 hours, causing day and night. The movements of the Earth in the Solar System determine the calendar. The length of a year – one complete orbit of the Earth around the Sun – is 365 days, 5 hours, 48 minutes and 46 seconds. Leap years prevent the calendar from becoming out of step with the solar year.

> The diagram below shows the planets around the Sun. The sizes of the planets are relative but the distances are not to scale. Closest to the Sun are dense rocky bodies, known as the terrestrial planets. They are Mercury, Venus, Earth, and Mars. Jupiter, Saturn, Uranus and Neptune are huge balls of gas. Pluto is a small, icy body.

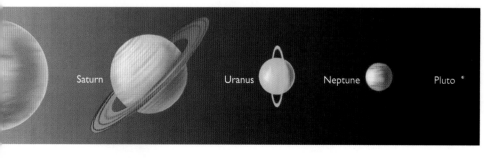

Saturn     Uranus     Neptune     Pluto

# The Changing Earth

THE SOLAR SYSTEM was formed around 4.7 billion years ago, when the Sun, a glowing ball of gases, was created from a rotating disk of dust and gas. The planets were then formed from material left over after the creation of the Sun.

After the Earth formed, around 4.6 billion years ago, lighter elements rose to the hot surface, where they finally cooled to form a hard shell, or crust. Denser elements sank, forming the partly liquid mantle, the liquid outer core, and the solid inner core.

## EARTH HISTORY

The oldest known rocks on Earth are around 4 billion years old. Natural processes have destroyed older rocks. Simple life forms first appeared on Earth around 3.5 billion years ago, though rocks formed in the first 4 billion years of Earth history contain little evidence of life. But

> Fold mountains, such as the Himalayan ranges which are shown above, were formed when two plates collided and the rock layers between them were squeezed upward into loops or folds.

rocks formed since the start of the Cambrian period (the first period in the Paleozoic era), about 590 million years ago, are rich in fossils. The study of fossils has enabled scientists to gradually piece together the long and complex story of life on Earth.

## THE PLANET EARTH

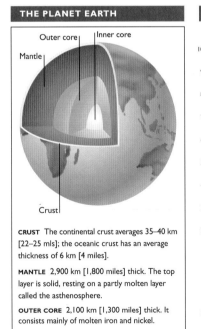

Outer core | Inner core
Mantle
Crust

**CRUST** The continental crust averages 35–40 km [22–25 mls]; the oceanic crust has an average thickness of 6 km [4 miles].

**MANTLE** 2,900 km [1,800 miles] thick. The top layer is solid, resting on a partly molten layer called the asthenosphere.

**OUTER CORE** 2,100 km [1,300 miles] thick. It consists mainly of molten iron and nickel.

**INNER CORE (DIAMETER)** 1,350 km [840 miles]. It is mainly solid iron and nickel.

## ELEMENTS

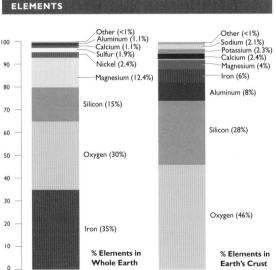

**% Elements in Whole Earth**
- Other (<1%)
- Aluminum (1.1%)
- Calcium (1.1%)
- Sulfur (1.9%)
- Nickel (2.4%)
- Magnesium (12.4%)
- Silicon (15%)
- Oxygen (30%)
- Iron (35%)

**% Elements in Earth's Crust**
- Other (<1%)
- Sodium (2.1%)
- Potassium (2.3%)
- Calcium (2.4%)
- Magnesium (4%)
- Iron (6%)
- Aluminum (8%)
- Silicon (28%)
- Oxygen (46%)

> The Earth contains about 100 elements, but eight of them account for 99% of the planet's mass. Iron makes up 35% of the Earth's mass, but most of it is in the core. The most common elements in the crust – oxygen and silicon – are often combined with one or more of the other common crustal elements, to form a group of minerals called silicates. The mineral quartz, which consists only of silicon and oxygen, occurs widely in such rocks as granites and sandstones.

## PLATE BOUNDARIES

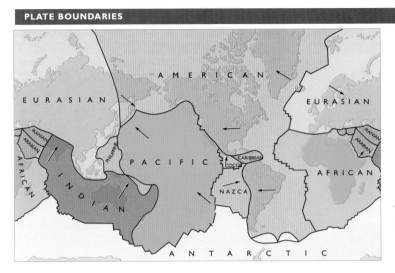

> The Earth's lithosphere
is divided into six huge
plates and several
small ones. Ocean
ridges, where plates
are moving apart, are
called constructive plate
margins. Ocean trenches,
where plates collide, are
subduction zones. These
are destructive plate
margins. The map shows
the main plates and the
directions in which they
are moving.

——— Plate boundaries

➡ Direction of
plate movements

## THE DYNAMIC EARTH

The Earth's surface is always changing because of a process called plate tectonics. Plates are blocks of the solid lithosphere (the crust and outer mantle), which are moved around by currents in the partly liquid mantle. Around 250 million years ago, the Earth contained one super-continent called Pangaea. Around 180 million years ago, Pangaea split into a northern part, Laurasia, and a southern part, Gondwanaland. Later, these huge continents, in turn, also split apart and the continents drifted to their present positions. Ancient seas disappeared and mountain ranges, such as the Himalayas and Alps, were pushed upward.

## PLATE TECTONICS

In the early 1900s, two scientists suggested that the Americas were once joined to Europe and Africa. Together they proposed the theory of continental drift to explain the similarities between rock structures on both sides of the Atlantic. But no one could offer an explanation as to how the continents moved.

Evidence from the ocean floor in the 1950s and 1960s led to the theory of plate tectonics, which suggested that the lithosphere is divided into large blocks, or plates. The plates are solid, but they rest on the partly molten asthenosphere, within the mantle. Long ridges on

the ocean floor were found to be the edges of plates which were moving apart, carried by currents in the asthenosphere. As the plates moved, molten material welled up from the mantle to fill the gaps. But at the ocean trenches, one plate is descending beneath another along what is called a subduction zone. The descending plate is melted and destroyed. This crustal destruction at subduction zones balances the creation of new crust along the ridges. Transform faults, where two plates are moving alongside each other, form another kind of plate edge.

## GEOLOGICAL TIME SCALE

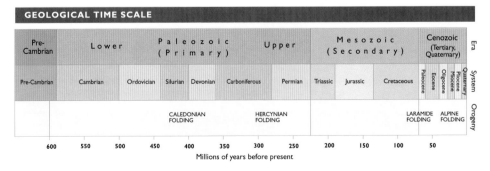

| | | | | | | | | | | | | |
|---|---|---|---|---|---|---|---|---|---|---|---|---|
| Pre-Cambrian | Lower | Paleozoic (Primary) | | | Upper | | Mesozoic (Secondary) | | | Cenozoic (Tertiary, Quaternary) | | **Era** |
| Pre-Cambrian | Cambrian | Ordovician | Silurian | Devonian | Carboniferous | Permian | Triassic | Jurassic | Cretaceous | Paleocene / Eocene / Oligocene | Miocene / Pliocene / Pleistocene | **System / Quaternary** |
| | | | CALEDONIAN FOLDING | | HERCYNIAN FOLDING | | | | | LARAMIDE FOLDING | ALPINE FOLDING | **Orogeny** |

| 600 | 550 | 500 | 450 | 400 | 350 | 300 | 250 | 200 | 150 | 100 | 50 |
|---|---|---|---|---|---|---|---|---|---|---|---|

Millions of years before present

# Earthquakes & Volcanoes

PLATE TECTONICS HELP us to understand such phenomena as earthquakes, volcanic eruptions, and mountain building.

## EARTHQUAKES

Earthquakes can occur anywhere, but they are most common near the edges of plates. They occur when intense pressure breaks the rocks along plate edges, making the plates lurch forward in a sudden movement.

| Major Earthquakes since 1900 ▼ | | | |
| --- | --- | --- | --- |
| Year | Location | Mag. | Deaths |
| 1906 | San Francisco, USA | 8.3 | 503 |
| 1906 | Valparaiso, Chile | 8.6 | 22,000 |
| 1908 | Messina, Italy | 7.5 | 83,000 |
| 1915 | Avezzano, Italy | 7.5 | 30,000 |
| 1920 | Gansu, China | 8.6 | 180,000 |
| 1923 | Yokohama, Japan | 8.3 | 143,000 |
| 1927 | Nan Shan, China | 8.3 | 200,000 |
| 1932 | Gansu, China | 7.6 | 70,000 |
| 1934 | Bihar, India/Nepal | 8.4 | 10,700 |
| 1935 | Quetta, Pakistan | 7.5 | 60,000 |
| 1939 | Chillan, Chile | 8.3 | 28,000 |
| 1939 | Erzincan, Turkey | 7.9 | 30,000 |
| 1960 | Agadir, Morocco | 5.8 | 12,000 |
| 1964 | Anchorage, Alaska | 8.4 | 131 |
| 1968 | Northeast Iran | 7.4 | 12,000 |
| 1970 | North Peru | 7.7 | 66,794 |
| 1976 | Guatemala | 7.5 | 22,778 |
| 1976 | Tangshan, China | 8.2 | 650,000 |
| 1978 | Tabas, Iran | 7.7 | 25,000 |
| 1980 | El Asnam, Algeria | 7.3 | 20,000 |
| 1980 | South Italy | 7.2 | 4,800 |
| 1985 | Mexico City, Mexico | 8.1 | 4,200 |
| 1988 | Northwest Armenia | 6.8 | 55,000 |
| 1990 | North Iran | 7.7 | 36,000 |
| 1993 | Maharashtra, India | 6.4 | 30,000 |
| 1994 | Los Angeles, USA | 6.4 | 57 |
| 1995 | Kobe, Japan | 7.2 | 5,000 |
| 1996 | Yunnan, China | 7.0 | 255 |

> The earthquake that struck Kobe in January 1995 was the worst one experienced in Japan since 1923. Japan lies alongside subduction zones.

> The section between the Pacific and Indian oceans shows a subduction zone under the American plate, with spreading ocean ridges in the Atlantic and Indian oceans. East Africa may one day split away from the rest of Africa as plate movements pull the Rift Valley apart.

Earthquakes are common along the mid-ocean ridges, but they are a long way from land and cause little damage. Other earthquakes occur near land in subduction zones, such as those that encircle much of the Pacific Ocean. These earthquakes often trigger off powerful sea waves, called tsunamis. Other earthquakes occur along transform faults, such as the San Andreas fault in California, a boundary between the North American and Pacific plates. Movements along this fault cause periodic disasters, such as the earthquakes in San Francisco (1906) and Los Angeles (1994).

## VOLCANOES & MOUNTAINS

Volcanoes are fueled by magma (molten rock) from the mantle. Some volcanoes, such as in Hawaii, lie above 'hot spots' (sources of heat in the mantle). But most volcanoes occur either along the ocean ridges or above subduction zones, where

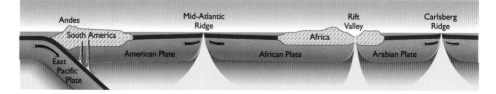

## EARTHQUAKES

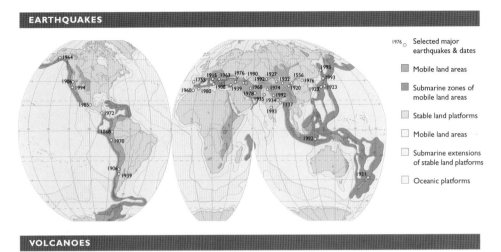

1976 ○ Selected major earthquakes & dates

▨ Mobile land areas

▨ Submarine zones of mobile land areas

▨ Stable land platforms

☐ Mobile land areas

☐ Submarine extensions of stable land platforms

☐ Oceanic platforms

## VOLCANOES

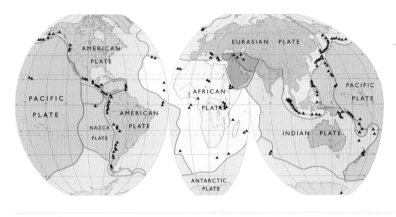

▲ Land volcanoes active since 1700

— Boundaries & tectonic plates

The maps show that the main earthquake zones follow plate edges. Most volcanoes are also in these zones, whereas some lie over 'hot spots', far from plate edges.

magma is produced when the descending plate is melted.

Volcanic mountains are built up by runny lava flows or by exploded volcanic ash. Fold mountains occur when two plates bearing land areas collide and the plate edges are buckled upward into fold mountain ranges. Plate movements also fracture rocks and block mountains are formed when areas of land are pushed upward along faults or between parallel faults. Blocks of land sometimes sink down between faults, creating deep rift valleys.

> Volcanoes occur when molten magma reaches the surface under pressure through long vents. 'Quiet' volcanoes emit runny lava (called pahoehoe). Explosive eruptions occur when the magma is sticky. Explosive gases shatter the magma into ash, which is hurled upwards into the air.

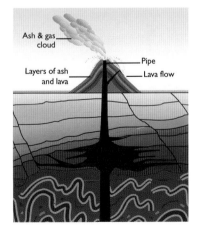

Ash & gas cloud

Pipe

Layers of ash and lava

Lava flow

# Water & Ice

A VISITOR FROM outer space might be forgiven for naming our planet 'Water' rather than 'Earth', because water covers more than 70% of its surface. Without water, our planet would be as lifeless as the Moon. Through the water cycle, fresh water is regularly supplied from the sea to the land. Most geographers divide the world's water into four main oceans: the Pacific, the Atlantic, the Indian and the Arctic. Together the oceans contain 97.2% of the world's water.

The water in the oceans is constantly on the move, even, albeit extremely slowly, in the deepest ocean trenches. The greatest movements of ocean water occur in the form of ocean currents. These are marked, mainly wind blown

> Ice breaks away from the ice sheet of Antarctica, forming flat-topped icebergs. The biggest iceberg ever recorded came from Antarctica. It covered an area larger than Belgium.

## EXPLANATION OF TERMS

**GLACIER** A body of ice that flows down valleys in mountain areas. It is usually narrow and hence smaller than ice caps or ice sheets.

**ICE AGE** A period of Earth history when ice sheets spread over large areas. The most recent Ice Age began about 1.8 million years ago and ended 10,000 years ago.

**ICEBERG** A floating body of ice in the sea. About eight-ninths of the ice is hidden beneath the surface.

**ICE SHEET** A large body of ice. During the last Ice Age, ice sheets covered large parts of the northern hemisphere.

**OCEAN** The four main oceans are the Pacific, the Atlantic, the Indian and the Arctic. Some

people classify a fifth southern ocean, but others regard these waters as extensions of the Pacific, Atlantic, and Indian oceans.

**OCEAN CURRENTS** Distinct currents of water in the oceans. Winds are the main causes of surface currents.

**SEA** An expanse of water, but smaller than an ocean.

## JANUARY TEMPERATURE AND OCEAN CURRENTS

(Northern Hemisphere – Winter)

ACTUAL SURFACE TEMPERATURE

°C
30
20
10
0
−10
−20
−30
−40

OCEAN CURRENTS
Cold  Warm  Speed (knots)
Less than 0.5
0.5 – 1.0
Over 1.0

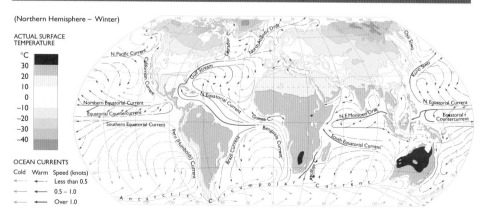

## CROSS SECTION OF ANTARCTICA

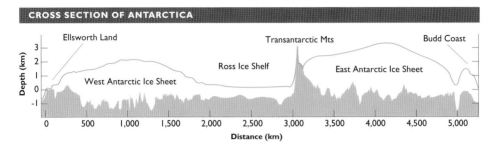

movements of water on or near the surface. Other dense, cold currents creep slowly across the ocean floor. Warm and cold ocean currents help to regulate the world's climate by transferring heat between the tropics and the poles.

### ICE

About 2.15% of the world's water is locked in two large ice sheets, several smaller ice caps and glaciers. The world's largest ice sheet covers most of Antarctica. The ice is up to 4,800 m [15,750 ft] thick and it represents 70% of the world's fresh water. The volume of ice is about nine times greater than that contained in the world's other ice sheet in Greenland. Besides these two ice sheets, there are some smaller ice caps in northern Canada, Iceland, Norway and Spitzbergen, and

many valley glaciers in mountain regions throughout the world, except Australia.

If global warming was to melt the world's ice, the sea level could rise by as much as 100 m [330 ft], flooding low-lying coastal regions. Many of the world's largest cities and most fertile plains would vanish beneath the waves.

> This section across Antarctica shows the concealed land areas in brown, with the top of the ice in blue. The section is divided into the West and East Antarctic Ice Sheets. The vertical scale has been exaggerated.

### Composition of Seawater ▾

The principal components of seawater, by percentage, excluding the elements of water itself:

| | | | |
|---|---|---|---|
| Chloride (Cl) | 55.04% | Potassium (K) | 1.10% |
| Sodium (Na) | 30.61% | Bicarbonate (HCO₃) | 0.41% |
| Sulfate (SO₄) | 7.69% | Bromide (Br) | 0.19% |
| Magnesium (Mg) | 3.69% | Strontium (Sr) | 0.04% |
| Calcium (Ca) | 1.16% | Fluorine (F) | 0.003% |

The oceans contain virtually every other element, the more important ones being lithium, rubidium, phosphorus, iodine and barium.

## JULY TEMPERATURE AND OCEAN CURRENTS

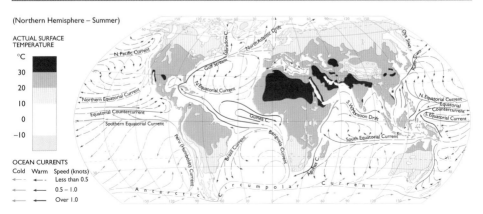

# Weather & Climate

WEATHER IS A description of the day-to-day state of the atmosphere. Climate, on the other hand, is weather in the long term: the seasonal pattern of temperature and precipitation averaged over time.

In some areas, the weather is so stable and predictable that a description of the weather is much the same as a statement of the climate. But in parts of the mid-latitudes, the weather changes from hour to hour. Changeable weather is caused mainly by low air pressure systems, called cyclones or depressions, which form along the polar front where warm subtropical air meets cold polar air.

The main elements of weather and

climate are temperature and rainfall. Temperatures vary because the Sun heats the Earth unequally, with the most intense heating around the Equator. Unequal heating is responsible for the general circulation of the atmosphere and the main wind belts.

Rainfall occurs when warm air containing invisible water vapor rises. As the rising air cools, the capacity of the air to hold water vapor decreases and so the water vapor condenses into droplets of water or ice crystals, which collect together to form raindrops or snowflakes.

> Lightning occurs in clouds and also between the base of clouds and the ground. Lightning that strikes the ground can kill people or start forest fires.

> The rainfall map shows areas affected by tropical storms, which are variously called hurricanes, tropical cyclones, willy willies and typhoons. Strong polar winds bring blizzards in winter.

## LIGHTNING

Lightning is a flash of light in the sky caused by a discharge of electricity in the atmosphere. Lightning occurs within cumulonimbus clouds during thunderstorms. Positive charges build up at the top of the cloud, while negative charges build up at the base. The charges are finally discharged as an electrical spark. Sheet lightning occurs inside clouds, while cloud to ground lightning is usually forked. Thunder occurs when molecules along the lightning channel expand and collide with cool molecules.

## ANNUAL RAINFALL

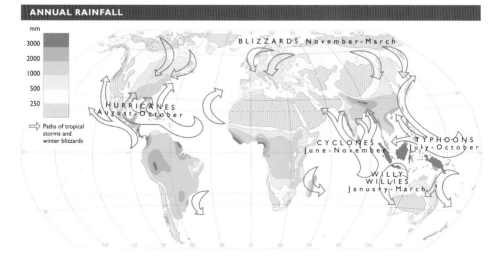

| mm | |
|---|---|
| 3000 | |
| 2000 | |
| 1000 | |
| 500 | |
| 250 | |

⇒ Paths of tropical storms and winter blizzards

BLIZZARDS November-March

HURRICANES August-October

CYCLONES June-November

TYPHOONS July-October

WILLY WILLIES January-March

## GLOBAL WARMING

The Earth's climates have changed many times during its history. Around 11,000 years ago, much of the northern hemisphere was buried by ice. Some scientists believe that the last Ice Age may not be over and that ice sheets may one day return. Other scientists are concerned that air

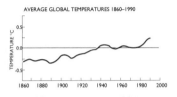

AVERAGE GLOBAL TEMPERATURES 1860–1990

pollution may be producing an opposite effect – a warming of the atmosphere. Since 1900, average world temperatures have risen by about 0.5°C [0.9°F] and increases are likely to continue. Global warming is the result of an increase in the amount of carbon dioxide in the atmosphere, caused by the burning of coal, oil, and natural gas, together with deforestation. Short-wave radiation from the Sun passes easily through the atmosphere. But, as the carbon dioxide content rises, more of the long-wave radiation that returns from the Earth's surface is absorbed and trapped by the carbon dioxide. This creates a 'greenhouse effect', which will change the world's climates with, perhaps, disastrous environmental consequences.

## CLIMATE

The world contains six main climatic types: hot and wet tropical climates; dry climates; warm temperate climates; cold temperate climates; polar climates; and mountain climates. These regions are further divided according to the character and amount of the rainfall and special features of the temperature, notably seasonal variations. Regions with temperate climates include Mediterranean areas with hot, dry summers and mild, moist winters. Because of its large size, the United States experiences a range of climates, from temperate on the east and west coasts, to dry in the interior.

## CLIMATIC REGIONS

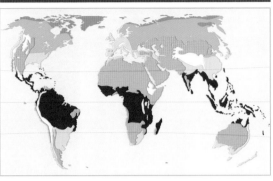

■ Tropical Climate (hot & wet)

▨ Dry Climate (desert & steppe)

☐ Temperate Climate (warm & wet)

▨ Continental Climate (cold & wet)

▨ Polar Climate (very cold & wet)

☐ Mountainous Areas (where altitude affects climate types)

## WORLD CLIMATIC RECORDS

**Highest Recorded Temperature**
Al Aziziyah, Libya: 136.4°F [58°C] on 13 September 1922

**Highest Mean Annual Temperature**
Dallol, Ethiopia: 94°F [34.4°C] from 1960–66

**Lowest Mean Annual Temperature**
Polus, Nedostupnosti, Pole of Cold, Antarctica: –72°F [–57.8 °C]

**Lowest Recorded Temperature (outside poles)**
Verkhoyansk, Siberia, Russia: –90°F [–68°C] on 6 February 1933

**Longest Heatwave**
Marble Bar, Western Australia: 162 days over 94°F [38°C], 23 October 1923 to 7 April 1924

**Driest Place**
Arica, northern Chile: only 0.03 in [0.8 mm] per year (60-year average)

**Longest Drought**
Calama, northern Chile: no recorded rainfall in 400 years to 1971

**Wettest Place (average)**
Tututendo, Colombia: mean annual rainfall 463 in [11,770 mm]

**Wettest Place (24 hours)**
Cilaos, Réunion, Indian Ocean: 73.6 in [1,870 mm] from 15–16 March 1952

**Wettest Place (12 months)**
Cherrapunji, Meghalaya, northeast India: 1,040 in [26,470 mm], August 1860 to1861. Cherrapunji also holds the record for rainfall in one month: 37 in [930 mm] in July 1861

**Heaviest Hailstones**
Gopalganj, central Bangladesh: up to 2.25 lbs [1.02 kg] in April 1986, which killed 92 people

**Heaviest Snowfall (continuous)**
Bessans, Savoie, France: 68 in [1,730 mm] in 19 hours over the period 5–6 April 1969

**Heaviest Snowfall (season/year)**
Paradise Ranger Station, Mt Rainer, Washington, USA: 1,224 in [31,102 mm] fell from 19 February 1971 to 18 February 1972

# Landscape & Vegetation

THE CLIMATE LARGELY determines the nature of soils and vegetation types throughout the world. The studies of climate and plant and animal communities are closely linked. For example, tropical climates are divided into tropical forest and tropical grassland climates. The tropical forest climate, which is hot and rainy throughout the year, is ideal for the growth of forests that contain more than half of the world's known plant and animal species. But tropical grassland, or savanna, climates have a marked dry season. As a result, the forest gives way to grassland, with scattered trees.

## CLIMATE & SCENERY
The climate also helps to shape the land. Frost action in cold areas splits boulders apart, while rapid temperature changes in hot deserts make rock surfaces peel away like the layers of an onion. These are examples of mechanical weathering.

Chemical weathering usually results from the action of water on rocks. For example, rainwater containing dissolved carbon dioxide is a weak acid, which reacts with limestone. This chemical process is responsible for the erosion of the world's most spectacular caves.

Running water and glaciers play a major part in creating scenery, while in

> The tropical broadleaf forests are rich in plant and animal species. The extinction of many species because of deforestation is one of the great natural disasters of our time.

## NATURAL VEGETATION

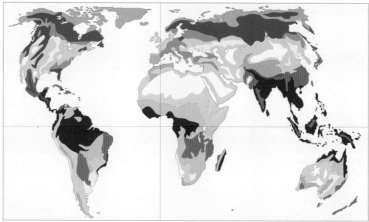

> Human activities, especially agriculture, have greatly modified plant and animal communities throughout the world. As a result, world vegetation maps show the natural 'climax vegetation' of regions – that is, the kind of vegetation that would grow in a particular climatic area, had that area not been affected by human activities. For example, the climax vegetation of western Europe is broadleaf, deciduous forest, but most of the original forest, together with the animals which lived in it, was destroyed long ago.

- Tundra & mountain vegetation
- Needleleaf evergreen forest
- Broadleaf deciduous forest
- Mixed needleleaf evergreen & broadleaf deciduous trees
- Mid-latitude grassland
- Semidesert scrub land
- Evergreen broadleaf & deciduous trees & scrub
- Desert
- Tropical grassland (savanna)
- Tropical broadleaf & monsoon rain forest
- Subtropical broadleaf & needleleaf forest

## DESERTIFICATION AND DEFORESTATION

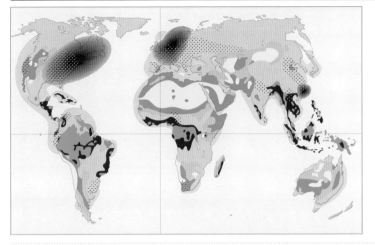

**Pollution**

☐ Polluted seas

▒ Main areas of sulfur & nitrogen emissions

■ Areas of acid rain

**Desertification**

☐ Existing deserts

■ Areas with a high risk of desertification

▦ Areas with a moderate risk of desertification

**Deforestation**

■ Former areas of rain forest

▨ Existing rain forest

dry areas, wind-blown sand is a powerful agent of erosion. Most landscapes seem to alter little in one person's lifetime. But geologists estimate that natural forces remove an average of 1.4 in [3.5 cm] from land areas every 1,000 years. Over millions of years, these forces reduce mountains to flat plains.

### HUMAN INTERFERENCE

Climate also affects people, though air conditioning and central heating now make it possible for us live in comfort almost anywhere in the world.

However, human activities are damaging our planet. Pollution is poisoning rivers and seas, while acid rain, caused by air pollution, is killing trees and acidifying lakes. The land is also harmed by such things as nuclear accidents and the dumping of toxic wastes.

Some regions have been overgrazed or so intensively farmed that once fertile areas have been turned into barren deserts. The clearance of tropical forests means that plant and animal species are disappearing before scientists have had a chance to study them.

### MOLDING THE LAND

Powerful forces inside the Earth buckle rock layers to form fold mountain ranges. But even as they rise, the forces of erosion wear them away. On mountain slopes, water freezes in cracks in rocks. Because ice occupies more space than the equivalent amount of water, this 'frost action' shatters rocks, and the fragments tumble downhill. Some end up on or inside moving glaciers. Other rocks are carried away by running water. The glaciers and streams not only transport rock fragments, but they also wear out valleys and so add to their load. The eroded material breaks down into fragments of sand, silt and mud, much of which reaches the sea, where it piles up on the sea floor in layers. These layers eventually become compacted into sedimentary rocks, such as sandstones and shales. These rocks may eventually be squeezed up again by a plate collision to form new fold mountains, so completing a natural cycle of mountain building and destruction.

### MAJOR FACTORS AFFECTING WEATHERING

| | WEATHERING RATE | | |
|---|---|---|---|
| | ◄ SLOW | | FAST ► |
| **Mineral solubility** | low (e.g. quartz) | moderate (e.g. feldspar) | high (e.g. calcite) |
| **Rainfall** | low | moderate | heavy |
| **Temperature** | cold | temperate | hot |
| **Vegetation** | sparse | moderate | lush |
| **Soil cover** | bare rock | thin to moderate soil | thick soil |

*Weathering is the breakdown and decay of rocks in situ. It may be mechanical (physical), chemical or biological.*

# Population

THE ADVENT OF agriculture began around 10,000 years ago, the invention of agriculture had a great impact on human society. People abandoned their nomadic way of life and settled in farming villages. With plenty of food, some people were able to pursue jobs unconnected with farming. These developments eventually led to rapid social changes, including the growth of cities and the emergence of civilization.

## THE POPULATION EXPLOSION

These changes had a major effect on the world's population, which rose from around 8 million in 8000 BC, to about 300 million by AD 1000. The rate of population increase then began to accelerate further, passing the 1 billion mark in the 19th century, the 2 billion mark in the 1920s and the 4 billion mark in the 1970s.

Today the world has a population of about 5.7 billion and experts forecast that it will reach around 11 billion by 2075. However, they then predict that it will stabilize or even decline a little toward 2100. Most of the expected increase will occur in developing countries in Africa, Asia and Latin America.

> Many cities in India, such as Bombay (also known as Mumbai), have grown so quickly that they lack sufficient jobs and homes for their populations. As a result, slums now cover large areas.

## POPULATION PYRAMIDS

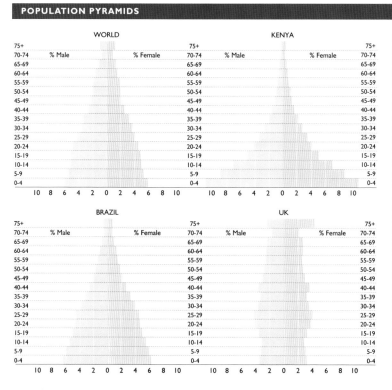

> The population pyramids compare the average age structures for the world with those of three countries at varying stages of development. Kenya, a developing country, had, until recently, one of the world's highest annual rates of population increase. As a result, a high proportion of Kenyans are aged under 15. Brazil has a much more balanced economy than Kenya's, and a lower rate of population increase. This is reflected in a higher proportion of people aged over 40. The UK is a developed country with a low rate of population growth, 0.3% per year between 1985–94, much lower than the world average of 1.6%. The UK has a far higher proportion of people over 60 years old.

## The World's Largest Cities ▼

By early next century, for the first time ever, the majority of the world's population will live in cities. Below is a list of the 20 largest cities (in thousands) based on 1995 figures.

| | | |
|---|---|---|
| 1 | New York, *USA* | 19,670 |
| 2 | Los Angeles, *USA* | 15,048 |
| = | Mexico City, *Mexico* | 15,048 |
| 4 | Bombay (Mumbai), *India* | 12,572 |
| 5 | Tokyo, *Japan* | 11,927 |
| 6 | Buenos Aires, *Brazil* | 11,256 |
| 7 | Calcutta, *India* | 10,916 |
| 8 | Seoul, *South Korea* | 10,628 |
| 9 | São Paulo, *Brazil* | 9,480 |
| 10 | Paris, *France* | 9,319 |
| 11 | Moscow, *Russia* | 8,957 |
| 12 | Shanghai, *China* | 8,930 |
| 13 | Chicago, *USA* | 8,410 |
| 14 | Jakarta, *Indonesia* | 8,259 |
| 15 | Delhi, *India* | 7,207 |
| 16 | Cairo, *Egypt* | 6,800 |
| 17 | Manila, *Philippines* | 6,720 |
| 18 | Beijing, *China* | 6,690 |
| 19 | Istanbul, *Turkey* | 6,620 |
| 20 | Lima–Callao, *Peru* | 6,601 |

This population explosion has been caused partly by better medical care, which has reduced child mortality and increased the average life expectancy at birth throughout the world. But it has also created problems. In some developing countries, nearly half of the people are children. They make no contribution to the economy, but they require costly education and health services. In richer countries, the high proportion of retired people is also a strain on the economy.

By the late 20th century, for the first time in 10,000 years, the majority of people are no longer forced to rely on farming for their livelihood. Instead, nearly half of them live in cities where many of them enjoy a high standard of living. But rapid urbanization also creates problems, especially in the developing world, with the growth of slums and an increase in crime.

## POPULATION BY CONTINENT

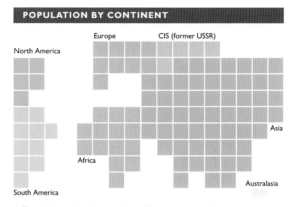

> The cartogram shows the populations of the continents in a diagrammatic way, with each square representing 1% of the world's population. For example, North America (colored turquoise) is represented by five squares, which means that it contains about 5% of the world's population, while Asia (in blue), the most populous continent even excluding the Asian part of the former USSR, is represented by 56 squares. By contrast, Australasia (yellow) is represented by less than half of a square because it contains only 0.45% of the world's population.

## WORLD DEMOGRAPHIC EXTREMES

| Fastest growing population; average annual % growth (1992–2000) | | Slowest growing population; average annual % growth (1992–2000) | |
|---|---|---|---|
| 1 | Nigeria ... 5.09 | 1 | Kuwait ... -1.39 |
| 2 | Afghanistan ... 4.21 | 2 | Ireland ... -0.24 |
| 3 | Ivory Coast ... 3.54 | 3 | St Kitts & Nevis ... -0.22 |
| 4 | Oman ... 3.52 | 4 | Bulgaria ... -0.13 |
| 5 | Syria ... 3.51 | 5 | Latvia ... -0.10 |

| Youngest populations; % aged under 15 years | | Oldest populations; % aged over 65 years | |
|---|---|---|---|
| 1 | Kenya ... 49.9 | 1 | Sweden ... 18.1 |
| 2 | Uganda ... 49.6 | 2 | Norway ... 16.4 |
| = | Yemen ... 49.6 | 3 | Denmark ... 15.4 |
| 4 | Botswana ... 49.3 | = | United Kingdom ... 15.4 |
| 5 | Tanzania ... 49.1 | 5 | Austria ... 15.0 |

| Highest urban populations; % of population living in urban areas | | Lowest urban populations; % of population living in urban areas | |
|---|---|---|---|
| 1 | Singapore ... 100.0 | 1 | Bhutan ... 5.3 |
| 2 | Macau ... 99.0 | 2 | Burundi ... 5.5 |
| 3 | Belgium ... 96.9 | 3 | Rwanda ... 7.7 |
| 4 | Kuwait ... 95.6 | 4 | Burkina Faso ... 9.0 |
| 5 | Hong Kong ... 94.1 | 5 | Nepal ... 9.6 |

| Most male populations; number of men per 100 women | | Most female populations; number of men per 100 women | |
|---|---|---|---|
| 1 | United Arab Emirates ... 206.7 | 1 | Russia ... 90.0 |
| 2 | Qatar ... 167.2 | 2 | Austria ... 91.2 |
| 3 | Bahrain ... 145.3 | = | Somalia ... 91.2 |
| 4 | Kuwait ... 128.3 | 4 | Germany ... 92.0 |
| 5 | Saudi Arabia ... 119.1 | 5 | Barbados ... 92.1 |

# Languages & Religions

ALL PEOPLE BELONG to one species, *Homo sapiens*, but within that species is a great diversity of cultures. Two of the main factors that give people an identity and sense of kinship with their neighbors are language and religion.

Definitions of languages vary and as a result estimates of the total number of languages in existence range from about 3,000 to 6,000. Many languages are spoken only by a small number of people. Papua New Guinea, for example, has only 4.2 million people but 869 languages.

The world's languages are grouped into families, of which the Indo-European is the largest. Indo-European languages are spoken in a zone stretching from

> Religion is a major force in Southeast Asia. About 94% of the people in Thailand are Buddhists, and more than 40% of men over the age of 20 spend some time, if only a few weeks, serving as Buddhist monks. Confucianism, Islam, Hinduism, and Christianity are also practiced in Thailand.

## THE WORLD'S LANGUAGES

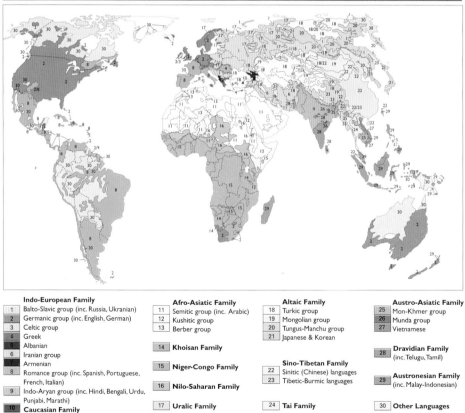

**Indo-European Family**
- 1 Balto-Slavic group (inc. Russia, Ukranian)
- 2 Germanic group (inc. English, German)
- 3 Celtic group
- 4 Greek
- 5 Albanian
- 6 Iranian group
- 7 Armenian
- 8 Romance group (inc. Spanish, Portuguese, French, Italian)
- 9 Indo-Aryan group (inc. Hindi, Bengali, Urdu, Punjabi, Marathi)
- 10 **Caucasian Family**

**Afro-Asiatic Family**
- 11 Semitic group (inc. Arabic)
- 12 Kushitic group
- 13 Berber group

- 14 **Khoisan Family**

- 15 **Niger-Congo Family**

- 16 **Nilo-Saharan Family**

- 17 **Uralic Family**

**Altaic Family**
- 18 Turkic group
- 19 Mongolian group
- 20 Tungus-Manchu group
- 21 Japanese & Korean

**Sino-Tibetan Family**
- 22 Sinitic (Chinese) languages
- 23 Tibetic-Burmic languages

- 24 **Tai Family**

**Austro-Asiatic Family**
- 25 Mon-Khmer group
- 26 Munda group
- 27 Vietnamese

- 28 **Dravidian Family** (inc. Telugu, Tamil)

- 29 **Austronesian Family** (inc. Malay-Indonesian)

- 30 **Other Languages**

## NATIVE SPEAKERS

> The chart shows the native speakers of major languages in millions. Mandarin Chinese is the language of 834 million, as compared with English, which has 443 million speakers. However, many other people speak English as a second language.

### Religious Adherents ▾

The world's major religions, with the number of adherents in millions (latest available year)

| | |
|---|---|
| **Christian** | 1,667 |
| Roman Catholic | 952 |
| Protestant | 337 |
| Orthodox | 162 |
| Anglican | 70 |
| Other Christian | 148 |
| | |
| **Muslim** | 881 |
| Sunni | 841 |
| Shia | 40 |
| | |
| **Hindu** | 663 |
| **Buddhist** | 312 |
| **Chinese folk** | 172 |
| **Ethnic/local** | 92 |
| **Jewish** | 18 |
| **Sikh** | 17 |

Europe, through southwestern Asia into the Indian subcontinent. In addition, during the period of European coloniz-ation, they spread throughout North and South America and also to Australia and New Zealand. Today about two-fifths of the world's people speak an Indo-European language, as compared with one-fifth who speak a language belong-ing to the Sino-Tibetan language.

The Sino-Tibetan language family includes Chinese, which is spoken as a first language by more people than any other. English is the second most important first language, but it is more important than Chinese in international affairs and business, because so many people speak it as a second language.

### RELIGIONS

Christianity is the religion of about a third of the world's population. Other major religions include Buddhism, Islam, Hinduism, Judaism, Chinese folk reli-gions and traditional tribal religions.

Religion is a powerful force in human society, establishing the ethics by which people live. It has inspired great music, painting, architecture and literature, yet at the same time religion and language have contributed to conflict between people throughout history. Even today, the cause of many of the conflicts around the world are partly the result of language and religious differences.

> Most languages have alphabetic systems of writing. The Greek alphabet uses some letters from the Roman alphabet, such as the A and B. Russians use the Cyrillic alphabet, which is based partly on Roman and partly on Greek letters. The Cyrillic alphabet is also used for Bulgarian. Serbs use either the Cyrillic or the Roman alphabet to write Serbo-Croat.

## ALPHABETS

**The Greek Alphabet**

Α Β Γ Δ Ε Ζ Η Θ Ι Κ Λ Μ Ν Ξ Ο Π Ρ Σ Τ Υ Φ Χ Ψ Ω

A  V/B  G  D  E  Z  E  TH  I  K  L  M  N  X  O  P  R  S  T  Y  F  CH  PS  O

**The Cyrillic Alphabet**

А Б В Г Д Е Ё Ж З И Й К Л М Н О П Р С Т У Ф Х Ц Ч Ш Щ Ю Я

A  B  V  G  D  E  YO  ZH  Z  I  Y  K  L  M  N  O  P  R  S  T  U  F  KH  TS  CH  SH  SHCH  YU  YA

# Agriculture & Industry

BECAUSE IT SUPPLIES so many basic human needs, agriculture is the world's leading economic activity. But its relative importance varies from place to place. In most developing countries, agriculture employs more people than any other activity. For example, the diagram at the bottom of this page shows that more than 90% of the people of Nepal are employed in farming.

Many farmers in developing countries live at subsistence level, producing barely enough to supply the basic needs of their families. Alongside the subsistence sector, some developing countries produce one or two cash crops that they export. Dependence on cash crops is precarious: when world commodity prices fall, the country is plunged into financial crisis.

In developed countries, by contrast, the proportion of people engaged in agriculture has declined over the last 200

> The cultivation of rice, one of the world's most important foods, is still carried out by hand in many areas. But the introduction of new strains of rice has greatly increased yields.

years. Yet, by using farm machinery and scientific methods, notably the selective breeding of crops and animals, the production of food has soared. For example, although agriculture employs only 3% of its workers, the United States is one of the world's top food producers.

## INDUSTRIALIZATION

The Industrial Revolution began in Britain in the late 18th century and soon spread to mainland Europe and other parts of the world. Industries first arose in areas with supplies of coal, iron ore, and cheap water power. But later, after oil and gas came into use as industrial fuels, factories could be set up almost anywhere.

The growth of manufacturing led to an increase in the number of industrial cities. The flight from the land was accompanied by an increase in efficiency in agriculture. As a result, manufacturing replaced agriculture as the chief source of

## EMPLOYMENT

The number of workers employed in manufacturing for every 100 workers engaged in agriculture (latest available year)

- ▨ Under 10
- ▨ 10 – 50
- ▨ 50 – 100
- ▨ 100 – 200
- ▨ 200 – 500
- ▨ Over 500

## DIVISION OF EMPLOYMENT

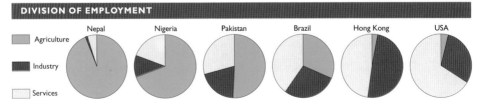

- Agriculture
- Industry
- Services

Nepal  Nigeria  Pakistan  Brazil  Hong Kong  USA

## PATTERNS OF PRODUCTION

> *The table shows how the economy breaks down (in terms of the Gross Domestic Product for 1993) in a selection of industrialized countries. Agriculture remains important in some countries, though its percentage share has steadily declined since the start of the Industrial Revolution. Industry, especially manufacturing, accounts for a higher proportion, but service industries account for the greatest percentage of the GDP in most developed nations. The figures for Manufacturing are shown separately from Industry because of their importance in the economy.*

| Country | Agriculture | Industry (excl. manufacturing) | Manufacturing | Services |
|---|---|---|---|---|
| Australia | 3% | 14% | 15% | 67% |
| Austria | 2% | 9% | 26% | 62% |
| Denmark | 4% | 7% | 20% | 69% |
| Finland | 5% | 3% | 28% | 64% |
| France | 3% | 7% | 22% | 69% |
| Germany | 1% | 11% | 27% | 61% |
| Greece | 18% | 12% | 20% | 50% |
| Hong Kong | 0% | 8% | 13% | 79% |
| Hungary | 6% | 9% | 19% | 66% |
| Ireland | 8% | 7% | 3% | 82% |
| Italy | 3% | 7% | 25% | 65% |
| Japan | 2% | 17% | 24% | 57% |
| Kuwait | 0% | 46% | 9% | 45% |
| Mexico | 8% | 8% | 20% | 63% |
| Netherlands | 4% | 9% | 19% | 68% |
| Norway | 3% | 21% | 14% | 62% |
| Singapore | 0% | 9% | 28% | 63% |
| Sweden | 2% | 5% | 26% | 67% |
| UK | 2% | 8% | 25% | 65% |
| USA | 3% | 9% | 25% | 63% |

income and employment in industrialized countries and rapidly widened the wealth gap between them and the poorer non-industrialized countries whose economies continued to rely on agriculture.

### SERVICE INDUSTRIES

Eventually, the manufacturing sector became so efficient that it could supply most of the things that people wanted to buy. Trade between industrialized countries also increased, so widening the choice for consumers in the developed world. These factors led to a further change in the economies of developed countries, namely a reduction in the relative importance of manufacturing and the growth of the service sector.

Service industries include such activities as government, transport, insurance, finance, and even the writing of computer software. In the United States, service industries now account for about two-thirds of the Gross National Product (GNP), while in Japan they account for more than half. But the wealth of both countries still rests on their massive industrial production.

## AGRICULTURE

Predominant type of farming or land use

- Nomadic herding
- Hunting, fishing & gathering
- Subsistence agriculture
- Commercial ranching
- Commercial livestock & grain farming
- Urban areas
- Forestry
- Unproductive land

# Trade & Commerce

TRADE HAS ALWAYS been an important human activity. It has widened the choice of goods available in any country, lowered prices and generally raised living standards. People regard any growth of world trade as a sign that the world economy is healthy, whereas a decline indicates a world recession.

Exports and imports are of two main kinds. Visible imports and exports include primary products, such as food and manufactures. Invisible imports and exports include services, such as banking, insurance, interest on loans, and money spent by tourists.

World trade, both visible and invisible, is dominated by the 25 members of the OECD (Organization for Economic Development), which includes the world's top trading nations, namely the United States, Germany, Japan, France, Italy, the United Kingdom and Canada, together with other European nations, as well as Australia, New Zealand and Mexico, which has close ties with the USA.

> The new port of the historic Italian city of Ravenna is linked to the Adriatic Sea by a canal. The port has large oil refining and petrochemical industries.

## CHANGING EXPORTS

From the late 19th century to the 1950s, primary products, including farm products, minerals, natural fibers, timber and, in the latter part of this period, oil

## DEBT AND AID

International debtors and the development aid they receive (1993)

The provision of aid by rich countries to developing countries is part of international politics. But the grants made to developing countries are often dwarfed by the burden of debt which the countries are expected to repay. In 1990, the debts of Mozambique, one of the world's poorest countries, were estimated to be 75 times its entire earnings from exports.

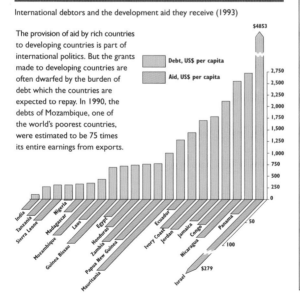

| The World's Largest Businesses ▼ |
| --- |

These are sales figures in billions of US$ and refer to the year ended 31 December 1992. They include sales of subsidiaries but exclude excise taxes collected by manufacturers.

| | | |
| --- | --- | --- |
| 1 | General Motors, *USA* | 132.8 |
| 2 | Exxon, *USA* | 103.5 |
| 3 | Ford Motor, *USA* | 100.8 |
| 4 | Royal Dutch Shell, *UK/Neths* | 98.9 |
| 5 | Toyota Motor, *Japan* | 79.1 |
| 6 | IRI, *Italy* | 67.5 |
| 7 | IBM, *USA* | 65.1 |
| 8 | Daimler-Benz, *Germany* | 63.3 |
| 9 | General Electric, *USA* | 62.2 |
| 10 | Hitachi, *Japan* | 61.5 |
| 11 | British Petroleum, *UK* | 59.2 |
| 12 | Matsushita Electric Ind., *Japan* | 57.5 |
| 13 | Mobil, *USA* | 57.4 |
| 14 | Volkswagen, *Germany* | 56.7 |
| 15 | Siemens, *Germany* | 51.4 |
| 16 | Nissan Motor, *Japan* | 50.2 |
| = | Philip Morris, *USA* | 50.2 |
| 18 | Samsung, *South Korea* | 49.6 |
| 19 | Fiat, *Italy* | 47.9 |
| 20 | Unilever, *UK/Neths* | 44.0 |

## TRADED PRODUCTS

The character of world trade has greatly changed in the last 50 years. While primary products were once the leading commodities, world trade is now dominated by manufactured products. Cars are the single most valuable traded product, followed by vehicle parts and engines. The next most valuable goods are high-tech products such as data processing (computer) equipment, telecommunications equipment, and transistors. Other items include aircraft, paper and board, trucks, measuring and control instruments, and electrical machinery. Trade in most manufactured products is dominated by the OECD countries. For example, the leading car exporter is Japan, which became the world's leading car manufacturer in the 1980s. The United States, Germany, the United Kingdom, France and Japan lead in the production of data processing equipment.

and natural gas, dominated world trade.

Many developing countries still remain dependant on exporting mineral ores, fossil fuels, or farm products such as cocoa or coffee whose prices fluctuate according to demand. But today, manufactured goods are the most important commodities in world trade. The OECD nations lead the world in exporting manufactured goods, though they are being challenged by a group of nations in eastern Asia, notably Hong Kong, Singapore, South Korea and Taiwan. Other rapidly industrializing countries in Asia include Indonesia, Malaysia and Thailand. The generally cheap labor costs of these countries have enabled them to produce manufactured goods for export at prices lower than those charged for similar goods made in Western countries.

Private companies carry on most of the world's trade. The small proportion handled by governments decreased recently with the collapse of Communist regimes in eastern Europe and the former Soviet Union.

## SHARE OF WORLD TRADE

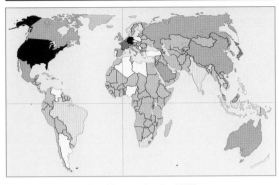

Percentage share of total world exports by value (1993)

| | | |
|---|---|---|
| ■ Over 10% | ■ 1 – 5% | □ 0.25 – 0.5% |
| ■ 5 – 10% | □ 0.5 – 1% | ▨ Under 0.25% |

## DEPENDENCE ON TRADE

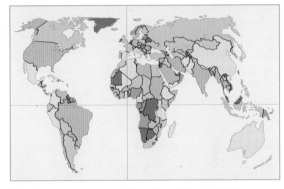

Value of exports as a percentage of Gross Domestic Product (1993)

| | | |
|---|---|---|
| ■ Over 50% GDP | ■ 30 – 40% GDP | □ 10 – 20% GDP |
| ■ 40 – 50% GDP | ■ 20 – 30% GDP | ▨ Under 10% GDP |

### Trade in Oil ▾

Major world trade in oil in millions of tons (1993)

| | |
|---|---|
| Middle East (Saudi Arabia, Iran, UAE & Kuwait) to W. Europe ..........180 | Nigeria to Western Europe ........ 30 |
| | Nigeria to USA .......................... 40 |
| Middle East to Japan .................139 | Canada to USA .......................... 46 |
| Middle East to Asia (not Japan) ...131 | Indonesia to Japan ...................... 20 |
| Latin America (Mexico & Venezuela) to Western Europe ...................110 | Latin America to W. Europe ...... 26 |
| | Western Europe (Norway & UK) |
| Middle East to USA ...................90 | to USA ...................................... 23 |
| Russia to Western Europe ......... 54 | Middle East to Latin America ...... 18 |
| Libya to Western Europe ...........52 | Total world trade ...................1,516 |

# Transport & Travel

ABOUT 200 YEARS ago, most people never traveled far from their birthplace. But adventurous travelers can now reach almost any part of the world.

Transport is concerned with moving goods and people around by land, water, and air. Land transport was once laborious, and was dependent on pack animals or animal-drawn vehicles. But during the Industrial Revolution, railroads played a vital role in moving bulky materials and equipment required by factories. They were also important in the opening up and development of remote areas around the world in North and South America, Africa, Asia and Australia.

Today, however, motor vehicles have taken over many of the functions once served by railroads. Unlike railroads, motor vehicles provide a door-to-door service and modern trucks can carry large loads. In the United States, however, the long distances between cities means that railroads still carry about 35% of the domestic freight traffic, with trucks accounting for just 25% (compared to 90% in Britain). However, automobiles account for more than 76% of intercity passenger traffic.

> Traffic jams and vehicle pollution have affected cities throughout the world. Many of Bangkok's beautiful old canals have been filled in to provide extra roads to cope with the enormous volume of traffic in the city.

## TRAVEL & TOURISM

Sea transport, which now employs huge bulk grain carriers, oil tankers and container ships, still carries most of the world's trade. But since the late 1950s, fewer passengers have traveled overseas by sea, because air travel is so much faster, though many former ocean liners now operate successfully as cruise ships.

Air travel has played a major part in the rapid growth of the tourist industry,

## AIR TRAVEL

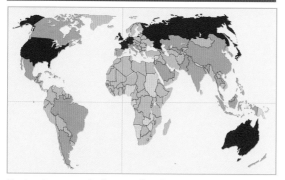

Number of passenger miles flown, in millions (1992). Passenger miles are the number of passengers (both international and domestic) multiplied by the distance flown by each passenger from airport of origin.

- ■ Over 60,000
- ■ 30,000 – 60,000
- ▨ 6,000 – 30,000
- ▨ 600 – 6,000
- ▢ 300 – 600
- ▢ Under 300

### The Busiest International Airports ▼

Number of international passengers, in thousands, (1993)

| | | |
|---|---|---|
| 1 | Heathrow, *London* | 40,848 |
| 2 | Frankfurt/Main, *Frankfurt* | 25,119 |
| 3 | Hong Kong Intl., *Hong Kong* | 24,421 |
| 4 | Charles de Gaulle, *Paris* | 23,336 |
| 5 | Schiphol, *Amsterdam* | 20,658 |
| 6 | New Tokyo Intl., *Tokyo* | 18,947 |
| 7 | Changi, *Singapore* | 18,796 |
| 8 | Gatwick, *London* | 16,656 |
| 9 | Kennedy, *New York* | 14,821 |
| 10 | Bangkok Intl., *Bangkok* | 12,789 |
| 11 | Miami Intl., *Miami* | 12,373 |
| 12 | Zürich, *Zürich* | 12,256 |
| 13 | Los Angeles Intl., *Los Angeles* | 11,945 |
| 14 | Chiang Kai-Shek, *Taipei* | 11,154 |
| 15 | Manchester, *Manchester* | 10,791 |

## The Longest Rail Networks ▼

Extent of rail network, in thousands of miles, (1993)

| | | |
|---|---|---|
| 1 | USA | 148.9 |
| 2 | Russia | 54.4 |
| 3 | India | 38.8 |
| 4 | China | 33.6 |
| 5 | Germany | 25.1 |
| 6 | Australia | 22.2 |
| 7 | Argentina | 21.2 |
| 8 | France | 20.3 |
| 9 | Mexico | 16.5 |
| 10 | Poland | 15.5 |

which accounted for 7.5% of world trade by the mid-1990s. Travel and tourism have greatly increased people's understanding and knowledge of the world, especially in the OECD countries, which account for about 7% of world tourism.

Some developing countries have large tourist industries which have provided employment and led to improvements in roads and other facilities. In some cases, tourism plays a vital role in the economy. For example, in Kenya, tourism provides more income than any other activity apart from the production and sale of coffee. However, too many tourists can damage fragile environments, such as the wildlife and scenery in national parks. Tourism can also harm local cultures.

## THE IMPORTANCE OF TOURISM

Nations receiving the most from tourism, millions of US$ (1993)

| | | |
|---|---|---|
| 1 | USA | 53,861 |
| 2 | France | 25,000 |
| 3 | Spain | 22,181 |
| 4 | Italy | 21,577 |
| 5 | UK | 13,683 |
| 6 | Austria | 13,250 |
| 7 | Germany | 10,982 |
| 8 | Switzerland | 7,650 |
| 9 | Hong Kong | 6,037 |
| 10 | Mexico | 5,997 |

Nations spending the most on tourism, millions of US$ (1993)

| | | |
|---|---|---|
| 1 | USA | 41,260 |
| 2 | Germany | 37,514 |
| 3 | Japan | 26,860 |
| 4 | UK | 17,244 |
| 5 | Italy | 13,053 |
| 6 | France | 12,805 |
| 7 | Canada | 10,629 |
| 8 | Netherlands | 8,974 |
| 9 | Austria | 8,180 |
| 10 | Taiwan | 7,585 |

Number of tourist arrivals, millions (1993)

| | | |
|---|---|---|
| 1 | France | 60,100 |
| 2 | USA | 45,793 |
| 3 | Spain | 40,085 |
| 4 | Italy | 26,379 |
| 5 | Hungary | 22,804 |
| 6 | UK | 19,186 |
| 7 | China | 18,982 |
| 8 | Austria | 18,257 |
| 9 | Poland | 17,000 |
| 10 | Mexico | 16,534 |

Fastest growing tourist destinations, % change in receipts (1994–95)

| | | |
|---|---|---|
| 1 | South Korea | 49% |
| 2 | Czech Republic | 27% |
| 3 | India | 21% |
| 4 | Russia | 19% |
| 5 | Philippines | 18% |
| 6 | Turkey | 17% |
| 7 | Thailand | 15% |
| 8 | Poland | 13% |
| 9 | China | 12% |
| 10 | Israel | 12% |

## THE WORLD'S VEHICLES

Proportion of the world's vehicles by region (1994)

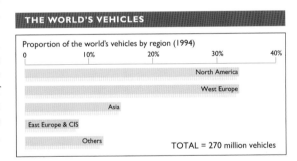

| | | | | |
|---|---|---|---|---|
| 0 | 10% | 20% | 30% | 40% |

North America

West Europe

Asia

East Europe & CIS

Others

TOTAL = 270 million vehicles

## CAR OWNERSHIP

Number of people per car (latest available year)

- ■ Over 1,000
- ■ 500 – 1,000
- ■ 100 – 500
- □ 25 – 100
- □ 5 – 25
- ▦ Under 5

Two-thirds of the world's vehicles are found in the developed countries of Europe and North America. Car ownership is also high in Australia and New Zealand, as well as in Japan, the world's leading car exporter. Car transport is the most convenient form of passenger travel, but air pollution caused by exhaust fumes is a serious problem in many large cities.

# International Organizations

IN THE LATE 1980s, people rejoiced at the collapse of Communist regimes in eastern Europe and the former Soviet Union, because this brought to an end the Cold War, a long period of hostility between East and West. But hope of a new era of peace was shattered when ethnic and religious rivalries led to civil war in Yugoslavia and in parts of the former Soviet Union.

In order to help maintain peace, many governments have formed international organizations to increase cooperation. Some, such as NATO (North Atlantic

> In the early 1990s, the United Nations peacekeeping mission worked to end the civil war in Bosnia-Herzegovina and also to bring aid to civilians affected by the fighting.

Treaty Organization), are defense alliances, while others aim to encourage economic and social cooperation. Some organizations such as the Red Cross are non-governmental organizations, or NGOs.

## UNITED NATIONS

The United Nations, the chief international organization, was formed in October 1945 and now has 185 member countries. The only independent nations that are not members are Kiribati, Nauru, Switzerland, Taiwan, Tonga, Tuvalu and the Vatican City.

### UN Contributions ▾

In 1994, the top ten contributing countries to the UN budget, which was US$2,749 million, were as follows:

| | | |
|---|---|---|
| 1 | USA | 25.0% |
| 2 | Japan | 12.5% |
| 3 | Germany | 8.9% |
| 4 | Russia | 6.7% |
| 5 | France | 6.0% |
| 6 | UK | 5.0% |
| 7 | Italy | 4.3% |
| 8 | Canada | 3.1% |
| 9 | Spain | 2.0% |
| 10 | Brazil | 1.6% |

## THE UNITED NATIONS

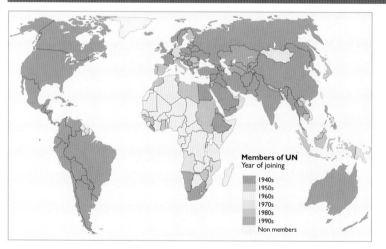

**Members of UN**
Year of joining

- 1940s
- 1950s
- 1960s
- 1970s
- 1980s
- 1990s
- Non members

> The membership of the UN has risen from 51 in 1945 to 185 in 1995. The first big period of expansion came in the 1960s when many former colonies achieved their independence. The membership again expanded rapidly in the 1990s when new countries were formed from the former Soviet Union and Yugoslavia. The most recent addition, Palau, is a former US trust territory in the Pacific Ocean and joined in 1994.

The United Nations was formed at the end of World War II to promote peace, international cooperation and security, and to help solve economic, social, cultural, and humanitarian problems. It promotes human rights and freedom and is a forum for negotiations between nations.

The main organs of the UN are the General Assembly, the Security Council, the Economic and Social Council, the Trusteeship Council, the International Court of Justice and the the Secretariat.

The UN also operates 14 specialized agencies concerned with particular issues, such as agriculture, education, working conditions, communications and health. For example, UNICEF (the United Nations International Children's Fund), established in 1946 to deliver postwar relief to children, now aims to provide basic health care to children and mothers worldwide. The ILO (International Labor Organization) seeks to improve working conditions, while the FAO (Food and Agricultural Organization) aims at improving the production and distribution of food. The WTO (World Trade Organization) was set up as recently as January 1995 to succeed GATT (General Agreements on Tariffs and Trade).

## THE UNITED NATIONS

**THE GENERAL ASSEMBLY** is the meeting of all member nations every September under a newly-elected president to discuss issues affecting development, peace, and security.

**THE SECURITY COUNCIL** has 15 members, of which five are permanent. It is responsible for maintaining international peace.

**THE SECRETARIAT** consists of the staff and employees of the UN, including the Secretary-General (appointed for a five-year term), who is the UN's chief administrator.

**THE ECONOMIC & SOCIAL COUNCIL** works with the specialized agencies to implement UN policies on improving living standards, health, cultural and educational cooperation.

**THE TRUSTEESHIP COUNCIL** was designed to bring several dependencies to independence. This work is now complete.

**THE INTERNATIONAL COURT OF JUSTICE**, or World Court, deals with legal problems and helps to settle disputes. Its headquarters are at The Hague, in the Netherlands.

## UN DEPARTMENTS

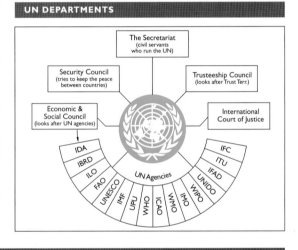

## UN PEACEKEEPING MISSIONS

The United Nations tries to resolve international disputes in several ways. It sends unarmed observer missions to monitor cease-fires or supervise troop withdrawals, and the Security Council members also send peacekeeping forces.

This first of these forces was sent in 1948 to supervise the cease-fire between Arabs and Jews in disputed parts of Palestine and, since then, it has undertaken more than 30 other missions. The 'Blue Berets', as the UN troops are called, must be impartial in any dispute and they can

fire only in self-defense. Hence, they can operate only with the support of both sides, which leaves them open to criticism when they are unable to prevent violence by intervening.

By the mid-1960s, the UN was involved in 15 world conflicts, was policing the boundary in partitioned Cyprus, and was seeking to enforce a peace agreement in Angola after 20 years of civil war. Other missions were in Burundi and Rwanda, El Salvador, Georgia, the Israeli-occupied Golan Heights, Haiti, Kuwait, southern

Lebanon, Liberia, Mozambique, Western Sahara and the former Yugoslavia. A force known as UNPROFOR (UN Protection Force) had been operating in Bosnia-Herzegovina and, by 1995, it accounted for 60% of the total UN peacekeeping budget of US$3 billion. In 1995, under a peace agreement, the UN approved the setting up of a new force (IFOR), composed of NATO and non-NATO members, to replace UNPROFOR, though small UN forces remained in Croatia and Macedonia.

## ECONOMIC ORGANIZATIONS

Over the last 40 years, many countries have joined common markets aimed at eliminating trade barriers and encouraging the free movement of workers and capital.

The best known of these is the European Union. Other organizations include ASEAN (the Association of Southeast Asian Nations), which aims at reducing trade barriers between its seven members: Brunei, Indonesia, Malaysia, the Philippines, Singapore, Thailand and Vietnam.

APEC (the Asia-Pacific Cooperation Group) was founded in 1989 and in-

> The European Parliament, one of the branches of the EU, consists of 626 members. The number of members for each country is based mainly on population.

cludes the countries of East and Southeast Asia, with the United States, Canada, Australia and New Zealand. APEC aims to create a free trade zone by 2020.

Together the United States, Canada and Mexico form NAFTA (North American Free Trade Agreement), which aims at eliminating trade barriers within 15 years of its foundation on 1 January 1994. Other economic groupings link the countries of Latin America.

Another economic group with more limited aims is OPEC (Organization of Petroleum Exporting Countries). It works to unify policies concerned with the sale of petroleum on world markets.

The central aim of the Colombo Plan is to provide economic development assistance for South and Southeast Asia.

## OTHER ORGANIZATIONS

Some organizations exist for consultation on matters of common interest. The Commonwealth of Nations grew out of the links created by the British Empire, while the OAS (Organization of American States) works to increase understanding throughout the Western Hemisphere. The OAU (Organization of

## THE EUROPEAN UNION

At the end of World War II (1939–45), many Europeans wanted to end the ancient emnities that had caused such destruction and rebuild the shattered continent. It was in this mood that Belgium, France, West Germany, Italy, Luxembourg and the Netherlands signed the Treaty of Paris in 1951. This set up the European Coal and Steel Community (ECSC), the forerunner of the European Union.

In 1957, through the Treaty of Rome, the same six countries created the European Economic Community (EEC) and the European Atomic Community (EURATOM). In 1967, the ECSC, the EEC and EURATOM merged to form the

single European Community (EC).

Another economic group, the European Free Trade Association (EFTA), was set up in 1960 by seven countries: Austria, Denmark, Norway, Portugal, Sweden, Switzerland, and the United Kingdom. However, Denmark, Ireland and the UK left to become members of the EC in 1973, followed by Greece in 1981, Spain and Portugal in 1986, and Austria, Finland and Sweden in 1995. The expansion of the EC to 15 members left EFTA with just four members: Iceland, Liechtenstein, Norway and Switzerland.

In 1993, following the signing of the Maastricht Treaty, the EC was reconstituted

as the European Union (EU). The aims of the EU include economic and monetary union, a single currency for all 15 countries, and closer cooperation on foreign and security policies and also on home affairs. This step has led to a debate. Some people would like the EU to develop into a federal Europe, but others fear that this would lead to a loss of national identity. Another matter of importance is the future enlargement of the EU. By 1995, formal applications for membership had been received from Turkey, Malta, Cyprus, Poland, Hungary, Slovakia and Romania. Other possible members include the Czech Republic, Estonia, Latvia and Lithuania.

## AUSTRALIA'S NEW ROLE

Most of the people who settled in Australia between 1788 and the mid-20th century came from the British Isles. However, the strong ties between Australia and Britain were weakened after Britain joined the European Community in 1973. Since 1973, many Australians have argued that their world position has changed and that they are part of a Pacific community of nations, rather than an extension of Europe. Some want closer integration with ASEAN, the increasingly powerful economic group formed by seven Southeast Asian nations. But in 1995, the prime minister of Malaysia, Dr Mahathir Mohamad, argued that Australia could not be regarded as Asian until at least 70% of its people were of ethnic Asian origin.

African Unity) has a similar role in Africa, while the Arab League is made up of Arabic-speaking North African and Middle Eastern states. The recently formed CIS (Commonwealth of Independent States) aims at maintaining links between 12 of the 15 republics which made up the Soviet Union.

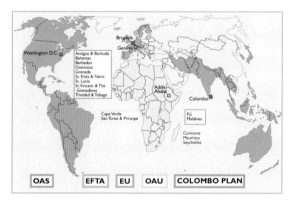

## NORTH–SOUTH DIVIDE

The deepest division in the world today is the divide between rich and poor nations. In international terms, this is called the North–South divide, because the North contains most of the world's developed countries, while the developing countries lie mainly in the South. The European Union recognizes this division and gives special trading terms to more than 60 former European dependencies, which form the ACP (African, Caribbean and Pacific) states. One organization containing a majority of developing countries is the Non-Aligned Movement. This Movement was created in 1961 during the Cold War as a political bloc allied neither to the East nor to the West. However, the aims of the 113 members who attended the movement's 11th gathering in 1995 were concerned mainly with economic matters. The 113 countries between them produce only about 7% of the world's gross output and they can speak for the poorer South.

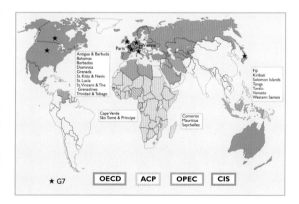

> The maps show the membership of major international organizations. One important grouping shown on the bottom map is the Group of Seven (often called G7), which was set up on 22 September 1985. This group of seven major industrial democracies (Canada, France, Germany, Italy, Japan, the United Kingdom and the United States) holds periodic meetings to discuss major problems, such as world recessions.

# Regions in the News

> The hoped-for era of peace following the end of the Cold War in Europe in the early 1990s was not to be. Former Yugoslavia, a federation of six republics ruled by a Communist government between 1946 and 1991, became a 'region in the news' when it split apart in 1991. First, Croatia, Slovenia and Macedonia declared themselves independent nations, followed by Bosnia-Herzegovina in 1992. This left two states, Serbia and Montenegro, to continue as Yugoslavia. The presence in Croatia and Bosnia-Herzegovina of Orthodox Christian Serbs, Roman Catholic Croats, and Muslims proved an explosive mixture. Fighting broke out first in Croatia and then in Bosnia-Herzegovina. Following a bitter civil war, accompanied by 'ethnic cleansing' (the slaughter and expulsion of rival ethnic groups), the signing of a peace agreement (the Dayton Peace Accord) in 1995 ended the war and affirmed Bosnia-Herzegovina as a single state with its capital at Sarajevo. But the new country is partitioned into a Muslim–Croat Federation (51% of the country) and a Serbian Republic (49%).

## Population breakdown ▼

Population totals and the proportion of ethnic groups (1995)

**Yugoslavia** .................................... 10,881,000
Serb 63%, Albanian 17%, Montenegrin 5%, Hungarian 3%, Muslim 3%

Serbia ............................................. 6,017,200
   Kosovo ...................................... 2,045,600
   Vojvodina ................................... 2,121,800
Montenegro .................................... 696,400

**Bosnia-Herzegovina** ............... 4,400,000
Muslim 49%, Serb 31%, Croat 17%

**Croatia** ...................................... 4,900,000
Croat 78%, Serb 12%

**Slovenia** .................................... 2,000,000
Slovene 88%, Croat 3%, Serb 2%

**Macedonia (F.Y.R.O.M.)** ............. 2,173,000
Macedonian 64%, Albanian 22%, Turkish 5%, Romanian 3%, Serb 2%

–·–·– International borders

–··–··– Republic boundaries

– – – – Province boundaries

———— Line of the Dayton Peace Accord

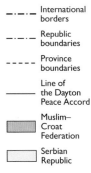

Muslim–Croat Federation

Serbian Republic

> Since its establishment in 1948, the State of Israel has seldom been out of the news. During wars with its Arab neighbors in 1948–49, 1956, 1967 and 1973, it occupied several areas. The largest of the occupied territories, the Sinai peninsula, was returned to Egypt in 1979 following the signing of an Egyptian–Israeli peace treaty. This left three Israeli-occupied territories: the Gaza Strip, the West Bank bordering Jordan, and the Golan Heights, a militarily strategic area overlooking southwestern Syria.

Despite the peace agreement with Egypt, conflict continued in Israel with the PLO (Palestine Liberation Organization), which claimed to represent Arabs in Israel and Palestinians living in exile. Finally, on 13 September 1993 Israel officially recognized the PLO, and Yasser Arafat, leader of the PLO, renounced terrorism and recognized the State of Israel. This led to an agreement signed by both sides in Washington, DC. In May 1994, limited Palestinian self-rule was established in the Gaza Strip and in parts of the occupied West Bank. A Palestinian National Authority (PNA) was created and took over from the Israeli military administration when Israeli troops withdrew from the Gaza Strip and the city of Jericho. On 1 July 1994 the Palestinian leader, Yasser Arafat, stepped on to Palestinian land for the first time in 25 years.

Many people hoped that these developments would eventually lead to the creation of a Palestinian state, which would coexist in peace with its neighbor Israel. But groups on both sides sought to undermine the peace process. In November 1995, a right-wing Jewish student assassinated the Israeli prime minister, Yitzhak Rabin, and then, in early 1996, Hamas, a Muslim group which aims at the overthrow of Israel and the creation of a Palestinian state in its place, launched a series of suicide bomb attacks in Israeli cities, killing many civilians and injuring hundreds more.

Meanwhile, Israel continues its long negotiations with Syria aimed at finding a resolution to the problem of the Golan Heights. This would hopefully form part of a general peace agreement between Israel and its Arab neighbors.

## Population breakdown ▾

Population totals and the proportion of ethnic groups (1995)

**Israel** .................................. **5,696,000**
Jewish 82%, Arab Muslim 14%, Arab
Christian 3%, Druse 2%
West Bank ........................................ 973,500
Palestinian Arab 97% (Arab Muslim 85%,
Christian 8%, Jewish 7%)
Gaza Strip ........................................ 658,200
Arab Muslim 98%

**Jordan** .................................. **5,547,000**
Arab 99% (Palestinian Arab 50%)

**Syria** .................................. **14,614,000**
Arab 89%, Kurdish 6%

THE NEAR EAST

—·—·— 1949 Armistice Line

----- 1974 Cease-fire Lines (Golan Heights)

*Efrata* Main Jewish settlements in the West Bank and Gaza Strip

Halhul Main Palestinian Arab towns in the West Bank and Gaza Strip
– under Palestinian control since May 1994 (Gaza and Jericho)
and 28 September 1995 (West Bank)

# World Flags

 Afghanistan

 Albania

 Algeria

 Angola

 Argentina

 Armenia

 Australia

 Austria

 Azerbaijan

 Bahamas

 Bahrain

 Bangladesh

 Belarus

 Belgium

 Benin

 Bhutan

 Bolivia

 Bosnia-Herzegovina

 Botswana

 Brazil

 Bulgaria

 Burkina Faso

 Burma (Myanmar)

 Burundi

 Cambodia

 Cameroon

 Canada

 Central African Rep.

 Chad

 Chile

 China

 Colombia

 Congo

 Costa Rica

 Croatia

 Cuba

 Cyprus

 Czech Republic

 Denmark

 Djibouti

 Dominican Republic

 Ecuador

 Egypt

 El Salvador

 Equatorial Guinea

 Eritrea

 Estonia

 Ethiopia

 Finland

 France

 Gabon

 Georgia

 Germany

 Ghana

 Greece

Guatemala

 Guinea

 Guinea–Bissau

 Guyana

 Haiti

 Honduras

 Hong Kong

 Hungary

 Iceland

 India

 Indonesia

 Iran

 Iraq

 Ireland

 Israel

 Italy

 Ivory Coast

 Jamaica

 Japan

 Jordan

 Kazakstan

 Kenya

 Korea, North

 Korea, South

 Kuwait

 Kyrgyzstan

 Laos

 Latvia

 Lebanon

 Lesotho

 Liberia

 Libya

 Liechtenstein

 Lithuania

 Luxembourg

 Macedonia

 Madagascar

 Malawi

 Malaysia

 Mali

 Malta

 Mauritania

 Mexico

 Moldova

 Mongolia

 Morocco

 Mozambique

 Namibia

 Nepal

 Netherlands

 New Zealand

 Nicaragua

 Niger

Nigeria

Norway

Oman

 Pakistan

 Panama

 Papua New Guinea

 Paraguay

 Peru

 Philippines

 Poland

 Portugal

 Puerto Rico

 Qatar

 Romania

 Russia

 Rwanda

 São Tomé & Príncipe

 Saudi Arabia

 Senegal

 Sierra Leone

 Singapore

 Slovak Republic

 Slovenia

 Somalia

 South Africa

 Spain

 Sri Lanka

 Sudan

 Surinam

 Swaziland

 Sweden

 Switzerland

 Syria

 Taiwan

 Tajikistan

 Tanzania

 Thailand

 Togo

 Trinidad & Tobago

 Tunisia

 Turkey

 Turkmenistan

 Uganda

 Ukraine

 UAE

 United Kingdom

 USA

Uruguay

Uzbekistan

Vatican City

Venezuela

Vietnam

Yemen

Yugoslavia

Zaïre

Zambia

Zimbabwe

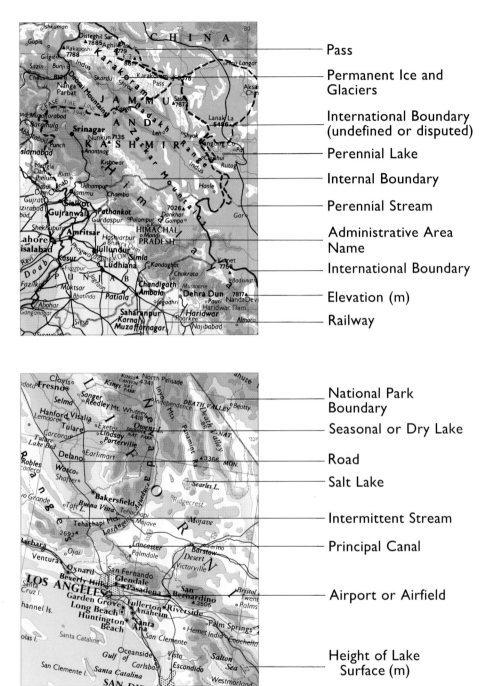

Pass

Permanent Ice and Glaciers

International Boundary (undefined or disputed)

Perennial Lake

Internal Boundary

Perennial Stream

Administrative Area Name

International Boundary

Elevation (m)

Railway

National Park Boundary

Seasonal or Dry Lake

Road

Salt Lake

Intermittent Stream

Principal Canal

Airport or Airfield

Height of Lake Surface (m)

## Settlements

Settlement symbols and type styles vary according to the scale of each map and indicate the importance of towns rather than specific population figures.

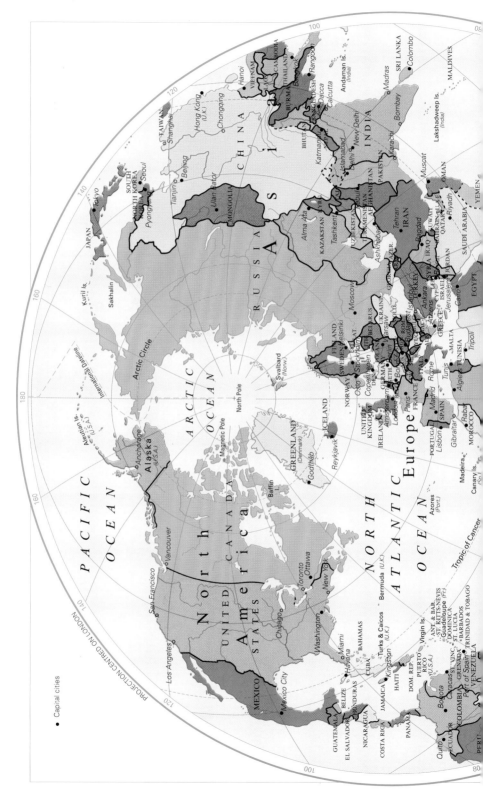

PROJECTION CENTRED ON LONDON

• Capital cities

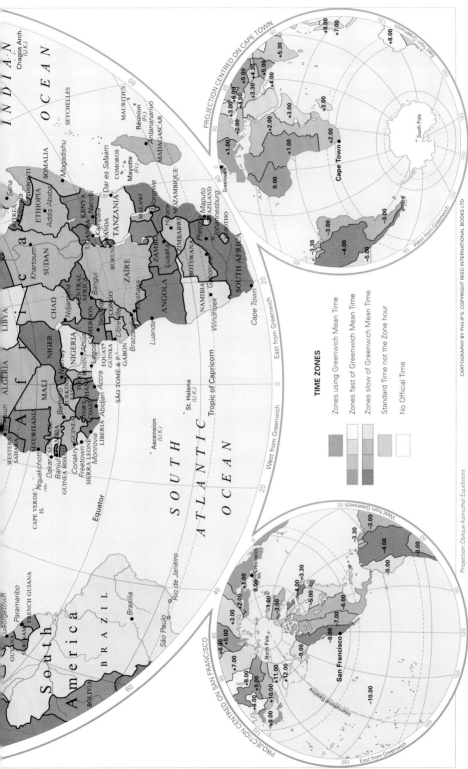

**TIME ZONES**

- Zones using Greenwich Mean Time
- Zones fast of Greenwich Mean Time
- Zones slow of Greenwich Mean Time
- Standard Time not the Zone hour
- No Official Time

PROJECTION CENTRED ON CAPE TOWN

PROJECTION CENTRED ON SAN FRANCISCO

Projection: Oblique Azimuthal Equidistant

CARTOGRAPHY BY PHILIP'S. COPYRIGHT REED INTERNATIONAL BOOKS LTD

INDIAN OCEAN

Chagos Arch.
(U.K.)

SEYCHELLES

MAURITIUS

Réunion
(Fr.)

Antananarivo

MADAGASCAR

Mayotte
(Fr.)

COMOROS

Dar es Salaam

Mogadishu

SOMALIA

DJIBOUTI

ETHIOPIA

Addis Ababa

Sana

ERITREA

Khartoum

SUDAN

KENYA

Nairobi

UGANDA

Kampala

TANZANIA

RWANDA

BURUNDI

MALAWI

Lilongwe

MOZAMBIQUE

ZAMBIA

Lusaka

Harare

ZIMBABWE

Maputo

Pretoria

SWAZILAND

Johannesburg

LESOTHO

Gaborone

BOTSWANA

SOUTH AFRICA

Cape Town

Windhoek

NAMIBIA

ANGOLA

Luanda

ZAIRE

Kinshasa

Brazzaville

CONGO

Libreville

GABON

EQUAT. GUINEA

SÃO TOMÉ & P.

CAMEROON

Yaoundé

CENTRAL AFRIC.

Bangui

Ndjamena

CHAD

NIGER

NIGERIA

Abuja

Lagos

BENIN

TOGO

GHANA

Accra

IVORY COAST

Abidjan

LIBERIA

Monrovia

Freetown

SIERRA LEONE

Conakry

GUINEA

GUINEA BISSAU

Banjul

Dakar

SENEGAL

GAMBIA

CAPE VERDE IS.

Nouakchott

MAURITANIA

MALI

Bamako

BURKINA

Niamey

Ouagadougou

ALGERIA

LIBYA

WESTERN SAHARA

Ascension
(U.K.)

St. Helena
(U.K.)

Tropic of Capricorn

Equator

SOUTH ATLANTIC OCEAN

SOUTH America

BRAZIL

BOLIVIA

Brasília

São Paulo

Rio de Janeiro

Paramaribo

SURINAM

FRENCH GUIANA

Georgetown

GUYANA

East from Greenwich

West from Greenwich

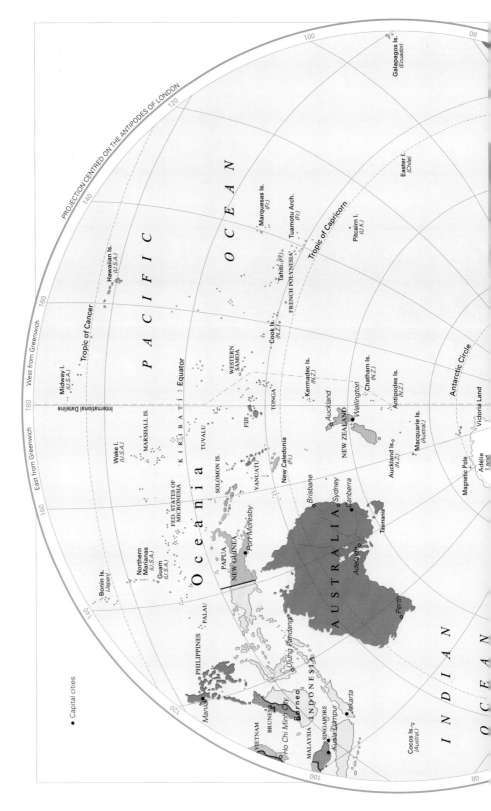

Galapagos Is.
(Ecuador)

PROJECTION CENTRED ON THE ANTIPODES OF LONDON

Easter I.
(Chile)

Marquesas Is.
(Fr.)

Tuamotu Arch.
(Fr.)

Tropic of Capricorn

Pitcairn I.
(U.K.)

PACIFIC OCEAN

Tahiti (Fr.)

FRENCH POLYNESIA

Tropic of Cancer

Cook Is.
(N.Z.)

Hawaiian Is.
(U.S.A.)

West from Greenwich

Antarctic Circle

Kermadec Is.
(N.Z.)

Chatham Is.
(N.Z.)

WESTERN
SAMOA

Victoria Land

Equator

International Dateline

Midway I.
(U.S.A.)

East from Greenwich

TONGA

FIJI

Auckland

Antipodes Is.
(N.Z.)

Wellington

Wake I.
(U.S.A.)

MARSHALL IS.

KIRIBATI

TUVALU

NEW ZEALAND

Macquarie Is.
(Austral.)

Magnetic Pole

Adélie
Land

Oceania

SOLOMON IS.

VANUATU

New Caledonia
(Fr.)

Auckland Is.
(N.Z.)

Bonin Is.
(Japan)

FED. STATES OF
MICRONESIA

Brisbane

Northern
Marianas
(U.S.A.)

Guam
(U.S.A.)

PAPUA
NEW GUINEA

Port Moresby

Sydney
Canberra

AUSTRALIA

Tasmania

PALAU

Adelaide

PHILIPPINES

Perth

INDIAN OCEAN

Ujung Pandang

Manila

Borneo

Jakarta

VIETNAM

BRUNEI

Ho Chi Minh City

INDONESIA

MALAYSIA

SINGAPORE

Kuala Lumpur

Cocos Is.
(Austral.)

• Capital cities

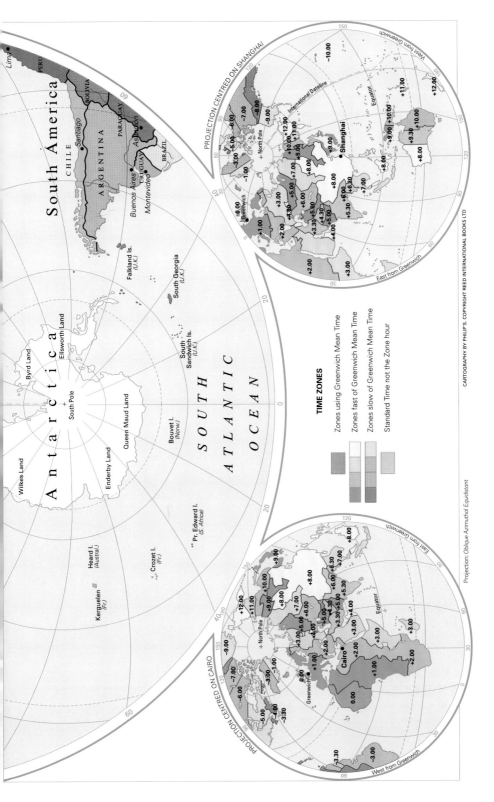

South America

Lima
PERU
BOLIVIA
Santiago
CHILE
ARGENTINA
PARAGUAY
Asunción
URUGUAY
Buenos Aires
Montevideo
BRAZIL

Falkland Is.
(U.K.)

South Georgia
(U.K.)

South
Sandwich Is.
(U.K.)

SOUTH
ATLANTIC
OCEAN

Bouvet I.
(Norw.)

Queen Maud Land

Enderby Land

** Pr. Edward I.
(S. Africa)

Crozet I.
(Fr.)

Heard I.
(Austral.)

Kerguelen
(Fr.)

Wilkes Land

Byrd Land

Ellsworth Land

Antarctica

South Pole

**PROJECTION CENTRED ON SHANGHAI**

Shanghai

International Dateline

North Pole

Greenwich

Equator

West from Greenwich

East from Greenwich

**PROJECTION CENTRED ON CAIRO**

North Pole

Greenwich

Cairo

Equator

East from Greenwich

West from Greenwich

**TIME ZONES**

Zones using Greenwich Mean Time

Zones fast of Greenwich Mean Time

Zones slow of Greenwich Mean Time

Standard Time not the Zone hour

CARTOGRAPHY BY PHILIP'S. COPYRIGHT REED INTERNATIONAL BOOKS LTD

Projection: Oblique Azimuthal Equidistant

**1: 20 000 000**

100   0   100   200   300   400   500 miles
100   0   200   400   600   800 km

10   11   12   13   14   15   16   17   18   19

*Hammerfest*

C

*Ob*

Murmansk

*Kiruna*

*White Sea*

Arkhangelsk

60

*Luleå*

*N. Dvina*

D

*Bothnia*

**FINLAND**

Kotlas

Perm   Nizhniy Tagil

*Vaasa*

*L. Onega*

Yekaterinburg

Tampere

Kirov

Chelyabinsk   55

Turku

Vyborg   *L. Ladoga*

Vologda

Ufa

Helsinki   ☐ ST. PETERSBURG

*Rybinsk Res.*

Yaroslavl   Kostroma

**R   U   S   S   I   A**

Kazan

Magnitogorsk

*kholm*

Tallinn

Ivanovo   Nizhniy Novgorod

E

*Sea*

**ESTONIA**

*L. Chudskoye*

**L A T V I A**

Riga

Simbirsk   Samara

Orenburg

Moscow ■

*W. Dvina*

**LITHUANIA**

Vitebsk

Smolensk

Tula

Penza

*Volga*

Uralsk

*Ural*

50

Kaunas

Mogilev

**K  A  Z  A  K  S  T  A  N**

*Kaliningrad (Russia)*

Vilnius

Minsk

Orel

Tambov

Saratov

**BELARUS**

Kursk

Voronezh

**A   N   D**

*Białystok*

Warsaw

Brest

Gomel

*Pripet*

Atyraū   F

Chernigov

Volgograd

Lublin

Zhitomir   Kiev   *Dnieper*

Kharkov

*Vistula*

Astrakhan   45

Kraków

Lvov

**U   K   R   A   I   N   E**

*Don*

*Caspian Sea*

**AK REP.**

*Dniester*

Dnepropetrovsk   Donetsk

*Bug*

Krivoy Rog   Zaporozhye   Taganrog

Rostov

Miskolc

**MOLDOVA**

Kherson

Stavropol

G

*dapest*

Debrecen

Kishinev

Nikolayev

Makhachkala

**RY**

Cluj-Napoca

Odessa

Krasnodar

**R   O   M   A   N   I   A**

Galati

Crimea

Timișoara

Brașov

Ploiești

Sevastopol

*Black   Sea*

**GEORGIA**

Tbilisi

**AZERBAIJAN**

Baku   40

Belgrade

Bucharest

Constanța

**ARMENIA**

**SERBIA**

*Danube*

Varna

Yerevan

*Araks*

Niš

**OSLAVIA**

**BULGARIA**

Sofia

Samsun

Erzurum

Tabriz   H

Skopje   Plovdiv

*Bosporus*

**MACEDONIA**

Thessaloníki

☐ İSTANBUL

**T   U   R   K   E   Y**

Diyarbakır

*a*

**IRAN**

**NIA**

Bursa

Ankara

Erzurum

**GREECE**

Kayseri

**A   S   I   A**

İzmir

Konya

*Aegean Sea*

Adana

Aleppo

*Euphrates*

**IRAQ**

*Tigris*

Pátrai

Athens

Antalya

**SYRIA**

Baghdad   J

Rhodes

**CYPRUS**   Nicosia

45

20   10   *Crete*   11   30   12   35   13   14   15

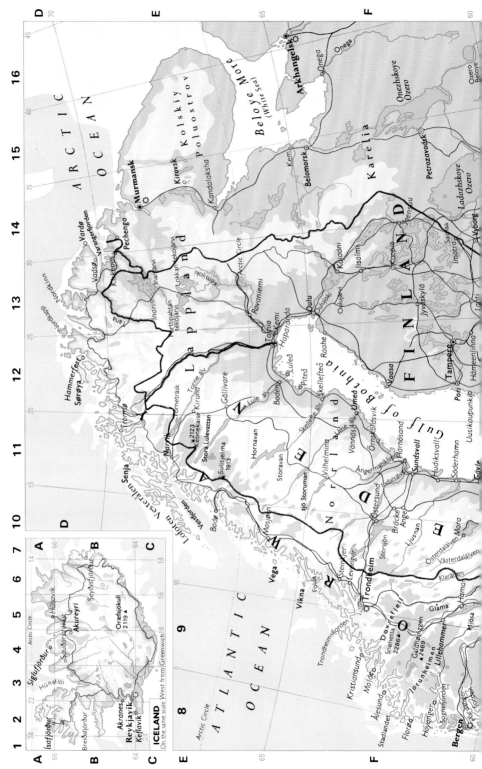

ARCTIC OCEAN

Beloye More
(White Sea)

Arkhangelsk

Onega
Onega
Onezhskoye
Ozero
Ozero
Beloye

Kolskiy Poluostrov

Kirovsk
Kandaloksha
Kem

Murmansk

Pechenga
Vardø
Vadsø
Varangerfjorden
Nordkinn

Belomorsk

Karelia

Petrozavodsk

Ladozhskoye
Ozero

Povenets

Vyborg

Kirkenes

Inari
Inarijärvi
Lokka tekojärvi
Porttipahtan tekojärvi
Ivalo

Kemijoki
Arctic Circle

L  a  p  p  l  a  n  d

Tana

Nordkapp

Hammerfest
Sørøya

Rovaniemi

Kuusamo
Suomussalmi

F  I  N  L  A  N  D

Tromsø
Senja

Torneträsk
Kiruna
2123
Kebnekaise 1913
Lulevatten
Stora
Sulitjelma

Torne älv

Gällivare

Tornio
Kemi
Haparanda

Oulu
Oulujoki
Oulujärvi

Kajaani

Iisalmi

Kuopio
Joensuu

Savonlinna
Imatra

Jyväskylä

Tahti

Hämeenlinna

Vaasa

Tampere

Pori
Uusikupunki

Narvik

Vesterålen
Lofoten

Luleå
Piteå

Boden
Lule älv

Hornavan

Storavan

Skellefteå
Raahe

Skellefte älv

Umeå

Vännäs
Vindeln

Örnsköldsvik

Härnösand

G  u  l  f    o  f    B  o  t  h  n  i  a

Ume älv

Vilhelmina
Ångermanälven

sjö Storuman

Sundsvall
Hudiksvall
Söderhamn

Gävle

Storjön
Bodø
Mosjøen
Vega

Vikna

Folda

Östersund
Indalsälven
Bräcke
Ånge
Ljusnan

Storsjön

N  o  r  r  l  a  n  d

Mora

Österdalälven
Västerdalälven

Steinkjer
Levanger

Trondheim

Vega

Kristiansund
Moldeo
Ålesund
Stadlandet
Florø

Trondheimsfjorden

Dovrefjell
Snøhetta
2286
Galdhøpiggen
2469
Jotunheimen
Lillehammer

Gudbrandsdalen

Glåma

Hamar

Mjøsa

Klaralven

Høyanger
Sognefjorden
Bergen
Hardanger
Skagerrak

E

N

D

O

M

R

W

A
B
C **ICELAND**
On the same scale. West from Greenwich 18

Ísafjörður
Siglufjörður
Húsavik
Akureyri
Seyðisfjörður
Saudárkrókur
Hünaflói
Breiðafjörður
Öræfajökull
2119
Akranes
Reykjavík
Keflavík

Arctic Circle

A  T  L  A  N  T  I  C    O  C  E  A  N

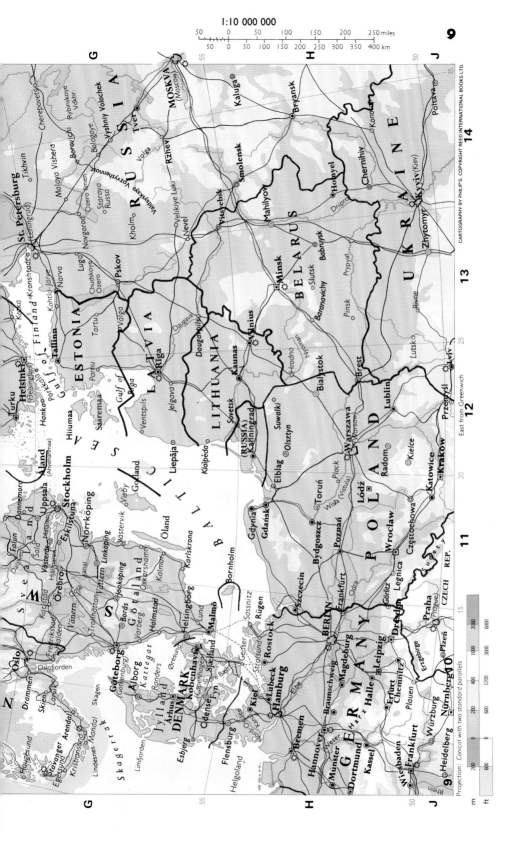

1:10 000 000

Projection: Conical with two standard parallels

East from Greenwich

**RUSSIA**

**MOSKVA** (Moscow)

Cherepovets
Rybinskoye
Vdkhr.
Rzhev
Volga
Kaluga
Bryansk
Konotop
POLTAVA

Tver
Vyshniy Volochek
Bologoye
Borovichi
Malaya Vishera
Staraya
Russa
Ozero Ilmen
Smolensk
Mahilyow
Hobyel
Chernihiv

St. Petersburg (Leningrad)
Kronshtadt
Tikhvin
Kokka
Narva
Pskov
Velikiye Luki
Nevel
Vitsebsk
Minsk
**BELARUS**
Babruysk
Pryp'yat
KYYIV (Kiev)

Turku
Helsinki (Helsingfors)
Gulf of Finland
Tallinn
**ESTONIA**
Tartu
**LATVIA**
Riga
**LITHUANIA**
Vilnius
Slutsk
Baranovichy
Pinsk
Rivne
Zhytomyr
**UKRAINE**
Lviv
Lutsk

Hanko
Hiiumaa
Saaremaa
Pärnu
Gulf of Riga
Daugava
Daugavpils
Hrodna
Kaunas
Białystok
Brest
Przemyśl

Åland (Ahvenanmaa)
Ventspils
Jelgava
Šiauliai
Sovetsk
Klaipėda
Suwałki
Lublin
Radom
Kielce

Stockholm
Uppsala
Gotland
Visby
Liepāja
Kaliningrad (RUSSIA)
Elbląg
Olsztyn
Warszawa (Warsaw)
**POLAND**
Kraków
Katowice

Örebro
Norrköping
Öland
Karlskrona
Gdynia
Gdańsk
Toruń
Łódź
Częstochowa
Wrocław

**SVERIGE** (Sweden)
Linköping
Jönköping
Kalmar
Bornholm
Bydgoszcz
Poznań
Legnica
Görlitz

Göteborg (Gothenburg)
Götaland
Halmstad
Helsingborg
Malmö
Szczecin
Frankfurt
Praha (Prague)
**CZECH REP.**

Oslo
Vänern
Borås
Varberg
Lund
Sjælland
Rügen
Rostock
**BERLIN**
Magdeburg
Dresden
Plzeň

**DENMARK**
København (Copenhagen)
Fyn
Stralsund
Lübeck
Hamburg
Leipzig
Chemnitz
Erzgebirge
Nürnberg

Esbjerg
Jylland
Århus
Odense
Kiel
Bremen
Braunschweig
Halle
Erfurt
Würzburg
Heidelberg

Flensburg
Helgoland
Hannover
Münster
Dortmund
Kassel
Wiesbaden
Frankfurt
**GERMANY**
Rhein

**BALTIC SEA**

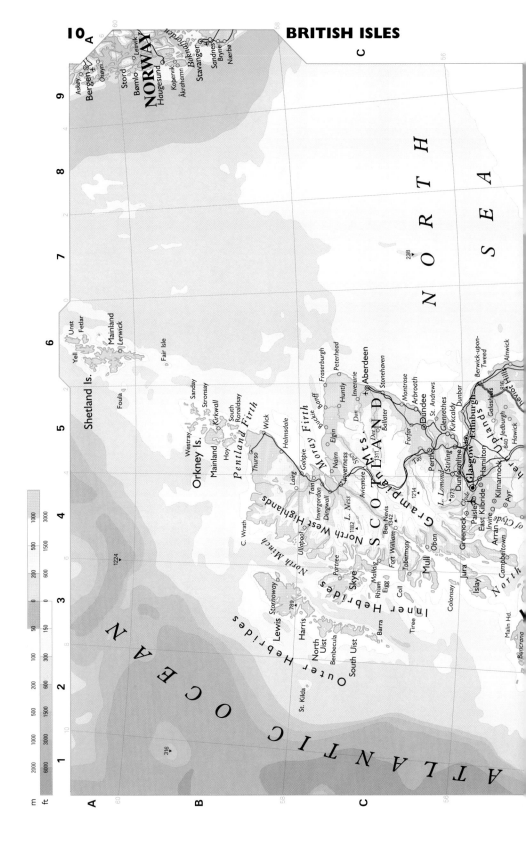

NORWAY
Bergen
Askøy
Osøyri
Stord
Bømlo
Kopervik
Åkrahamn
Haugesund
Stavanger
Sandnes
Bryne
Nærbø
Bokn
Hjelmeland
Leirvik

NORTH SEA

N O R T H

S E A

ATLANTIC OCEAN

A T L A N T I C   O C E A N

Shetland Is.
Unst
Fettar
Yell
Mainland
Lerwick
Fair Isle
Foula

Orkney Is.
Westray
Sanday
Stronsay
Kirkwall
South Ronaldsay
Mainland
Hoy
Pentland Firth

Wick
Helmsdale
Thurso
Golspie
Lairg
Tain
Invergordon
Dingwall
C. Wrath
Ullapool
Inverness
Nairn
Elgin
Aviemore
L. Ness
Ben Nevis 1342
Fort William
Spey
Huntly
Banff
Fraserburgh
Peterhead
Aberdeen
Stonehaven
Montrose
Arbroath
Dundee
St. Andrews
Forfar
Ballater
Dee
311
Don
Moray Firth
Grampian Mts.
SCOTLAND
North West Highlands
1182
1224
316
789
238

Stornoway
Lewis
Harris
North Uist
Benbecula
South Uist
Barra
St. Kilda
Outer Hebrides
North Minch
Skye
Portree
Rhum
Eigg
Coll
Tiree
Mallaig
Tobermory
Oban
Mull
Colonsay
Jura
Islay
Inner Hebrides

Perth
Stirling
Dunfermline
Glenrothes
Kirkcaldy
Edinburgh
Dunbar
Galashiels
Jedburgh
Hawick
840
Berwick-upon-Tweed
Alnwick
Cheviot Hills
316
Southern Uplands
Glasgow
Paisley
Greenock
Clyde
L. Lomond
973
East Kilbride
Hamilton
Kilmarnock
Irvine
Ayr
Arran
Campbeltown
Firth of Clyde
North
Malin Hd.
Buncrana

Tay
1214
1342

m    ft
2000  6000
1000  3000
500   1500
200   600
100   300
50    150
0     0
0     0
50    150
200   600
500   1500
1000  3000

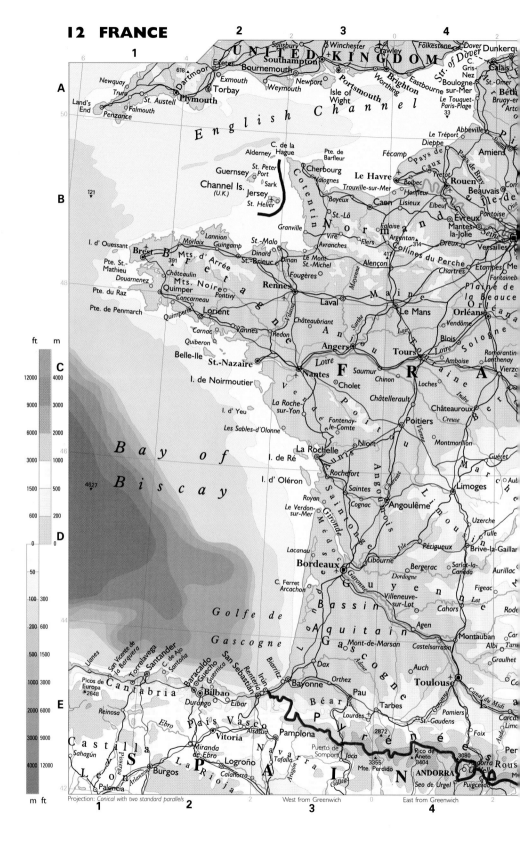

**UNITED KINGDOM**

Newquay · Truro · Dartmoor · 618 · Exeter · Bournemouth · Salisbury · Winchester · Crawley · Folkestone · Dover · Dunkerqu

Land's End · St. Austell · Plymouth · Torbay · Exmouth · Weymouth · Newport · Portsmouth · Brighton · Worthing · Eastbourne · sur-Mer · C. Gris-Nez · Boulogne- · Calais

Penzance · Falmouth · Isle of Wight · Le Touquet-Paris-Plage · 33 · Bruay-la-Arto · Béth

**English** Channel

121 · C. de la Hague · Alderney · Pte. de Barfleur · Fécamp · Le Tréport · Dieppe · Pays de Caux · Amiens · Abbeville

Channel Is. (U.K.) · St. Peter Port · Guernsey · Sark · Cherbourg · Valognes · Trouville-sur-Mer · Le Havre · Bolbec · Yvetot · Rouen · Beauvais

Jersey · St. Helier · Bayeux · Caen · Honfleur · Elbeuf · Evreux · Pontoise · Île-de- · Oise

I. d' Ouessant · Granville · St.-Lô · Vire · Lisieux · Falaise · Argentan · Dreux · Versailles · Mantes-la-Jolie · Seine

Pte. St-Mathieu · Brest · Morlaix · Lannion · Guingamp · St.-Malo · Dinard · Avranches · Le Mont St.-Michel · Flers · 314 · Collines du Perche · Étampes · Me

Douarnenez · Mts. d'Arrée · 391 · St.-Brieuc · Dinan · Fougères · Alençon · 417 · Chartres · Fontaineb

Pte. du Raz · Châteaulin · Mts. Noire · Pontivy · Rennes · Laval · Le Mans · Orléans · Vendôme · Plaine de la Beauce · Orléan

Pte. de Penmarch · Quimper · Concarneau · Quimperlé · Lorient · Châteaubriant · Sarthe · Maine · Blois · Sologne

Carnac · Vannes · Redon · Angers · Saumur · Tours · Amboise · Romorantin-Lanthenay · Vierzo

Belle-Île · St.-Nazaire · Quiberon · Nantes · Cholet · Chinon · Loches · Châteauroux · Ber

I. de Noirmoutier · Châtellerault · Indre

I. d' Yeu · La Roche-sur-Yon · Fontenay-le-Comte · Poitiers · Vienne · Creuse

Les Sables-d'Olonne · Niort · Montmorillon · Guéret

**Bay of** · La Rochelle · I. de Ré · Rochefort · Aunis · Angoumois · Mar

**Biscay** · 4627 · I. d' Oléron · Saintes · Cognac · Angoulême · Limoges · Uzerche

Royan · Médoc · Charente · Périgueux · Brive-la-Gaillar · Tulle

Le Verdon-sur-Mer · Libourne · Sarlat-la- · Aurillac

Lacanau · Bordeaux · Dordogne · Bergerac · Canéda · Figeac · Rode

C. Ferret · Arcachon · Garonne · Guyen · Villeneuve-sur-Lot · Cahors · Lot

**Golfe de** · Bassin · Agen · Montauban · Albi · Tarn

**Gascogne** · Aquitain · Mont-de-Marsan · Castelsarrasin · Graulhet · Ca

Llanes · San Vicente de la Barquera · Torrelavega · Santander · C. de Ajo · Santoña · Baracaldo · San Sebastián · Biarritz · Dax · Adour · Auch · Toulouse · Canal du Midi

Picos de Europa · 2648 · Cantabria · Bilbao · Guecho · Guernica · Irún · Renteria · Bayonne · Orthez · Pau · Tarbes · Pamiers · Carca

Reinosa · Durango · Eibar · Alsasua · Pamplona · Béarn · Lourdes · St.-Gaudens · Foix · Lim

Ebro · País Vasco · Vitoria · Navarra · 2872 · Pyréné · Per

Sahagún · Miranda de Ebro · Logroño · Tafalla · Puerto de Somport · Jaca · Rico de Aneto · 3404 · 3080 · Rous

Castilla · León · Burgos · Calahorra · La Rioja · A · Aragón · 3355 · Mte. Perdido · ANDORRA · Andorra la Vella · Puigcerda

León · Palencia · Arlanzón · Pisuerga · Gállego · Seo de Urgel · N

| ft | m |
|---|---|
| 12000 | 4000 |
| 9000 | 3000 |
| 6000 | 2000 |
| 3000 | 1000 |
| 1500 | 500 |
| 600 | 200 |
| 0 | 0 |

| m | ft |
|---|---|
| 0 | 0 |
| 50 | |
| 100 | 300 |
| 200 | 600 |
| 500 | 1500 |
| 1000 | 3000 |
| 2000 | 6000 |
| 3000 | 9000 |
| 4000 | 12000 |

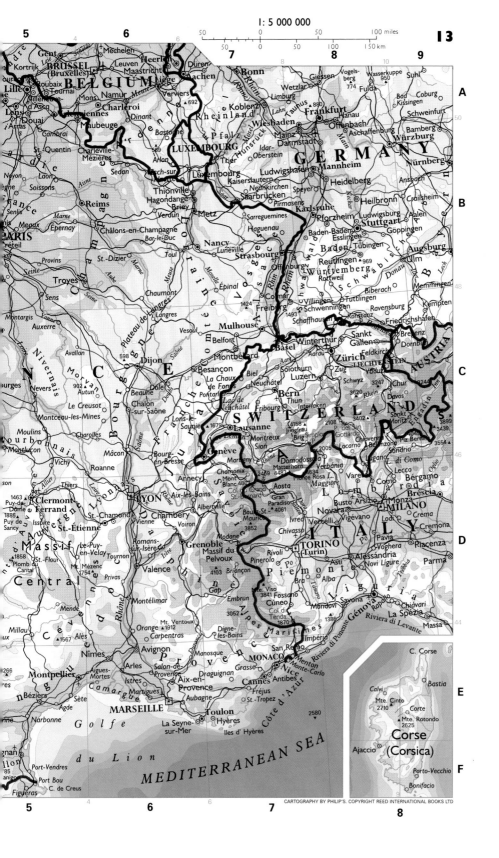

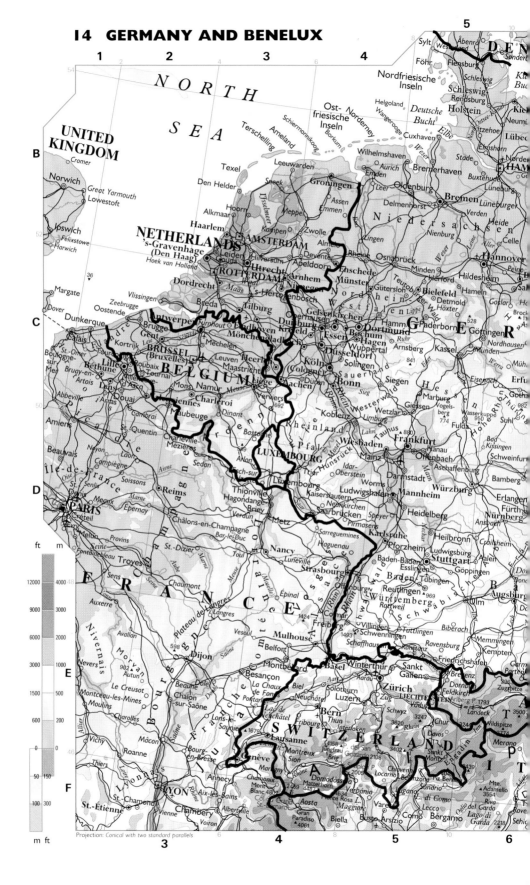

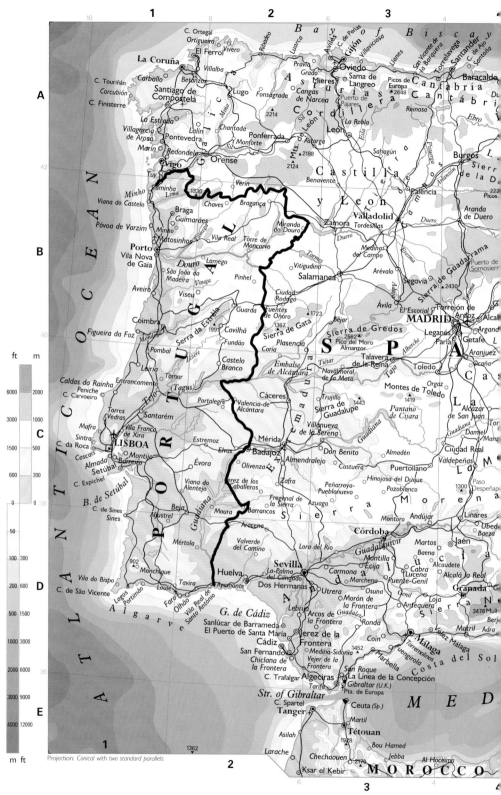

**18 SPAIN AND PORTUGAL**

Bay of Biscay

**ATLANTIC OCEAN**

C. Ortegal
Ortigueira
El Ferrol
Vivero
C. de Peñas
Avilés
Llanes
San Vicente de la Barquera
Santander
C. de Ajo
Santoña

La Coruña
Carballo
Betanzos
Villalba
Luarca
Ribadeo
Gijón
Villaviciosa
Torrelavega

C. Touriñán
Corcubión
C. Finisterre
Santiago de Compostela
Lugo
Fonsagrada
Pravia
Grado
Mieres
Oviedo
Sama de Langreo
Cangas de Narcea
Picos de Europa
Puerto de Pajares
▲2648
Cantabria
Cordillera
Cantábrica
Baracaldo
Reinosa

La Estrada
Chantada
▲2214
▲
Minho
Sil
Ponferrada
Astorga
León
La Robla
Sahagún
Ebro
Burgos
Sierra de la D

Villagarcía de Arosa
Pontevedra
Marín
Redondela
Lalín
Monforte
Sil
Orense
▲2188
▲2124
Benavente
Castilla
Palencia
Aranda de Duero
222

Vigo
Tuy
Galicia
Verín
y León
Valladolid
Tordesillas
Duero
Picos

Camiña
Minho
Lima
1330
Chaves
Bragança
Miranda do Douro
Zamora
Medina del Campo
Duero
Tresma
Segovia
Sierra de Guadarrama
Puerto de Somosierr

Viana do Castelo
Braga
Guimarães
Vila Real
Torre de Moncorvo
Vitigudino
Salamanca
Arévalo
Ávila
▲2430

Póvoa de Varzim
Matosinhos
Minho
Douro
Lamego
Pinhel
Ciudad Rodrigo
Fuentes de Oñoro
Segovia
El-Escorial
Torrejón de Ardoz
Alca

Porto
Vila Nova de Gaia
São João da Madeira
Vouga
Viseu
Guarda
▲1723
Béjar
MADRID
Leganés
Argand

Aveiro
Douro
PORTUGAL
1367
Covilhã
Sierra de Gata
Coria
Plasencia
Pico del Moro Almanzor
▲2592
Sierra de Gredos
Tiétar
Parla
Getafe
SPA

Coimbra
Figueira da Foz
Serra da Estrela
1991
Fundão
Castelo Branco
Navalmoral de la Mata
Talavera de la Reina
Tajo
Toledo
Aranjuez
Ocaña

Leiria
Tomar
(Tagus)
Embalse de Alcántara
Montes de Toledo
Orgaz
CA

Caldas da Rainha
Peniche
C. Carvoeiro
Entroncamento
Tejo
Portalegre
Valencia de Alcántara
Cáceres
Trujillo
▲1443
▲1419
Alcázar de San Juan

Torres Vedras
Santarém
Vila Franca de Xira
Estremoz
Elvas
Mérida
Villanueva de la Serena
Sierra de Guadalupe
Pantano de Cíjara
Guadiana
Damiel
Tor

Mafra
Sintra
C. da Roca
Cascais
LISBOA
Almada
Barreiro
Montijo
Setúbal
Évora
Olivenza
Badajoz
Don Benito
Almendralejo
Castuera
Almadén
Ciudad Real
Valdepeñas

C. Espichel
B. de Setúbal
C. de Sines
Sines
Beja
Aljustrel
Viana do Alentejo
Jerez de los Caballeros
Zafra
Peñarroya-Pueblonuevo
Hinojosa del Duque
Pozoblanco
Puertollano
1300
Paso Despeñap
M

Guadiana
Moura
Barrancos
Fregenal de la Sierra
Azuaga
Sierra
Morena

Mértola
Valverde del Camino
Aracena
Lora del Río
Montoro
Andújar
Linares
Úbed
Baeza

Monchique
902
Huelva
La Palma del Condado
Carmona
Écija
Montilla
Baena
Córdoba
Guadalquivir
Martos
Jaén
Lucena
Cabra
Alcaudete
Alcalá la Real

Vila do Bispo
C. de São Vicente
Loulé
Tavira
Ayamonte
Dos Hermanas
Utrera
Morón de la Frontera
Osuna
Marchena
Puente-Genil
Genil
Loja
Granada
3478
Sierra

Algarve
Lagos
Portimão
Faro
Olhão
Vila Real de Santo António
Sevilla
Lebrija
Arcos de la Frontera
Guadalete
Ronda
Coín
Antequera
Velez Málaga
Berje

G. de Cádiz
Sanlúcar de Barrameda
El Puerto de Santa María
Cádiz
San Fernando
Chiclana de la Frontera
Jerez de la Frontera
Medina-Sidonia
Vejer de la Frontera
1452
Marbella
Torremolinos
Fuengirola
Málaga
Costa del Sol
Matril

C. Trafalgar
Tarifa
Algeciras
San Roque
La Línea de la Concepción
Gibraltar (U.K.)
Pta. de Europa

Str. of Gibraltar
C. Spartel
Tanger
Ceuta (Sp.)
MED

Asilah
Martil
Tétouan
1928
Bou Hamed

1362
Larache
Chechaouen
▲2170
Jebba
Al Hoceima

Ksar el Kebir
**MOROCCO**

ft | m
---|---
6000 | 2000
3000 | 1000
1500 | 500
600 | 200
0 | 0
 | 
50 | 
100 | 300
200 | 600
500 | 1500
1000 | 3000
2000 | 6000
3000 | 9000
4000 | 12000
m ft |

42
40
38
36

10 8 6 4

1 2 3

Projection: Conical with two standard parallels

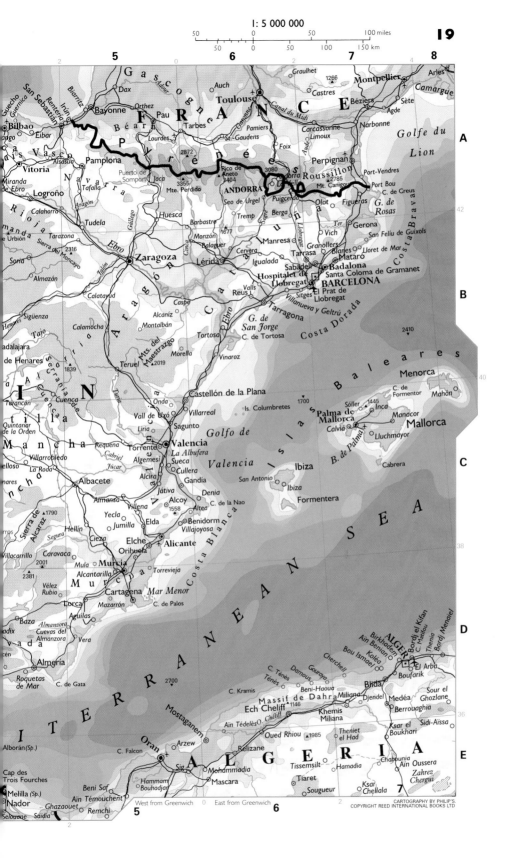

**I: 5 000 000**

50    0    50    100 miles

50  0  50   100   150 km

**5**      **6**      **7**      **8**

G   a   s   c   o   g   n   e

Graulhet   1266   **Montpellier**   Arles

Auch   Castres   **Camargue**

San Sebastián   Dax   **Toulouse**   Béziers   Sète

Biarritz   Bayonne   Orthez   Pau   Tarbes   Canal du Midi   Agde

Irún   F   R   A   N   C   E

Bilbao   Béarn   Pamiers   Carcassonne   Narbonne   **Golfe du**

Eibar   Lourdes   St.-Gaudens   Limoux   **Lion**

Vitoria   Alsasua   Pamplona   P   y   r   é   n   é   e   s   Foix   Perpignan   Port-Vendres

Navarra   2872   Rico de   3080   Roussillon   2785   Port Bou

Miranda   Tafalla   Puerto de   Aneto   Mt. Canigou   C. de Creus

de Ebro   Logroño   Somport   Jaca   8404   **ANDORRA**   Olot   Figueras   G. de

Rioja   Aragón   3855   Mte. Perdido   Seo de Urgel   Puigcerdá   Rosas

Calahorra   Mte. Perdido   Berga   Olot   Gerona   Costa

manda   Tudela   Huesca   Tremp   Vich   San Feliu de Guixols   Brava

de Urbión   Sierra del Moncayo   Barbastro   1677   Manresa   Granollers   Blanes   Lloret de Mar

Soria   2316   Tarazona   Monzón   Cervera   Tarrasa   Mataró

Almazán   Ebro   Zaragoza   Balaguer   Igualada   Sabadell   **Badalona**

Calatayud   Lérida   Reus   **Hospitalet de**   Santa Coloma de Gramanet

Sigüenza   Caspe   Valls   **Llobregat**   **BARCELONA**

adalajara   Calamocha   Alcañiz   Villanueva y Geltrú   El Prat de Llobregat

de Henares   Montalbán   G. de   Sitges   Costa

1839   Tortosa   San Jorge   2410

Tajo   Morella   C. de Tortosa   Costa Dorada

Teruel   2019   Vinaroz

I   N   Castellón de la Plana   B   a   l   e   a   r   e   s

Tarancón   Cuenca   Onda   Villarreal   1700   C. de   **Menorca**

Cuenca   Vall de Uxó   Is. Columbretes   Formentor   Mahón

tilla   Liria   Sagunto   **Palma de**   Sóller   1445   Inca

Quintanar   Requena   Cabriel   **Mallorca**   Calviá   Manacor

de la Orden   Torrente   **Valencia**   Golfo de   Caliá   **Mallorca**

M   a   n   c   h   a   Algemesí   Júcar   Sueca   I   s   l   a   s   Lluchmayor   B. de   Cabrera

Villarrobledo   La Albufera   Cullera   **Valencia**   Palma

lloso   La Roda   Alcira   Gandía   Ibiza

nares   Albacete   Játiva   San Antonio   Ibiza

Almansa   Denia   Formentera

Sierra de   Yecla   Alcoy   C. de la Nao

Alcaraz   1790   1558   Altea

Hellín   Jumilla   Elda   Benidorm

Cieza   Villajoyosa

Villacarrillo   Caravaca   Elche   **Alicante**

2001   Mula   **Murcia**   Orihuela   Costa Blanca

2381   Alcantarilla   Torrevieja

Vélez   M   u   r   c   i   a   Torrevieja

Rubio   Lorca   Cartagena   Mar Menor

Baza   Aguilas   Mazarrón   C. de Palos

adix   Almanzora   M   E   D   I   T   E   R   R   A   N   E   A   N   S   E   A

v   a   d   a   Cuevas del   Vera

cen   Almanzora

Almería   2700

Roquetas   C. de Gata   C. Kramis

de Mar   Cherchell

I   T   E   R   R   Damous   Gouraya   **ALGER**   Bordj el Kifán

Mostaganem   C. Ténès   Beni-Haoua   Kolea   El Arba

Ech Cheliff   Ténès   Boufarik

Alborán (Sp.)   Massif de Dahra   1146   Miliana   **Blida**   Sour el

Ain Tédelès   O. Chéliff   Djendel   Medéa   Ghozlane

Cap des   Oran   Arzew   Oued Rhiou   1985   Khemis   Berrouaghia

Trois Fourches   Relizane   Miliana   Ksar el   Sidi-Aïssa

Melilla (Sp.)   Sig   **A   L   G   E   R   I   A**   Tissemsilt   Hamadia   Boukhari

Nador   Mohammadia   Chabounia   Ain Oussera

Beni Saf   Hammam   Mascara   Tiaret   Zahrez

Ghazaouet   Bouhadjan   Sougueur   Ksar   Chergui

Saidía   Aïn Témouchent   Remchi   Chellala

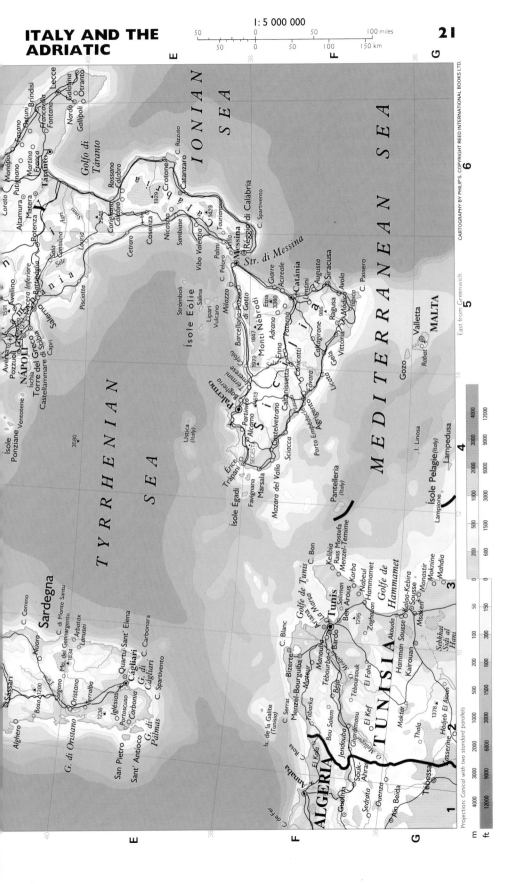

1: 5 000 000

Projection: Conical with two standard parallels

East from Greenwich

## TYRRHENIAN SEA

## IONIAN SEA

## MEDITERRANEAN SEA

Golfo di Táranto

Str. di Messina

Sardegna

MALTA

TUNISIA

ALGERIA

Isole Eólie

Isole Pelagie (Italy)

Golfe de Tunis

Golfe de Hammamet

NÁPOLI

Palermo

Catánia

Tunis

Cagliari

Sássari

m ft

4000  12000
3000  9000
2000  6000
1000  3000
500   1500
200   600
0     0

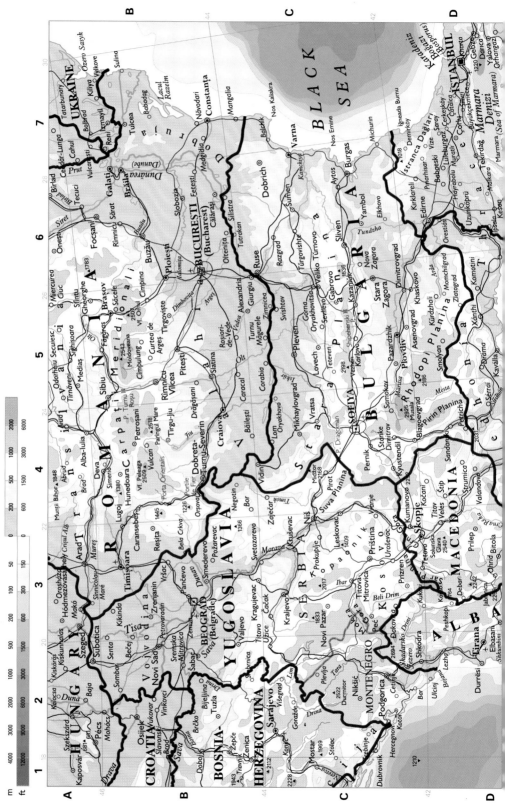

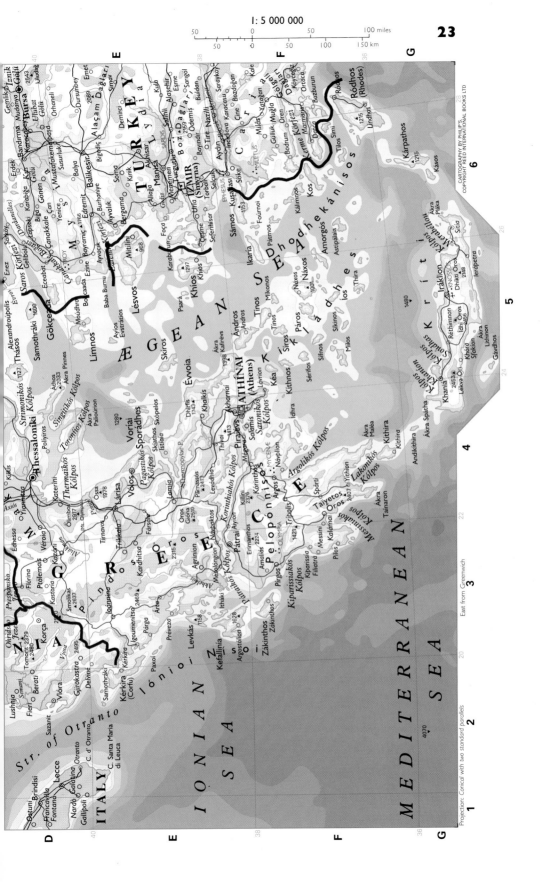

1: 5 000 000

50    0    50    100 miles
50    0    50    100    150 km

East from Greenwich

Projection: Conical with two standard parallels

ITALY

Brindisi
Ostuni
Francavilla
Fontana
Lecce
Galatina
Nardo
Gallipoli
Otranto
C. Santa Maria
di Leuca

ALBANIA
Lushnja
Fieri
Semuni
Berati 2480
Tomorrit 2495
Vlóra
Delvinë
Gjirokastra
Smollkas 2637
Tepelene
Vjosë

Str. of Otranto

Sazani

IONIAN SEA

Kérkira (Corfu)
Samothráki
Paxoi

Ióni oi

Leukás
Préveza
Árta
Párga
Igoumenitsa
Ioánnina
1628
1158
Zákinthos
Zákinthos
Kefallinía
Argostólion

MEDITERRANEAN SEA

4070

GREECE

Ohridsko J. Jezer
Prespansko
Korça
Florina
Kastoria 2480
2469
Ptolemais
Kozáni
2512
Veroia
Édhessa
Axios
Yiannitsa
Náoussa
Olimbos (Mt. Olympus) 2917
Katerini
Servia
Kardhitsa
Tirnavos
Tríkkala
Lárisa
Vólos
2315
Ossa 1978
Lamía
Ágrinion
Mesolóngion
Naupaktos
Pátrai Aíyion
Amaliás
Pírgos
OLYMPIA
Filiátra

Thessaloniki

Pindhos Óros

Erimanthos 2224
Trípolis
Sparti
Taïyetos Óros 2407
Kalamái
Pilos
Messini
Kiparissía

Peloponnísos

Olympus

Strimonikós Kólpos
Singitikós Kólpos
Sithonía
Toronikós Kólpos
Thermaïkós Kólpos
Pagastikós Kólpos

Thásos
1127
Athos 2033
Akra Pinnes
Polívyros

Athos

Samothráki

Vóriai Sporádhes
Skíathos
Skópelos
Istiáa
1280
Évvoia
Khalkís
Dhírfis 1743
Levádhia
Thívai
413
Megára
Kórinthos
MYCENE
Argos
Návplion
Argolikós Kólpos
Lakonikós Kólpos
Yíthion
Akra Maléa
Kithira
Kithira

ATHINAI (Athens)
Peiraiévs
Salamis
Lávrion
Aíyina
Saronikós Kólpos
Andikíthira

Thermopílai-P.
Akra Kafirévs

Skíros

Voïiai

ÆGEAN SEA

Limnos
Ayios Evstrátios

Lésvos
Mitilíni
968

Psará
Khíos
1297
Khíos

Kikládhes

Ándros
Andros
Kéa
Kíthnos
Kíthnos
Síros
Tínos
Tínos
Míkonos
Náxos
Páros
Náxos 1001
Íos
Amorgós
Astipálaia
Síkinos
Thíra
Sérifos
Sífnos
Mílos

Ikaría
Fournoí
Sámos
1153
Pátmos
Kálimnos
Leros
Kos

Dhodhekánisos

Kos
Sími
Tílos
Astipálaia

TURKEY

Gemlik Iznik
İznik Gölü 2543
Bandirma Mudanya Bursa
Karacabey
Uludağ
Susurluk
Orhaneli
M. Kemalpaşa
İnegöl
Gönen
Biga
Yenice
Can
Balikesir
Soma
Bergama
Ayvalık
Edremit Körfezi
Edremit
Burhaniye
Ayvacık
Bayramiç
Ezine
TROY
Çanakkale
Çan
Gelibolu (Dardanelles)
Eceabat
Boğazı (Dardanelles)
Kilitbahir
Gökçeada

MYSIA

AEOLIS

Alaçam Dağları
Demirci
Simav
Kula
Eşme
Selendi
İzmir (Smyrna)
Menemen
Turgutlu
Manisa
Salihli
Alaşehir
Boz Dağları 2159
Ödemis
Tire Nazilli
Sarıgöl
Buldan
Nazilli
Aydın
Germencik
İnci İrova
Söke
MILETUS
Kuşadası
EPHESUS
Seferihisar
Torbalı
Selçuk
Çeşme
Foça

LYDIA

CARIA

Karacasu
Çine
Tavas
Muğla
Yatağan
Ören
Milás
Gökova Körfezi
Bodrum
Güllük
Marmaris
Datça
Köyceğiz
Ortaca
Bozburun

Ródhos (Rhodes)
Rhodos
Líndhos
1215

Kárpathos
1215
Kásos

KRÍTI

Kólpos Mérabéllou
Sitía
Iráklion
KNOSSOS
Dhíkti Óros 2148
Lithínon
Ierápetra
Akra Plaka
Akra Líthinon
Akra Síderos

Khaniá
Réthimnon
Ídhi Óros 2456
Léfka Óri 2453
Akra Spátha
Soúdhas
Kólpos Kíssamou
Kólpos Khanion
Gávdhos
Khorá Sfakíon

E G E A N   S E A

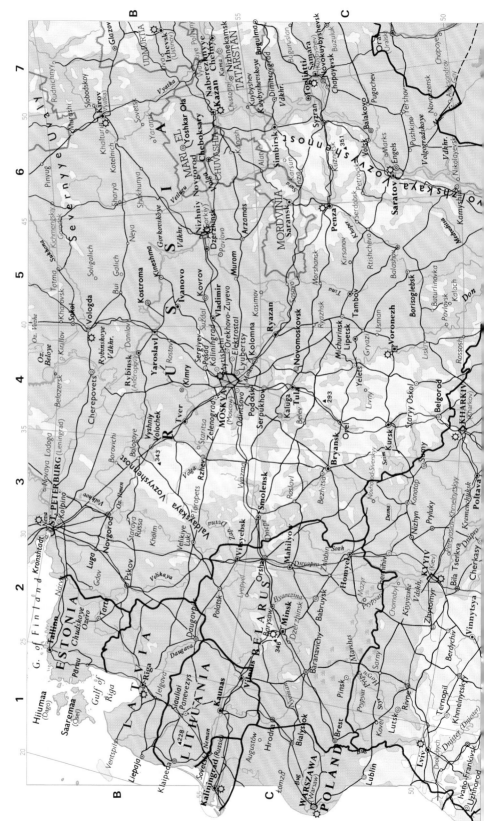

1: 10 000 000

Projection: Conical with two standard parallels 30    35 East from Greenwich

CARTOGRAPHY BY PHILIP'S. COPYRIGHT REED INTERNATIONAL BOOKS LTD.

1. Karachey-Cherkessia
2. Kabardino-Balkaria
3. North Ossetia
4. Ingushetia

D

ATLANTIC OCEAN

GREENLAND

ICELAND

Arctic Circle

Svalbard

ARCTIC

Barents Sea

Novaya Zemlya

Kara Sea

UNITED KINGDOM

NORWAY

50

North Sea

White Sea

Murmansk

Vorkuta

Salekhard

Yenisei

R U

LONDON

SWEDEN

FINLAND

Arkhangelsk

Ob

50

E

FRANCE

PARIS

E

GERMANY

Berlin

Prague

Vienna

Warsaw

ST. PETERSBURG

MOSCOW

Nizhniy Novgorod

Perm

Yekaterinburg

Irtysh

Kazan

Ufa

Chelyabinsk

Omsk

Pavlodar

40

ITALY

Rome

o p e

U K R A I N E

Belgrade

Odessa

Danube

Volga

Samara

Rostov

KAZAKSTAN

Karaganda

Semey

F

Mediterranean Sea

Athens

B l a c k  S e a

ISTANBUL

Bursa

Izmir

Konya

Ankara

GEORGIA

Tbilisi

Yerevan

ARMENIA

AZERBAIJAN

Baku

Caspian Sea

Aral Sea

Syr Dar'ya

L. Balkhash

30

Don

Volgograd

Astrakhan

UZBEKISTAN

Tashkent

Bishkek

Alma Ata

KYRGYZSTAN

SINK

Nicosia

CYPRUS

Beirut

LEBANON

Adana

Aleppo

TURKEY

Mosul

Tabriz

TURKMENISTAN

Samarkand

TAJIKISTAN

Kashi

UIG

G

LIBYA

Alexandria

ISRAEL

CAIRO

Damascus

SYRIA

Euphrates

Ashkhabad

Dushanbe

Hotan

EGYPT

Suez

Jerusalem

Amman

JORDAN

Baghdad

IRAQ

Basra

TEHRĀN

IRAN

Mashhad

Herāt

Kābul

Islamabad

JAMMU & KASHMIR

Lahore

T

20

Nile

Esfahān

KUWAIT

Kuwait

The Gulf

Shirāz

Zāhedān

Qandahār

AFGHANISTAN

Faisalabad

PAKISTAN

DELHI

New Delhi

NE

H

Aswān

Port Sudan

SAUDI

Jedda

Medina

Mecca

Riyadh

ARABIA

BAHRAIN

Al Manāmah

QATAR

Doha

Abu Dhabi

UNITED ARAB EMIRATES

G. of Oman

Muscat

KARACHI

Indus

Jaipur

Lucknow

Kanpur

Varanasi

I N D I

10

SUDAN

Khartoum

Red Sea

ERITREA

OMAN

Ahmadabad

Vadodara

Surat

Indore

Bhopal

Nagpur

BOMBAY

Pune

Hyderabad

DJIBOUTI

Sana'

YEMEN

Aden

G. of Aden

Socotra (Yemen)

A r a b i a n

S e a

Lakshadweep Is. (India)

J

A

Addis Ababa

ETHIOPIA

SOMALI

Bangalore

MADR

0

UGANDA

L. Victoria

KENYA

REP.

a

Mogadishu

Equator

I N D I A N

Madurai

Colombo

SRI L

MALDIVES

Male

O C

K

ZAÏRE

Nairobi

TANZANIA

Mombasa

10

Dar es Salaam

SEYCHELLES

Victoria

L

ZAMBIA

MALAWI

Aldabra Is. (Seychelles)

Amirante Is. (Seychelles)

Chagos Arch. (U.K.)

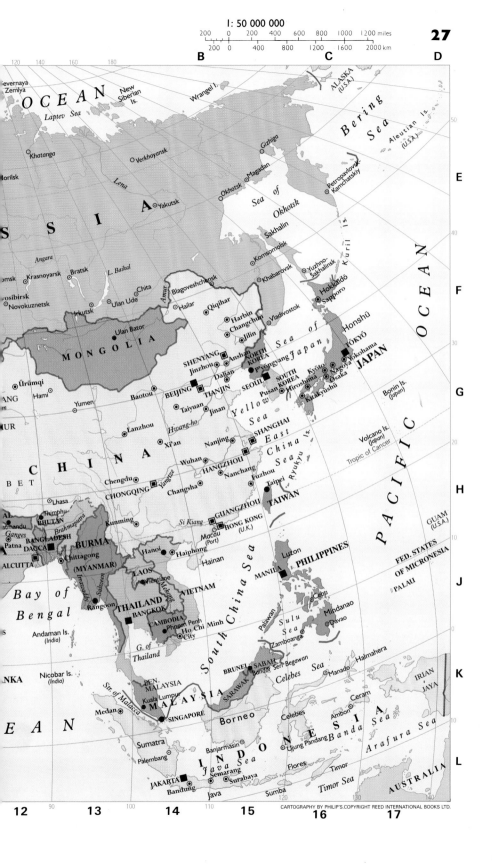

200   0   200   400   600   800   1000   1200 miles
200   0   400   800   1200   1600   2000 km

B   C   D

120   140   160   180

O C E A N

evernaya
Zemlya

New
Siberian
Is.

Wrangel I.

ALASKA
(U.S.A.)

Laptev Sea

Bering

Sea

E   50

Khatanga

Verkhoyansk

Okhotsk Magadan

Aleutian Is.
(U.S.A.)

lorilsk

Lena

Yakutsk

Sea of

Okhotsk

Petropavlovsk-
Kamchatskiy

40

S   S   I   A

Angara

Bratsk

Komsomolsk

Sakhalin

Kuril Is.

OCEAN

F

omsk   Krasnoyarsk

L. Baikal

Khabarovsk

Yuzhno-
Sakhalinsk

osibirsk   Irkutsk   Ulan Ude   Chita

Amur

Blagoveshchensk

Hokkaido   30

Novokuznetsk

Hailar

Qiqihar

Harbin

Vladivostok

Sapporo

Honshū

Ulan Bator

Changchun

Sea of

TŌKYŌ

M O N G O L I A

Jilin

Japan

Yokohama   JAPAN   G

Ürümqi   Hami

SHENYANG   Anshan

NORTH
KOREA

Kyōto

Nagoya   30

Jinzhou

Pyongyang

Osaka

Yumen

Baotou

Dalian

SEOUL

Pusan

Hiroshima

ANG

BEIJING   TIANJIN

SOUTH
KOREA

Kitakyūshū

Bonin Is.
(Japan)

Lanzhou

Taiyuan

Jinan

Yellow

Kyūshū

UR

Hwang-ho

Sea

Volcano Is.
(Japan)

20

C H I N A

Xi'an

Nanjing

SHANGHAI

East

Tropic of Cancer

BET

Chengdu

Wuhan

HANGZHOU

China

Ryukyu Is.

H

Lhasa

CHONGQING

Yangtze

Nanchang

Sea

Fuzhou

AL   Thimphu

Changsha

Taipei

Volcano Is.

atmandu   BHUTAN

Brahmaputra

Kunming

GUANGZHOU

TAIWAN   10

Ganges

Si Kiang

BANGLADESH

HONG KONG

GUAM
(U.S.A.)

Patna

DACCA

Macau
(Port)

(U.K.)

ALCUTTA

Chittagong

Hanoi

Haiphong

Hainan

Luzon

FED. STATES   J

BURMA

LAOS

PHILIPPINES

OF MICRONESIA

(MYANMAR)

MANILA

PALAU

Bay   of

Irrawaddy

Vientiane

VIETNAM

Andaman Is.
(India)

Rangoon

THAILAND

Mekong

South

Cebu

Bengal

BANGKOK

CAMBODIA

China Sea

Mindanao

Phnom Penh

Davao

G. of

Ho Chi Minh
City

Sulu

NKA   Nicobar Is.
(India)

Thailand

Palawan

Sea

Zamboanga

IRIAN   K

BRUNEI   SABAH

Celebes

Manado

Halmahera

JAYA

PEN.
MALAYSIA

Bandar Seri Begawan

Sea

Str. of Malacca

SARAWAK

Ceram

Medan

Kuala Lumpur

Celebes

Ambon

EA N   MALAYSIA

Borneo

I   N   D   O   N   E   S   I   A   10

SINGAPORE

Banda

Sumatra

Banjarmasin

Ujung Pandang   Sea

Arafura Sea

Palembang

Java Sea

Flores

Timor

L

JAKARTA

Semarang

AUSTRALIA

Bandung

Surabaya

Sumba

Timor Sea

Java

12   90   13   100   14   110   15   16   130   17   140

CARTOGRAPHY BY PHILIP'S.COPYRIGHT REED INTERNATIONAL BOOKS LTD.

RUSSIA
1. Adygea
2. Karachey-Cherkessia
3. Kabardino-Balkaria
4. North Ossetia
5. Ingushetia
6. Chechenia
7. Dagestan
8. Mordvinia
9. Chuvashia
10. Mari El
11. Tatarstan
12. Udmurtia
13. Khakassia

AZERBAIJAN
14. Naxçıvan

GEORGIA
15. Ajaria
16. Abkhazia

UKRAINE
17. Crimea

1: 20 000 000

100   0   100   200   300   400   500 miles
100   0   200   400   600   800 km

Projection: Conical Orthomorphic with two standard parallels

East from Greenwich

m    ft
600
200      600
0        0
1200
3000
6000
12 000
2000
4000

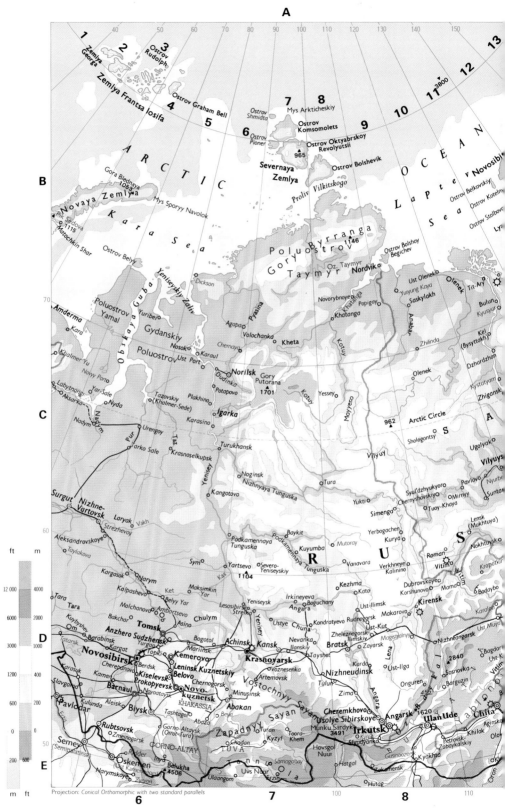

A

1  2  Ostrov 3
Zemlya  Rudolph
Georga  Zemlya Frantsa Iosifa  4
Ostrov Graham Bell  5
7  8  10  11  3800  12  13

A R C T I C  6  Ostrov
Ostrov  Mys Arktcheskiy
Shmidta  Ostrov
Komsomolets  9
Ostrov
Pioner  Ostrov Oktyabrskoy
Revolyutsii  O C E A N
965  Ostrov Bolshevik
Severnaya
Zemlya
Proliv Vilkitskogo  L a p t e v  Novosib
Ostrov Belkovskiy
Gora Blednaya  Sea  Ostrov Kotel
108  Ostrov Stolbov
B  Mys Sporyy Navolok
N o v a y a  Z e m l y a  Ly
Medova  K a r a  S e a  P o l u o s t r o v  Ostrov Bolshoy
1115  Goryu Byrranga  1146  Begichev
Matochkin Shar  T a y m y r  Oz. Taymyr  Nordvik  Ust Olenek  Olenek  Tit-Ary
Ostrov Belyy  Dickson  Agapa  Pyasina  Khatanga  Yunyung Kaya  Saskylakh  Bulun
Amderma  Yeniseyskiy Zaliv  Novorybnoye  Popigay  Kyusyur
Poluostrov  Yuribey  Volochanka  Kheta  Khatanga  Anabar  Zhilinda  Kel
70  Yamal  Karaul  Kotuy  (Bysyttakh)
Kara  Nosoko  Olenek  Dzhardzhan
Khalmer Yu  Gydanskiy  Ust Port  Olenek
Novyy Porto  Poluostrov  Dudinka  Gory  Yessey  Kystatyam
Yar-Sale  Potapovo  Putorana  Moyyero  Zhigansk
Labytnangi  Nyda  Plakhino  Igarka  1701  962  Arctic Circle  A
Aksarka  Tazovskiy  Kotuy  Shologontsy  S
C  (Khalmer-Sede)  Karasino  Ugolyak
Nadym  Urengoy  Turukhansk  Vilyuy  Vilyuy
Pur  Tarko Sale  Syul'dzhukyoro  Pavlovo  Nyurbe
Taz  Krasnoselkupsk  Noginsk  Tura  Yukti  Chernyshovskiy  Mirnyy  Suntar
Surgut  Nizhnyaya Tunguska  Tuoy-Khaya
Nizhne-  Laryak  Vakh  Kangotovo  Simenga  Lensk
Vartovsk  Strezhevoy  (Mukhtuya)
60  Aleksandrovskoye  Baykit  Yerbogachen  Nokhtuysk
Taylakova  Podkamennaya  Kuyumba  Verkhneye  Roman  Vitim
Kargasok  Sym  Tunguska  Podkamennaya Tunguska  Mutoray  Kalinino  Kropotkin
Narym  Yartsevo  Severo-  Vanavara  Kurya  R  Bodaybo
ft  m  Kolpashevo  Ket  Kas  1104  Yeniseyskiy  Kata  Dubrovskoye  Mama
Tara  Tara  Maksimkin  Kezhma  Korshunovo  Karalon
Molchanovo  Yar  Lesosibirsk  Irkineyeva  Boguchany  Ust-Ilimsk  Makarovo  Kirensk  Ust Muyu
12 000  4000  Bakchar  Ambartsevo  Belyy Yar  Strelka  Yeniseysk  Angara  Kondratyevo  Rudnogorsk  Makarovo  Ust-Kut  Nizhneangarsk  Bagdari
Om  Barabinsk  Asino  Chulym  Ustye Chuna  Ilimskiy  Magistralnyy
Kuybyshev  Kargat  Yurga  Bogotol  Achinsk  Kansk  Nevanka  Zheleznogorsk-  Ust-Kut  Sosnovka  Vitim
6000  2000  Anzhero Sudzhensk  Tomsk  Tayshet  Mogistralnyy  2840  Bagdari
D  Novosibirsk  Topki  Kemerovo  Krasnoyarsk  Ilanskiy  Bratsk  Zayarsk  Ust-Iga  Onguren  Barguzin  Vitim
Tatarsk  Cherepanovo  Berdsk  Leninsk Kuznetskiy  Voznesenka  Artemovsk  Nizhneudinsk  Tulun  455
3000  1000  Karasuk  Belovo  Chernogorsk  Zima  Angara
Slavgorod  Kamen  Novo-  Minusinsk  Vostochnyy  Sayan  Cheremkhovo  Angarsk  1620  Chita
1200  400  Pavlodar  Kulunda  Barnaul  Novoaltaysk  kuznetsk  Abakan  Usolye Sibirskoye  Ulan Ude  Aginsk
Aleisk  Biysk  KHAKASSIA  Munku Sardyk  Irkutsk  Kyren  Petrovsk  Olo
600  200  Rubtsovsk  Tashtagol  Zapadnyy  Toora-  3491  Listvyanka  Zabaykalskiy  Khilok
Zmeinogorsk  Gorno-Altaysk  Abaza  Bely  Kyzyl  Khem  Hovsgol  Kyakhta  Ol
0  0  Semey  (Oirot-Tura)  Sayan  Chadan  Nuur  Gusinoozersk  U
(Semipalatinsk)  GORNO-ALTAY  T U V A  Munku Sardyk  Naushki
50  Oskemen  Imra  Belukha  Samagaltay  Hatgal  Kyakhta  Or
200  600  (Ust Kamenog..)  4506  Uvs Nuur  Erzin  Hutag
E  Narymskoye  Zyryan  Ulaangom  l a

m  ft  Projection: Conical Orthomorphic with two standard parallels

6  7  100  8  110

1: 20 000 000

100    0    100    200    300    400    500 miles
100    0    200    400    600    800 km

East from Greenwich

CARTOGRAPHY BY PHILIP'S.
COPYRIGHT REED INTERNATIONAL BOOKS LTD.

14    B    15    C    16

9    10    11

Mys Dezhneva
(East C.)

Chukchi Sea

St. Lawrence I.
(U.S.A.)

Anadyrskiy Zaliv

Bering Sea

East Siberian Sea

Ostrov Vrangelya

Ostrov Henrietta
Jeanette
Ostrova Delong
Ostrov Zhokhova

kiye Ostrova
Ostrov Faddeyevskiy
Ostrov Novaya Sibir

Ostrov Bennett

Ostrov Medvezhi

Ostrov Ayon

Uelen
Lavrentiya
Lorino
Providefinya
Beringovskiy

Anadyr

Chukotskoye Nagorye

▲1843

▲1883

1742

Bolshoy Anyuy

Koryakskoye Nagorye

▲2562

Ostrova Malyy
Lyakhovskiy
Ostrov Bolshoy
Lyakhovskiy

▲374

skiye Ostrova Dmitriya Lapteva

Proliv Dmitriya Lapteva

Mys Buorkhaya

Yana

Batagay

Verkhoyansk

▲2389

Verkhoyanskiy Khrebet

K
H

Kolmskoye Nagorye

Omolon

Gizhiga
Penzhinskaya Guba

Sredinnyy

Poluostrov
Kamchatka

▲4750

Ust-Kamchatsk

Komandorskiye
Ostrova

Nikolskoye

Indigirka
Srednekolymsk

Kolyma

Pobeda
▲3147

Gora Chen
▲2882

Khrebet Cherskogo

Yakutsk
Pokrovsk

Magadan

Zaliv
Shelikhova

Petropavlovsk-
Kamchatskiy
▲3486

Sea of Okhotsk

1780

Ostrov
Paramushir

Ostrov
Onekotan

Aldan

Stanovoy Khrebet

Olekminsk
Tommot

Aldan

▲2246

▲2482

Khrebet Dzhugdzur

Okhotsk

Ostrov Bolshoy
Shantar

Sakhalinskiy
Zaliv

Nikolayevsk-
nd-Am.

Sakhalin
Okha

▲1609

Kurilskiye Ostrova

Ostrov
Simushir

Ostrov
Urup

Chara
Ust-Nyukzha

Khrebet

Tynda
Zeya

Komsomolsk

Sovetskaya Gavan
Yuzhno-Sakhalinsk

Ostrov Iturup

Ostrov
Kunashir

Blagoveshchensk

Da Hinggan Ling

Birobidzhan
Khabarovsk

Khrebet Sikhote Alin

▲3669

Hokkaidō

▲2290

Sapporo

Qiqihar

Harbin

Jiamusi

Ussuriysk
Vladivostok
Nakhodka

JAPAN

Hakodate

Muroran

Hulun Nur

MAN
CHU
RIA

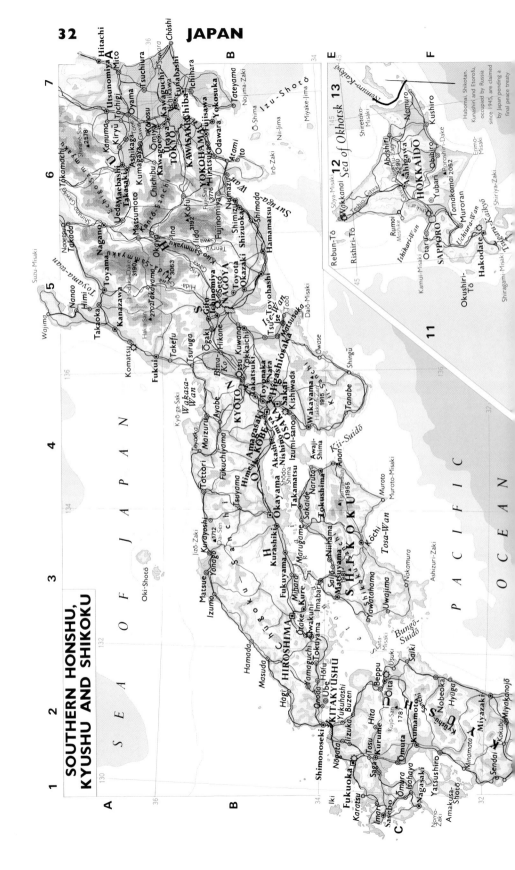

## SOUTHERN HONSHU, KYUSHU AND SHIKOKU

SEA OF JAPAN

PACIFIC OCEAN

Sea of Okhotsk

Habomai, Shikotan, Kunashiri and Etorofu, occupied by Russia since 1945, are claimed by Japan pending a final peace treaty

HOKKAIDO

SAPPORO

TOKYO

YOKOHAMA

KAWASAKI

NAGOYA

KYOTO

OSAKA

KOBE

HIROSHIMA

KITAKYUSHU

Fukuoka

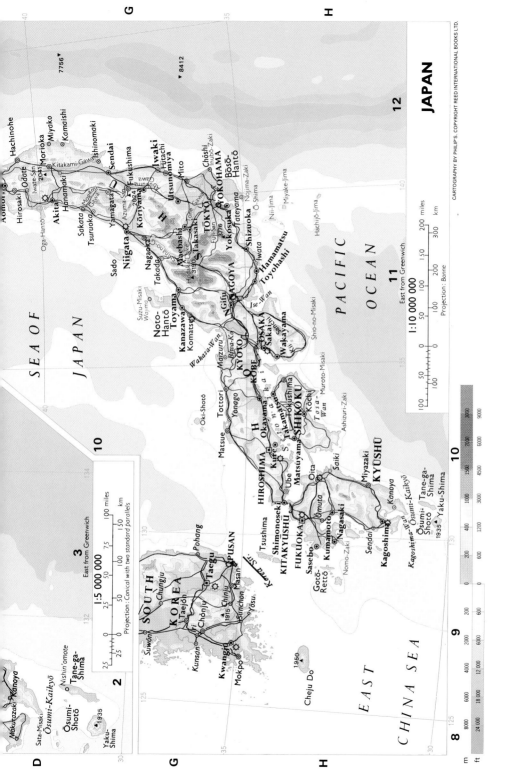

JAPAN

SEA OF

JAPAN

PACIFIC

OCEAN

EAST

CHINA SEA

SOUTH

KOREA

KYŪSHŪ

SHIKOKU

HIROSHIMA

NAGOYA

TŌKYŌ

YOKOHAMA

ŌSAKA

KYŌTO

KOBE

CARTOGRAPHY BY PHILIP'S. COPYRIGHT REED INTERNATIONAL BOOKS LTD.

1:5 000 000

East from Greenwich

0    25   50   75   100 miles

25  0   25   50       150    km

Projection: Conical with two standard parallels

1:10 000 000

East from Greenwich

0     50    100   150   200 miles

0    100   200        300   km

Projection: Bonne

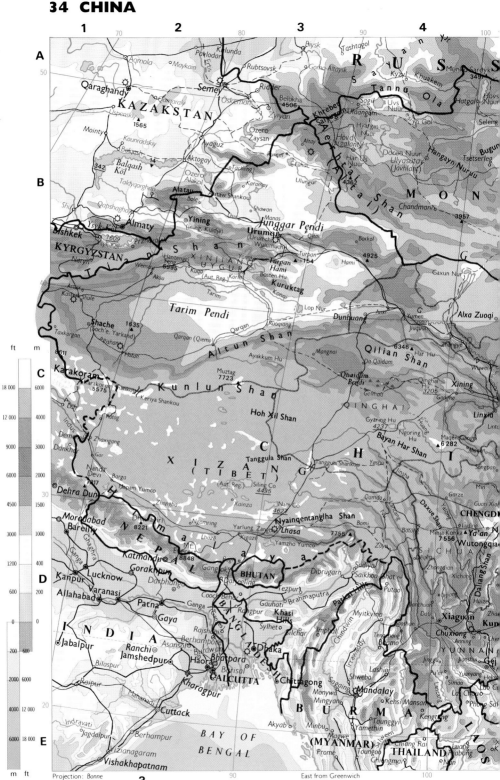

**1**    70    **2**    80    **3**    90    **4**    100

A

50

Aqmola   Maykain   Pavlodar   Kulunda   Rubtsovsk   Biysk   Tashtagol   Gorno-Altaysk   R U S S

Qaraghandy   Semey   Öskemen   Ridder   Belukha 4506   Khrebet   Kyzyl   Khuakem   Munku Sardyk   3491

K A Z A K S T A N   1565   Zhyan   Ozero   Zaysan   Altay   Uvs Nuur   Tannu Ola   Hatgal   Nuur   Seleng

Mointy   Kaunradskiy   Ayaguz   Tacheng   Bürqin   Har Us Nuur   Döröö Nuur   Hangayn Nuruu   Tsetserleg   M O N

Balqash Köl   14   Aktogay   Ulungur   4362   3957   Chandmani   Bugun

B

342   Taldyqorghan   Ozero Alakol   Usu   Karamay   Manas   Shawan   Barkol   4925   G

Qapshaghay   Alatau   Dataw Shankou   Bole   Junggar Pendi   Qitai   Hami   Gaxun Nur

Bishkek   Almaty   Ysyk   Yining (Ining, Kuldja)   Ürümqi (Urumchi) Wulumuchi   Turpan Hami   Alxa Zuoqi

KYRGYZSTAN   Ysyk Köl   1609   Shan   Hantengri Feng 6995   X I N J I A N G   UYGUR (Aut. Reg.)   Bosten Hu   Turpan -154   Kuruktag

Naryn   Wensu   Aksu   Kuqa   Korla   Kongi

40   Kashgar shule   Tarim   Lop Nur   Dunhuang   Yumen   Zhangye

Taxkorgan   Shache (Soch'e, Yarkand) 1635   Tarim Pendi   Qargan (Qiemo)   Ruoqiang   Anxi   Jiuquan   6346 Har Hu   Qilian Shan   Da Qaidam   Wuwei

8611   Karakoram   Karakorum   5575   Tankou   Keriya Shankou   Altun Shan   Ayakkum Hu   Mangnai   Qaidam Pendi   Qinghai Hu 3205   Xining   Linxia

C

18 000   6000   Karakoram   Muztag 7723   K u n l u n   S h a n   Golmud   Gyaring Hu 4237   Maqên Gangri 6282   Magê   Songpan

12 000   4000   Leh   Firdog   Hoh Xil Shan   Q I N G H A I   Ngoring Hu   Bayan Har Shan   Min

9000   3000   Demo   Zhaxigang   X I Z A N G   Tanggula Shan   Tanggula Shankou   Yushu   Jinsha   Garze

Darikha   Barga   (T I B E T) (Aut. Reg.)   Siling Co 4495   Qamdo   Daxue Shan   Guon Xian   CHENGDU

6000   2000   Nanda Devi 7817   Mapam Yumco   Zhongba   Xainza   Nam Co 4622   S I C H U A N   Min Konka 7556   Ya'an   Wutongqia

30   4500   1500   Dehra Dun   Zhongba   Ngamring   Nyainqentanglha Shan   Lhasa   7755   Batong   Zhongdian   Xichang

Moradabad   Dhaulagiri 8221   N E P A L   Lhazê   Xigazê   Yarlung Zangbo   Bomi   Zaya   DALI   Huize   Zha

Bareilly   3000   1000   Mt. Everest 8848   Gangtok   Yamzho Yumco   Parker Pass   Xiaguan   Kun

D

1200   400   Kanpur   Lucknow   Katmandu   Gorakhpur   Darbhanga   BHUTAN   Dibrugarh   Saikhoa Ghat   Putao   Chuxiong   Y U N N A N   Gej

600   200   Varanasi   Ganga   Cooch Behar   Darjeeling   Tezpur   Brahmaputra   Myitkyina   Tengchong   Dali   Anning   Jianshui   Yuanyang   Mengzi

Allahabad   Patna   Ganga   Rajshahi   Gauhati   Khasi Hills   Silchar   Imphal   Chindwin   Bhamo   Jinggu   Pu'er   Luo Co

0   0   I N D I A   Gaya   Berhampore   Rangpur   Sylhet   B A N G L A D E S H   Lashio   Shweba   Simao   La Chiou   Phong Sal

Jabalpur   Ranchi   Asansol   Burdwan   Dhaka   Irrawaddy   Monywa   Mandalay   Kehsi Mansam   Kengtung

200   600   Bilaspur   Jamshedpur   Haora   Bhatpara   Barisal   Chittagong   Mingyan   Sagaing   LAOS

Raipur   CALCUTTA   Kharagpur   B U R M A   Taunggyi   Chiang Rai   Luang Prabang

2000   6000   Mahanadi   Cuttack   (M Y A N M A R)   Minbu   Magwe   Yamethin

20   4000   12 000   Indravati   Jagdalpur   Berhampur   Akyab   Prome   Toungoo   THAILAND   Chiangmai

E

6000   18 000   Vizianagaram   B A Y   O F   B E N G A L   Vishakhapatnam

m   ft     Projection: *Bonne*    **3**    90    East from Greenwich    **4**    100

1 : 20 000 000

100   0   100   200   300   400   500 miles
100   0   200   400   600   800 km

5 · 110 · 6 · 120 · 7 · 130 · 8

Cheremkhovo 1620
Angarsk
Irkutsk                455
Ulan Ude   Khilok   Chita   Sretensk   Shimanovsk   Svobodnyy   Chegdomyn
Babushkin   Petrovsky   Olovyannaya   Borzya   Shika   Nerchinsk   Aihui   Blagoveshchensk   Bureya   2640   Ozero
Kyakhta Zabaykalsky   Yablonovyy Khrebet   Argun   Yilehuli Shan   Poyarkovo   Raychikhinsk   Bolon
Suhbaatar   Alfanbulag   Manzhouli   Borzya   Xiao   Hinggan Ling   Furao   Tongjiang   Khabarovsk
Orhon   Kerulen   Hulun Nur   Hailar   Bugt   Nenjiang   Baian   Yichun   Hegang   Bikin
A

MONGOLIA
Hentiyn   Nuruu   Ulaanbaatar (Ulan Bator)   Ondörhaan   Choybalsan   Buir   Nur   Xin Barag   Arxan   Solon   Qiqihar   Hailun   Yilan   Jiamusi   Shuangyashan   Dalnerechensk   Mishan
Dzuunmod                Matad   Tamsagbulag                Horqin Youyi Qianqi   Baicheng   Songhua   HEILONGJIANG   HARBIN   Suihua   B
Bulgan   1949   Da Hinggan Ling   Ang'angxi   Da'an   Fuyu   Mudanjiang   Suifenhe   Ussurisk
Bayanhongor   Saynshand   Dzamin Üüd   Erenhot   Sonid Youqi   Linxi   Duolun   Tongliao   Shuangliao   Changchun   Jilin   Vladivostok   Artem
Dalandzadgad   Bayan Bo   Mumingan Lianheqi   NEI   MONGGOL (Aut. Reg.)   Chifeng   Siping   Liaoyuan   Dunhua   Yanji   Hunchun   Najin
Chongjin
NORTH
KOREA
Hohhot   Jining   Zhangjiakou   Xuanhua   Chengde   Fuxin   Fushun   Tonghua   Hamhung   Hungnam
BAOTOU   Datong   Tong Xian   Qinhuangdao   Jinzhou   SHENYANG   Benxi   Anshan   Dandong   Sinuiju   Anju   Wonsan
Mu Us Shamo   3015   Beijing (Peking)   Liaoyang   Liaodong Wan   Korea Bay   Chinnampo   P'yongyang   Hoeju
Yinchuan   THE GREAT WALL   Yulin   Shijiazhuang   Baoding   TIANJIN (Tientsin)   Tangshan   Bo Hai   DALIAN   Kaesong   SEOUL   Kangnung
NINGXIA HUIZAI   2894   Taiyuan   Yangquan   Yuci   Baoding   Bozhen   Longkou   Yantai   Weihai   Inch'on   SOUTH   Taejon   KOREA   Taegu
Wuzhong   Fenyang   Xingtai   Jinan   Zibo   Weifang   Kunsan   Chonju   Pusan   Masan
Baiyin   Lanzhou   Qingyang   Changzhi   Handan   Boshan   Yao Xian   QINGDAO   YELLOW   SEA   Kwangju   Tsushima Str.
Pingliang   Tongchuan   Xinxiang   Anyang   Jining   SHANDONG   Yanzhou   Mokpo   Fukuoka   Sasebo
Tianshui   Baoji   Yongji   Jiaozuo   Huang   Kaifeng   Shangqiu   Lianyungang   Cheju   Cheju Do   1950   Nagasaki
Min Xian   Dali   Luoyang   Zhengzhou   Xuzhou   Hai'an   JIANGSU   Korea Str.
XI'AN   Xuchang   HENAN   Shangshui   Guannan   JAPAN
Hanzhong   Ankang   Nanyang   Zhumadian   Huainan   Bengbu   Zhenjiang   Changzhou   Chang
Langzhong   Daba Shan   Xiangfan   Xinyang   Hefei   Ma'anshan   Wuxi   Suzhou   SHANGHAI
Daxian   Fengjie   Zigui   Yichang   HUBEI   ANHUI   Anqing   Wuhu   Jiaxing
Nanchong   Wanxian   Chang   WUHAN   Huangshi   Hangzhou   Shaoxing   EAST
Beibei   Jinshi   Jiujiang   Poyang Hu   Tunxi   Jingdezhen   Ningbo   CHINA
Zigong   CHONGQING   Changde   Dongting Hu   Nanchang   Shangrao   Qu Xian   Linhai   SEA
Luzhou   Yiyang   Yichun   Yingtan   2120   Wenzhou
Yibin   Changsha   Xiangtan   JIANGXI   Shaowu   Xiapu
Zunyi   2494   Zhuzhou   Ji'an   Wuyi Shan   Tian'ou   Ningde   Ryūkyū-Rettō   Okinawa 7507
GUIZHOU   Zhenyuan   Hengyang   HUNAN   Nanping   Min   Fuzhou
Guiyang   Hongjiang   Shaoyang   Chen Xian   Changting   FUJIAN   Taibei (Taipei)   Jilong
Anshun   Duyun   Guilin   Shaoguan   Chongting   Quanzhou   Xinzhu   Miaoli   Yilan
Xingren   Hechi   Mei Xian   Zhangzhou   Xiamen   Taizhong   TAIWAN   Tropic of Cancer
Lingyun   Liuzhou   GUANGDONG   Chao'an   Zhanghua   Jiayi   Sakishima-Guntō
GUANGXI ZHUANGZU   Guiping   GUANGZHOU (Canton)   Shantou   Chaoyang   Yu Shan 3950   Tainan   Taidong
Nanning   Wuzhou   Sanshui   Foshan   Shilong   Gaoxiong   Pingdong
Pingxiang   Qinzhou   Jiangmen   Macao (PORT.)   Kowloon   Bashi Channel
Lang Son   Beihai   Maoming   Hong Kong (Br.)   Batan Is.
HANOI   G. of Tonkin   Zhanjiang   Leizhou Bandao   SOUTH CHINA
Haiphong   Changjiang   Haikou   Hainan Dao   SEA   PHILIPPINES
Vinh   Huangliu   1867   HAINAN   Luzon   Laoag

40
30
20

A
B
C
D
E

5 · 110 · 6 · 7

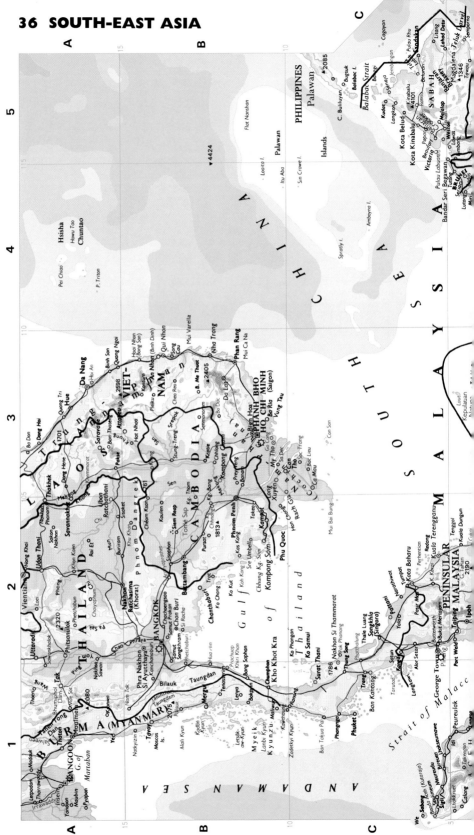

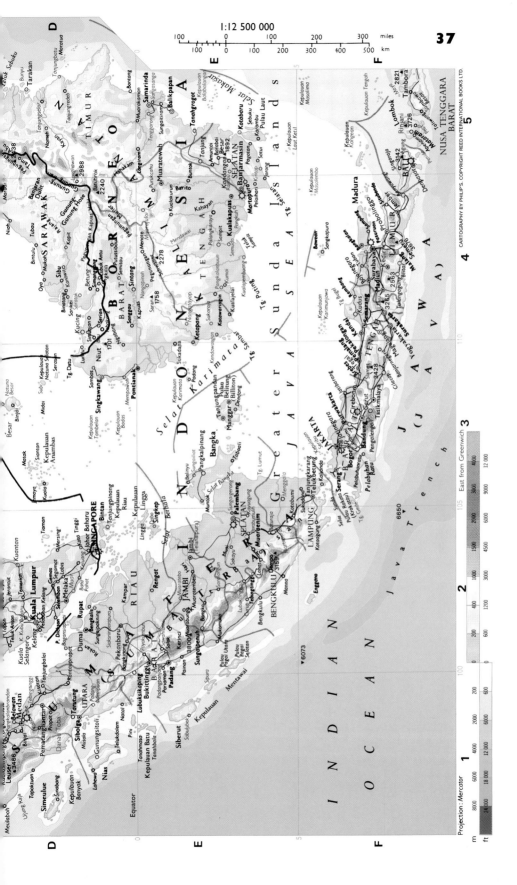

37

1:12 500 000

Projection : Mercator

East from Greenwich

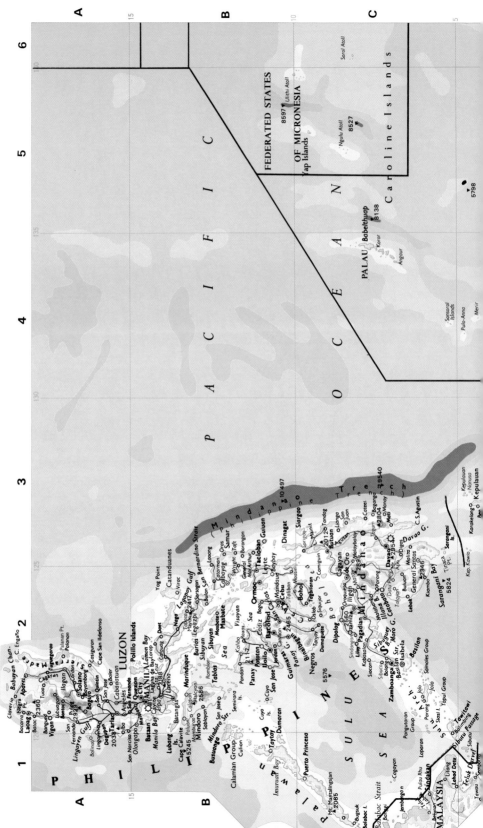

1:12 500 000

100    0    100    200    300    miles
100    0    100    200    300    400    500    km

P A P U A   N E W   G U I N E A

I R I A N   J A Y A

Equator

B A N D A   S E A

A R A F U R A   S E A

C E L E B E S   S E A

S E R A M   S E A

M O L U C C A   S E A

SULAWESI (CELEBES)

Halmahera

MALUKU

F L O R E S   S E A

Lesser Sunda Islands

S A W U   S E A

Selat Makasar

Projection: Mercator

East from Greenwich

CARTOGRAPHY BY PHILIP'S. COPYRIGHT REED INTERNATIONAL BOOKS LTD.

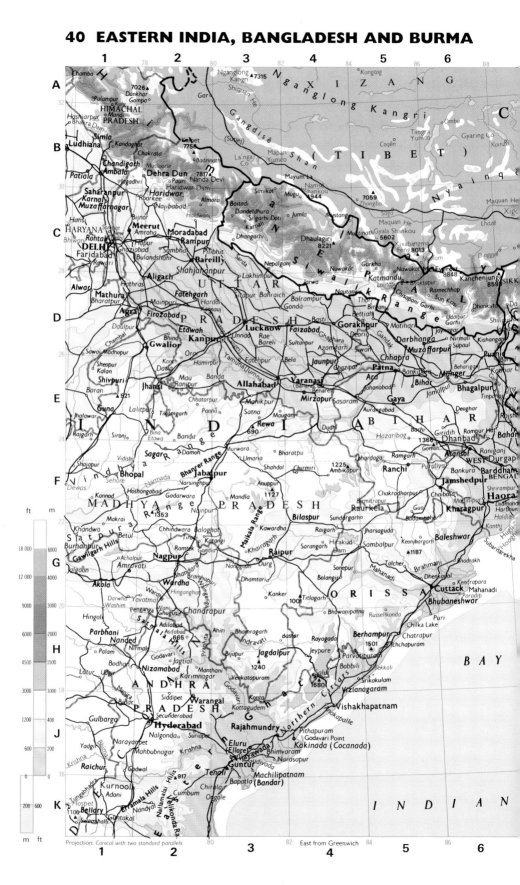

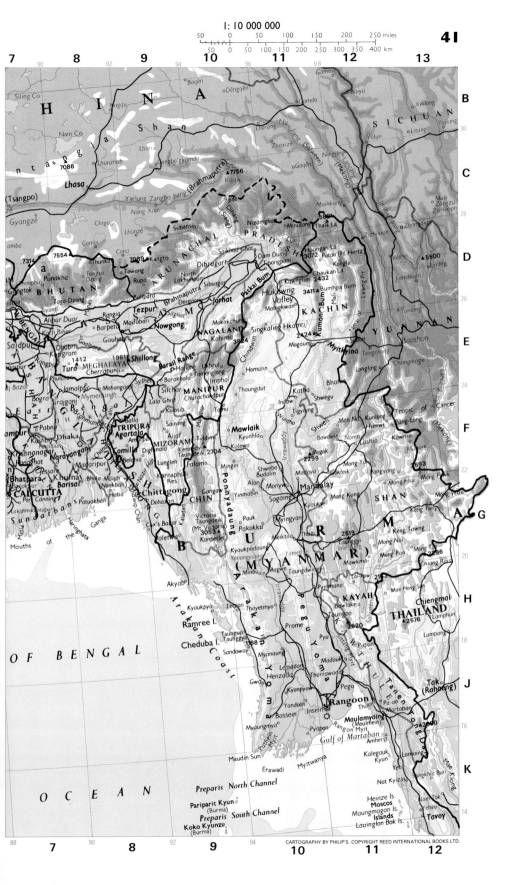

7    8    9    10    11    12    13

C H I N A

H    Siling Co    Bagên    Dêngqên    Gamtog    Baiyu    B

Ngagla    Shan    SICHUAN    Xinlong

Nam Co    Damdo    Litang    Yaxing

Lhasa    Lhünzhub    Gongbo'gyamda    Nu Jiang (Salween)    Ningjing    Zhaxizê    Gogên    Markan    Zhongdian    Mainkung    Muli Zizzhu    Zizixtan    5500    D

7088    Riga    7756    Jido    Nizamghat    Thala La    Hpungan La    Putao (Ft. Hertz)    Konglu    Jianchuan    Lijiang

Yarlung Zangbo Jiang (Brahmaputra)    Nang Xian    ARUNACHAL PRADESH    Minutang    3072    Welxi    Yuanqing

(Tsangpo)    Lhünzê    Subansin    Sang    Dihang    Saikhoa Ghat    5891    Chaukan La    Lawng Pit    Baoshan    E

Gyangzê    Chigu    Cona    Thunkar    7089    Kangto    Dibrugarh    Dam Duma    Ibongpani    3411    Bumhpa Bum    Yunlong    Tengchong

Comai    7554    Towang    Rupa    North    Kawngtim    2432    Changningo

7314    a    Punakha    Tongsa Dzong    Balipara    Lakhimpur    Hukawng    2424 Bum    KACHIN    YUNNAN

BHUTAN    Toga-Dzong    Rangia    Brahmaputra    Dergaon    Valley    Mogaung    Myitkyina    Longling    Baoshan    F

Gongtok    Jayanti    Alipur Duar    Mairabari    Sibsagar    Singkaling Hkamti    Homalin

Koch Bihar    Barpeta    Gauhati    3824    Chindwin    Mong Yu

Saidpur    Dhubri    Kohima    Thaungdut    Katha    Shwegu    Hsenwi    Lashio    Kawnro

Rangpur    1412    1961    Shillong    Barail Range    Haflong    Ukhrul    Tamenglong    Ingbw    Shweli    Man Na    Kunlong    Pung-Long    Tropic of Cancer

Tura    Cherrapunji    MEGHALAYA    Sylhet    Barakhola    Imphal    Mokokchung    Wuntho    Tigyaing    Bawdwin    Namtu    Mong Yo    Mong Hsu    693    G

Bogra    Jamalpur    Mohanganj    MANIPUR    Churachandpur    Tamu    Mogok    2299    Mong Kung    SHAN    Mong Yo

Sirajganj    Mymensingh    Silchar    Lala Ghat    Kolasib    Sairang    Kyunhla    Kalewa    Madaya    Gokteik    Pangyang    Mong Yaw

CALCUTTA    Pabna    Dhaka    TRIPURA    Agartala    Aijal    MIZORAM    Tiddim    Mingin    Shwebo    Mandalay    Mong Kung    Keng Tung

Narayanganj    Comilla    Dighnala    Kemrep    2704    Falam    Alon    Monywa    Kyaukse    Mong Hsu

Khulna    Barisal    Bhola    Hatia    Lungleh    Karnaphuli Res.    Yinmabin    Sagaing    Thazi    2519    Keng Tawng    2296    G

Bhatpara    Chittagong    CHIN    Gangaw    Pakokku    Myingyan    Taunggyi    Mong Nai    Chiang Rai    A

Jessore    Dohazari    Victoria    Pauk    Meiktila    MYANMAR    Mong Pan    Mong Tu

Lakshmikantapur    Cox's Bazar    Taungdeik    (Mt. Victoria)    Kyaukpadaung    Yamethin    Mawkmai

Pari Canning    Sundarbans    3053    Kanpetlet    Yenangyaung    Magwe    Taungdwingyi    Loi-kaw    216    Mae Hong Son

Mouths    of    the Ganga    Ghata    Akyab    Minbu    Pyinmana    KAYAH    Chiengmai    H

OF BENGAL    Kyaukpyu    Letpan    Thayetmyo    Taungup    Toungoo    2620    Bawlake    2576    THAILAND    Lamphun

Ramree I.    Sandoway    Myanaung    Prome    Pyu    Lampang

Cheduba I.    1168    Henzada    Madauk    Pegu    Tak (Rahaeng)    J

Gwa    Kyonpyaw    Thatbyin    Thanatpin    Pa-an

Bassein    Inseine    Rangoon    Thaton    Martaban

Myaungmya    Rangon Myit    Maulamyaing (Moulmein)    2060    K

OCEAN    Maudin Sun    Myitwanya    Amherst    Kalegauk    Nat Kyizing    Lamaing    Sangkhla Buri

Erawadi    Kyun    Yebyu    Mae Klong

Preparis North Channel    Heinze Is.

Pariparit Kyun (Burma)    Moscos    Maungmagan Is.    Nam Tok

Preparis South Channel    Islands    Tavoy    K

Koko Kyunzu (Burma)    Laungion Bok Is.

88    7    90    8    92    9    94    10    11    12

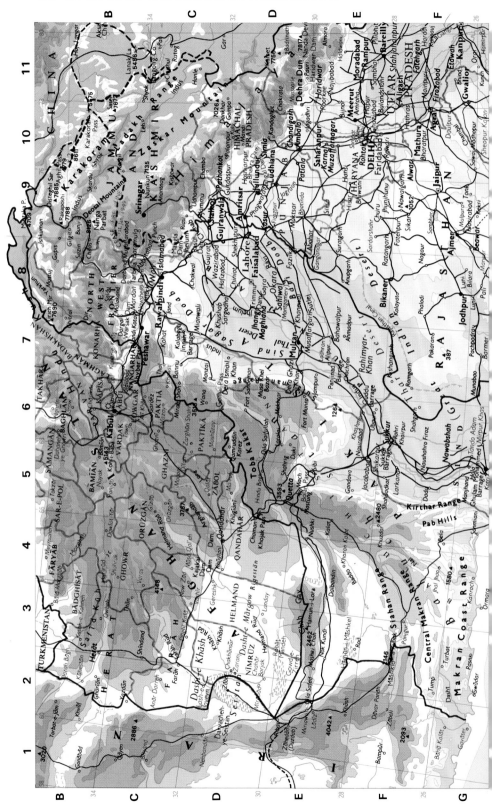

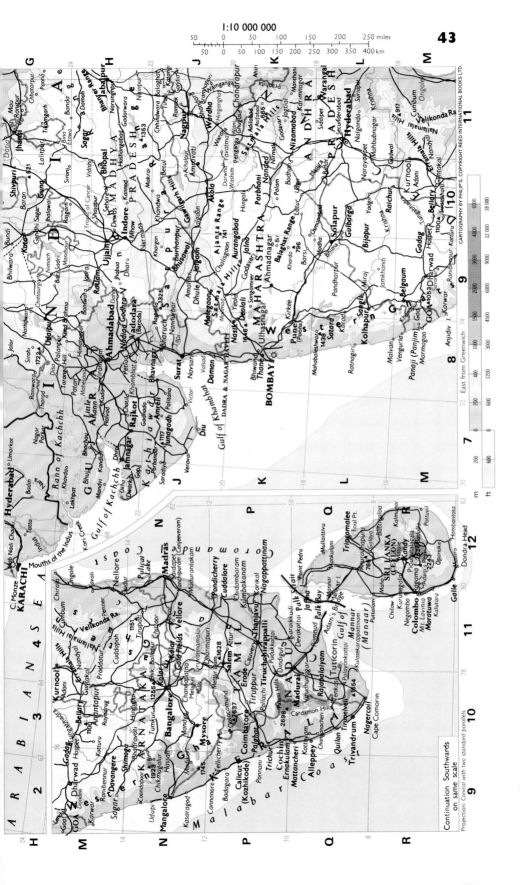

1:10 000 000

50   0   50   100   150   200   250 miles

50   0   50   100   150   200   250   300   350   400 km

CARTOGRAPHY BY PHILIP'S. COPYRIGHT REED INTERNATIONAL BOOKS LTD.

East from Greenwich

Continuation Southwards
on same scale

Projection: Conical with two standard parallels

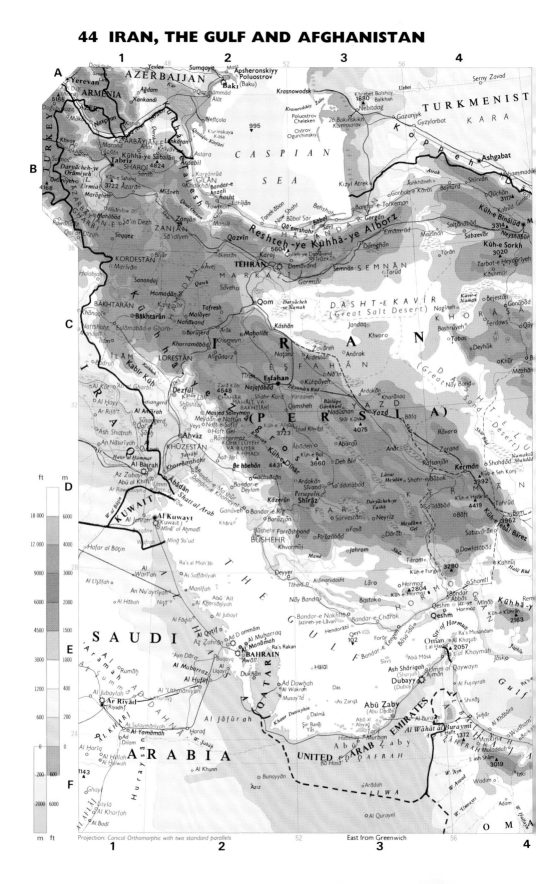

Projection: Conical Orthomorphic with two standard parallels

East from Greenwich

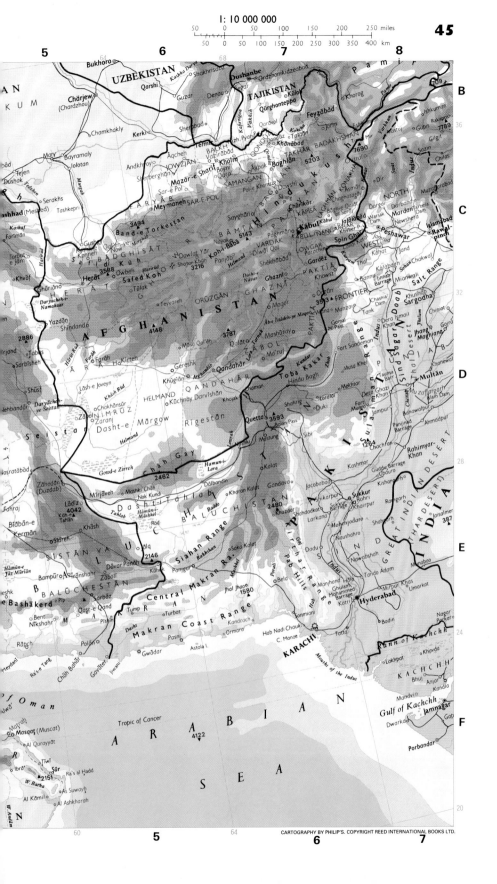

1: 10 000 000

50   0   50   100   150   200   250 miles
50   0   50   100   150   200   250   300   350   400 km

**5**        **6**        **7**        **8**

UZBEKISTAN

Bukhoro
Chärjew
(Chardzhou)
KUM
Qarshi
Shakhrisabz
Kashka-Darya
Denau
Dushanbe
Ordzhonikidzeabad
Guzar
TAJIKISTAN
Külob
Pamir
Khorog
Chamkhakly
Sherabad
Qürghonteppa
Feyzābād
Ishkuman
709
Kerki
Termiz
Qaravol
Kokcha
Jürm
KVakhan
Gupis
Gilgit
Rakaposhi
7789
Mary
Bayramaly
Iolotan
Andkhvoy
Āqcheh
Khānābād
BADAKHSHAN
Darkot
Chilas
Murgab
Sherberghān
BALKH
Vazirābād
Kholm
Qondūz
Taluqan
Dir
Muzaffarabad
Serakhs
Tashkepri
Sar-e Pol
Pol-e Khomri
Dowshi
5203
NORTH
Mardan
Darband
Nowshera
hhad (Meshed)
FĀRYĀB
SAMANGAN
Kashaf
Meymaneh
SAR-E-POL
Sayghān
BĀMIĀN
Charikār
KĀPISA
Asmar
Darra
WEST
Peshawar
Islamabad
Rawal-pinch
Fariman
Band-e Torkestan
3494
Dowlat Yar
Koh-i-Baba
Nayak
5143
Paghman
KĀBUL
NANGAR.
Jalalabad
Khyber P.
Spin Ghar
Kohat
Torbat-e Jām
Owbeh
Hariröd
Shotor Khan
Panjāb
Diwāl Qol
LOWGAR
Paroachinar
Thal
Herāt
3588
Safed Koh
3216
Shēkhābād
Gardēz
Jand
Bannu
Kālābagh
HERĀT
Tülak
Dasht-e-Nāwar
Ghazni
PAKTIĀ
Khowst
Mianwali
Salt Range
Chakwal
Khushab
Ghüriān
Teyvareh
ORŪZGĀN
GHAZNĪ
Mogor
353
Khost
FRONTIER
Barra
Chasnia
Dam
Sargodha
Daryacheh-i-Namaksar
Yazdān
Shindand
4148
Müsa Qal'eh
Qalāt
3787
Āb-e Istādeh-ye Moqor
Gemal
Pass
Manzan
Tank
Chinioi
Shūsf
2886
Tabas
Fajak
Farāh
ōlās
Gereshk
Qalāt
BOL
Mashütay
Karatu
Fort Sandeman
Zhob
Musa Khel
Jhang
Maghiana
Sarbīsheh
Khvāf
HīrūRūd
FĀRĀ
Hokirteh
Khūgiānī
Qandahār
Archandāb
Toba Kakar
Mekhtar
Ghazi
Khan
Dera Ismail
Khanewal
Lāsh-e Joveyn
Khāsh Rūd
Chakhānsūr
HELMAND
Kūchnay Darvishān
Chaman
Shahrig
Duki
Multan
Daryacheh-ye Seistan
Zābol
NIMRŪZ
Zaranj
Dasht-e Mārgow
Kandil
Hindu Bogh
Quetta
3593
Bolan Pass
Sibi
Fort Panjānr
Bahawalpur
Panjnad
Barrage
Ahmadpur
lenbandān
Daryacheh-ye Seistan
Helmand
Rigestān
Müshki
Müstung
Bolan Pass
1264
Kachhan
Rahimyar-Khan
Nosratābād
Seistan
Gowd-e Zirreh
Chāh Gay
Hamun-i-Lora
Kalat
Kashmor
Guddu Barrage
Ubduro
Fahraj
Zāhedān
(Duzdab)
2462
Dālbandan
Kharan Kalat
Gandava
Jacobabad
Kashangarh
Ladiz
4042
Koh-i-Taftān
Mirjāveh
Mashki Chāh
Nok Kundi
Baddo
Khuzdar
Shahdadkot
Shikarpur
Sukkur
Rohri
Rahimyar-Khan
Jaisalmer
387
Bfābān-e
Kermān
Khāsh
Tahlab
Hamūn-i-Māshkel
Rod
BALUCHISTAN
2480
Larkana
Mohenjodaro
Naushahro
Khairpur
THAR DESERT
Dilārām
INDIA
Gotāreh
Jalq
2146
Siahan Range
Saka Kalat
Kalat
Dadu
Nawabshah
GREAT INDIAN DESERT
SISTĀN VA
Hāmūn-e Jāz Mūriān
Bampūr
Trānshahr
Dāvar Panāh
Zābolī
Kahak
Panjgur
Rakhshan
Jhal Jhao
1580
Pab Hills
Manjhand
Tando Adam
Mirpur Khas
Umarkot
Bashākerd
BALÜCHESTAN
Bent
Nikshahr
Qasr-e Qand
Sorbāz
Tump
Central
Makran
Coast
Range
Turbat
Kandrach
Bela
Ghulam Mohammad Barrage
Kottri
Hyderabad
Nagar
Parkar
Rārgh
Polān
M
Pishin
Dasht
Pasni
Ormara
Hab Nadi Chauk
C. Monze
Sonmiani
Tatta
Badin
Rann of Kachchh
Khavda
KACHCHH
Mandvi
Ra'se Tang
Chāh Bahār
Govāter
Jiwani
Gwādar
Astola I.
KARACHI
Mouths of the Indus
Lakhpat
Bhuj
Anjar
Kandla
of OMAN
Meydani
Masqat (Muscat)
Al Qurayyāt
Tropic of Cancer
4122
ARABIAN
Gulf of Kachchh
Dwarka
Jamnagar
Gop
Ibrā
Tiwi
Ṣūr
Ra's al Hadd
W. Batha
2151
SEA
Porbandar
Al Kāmil
As Suwayh
Al Ashkharah
N

60          64          **5**          **6**          **7**

B
C
D
E
F

36
32
28
24
20

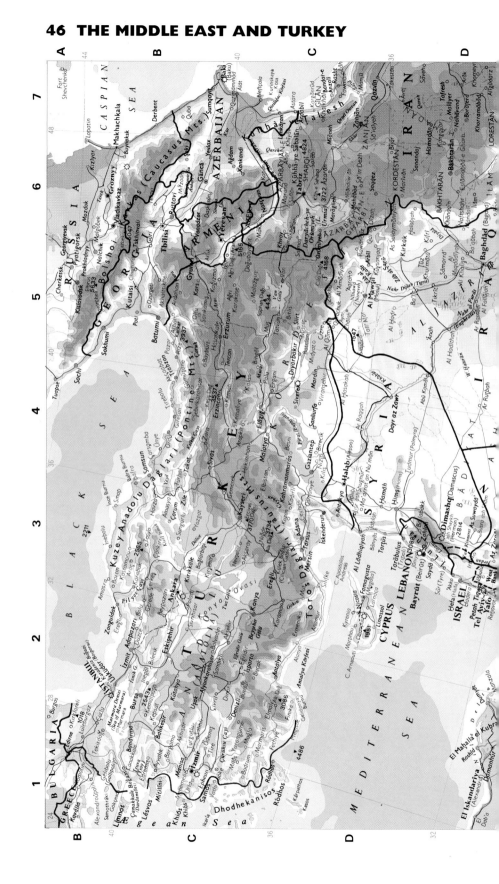

1:10 000 000

50    0    50    100    150    200    250 miles

50  0  50  100  150  200  250  300  350  400 km

THE GULF

KHŪZESTĀN (ARABISTĀN)

Dezfūl

Ahvāz

Shatt al Arab

Ābādān

Kabīr Kūh

MESOPOTAMIA

KUWAIT

Al Kuwayt

AL HASĀ

Ar Riyāḍ
Riyadh

S A U D I  A R A B I A

DAHNĀ

SUDAYR

AL ĀRIḌ

NAJD

A L   H I J Ā Z

AN NAFŪD

J A B A L   S H A M M A R

Ṣafājah

Harrat Khaybar

Al Madīnah

Makkah (Mecca)

2565 Al Ṭā'if

Jiddah

R E D   S E A

JORDAN

Ammān

Jerusalem (Al Quds)

Dead Sea -403

AL ḤIJĀZ

SINAI

Gebel el Tih

Suez Canal

EL QĀHIRA (CAIRO)

El Gîza

Pyramids

Tanta

Bûr Saʿîd (Port Said)

E G Y P T

Es Sahrâ el Sharqiya

Esh Sharqiya

Aswân

El Wâhât el Khârga

S U D A N

Buḥeiret en Naser (Lake Nasser)

ES SAHRÂ EN NÛBÎYA (NUBIAN DESERT)

Nahr en Nîl (Nile)

East from Greenwich

CARTOGRAPHY BY PHILIP'S. COPYRIGHT REED INTERNATIONAL BOOKS LTD.

Projection: Conical Orthomorphic with two standard parallels

--- Division between Greeks and Turks
    in Cyprus; Turks to the North.

| m | ft |
|---|---|
| 4000 | 12 000 |
| 3000 | 9000 |
| 2000 | 6000 |
| 1500 | 4500 |
| 1000 | 3000 |
| 600 | 1800 |
| 0 | 0 |
| 200 | 600 |
| 2000 | 6000 |

1128

1814

1143

2216 G. Kāterīna

1977 G. Ḥamāta

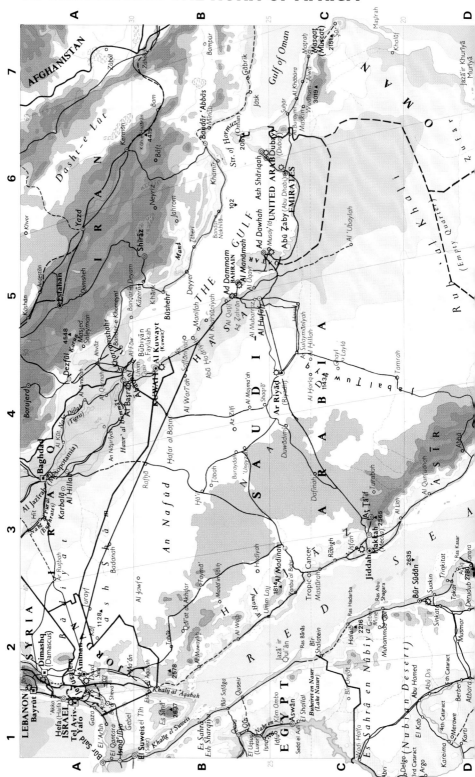

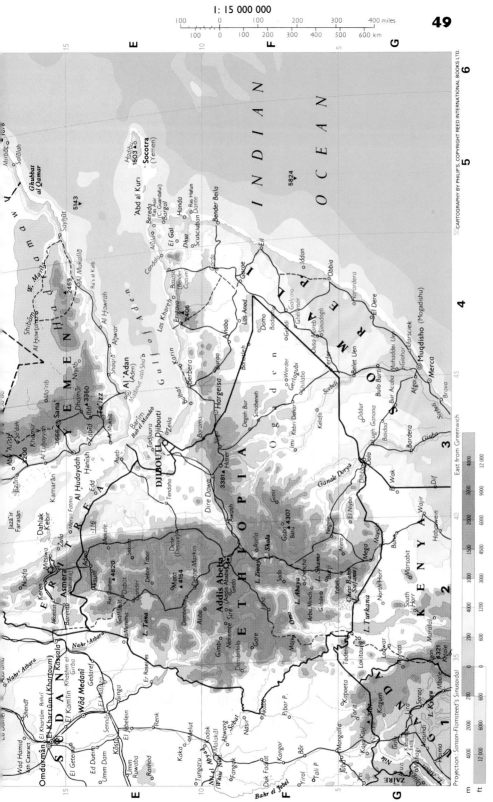

I: 15 000 000

100    0    100    200    300    400 miles
100  0  100  200  300  400  500  600 km

6

5

4

3

2

1

East from Greenwich

Projection: Sanson-Flamsteed's Sinusoidal

m    ft
4000  12 000
3000  9000
2000  6000
1500  4500
1000  3000
600   1800
200   600
0     0
4000  12 000

INDIAN

OCEAN

Socotra
(Yemen)
Hadibu
1503

5824

Abd al Kuri

El Gal
Dhui
Candala
Alula
Bereda
(C. Guardafui)
Ras Asir
Borgal
Scusciuban
Bender Bella
Dante

Bosaso
(Bender Cassim)
Gardo
Gacoe
Eil
Iddan

Obbia

Galcaio
Farardera

El Dere

S    O    M    A    L    I    A

Eringavo
2406
Las Khoreh

Cossim

Bodule
Domo
Goldii
Scebeli
Bulo Burti

Werder
Gerlogubi
Shilabo

Dusa Mareb
Sinadogo

Mahaddei Uen
Warsciek
Giohar
Muqdisho (Mogadishu)
Merca

Ras Hafun

YEMEN

W. Masila
Shibam
Al Huwaymah
2469
Sayhut
5143
Mirbat
Taqa

Ghubbat
al Qamar

Nisab
Dhamar
3360
3666
Sana
Ta'izz
Khamir
Al Lubayyah
Abu 'Arish
5200
Jizan

Mukalla
Ras al Kalb
Al Hawrah
Ajwar
Shaqra
Madinat ash Sha'b
Al 'Adan (Aden)

Jazirat
Farasan
Kamaran
Al Hudaydah
Hanish
Zabid

Baha
Barim
Bab el Mandeb
Mukha
Zeila
Tadjoura
DJIBOUTI
Obock

Aseb
Edd
Mersa Fatma
Zula

Berbera
Karin
Bulhar
Hargeisa
Sharbeneh
Degeh Bur

O    g    a    d    e    n

Anabo
Burao
Scebeli
Harer
Giggi
Kebri Dehar
Imi
Kelafo
Qoddur

Dolo
Lugh Ganana
Baidoa
Bardera
Giuba
Bur Acaba
Afgoi
Brava

Sceek

Dif

El Wak

Wajir
Habaswein

K    E    N    Y    A

L. Turkana
North Horr
South Horr
Marsabit
Buhera
Mega

Dire Dawa
3381
Harer
Borama

Aysha
Gimir
4307
Batu
Goba

Asela
Ginir
Shala
Chafa Bahir
L. Stefanie

Nazele
El Nijbo

Ganale Dorya

ETHIOPIA

Addis Abeba
(Addis Ababa)
Debre Markos
4620
Gonder
Aksum
4154
Ras Dashen
Dabat
Debre Tabor
Dese
(Dessye)
Sekota
Adua
Gabbat

Meqele
Aduba

L. Tana

Nekemte
Gimbi
Gedo
Jima
L. Ziway
L. Abaya
Mula
L. Shamo
Sodo
Yabelo
Gore
Dembidolo
Debarek

Meremi
Adwa
Aduba

ERITREA

Asmera
Keren
Nakfa
Mitsiwa
Dahlak
Kebir
Kordam
Barentu
Agordat

-116
Melele

Todenyan
Kapoeta
Lokitaung
Lodwar
Todem
Kaga
Maralal
Kakuma
L. Koaga
Mbale
4321
Kitale
Soroti

U    G    A    N    D    A

Kitgum
Tarit
Mongalla
Juba

ZAIRE

S    U    D    A    N

Omdurman
El Khartum (Khartoum)
Khartum Bahri
Kassala
Gedaref
Wad Medani
Er Roseyres
Singa
Sennar
Kosti
El Dueim
Umm Ruwaba
Ed Duem
Rashad
Malakal
Kodok
Abwong
Fangak
Nasir
Sobat
Kongor
Bor
Tali P
Yirol
Duk Fadat
Jonglei
Pibor P.
Mandalla

Nahr Atbara
Nahr Atbara
Shendi
El Kamlin
Khoshm el Girba
Girba
El Fasher
El Abelein
Umm Dam

Atbara
Wad Hamid

Wad Hamid
El Geteina

White Nile
Bahr el Jebel

Tungaru

Shilluk

E

F

G

15

10

10

5

5

50

45

40

35

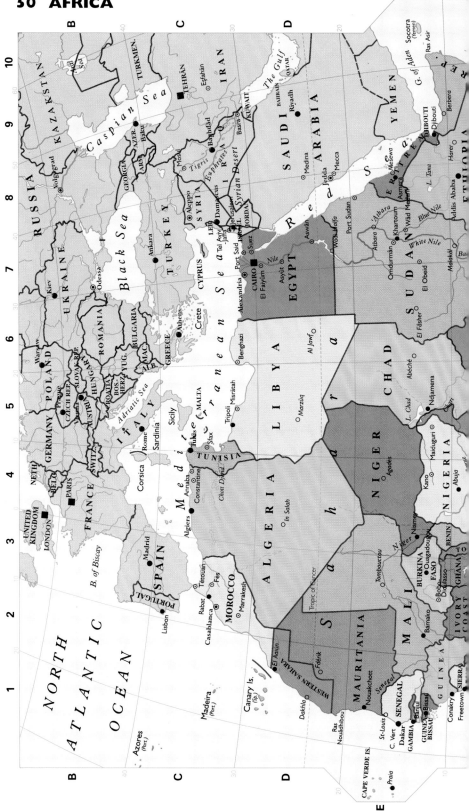

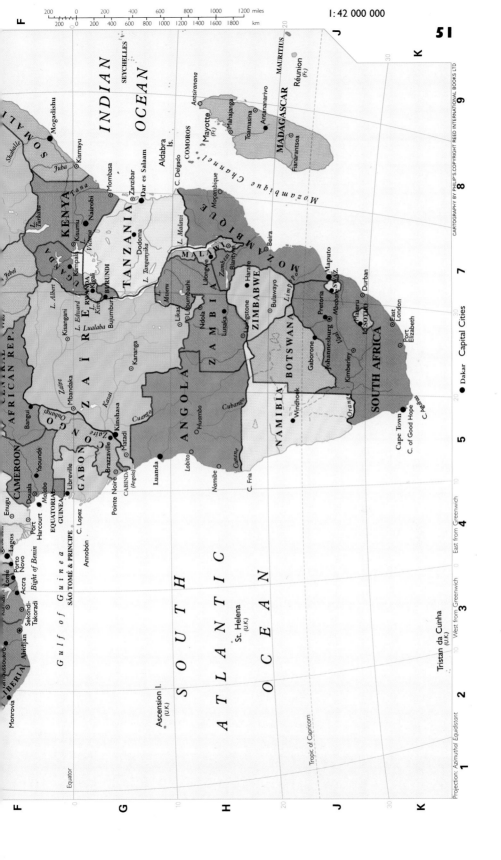

**51**

1:42 000 000

INDIAN OCEAN

SOUTH ATLANTIC OCEAN

**Capital Cities**

● Dakar

Projection: Azimuthal Equidistant

East from Greenwich

West from Greenwich

Equator

Tropic of Capricorn

SOMALI

KENYA

TANZANIA

ZAÏRE

UGANDA

RWANDA

BURUNDI

ANGOLA

ZAMBIA

MALAWI

MOZAMBIQUE

ZIMBABWE

NAMIBIA

BOTSWANA

SOUTH AFRICA

LESOTHO

SWAZ.

MADAGASCAR

COMOROS

SEYCHELLES

MAURITIUS

Réunion (Fr.)

Mayotte (Fr.)

CENTRAL AFRICAN REP.

CAMEROON

GABON

CONGO

EQUATORIAL GUINEA

SÃO TOMÉ & PRÍNCIPE

LIBERIA

Mogadishu

Kismayu

Mombasa

Nairobi

Kisumu

Kampala

Dodoma

Dar es Salaam

Zanzibar

C. Delgado

Antsiranana

Mahajanga

Toamasina

Antananarivo

Fianarantsoa

Aldabra Is.

Juba

Kisangani

Bangui

Yaoundé

Douala

Malabo

Libreville

Brazzaville

Kinshasa

Matadi

Pointe Noire

C. Lopez

Annobón

Luanda

CABINDA (Angola)

Lobito

Namibe

C. Fria

Huambo

Mbandaka

Kananga

Lubumbashi

Likasi

Ndola

Lusaka

Lilongwe

Blantyre

Harare

Beira

Bulawayo

Livingstone

Gaborone

Windhoek

Johannesburg

Pretoria

Mbabane

Maseru

Kimberley

Maputo

Durban

East London

Port Elizabeth

Cape Town

C. of Good Hope

Porto Novo

Lagos

Porto Novo

Accra

Sekondi-Takoradi

Abidjan

Monrovia

Enugu

Port Harcourt

Bight of Benin

Gulf of Guinea

Ascension I. (U.K.)

St. Helena (U.K.)

Tristan da Cunha (U.K.)

Mozambique Channel

L. Turkana

L. Victoria

L. Albert

L. Edward

L. Kivu

L. Tanganyika

L. Malawi

L. Mweru

Zambezi

Limpopo

Orange

Zaïre

Kasai

Cuango

Cubango

Cunene

Cuanza

Lualaba

Shabelle

Juba

Tana

Jebel

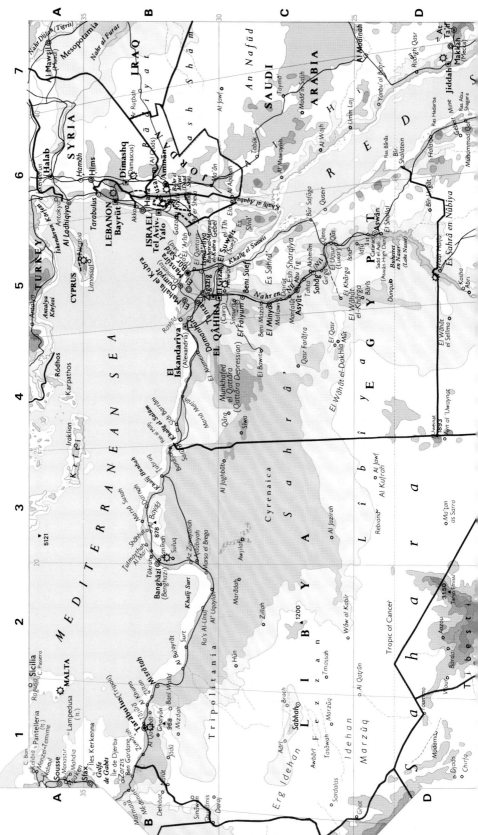

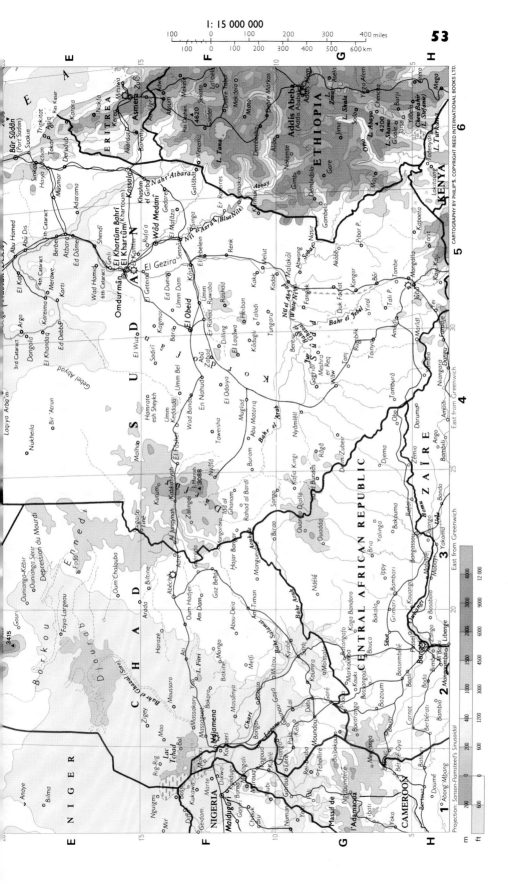

**1: 15 000 000**

53

Projection: Sanson-Flamsteed's Sinusoidal

CARTOGRAPHY BY PHILIP'S. COPYRIGHT REED INTERNATIONAL BOOKS LTD.

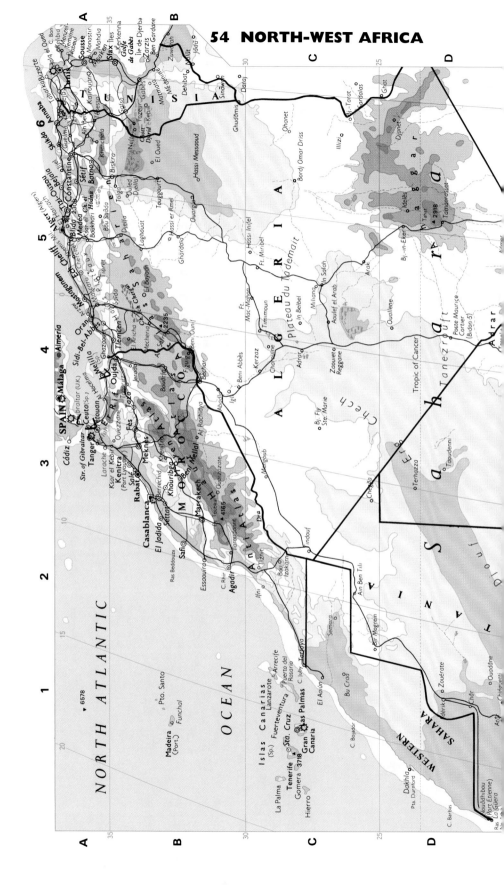

# 54 NORTH-WEST AFRICA

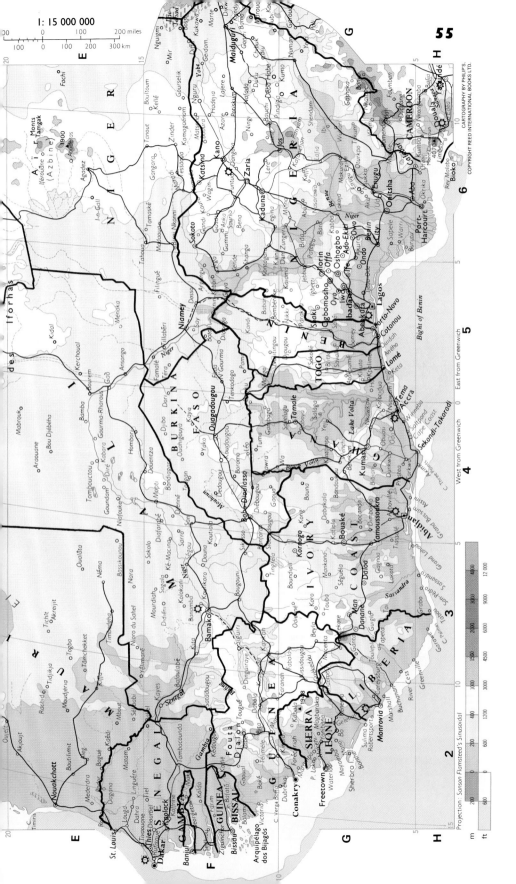

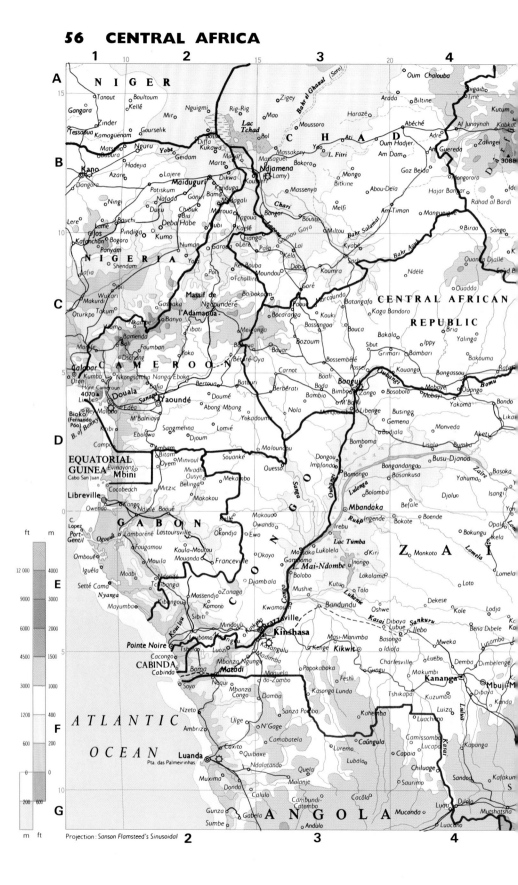

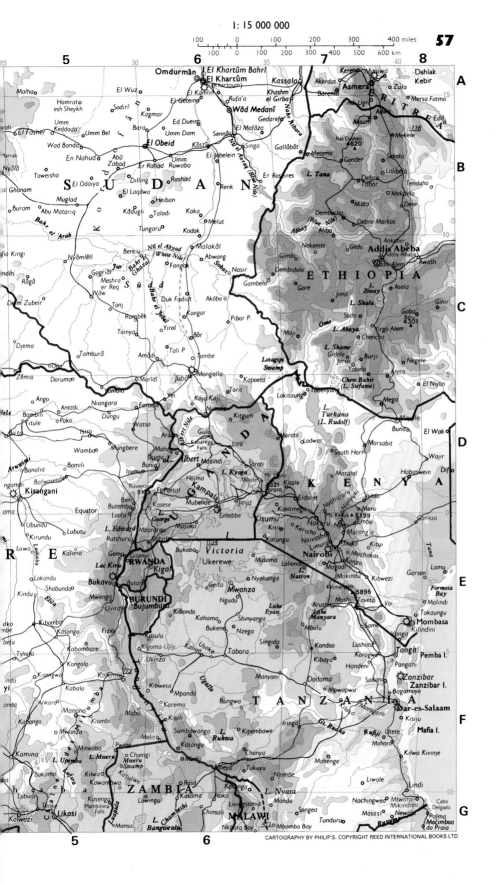

1 : 15 000 000

100    0    100    200    300    400 miles
100    0    100    200    300    400    500    600 km

**5** · 30 · **6** · 35 · **7** · 40 · **8**

Omdurmân  El Khartûm Bahrî  Kassala  Kereno  Musiwa  Dahlak Kebir
El Khartûm  Akordat  Asmera  Zula  Mersa Fatma
(Khartoum)  Barento  E R I T R E A  Edd
Malhao  Hamrat esh Sheykh  El Wuz  El Kamlin  Khashm el Girba  Keren  **A** 15
Sodirî  El Geteina  Rufa'a  Agordat  Aksum  -116
El Fasher  Kagmar  Wâd Medanî  Gedaref  Ras Dashen  Mekele
Umm Keddada  Bara  Ed Dueim  El Mafâza  4620  Sokota
Umm Bel  Umm Dam  Sennâr  Gallâbât  Metema  Gonder  Lalibela  **B**
Wad Banda  El Obeid  Kôstí  Singa  Debre Tabor  Tendaho
En Nahud  Er Rahad  Umm Ruwaba  El Jabelein  L. Tana  Mekela
Nyâlâ  Abû Zabad  Renk  Er Roseires  Ankober  Dese
Taweisha  Dilling  Rashad  Ras Rahad  Mota  Debre Markos
Muglad  El Odaiya  Heiban  Kaka  Abbay  Aliba
Buram  Abu Matariq  El Laqâwa  Talodi  Melut  Nekemte  Gedo  Addis Abeba  **B** 10
Bahr el 'Arab  Kâdugli  Tungaru  Kodok  (Addis Ababa)  Awash
Gogrial  Malakâl  Gimbo  Addis-Alem
Bentiu  Nil el Abyad  Dembidolo  ETHIOPIA
Nyamlèll  White Nile  Abwong  Gore  L. Ziway
Bahr el Ghazal  Fangak  Nasir  Gambela  Jima  Asela
Meshra er Req  Akôbo  Jarso  Soda  Goba  **C**
Tonj  Duk Fadiat  Kongor  L. Abaya  Yirga Alem  4307  Ginir
Rumbêk  Pibor P.  Omo  Chencha
Toinya  Nil el Jebel  Yirol  Bôr  L. Shamo  Gidole  Burji
Tamburâ  Amadi  Tali P  Tombe  Jarso  Negele
Djema  Mongalla  Lotagipi Swamp  Chew Bahir  Arero
Jûba  Kapoeta  (L. Stefanie)  El Niybo  **C**
Zémio  Dorumo  Marîdi  Torit  Loiyangalani  Mega
Ango  Amadi  Yei  Kaja Kaji  Lokitaung  L. Turkana  Bunao  El Wak  **D**
Niangara  Faradje  Kitgum  (L. Rudolf)
Bambili  Poko  Watsa  Aru  Gulu  Moroto  Moyale
Isiro  Dûngu  Lira  Lodwar  Marsabit  Wajir
Wambo  Mungbere  Mahagi  Kabarega Falls  South Horn  Habaswein  Dif  **D**
Kisangani  Bunia  L. Albert  Soroti  Mt. Elgon  Kitale  Mardial
Beni  Irumu  Mosindi  L. Kyoga  4321  Eldoret  Meru
Butembo  Ruwenzori  Hoima  Mbale  Gororo  Nyahururu  Ysiolo
Equator  5109  El Portal  Mubende  Jinja  Kakamega  Mt. Kenya  5199  Garissa
Ubundu  Kasese  Kampala  Entebbe  Kisumu  Nakuru  Embu
Lubutu  Luofu  George  Masaka  Kisii  Kericho  Nyeri  **E**
L. Edward  Mbarara  Bukoba  Karungu  Naivasha  Limuru  Thika  Kitui
Rutshuru  Kabali  Victoria  Musoma  Nairobi  Machakos  Lamu
Kirundu  Goma  Gisenyi  1134  Ukerewe  Nyahanga  Loliondo  Magadi  Konza  Garsen
Kalima  Lac Kivu  RWANDA  Kigali  I.  Mwanza  Natron  Makindu  Kibwezi
Lowa  Bukavu  Butare  Geita  Mûsoma  5895  Katimani  Formosa Bay  **E**
Lokandu  Mwenga  BURUNDI  Ngudu  L. Eyasi  Arusha  Voi  Malindi
Shabunda  Uvira  Bujumbura  Kibondo  Shinyanga  Moshi  Taveta  Takaungu
Kindu  Fizi  Kahama  Nzega  Mbulu  Same  Mombasa
Kibombo  Kasongo  Kigoma-Ujiji  Ukoke  Singida  Kondoa  Lushoto  Kilindini
Kongolo  Kabambare  Uvinza  Tabora  Korogwe  Pemba I.  Tanga
Kongola  Kaliua  Manyoni  Kibaya  Handeni  Pangani
Kabalo  Kibwesa  Ufalla  Dodoma  Mpwapwa  Sadani  Zanzibar  Zanzibar I.
Manono  Mpanda  Karema  Rungwa  Morogoro  Bagamoyo
Ankoro  Kiambi  Maba  TANZANIA  Dar-es-Salaam  **F**
Kapongo  Molira  Sumbawanga  L. Rukwa  Kipembawe  Iringa  Rufiji  Kisiju
Mwanza  Kalomo  Chunya  Mahenge  Mafia I.
Kamina  Mitwaba  L. Mweru  Chiengi  Mbeya  Tukuyu  Njombe  Kilwa Kivinje
Bukama  Mweru Swamp  Kaluiwe  Rosa  Manda  Liwale  Lindi
ZAMBIA  Kasenga  Mansa  Luwingu  Kasama  Songea  Tunduru  Nachingwea  Mtwara  **G**
Likasi  Mambilima Falls  Chambeshi  Chinsali  Livingstonia  L. Nyasa  Masasi  Mikindani  Cabo Delgado
Kolwezi  Bangweulu  Nkhata Bay  MALAWI  Mbamba Bay  Ruvuma  Palma  Moçimboa da Praia  **G** 10

**5** · **6**

CARTOGRAPHY BY PHILIP'S. COPYRIGHT REED INTERNATIONAL BOOKS LTD

**ATLANTIC OCEAN**

**ANGOLA**

Lobito
Benguela
Bailundo
Camacupa
Luena
Mwinilunga
Cazombo
Chavuma
Macond
Caundo
Zambezi

2619
Nova Lisboa
Bié
Munhango
Luvuei
Huambo
Cuima
Catata
Lumai
Zambezi
Lucira
Ganda
Chitembo
Quilengues
Ecunda
Galangue
Cubango
Lumbala N'guimbo
Libonda
Bibala
Lubango
Kipungo
Cuchi
Menongue
Kalabo
Mongu
Namibe
Chibia
Cassinga
Caiundo
Mavinga
Senanga
Tombua
Chianje
Chibemba
Mupa
Sioma
Oncocua
Xangongo
Cunene
Katima Mulilo
Chitado
Ondjiva
Cuito
Cuangar
Luiana
Shi
Cunene
Cubango (Okavango)
Dirico
C. Fria
Ondangua
Rundu
Andara
Caprivi Strip
Sesfontein
Ovamboland
Etosha Pan
Namutoni
Okaukuejo
Tsumeb
Okavango Swamps
Maun
Botswana
Otavi
Grootfontein
Tsau
Toteng
Botle E
Outjo
Otjiwarongo
Sehitwa
Ngami Depression
Ngami
Damaraland
Omatako
Omaruru
Epukiro
Ghanzi
Usakos
Okahandja
Karibib
Gobabis
BOTSWANA
Swakopmund
Windhoek
Tshwane
Kalahari
Walvisbaai
2483
Rehoboth
Tshane
Molep
Tropic of Capricorn
NAMIBIA
Tsumis
Namib Desert
Kalkrand
Aranos
Khakhea
Hardap Dam
Mariental
Maltahöhe
Namaland
Gochas
Werda
Lob
Gibeon
Koes
Tshabong
Mmabat
Li
Bethanie
Keetmanshoop
Lüderitz
Aus
Seeheim
Aroab
Rietfontein
Molopo
Vryburg
Fish
Kuruman
Nakop
Upington
Kimberley
Karasburg
Kakamas
Warrenton
Oranjemund
Warmbad
Orange
Pofadder
Kenhardt
Alexander Bay
Port Nolloth
Okiep
Prieska
Hopetown
Springbok
Britstown
De Aar
Hondeklipbaai
Brandvlei
Carnarvon
Springfonte
Bitterfontein
Sakrivier
Victoria W.
Noupoort
5283
Calvinia
SOUTH
AFRI
Vanrhynsdorp
Klawer
Nuweveldberge
Graaff-Reinet
Clanwilliam
Beaufort West
Somerset E
St. Helena B.
Piketberg
Ceres
Willowmore
Vredenburg
Worc
Oudtshoorn
Alice
Saldanha
Tafelbaai
Paarl
Robertson
George
Uitenhage
Cape Town
Stellenbosch
Swellendam
St
(Kaapstad)
Strand
Riversdale
Mosselbaai
Francis
Table Mt.
Caledon
Kaap die Goeie Hoop
Bredasdorp
(C.of Good Hope)
False
Danger Pt.
C. Agulhas

**ft m**

| 9000 | 3000 |
| 6000 | 2000 |
| 4500 | 1500 |
| 3000 | 1000 |
| 1200 | 400 |
| 600 | 200 |
| 0 | 0 |
| 200 | 600 |

m ft

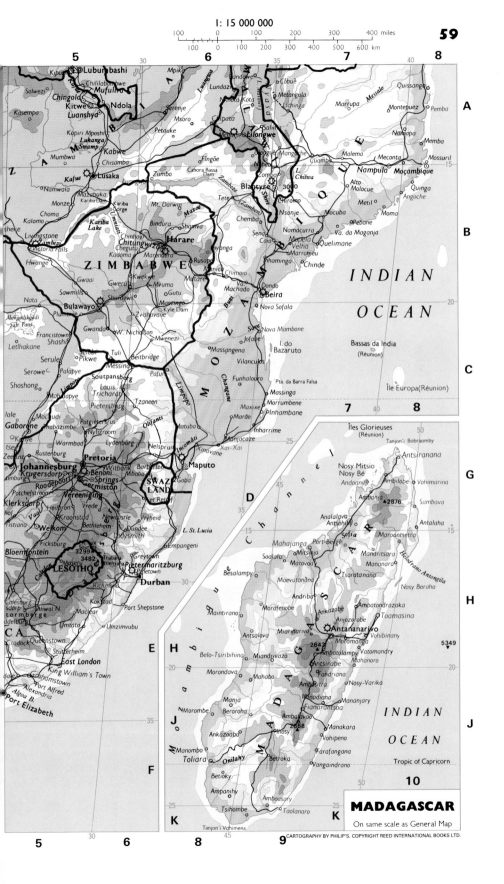

100    0    100    200    300    400 miles
100    0    100   200   300   400   500   600 km

5                    6                    7                    8

**INDIAN**

**OCEAN**

Bassas da India
(Réunion)

Île Europa(Réunion)

ZAMBIA

Lubumbashi
Chililabombwe
Mufulira
Solwezi
Chingola
Kitwe    Ndola
Luanshya
Kasempa
Kopiri Mposhi
Lukanga    Kabwe
Swamp
Mumbwa    Chisamba
Kafue    Lusaka
Namwala
Mazabuka
Monze    Kariba
Choma    Gorge
Kalomo    Kariba
Livingstone    Lake
Victoria Falls
Hwange

Kipushi        Mpika
                Lundazi
Katete        Nkhota-Kota
Serenje        Chipata
Msoro        Salima        Lilongwe
Petauke        Mangochi    Cuamba
            Fingõe    Mchinji
Zumbo    Cahora Bassa
            Dam    Zomba    Blantyre    3000
                    Tete    Chiromo
Mt. Darwin    Nsanje
Bindura    Shamva    Chembo
Chinhoyi    Caia
Chegutu    Harare    Senga
Kadoma    Marondera    Namacurra
Kwekwe    Rusape    Mopeia
Gweru    Mutoko    Velha
Shurugwi    Mutare    Chinde
Gutu    Chimoio
Masvingo    Dondo
Zvishavane    Beira
Mberengwa    Nova Sofala

ZIMBABWE

Gwaai
Sawmills
Nata
Makgadikgadi
Salt Pans
Bulawayo
Plumtree
Gwanda    W. Nicholson
Francistown    Mwenezi
Shashi    Tuli    Beitbridge
Letlhakane    Messina
Serule    Pikwe
Gaborone    Soutpansberg
Kanye    Louis    Pietersburg
Thabazimbi    Trichardt
Mochudi    Nylstroom
Warmbad    Lydenburg
Rustenburg    Nelspruit
Johannesburg    Witbank    Komatipoort
Krugersdorp    Benoni    Barberton
Roodepoort    Springs    Mbabane
Potchefstroom    Germiston    SWAZI
Klerksdorp    Vereeniging    LAND
Vaal    Heilbron    Piet Retief
Kroonstad    Vrede    Volksrust
Welkom    Newcastle    Vryheid
Bethlehem    Dundee    Empangeni
Ficksburg    Ladysmith    L. St. Lucia
Bloemfontein    Maseru    3299
LESOTHO    3482    Greytown
Thaba Ntlenyana    Pietermaritzburg
Richmond    Pinetown
Kokstad    Durban
Aliwal N    Port Shepstone
Umtata    Umzimvubu
Cradock    Queenstown
Stutterheim    East London
King William's Town
Grahamstown
Port Alfred
Algoa B.
Port Elizabeth

M O Z A M B I Q U E

Cóbuè
Metangula
Lichinga    Marrupa    Messalo
Montepuez
Nacala
Alto    Nampula    Moçambique
Molocue    Quinga
Metil    Angoche
Moma
Pebane
Va. da Maganja
Quelimane
L. Chilwa

Marrupa
Pemba
Memba
Mossuril

I.do
Bazaruto
Pta. da Barra Falsa
Massinga
Morrumbene
Maxixe    Inhambane
Mardo
Vilanculos
Funhalouro
Massangena
Mabote
Sofala
Nova Mambone

Massinga
Maxixe
Mardo    Inharrime
Manjacaze    Xai-Xai
Maputo    Incomati
Goba
Matuba
Chibuto
Manzini

Mozambique
Channel

**MADAGASCAR**

Îles Glorieuses
(Réunion)
Tanjon'i Bobraomby
Nosy Mitsio    Antsiranana
Nosy Bé
Andoany    Ambilobe    Vohimarina
Ambanja    2876
Analalava    Sambava
Antsohihy    Sofia    Antalaha
Maroantsetra
Port-Bergé    Mandritsara
Mahajanga    Mananara
Mitsinjo    Tsaratanana
Soalala    Marovoay    Nosy Boraha
Maevatanana    Andriba
Besalampy    Ankazobe
Morafenobe    Anjozorobe    Toamasina
Maintirano    Ambatondrazaka
Antsalova    Ankazobe
Antananarivo
Miarinarivo    Moramanga
Belo-Tsiribihina    Ambatolampy    Vohibinany
Miandrivazo    2643    Vatomandry
Antsirabe    Mahanoro
Morondava    Fandriana
Mahabo    Ambositra    Nosy-Varika
Ambatofinandrahana
Manja    Ifanadiana    Mananjary
Beroroha    Fianarantsoa
N'Morombe    Ambalavao    Manakara
Ankazoabo    2688    Vohipeno
Ihosy    Farafangana
Manombo    Betioky    Vangaindrano
Toliara    Onilahy    Betroka
Betioky
Ampanihy    Ambovombe
Tsihombe    Taolanara
Tanjon'i Vohimena

5349

**INDIAN**

**OCEAN**

Tropic of Capricorn

10

**MADAGASCAR**
On same scale as General Map

CARTOGRAPHY BY PHILIP'S. COPYRIGHT REED INTERNATIONAL BOOKS LTD.

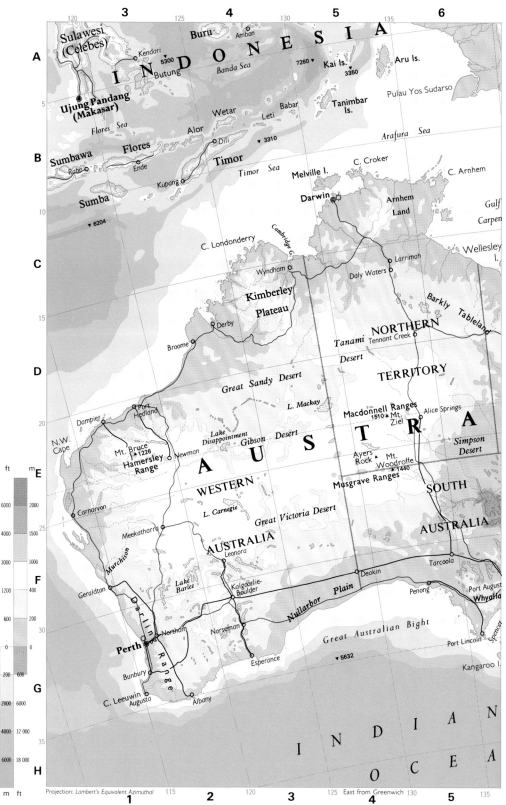

Sulawesi (Celebes)
Buru
Ambon
INDONESIA
Kendari
5300
Butung
Banda Sea
7260
Kai Is.
3350
Aru Is.
Pulau Yos Sudarso

Ujung Pandang (Makasar)
Wetar
Leti
Babar
Tanimbar Is.
Arafura Sea

Flores Sea
Alor
Dili
3310

Sumbawa
Flores
Timor
Timor Sea
Melville I.
C. Croker
C. Arnhem

Raba
Ende
Kupang
Darwin
Arnhem Land
Gulf Carpen

Sumba
6204
C. Londonderry
Cambridge G.
Arnhem Land
Wellesley I.

Wyndham
Larrimah
Daly Waters
Barkly Tableland

Derby
Kimberley Plateau
NORTHERN
Tanami Desert
Tennant Creek

Broome
Great Sandy Desert
L. Mackay
TERRITORY
Macdonnell Ranges
1510 Mt. Ziel
Alice Springs

Dampier
Port Hedland
Lake Disappointment
Gibson Desert
AUSTRA
Simpson Desert

N.W. Cape
Mt. Bruce 1226
Hamersley Range
Newman
Ayers Rock
Mt. Woodroffe 1440

Carnarvon
WESTERN
L. Carnegie
Musgrave Ranges
SOUTH

Meekatharra
Great Victoria Desert
AUSTRALIA

Murchison
AUSTRALIA
Leonora
Tarcoola

Geraldton
Lake Barlee
Kalgoorlie-Boulder
Deakin
Penong
Port August
Whyalla

Darling Range
Northam
Norseman
Nullarbor Plain
Great Australian Bight
Port Lincoln
Spencer

Perth
Esperance
5632
Kangaroo I.

Bunbury
C. Leeuwin Augusta
Albany
INDIAN

OCEA

ft    m
6000    2000
4000    1500
3000    1000
1200    400
600    200
0    0
200    600
2000    6000
4000    12 000
6000    18 000
m    ft

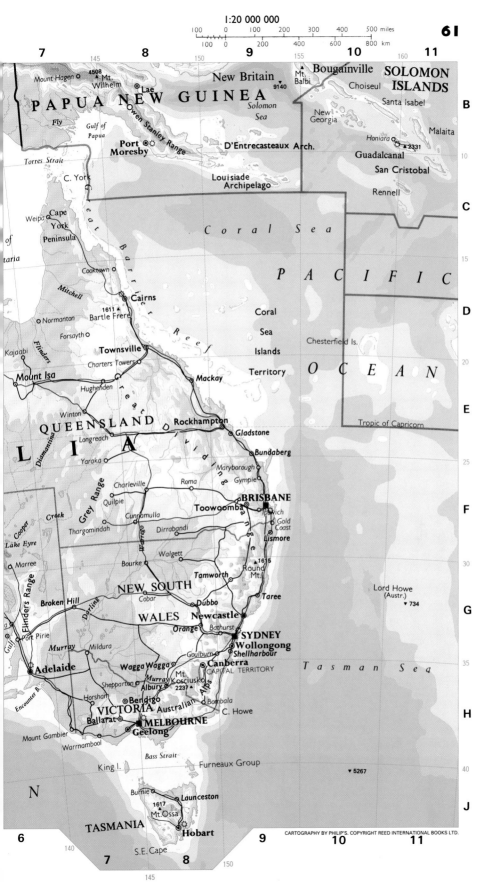

1:20 000 000

100    0    100    200    300    400    500 miles
100    0    200    400    600    800 km

**7**        145        **8**        150        **9**        155        **10**        160        **11**

Mount Hagen    ▲4508 ▲Mt.    New Britain        Mt.    Bougainville    **SOLOMON**
                    Wilhelm    ◎Lae        ▼Balbi            **ISLANDS**
**PAPUA NEW GUINEA**        9140    Choiseul    Santa Isabel        B

Fly    Gulf of        Solomon        New        Malaita
        Papua        Sea        Georgia

Port ◎☼        D'Entrecasteaux Arch.        Honiara ☼ ▲2331

Torres Strait    Moresby            Guadalcanal            10
                        San Cristobal
C. York        Louisiade        Rennell
                Archipelago                        C

Weipa    Cape        C o r a l   S e a
        York
        Peninsula                        15

        Cooktown                P A C I F I C

Mitchell    ◎Cairns    Coral            D
        1611▲
        Bartle Frere    Sea    Chesterfield Is.

Normanton        Islands            O C E A N        20
Forsayth

Kajaabi    Townsville    Territory

Mount Isa    Charters Towers            Tropic of Capricorn    E

        Hughenden        Mackay        Lord Howe    25
                                (Austr.)
Winton    QUEENSLAND    Rockhampton        ▼734
Longreach        Gladstone
L I A    Yaraka    Bundaberg            G

Charleville    Roma    Maryborough
        Gympie        T a s m a n   S e a    30
Quilpie    Cunnamulla    BRISBANE
Thargomindah        Toowoomba    Ipswich
Cooper    Creek        Gold            ▼5267    40
Lake Eyre        Dirrabandi    Coast
                Lismore
Marree        Walgett
                Round    1615
        Bourke    Tamworth    Mt.
NEW SOUTH
Broken Hill    Cobar    Dubbo    Taree
        Darling    WALES    Newcastle    J
Port Pirie    Orange    Bathurst
Murray    Mildura        SYDNEY
Adelaide            Canberra    Wollongong
        Wagga Wagga    CAPITAL TERRITORY    Shellharbour    35
Shepparton    Albury    Mt.
        Murray    Kosciusko
Horsham    Bendigo    2237▲
VICTORIA    Australian    Bombala
Ballarat    MELBOURNE    C. Howe
Mount Gambier    Geelong            H
Warrnambool
        Bass Strait    Furneaux Group
King I.
N        Burnie    Launceston        40
        1617▲
        Mt.Ossa
TASMANIA    Hobart            J
6    140    S.E. Cape    9    10    11
7    8
145    150

CARTOGRAPHY BY PHILIP'S. COPYRIGHT REED INTERNATIONAL BOOKS LTD.

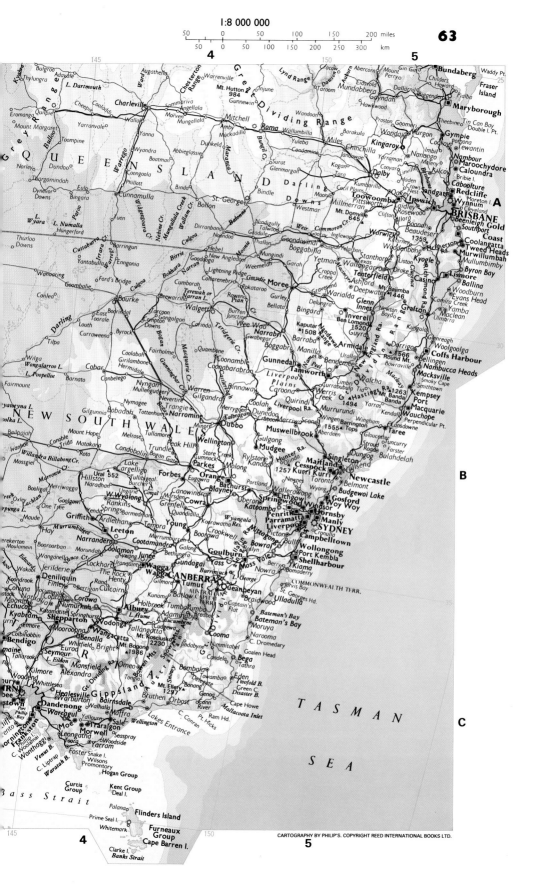

1:8 000 000

50   0   50   100   150   200 miles
50  0  50 100 150 200 250 300 km

**4**   **5**

CARTOGRAPHY BY PHILIP'S. COPYRIGHT REED INTERNATIONAL BOOKS LTD.

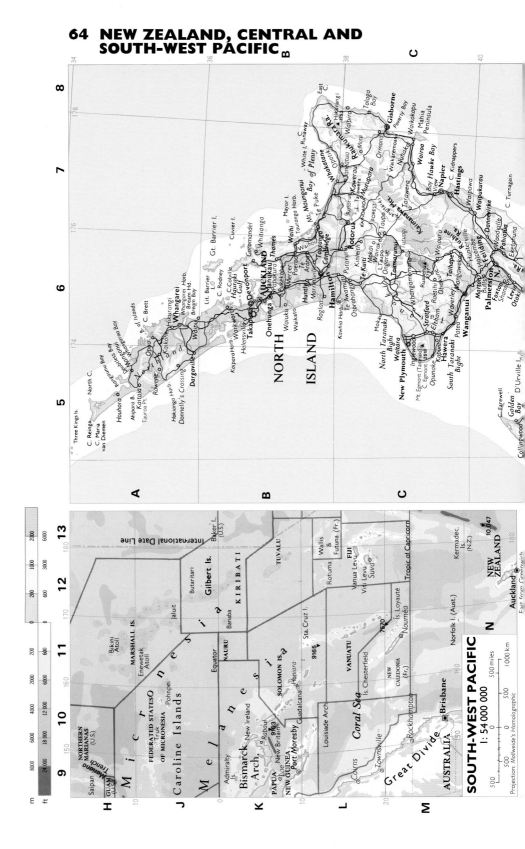

## NORTH ISLAND

Three Kings Is.
C. Reinga
C. Maria van Diemen
North C.
Houhora
Ahipara B.
Kaitaia
Tauroa Pt.
Rangaunu Bay
Doubtless Bay
B. of Islands
C. Brett
Hokianga Harb.
Donnelly's Crossing
Dargaville
Rawene
Opua
Waikohu
Northland
Kaipara Harb.
Helensville
Waikato
Waiuku
Waipa
Workworth
C. Rodney
Lit. Barrier I.
Gt. Barrier I.
Cuvier I.
C. Colville
Coromandel
Whitianga
Whangarei
Whangarei Harb.
Hikurangi
Bream Hd.
Bream Bay
Waipu
Devonport
Takapuna
AUCKLAND
Hauraki Gulf
Manukau
Onehunga
Thames
Paeroa
Waihi
Waihou
Wairoa
Mercer
Huntly
Ngaruawahia
Hamilton
Cambridge
Te Aroha
Morrinsville
Matamata
Tauranga
Mayor I.
Bay of Plenty
White I.
East C.
Opotiki
Te Puke
Mt. Maunganui
Tauranga Harb.
Whakatane
Mt. Edgecumbe
Raglan
Kawhia Harb.
Otorohanga
Te Kuiti
Te Awamutu
Putaruru
Tokoroa
Rotorua
L. Rotorua
Kaingaroa Forest
Murupara
Waikaremoana
Ruatahuna
Wairoa
Mahia Peninsula
Waikokopu
Gisborne
Poverty Bay
Tolaga Bay
Hikurangi
Raukumara Ra.
Waipiro
Ruatoria
Kawerau
Tarawera
Kaokaoroa
Ormond
Taneatua
NORTH ISLAND
Mokau
Awakino
North Taranaki Bight
New Plymouth
Mt. Egmont (Taranaki)
C. Egmont
Inglewood
Stratford
Eltham
Opunake
Kapuni
Hawera
Patea
South Taranaki Bight
Wanganui
Waverley
Mangaweka
Taumarunui
L. Taupo
Taupo
Tongariro
Ngaruahoe
Ruapehu
Ohakune
Raetihi
Waiouru
Taihape
Rangitikei
Marton
Bulls
Feilding
Palmerston N.
Shannon
Levin
Otaki
Foxton
Ruahine Ra.
Dannevirke
Woodville
Pahiatua
Eketahuna
Napier
Hastings
Waipawa
Waipukurau
Hawke Bay
C. Kidnappers
Havelock North
Takapau
Kaweka Ra.
Kaimanawa Mts.
Waiotapu

## SOUTH-WEST PACIFIC

NORTHERN MARIANAS (U.S.)
Saipan
GUAM (U.S.)
Mariana Trench
Micronesia
Caroline Islands
FEDERATED STATES OF MICRONESIA
Truk
Pohnpei
Yap
MARSHALL IS.
Bikini Atoll
Enewetak Atoll
Jaluit
Melanesia
Admiralty Is.
Bismarck Arch.
New Ireland
New Britain
Rabaul
Lae
PAPUA NEW GUINEA
Port Moresby
Louisiade Arch.
SOLOMON IS.
Guadalcanal
Honiara
9165
Equator
NAURU
Banaba
KIRIBATI
Gilbert Is.
Butaritari
Baker I. (U.S.)
TUVALU
Rotuma
Sta. Cruz I.
VANUATU
Chesterfield
NEW CALEDONIA (Fr.)
Nouméa
Is. Loyauté
7570
Coral Sea
Townsville
Cairns
Rockhampton
AUSTRALIA
Brisbane
Great Divide
Norfolk I. (Aust.)
Wallis & Futuna (Fr.)
FIJI
Vanua Levu
Viti Levu
Suva
Tropic of Capricorn
Kermadec Is. (N.Z.)
10 047
NEW ZEALAND
Auckland

International Date Line

**SOUTH-WEST PACIFIC**
1: 54 000 000

500 0 500 1000 km
500 0 500 miles

Projection: Mollweide's Homolographic

East from Greenwich

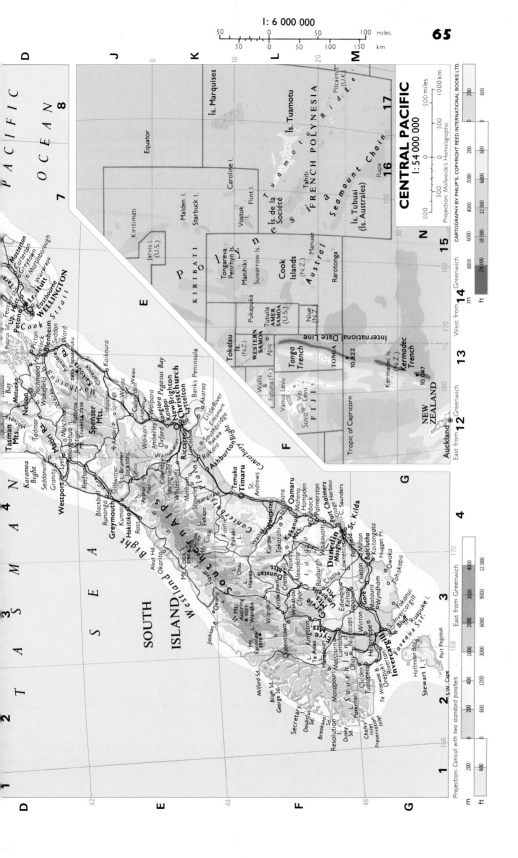

1: 6 000 000

50    0    50    100 miles
50    0    50    100    150    km

CENTRAL PACIFIC
1: 54 000 000

500    0    500    1000 km
500    0    500 miles

Projection: Mollweide's Homolographic
CARTOGRAPHY BY PHILIP'S. COPYRIGHT REED INTERNATIONAL BOOKS LTD.

PACIFIC OCEAN

Is. Marquises

Equator

Is. Tuamotu

FRENCH POLYNESIA

Pitcairn I.

Seamount Chain

Rapa

Tahiti

Caroline I.

Malden I.
Starbuck I.

Is. de la Société

Vostok
Flint I.

Kiritimati

Tubuai (Is. Australes)

Jarvis I. (U.S.)

KIRIBATI

Tongareva
Penrhyn I.

Suwarrow Is.

Manuae

Manihiki

Cook Islands (N.Z.)

Rarotonga

Austral

Pukapuka

Tutuila
AMER. SAMOA (U.S.)

Niue (N.Z.)

Tokelau (N.Z.)

WESTERN SAMOA    Apia

International Date Line

Wallis & Futuna (Fr.)

Vanua Levu

Tonga Trench

10.822

TONGA

FIJI

Suva    Viti Levu

Kermadec Is. (N.Z.)

10.047

Kermadec Trench

Tropic of Capricorn

Auckland

NEW ZEALAND

West from Greenwich

East from Greenwich

TASMAN SEA

SOUTH ISLAND

Cook Strait

WELLINGTON
Petone    Lr. Hutt
Eastbourne

Masterton
Carterton
Greytown
Martinborough
Featherston

Blenheim
Picton
Havelock
Seddon
Ward

Nelson
Richmond
Wakefield
Motueka

Tasman Mts.
Tasman Bay

Spenser Mts.
2885
Travers 2338
Tapuaenuku

Marlborough

Kaikoura

Golden Bay

Karamea Bight

Westport
Granity
Seddonville
Denniston

Reefton
Murchison
Maruia
Lyell

Maruia

Murchison

Greymouth
Runanga
Blackball
Kumara

Hokitika
Ross

Okarito

Abut Hd.

SOUTH WEST LAND

South Island

Mt. Cook 3764
3753

Banks Peninsula

Christchurch
New Brighton
Riccarton
Lyttelton

Rangiora Pegasus Bay
Oxford
Kaiapoi
Amberley

Waiau
Culverden
Waipara

Hanmer
Springs

Hurunui

Waikari

Southern Alps

Arthur's Pass

L. Brunner

Jacksons

Otira

Rakaia
Methven
Springfield
Whitecliffs
Coleridge

Darfield

Ashburton

Temuka
Timaru
St. Andrews

Geraldine
Fairlie
Pleasant Pt.

L. Tekapo

Mt. Cook

L. Pukaki

L. Ohau

Twizel

Omarama

Kurow
Waitaki

Oamaru
Moeraki
Hampden

Palmerston
Dunback
Waikouaiti
Port Chalmers

Dunedin
Mosgiel
St. Kilda

Ranfurly
Middlemarch

Alexandra
Clyde
Cromwell

Roxburgh
Ettrick
Lawrence

Milton
Kaitangata
Balclutha

Taieri

Owaka

Nugget Pt.

Clinton
Waipahi

Gore
Mataura
Wyndham

Edendale

Invercargill
Bluff

Winton
Otautau

Nightcaps

Lumsden

Mossburn

Te Anau
L. Te Anau

Kingston
Queenstown

Wanaka
L. Wanaka

Mt. Aspiring 3027

Mt. Earnslaw 2819

Manapouri
L. Manapouri

Jackson B.

Milford Sd.

Bligh Sd.
George Sd.

Secretary I.

Doubtful Sd.

Breaksea Sd.

Dusky Sd.
Resolution I.

Chalky Inlet

Preservation Inlet

SOUTHLAND

Riverton

Foveaux Str.

Ruapuke I.

Stewart I.

Halfmoon Bay

S.W. Cape

Port Pegasus

Projection: Conical with two standard parallels

m    ft

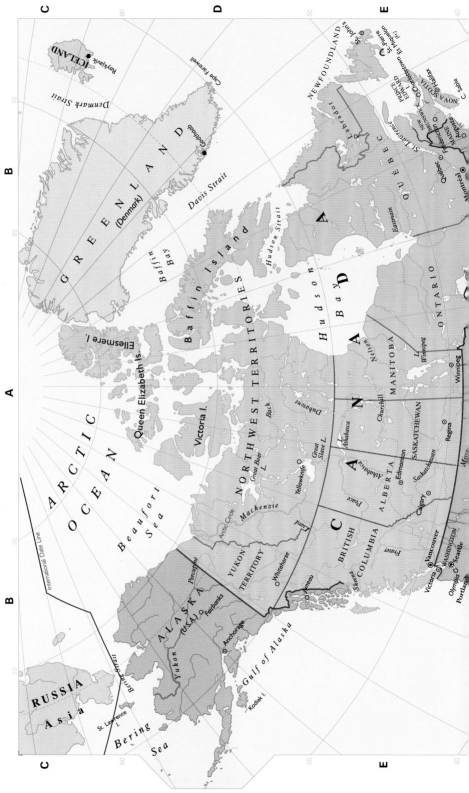

ICELAND
Reykjavik

Denmark Strait

Cape Farewell

NEWFOUNDLAND
St. John's
St. Pierre
Charlottetown Et Miquelon (Fr.)
PRINCE
EDWARD I.
NOVA SCOTIA Halifax
Cape Sable
NEW BRUNSWICK
Fredericton
MAINE
Augusta

GREENLAND
(Denmark)

Godthaab

Davis Strait

Baffin
Bay

Labrador

St. Lawrence

QUEBEC

Québec Montréal

Hudson Strait

Baffin Island

Ellesmere I.

Queen Elizabeth Is.

Victoria I.

ARCTIC

OCEAN

International Date Line

Beaufort
Sea

Arctic Circle

Great Bear
L.

Yellowknife

Great
Slave L.

Mackenzie

NORTHWEST TERRITORIES

Back

Dubawnt

Hudson

Bay

Nelson

Eastmain

ONTARIO

MANITOBA

L.
Winnipeg

Winnipeg

Churchill

C A N A D A

SASKATCHEWAN

Athabasca

L.
Athabasca

Saskatchewan

Regina

Peace

Edmonton

ALBERTA

Calgary

Miss

Liard

YUKON
TERRITORY

Whitehorse

BRITISH
COLUMBIA

Fraser

Vancouver

Skeena

Victoria

WASHINGTON
Seattle
Olympia
Portla

RUSSIA
Asia

Bering Strait

St. Lawrence
I.

Bering

Sea

A L A S K A
(U.S.A.)

Porcupine

Fairbanks

Yukon

Anchorage

Gulf of Alaska

Kodiak I.

Juneau

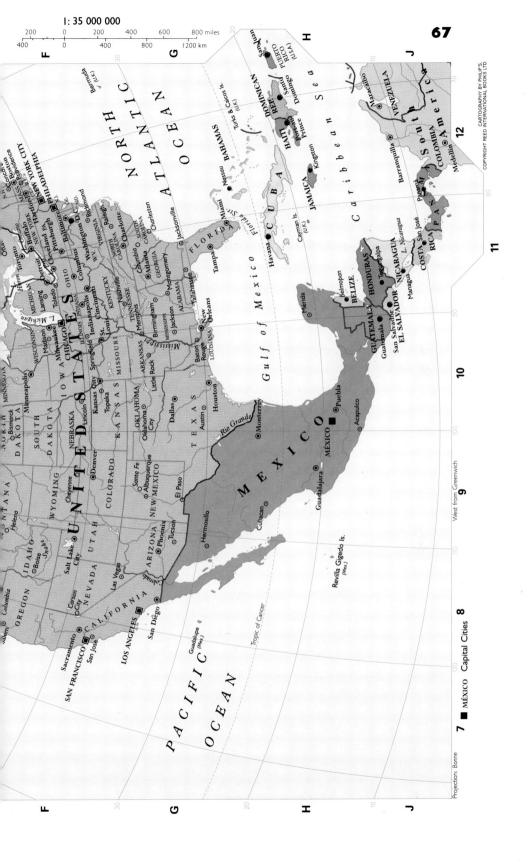

1:35 000 000

200    0    200    400    600    800 miles
400    0    400    800    1200 km

NORTH ATLANTIC OCEAN

Bermuda (U.K.)

NORTH
N.Concord O Boston
O Providence
MASS. NEW YORK CITY
NEW YORK Hartford
CT.
PHILADELPHIA
Buffalo O N.J.
PENNSYLVANIA
Cleveland O Pittsburgh
OHIO MD. Baltimore
Washington D.C.
Columbus W. VIRGINIA
Cincinnati VIRGINIA
KENTUCKY Richmond
Raleigh
NORTH CAROLINA
Nashville Charlotte
TENNESSEE SOUTH CAROLINA
Columbia
Memphis Atlanta
ALABAMA GEORGIA
Birmingham Montgomery Jacksonville
Jackson
MISSISSIPPI FLORIDA
New Orleans Tallahassee
LOUISIANA Tampa
Baton Rouge

Detroit O
MICHIGAN
Lansing O
Toledo
INDIANA
Indianapolis
ILLINOIS
Springfield
St. Louis
MISSOURI

Toronto O
Huron L.
L. Michigan
Milwaukee
CHICAGO
Madison
WISCONSIN
IOWA

Ott L.
Ottawa

MINNESOTA
Minneapolis
NORTH DAKOTA
Bismarck
SOUTH DAKOTA

MONTANA
Helena
IDAHO
Boise
Snake
WYOMING
Cheyenne
NEBRASKA
Lincoln
Denver
COLORADO
KANSAS
Topeka
Kansas City
OKLAHOMA
Oklahoma City
Little Rock
ARKANSAS

UNITED STATES

NEVADA
Carson City
Salt Lake City
UTAH
Santa Fe
Albuquerque
NEW MEXICO
ARIZONA
Phoenix
Tucson
El Paso
TEXAS
Dallas
Austin
Houston
San Antonio

OREGON
Salem
Columbia
Sacramento
San Francisco
San Jose
CALIFORNIA
LOS ANGELES
Las Vegas
San Diego
Colorado

Hermosillo
Culiacan

Guadalupe (Mex.)

Tropic of Cancer

Revilla Gigedo Is. (Mex.)

PACIFIC OCEAN

MEXICO

Rio Grande
Monterrey
Guadalajara
MÉXICO
Puebla
Acapulco
Mérida

Gulf of Mexico

Havana
CUBA
Florida Str.
Miami
Nassau
BAHAMAS

Turks & Caicos Is. (U.K.)

Cayman Is. (U.K.)

Kingston
JAMAICA

Caribbean Sea

San Juan
PUERTO RICO (U.S.A.)
DOMINICAN REP.
Santo Domingo
HAITI Port-au-Prince

Belmopan
BELIZE
GUATEMALA
Guatemala
San Salvador
EL SALVADOR
HONDURAS
Tegucigalpa
NICARAGUA
Managua
L. Nicaragua
COSTA RICA
San José
PANAMA
Panamá

VENEZUELA
Maracaibo
Barranquilla
COLOMBIA
Medellín
South America

West from Greenwich

Projection: Bonne

7    ■ MÉXICO    Capital Cities    8

**69**

1 : 15 000 000

100   0   100   200   300   400 miles

100   0   100   200   300   400   500   600 km

CARTOGRAPHY BY PHILIP'S. COPYRIGHT REED INTERNATIONAL BOOKS LTD.

Projection: Bonne

1: 15 000 000

100    0    100    200    300    400 miles
100    0    100    200    300    400    600 km

Projection: Bonne

ALASKA
1: 30 000 000

100    0    100    200    300 miles
100    0    100    200    300    400 km

West from Greenwich

| m | ft |
|---|---|
| 3000 | 9000 |
| 2000 | 6000 |
| 1500 | 4500 |
| 1000 | 3000 |
| 400 | 1200 |
| 200 | 600 |
| 0 | 0 |
| 200 | 600 |
| 2000 | 6000 |

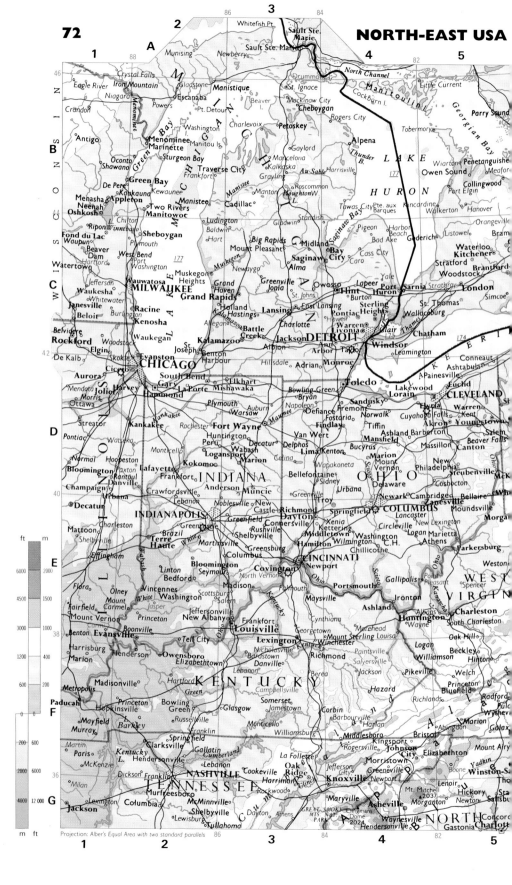

Projection: Alber's Equal Area with two standard parallels

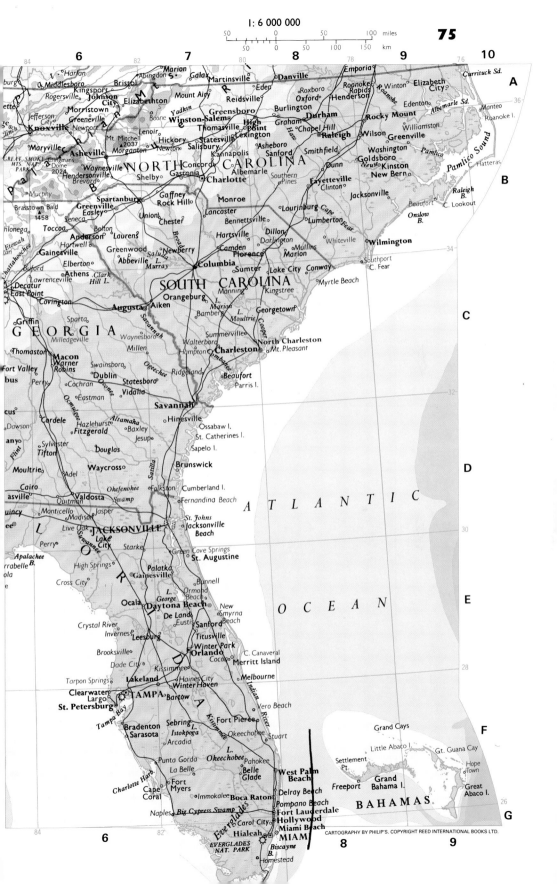

1: 6 000 000

50    0    50    100 miles
50  0  50  100  150 km

**A**

Currituck Sd.
Harlan    Marion
Middlesboro    Galax  Martinsville    Danville    Emporia    Roanoke    Elizabeth    Manteo
Rogersville    Abington    Eden    Roxboro    Winton    City
Johnson    Bristol    Mount Airy    Reidsville    Oxford    Roanoke    Edenton    Roanoke I.
Jefferson    City    Elizabethton    Boone    Yadkin    Greensboro    Burlington    Henderson    Albemarle Sd.
City    Morristown    Lenoir    Thomasville    High    Graham    Durham    Rocky Mount    Williamston
Greeneville    Newport    Hickory    Statesville    Point    Lexington    Chapel Hill    Raleigh    Wilson    Greenville
Knoxville    Mt. Mitchell    Morganton    Newton    Salisbury    Asheboro    Smithfield    Washington    Pamlico
Maryville    2037    Kannapolis    Sanford    Dunn    Goldsboro    Kinston    Hatteras
Asheville    Cleveland    Concord    NORTH  CAROLINA    New Bern
Waynesville    Dome    Shelby    Gastonia    Albemarle    Southern    Clinton    Jacksonville
Hendersonville    2024    Charlotte    Pines    Fayetteville
Brevard

**B**

Murphy    Gaffney    Monroe    Laurinburg    Cape    Onslow    Raleigh
Brasstown Bald    Spartanburg    Rock Hill    Lancaster    Lumberton    Fear    B.    C. Lookout
1458    Greenville    Easley    Union    Chester    Bennettsville    Whiteville    Wilmington    Beaufort
Toccoa    Seneca    Hartsville    Dillon
Anderson    Laurens    Darlington    Mullins
Hartwell    Greenwood    Newberry    Camden    Florence    Marion    Southport
Gainesville    Abbeville    Saluda    Columbia    Sumter    Lake City    Conway    C. Fear
Elberton    L.    Murray    SOUTH  CAROLINA    Myrtle Beach
Buford    Athens    Clark
Lawrenceville    Hill L.    Orangeburg    Manning    Kingstree
Decatur    Covington    Augusta    Aiken    Bamberg    L.    Georgetown
East Point    Griffin    Sparta    Waynesboro    Moultrie    Cooper

**C**

GEORGIA    Milledgeville    Millen    Summerville    North Charleston
Thomaston    Macon    Warner    Swainsboro    Walterboro    Charleston    Mt. Pleasant
Fort Valley    Robins    Dublin    Ridgeland    Beaufort
Perry    Cochran    Statesboro    Vidalia    Parris I.
Dawson    Cordele    Hazlehurst    Altamaha    Savannah
Sylvester    Fitzgerald    Baxley    Hinesville    Ossabaw I.
Tifton    Jesup    St. Catherines I.
Moultrie    Adel    Douglas    Waycross    Sapelo I.

**D**

Cairo    Okefenokee    Brunswick
asville    Quitman    Swamp    Folkston    Cumberland I.
quincy    Monticello    Jasper    Fernandina Beach
Madison    Live Oak    St. Johns    ATLANTIC
Perry    Lake    Jacksonville    Jacksonville    Beach
Apalachee    City    Green  Cove  Springs
rrabelle B.    High Springs    Starke    St. Augustine

**E**

Cross City    Palatka    Bunnell
Gainesville    Ormond
Ocala    L.    Beach    OCEAN
George    Daytona Beach
Crystal River    De Land    New    Smyrna
Inverness    Eustis    Sanford    Beach
Leesburg    Titusville
Brooksville    Winter  Park
Dade City    Orlando    C. Canaveral
Tarpon Springs    Kissimmee    Cocoa    Merritt Island

**F**

Lakeland    Haines  City    Melbourne
Clearwater    Winter  Haven
Largo    TAMPA    Bartow    Indian
St. Petersburg    Vero Beach    Grand Cays
Bradenton    Sebring    Fort Pierce    Little Abaco I.    Gt. Guana Cay
Tampa Bay    Sarasota    Istokpoga    Okeechobee    Stuart    Hope
Arcadia    L.    Settlement    Town
Punta Gorda    Okeechobee    Pahokee    Pt.    Freeport    Grand    Great
La Belle    Belle    West Palm    Bahama I.    Abaco I.
Charlotte Harb.    Fort    Glade    Beach
Cape    Myers    Immokalee    Delray Beach    BAHAMAS
Coral    Boca Raton
Naples    Big Cypress Swamp    Pompano Beach

**G**

Fort Lauderdale
Everglades    Carol City    Hollywood
Hialeah    Miami Beach
EVERGLADES    MIAM
NAT. PARK    Biscayne
B.
Homestead

FLORIDA

CARTOGRAPHY BY PHILIP'S. COPYRIGHT REED INTERNATIONAL BOOKS LTD.

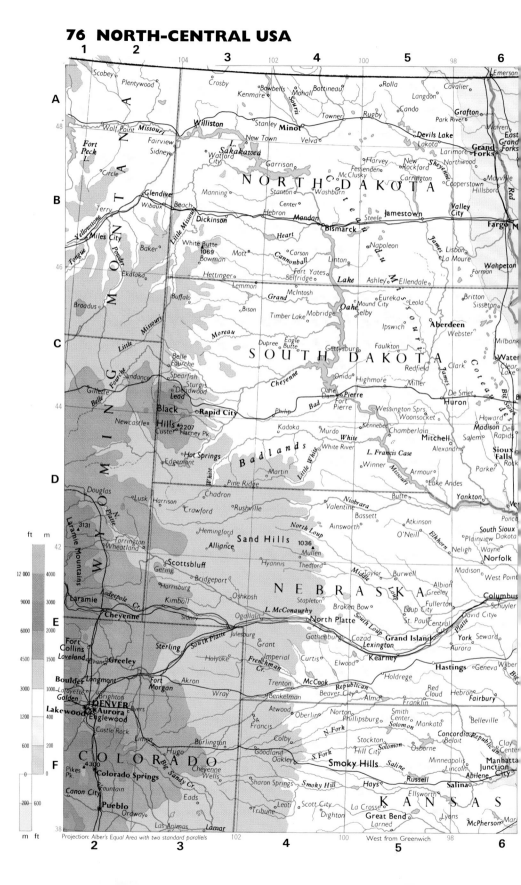

Projection: Alber's Equal Area with two standard parallels

West from Greenwich

1: 6 000 000

50   0   50   100 miles
50   0   50   100   150 km

7 8 9 10 11

**CANADA**

Lake of the Woods
Roseau
Warroad
Rainy River
Baudette
International Falls
Rainy
Rainy Lake
Fort Frances
Atikokan
Lac la Croix
**Thunder Bay**
Isle Royale
183

Thief River Falls
Upper Red L.
Red Lake Falls
Lower Red
Crookston
Grand Marais
**LAKE SUPERIOR**
Copper Harbor
Keweenaw Pt.
Keweenaw Pen.
Keweenaw B.

Ada
Fosston
Bagley
Bemidji
Mahnomen
Cass Lake
Winnibigoshish
Leech L.
Walker
Park Rapids
Hibbing
Eveleth
Virginia
St. Louis
Two Harbors
Apostle Is.
Hancock
Houghton
Ontonagon
L'Anse
604
Ishpeming Marquette
Negaunee

oorhead
Hawley
Detroit Lakes
Perham
Wadena
Staples
Grand Rapids
Mille Lacs L.
Moose Lake
**Duluth**
Superior
Washburn
Ashland
Hurley
Bessemer
Ironwood
**MICHIGAN**
Crystal Falls

Barnesville
Breckenridge
Fergus Falls
Little Falls
Brainerd
Aitkin
Cloquet
Hayward
Park Falls
Eagle River
Iron Mountain
Niagara
Powers

Alexandria
Morris
Wheaton
Glenwood
Milaca
Mora
Pine City
Grantsburg
Spooner
Phillips
Rhinelander
Crandon
Menominee

**MINNESOTA**
Sauk Rapids
St. Cloud
Mississippi
Cambridge
Rice Lake
Ladysmith
Cornell
Medford
Merrill
Antigo
Green Bay
Marinette

town
Willmar
Litchfield
Montevideo
Hutchinson
Glencoe
**MINNEAPOLIS**
St. Paul
Bloomington
Hastings
Anoka
Stillwater
Hudson
Menomonie
Chippewa Falls
Eau Claire
**WISCONSIN**
Marshfield
Wausau
Stevens Point
Shawano
Oconto
Sturgeon Bay
**Green Bay**
Kewaunee

Granite Falls
Canby
Redwood Falls
Marshall
New Ulm
Northfield
Red Wing
Lake City
Alma
Whitehall
Wisconsin Rapids
Waupaca
Menasha
Neenah
Appleton
De Pere
Kaukauna
Two Rivers
**Manitowoc**

rookings
St. Peter
Faribault
Mankato
Owatonna
Winona
Rochester
Black River Falls
Wautoma
Oshkosh
L. Winnebago
Chilton
Sheboygan

Flandreau
Waseca
St. James
Preston
Sparta
Tomah
Montello
Ripon
Fond du Lac
Waupun
Plymouth

Pipestone
Windom
Albert Lea
Austin
Onalaska
**La Crosse**
Viroqua
Reedsburg
Baraboo
Portage
Beaver Dam
Hartford
West Bend
Port Washington

Worthington
Jackson
Fairmont
Northwood
Preston
Richland Center
Wisconsin
Watertown
Jefferson
Wauwatosa
**MILWAUKEE**
**MICHIGAN**
**LAKE**

Rapids
Canton
Sibley
Estherville
Spencer
Emmetsburg
Forest City
Osage
Decorah
Waukon
Prairie du Chien
Dodgeville
Lancaster
Darlington
Madison
Waukesha
Whitewater
**Racine**

million
Sheldon
Le Mars
Cherokee
Algona
Garner
Hampton
Charles City
New Hampton
Monroe
Janesville
Beloit
Burlington
Kenosha

City
Sioux City
Storm Lake
Pocahontas
Clarion
Waverly
Oelwein
Wisconsin
Dubuque
Freeport
Woodstock
Belvidere
Waukegan

Little Sioux
Ida Grove
Sac City
Fort Dodge
Webster
Iowa Falls
Cedar Falls
Waterloo
Independence
Wapsipinicon
Maquoketa
Rockford
Elgin
Skokie
Evanston
**CHICAGO**

Onawa
Denison
Carroll
Boone
Ames
**IOWA**
Marshalltown
Vinton
Marion
**Cedar Rapids**
Clinton
Sterling
Dixon
De Kalb
Aurora
Cicero
Harvey

Tekamah
Blair
Audubon
Perry
Newton
Grinnell
Marengo
Iowa City
**Davenport**
Moline
Rock Island
Mendota
Princeton
Morris
Joliet
Ottawa

Fremont
Harlan
W. Des Moines
**Des Moines**
Montezuma
Muscatine
Kewanee
Peru
Streator
Kankakee

**Omaha**
Wahoo
Atlantic
Winterset
Indianola
Pella
Washington
L. Red Rock
Aledo
Galesburg
Chillicothe
Pontiac

Council Bluffs
Greenfield
Knoxville
Oskaloosa
Ottumwa
Fairfield
Monmouth
Peoria
Pekin
Normal
Paxton

Plattsmouth
Glenwood
Red Oak
Creston
Osceola
Albia
Mt. Pleasant
**Burlington**
Canton
Bloomington
Rantoul

**Lincoln**
Nebraska
Shenandoah
Corning
Bedford
Leon
Centerville
Fort Madison
Macomb
Lincoln
Champaign

Auburn
Clarinda
Bloomfield
Keokuk
Rushville
Decatur

Beatrice
Rockport
Grant City
Princeton
Unionville
Kahoka
**ILLINOIS**

Pawnee City
Blue
Bethany
Milan
Kirksville
Edina
Beardstown
Taylorville
Pana
Shelbyville

Falls City
Savannah
Trenton
Chillicothe
Palmyra
**Quincy**
Springfield
Jacksonville
Mattoon

Hiawatha
Troy
Brookfield
**Hannibal**
Carlinville
Litchfield
Effingham

Marysville
Holton
Atchison
St. Joseph
Excelsior Sprs.
Carrollton
Macon
Moberly
Carrollton
Jerseyville
Vandalia

Leavenworth
Richmond
Independence
Fayette
Mexico
Troy
**Alton**
Greenville

Kansas
Alma
Topeka
**Kansas City**
Lexington
Marshall
Columbia
Fulton
St. Charles
Granite City
St. Louis
Centralia

Lawrence
Olathe
Warrensburg
Sedalia
Boonville
Jefferson City
Hermann
Union
**ST. LOUIS**
East St. Louis
Belleville
Fairfield

Council Grove
Ottawa
Paola
Harrisonville
Missouri
Osage
Sullivan
Waterloo
Mount Vernon

Emporia
Garnett
Butler
Clinton
Lake of the Ozarks
De Soto
Ste. Genevieve
Pinckneyville
Du Quoin
Benton

Burlington
**MISSOURI**

CARTOGRAPHY BY PHILIP'S. COPYRIGHT REED INTERNATIONAL BOOKS LTD.

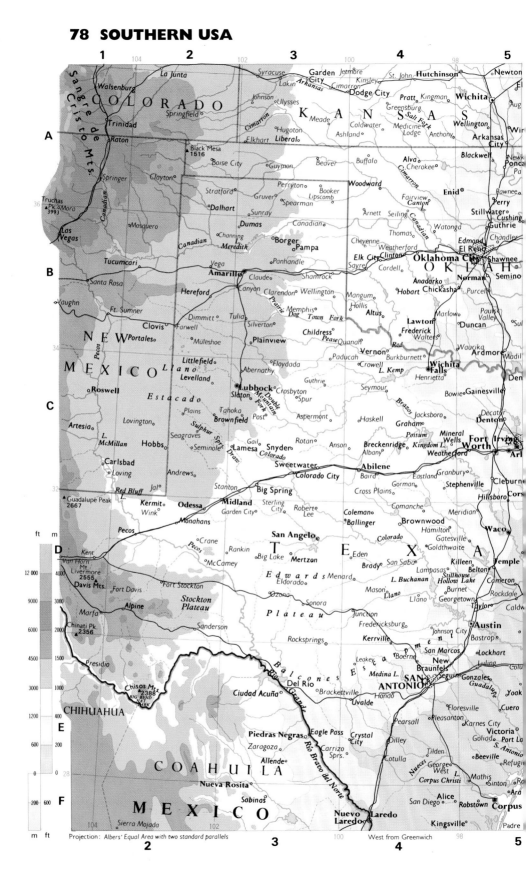

Projection: Albers' Equal Area with two standard parallels

West from Greenwich

1: 6 000 000

50    0    50    100 miles

50    0    50    100    150 km

GULF    OF

MEXICO

Continuation
Southwards
on same scale

CARTOGRAPHY BY PHILIP'S. COPYRIGHT REED INTERNATIONAL BOOKS LTD.

Projection: Alber's Equal Area with two standard parallels

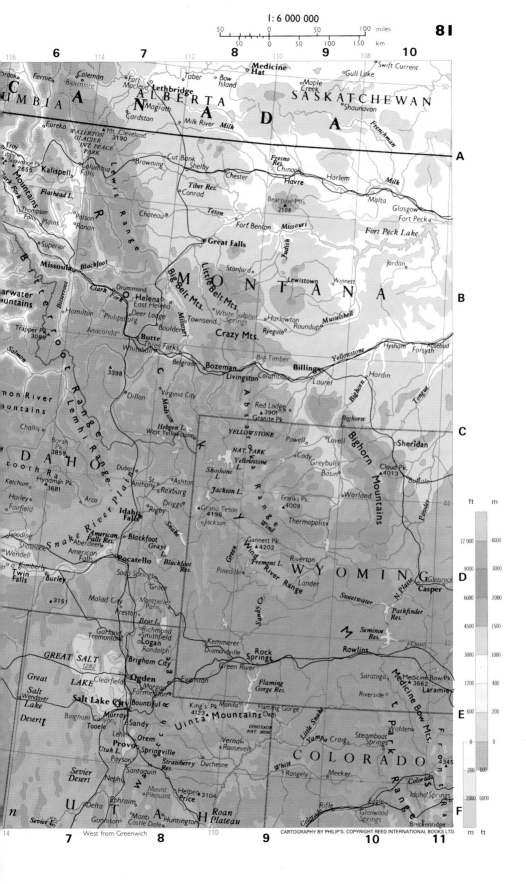

1: 6 000 000

50  0  50  100 miles
50  0  50  100  150 km

**6**     **114**     **7**     112     **8**     110     **9**     108     **10**

CANADA

C—LUMBIA  Brooke  Fernie  Coleman  Blairmore  Fort  Macleod  Lethbridge  Taber  Bow  Island  Medicine  Hat  Maple  Creek  Gull Lake  Swift Current  50

A  N  Magrath  ALBERTA  Cardston  Milk River  Milk  SASKATCHEWAN  Shaunavon  A

Troy  Eureka  WATERTON  GLACIER  INT PEACE  PARK  Mt. Cleveland  3190  Frenchman  A

Libby  Snowshoe Pk  2655  Kalispell  Columbia  Falls  Browning  Cut Bank  Shelby  Chester  Fresno  Res.  Chinook  Havre  Harlem  Milk

Clark Fork  Flathead L.  Lewis  Range  Conrad  Tiber Res.  Conrad  Bearpaw Mts.  2108  Malta  Glasgow  Fort Peck  B

Thompson  Falls  Plains  Polson  Ronan  Choteau  Teton  Fort Benton  Missouri  Judith  Jordan  Fort Peck Lake

Superior  Great Falls  Stanford  Lewistown  Winnett

Missoula  Blackfoot  Big  Belt Mts.  MONTANA  B

arwater  untains  Clark Fork  Drummond  Helena  East Helena  Deer Lodge  Philipsburg  Townsend  White Sulphur  Springs  Harlowton  Ryegate  Roundup  Musselshell

Hamilton  Anaconda  Boulder  Crazy Mts.  Hysham  Rosebud  Forsyth

Trapper Pk  3098  Butte  Three Forks  Whitehall  Belgrade  Big Timber  Yellowstone

Salmon  3398  Bozeman  Livingston  Columbus  Billings  Laurel  Hardin  C

IDAHO  Lemhi Range  Dillon  Virginia City  Red Lodge  3901  Granite Pk.  Bighorn  Sheridan

Challis  Hebgen L.  West Yellowstone  YELLOWSTONE  NAT. PARK  Powell  Lovell  Bighorn  Cloud Pk.  4013  Buffalo

Borah Pk  3859  Dubois  St.  Anthony  Yellowstone  L.  Cody  Greybull  Basin  Worland  C

Ketchum  Hyndman Pk.  3681  Arco  Rexburg  Shoshone  L.  Franks Pk.  4009  Thermopolis

Hailey  Fairfield  Driggs  Jackson L.  Grand Teton  4196  Wind  Riverton  Powder  44

Gooding  Idaho  Falls  Rigby  Jackson  Gannett Pk.  4202  Lander  Bighorn  Mountains

Shoshone  American  Falls Res.  Blackfoot  Grays  L.  Green  Wind River Range  Fremont L.  Riverton

Wendell  Aberdeen  Blackfoot  Res.  Pinedale  Lander  WYOMING  Glenrock  D

Twin  Falls  Burley  Soda Springs  Grace  Sweetwater  N. Platte  Casper

3151  Malad City  Montpelier  Paris  Pathfinder  Res.

Garland  Tremonton  Preston  Bear L.  Kemmerer  Seminoe  Res.  Hanna

GREAT SALT  1282  Richmond  Smithfield  Logan  Randolph  Diamondville  Rock  Springs  Rawlins  Saratoga  Medicine Bow Pk  3662  Laramie

Great  Salt  Clearfield  Brigham City  Green River  Riverside  42

LAKE  Ogden  Evanston  Flaming  Gorge Res.  Medicine Bow Mts.

Salt Lake  Wendover  Lake  Morgan  Farmington  King's Pk  4123  Manila  Flaming Gorge  Dam  Waldena  4345  E

Desert  Salt Lake City  Bountiful  Uinta Mountains  DINOSAUR  NAT. MON.  Yampa  Craig  Steamboat  Springs  Front

Bingham Canyon  Murray  Sandy  Vernala  Roosevelt  Walden  Range

Tooele  Orem  Provo  Springville  Payson  Vernal  COLORADO

Sevier  Desert  Santaquin  Strawberry  Res.  Duchesne  White  Meeker  Colorado  Idaho Springs

Nephi  Mount  Pleasant  Helper  Price  3104  Rangely  Eagle  Rifle  Glenwood  Springs  F

Delta  Ephraim  Manti  Castle Dale  Huntington  Roan  Plateau  Colorado  Breckenridge

n  Sevier L.  UTAH  Gunnison  Colorado

**7**  West from Greenwich  **8**  110  **9**  **10**  **11**

CARTOGRAPHY BY PHILIP'S. COPYRIGHT REED INTERNATIONAL BOOKS LTD.

ft    m

12 000    4000

9000    3000

6000    2000

4500    1500

3000    1000

1200    400

600    200

0    0

200    600

2000    6000

m    ft

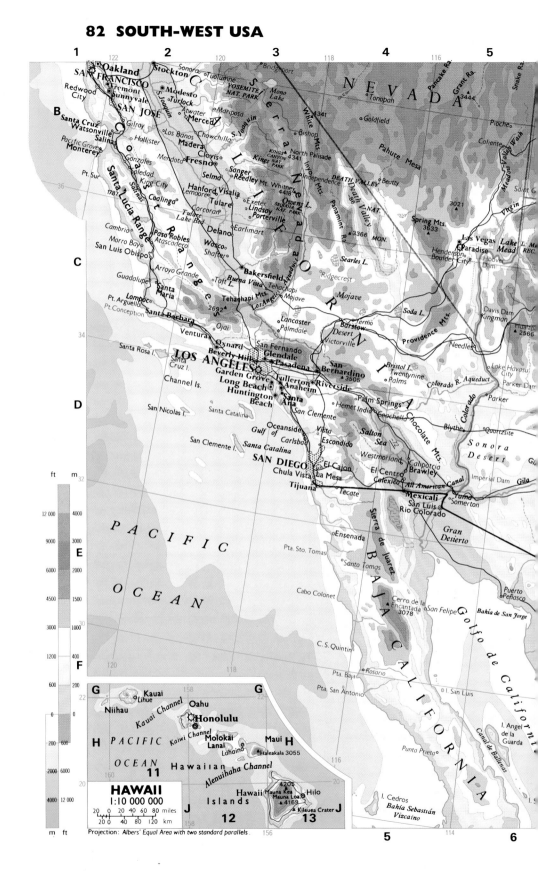

**82 SOUTH-WEST USA**

1  2  3  4  5

**NEVADA**

Bridgeport
Sonora
Tuolumne
Mono Lake
Tonopah
Pancake Ra.
Grant Ra.
3444
Snake Ra.

Oakland
Stockton
SAN FRANCISCO
Fremont
Redwood City
Sunnyvale
SAN JOSE
Modesto
Turlock
Atwater
Merced
Mariposa
YOSEMITE NAT. PARK
White Mts.
4341
Bishop
Goldfield
Pioche
Caliente
Meadow Valley Wash

Santa Cruz
Watsonville
Salinas
Gilroy
Hollister
Los Banos
Chowchilla
San Joaquin
North Palisade 4341
Independence Mts.
Owens L.
Saint G

Pacific Grove
Monterey
Gonzales
Soledad
Mendota
Madera
Clovis
Fresno
Sanger
Reedley
Selma
KINGS CANYON 4341
KINGS NAT. PARK
Mt. Whitney 4418
DEATH VALLEY
Beatty
DEATH VALLEY NAT.
3021

Pt. Sur
King City
Coalinga
Hanford
Lemoore
Visalia
Exeter
SEQUOIA NAT. PARK
Owens L.
Vgin

Santa Lucia Range
Salinas
1787
Tulare
Corcoran
Lindsay
Porterville
Panamint Ra.
3366 MON.
Spring Mts. 3633
Las Vegas
Lake Mead
L. Me REC.

Cambria
Morro Bay
Paso Robles
Atascadero
Tulare Lake Bed
Delano
Earlimart
Searles L.
Henderson
Paradise
Boulder City
Hoover Dam

San Luis Obispo
Arroyo Grande
Shafter
Wasco
Ridgecrest
Mojave
Davis Dam
Kingman
Hualapai 2566

Guadalupe
Santa Maria
Lompoc
Pt. Arguello
Pt. Conception
Santa Barbara
Taft
Buena Vista
Bakersfield
Tehachapi Mts.
2692
Tehachapi
Los Angeles Aqueduct
Mojave
Soda L.
Providence Mts.
Needles
Lake Havasu City
Parker Dam

Santa Rosa I.
Ventura
Ojai
Lancaster
Palmdale
Barstow
Termo
Victorville
Bristol L.
Twentynine Palms
Colorado R. Aqueduct
Parker

LOS ANGELES
Beverly Hills
Glendale
Pasadena
San Fernando
Oxnard
Santa Cruz I.
Channel Is.
San Bernardino 3505
Palm Springs
Chocolate Mts.
Blythe
Quartzsite
Parker

Garden Grove
Long Beach
Huntington Beach
Fullerton
Anaheim
Santa Ana
Riverside
San Clemente
Hemet
Indio
Coachella
Colorado
Sonora Desert

San Nicolas I.
Santa Catalina
San Clemente I.
Oceanside
Carlsbad
Vista
Escondido
Salton Sea
Westmorland
Calipatria
Brawley
Imperial Dam
Gila

SAN DIEGO
Chula Vista
La Mesa
El Cajon
El Centro
Calexico
All American Canal
Yuma
Somerton

Tijuana
Tecate
Mexicali
San Luis Rio Colorado
Gran Desierto

**PACIFIC OCEAN**

Ensenada
Sierra de Juarez
BAJA

Pta. Sto. Tomas
Santa Tomas
Cerro de la Encantada 3078
San Felipe
Bahía de San Jorge
Puerto Peñasco
Golfo de California

Cabo Colonet
C. S. Quintin
Rosario
CALIFORNIA
I. San Luis
I. Angel de la Guarda

Pta. Baja
Pta. San Antonio
Punta Prieta
Canal de Ballenas

I. Cedros
Bahía Sebastián Vizcaíno

**Elevation scale**

| ft | m |
|---|---|
| 12 000 | 4000 |
| 9000 | 3000 |
| 6000 | 2000 |
| 4500 | 1500 |
| 3000 | 1000 |
| 1200 | 400 |
| 600 | 200 |
| 0 | 0 |
| 200 | 600 |
| 2000 | 6000 |
| 4000 | 12 000 |

## HAWAII
### 1:10 000 000

Kauai
Lihue
Niihau
Kauai Channel
Oahu
Honolulu
Molokai
Lanai
Lahaina
Maui
Haleakala 3055
PACIFIC OCEAN
Hawaiian
Alenuihaha Channel
Kaiwi Channel
Hawaii
Islands
Mauna Kea 4205
Mauna Loa 4169
Hilo
Kilauea Crater

20 0 20 40 60 80 miles
20 0 40 80 120 km

Projection: Albers' Equal Area with two standard parallels.

1 : 6 000 000

50   0   50   100 miles
50   0   50   100   150 km

**COLORADO**

**UTAH**

Fillmore
Richfield
Monroe
Milford
Beaver
Loa
3710 Junction
Parowan
Cedar City
Panguitch
Zion Nat. Park
Santa Clara
Hurricane
Washington
Kanab
Fredonia
Mt. Trumbull 2447
Colorado

Grand Junction
Leadville
Mt. Elbert 4399
Aspen
Fairplay
Gunnison
Delta
Paonia
Mt. Antero 4349
Buena Vista
Moab
Mt. Peale 3877
Montrose
Blue Mesa Res.
Uncompahgre Pk. 4359
Ouray
Lake City
Saguache
Silverton
Creede
Rio Grande
Telluride
Del Norte
Blanca Pk. 4378
Alamosa
San Luis
Wheeler Pk. 4011
Taos

Green River
Moab
Canyonlands Nat. Park
Monticello
Dove Creek
Blanding
Glen Canyon Nat. Rec. Area
Glen L. Powell
Glen Canyon Dam
Page
San Juan
Cortez
Durango
Pagosa Springs
Antonito

**A**

**B**

Shiprock
Aztec
Navajo Res.
Farmington
Bloomfield
Tierra Amarilla
Kayenta
Roof Butte 2989
Chinle
Tuba City
Ganado
Los Alamos
Truchas Pk. 3993
Mora
Santa Fe
Las Vegas
Bernalillo
Alameda
Albuquerque
Isleta
Los Lunas
Moriarty
Estancia
Vaughn

Grand Canyon
Painted Desert
Little Colorado
Humphreys Pk. 3851
Williams
Flagstaff
Chino Valley
Clarkdale
Cottonwood
Prescott
Winslow
Holbrook
Hough
Gallup
Mt. Taylor 3445
Grants
Zuni
Belen
Mountainair

**C**

**ARIZONA**

**NEW MEXICO**

Mogollon Rim
Snowflake
Little Colorado
St. Johns
Show Low
Payson
Lakeside
Pinetop
Springerville
3476 Baldy Pk.
Reserve
Magdalena
South Baldy 3287
Socorro
Carrizozo

Wickenburg
Sun City
Glendale
PHOENIX
Tempe
Mesa
Chandler
Miami
Globe
San Carlos
Roosevelt Res.
Salt
Whitewater Baldy 3321
Gila
Black Ra.
Elephant Butte Res.
Truth or Consequences
Sierra Blanca Pk. 3659
Ruidoso

Bend Mts.
Gila Bend
Casa Grande
Coolidge
Florence
Hayden
Coolidge Dam
San Carlos L.
Bylas
Clifton
Silver City
Central
Hurley
Hatch
Tularosa
Alamogordo

**D**

Eloy
Mammoth
Oracle
Pima
Thatcher
Safford
Mt. Graham 3267
Galiuro Mts.
Marana
Tucson
Willcox
Lordsburg
Deming
Las Cruces
Mesilla
Sacramento Mts.
San Andres Mts.

Sells
Sonoyta
Mt. Wrightson 2881
Benson
Chiricahua Pk. 2986
Tombstone
Sierra Vista
Bisbee
Douglas
Las Palomas
Ciudad Juárez
Anthony
El Paso
2667 Guadalupe Pk.
Clint
Fabens

Nogales
Nogales
Agua Prieta
**TEXAS**

**E**

Heroica Caborca
Altar
Imuris
Cananea
Magdalena
Santa Ana
Nacozari
Arizpe
Guadalupe
Bravos
El Porvenir
Rio Grande
Sierra Blanca
L. de Sta. María
Villa Ahumada
L. de Palos
Rio Bravo del Norte

Benjamin Hill
Cumpas
Moctezuma
Nuevo Casas Grandes
Buenaventura
El Sueco

**MEXICO**

**SONORA**

**CHIHUAHUA**

**F**

Desierto de Altar
Tiburón
San Esteban
Lorenzo
Hermosillo
Ures
Sonora
Mazatán
Suaqui
Sahuaripa
Torres
Temosachic
Chihuahua
Aquiles Serdán

West from Greenwich

CARTOGRAPHY BY PHILIP'S. COPYRIGHT REED INTERNATIONAL BOOKS LTD.

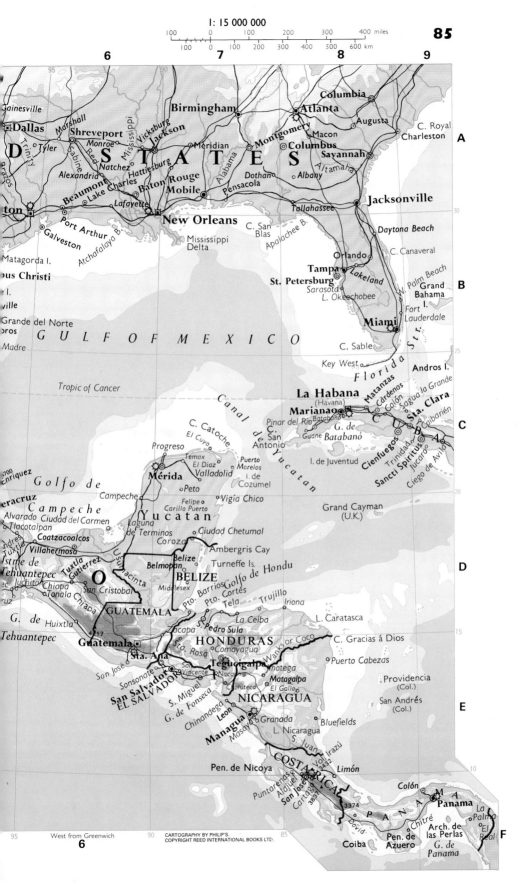

1: 15 000 000

100   0   100   200   300   400 miles
100   0   100   200   300   400   600 km

**6**     **7**     **8**     **9**

Gainesville

☐Dallas
Marshall
Shreveport
Tyler
Monroe      Vicksburg  Jackson
Natchez   Hattiesburg   Meridian
Alexandria         Baton Rouge
Beaumont  Lake Charles
ton   Port Arthur   Lafayette   Mobile   Pensacola
Galveston

**D**
**S**    **T**   **A**   **T**   **E**   **S**

Birmingham
Atlanta
Columbia
Augusta
Macon         C. Royal
Charleston
Montgomery
Columbus      Savannah
Dothan
Albany
Altamaha

Jacksonville

Matagorda I.

us Christi

e I.
ville

Grande del Norte
ros
Madre

**A**

Tallahassee

New Orleans
C. San Blas
Apalachee B.
Mississippi Delta

Daytona Beach

Orlando      C. Canaveral
Tampa   Lakeland
St. Petersburg   W. Palm Beach
Sarasota      Grand Bahama I.
L. Okeechobee
Fort Lauderdale
Miami

**B**

**G U L F     O F     M E X I C O**

C. Sable

Key West      Andros I.

30

25

Tropic of Cancer

Florida Str.

La Habana (Havana)     Matanzas
Marianao      Cárdenas
Pinar del Rio   Batabanó   Colón   Sagua la Grande
C. San Antonio   Guane   G. de   Sta. Clara   Caibarién
Batabanó
Cienfuegos   Trinidad   Sancti Spíritus   Júcaro
I. de Juventud      Ciego de Avila

**C**

Canal de Yucatan

C. Catoche
El Cuyo
Progreso   Temax   Puerto
El Diaz   Morelos
Mérida   Valladolid   I. de Cozumel
Peto

Golfo de

Enriquez
700

eracruz
Campeche
Alvarado   Ciudad del Carmen
Tlacotalpan
Coatzacoalcos
Tuxtla   Villahermosa
Istme de
Tehuantepec   Gutierrez
Juchitán   Chiapa   San Cristobal
Tonalá   Chiapa
G. de   Huixtla
Tehuantepec

**O**

Campeche   Felipe
Carillo Puerto   Vigía Chico

**Y u c a t a n**

Laguna de Terminos
Corozal   Ciudad Chetumal
Ambergris Cay
Belize   Turneffe Is.
Belmopan   Middlesex
**BELIZE**
Pto. Barrios   Golfo de Hondu
Pto. Cortés
**GUATEMALA**
Zacapa   Tela   Trujillo
Sta. Rosa   S. Pedro Sula   La Ceiba   Iriona
Guatemala   **HONDURAS**
4217   Comayagua      L. Caratasca
Sta. Ana   Tegucigalpa   or Coco   C. Gracias á Dios
San José   S. Vicente   Jinotega   Wanks
Sonsonate   San Salvador   Matagalpa   El Gallo   Puerto Cabezas
**EL SALVADOR**   S. Miguel   Coluteca   **NICARAGUA**
G. de Fonseca   Chinandega   León

Grand Cayman (U.K.)

Providencia (Col.)
San Andrés (Col.)

20

15

**D**

**E**

Managua   Granada   Bluefields
Masaya   L. Nicaragua
S. Juan   Irazú
Pen. de Nicoya   **COSTA RICA**   Limón
Puntarenas   3432
Alajuela   San José   Colón   Panama
Cartago   3837   **Panama**   La
3374   **P  A  N  A  M  A**   Palma
Dávid   Chitré   El Real
Coiba   Pen. de Azuero   Arch. de las Perlas
G. de Panama

10

**F**

95      West from Greenwich      90

CARTOGRAPHY BY PHILIP'S.
COPYRIGHT REED INTERNATIONAL BOOKS LTD.

85

# 86 CARIBBEAN AND CENTRAL AMERICA

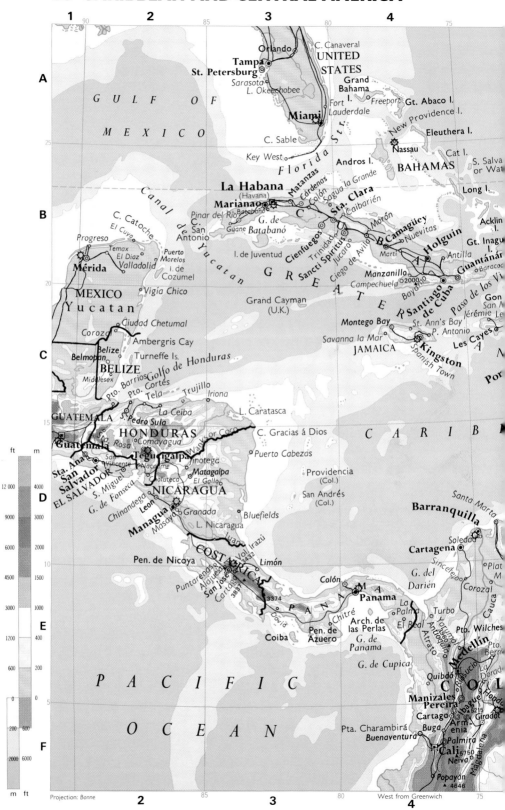

GULF OF MEXICO

UNITED STATES

Orlando
C. Canaveral
Tampa
St. Petersburg
Sarasota
L. Okeechobee
Grand Bahama I.
Fort Lauderdale
Freeport
Gt. Abaco I.
Miami
New Providence I.
C. Sable
Key West
Nassau
Eleuthera I.
Cat I.
S. Salva or Wat
Florida
Andros I.
BAHAMAS

C. Catoche
C. Cuyo
El Diaz
Progreso
Temax
Puerto Morelos
Mérida
Valladolid
I. de Cozumel
MEXICO
Yucatan
Vigía Chico
Corozal
Ciudad Chetumal
Ambergris Cay
Belize
Belmopan
Turneffe Is.
BELIZE
Middlesex
Pto. Barrios
Golfo de Honduras
Pto. Cortés
Tela
Trujillo
Iriona
La Ceiba
L. Caratasca
GUATEMALA
S. Pedro Sula
HONDURAS
Guatemala
Rosa
Comayagua
Sta. Ana
San Vicente
Tegucigalpa
San Salvador
S. Miguel
Nacaome
EL SALVADOR
Jinotega
G. de Fonseca
Matagalpa
El Gallo
Chinandega
Choluteca
León
NICARAGUA
Masaya
Granada
Managua
Bluefields
L. Nicaragua
Pen. de Nicoya
COSTA RICA
Vol. Irazú
Limón
Puntarenas
Alajuela
San José
Cartago
Coiba
Pen. de Azuero
Colón
Panama
Arch. de las Perlas
G. de Panama
G. de Cupica
Pta. Charambirá
Buenaventura

Canal de Yucatan
I. de Juventud
La Habana
(Havana)
Marianao
Pinar del Río
C. San Antonio
G. de Guane Batabanó
Matanzas
Cárdenas
Colón
Sagua la Grande
Sta. Clara
Caibarién
Cienfuegos
Trinidad
Sancti Spíritus
Ciego de Avila
Morón
Jucaro
Camagüey
Nuevitas
Holguin
Martí
Antilla
Gt. Inagu I.
Acklin
Manzanillo
Campechuela
Bayamo
Santiago de Cuba
Guantána
Baracoa
Paso de los Vi
Grand Cayman (U.K.)
Montego Bay
Savanna la Mar
JAMAICA
Spanish Town
St. Ann's Bay
Kingston
P. Antonio
Les Cayes
Jérémie
GREATER
Long I.

CARIBB
Providencia (Col.)
San Andrés (Col.)
Santa Marta
Barranquilla
Soledad
Cartagena
G. del Darién
Corozal
La Palma
Turbo
El Real
Pto. Wilches
Quibdó
Medellín
COL
Manizales
Pereira
Cartago
Buga
Armenia
Palmira
Cali
Neiva
Popayán

PACIFIC OCEAN

C. Gracias á Dios
Puerto Cabezas

Projection: Bonne

West from Greenwich

| ft | m |
|---|---|
| 12 000 | 4000 |
| 9000 | 3000 |
| 6000 | 2000 |
| 4500 | 1500 |
| 3000 | 1000 |
| 1200 | 400 |
| 600 | 200 |
| 0 | 0 |
| 200 | 600 |
| 2000 | 6000 |

m    ft

1 : 15 000 000

100    0    100    200    300    400 miles

100  0  100 200 300 400 500 600 km

5        6              7              8

A

A T L A N T I C

O C E A N

B

Tropic of Cancer                                                    25

or
ings I.

Mayaguana
Caicos I. (U.K.)
Turks Is. (U.K.)                                                    20

S. Francisco de Macoris
Port de Paix
Cap Haitien
Monte Cristi
Valverde
Pto. Plata
Santiago
Vega
Sánchez
Canal de la Mona
PUERTO RICO (U.S.A.)
San Juan
St. Thomas (U.S.A.)
Charlotte Amalie
Virgin Is. (U.K.)
Sombrero (U.K.)
Anguilla (U.K.)
St. Martin (Fr. & Neth.)                                           C
ives I.
arco
gane
DOMINICAN
REP.
La Romana
Aguadilla
Arecibo
Caguas
Ponce
St. Croix (U.S.A.)
ST. CHRISTOPHER -
NEVIS
ANTIGUA &
BARBUDA
au Prince
Jacmel
Bani
Azua
Barahona
Duverge
S. Pedro de Macoris
1338
Guayama
Mayagüez
Christiansted
Basseterre
Charlestown
St. John's
Plymouth  Montserrat (U.K.)
Guadeloupe (Fr.)
Pointe à Pitre
Santo Domingo
Hispaniola
T I L L E S
Leeward
Islands
DOMINICA
Roseau
LESSER
Martinique (Fr.)
Fort de France
Castries
ST. LUCIA
BARBADOS
Bridgetown
E A N     S E A
ANTILLES
Windward
ST. VINCENT
& Kingstown
THE GRENADINES
Islands
GRENADA
St. George's                                                       D

Pta. Gallinas
Pen. de la
Guajira
Golfo de Venezuela
Aruba (Neth.)
Curaçao
Willemstad
Bonaire
La Blanquilla
(Ven.)
Margarita
La Asunción
NETH.
ANTILLES
Pto. Cabello
Maiquetía
La Tortuga (Ven.)
Carúpano
Tobago
Port of Spain
TRINIDAD & TOBAGO
San Fernando                                                       E
Rhoacha
Coro
Dabajuro
Maracay
Caracas
Barcelona
Cumaná
G. de
Paria
5800
Sa. Nevada
de S. Marta
Maracaibo
Cabimas
San Felipe
Valencia
2596
Caripito
Maturín
El Tigre
Tucupita
Ciudad
Guayana
L. de
Maracaibo
Trujillo
Barquisimeto
Las Mercedes
Cúcuta
Ocaña
5007
Cord. de Mérida
Guanare
Portuguesa
San Fernando
de Apure
Orinoco
Ciudad Bolívar
El Callao
Tumeremo
Georgetown
San Cristóbal
Apure
Caicara
Parguaza
Barticao
Amsterdam
Wismar
4100
Rubio
Pamplona
Arauca
Arauca
V E N E Z U E L A
Caura
2560
Roraima
Cuyuni
New
Corentyne
Barrancabermeja
Bucaramanga
Pto. Páez
Pto. Carreño
2285
Pto. Ayacucho
Meta
G U Y A N A
2810
Essequibo
SURINAM
1280
Tunja
O M B I A
Sierra Pacaraima
Zipaquirá
Bogotá
Casiquiare
Guaviare
B R A Z I L                                                        F

5        70        6        65        7              8

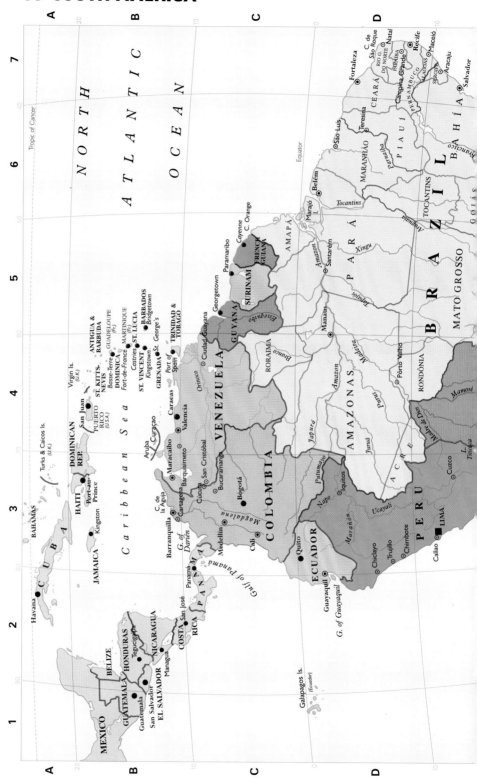

NORTH

ATLANTIC

OCEAN

Tropic of Cancer

Equator

**BRAZIL**

**MATO GROSSO**

**PARÁ**

**AMAPÁ**

**AMAZONAS**

**RORAIMA**

**RONDÔNIA**

**MARANHÃO**

**PIAUI**

**CEARÁ**

**BAHÍA**

GOIÁS

TOCANTINS

ACRE

PERNAMBUCO

PARAÍBA

RIO G. DO NORTE

ALAGOAS

SERGIPE

**VENEZUELA**

**COLOMBIA**

**ECUADOR**

**PERU**

**GUYANA**

**SURINAM**

**FRENCH GUIANA**

**BAHAMAS**

**CUBA**

**HAITI**

**DOMINICAN REP.**

**JAMAICA**

**MEXICO**

**GUATEMALA**

**BELIZE**

**HONDURAS**

**EL SALVADOR**

**NICARAGUA**

**COSTA RICA**

**PANAMA**

Caribbean Sea

Gulf of Panama

G. of Guayaquil

Turks & Caicos Is. (U.K.)

Virgin Is. (U.K.)

PUERTO RICO (USA)

ST. KITTS-NEVIS

ANTIGUA & BARBUDA

GUADELOUPE (Fr.)

DOMINICA

MARTINIQUE (Fr.)

ST. LUCIA

ST. VINCENT

BARBADOS

GRENADA

TRINIDAD & TOBAGO

Galapagos Is. (Ecuador)

Havana

Kingston

Port-au-Prince

San Juan

Basse-Terre

Fort-de-France

Castries

Kingstown

Bridgetown

St. George's

Port of Spain

Guatemala

San Salvador

Tegucigalpa

Managua

San José

Panamá

Barranquilla

Cartagena

Maracaibo

Barquisimeto

Valencia

Caracas

Bucaramanga

San Cristóbal

Cúcuta

Bogotá

Medellín

Cali

Quito

Guayaquil

Quitos

Chiclayo

Trujillo

Chimbote

Callao

LIMA

Cuzco

Georgetown

Paramaribo

Cayenne

Ciudad Guayana

Belém

Marajó

Santarém

Manaus

Pôrto Velho

São Luís

Teresina

Fortaleza

Natal

Campina Grande

Recife

Maceió

Aracaju

Salvador

C. de Orange

C. de São Roque

C. de la Aguja

G. of Darién

Curaçao

Aruba

Orinoco

Magdalena

Marañón

Napo

Putumayo

Japurá

Negro

Branco

Essequibo

Casiquiare

Amazon

Purus

Juruá

Madeira

Madre de Dios

Ucayali

Mamoré

Beni

Tapajós

Xingu

Tocantins

Marajó

Parnaíba

São Francisco

Amazon

Teruána

L. Titicaca

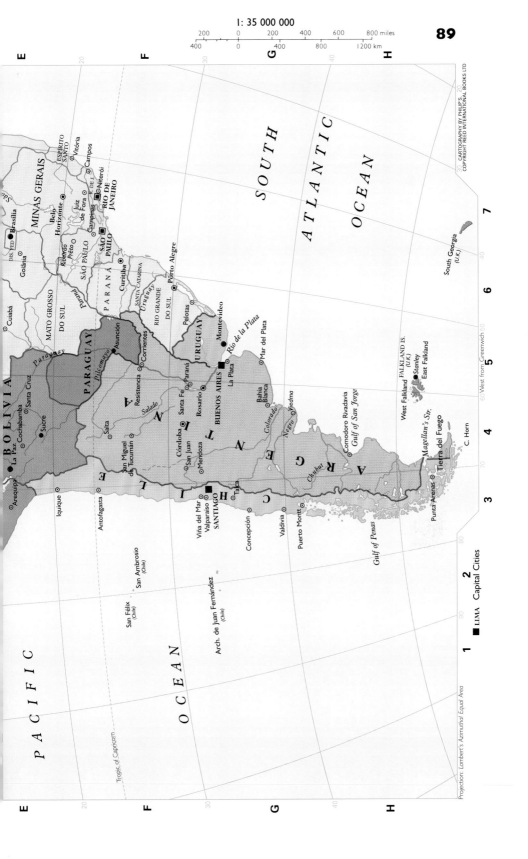

1: 35 000 000

**89**

CARTOGRAPHY BY PHILIP'S.
COPYRIGHT REED INTERNATIONAL BOOKS LTD

200   0   200   400   600   800 miles
400   0   400   800   1200 km

■ LIMA   Capital Cities

Projection: Lambert's Azimuthal Equal Area

PACIFIC

OCEAN

Tropic of Capricorn

San Félix (Chile)

San Ambrosio (Chile)

Arch. de Juan Fernández (Chile)

Iquique

Antofagasta

Arequipa

BOLIVIA
La Paz
Cochabamba
Sucre
Santa Cruz

Salta

San Miguel de Tucumán

San Juan

Córdoba

Mendoza

C H I L E

Viña del Mar
Valparaíso
SANTIAGO

Talca

Concepción

Valdivia

Puerto Montt

Gulf of Penas

PARAGUAY
Asunción

Pilcomayo

Paraguay

Resistencia

Santa Fe

Paraná

Rosario

Salado

BUENOS AIRES

La Plata

Bahía Blanca

A R G E N T I N A

Colorado

Negro

Viedma

Chubut

Comodoro Rivadavia
Gulf of San Jorge

Magellan's Str.

Punta Arenas

Tierra del Fuego

C. Horn

MATO GROSSO
DO SUL

Cuiabá

Goiânia

Brasília
DIST. FED.

MINAS GERAIS

Belo Horizonte

Juiz de Fora

Ribeirão Prêto

SÃO PAULO

SÃO PAULO

ESPÍRITO SANTO
Vitória

Campos

Niterói
RIO DE JANEIRO

PARANÁ

Paraná

Curitiba

SANTA CATARINA

RIO GRANDE DO SUL

Uruguay

Pôrto Alegre

Pelotas

Corrientes

URUGUAY
Montevideo

Rio de la Plata

Mar del Plata

SOUTH

ATLANTIC

OCEAN

South Georgia (U.K.)

FALKLAND IS. (U.K.)

West Falkland
Stanley
East Falkland

West from Greenwich

E   F   G   H

1   2   3   4   5   6   7

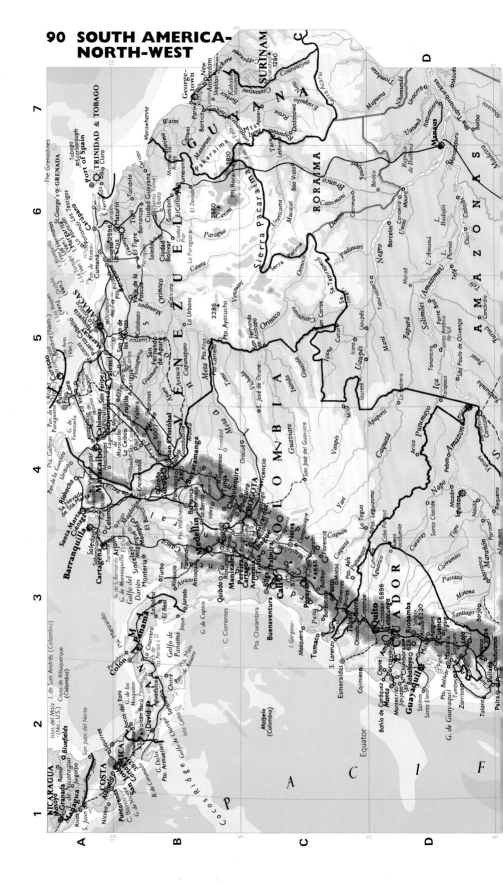

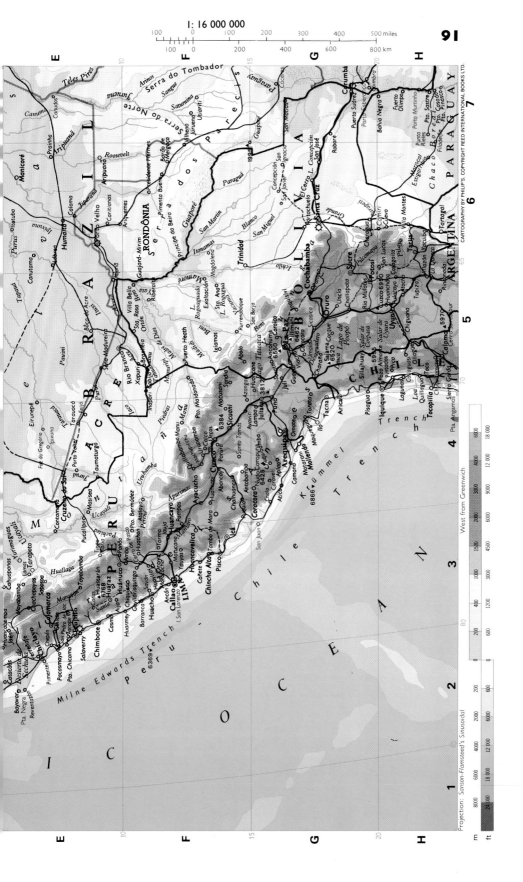

1:16 000 000

Projection: Sanson-Flamsteed's Sinusoidal

West from Greenwich

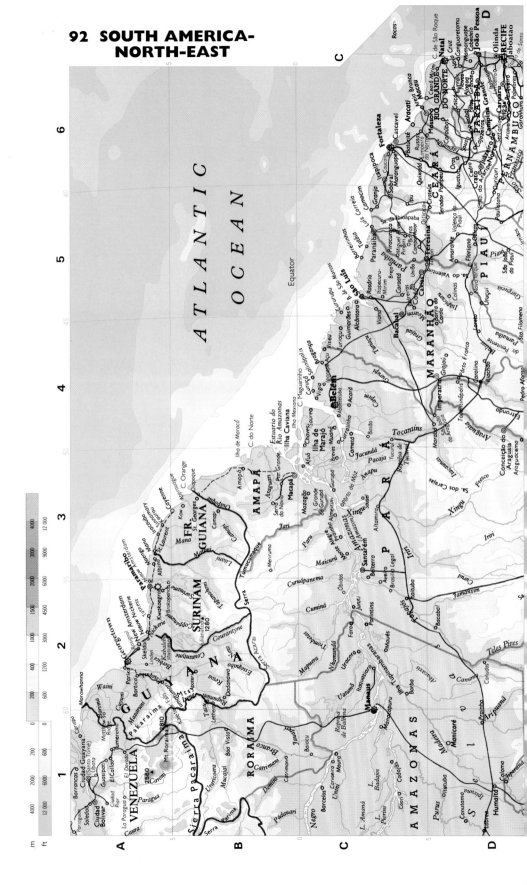

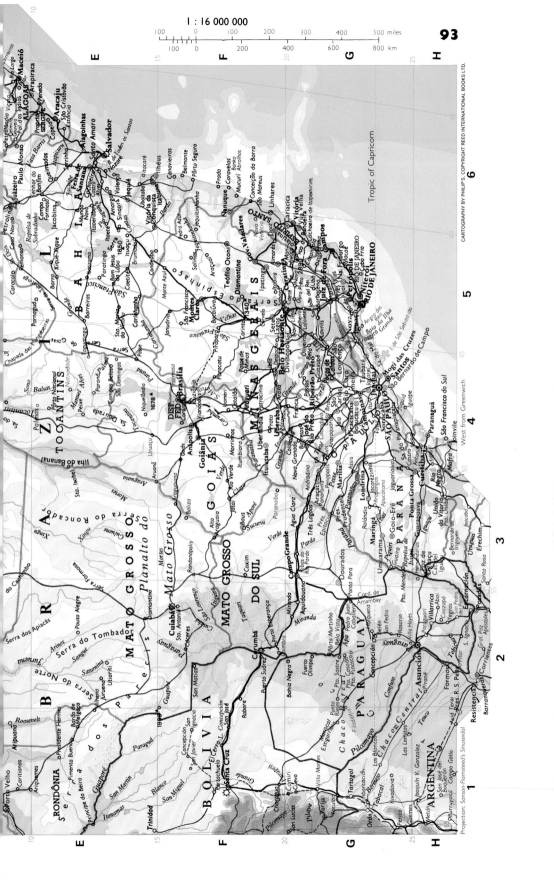

1 : 16 000 000

100    0    100    200    300    400    500 miles
100    0    200    400    600    800 km

Projection: Sanson-Flamsteed's Sinusoidal

West from Greenwich

Tropic of Capricorn

B    R    A    Z    I    L

RONDÔNIA

MATO GROSSO

Planalto do
Mato Grosso

MATO GROSSO
DO SUL

GOIÁS

TOCANTINS

BAHIA

DIST.
FED.
Brasília

MINAS GERAIS

SÃO PAULO

PARANÁ

SANTO

RIO DE JANEIRO

BOLIVIA

PARAGUAY

ARGENTINA

Porto Velho
Santa Cruz
Asunción
Curitiba
SÃO PAULO
Santos
RIO DE JANEIRO
Belo Horizonte
Goiânia
Anápolis
Salvador
Maceió
Aracaju

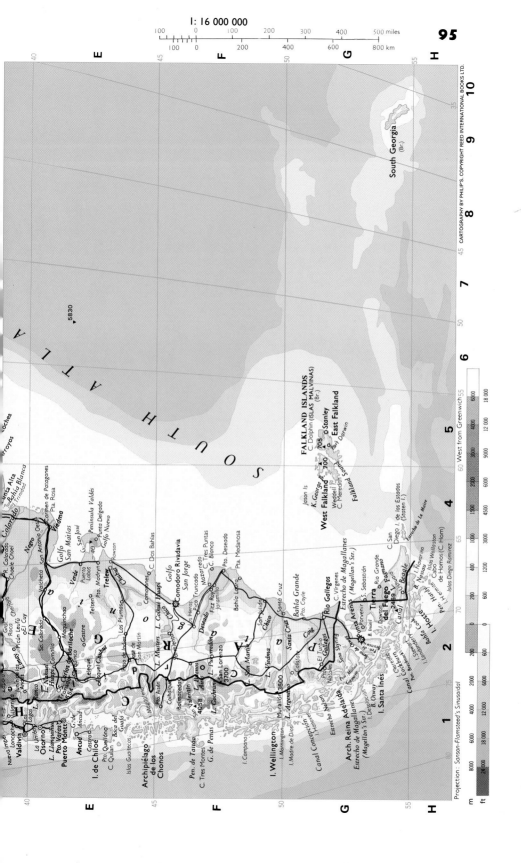

1: 16 000 000

```
100      0      100    200    300    400    500 miles
100   0      200      400      600      800 km
```

Projection: Sanson-Flamsteed's Sinusoidal

S O U T H   A T L A

South Georgia
(Br.)

FALKLAND ISLANDS
(ISLAS MALVINAS)
(Br.)
C. Dolphin    O Stanley
Jason Is            705
K. George            East Falkland
West Falkland        Darwin
C. Meredith    Port
Weddell        Falkland S.

West from Greenwich

Bahía Alta
Bahía Blanca
Pta. Trinidad
Carmen de Patagones
Pta. Rosa
Viedma
San José
Golfo
San Matías
Península Valdés
Punta Delgada
Golfo Nuevo
Puerto
Madryn
Rawson
Trelew
C. Dos Bahías
Camarones
Golfo
San Jorge
Comodoro Rivadavia
C. Tres Puntas
Mazarredo
C. Blanco
Pto. Deseado
Bahía Laura
Pto. Medanosa
Santa Cruz
C. San
Diego I. de los Estados
(Staten I.)
Bahía Grande
Río Gallegos
Estrecho de Magallanes
(Magellan's Str.)
C. Vírgenes
Tierra
del Fuego
I. Navarino
Cabo
de Hornos (C. Horn)
Islas Diego Ramírez

5830

Valdivia
Osorno
Pto. Varas
Puerto Montt
Ancud
I. de Chiloé
Castro
Pto. Quellón
Quilán
Guafo
Islas Guaitecas
Archipiélago
de los
Chonos
Pen. de Taitao
C. Tres Montes
G. de Penas
I. Campana
I. Wellington
I. Morninton
I. Madre de Dios
Pen. de Tres Montes
Arch. Reina Adelaida
Estrecho de Magallanes
(Magellan's Str.)

m       ft
8000    24000
6000    18000
4000    12000
2000    6000
        0
```
        6000    18000
        4000    12000
        3000    9000
        2000    6000
        1500    4500
        1000    3000
        400     1200
        200     600
        0
        200     600
```

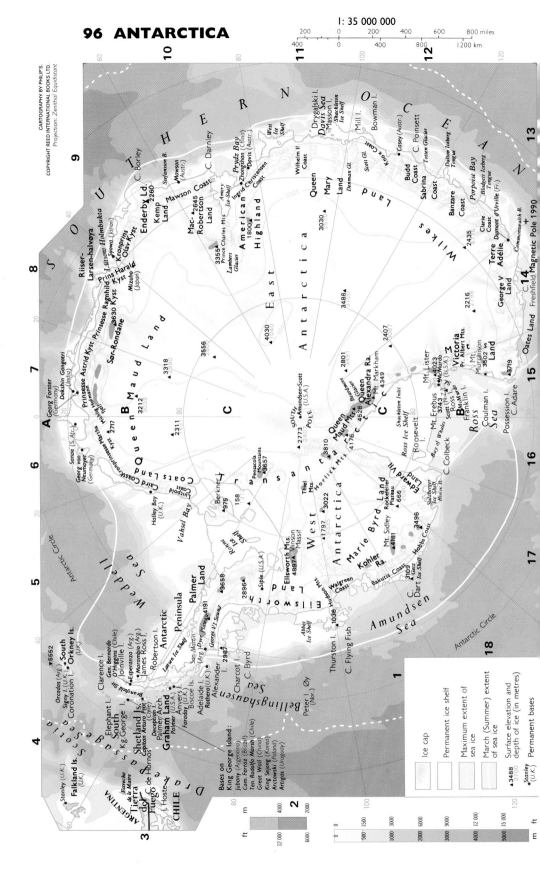

# Index to Map Pages

The index contains the names of all principal places and features shown on the maps. Physical features composed of a proper name (Erie) and a description (Lake) are positioned alphabetically by the proper name. The description is positioned after the proper name and is usually abbreviated:

Erie, L. . . . . . . **72** **C5**

Where a description forms part of a settlement or administrative name however, it is always written in full and put in its true alphabetical position:

Lake Charles **79** **D7**

Names beginning St. are alphabetized under Saint, but Sankt, Sint, Sant, Santa and San are all spelt in full and are alphabetized accordingly.

The number in bold type which follows each name in the index refers to the number of the map page where that feature or place will be found. This is usually the largest scale at which the place or feature appears.

The letter and figure which are in bold type immediately after the page number give the grid square on the map page, within which the feature is situated.

Rivers carry the symbol ➔ after their names. A solid square ■ follows the name of a country while an open square □ refers to a first order administrative area.

## A

A Coruña = La
  Coruña . . . . . **18** **A1**
Aachen . . . . . . **14** **C4**
Aalborg =
  Ålborg . . . . . **9** **G9**
Aalen . . . . . . . . **14** **D6**
Aarau . . . . . . . . **13** **C8**
Aare ➔ . . . . . . **13** **C8**
Aarhus = Århus **9** **G10**
Aba . . . . . . . . . . **55** **G6**
Ābādān . . . . . . **47** **E7**
Ābādeh . . . . . . **44** **D3**
Abadla . . . . . . . **54** **B4**
Abaetetuba . . . **92** **C4**
Abakan . . . . . . . **30** **D7**
Abancay . . . . . . **91** **F4**
Abarqū . . . . . . . **44** **D3**
Abashiri . . . . . . **32** **F12**
Abay . . . . . . . . . **29** **E8**
Abaya, L. . . . . . **53** **G6**
Abbay = Nîl el
  Azraq ➔ . . . **53** **E5**
Abbeville . . . . . **12** **A4**
Abbieglassie . . **63** **A4**
Abbot Ice Shelf **96** **B2**
Abbottabad . . . **42** **B8**
Abd al Kūrī . . . **49** **E5**
Abéché . . . . . . . **53** **F3**
Abeokuta . . . . . **55** **G5**
Abercorn =
  Mbala . . . . . . **57** **F6**
Abercorn . . . . . **63** **A5**
Aberdeen,
  Australia . . . . **63** **B5**
Aberdeen, U.K. **10** **C5**
Aberdeen,
  S. Dak., U.S.A. **76** **C5**

Aberdeen,
  Wash., U.S.A. **80** **B2**
Aberystwyth . . **11** **E4**
Abidjan . . . . . . **55** **G4**
Abilene . . . . . . . **78** **C4**
Abitibi L. . . . . . **69** **D3**
Abkhaz
  Republic □ =
  Abkhazia □ . **25** **E5**
Abkhazia □ . . . **25** **E5**
Abminga . . . . . **62** **A1**
Åbo = Turku . . **9** **F12**
Abohar . . . . . . . **42** **D9**
Abomey . . . . . . **55** **G5**
Abong-Mbang . **56** **D2**
Abou-Deïa . . . . **53** **F2**
Abri . . . . . . . . . . **52** **D5**
Abrolhos, Banka **93** **F6**
Abrud . . . . . . . . **17** **E6**
Absaroka Range **81** **C9**
Abū al Khaşīb . **47** **E6**
Abū 'Alī . . . . . . **47** **F7**
Abu 'Arīsh . . . . **49** **D3**
Abu Dhabi =
  Abū Ẕaby . . . **44** **E3**
Abū Dīs . . . . . . **53** **E5**
Abu Hamed . . . **53** **E5**
Abū Kamāl . . . . **46** **D5**
Abū Madd, Ra's **47** **F4**
Abū Mataríq . . **53** **F4**
Abu Rudeis . . . **47** **E3**
Abu Tig . . . . . . **52** **C5**
Abû Zabad . . . . **53** **F4**
Abū Ẕaby . . . . **44** **E3**
Abuja . . . . . . . . **55** **G6**
Abukuma-
  Gawa ➔ . . . **33** **G12**
Abunã . . . . . . . **91** **E5**
Abunã ➔ . . . . . **91** **E5**

Abut Hd. . . . . . **65** **E4**
Abwong . . . . . . **53** **G5**
Acaponeta . . . . **84** **C3**
Acapulco . . . . . **84** **D5**
Acarigua . . . . . **90** **B5**
Accra . . . . . . . . **55** **G4**
Aceh □ . . . . . . **36** **D1**
Achalpur . . . . . **43** **J10**
Achill I. . . . . . . **11** **E1**
Achinsk . . . . . . **30** **D7**
Acireale . . . . . . **21** **F5**
Acklins I. . . . . . **86** **B5**
Aconcagua,
  Cerro . . . . . . **94** **C3**
Aconquija, Mt. . **94** **B3**
Açores, Is. dos
  = Azores . . . **50** **C1**
Acraman, L. . . . **62** **B2**
Acre = 'Akko . **46** **D3**
Acre □ . . . . . . . **91** **E4**
Acre ➔ . . . . . . **91** **E5**
Ad Dahnā . . . . **47** **F7**
Ad Dammām . . **47** **F7**
Ad Dawhah . . . **44** **E2**
Ad Dilam . . . . . **47** **G6**
Ad Dīwānīyah . **47** **E6**
Ada . . . . . . . . . . **79** **B5**
Adaja ➔ . . . . . **18** **B3**
Adam . . . . . . . . **44** **F4**
Adamaoua,
  Massif de l' . **53** **G1**
Adamawa
  Highlands =
  Adamaoua,
  Massif de l' . **53** **G1**
Adamello, Mte. . **20** **A3**
Adaminaby . . . **63** **C4**
Adam's Bridge **43** **Q11**
Adams Mt. . . . . **80** **B3**

Adana . . . . . . . . **46** **C3**
Adapazarı . . . . . **46** **B2**
Adarama . . . . . . **53** **E5**
Adare, C. . . . . . **96** **B15**
Adaut . . . . . . . . **39** **F4**
Adavale . . . . . . **63** **A3**
Adda ➔ . . . . . . **20** **B2**
Addis Ababa =
  Addis Abeba **53** **G6**
Addis Abeba . . **53** **G6**
Addis Alem . . . **53** **G6**
Adelaide . . . . . . **62** **B2**
Adelaide I. . . . . **96** **A3**
Adelaide Pen. . **70** **B10**
Adélie, Terre . . **96** **A14**
Adélie Land =
  Adélie, Terre **96** **A14**
Aden = Al
  'Adan . . . . . **49** **E4**
Aden, G. of . . . **49** **E4**
Adi . . . . . . . . . . **39** **E4**
Adi Ugri . . . . . . **53** **F6**
Adige ➔ . . . . . **20** **B4**
Adilabad . . . . . **43** **K11**
Adirondack Mts. **73** **C8**
Admer . . . . . . . . **54** **D6**
Admiralty I. . . . **71** **C6**
Admiralty Is. . . **64** **K9**
Ado-Ekiti . . . . . **55** **G6**
Adonara . . . . . . **39** **F2**
Adoni . . . . . . . . **43** **M10**
Adour ➔ . . . . . **12** **E3**
Adra . . . . . . . . . **18** **D4**
Adrano . . . . . . . **21** **F5**
Adrar . . . . . . . . **54** **C4**
Adré . . . . . . . . . **53** **F3**
Adrī . . . . . . . . . **52** **C1**
Adriatic Sea . . . **20** **C5**
Adua . . . . . . . . . **39** **E3**

97

Adwa ........ 53 F6
Adzhar
  Republic □ =
  Ajaria □ .... 25 E5
Ægean Sea .. 23 E5
Aerhtai Shan .. 34 B4
Afghanistan ■ . 45 C6
Afgoi ........ 49 G3
'Afif ....... 47 G5
Afognak I. .... 71 C4
Afuá ......... 92 C3
Afyonkarahisar 46 C2
Agadès =
  Agadez ..... 55 E6
Agadez ....... 55 E6
Agadir ....... 54 B3
Agapa ........ 30 B6
Agartala ..... 41 F8
Agats ........ 39 F5
Agboville ..... 55 G4
Agde ......... 13 E5
Agen ......... 12 D4
Agra ......... 42 F10
Agri ~► ...... 21 D6
Ağrı Dağı .... 46 C6
Ağrı Karakose . 46 C5
Agrigento ..... 21 F4
Agrinion ...... 23 E3
Água Clara ... 93 G3
Agua Prieta .. 84 A3
Aguadas ...... 90 B3
Aguadilla .... 87 C6
Aguarico ~► .. 90 D3
Aguas Blancas 94 A3
Aguascalientes 84 C4
Aguilas ....... 19 D5
Agulhas, C. .. 58 E4
Agung ........ 37 F5
Agusan ~► ... 38 C3
Ahaggar ...... 54 D6
Ahar ......... 46 C6
Ahipara B. ... 64 A5
Ahiri ........ 43 K12
Ahmadabad .. 43 H8
Ahmadnagar .. 43 K9
Ahmadpur .... 42 E7
Ahmedabad =
  Ahmadabad . 43 H8
Ahmednagar =
  Ahmadnagar 43 K9
Ahvāz ....... 47 E7
Ahvenanmaa =
  Åland ...... 9 F11
Ahwar ....... 49 E4
Aigues-Mortes . 13 E6
Aihui ........ 35 A7
Aija ......... 91 E3
Aiken ........ 75 C7
Aimere ....... 39 F2
Aimorés ...... 93 F5
Ain Banaiyan . 44 F2
Aïn Beïda .... 54 A6
Aïn Ben Tili .. 54 C3
Aïn-Sefra .... 54 B4
Ainabo ....... 49 F4
Aïr .......... 55 E6
Aisne ~► ..... 13 B5
Aiud ......... 17 E6
Aix-en-Provence 13 E6
Aix-la-Chapelle
  = Aachen ... 14 C4
Aix-les-Bains . 13 D6
Aiyion ....... 23 E4
Aizawl ....... 41 F9
Ajaccio ...... 13 F8
Ajanta Ra. ... 43 J9
Ajari Rep. =
  Ajaria □ .... 25 E5
Ajaria □ ...... 25 E5

Ajdâbiyah .... 52 B3
Ajka ......... 16 E3
'Ajmān ....... 44 E3
Ajmer ........ 42 F9
Ajo, C. de ... 18 A4
Akaroa ....... 65 E5
Akashi ....... 32 B4
Akelamo ..... 39 D3
Aketi ........ 56 D4
Akharnaí ..... 23 E4
Akhelóös ~► .. 23 E3
Akhisar ...... 23 E6
Akhmîm ...... 52 C5
Akimiski I. .... 69 C2
Akita ........ 33 G12
Akjoujt ...... 55 E2
'Akko ........ 46 D3
Akkol ........ 29 E8
Aklavik ...... 70 B6
Akmolinsk =
  Aqmola .... 29 D8
Akobo ~► .... 53 G5
Akola ........ 43 J10
Akordat ...... 53 E6
Akpatok I. .... 68 B4
Akreïjit ...... 55 E3
Akron ........ 72 D5
Aksai Chin ... 42 B11
Aksaray ...... 46 C3
Aksarka ...... 28 C7
Akşehir ...... 46 C2
Aksu ......... 34 B3
Aksum ....... 53 F6
Aktogay ...... 29 E8
Aktsyabrski .. 17 B9
Aktyubinsk =
  Aqtöbe .... 29 D6
Aku .......... 55 G6
Akure ........ 55 G6
Akyab = Sittwe 41 G9
Al 'Adan ..... 49 E4
Al Aḥsā ...... 47 F7
Al Amādīyah .. 46 C5
Al Amārah .... 47 E6
Al 'Aqabah ... 47 E3
Al 'Aramah ... 47 F6
Al Ashkhara .. 45 F4
Al Badī' ..... 47 G6
Al Baṣrah .... 47 E6
Al Baydā ..... 52 B3
Al Bu'ayrāt al
  Ḥasūn ...... 52 B2
Al Fallūjah ... 46 D5
Al Fāw ....... 47 E7
Al Fujayrah ... 44 E4
Al Hābah ..... 47 F6
Al Haddār .... 47 G6
Al Hāmad .... 47 E4
Al Ḥamar .... 47 G6
Al Ḥamrā' .... 47 F4
Al Ḥarīq ..... 47 G6
Al Ḥasakah .. 46 C5
Al Ḥawrah ... 49 E4
Al Ḥayy ...... 47 D6
Al Ḥijāz ...... 47 F4
Al Ḥillah, Iraq . 47 D6
Al Ḥillah,
  Si. Arabia ... 47 G6
Al Hindīyah .. 47 D6
Al Hoceïma ... 54 A4
Al Ḥudaydah .. 49 E3
Al Hufūf ..... 47 F7
Al Ḥulwah ... 47 G6
Al Ittihad =
  Madīnat ash
  Sha'b ...... 49 E3
Al Jāfūrah ... 47 F7
Al Jaghbūb ... 52 C3
Al Jahrah .... 47 E6

Al Jalāmīd .... 47 E4
Al Jawf, Libya . 52 D3
Al Jawf,
  Si. Arabia ... 47 E4
Al Jazirah, Iraq 46 D5
Al Jazirah, Libya 52 C3
Al Jubayl .... 47 F7
Al Jubaylah ... 47 F6
Al Junaynah .. 53 F3
Al Khābūra ... 44 F4
Al Khalīl ..... 47 E3
Al Kharfah ... 47 G6
Al Kharj ..... 47 F6
Al Khasab .... 44 E4
Al Kufrah .... 52 D3
Al Kūt ....... 47 D6
Al Kuwayt .... 47 E7
Al Lādhiqīyah . 46 D3
Al Luḥayyah .. 49 D3
Al Madīnah ... 47 F4
Al Majma'ah .. 47 F6
Al Manāmah .. 44 E2
Al Marj ...... 52 B3
Al Mawṣil .... 46 C5
Al Midhnab ... 47 F6
Al Mish'āb ... 47 E7
Al Mubarraz .. 47 F7
Al Muḥarraq .. 44 E2
Al Mukallā ... 49 E4
Al Mukhā .... 49 E3
Al Musayyib .. 47 D6
Al Muwayliḥ .. 47 F3
Al Qadīmah .. 47 G4
Al Qā'iyah ... 47 F5
Al Qāmishli .. 46 C5
Al Qaşabát ... 52 B1
Al Qaşīm .... 47 F5
Al Qaţif ...... 47 F7
Al Qaţrūn .... 52 D2
Al Qayşūmah . 47 E6
Al Quaisūmah . 47 E6
Al Quds =
  Jerusalem .. 47 E3
Al Qurayyāt .. 45 F4
Al Qurnah .... 47 E6
Al 'Ulā ...... 47 F4
Al Uqaylah ash
  Sharqīgah .. 52 B2
Al Uqayr ..... 47 F7
Al 'Uthmānīyah 47 F7
Al 'Uwaynid .. 47 F6
Al 'Uwayqīlah . 47 E5
Al 'Uyūn ..... 47 F5
Al Wakrah .... 44 E2
Al Wari'āh ... 47 F6
Al Yamāmah . 47 F6
Alabama □ ... 74 C4
Alabama ~► .. 74 D4
Alaçam Dağları 23 E7
Alagoa Grande 92 D6
Alagoas □ .... 93 D6
Alagoinhas ... 93 E6
Alajuela ...... 86 D3
Alamosa ..... 83 B10
Åland ........ 9 F11
Alania = North
  Ossetia □ ... 25 E5
Alanya ....... 46 C2
Alapayevsk ... 29 D7
Alaşehir ...... 23 E7
Alaska □ ..... 71 B4
Alaska, G. of . 71 C5
Alaska Peninsula 71 C4
Alaska Range . 71 B4
Alataw Shankou 34 B3
Alatyr ....... 24 C6
Alausi ....... 90 D3
Alawoona .... 62 B3
Alba ......... 20 B2

Alba-Iulia .... 17 E6
Albacete ..... 19 C5
Albacutya, L. .. 62 C3
Albania ■ .... 23 D3
Albany,
  Australia .... 60 H2
Albany, Ga.,
  U.S.A. ...... 75 D5
Albany, N.Y.,
  U.S.A. ...... 73 C9
Albany, Oreg.,
  U.S.A. ...... 80 C2
Albany ~► .... 69 C2
Albardón ..... 94 C3
Albemarle .... 75 B7
Alberche ~► .. 18 C3
Albert, L. .... 62 C2
Albert L. ..... 57 D6
Albert Nile ~► . 57 D6
Albertville ... 13 D7
Albi ......... 12 E5
Albina ....... 92 A3
Alborán ...... 18 E4
Ålborg ....... 9 G9
Alborz, Reshteh-
  ye Kūhhā-ye . 44 B3
Albuquerque . 83 C9
Albury ....... 63 C4
Alcalá de
  Henares .... 18 B4
Alcalá la Real . 18 D4
Alcamo ...... 21 F4
Alcaniz ...... 19 B5
Alcântara .... 92 C5
Alcántara,
  Embalse de . 18 C2
Alcantarilla .. 19 D5
Alcaraz, Sierra
  de ......... 19 C4
Alcaudete .... 18 D3
Alcázar de San
  Juan ....... 18 C4
Alchevsk ..... 25 D4
Alcira ....... 19 C5
Alcoy ........ 19 C5
Aldabra Is. ... 51 G8
Aldan ....... 31 C10
Alderney .... 11 G5
Aleg ......... 55 E2
Alegrete ..... 94 B5
Aleisk ....... 29 D9
Aleksandriya =
  Oleksandriya 17 C8
Aleksandrovskoye
  ............ 29 C8
Alemania .... 94 B3
Alençon ...... 12 B4
Aleppo = Ḥalab 46 C4
Alès ......... 13 D6
Alessándria .. 20 B2
Ålesund ...... 8 F9
Aleutian Is. ... 71 C2
Alexander Arch. 71 C6
Alexander I. .. 96 A3
Alexandra,
  Australia .... 63 C4
Alexandra, N.Z. 65 F3
Alexandria = El
  Iskandarīya .. 52 B4
Alexandria,
  Canada ..... 71 C7
Alexandria,
  Romania .... 22 C5
Alexandria,
  S. Africa .... 59 E5
Alexandria, La.,
  U.S.A. ...... 79 D7
Alexandria, Va.,
  U.S.A. ...... 73 E7

Alexandrina, L. 62 C2
Alexandroúpolis 22 D5
Alga 29 E6
Algarve 18 D1
Algeciras 18 D3
Algemesí 19 C5
Alger 54 A5
Algeria ■ 54 C5
Alghero 21 D2
Algiers = Alger 54 A5
Algoa B. 59 E5
Alhucemas = Al
  Hoceïma 54 A4
'Alī al Gharbī 47 D6
'Alī Khēl 42 C6
Aliağa 23 E6
Alibo 53 G6
Alicante 19 C5
Alice Springs 60 E5
Aligarh 42 F11
Alīgūdarz 46 D7
Alipur 42 E7
Alipur Duar 41 D7
Aliwal North 59 E5
Aljustrel 18 D1
Alkmaar 14 B3
All American
  Canal 82 D5
Allahabad 40 E3
Allanmyo 41 H10
Allegheny ➤ 73 D5
Allegheny
  Plateau 73 F5
Allentown 73 D8
Alleppey 43 Q10
Aller ➤ 14 B5
Allier ➤ 13 C5
Allora 63 A5
Alma Ata =
  Almaty 29 E8
Almada 18 C1
Almadén 18 C3
Almansa 19 C5
Almanzor, Pico
  del Moro 18 B3
Almanzora ➤ 19 D5
Almaty 29 E8
Almazán 19 B4
Almeirim 92 C3
Almelo 14 B4
Almendralejo 18 C2
Almería 19 D4
Almora 42 E11
Alnwick 10 D6
Alon 41 F10
Alor 39 F2
Alor Setar 36 C2
Alps 14 E5
Alsace 13 B7
Alsask 71 C9
Alsásua 19 A4
Alta Gracia 94 C4
Altagracia 90 A4
Altai = Aerhtai
  Shan 34 B4
Altamira 92 C3
Altamura 21 D6
Altanbulag 35 A5
Altay 34 B3
Altea 19 C5
Alto Araguaia 93 F3
Alto Molocue 59 B7
Alton 77 F9
Alton Downs 62 A2
Altoona 73 D6
Altun Shan 34 C3
Alùla 49 E5
Alusi 39 F4
Alvarado 85 D5

Alvear 94 B5
Alvie 62 C3
Alwar 42 F10
Alxa Zuoqi 35 C5
Am Dam 53 F3
Am-Timan 53 F3
Amâdi, Sudan 53 G5
Amadi, Zaïre 57 D5
Amadjuak 68 B3
Amadjuak L. 68 B3
Amagasaki 32 B4
Amakusa-Shotō 32 C2
Amaliás 23 F3
Amalner 43 J9
Amambay,
  Cordillera de 94 A5
Amangeldy 29 D7
Amapá 92 B3
Amapá □ 92 B3
Amarante 92 D5
Amargosa 93 E6
Amarillo 78 B3
Amaro, Mte. 20 C5
Amasra 46 B3
Amasya 46 B3
Amazon =
  Amazonas ➤ 92 C3
Amazonas □ 90 D5
Amazonas ➤ 92 C3
Ambala 42 D10
Ambalavao 59 J9
Ambam 56 D2
Ambanja 59 G9
Ambartsevo 29 D9
Ambato 90 D3
Ambatolampy 59 H9
Ambatondrazaka 59 H9
Amberg 15 D6
Ambergris Cay 85 D7
Amberley 65 E5
Ambikapur 40 F4
Ambilobé 59 G9
Ambo 91 F3
Amboise 12 C4
Ambon 39 E3
Ambositra 59 J9
Amboyna I. 36 C4
Ambriz 56 F2
Amby 63 A4
Amchitka I. 71 C1
Amderma 28 C7
Ameca 84 C4
Ameland 14 B3
American
  Highland 96 B10
American
  Samoa ■ 65 L13
Americus 75 C5
Amery 71 C10
Amery Ice Shelf 96 A10
Amherst, Burma 41 J11
Amherst,
  Canada 69 D4
Amiata, Mte. 20 C3
Amiens 12 B5
Amirante Is. 26 K9
'Ammān 47 E3
Amorgós 23 F5
Amoy = Xiamen 35 D6
Ampanihy 59 J8
Ampenan 37 F5
Amper ➤ 15 D6
Amravati 43 J10
Amreli 43 J7
Amritsar 42 D9
Amroha 42 E11
Amsterdam 14 B3
Amstetten 15 D8

Amudarya ➤ 29 E6
Amundsen Gulf 70 A7
Amundsen Sea 96 B1
Amuntai 37 E5
Amur ➤ 31 D12
Amurang 39 D2
Amuri Pass 65 E5
Amyderya =
  Amudarya ➤ 29 E6
An Nafūd 47 E5
An Najaf 47 D6
An Nhon 36 B3
An Nu'ayrīyah 47 F7
Anabar ➤ 30 B9
Anaconda 81 B7
Anadolu 46 C2
'Ānah 46 D5
Anaheim 82 D4
Anakapalle 40 J4
Analalava 59 G9
Anambas,
  Kepulauan 37 D3
Anambas Is. =
  Anambas,
  Kepulauan 37 D3
Anamur 46 C3
Anan 32 C4
Anantnag 42 C9
Ananyiv 17 E9
Anápolis 93 F4
Anār 44 D3
Anārak 44 C3
Anatolia =
  Anadolu 46 C2
Añatuya 94 B4
Anaye 53 E1
Anchorage 71 B5
Ancohuma,
  Nevada 91 G5
Ancón 91 F3
Ancona 20 C4
Ancud 95 E2
Ancud, G. de 95 E2
Andalgalá 94 B3
Andalucía □ 18 D3
Andalusia 74 D4
Andalusia □ =
  Andalucía □ 18 D3
Andaman Is. 27 H13
Andaman Sea 36 B1
Andara 58 B4
Anderson 72 D3
Anderson ➤ 70 B7
Andes = Andes,
  Cord. de los 91 G4
Andes, Cord. de
  los 91 G4
Andhra
  Pradesh □ 43 L11
Andijon 29 E8
Andikíthira 23 G4
Andizhan =
  Andijon 29 E8
Andkhvoy 45 B6
Andoany 59 G9
Andorra ■ 19 A6
Andorra La Vella 19 A6
Andreanof Is. 71 C2
Andrewilla 62 A2
Ándria 20 D6
Andriba 59 H9
Andropov =
  Rybinsk 24 B4
Ándros 23 F5
Andros I. 86 B4
Andújar 18 C3
Andulo 56 G3
Aného 55 G5
Aneto, Pico de 19 A6

Angamos, Punta 94 A2
Ang'angxi 35 B7
Angara ➤ 30 D7
Angarsk 30 D8
Angaston 62 B2
Ånge 8 F11
Angeles 38 A2
Angellala 63 A4
Ångermanälven ➤
  8 F11
Angers 12 C3
Anglesey 11 E4
Ango 57 D5
Angola ■ 58 A3
Angoulême 12 D4
Angoumois 12 D4
Angra dos Reis 94 A8
Angren 29 E8
Anguilla ■ 87 C7
Anhui □ 35 C6
Anhwei □ =
  Anhui □ 35 C6
Anjidiv I. 43 M9
Anjou 12 C3
Anjozorobe 59 H9
Anju 35 C7
Anka 55 F6
Ankang 35 C5
Ankara 46 C3
Ankazoabo 59 J8
Ankazobe 59 H9
Ankoro 57 F5
Ann Arbor 72 C4
Annaba 54 A6
Annan 11 D5
Annapolis 73 E7
Annecy 13 D7
Anning 34 D5
Anniston 74 C5
Annobón 51 G4
Annuello 62 B3
Anqing 35 C6
Ansbach 14 D6
Anshan 35 B7
Anshun 35 D5
Ansirabe 59 H9
Ansongo 55 E5
Ansudu 39 E5
Antabamba 91 F4
Antakya 46 C4
Antalaha 59 G10
Antalya 46 C2
Antalya Körfezi 46 C2
Antananarivo 59 H9
Antarctic Pen. 96 A4
Antarctica 96 C
Antequera 18 D3
Anti Atlas 54 C3
Antibes 13 E7
Anticosti, I. d' 69 D4
Antigua &
  Barbuda ■ 87 C7
Antilla 86 B4
Antioquia 90 B3
Antofagasta 94 A2
Antofagasta de
  la Sierra 94 B3
Antongila,
  Helodrano 59 H9
Antonina 94 B7
Antrim 11 D3
Antsalova 59 H8
Antsiranana 59 G9
Antsohihy 59 G9
Antwerp =
  Antwerpen 14 C3
Antwerpen 14 C3
Anupgarh 42 E8
Anvers =
  Antwerpen 14 C3

# Anvers I.

| | | |
|---|---|---|
| Anvers I. | 96 | A3 |
| Anxi | 34 | B4 |
| Anxious B. | 62 | B1 |
| Anyang | 35 | C6 |
| Anzhero-Sudzhensk | 29 | D9 |
| Ánzio | 20 | D4 |
| Aomori | 33 | F12 |
| Aosta | 20 | B1 |
| Aoudéras | 55 | E6 |
| Aoulef el Arab | 54 | C5 |
| Apalachicola ⇀ | 74 | E5 |
| Apaporis ⇀ | 90 | D5 |
| Aparri | 38 | A2 |
| Apeldoorn | 14 | B3 |
| Apennines = Appennini | 20 | B3 |
| Apia | 65 | L13 |
| Apiacás, Serra dos | 91 | E7 |
| Aplao | 91 | G4 |
| Apo, Mt. | 38 | C3 |
| Apollonia = Marsá Susah | 52 | B3 |
| Apolo | 91 | F5 |
| Apoteri | 90 | C7 |
| Appalachian Mts. | 73 | F5 |
| Appennini | 20 | B3 |
| Appleton | 72 | B1 |
| Approuague | 92 | B3 |
| Aprília | 20 | D4 |
| Apucarana | 94 | A6 |
| Apure ⇀ | 90 | B5 |
| Apurimac ⇀ | 91 | F4 |
| Aqabah = Al 'Aqabah | 47 | E3 |
| 'Aqabah, Khalīj al | 47 | E3 |
| Āqcheh | 45 | B6 |
| Aqīq | 53 | E6 |
| Aqmola | 29 | D8 |
| Aqrah | 46 | C5 |
| Aqtöbe | 29 | D6 |
| Aquidauana | 93 | G2 |
| Aquitain, Bassin | 12 | D3 |
| Ar Rachidiya | 54 | B4 |
| Ar Ramādī | 46 | D5 |
| Ar Raqqah | 46 | D4 |
| Ar Rass | 47 | F5 |
| Ar Rifā'ī | 47 | E6 |
| Ar Riyāḍ | 47 | F6 |
| Ar Ruṭbah | 46 | D5 |
| Ar Ruwayḍah | 47 | G6 |
| Ara | 40 | E5 |
| 'Arab, Bahr el ⇀ | 53 | G4 |
| Arab, Shatt al ⇀ | 47 | E7 |
| Arabian Desert = Es Sahrâ' Esh Sharqîya | 52 | C5 |
| Arabian Gulf = Gulf, The | 44 | E2 |
| Arabian Sea | 26 | H10 |
| Araç | 46 | B3 |
| Aracaju | 93 | E6 |
| Aracataca | 90 | A4 |
| Aracati | 92 | C6 |
| Araçatuba | 93 | G3 |
| Aracena | 18 | D2 |
| Araçuaí | 93 | F5 |
| Arad | 16 | E5 |
| Arada | 53 | F3 |
| Arafura Sea | 39 | F4 |
| Aragón □ | 19 | B5 |
| Aragón ⇀ | 19 | A5 |
| Araguacema | 92 | D4 |
| Araguaia ⇀ | 92 | D4 |
| Araguari | 93 | F4 |
| Araguari ⇀ | 92 | B4 |
| Arak | 54 | C5 |
| Arakan Coast | 41 | H9 |
| Arakan Yoma | 41 | H10 |
| Araks = Aras, Rūd-e ⇀ | 46 | B7 |
| Aral | 29 | E7 |
| Aral Sea | 29 | E6 |
| Aral Tengizi = Aral Sea | 29 | E6 |
| Aralsk = Aral | 29 | E7 |
| Aralskoye More = Aral Sea | 29 | E6 |
| Aran I. | 10 | D2 |
| Aran Is. | 11 | E2 |
| Aranda de Duero | 18 | B4 |
| Aranjuez | 18 | B4 |
| Aranos | 58 | C3 |
| Araouane | 55 | E4 |
| Arapgir | 46 | C4 |
| Arapiraca | 93 | D6 |
| Arapongas | 94 | A6 |
| Araranguá | 94 | B7 |
| Araraquara | 93 | G4 |
| Ararat | 62 | C3 |
| Ararat, Mt. = Ağrı Dağı | 46 | C6 |
| Araripe, Chapada do | 92 | D6 |
| Aras, Rūd-e ⇀ | 46 | B7 |
| Arauca | 90 | B4 |
| Arauca ⇀ | 90 | B5 |
| Arauco | 94 | D2 |
| Araxá | 93 | F4 |
| Araya, Pen. de | 90 | A6 |
| Arbatax | 21 | E2 |
| Arbīl | 46 | C6 |
| Arbroath | 10 | C5 |
| Arcachon | 12 | D3 |
| Archangel = Arkhangelsk | 28 | C5 |
| Arcila = Asilah | 54 | A3 |
| Arckaringa | 62 | A1 |
| Arckaringa Cr. ⇀ | 62 | A2 |
| Arcos de la Frontera | 18 | D3 |
| Arcot | 43 | N11 |
| Arcoverde | 92 | D6 |
| Arctic Bay | 68 | A2 |
| Arctic Red River | 70 | B6 |
| Arda ⇀ | 22 | D6 |
| Ardabīl | 46 | C7 |
| Ardahan | 46 | B5 |
| Ardakān = Sepīdān | 44 | D3 |
| Ardenne | 14 | D3 |
| Ardennes = Ardenne | 14 | D3 |
| Ardestān | 44 | C3 |
| Ardlethan | 63 | B4 |
| Ardmore | 78 | B5 |
| Ardrossan | 62 | B2 |
| Arecibo | 87 | C6 |
| Areia Branca | 92 | C6 |
| Arendal | 9 | G9 |
| Arequipa | 91 | G4 |
| Arero | 53 | H6 |
| Arévalo | 18 | B3 |
| Arezzo | 20 | C3 |
| Argamakmur | 37 | E2 |
| Arganda | 18 | B4 |
| Argentan | 12 | B3 |
| Argentário, Mte. | 20 | C3 |
| Argentina ■ | 94 | D3 |
| Argentina Is. | 96 | A3 |
| Argentino, L. | 95 | G2 |
| Argeş ⇀ | 22 | B6 |
| Arghandab ⇀ | 42 | D4 |
| Argo | 53 | E5 |
| Argolikós Kólpos | 23 | F4 |
| Árgos | 23 | F4 |
| Argostólion | 23 | E3 |
| Argungu | 55 | F5 |
| Århus | 9 | G10 |
| Arica, Chile | 91 | G4 |
| Arica, Colombia | 90 | D4 |
| Aridh | 47 | F6 |
| Arinos ⇀ | 91 | F7 |
| Aripuanã | 91 | E6 |
| Aripuanã ⇀ | 90 | E6 |
| Ariquemes | 91 | E6 |
| Arizona | 94 | D3 |
| Arizona □ | 83 | C7 |
| Arjona | 90 | A3 |
| Arkalyk = Arqalyk | 29 | D7 |
| Arkansas □ | 79 | B7 |
| Arkansas ⇀ | 79 | C8 |
| Arkansas City | 78 | A5 |
| Arkhangelsk | 28 | C5 |
| Arklow | 11 | E3 |
| Arkticheskiy, Mys | 30 | A7 |
| Arlanzón ⇀ | 18 | A3 |
| Arlberg P. | 14 | E6 |
| Arles | 13 | E6 |
| Arlington, Va., U.S.A. | 73 | E7 |
| Arlington, Wash., U.S.A. | 80 | A2 |
| Arlon | 14 | D3 |
| Armagh | 11 | D3 |
| Armavir | 25 | D5 |
| Armenia | 90 | C3 |
| Armenia ■ | 25 | E5 |
| Armidale | 63 | B5 |
| Armstrong | 69 | C2 |
| Arnaud ⇀ | 68 | B3 |
| Arnauti, C. | 46 | D3 |
| Arnhem | 14 | C3 |
| Arnhem, C. | 60 | C6 |
| Arnhem Land | 60 | C5 |
| Arno ⇀ | 20 | C3 |
| Arno Bay | 62 | B2 |
| Arnsberg | 14 | C5 |
| Aroab | 58 | D3 |
| Arqalyk | 29 | D7 |
| Arrabury | 62 | A3 |
| Arrah = Ara | 40 | E5 |
| Arran | 10 | D4 |
| Arras | 13 | A5 |
| Arrecife | 54 | C2 |
| Arrée, Mts. d' | 12 | B2 |
| Arrowtown | 65 | F3 |
| Árta | 23 | E3 |
| Arthur ⇀ | 62 | D3 |
| Arthur's Pass | 65 | E4 |
| Artigas | 94 | C5 |
| Artois | 12 | A5 |
| Artsyz | 17 | E9 |
| Artvin | 46 | B5 |
| Aru, Kepulauan | 39 | F4 |
| Aru Is. = Aru, Kepulauan | 39 | F4 |
| Arua | 57 | D6 |
| Aruanã | 93 | E3 |
| Aruba ■ | 87 | D6 |
| Arumpo | 62 | B3 |
| Arunachal Pradesh □ | 41 | C10 |
| Arusha | 57 | E7 |
| Aruwimi ⇀ | 56 | D4 |
| Arxan | 35 | B6 |
| Arys | 29 | E7 |
| Arzamas | 24 | B5 |
| Arzew | 54 | A4 |
| 'As Saffānīyah | 47 | E7 |
| As Samāwah | 47 | E6 |
| As Sulaymānīyah, Iraq | 46 | D6 |
| As Sulaymānīyah, Si. Arabia | 47 | F6 |
| As Summān | 47 | F6 |
| As Sūq | 47 | G5 |
| As Suwaydā' | 46 | D4 |
| As Suwayh | 45 | F4 |
| As Ṣuwayrah | 47 | D6 |
| Asahigawa | 32 | F12 |
| Asansol | 40 | F6 |
| Ascension I. | 51 | G2 |
| Aschaffenburg | 14 | D5 |
| Aschersleben | 15 | C6 |
| Áscoli Piceno | 20 | C4 |
| Ascope | 91 | E3 |
| Aseb | 49 | E3 |
| Asela | 53 | G6 |
| Asenovgrad | 22 | C5 |
| Ash Shām, Bādiyat | 47 | D4 |
| Ash Shāmīyah | 47 | E6 |
| Ash Shāriqah | 44 | E3 |
| Ash Shaṭrah | 47 | E6 |
| Ash Shaykh, J. | 46 | D3 |
| Ash Shu'aybah | 47 | F6 |
| Ash Shu'bah | 47 | E6 |
| Ashburton | 65 | E4 |
| Ashcroft | 71 | C7 |
| Asheville | 75 | B6 |
| Ashford, Australia | 63 | A5 |
| Ashford, U.K. | 11 | F7 |
| Ashgabat | 29 | F6 |
| Ashikaga | 32 | A6 |
| Ashizuri-Zaki | 32 | C3 |
| Ashkhabad = Ashgabat | 29 | F6 |
| Ashmyany | 17 | A7 |
| Ashqelon | 47 | E3 |
| Ashtabula | 72 | D5 |
| Ashuanipi, L. | 69 | C4 |
| Asia, Kepulauan | 39 | D4 |
| Asifabad | 43 | K11 |
| Asike | 39 | F6 |
| Asilah | 54 | A3 |
| Asinara | 20 | D2 |
| Asinara, G. dell' | 20 | D2 |
| Asino | 29 | D9 |
| Asipovichy | 17 | B9 |
| 'Asīr □ | 48 | D3 |
| Asir, Ras | 49 | E5 |
| Asmara = Asmera | 53 | E6 |
| Asmera | 53 | E6 |
| Aspiring, Mt. | 65 | F3 |
| Assam □ | 41 | D9 |
| Assen | 14 | B4 |
| Assini | 55 | G4 |
| Assiniboia | 71 | D9 |
| Assiniboine ⇀ | 71 | D10 |
| Assis | 94 | A6 |
| Assisi | 20 | C4 |
| Asti | 20 | B2 |
| Astipálaia | 23 | F6 |
| Astorga | 18 | A2 |
| Astoria | 80 | B2 |
| Astrakhan | 25 | D6 |
| Astrakhan-Bazàr | 25 | F6 |
| Asturias □ | 18 | A3 |
| Asunción | 94 | B5 |
| Aswân | 52 | D5 |
| Aswân High Dam = Sadd el Aali | 52 | D5 |

Asyût ........ 52 C5
At Ţafilah ..... 47 E3
At Ţā'if ..... 48 C3
Atacama,
  Desierto de . 94 A3
Atacama, Salar
  de ......... 94 A3
Atakpamé .... 55 G5
Atalaya ....... 91 F4
Atami ........ 32 B6
Atapupu ...... 39 F2
Atâr ......... 54 D2
Atasu ........ 29 E8
Atauro ....... 39 F3
Atbara ....... 53 E5
'Atbara →   . 53 E5
Atbasar ...... 29 D7
Athabasca ... 71 C8
Athabasca → . 70 C8
Athabasca, L. . . 70 C8
Athens =
  Athínai ..... 23 F4
Athens, Ala.,
  U.S.A. ..... 74 B4
Athens, Ga.,
  U.S.A. ..... 75 C6
Athínai ....... 23 F4
Athlone ...... 11 E3
Áthos ........ 23 D5
Athy ......... 11 E3
Ati .......... 53 F2
Atico ......... 91 G4
Atlanta ....... 75 C5
Atlantic City ... 73 E8
Atlas Mts. =
  Haut Atlas .. 54 B3
Atrak =
  Atrek → ... 44 B3
Atrek → ..... 44 B3
Attawapiskat → 69 C2
Attock ....... 42 C8
Attopeu ...... 36 B3
Attur ........ 43 P11
Atuel → ..... 94 D3
Atyraū ....... 29 E6
Aubagne ..... 13 E6
Aube → ..... 13 B5
Auburn ...... 74 C5
Auburn Ra. ... 63 A5
Aubusson ... 12 D5
Auch ........ 12 E4
Auckland ..... 64 B6
Aude → .... 13 E5
Augathella ... 63 A4
Augsburg ..... 14 D6
Augusta, Italy . 21 F5
Augusta, Ga.,
  U.S.A. ..... 75 C7
Augusta, Maine,
  U.S.A. ..... 73 B11
Aunis ........ 12 C3
Auponhia .... 39 E3
Aurangabad,
  Bihar, India . 40 E5
Aurangabad,
  Maharashtra,
  India ....... 43 K9
Aurich ....... 14 B4
Aurillac ...... 12 D5
Aurora, Colo.,
  U.S.A. ..... 76 F2
Aurora, Ill.,
  U.S.A. ..... 72 D1
Aus .......... 58 D3
Auschwitz =
  Oświęcim ... 16 C4
Austin, Minn.,
  U.S.A. ..... 77 D8
Austin, Tex.,
  U.S.A. ..... 78 D5

Austral Is. =
  Tubuai Is. ... 65 M16
Austral
  Seamount
  Chain ...... 65 M16
Australia ■ ... 60 E6
Australian Alps 63 C4
Australian
  Capital
  Territory □ .. 63 C4
Austria ■ ..... 15 E8
Autun ........ 13 C6
Auvergne .... 13 D5
Auvergne, Mts.
  d' .......... 13 D5
Auxerre ...... 13 C5
Avallon ....... 13 C5
Aveiro, Brazil . 92 C2
Aveiro, Portugal 18 B1
Āvej ......... 46 D7
Avellaneda .... 94 C5
Avellino ...... 21 D5
Aversa ....... 21 D5
Avezzano ..... 20 C4
Aviá Terai .... 94 B4
Aviemore .... 10 C5
Avignon ...... 13 E6
Ávila ......... 18 B3
Avilés ........ 18 A3
Avoca → .... 62 C3
Avola ........ 21 F5
Avranches .... 12 B3
'Awālī ....... 44 E2
Awash ....... 49 F3
Awatere → .. 65 D6
Awbārī ...... 52 C1
Awjilah ...... 52 C3
Axim ........ 55 H4
Axiós → .... 23 D4
Ayabaca ..... 90 D3
Ayabe ....... 32 B4
Ayacucho,
  Argentina ... 94 D5
Ayacucho, Peru 91 F4
Ayaguz ...... 29 E9
Ayamonte .... 18 D2
Ayaviri ....... 91 F4
Āybak ....... 45 B7
Aydın ........ 23 F6
Ayers Rock .. 60 F5
Áyios Evstrátios 23 E5
Aylmer, L. .... 70 B8
Ayn Dār ..... 47 F7
Ayn Zālah ... 46 C5
Ayr .......... 10 D4
Aytos ........ 22 C6
Ayu, Kepulauan 39 D4
Ayutla ....... 84 D5
Ayvacık ...... 23 E6
Ayvalık ...... 23 E6
Aẕ Ẕahrān ... 47 F7
Az Zarqā .... 46 D4
Az-Zilfī ...... 47 F6
Az Zubayr ... 47 E6
Az Zuwaytīnah 52 B3
Azamgarh .... 40 D4
Azärbayjan =
  Azerbaijan ■ 25 E6
Āzarbāyjān-e
  Gharbī □ .. 46 C5
Āzarbāyjān-e
  Sharqī □ .... 46 C6
Azare ....... 55 F7
Azbine = Aïr . 55 E6
Azerbaijan ■ .. 25 E6
Azerbaijchan =
  Azerbaijan ■ 25 E6
Azogues ..... 90 D3
Azores ....... 50 C1

Azov ......... 25 D4
Azov, Sea of .. 25 D4
Azovskoye More
  = Azov, Sea
  of ......... 25 D4
Azovy ........ 28 C7
Azúa ......... 87 C5
Azuaga ....... 18 C3
Azuero, Pen. de 86 E3
Azul ......... 94 D5

B

Ba Don ....... 36 A3
Ba Ria ....... 36 B3
Bab el Mandeb 49 E3
Baba Burnu .. 23 E6
Babadag ..... 22 B7
Babadayhan .. 29 F7
Babaeski .... 22 D6
Babahoyo .... 90 D3
Babana ...... 55 F5
Babar ........ 39 F3
Babo ........ 39 E4
Bābol ........ 44 B3
Bābol Sar .... 44 B3
Baboua ...... 56 C2
Babruysk .... 17 B9
Babura ...... 55 F6
Babuyan Chan. 38 A2
Babylon ...... 47 D6
Bacabal ..... 92 C5
Bacan,
  Kepulauan . 39 E3
Bacan, Pulau . 39 E3
Bacarra ..... 38 A2
Bacău ....... 17 E8
Bachelina ... 29 D7
Back → ..... 70 B9
Backstairs
  Passage ... 62 C2
Bacolod ..... 38 B2
Bad Ischl .... 15 E7
Bad Kissingen . 14 C6
Bad Lands ... 76 D3
Badagara .... 43 P9
Badajoz ..... 18 C2
Badalona .... 19 B7
Badalzai ..... 42 E4
Badampahar .. 40 F6
Badanah ..... 47 E5
Badarinath .. 42 D11
Badas ....... 36 D4
Badas,
  Kepulauan .. 37 D3
Baddo → ... 42 E4
Bade ........ 39 F5
Baden ....... 15 D9
Baden-Baden .. 14 D5
Baden-
  Württemberg □
  ........... 14 D5
Badgastein ... 15 E7
Bādghīsāt □ .. 42 B3
Badin ....... 43 G6
Baduen ...... 49 F4
Baena ....... 18 D3
Baeza ....... 18 D4
Bafatá ...... 55 F2
Baffin B. .... 68 A4
Baffin I. ..... 68 B3
Bafia ....... 56 D2
Bafing → ... 55 F2
Bafoulabé ... 55 F2
Bāfq ........ 44 D3
Bafra ....... 46 B3

Bāft ......... 44 D4
Bafwasende .. 57 D5
Bagamoyo ... 57 F7
Baganga ..... 38 C3
Bagansiapiapi . 37 D2
Bagdarin .... 30 D9
Bagé ........ 94 C6
Baghdād .... 46 D6
Bagheria .... 21 E4
Baghlān .... 42 A6
Baghlān □ ... 45 C7
Baguio ...... 38 A2
Bahamas ■ .. 86 A4
Baharampur .. 40 E7
Bahawalpur ... 42 E7
Bahía =
  Salvador .... 93 E6
Bahía □ ..... 93 E5
Bahía Blanca .. 94 D4
Bahía de
  Caráquez ... 90 D2
Bahía Laura .. 95 F3
Bahía Negra . 91 H7
Bahr Aouk → . 56 C3
Bahr
  Salamat → . 53 G2
Bahraich ..... 40 D3
Bahrain ■ .... 44 E2
Baia Mare ... 17 E6
Baïbokoum .. 53 G2
Baidoa ...... 49 G3
Baie Comeau . 69 D4
Ba'ijī ....... 46 D5
Baikal, L. =
  Baykal, Oz. . 30 D8
Baile Atha Cliath
  = Dublin .... 11 E3
Bāilești ..... 22 B4
Bailundo .... 58 A3
Bā'ir ....... 47 E4
Baird Mts. ... 71 B3
Bairnsdale ... 63 C4
Baitadi ...... 40 C3
Baiyin ...... 35 C5
Baja ........ 16 E4
Baja, Pta. .... 84 B1
Baja California . 84 A1
Bajimba, Mt. .. 63 A5
Bakala ...... 56 C4
Bakchar .... 29 D9
Bakel ....... 55 F2
Baker, L. .... 70 B10
Baker I. ..... 64 J13
Baker Lake .. 70 B10
Baker Mt. ... 80 A3
Baker's Dozen
  Is. ........ 69 C3
Bakersfield .. 82 C3
Bākhtarān ... 46 D6
Baki = Bakı .. 25 E6
Bakony Forest =
  Bakony
  Hegyseg ... 16 E3
Bakony Hegyseg 16 E3
Bakouma .... 56 C4
Baku = Bakı .. 25 E6
Bakutis Coast . 96 B1
Baky = Bakı .. 25 E6
Balabac I. ... 36 C5
Balabac Str. .. 36 C5
Balabalangan,
  Kepulauan .. 37 E5
Balaghat Ra. .. 43 K10
Balaguer .... 19 B6
Balaklava,
  Australia ... 62 B2
Balaklava,
  Ukraine ..... 25 E3
Balakovo .... 24 C6

Balashov . . . . . 24 C5
Balasore =
Baleshwar . . 40 G6
Balaton . . . . . . . 16 E3
Balbina, Reprêsa
de . . . . . . . . 90 D7
Balchik . . . . . . . 22 C7
Balclutha . . . . . 65 G3
Baleares, Is. . . 19 C7
Balearic Is. =
Baleares, Is. . 19 C7
Baler . . . . . . . . 38 A2
Baleshwar . . . 40 G6
Bali, Cameroon 55 G7
Bali, Indonesia 37 F5
Bali □ . . . . . . . 37 F5
Balikeşir . . . . . . 23 E6
Balikpapan . . . . 37 E5
Balimbing . . . 38 C1
Balipara . . . . . 41 D9
Baliza . . . . . . . . 93 F3
Balkan Mts. =
Stara Planina 22 C4
Balkh . . . . . . . . 45 B6
Balkhash =
Balqash . . . . 29 E8
Balkhash, Ozero
= Balqash Köl 29 E8
Balla . . . . . . . . 41 E8
Ballarat . . . . . . . 62 C3
Ballater . . . . . . 10 C5
Ballina, Australia 63 A5
Ballina, Ireland 11 D2
Ballinasloe . . . . 11 E2
Ballymena . . . 11 D3
Balmaceda . . . . 95 F2
Balmoral . . . . . 62 C3
Balonne → . . 63 A4
Balqash . . . . . 29 E8
Balqash Köl . . . 29 E8
Balrampur . . . . 40 D4
Balranald . . . . 62 B3
Balsas → . . . 84 D4
Balta . . . . . . . . 17 D9
Bălţi . . . . . . . . 17 E8
Baltic Sea . . . . 9 G11
Baltimore . . . . 73 E7
Baluchistan □ . 42 F4
Balya . . . . . . . . 23 E6
Bam . . . . . . . . 44 D4
Bama . . . . . . . . 53 F1
Bamako . . . . . 55 F3
Bamba . . . . . . 55 E4
Bambari . . . . . 56 C4
Bamberg . . . . . 14 D6
Bambili . . . . . . 57 D5
Bamenda . . . . 55 G7
Bāmiān □ . . . 42 B5
Bampūr . . . . . 45 E5
Ban Don =
Surat Thani . 36 C1
Ban Mê Thuôt =
Buon Me
Thuot . . . . 36 B3
Banaba . . . . . . 64 K11
Banalia . . . . . . 57 D5
Banam . . . . . . 36 B3
Banamba . . . . 55 F3
Bananal, I. do . 93 E3
Banaras =
Varanasi . . . 40 E4
Band-e
Torkestān . . 45 C6
Banda,
Kepulauan . . 39 E3
Banda Aceh . . . 36 C1
Banda Banda,
Mt. . . . . . . . . 63 B5
Banda Elat . . . . 39 F4

Banda Is. =
Banda,
Kepulauan . . 39 E3
Banda Sea . . . . 39 F3
Bandanaira . . . 39 E3
Bandar =
Machilipatnam 40 J3
Bandār 'Abbās 44 E4
Bandar-e Anzalī 46 C7
Bandar-e
Bushehr =
Būshehr . . . 44 D2
Bandar-e Chārak 44 E3
Bandar-e
Deylam . . . . . 47 E7
Bandar-e
Khomeynı . . 47 E7
Bandar-e
Lengeh . . . 44 E3
Bandar-e
Ma'shur . . . 47 E7
Bandar-e
Nakhīlū . . . . . 44 E3
Bandar-e Rīg . . 44 D2
Bandar-e
Torkeman . . 44 B3
Bandar
Maharani =
Muar . . . . . 37 D2
Bandar
Penggaram =
Batu Pahat . . 37 D2
Bandar Seri
Begawan . . . 36 D5
Bandawe . . . 59 A6
Bandeira, Pico
da . . . . . . . . . 93 G5
Bandera . . . . 94 B4
Bandiagara . . . 55 F4
Bandırma . . . . . 23 D7
Bandon . . . . . 11 F2
Bandundu . . . . 56 E3
Bandung . . . . 37 F3
Banff, Canada . 71 C8
Banff, U.K. . . . 10 C5
Banfora . . . . . 55 F4
Bang Saphan . 36 B1
Bangalore . . . 43 N10
Bangassou . . . . 56 D4
Banggai,
Kepulauan . . 39 E2
Banggi, P. . . . 36 C5
Banghāzī . . . . 52 B3
Bangka, P.,
Sulawesi,
Indonesia . . . 39 D3
Bangka, P.,
Sumatera,
Indonesia . . 37 E3
Bangka, Selat . 37 E3
Bangkinang . . . 37 D2
Bangko . . . . . . . 37 E2
Bangkok . . . . 36 B2
Bangladesh ■ . 41 E7
Bangong Co . . 42 B11
Bangor, Down,
U.K. . . . . . . . . 11 D4
Bangor,
Caerns. & Mers.,
U.K. . . . . . . 11 E4
Bangor, U.S.A. 73 B11
Bangued . . . . . 38 A2
Bangui . . . . . 56 D3
Bangweulu, L. . 57 G6
Bani . . . . . . . . 87 C5
Banī Walīd . . 52 B1
Banīnah . . . . 52 B3
Bāniyās . . . . . 46 D3
Banja Luka . . . . 20 B6

Banjarmasin . . 37 E4
Banjul . . . . . . . 55 F1
Bankipore . . . 40 E5
Banks I. . . . . . 70 A7
Banks Pen. . . . 65 E5
Banks Str. . . . 62 D4
Bankura . . . . . 40 F6
Banningville =
Bandundu . . 56 E3
Bannu . . . . . . 42 C7
Banská Bystrica 16 D4
Banswara . . . 43 H9
Bantry . . . . . . 11 F2
Banu . . . . . . . 42 B6
Banyak,
Kepulauan . . 37 D1
Banyo . . . . . . 55 G7
Banzare Coast . 96 A13
Banzyville =
Mobayi . . . . 56 D4
Baoding . . . . 35 C6
Baoji . . . . . . . 35 C5
Baoshan . . . . 34 D4
Baotou . . . . . 35 B6
Bapatla . . . . . 40 K3
Ba'qūbah . . . 46 D6
Bar,
Montenegro, Yug.
. . . . . . . . . . 22 C2
Bar, Ukraine . . 17 D8
Bar-le-Duc . . . 13 B6
Barabai . . . . . . 37 E5
Barabinsk . . . 29 D8
Baracaldo . . . 19 A4
Baracoa . . . . 86 B5
Barahona . . . 87 C5
Barail Range . . 41 E9
Barakhola . . . 41 E9
Barakpur . . . 41 F7
Barakula . . . 63 A5
Baramula . . . 42 B9
Baran . . . . . 43 G10
Baranavichy . . 17 B8
Baranof I. . . . . 71 C6
Barão de
Melgaço . . . 91 F6
Barapasi . . . . 39 E5
Barat Daya,
Kepulauan . . 39 F3
Barbacena . . . 93 G5
Barbacoas . . . 90 C3
Barbados ■ . . 87 D8
Barbastro . . . 19 A6
Barberton . . . 59 D6
Barcellona Pozzo
di Gotto . . . 21 E5
Barcelona, Spain 19 B7
Barcelona,
Venezuela . . 90 A6
Barcelos . . . . 90 D6
Bardai . . . . . 52 D2
Barddhaman . . 40 F6
Bardejov . . . 16 D5
Bardera . . . . 49 G3
Bardi, Ra's . . 47 F4
Bardīyah . . . 52 B4
Bareilly . . . . 42 E11
Barentu . . . . 53 E6
Barfleur, Pte. de 12 B3
Barga . . . . . 34 C3
Bargal . . . . 49 E5
Barhi . . . . . 40 E5
Bari . . . . . . 20 D6
Bari Doab . . 42 D8
Barīm . . . . . 49 E3
Bârîs . . . . . 52 D5
Barisal . . . . 41 F8
Barisan, Bukit . 37 E2

Barito → . . . . . 37 E4
Barkly Tableland 60 D6
Barlee, L. . . . 60 F2
Barletta . . . . 20 D6
Barmedman . . 63 B4
Barmer . . . . . 42 G7
Barmera . . . . 62 B3
Barnato . . . . 63 B4
Barnaul . . . . 29 D9
Barnsley . . . 11 E6
Barnstaple . . . 11 F4
Baro . . . . . 55 G6
Baroda =
Vadodara . . . 43 H8
Barpeta . . . . 41 D8
Barquísimeto . . 90 A5
Barra, Brazil . . 93 E5
Barra, U.K. . . . 10 C3
Barra do Corda 92 D4
Barra do Piraí . 93 G5
Barra Falsa, Pta.
da . . . . . . . . 59 C7
Barraba . . . . 63 B5
Barrackpur =
Barakpur . . . . 41 F7
Barraigh =
Barra . . . . . 10 C3
Barranca, Lima,
Peru . . . . . . 91 F3
Barranca,
Loreto, Peru . 90 D3
Barrancabermeja
. . . . . . . . . . 90 B4
Barrancas . . . 90 B6
Barrancos . . . 18 C2
Barranqueras . 94 B5
Barranquilla . . 90 A4
Barras . . . . . 92 C5
Barreiras . . . 93 E5
Barreirinhas . . 92 C5
Barreiro . . . . 18 C1
Barreiros . . . 92 D6
Barretos . . . 93 G4
Barrier Ra. . . . 62 B3
Barrington Tops 63 B5
Barringun . . . 63 A4
Barrow . . . . 71 A4
Barrow-in-
Furness . . . 11 D5
Barry . . . . . 11 F5
Barsi . . . . . 43 K9
Barsoi . . . . 40 E6
Barstow . . . 82 C4
Bartica . . . . 90 B7
Bartin . . . . 46 B3
Bartle Frere . . 61 D8
Bartlesville . . . 79 A6
Barysaw . . . 17 A9
Bāsa'idū . . . 44 E3
Basankusa . . 56 D3
Basarabeasca . 17 E9
Basel . . . . 13 C7
Bashi Channel . 35 D7
Bashkir Republic
=
Bashkortostan □
. . . . . . . . . . 29 D6
Bashkortostan □ 29 D6
Basilan . . . . 38 C2
Basilan Str. . . . 38 C2
Basildon . . . 11 F7
Basim =
Washim . . . 43 J10
Basingstoke . . 11 F6
Basle = Basel . 13 C7
Basoka . . . . . 56 D4
Basongo . . . 56 E4
Basque
Provinces =
País Vasco □ . 19 A4

Basra = Al
Başrah ..... 47 E6
Bass Str. .... 61 H8
Bassano ...... 71 C8
Bassano del
Grappa .... 20 B3
Bassas da India 59 C7
Bassein ...... 41 J10
Basseterre .... 87 C7
Bassikounou .. 55 E3
Bastak ....... 44 E3
Bastar ........ 40 H3
Basti ........ 40 D4
Bastia ........ 13 E8
Bastogne ..... 14 C3
Bata ......... 56 D1
Bataan ....... 38 B2
Batabanó ..... 86 B3
Batabanó, G. de 86 B3
Batac ........ 38 A2
Batagoy ...... 31 C11
Batamay ...... 31 C10
Batang ....... 34 C4
Batangafo .... 56 C3
Batangas ..... 38 B2
Batanta ...... 39 E4
Bateman's B. .. 63 C5
Batemans Bay . 63 C5
Bath ........ 11 F5
Bathurst,
Australia .... 63 B4
Bathurst,
Canada ..... 69 D4
Bathurst, C. ... 70 A7
Bathurst Harb. . 62 D4
Bathurst Inlet .. 70 B9
Batinah ....... 44 F4
Batlow ....... 63 C4
Batman ....... 46 C7
Batna ........ 54 A6
Baton Rouge .. 79 D8
Batouri ...... 56 D2
Battambang ... 36 B2
Battipáglia ... 21 D5
Battle Creek .. 72 C3
Battle Harbour . 69 C5
Battleford .... 71 C9
Batu ......... 49 F2
Batu, Kepulauan 37 E1
Batu Is. = Batu,
Kepulauan .. 37 E1
Batu Pahat ... 37 D2
Batuata ....... 39 F2
Batumi ....... 25 E5
Baturaja ...... 37 E2
Baturité ...... 92 C6
Bau .......... 37 D4
Baubau ....... 39 F2
Bauchi ....... 55 F6
Bauer, C. ..... 62 B1
Baukau ....... 39 F3
Bauru ........ 93 G4
Baús ......... 93 F3
Bautzen ...... 15 C8
Bavaria =
Bayern □ ... 15 D6
Bawdwin ..... 41 F11
Bawean ....... 37 F4
Bawku ....... 55 F4
Bawlake ...... 41 H11
Bay, L. de .... 38 B2
Bay City ..... 72 C4
Bay View ..... 64 C7
Bayamo ...... 86 B4
Bayan Har Shan 34 C4
Bayan Hot =
Alxa Zuoqi .. 35 C5
Bayanaũyl .... 29 D8
Bayanhongor .. 35 B5

Bayázeh ...... 44 C3
Baybay ....... 38 B2
Bayburt ...... 46 B5
Bayern □ ..... 15 D6
Bayeux ....... 12 B3
Bayındır ..... 23 E6
Baykal, Oz. ... 30 D8
Baykit ........ 30 C7
Baykonur =
Bayqongyr .. 29 E7
Bayombong ... 38 A2
Bayonne ...... 12 E3
Bayovar ...... 91 E2
Bayqongyr .... 29 E7
Bayram-Ali =
Bayramaly . 29 F7
Bayramaly ... 29 F7
Bayramiç ..... 23 E6
Bayreuth ..... 15 D6
Bayrūt ....... 46 D3
Baytown ...... 79 E6
Baza ......... 19 D4
Bazaruto, I. do . 59 C7
Beachport .... 62 C2
Beagle, Canal . 95 G3
Beardmore
Glacier ..... 96 C14
Béarn ........ 12 E3
Beauce, Plaine
de la ....... 12 B4
Beaudesert ... 63 A5
Beaufort ..... 36 C5
Beaufort Sea .. 66 B6
Beaufort West . 58 E4
Beaumont .... 79 D6
Beaune ....... 13 C6
Beauvais ..... 12 B5
Beauval ...... 71 C9
Beaver ....... 71 B5
Beaver → .... 71 C9
Beawar ...... 42 F9
Bečej ........ 22 B3
Béchar ....... 54 B4
Bedford ...... 11 E6
Beenleigh .... 63 A5
Be'er Sheva ... 47 E3
Beersheba =
Be'er Sheva . 47 E3
Befale ........ 56 D4
Bega ......... 63 C4
Behbehān ..... 47 E7
Behshahr ..... 44 B3
Bei Jiang → .. 35 D6
Bei'an ....... 35 B7
Beibei ....... 35 D5
Beihai ....... 35 D5
Beijing ....... 35 C6
Beilpajah .... 63 B3
Beinn na
Faoghla =
Benbecula .. 10 C3
Beira ........ 59 B6
Beirut = Bayrūt 46 D3
Beitbridge ... 59 C6
Beja, Portugal . 18 C2
Béja, Tunisia . 54 A6
Bejaia ....... 54 A6
Béjar ........ 18 B3
Bejestān ..... 44 C4
Békéscsaba ... 16 E5
Bela, India ... 40 E4
Bela, Pakistan . 42 F5
Bela Crkva ... 22 B3
Bela Vista ... 94 A5
Belarus ■ ..... 24 C2
Belau = Palau ■ 38 C4
Belawan ...... 37 D1
Belaya Tserkov
= Bila Tserkva 17 D10

Belcher Is. .... 69 C3
Belém ........ 92 C4
Belén ........ 94 A5
Belet Uen ..... 49 G4
Belev ........ 24 C4
Belfast ....... 11 D4
Belfort ....... 13 C7
Belgaum ..... 43 M9
Belgium ■ .... 14 C3
Belgorod ..... 24 C4
Belgorod-
Dnestrovskiy
= Bilhorod-
Dnistrovskyy 25 D3
Belgrade =
Beograd .... 22 B3
Beli Drim → .. 22 C3
Belinga ...... 56 D2
Belinyu ...... 37 E3
Beliton Is. =
Belitung .... 37 E3
Belitung ..... 37 E3
Belize ■ ...... 85 D7
Belize City ... 85 D7
Belkovskiy,
Ostrov .... 30 B11
Bell Bay ...... 62 D4
Bell Peninsula . 68 B2
Bell Ville ..... 94 C4
Bella Unión ... 94 C5
Bella Vista ... 94 B5
Bellary ....... 43 M10
Bellata ....... 63 A4
Belle-Ile ..... 12 C2
Belle Isle .... 69 C5
Belle Isle, Str. of 69 C5
Belleville,
Canada .... 69 D3
Belleville, U.S.A. 77 F10
Bellin =
Kangirsuk ... 68 C4
Bellingen .... 63 B5
Bellingham .. 80 A2
Bellingshausen
Sea ....... 96 A2
Bellinzona ... 13 C8
Belluno ...... 20 A4
Belmont ..... 63 B5
Belmonte .... 93 F6
Belmopan .... 85 D7
Belo Horizonte . 93 F5
Belo-Tsiribihina 59 H8
Beloit ........ 77 D10
Belokorovichi . 17 C9
Belomorsk ... 28 C4
Belonia ...... 41 F8
Belorussia ■ =
Belarus ■ ... 24 C2
Belovo ....... 29 D9
Beloye, Ozero . 24 A4
Beloye More .. 28 C4
Belozersk .... 24 A4
Beltana ...... 62 B2
Belterra ...... 92 C3
Beltsy = Bălţi . 17 E8
Belukha ...... 29 E9
Beluran ...... 36 C5
Belyy, Ostrov . 28 B8
Belyy Yar .... 29 D9
Bembéréke ... 55 F5
Bemidji ...... 77 B7
Ben Gardane .. 52 B1
Ben Lomond,
N.S.W.,
Australia .... 63 B5
Ben Lomond,
Tas., Australia 62 D4
Ben Nevis .... 10 C4
Bena ........ 55 F6

Bena Dibele ... 56 E4
Benagerie .... 62 B3
Benalla ...... 63 C4
Benambra, Mt. . 63 C4
Benares =
Varanasi .... 40 E4
Benavente .... 18 A3
Benbecula .... 10 C3
Benbonyathe .. 62 B2
Bend ........ 80 C3
Bender Beila .. 49 F5
Bendery =
Tighina ..... 17 E9
Bendigo ...... 63 C3
Benevento ... 20 D5
Bengal, Bay of . 41 J7
Bengbu ...... 35 C6
Benghazi =
Banghāzī ... 52 B3
Bengkalis .... 37 D2
Bengkulu .... 37 E2
Bengkulu □ .. 37 E2
Benguela .... 58 A2
Beni ........ 57 D5
Beni → ...... 91 F5
Beni Abbès ... 54 B4
Beni Mazâr ... 52 C5
Beni Mellal ... 54 B3
Beni Ounif ... 54 B4
Beni Suef ..... 52 C5
Benidorm .... 19 C5
Benin ■ ...... 55 G5
Benin, Bight of 55 H5
Benin City .... 55 G6
Benjamin
Constant .... 90 D4
Benoni ...... 59 D5
Bent ........ 44 E4
Benteng ...... 39 F2
Benton Harbor 72 C2
Benue → ..... 55 G6
Benxi ........ 35 B7
Beo .......... 38 D3
Beograd ...... 22 B3
Beppu ....... 32 C2
Berati ....... 23 D2
Berau, Teluk .. 39 E4
Berber ....... 53 E5
Berbera ...... 49 E4
Berbérati .... 56 D3
Berbice → .... 90 B7
Berdichev =
Berdychiv ... 17 D9
Berdsk ....... 29 D9
Berdyansk ... 25 D4
Berdychiv ... 17 D9
Berebere .... 39 D3
Bereda ....... 49 E5
Berehove .... 17 D6
Berekum ..... 55 G4
Berestechko .. 17 C7
Bereza ....... 17 B7
Berezhany ... 17 D7
Berezina =
Byarezina → 17 B10
Berezniki .... 28 D6
Berezovo .... 28 C7
Berga ........ 19 A6
Bergama ..... 23 E6
Bérgamo ..... 20 B2
Bergen ....... 8 F9
Bergerac ..... 12 D4
Berhala, Selat . 37 E2
Berhampore =
Baharampur . 40 E7
Berhampur ... 40 H5
Bering Sea ... 71 C1
Bering Strait .. 71 B3
Berja ........ 19 D4

# Berkeley

Berkeley ...... 80 G2
Berkner I. ..... 96 B4
Berlin ........ 15 B7
Bermejo →,
Formosa,
Argentina .. 94 B5
Bermejo →,
San Juan,
Argentina ... 94 C3
Bermuda ■ ... 67 F13
Bern ......... 13 C7
Bernardo de
Irigoyen .... 94 B6
Bernburg ..... 15 C6
Berne = Bern . 13 C7
Bernina, Piz .. 13 C8
Beroroha ..... 59 J9
Beroun ....... 16 D2
Berrechid ..... 54 B3
Berri ......... 62 B3
Berry, Australia 63 B5
Berry, France .. 12 C5
Bershad ...... 17 D9
Bertoua ...... 56 D2
Berwick-upon-
Tweed ..... 10 D6
Besalampy .... 59 H8
Besançon .... 13 C7
Besar ........ 37 E5
Besni ........ 46 C4
Bessarabiya .. 17 E9
Bessarabka =
Basarabeasca 17 E9
Bessemer ..... 74 C4
Betanzos ..... 18 A1
Bétaré Oya .... 56 C2
Bethanien ... 58 D3
Bethel ....... 71 B3
Bethlehem,
S. Africa .... 59 D5
Bethlehem,
U.S.A. .... 73 D8
Béthune ...... 13 A5
Bethungra .... 63 B4
Betioky ...... 59 J8
Betroka ...... 59 J9
Betsiamites ... 69 D4
Bettiah ...... 40 D5
Betul ......... 43 J10
Betung ....... 37 D4
Beverley ..... 11 E6
Beverly Hills .. 82 C3
Beyla ........ 55 G3
Beyneu ....... 29 E6
Beypazarı ..... 46 B2
Beyşehir Gölü . 46 C2
Bezhitsa ..... 24 C3
Béziers ....... 13 E5
Bezwada =
Vijayawada . 40 J3
Bhachau ..... 43 H7
Bhadrakh ..... 40 G6
Bhadravati .... 43 N9
Bhagalpur ... 40 E6
Bhakra Dam ... 42 D10
Bhamo ....... 41 E11
Bhandara ..... 43 J11
Bhanrer Ra. ... 43 H11
Bharat =
India ■ ..... 43 J10
Bharatpur .... 42 F10
Bhatpara ..... 41 F7
Bhaunagar =
Bhavnagar . 43 J8
Bhavnagar .... 43 J8
Bhawanipatna . 40 H3
Bhilsa = Vidisha 43 H10
Bhilwara ...... 43 G9
Bhima → .... 43 L10

Bhimavaram .. 40 J3
Bhind ........ 42 F11
Bhiwandi ..... 43 K8
Bhiwani ...... 42 E10
Bhola ........ 41 F8
Bhopal ....... 43 H10
Bhubaneshwar 40 G5
Bhuj ......... 43 H6
Bhumiphol Dam
= Phumiphon,
Khuan ...... 36 A1
Bhusaval ..... 43 J9
Bhutan ■ ..... 41 D8
Biafra, B. of =
Bonny, Bight
of ......... 56 D1
Biak ......... 39 E5
Biała Podlaska . 17 B6
Białogard ..... 16 A2
Białystok ..... 17 B6
Biaro ........ 39 D3
Biarritz ...... 12 E3
Bibala ........ 58 A2
Biberach ..... 14 D5
Bibiani ....... 55 G4
Bida ......... 55 G6
Bidar ........ 43 L10
Biddeford .... 73 C10
Bidon 5 = Poste
Maurice
Cortier ..... 54 D5
Bié, Planalto de 58 A3
Biel ......... 13 C7
Bielefeld ...... 14 B5
Biella ........ 20 B2
Bielsk Podlaski 17 B6
Bielsko-Biała .. 16 D4
Bien Hoa ..... 36 B3
Bienne = Biel . 13 C7
Bienville, L. ... 69 C3
Big Horn Mts. =
Bighorn Mts. 81 C10
Big Spring .... 78 C3
Big Trout L. ... 69 C2
Biğa ......... 23 D6
Bigadiç ...... 23 E7
Biggar ....... 71 C9
Biggenden .... 63 A5
Bighorn → ... 81 B10
Bighorn Mts. .. 81 C10
Bihać ........ 20 B5
Bihar ........ 40 E5
Bihar □ ...... 40 E5
Bihor, Munţii . 17 E6
Bijagós,
Arquipélago
dos ...... 55 F1
Bijapur,
Karnataka,
India ...... 43 L9
Bijapur, Mad. P.,
India ...... 40 H3
Bijār ........ 46 D6
Bijeljina ..... 20 B7
Bijnor ....... 42 E11
Bikaner ...... 42 E8
Bikini Atoll .... 64 H11
Bila Tserkva ... 17 D10
Bilara ....... 42 F8
Bilaspur ...... 40 F4
Bilauk Taungdan 36 B1
Bilbao ....... 19 A4
Bilbo = Bilbao . 19 A4
Bilecik ....... 46 B2
Bilhorod-
Dnistrovskyy 25 D3
Bilir ......... 31 C11
Billings ...... 81 C9
Billiton Is. =
Belitung .... 37 E3

Bilma ........ 53 E1
Biloxi ....... 79 D9
Biltine ....... 53 F3
Bima ......... 39 F1
Bimbo ....... 56 D3
Bina-Etawah .. 43 G11
Binalbagan ... 38 B2
Binalong ..... 63 B4
Bīnālūd, Kūh-e 44 B4
Binatang ..... 37 D4
Binda ........ 63 A4
Bindle ....... 63 A4
Bindura ...... 59 B6
Bingara, N.S.W.,
Australia .... 63 A5
Bingara,
Queens.,
Australia .... 63 A3
Bingham
Canyon ... 81 E7
Binghamton .. 73 C8
Bingöl ....... 46 C5
Binh Dinh = An
Nhon ..... 36 B3
Binh Son .... 36 A3
Binjai ........ 37 D1
Binnaway .... 63 B4
Binongko .... 39 F2
Bintan ....... 37 D2
Bintulu ...... 37 D4
Bintuni ...... 39 E4
Binzert = Bizerte 54 A6
Bioko ........ 56 D1
Bir .......... 43 K9
Bir Autrun .... 53 E4
Bir Mogrein .. 54 C2
Bîr Ungât .... 52 D5
Bira ......... 39 E4
Birao ........ 53 F3
Birch ip ...... 62 C3
Birecik ...... 46 C4
Bireuen ...... 36 C1
Bîrlad ....... 17 E8
Bîrlad → ..... 17 F8
Birmingham,
U.K. ....... 11 E6
Birmingham,
U.S.A. .... 74 C4
Birmitrapur .. 40 F5
Birni Nkonni .. 55 F6
Birnin Kebbi .. 55 F5
Birr ......... 11 E3
Birrie → ..... 63 A4
Birsk ........ 29 D6
Birur ........ 43 N9
Bisa ......... 39 E3
Biscay, B. of .. 12 D2
Biscoe Bay ... 96 B17
Biscoe Is. .... 96 A3
Bishkek ...... 29 E8
Biskra ....... 54 B6
Bislig ........ 38 C3
Bismarck ..... 76 B4
Bismarck Arch. 64 K9
Bissagos =
Bijagós,
Arquipélago
dos ...... 55 F1
Bissau ....... 55 F1
Bistriţa ...... 17 E7
Bistriţa → .... 17 E8
Bitam ........ 56 D2
Bitkine ...... 53 F2
Bitlis ........ 46 C5
Bitola ........ 22 D3
Bitolj = Bitola . 22 D3
Bitter L. =
Buheirat-
Murrat-el-
Kubra ...... 52 B5

Bitterfontein .. 58 E3
Bitterroot Range 81 B6
Biu ......... 53 F1
Biwa-Ko ..... 32 B5
Biysk ........ 29 D9
Bizerte ....... 54 A6
Bjelovar ...... 20 B6
Black Forest =
Schwarzwald 14 D5
Black Hills ... 76 D3
Black Sea ..... 25 E3
Black Volta → . 55 G4
Blackball ..... 65 E4
Blackburn ..... 11 E5
Blackpool .... 11 E5
Blackwater → . 11 E2
Blagodarnoye =
Blagodarnyy . 25 D5
Blagodarnyy .. 25 D5
Blagoevgrad .. 22 C4
Blagoveshchensk
............ 31 D10
Blairmore ..... 71 D8
Blanc, Mont .. 13 D7
Blanca, B. ... 95 D4
Blanca Peak .. 83 B10
Blanche, C. ... 62 B1
Blanche, L. ... 62 A2
Blanes ....... 19 B7
Blantyre ..... 59 B6
Blayney ...... 63 B4
Blednaya, Gora 28 B7
Blenheim ..... 65 D5
Blida ........ 54 A5
Bligh Sound .. 65 F2
Blitta ........ 55 G5
Blodgett Iceberg
Tongue .... 96 A13
Bloemfontein . 59 D5
Bloemhof .... 59 D5
Blois ........ 12 C4
Bloomington,
Ill., U.S.A. .. 77 E10
Bloomington,
Ind., U.S.A. .. 72 E2
Blue Mts., Oreg.,
U.S.A. .... 80 C4
Blue Mts., Pa.,
U.S.A. .... 73 D7
Blue Nile = Nîl
el Azraq → . 53 E5
Blue Ridge Mts. 75 A7
Bluefields .... 86 D3
Bluff ........ 65 G3
Blumenau .... 94 B7
Bo ......... 55 G2
Bo Duc ...... 36 B3
Bo Hai ....... 35 C6
Boa Vista .... 90 C6
Boatman ..... 63 A4
Bobadah ..... 63 B4
Bobbili ....... 40 H4
Bobo-Dioulasso 55 F4
Bóbr → ...... 16 B2
Bobraomby,
Tanjon' i ... 59 G9
Bobruysk =
Babruysk ... 17 B9
Bôca do Acre . 91 E5
Boca Raton ... 75 F7
Bocaiúva ..... 93 F5
Bocanda ..... 55 G4
Bocaranga ... 56 C3
Bochnia ..... 16 D5
Bochum ..... 14 C4
Boda ........ 56 D3
Bodaybo ..... 30 D9
Boden ....... 8 E12
Bodensee .... 13 C8
Bodhan ...... 43 K10

Bodø ......... 8 E10
Bodrog → .... 16 D5
Bodrum ....... 23 F6
Boende ....... 56 E4
Boffa ........ 55 F2
Bogalusa ..... 79 D9
Bogan Gate ... 63 B4
Boggabilla .... 63 A5
Boggabri ..... 63 B5
Bogo ........ 38 B2
Bogong, Mt. .. 63 C4
Bogotá ....... 90 C4
Bogotol ...... 29 D9
Bogra ........ 41 E7
Bogué ........ 55 E2
Bohemian
  Forest =
  Böhmerwald . 15 D7
Bohena Cr. → . 63 B4
Böhmerwald .. 15 D7
Bohol ........ 38 C2
Bohol Sea .... 38 C2
Bohotleh ..... 49 F4
Boise ........ 80 D5
Boise City ... 78 A2
Bojador C. ... 54 C2
Bojana → .... 22 D2
Bojnürd ...... 44 B4
Boké ........ 55 F2
Bokhara → ... 63 A4
Bokoro ....... 53 F2
Bokote ....... 56 E4
Bokungu ...... 56 E4
Bol .......... 53 F1
Bolama ....... 55 F1
Bolan Pass .... 42 E5
Bolbec ....... 12 B4
Bole ......... 34 B3
Bolekhiv ..... 17 D6
Bolekhov =
  Bolekhiv .... 17 D6
Bolesławiec ... 16 C2
Bolgrad =
  Bolhrad .... 17 F9
Bolhrad ...... 17 F9
Bolinao C. .... 38 A1
Bolívar,
  Argentina ... 94 D4
Bolívar,
  Colombia ... 90 C3
Bolivia ■ ..... 91 G6
Bollon ....... 63 A4
Bolobo ....... 56 E3
Bologna ...... 20 B3
Bologoye ..... 24 B3
Bolomba ...... 56 D3
Bolong ....... 38 C2
Bolsena, L. di . 20 C3
Bolshereche ... 29 D8
Bolshevik,
  Ostrov ...... 30 B8
Bolshoi Kavkas
  = Caucasus
  Mountains .. 25 E5
Bolshoy Atlym 28 C7
Bolshoy
  Begichev,
  Ostrov ...... 30 B9
Bolshoy
  Lyakhovskiy,
  Ostrov ...... 31 B12
Bolton ....... 11 E5
Bolu ......... 46 B2
Bolvadin ..... 46 C2
Bolzano ...... 20 A3
Bom Despacho 93 F4
Bom Jesus da
  Lapa ....... 93 E5
Boma ........ 56 F2
Bomaderry .... 63 B5

Bombala ..... 63 C4
Bombay ...... 43 K8
Bomboma .... 56 D3
Bomili ....... 57 D5
Bomongo ..... 56 D3
Bomu → ..... 56 D4
Bon, C. ...... 52 A1
Bonaire ...... 87 D6
Bonang ...... 63 C4
Bonavista .... 69 D5
Bondo ....... 56 D4
Bondoukou ... 55 G4
Bone, Teluk .. 39 E2
Bonerate ..... 39 F2
Bonerate,
  Kepulauan .. 39 F2
Bong Son =
  Hoai Nhon . 36 B3
Bongandanga . 56 D4
Bongor ....... 53 F2
Bonifacio .... 13 F8
Bonn ........ 14 C4
Bonney, L. ... 62 C3
Bonny, Bight of 56 D1
Bonoi ........ 39 E5
Bontang ...... 37 D5
Bonthain ..... 39 F1
Bonthe ...... 55 G2
Bontoc ...... 38 A2
Boolaboolka L. 62 B3
Booligal ..... 63 B3
Boonah ...... 63 A5
Boorindal .... 63 B4
Boorowa ..... 63 B4
Boothia, Gulf of 68 A2
Boothia Pen. .. 70 A10
Booué ....... 56 E2
Bor,
  Serbia, Yug. . 22 B4
Bôr, Sudan ... 53 G5
Borama ...... 49 F3
Borås ........ 9 G10
Borāzjān .... 44 D2
Borba ........ 90 D7
Borda, C. .... 62 C2
Bordeaux .... 12 D3
Bordertown ... 62 C3
Bordj Fly Ste.
  Marie ...... 54 C4
Bordj-in-Eker . 54 D6
Bordj Omar
  Driss ....... 54 C6
Bordj-Tarat .. 54 C6
Borger ....... 78 B3
Borisoglebsk .. 24 C5
Borisov =
  Barysaw ... 17 A9
Borja ........ 90 D3
Borkou ...... 53 E2
Borkum ...... 14 B4
Borley, C. .... 96 A9
Borneo ...... 37 D4
Bornholm .... 9 G11
Boromo ...... 55 F4
Borongan .... 38 B3
Borovichi .... 24 B3
Borşa ........ 17 E7
Borūjerd .... 46 D7
Boryslav ..... 17 D6
Bosa ........ 21 D2
Bosanska
  Gradiška ... 20 B6
Bosaso ...... 49 E4
Boshan ...... 35 C6
Boshrūyeh ... 44 C4
Bosna → ..... 20 B7
Bosna i
  Hercegovina
  = Bosnia-
  Herzegovina ■ 20 B6

Bosnia-
  Herzegovina ■ 20 B6
Bosnik ....... 39 E5
Bosobolo .... 56 D3
Bosporus =
  Karadeniz
  Boğazı .... 22 D7
Bossangoa .... 56 C3
Bossembélé .. 53 G2
Bosso ....... 53 F1
Bosten Hu .... 34 B3
Boston, U.K. .. 11 E6
Boston, U.S.A. . 73 C10
Botany B. .... 63 B5
Bothnia, G. of . 8 F12
Bothwell ..... 62 D4
Botletle → ... 58 C4
Botoşani ..... 17 E8
Botswana ■ .. 58 C4
Botucatu ..... 94 A7
Bou Djébéha . 55 E4
Bou Izakarn ... 54 C3
Bouaké ...... 55 G3
Bouar ........ 56 C3
Bouârfa ...... 54 B4
Bouca ....... 56 C3
Bougie = Bejaia 54 A6
Bougouni .... 55 F3
Boulder ...... 76 E2
Boulder Dam =
  Hoover Dam 82 B5
Boulogne-sur-
  Mer ........ 12 A4
Boultoum .... 55 F7
Bouna ....... 55 G4
Boundiali .... 55 G3
Bourbonnais .. 13 C5
Bourem ...... 55 E4
Bourg-en-Bresse 13 C6
Bourg-St.-
  Maurice .... 13 D7
Bourges ..... 12 C5
Bourgogne .... 13 C6
Bourke ...... 63 B4
Bournemouth . 11 F6
Bousso ...... 53 F2
Boutilimit .... 55 E2
Bowen Mts. .. 63 C4
Bowman I. ... 96 A12
Bowmans .... 62 B2
Bowral ....... 63 B5
Bowraville ... 63 B5
Boyne → .... 11 E3
Boyni Qara ... 45 B6
Boz Dağları .. 23 E7
Bozburun .... 23 F7
Bozcaada .... 23 E6
Bozdoğan .... 23 F7
Bozeman .... 81 C8
Bozen =
  Bolzano ... 20 A3
Bozoum ...... 56 C3
Bra .......... 20 B1
Brač ........ 20 C6
Bracciano, L. di 20 C4
Brach ........ 52 C1
Bräcke ....... 8 F11
Brad ........ 17 E6
Bradenton .... 75 F6
Bradford ..... 11 E6
Braemar ..... 62 B2
Braga ........ 18 B1
Bragança, Brazil 92 C4
Bragança,
  Portugal .... 18 B2
Brahmanbaria . 41 F8
Brahmani → .. 40 G6
Brahmaputra → 41 F7
Braidwood .... 63 C4

Brăila ........ 17 F8
Branco → .... 90 D6
Brandenburg =
  Neubrandenburg
  .......... 15 B7
Brandenburg .. 15 B7
Brandenburg □ 15 B7
Brandon ...... 71 D10
Brandvlei .... 58 E4
Braniewo .... 16 A4
Bransfield Str. . 96 A4
Brantford .... 69 D2
Branxholme ... 62 C3
Brasiléia ..... 91 F5
Brasília ...... 93 F4
Braşov ....... 17 F7
Brassey,
  Banjaran ... 36 D5
Bratislava .... 16 D3
Bratsk ....... 30 D8
Braunau ..... 15 D7
Braunschweig . 14 B6
Brava ........ 49 G3
Bravo del Norte,
  R. → =
  Grande,
  Rio → ..... 79 F5
Brawley ...... 82 D5
Bray ......... 11 E3
Bray, Pays de . 12 B4
Brazil ■ ...... 93 E4
Brazos → .... 79 E6
Brazzaville ... 56 E3
Brčko ....... 20 B7
Breaksea Sd. .. 65 F2
Bream B. ..... 64 A6
Bream Hd. ... 64 A6
Brecon ...... 11 F5
Breda ........ 14 C3
Bredasdorp ... 58 E4
Bredbo ...... 63 C4
Bregenz ..... 14 E5
Brejo ........ 92 C5
Bremen ...... 14 B5
Bremerhaven . 14 B5
Bremerton ... 80 B2
Brenner P. ... 15 E6
Bréscia ...... 20 B3
Breslau =
  Wrocław ... 16 C3
Bressanone ... 20 A3
Brest, Belarus . 17 B6
Brest, France .. 12 B1
Brest-Litovsk =
  Brest ....... 17 B6
Bretagne .... 12 B2
Brett, C. ..... 64 A6
Brewarrina .... 63 A4
Brezhnev =
  Naberezhnyye
  Chelny .... 29 D6
Bria ......... 56 C4
Briançon .... 13 D7
Bribie I. ..... 63 A5
Bridgeport ... 73 D9
Bridgetown ... 87 D8
Bridgewater ... 69 D4
Bridgewater, C. 62 C3
Bridlington ... 11 D6
Bridport ..... 62 D4
Brig ......... 13 C7
Brigham City .. 81 E7
Bright ....... 63 C4
Brighton,
  Australia .... 62 C2
Brighton, U.K. . 11 F6
Bríndisi ...... 21 D6
Brinkworth ... 62 B2
Brisbane ..... 63 A5
Brisbane → .. 63 A5

Bristol, *U.K.* . . . 11 F5
Bristol, *U.S.A.* . 75 A6
Bristol B. . . . . . . 71 C3
Bristol Channel . 11 F4
Britstown . . . . . 58 E4
Brittany =
Bretagne . . . . 12 B2
Brive-la-
Gaillarde . . . . 12 D4
Brixen =
Bressanone . 20 A3
Brlik . . . . . . . . 29 E8
Brno . . . . . . . 16 D3
Brocken . . . . . . 14 C6
Brodeur Pen. . . 68 A2
Brodnica . . . . . 16 B4
Brody . . . . . . . . 17 C7
Broken Hill =
Kabwe . . 59 A5
Broken Hill . . . . 62 B3
Bronte Park . . . 62 D4
Brooks Ra. . . . . 71 B5
Brooloo . . . . . 63 A5
Broome . . . . . . 60 D3
Broughton
Island . . . . . 68 B4
Brown, Pt. . . . . 62 B1
Brownsville . . 78 B5
Brownwood . . 78 D4
Bruay-en-Artois 13 A5
Bruce, Mt. . . . 60 E2
Bruck an der
Mur . . . . . . . . 15 E8
Bruges =
Brugge . . . . 14 C2
Brugge . . . . . . 14 C2
Brumado . . . . 93 E5
Brunei = Bandar
Seri Begawan 36 D5
Brunei ■ . . . 36 D4
Brunner, L. . . . 65 E4
Brunswick =
Braunschweig 14 B6
Brunswick . . . 75 D7
Brunswick, Pen.
de . . . . . . . . 95 G2
Brusque . . . . 94 B7
Brussel . . . . . 14 C3
Brussels =
Brussel . . . . 14 C3
Bruthen . . . . 63 C4
Bruxelles =
Brussel . . . . 14 C3
Bryan . . . . . . 79 D5
Bryan, Mt. . . . 62 B2
Bryansk . . . . 24 C3
Bu Craa . . . . 54 C2
Buapinang . . . 39 E2
Buayan . . . . . 38 C3
Bucak . . . . . . 46 C2
Bucaramanga . 90 B4
Buchach . . . 17 D7
Buchanan . . . 55 G2
Buchans . . . 69 D5
Bucharest =
Bucureşti . . 22 B6
Buckie . . . . . . 10 C5
Buckleboo . . . 62 B2
Bucureşti . . . 22 B6
Budalin . . . . . 41 F10
Budapest . . . 16 E4
Budd Coast . . 96 A12
Bude . . . . . . . 11 F4
Budennovsk . . 25 E5
Budgewoi . . . 63 B5
Budjala . . . . . 56 D3
Buenaventura . 90 C3
Buenos Aires . 94 C5
Buenos Aires, L. 95 F2
Buffalo . . . . . . 73 C6

Bug →■ =
Buh → . . . . . 25 D3
Bug →■ . . . . . 16 B5
Buga . . . . . . . . 90 C3
Bugel, Tanjung 37 F4
Bugsuk . . . . . 36 C5
Bugun Shara . . 35 B5
Buguruslan . . . 29 D6
Buh → . . . . . 25 D3
Buheirat-Murrat-
el-Kubra . . . . 52 B5
Buir Nur . . . . 35 B6
Bujumbura . . . 57 E5
Bukama . . . . . 57 F5
Bukavu . . . . . 57 E5
Bukene . . . . . 57 E6
Bukhara =
Bukhoro . . . 29 F7
Bukhoro . . . . 29 F7
Bukittinggi . . 37 E2
Bukoba . . . . . 57 E6
Bula . . . . . . . . 39 E4
Bulahdelah . . . 63 B5
Bulan . . . . . . 38 B2
Bulandshahr . . 42 E10
Bulawayo . . . 59 C5
Buldan . . . . . . 23 E7
Bulgan . . . . . 35 B5
Bulgaria ■ . . . 22 C5
Bulgroo . . . . . 63 A3
Bulgunnia . . . 62 B1
Bulhar . . . . . . 49 E3
Buli, Teluk . . . 39 D3
Buliluyan, C. . . 36 C5
Bulli . . . . . . . . 63 B5
Bulloo →■ . . . 63 A3
Bulloo Downs . 62 A3
Bulloo L. . . . . 62 A3
Bulls . . . . . . . . 64 D6
Bulo Burti . . . 49 G4
Bulsar = Valsad 43 J8
Bulukumba . . . 39 F2
Bulun . . . . . . 30 B10
Bumba . . . . . 56 D4
Bumhpa Bum . 41 D11
Buna . . . . . . . 57 D7
Bunbah, Khalīj . 52 B3
Bunbury . . . . 60 G2
Buncrana . . . 11 D3
Bundaberg . . 63 A5
Bundi . . . . . . 43 G9
Bundoran . . . 11 D2
Bungo-Suidō . 32 C3
Bunia . . . . . . 57 D6
Bunji . . . . . . . 42 B9
Buntok . . . . . 37 E4
Bunyu . . . . . . 37 D5
Buol . . . . . . . . 39 D2
Buon Me Thuot 36 B3
Buorkhaya, Mys 31 B11
Buqayq . . . . . 47 F7
Bur Acaba . . . 49 G3
Bûr Safâga . . 52 C5
Bûr Sa'îd . . . 52 B5
Bûr Sûdân . . 53 E6
Burao . . . . . . 49 F4
Buraydah . . . 47 F6
Buraymī, Al
Wāhāt al . . 44 E3
Burcher . . . . . 63 B4
Burdur . . . . . . 46 C2
Burdwan =
Barddhaman 40 F6
Burgas . . . . . . 22 C6
Burgersdorp . . 59 E5
Burgos . . . . . 18 A4
Burgundy =
Bourgogne . 13 C6
Burhaniye . . . 23 E6
Burhanpur . . . 43 J10

Burias . . . . . . . 38 B2
Buriram . . . . . . 36 A2
Burji . . . . . . . . 53 G6
Burkina Faso ■ 55 F4
Burlington,
*Iowa, U.S.A.* . 77 E9
Burlington, *N.C.,*
*U.S.A.* . . . . . 75 A8
Burlington, *Vt.,*
*U.S.A.* . . . . . 73 B9
Burlyu-Tyube . . 29 E8
Burma ■ . . . . 41 G11
Burnie . . . . . . 62 D4
Burnley . . . . . 11 E5
Burnside →■ . . 70 B9
Burqān . . . . . 47 E6
Burqin . . . . . . 34 B3
Burra . . . . . . . 62 B2
Burren Junction 63 B4
Burrendong
Dam . . . . . . 63 B4
Burrinjuck Res. 63 C4
Burruyacú . . . 94 B4
Bursa . . . . . . 23 D7
Burtundy . . . . 62 B3
Buru . . . . . . . 39 E3
Burundi ■ . . . 57 E6
Burutu . . . . . . 55 G6
Bury St.
Edmunds . . 11 E7
Buşayyah . . . 47 E6
Büshehr . . . . 44 D2
Büshehr □ . . . 44 D2
Bushire =
Büshehr . . . 44 D2
Businga . . . . 56 D4
Busra ash Shām 46 D4
Busto Arsízio . 20 B2
Busu-Djanoa . 56 D4
Busuanga . . . 38 B1
Buta . . . . . . . 57 D4
Butare . . . . . . 57 E5
Butaritari . . . . 64 J12
Butembo . . . . 57 D5
Butha Qi . . . . 35 B7
Buton . . . . . . 39 E2
Butte . . . . . . . 81 B7
Butterworth . . 36 C2
Butuan . . . . . 38 C3
Butung = Buton 39 E2
Buturlinovka . . 24 C5
Buxtehude . . . 14 B5
Buy . . . . . . . . 24 B5
Büyük
Menderes →■ 23 F6
Büyükçekmece 22 D7
Buzău . . . . . . 17 F8
Buzău →■ . . . 17 F8
Buzen . . . . . . 32 C2
Buzi →■ . . . . . 59 B6
Buzuluk . . . . . 29 D6
Byarezina →■ . 17 B10
Bydgoszcz . . . 16 B3
Byelarus =
Belarus ■ . . 24 C2
Byelorussia =
Belarus ■ . . 24 C2
Bykhaw . . . . . 17 B10
Bykhov =
Bykhaw . . . 17 B10
Bylot I. . . . . . 68 A3
Byrd, C. . . . . . 96 A3
Byrock . . . . . . 63 B4
Byron Bay . . . 63 A5
Byrranga, Gory 30 B8
Byrranga Mts. =
Byrranga,
Gory . . . . . 30 B8
Bytom . . . . . 16 C4
Bytów . . . . . . 16 A3

## C

Ca Mau = Quan
Long . . . . . . . 36 C3
Caála . . . . . . . 58 A3
Cabanatuan . . . 38 A2
Cabedelo . . . . 92 D7
Cabimas . . . . 90 A4
Cabinda . . . . . 56 F2
Cabinda □ . . . . 56 F2
Cabinet Mts. . . 81 B6
Cabo Blanco . . 95 F3
Cabo Frio . . . . 93 G5
Cabo Pantoja . 90 D3
Cabonga,
Réservoir . . . 69 D3
Caboolture . . . 63 A5
Cabora Bassa
Dam =
Cahora Bassa
Dam . . . . . 59 B6
Cabot Str. . . . 69 D5
Cabra . . . . . . 18 D3
Cabrera . . . . . 19 C7
Cabriel →■ . . . 19 C5
Čačak . . . . . . 22 C3
Cáceres, *Brazil* 91 G7
Cáceres, *Spain* 18 C2
Cachimbo, Serra
do . . . . . . . 93 D2
Cachoeira . . . 93 E6
Cachoeira de
Itapemirim . . 93 G5
Cachoeira do
Sul . . . . . . . 94 C6
Cacólo . . . . . . 56 G3
Caconda . . . . 58 A3
Cacongo . . . . 56 F2
Cadibarrawirracanna,
L. . . . . . . . . 62 A2
Cádiz, *Phil.* . . 38 B2
Cádiz, *Spain* . 18 D2
Cádiz, G. de . . 18 D2
Cadney Park . . 62 A1
Caen . . . . . . . 12 B3
Caeté . . . . . . 93 F5
Caetité . . . . . 93 E5
Cagayan →■ . . 38 A2
Cagayan de Oro 38 C2
Cágliari . . . . . 21 E2
Cágliari, G. di . 21 E2
Caguas . . . . . 87 C6
Cahora Bassa
Dam . . . . . 59 B6
Cahors . . . . . 12 D4
Cahuapanas . . 91 E3
Cahul . . . . . . 17 F9
Caia . . . . . . . 59 B7
Caibarién . . . . 86 B4
Caicara . . . . . 90 B5
Caicó . . . . . . 92 D6
Caicos Is. . . . 87 B5
Caird Coast . . 96 B5
Cairns . . . . . . 61 D8
Cairo = El
Qâhira . . . 52 B5
Cairo . . . . . . 79 A9
Caiundo . . . . 58 B3
Caiza . . . . . . 91 H5
Cajamarca . . . 91 E3
Cajàzeiras . . . 92 D6
Calabar . . . . . 55 H6
Calábria □ . . . 21 E6
Calafate . . . . 95 G2
Calahorra . . . 19 A5
Calama, *Brazil* . 91 E6
Calama, *Chile* . 94 A3

Calamar,
  Bolívar,
  Colombia ... 90 A4
Calamar,
  Vaupés,
  Colombia ... 90 C4
Calamian Group 38 B1
Calamocha .... 19 B5
Calang ....... 36 D1
Calapan ...... 38 B2
Călăraşi ...... 22 B6
Calatayud .... 19 B5
Calauag ...... 38 B2
Calavite, C. ... 38 B2
Calbayog .... 38 B2
Calca ........ 91 F4
Calcutta ...... 41 F7
Caldas da
  Rainha .... 18 C1
Caldera ...... 94 B2
Caldwell ...... 80 D5
Caledon ...... 58 E3
Caledon ➤ ... 59 E5
Calgary ...... 71 C8
Cali ......... 90 C3
Calicut ....... 43 P9
California □ ... 82 B3
California, G. de 84 B2
Calingasta ... 94 C3
Callabonna, L. . 62 A3
Callao ........ 91 F3
Caloundra .... 63 A5
Caltagirone .. 21 F5
Caltanissetta .. 21 F5
Calulo ........ 56 G2
Calunda ...... 58 A4
Calvi ......... 13 E8
Calviá ....... 19 C7
Calvinia ...... 58 E3
Camabatela ... 56 F3
Camacupa .... 58 A3
Camagüey ... 86 B4
Camaná ...... 91 G4
Camargo .... 91 H5
Camargue .... 13 E6
Camarones ... 95 E3
Cambay =
  Khambhat . 43 H8
Cambay, G. of =
  Khambat, G.
  of ......... 43 J8
Cambodia ■ .. 36 B3
Cambrai ...... 13 A5
Cambrian Mts. 11 E4
Cambridge, N.Z. 64 B6
Cambridge, U.K. 11 E7
Cambridge,
  U.S.A. ... 73 C10
Cambridge Bay 70 B9
Cambridge G. . 60 C4
Cambundi-
  Catembo .... 56 G3
Camden, Ark.,
  U.S.A. .... 79 C7
Camden, N.J.,
  U.S.A. .... 73 E8
Cameroon ■ .. 56 C2
Cameroun, Mt. 56 D1
Cametá ...... 92 C4
Caminha .... 18 B1
Camira Creek .. 63 A5
Camissombo .. 56 F4
Camocim .... 92 C5
Camopi .... 92 B3
Campana, I. ... 95 F1
Campánia □ .. 21 D5
Campbell Town 62 D4
Campbellton .. 69 D4
Campbelltown . 63 B5

Campbeltown . 10 D4
Campeche .... 85 D6
Campeche, B. de 85 D6
Camperdown .. 62 C3
Campina Grande 92 D6
Campinas ..... 94 A7
Campo ....... 56 D1
Campo Belo ... 93 G4
Campo Formoso 93 E5
Campo Grande . 93 G3
Campo Maíor . 92 C5
Campo Mourão 93 G3
Campoalegre .. 90 C3
Campobasso .. 20 D5
Campos ...... 93 G5
Campos Belos . 93 E4
Campuya ➤ .. 90 D4
Camrose ..... 71 C8
Çan ......... 23 D6
Can Tho ...... 36 B3
Canada ■ ..... 70 C8
Cañada de
  Gómez .... 94 C4
Çanakkale .... 23 D6
Çanakkale
  Boğazı ...... 23 D6
Cananea ..... 84 A2
Canarias, Is. ... 54 C1
Canary Is. =
  Canarias, Is. . 54 C1
Canavieiras ... 93 F6
Canbelego ... 63 B4
Canberra ..... 63 C4
Candala ...... 49 E4
Candelo ..... 63 C4
Candia =
  Iráklion ... 23 G5
Canea = Khaniá 23 G5
Canelones .... 94 C5
Cañete, Chile . 94 D1
Cañete, Peru .. 91 F3
Cangas de
  Narcea ..... 18 A2
Canguaretama . 92 D6
Canguçu ..... 94 C6
Canicattì ..... 21 F4
Canigou, Mt. .. 12 E5
Canipaan ..... 36 C5
Çankırı ...... 46 B3
Cann River .... 63 C4
Cannanore ... 43 P9
Cannes ....... 13 E7
Canoas ...... 94 B6
Canora ...... 71 C9
Canowindra ... 63 B4
Cantabria □ ... 18 A4
Cantabrian Mts.
  = Cantábrica,
  Cordillera ... 18 A3
Cantábrica,
  Cordillera ... 18 A3
Cantal, Plomb
  du ......... 13 D5
Canterbury .... 11 F7
Canterbury □ . 65 E4
Canterbury
  Bight ....... 65 F4
Canterbury
  Plains ...... 65 E4
Canton =
  Guangzhou . 35 D6
Canton ...... 72 D5
Canudos .... 91 E7
Canutama ... 91 E6
Cap-Haïtien .. 87 C5
Cap St.-Jacques
  = Vung Tau . 36 B3
Capaia ...... 56 F4
Capanaparo ➤ 90 B5
Cape Barren I. . 62 D4

Cape Breton I. . 69 D4
Cape Coast ... 55 G4
Cape Dorset .. 68 B3
Cape Dyer .... 68 B4
Cape Girardeau 79 A9
Cape Jervis ... 62 C2
Cape Town ... 58 E3
Cape Verde Is. ■ 50 E1
Cape York
  Peninsula .. 61 C7
Capela ....... 93 E6
Capim ➤ .... 92 C4
Capraia ...... 20 C2
Capri ........ 21 D5
Caprivi Strip .. 58 B4
Captain's Flat . 63 C4
Caquetá ➤ ... 90 D5
Caracal ...... 22 B5
Caracas ..... 90 A5
Caracol ...... 93 D5
Caradoc ..... 62 B3
Carajás, Serra
  dos ........ 92 D3
Carangola .... 93 G5
Caransebeş ... 17 F6
Caratasca, L. .. 86 C3
Caratinga .... 93 F5
Caraúbas .... 92 D6
Caravaca .... 19 C5
Caravelas .... 93 F6
Caraveli ...... 91 G4
Carballo ..... 18 A1
Carbonara, C. . 21 E2
Carbondale ... 79 A9
Carbonear .... 69 D5
Carbonia ..... 21 E2
Carcassonne .. 12 E5
Carcross ..... 70 B6
Cardamon Hills 43 Q10
Cárdenas .... 86 B3
Cardiff ....... 11 F5
Cardigan B. ... 11 E4
Cardston .... 71 D8
Carei ........ 17 E6
Careysburg ... 55 G2
Carhué ...... 94 D4
Caria ........ 23 F7
Cariacica .... 93 G5
Caribbean Sea . 86 D5
Cariboo Mts. .. 71 C7
Carinda ...... 63 B4
Carinhanha .. 93 E5
Carinthia □ =
  Kärnten □ .. 15 E7
Caripito ...... 90 A6
Caritianas .... 91 E6
Carlisle ...... 11 D5
Carlow ....... 11 E3
Carlsbad ..... 78 C1
Carmacks .... 70 B6
Carman ...... 71 D10
Carmarthen ... 11 F4
Carmaux ..... 12 D5
Carmelo ..... 94 C5
Carmen ...... 90 B3
Carmen de
  Patagones .. 95 E4
Carmona .... 18 D3
Carnac ...... 12 C2
Carnarvon,
  Australia .... 60 E1
Carnarvon,
  S. Africa .... 58 E4
Carnegie, L. ... 60 F3
Carnic Alps =
  Karnische
  Alpen ...... 20 A4
Carniche Alpi =
  Karnische
  Alpen ...... 20 A4

Carnot ....... 56 D3
Carnot, C. ..... 62 B2
Carolina ..... 92 D4
Carolina ..... 92 D4
Caroline I. .... 65 K15
Caroline Is. ... 64 J10
Caroni ➤ .... 90 B6
Caroníe =
  Nébrodi,
  Monti ..... 21 F5
Caroona ..... 63 B5
Carpathians ... 16 D5
Carpaţii
  Meridionali .. 17 F7
Carpentaria, G.
  of ......... 60 C6
Carpentras ... 13 D6
Carpi ........ 20 B3
Carpolac =
  Morea ..... 62 C3
Carrara ...... 20 B3
Carrauntoohill . 11 E2
Carrick-on-Suir 11 E3
Carrieton .... 62 B2
Carrizal Bajo .. 94 B2
Çarşamba .... 46 B4
Carson City ... 80 F4
Cartagena,
  Colombia ... 90 A3
Cartagena,
  Spain ...... 19 D5
Cartago,
  Colombia ... 90 C3
Cartago,
  Costa Rica .. 86 E3
Carterton .... 65 D6
Carthage .... 79 A6
Cartwright ... 68 C5
Caruaru ..... 92 D6
Carúpano .... 90 A6
Carvoeiro .... 90 D6
Carvoeiro, C. . 18 C1
Casablanca .. 54 B3
Cascade Ra. .. 80 B3
Cascais ..... 18 C1
Cascavel .... 94 A6
Cáscina ..... 20 C3
Caserta ...... 20 D5
Casiguran ... 38 A2
Casilda ...... 94 C4
Casino ...... 63 A5
Casiquiare ➤ . 90 C5
Casma ...... 91 E3
Caspe ....... 19 B5
Casper ...... 81 D10
Caspian Sea .. 29 E6
Cassinga .... 58 B3
Castellammare
  di Stábia .. 21 D5
Castellón de la
  Plana ....... 19 C5
Castelo Branco 18 C2
Castelsarrasin . 12 D4
Castelvetrano . 21 F4
Casterton .... 62 C3
Castilla La
  Mancha □ .. 18 C4
Castilla y
  Leon □ .... 18 A3
Castlebar .... 11 E2
Castleblaney .. 11 D3
Castlemaine .. 63 C3
Castlereagh ➤ 63 B4
Castres ..... 12 E5
Castries ..... 87 D7
Castro ...... 95 E2
Castro Alves .. 93 E6
Castuera .... 18 C3
Cat I. ........ 86 B4
Catacáos .... 91 E2

# Catalão

| | | | | | | | | | | | |
|---|---|---|---|---|---|---|---|---|---|---|---|
| Catalão | 93 | F4 | Česka Republika | | | Channel Is. | 11 | G5 | Chekiang = | | |
| Çatalca | 22 | D7 | = Czech | | | Chantada | 18 | A2 | Zhejiang □ | 35 | D7 |
| Catalonia = | | | Rep. ■ | 16 | D2 | Chanthaburi | 36 | B2 | Cheleken | 29 | F6 |
| Cataluña □ | 19 | B6 | České | | | Chantrey Inlet | 70 | B10 | Chelforó | 95 | D3 |
| Cataluña □ | 19 | B6 | Budějovice | 16 | D2 | Chanute | 79 | A6 | Chelkar = | | |
| Catamarca | 94 | B3 | Ceskomoravská | | | Chao Phraya ➤ | 36 | B2 | Shalqar | 29 | E6 |
| Catanduanes | 38 | B2 | Vrchovina | 16 | D2 | Chao'an | 35 | D6 | Chelkar Tengiz, | | |
| Catanduva | 93 | G4 | Çeşme | 23 | E6 | Chaoyang | 35 | D6 | Solonchak | 29 | E7 |
| Catánia | 21 | F5 | Cessnock | 63 | B5 | Chapala, L. de | 84 | C4 | Chełm | 17 | C6 |
| Catanzaro | 21 | E6 | Cetinje | 22 | C2 | Chapayevsk | 24 | C6 | Chełmno | 16 | B4 |
| Catarman | 38 | B2 | Cetraro | 21 | E5 | Chapra = | | | Chelmsford | 11 | F7 |
| Cateel | 38 | C3 | Ceuta | 18 | E3 | Chhapra | 40 | E5 | Cheltenham | 11 | F5 |
| Catoche, C. | 85 | C7 | Cévennes | 13 | D5 | Châr | 54 | D2 | Chelyabinsk | 29 | D7 |
| Catrimani | 90 | C6 | Ceyhan | 46 | C3 | Chara | 31 | D9 | Chemnitz | 15 | C7 |
| Catskill Mts. | 73 | C8 | Ceylon = Sri | | | Charadai | 94 | B5 | Chen Xian | 35 | D6 |
| Cauca ➤ | 90 | B4 | Lanka ■ | 43 | R12 | Charagua | 91 | G6 | Chenab ➤ | 42 | D7 |
| Caucaia | 92 | C6 | Chachapoyas | 91 | E3 | Charaña | 91 | G5 | Chencha | 53 | G6 |
| Caucasus | | | Chachran | 42 | E7 | Chardara | 29 | E7 | Chenchiang = | | |
| Mountains | 25 | E5 | Chad ■ | 53 | E2 | Chardzhou = | | | Zhenjiang | 35 | C6 |
| Caúngula | 56 | F3 | Chad, L. = | | | Chärjew | 29 | F7 | Chengchou = | | |
| Cauquenes | 94 | D2 | Tchad, L. | 53 | F1 | Charente ➤ | 12 | D3 | Zhengzhou | 35 | C6 |
| Caura ➤ | 90 | B6 | Chadileuvú ➤ | 94 | D3 | Chari ➤ | 53 | F1 | Chengde | 35 | B6 |
| Cauvery ➤ | 43 | P11 | Chadyr-Lunga = | | | Chārīkār | 42 | B6 | Chengdu | 35 | C5 |
| Caux, Pays de | 12 | B4 | Ceadâr-Lunga | 17 | E9 | Chärjew | 29 | F7 | Chengjiang | 34 | D5 |
| Cavan | 11 | D3 | Chagai Hills | 42 | E3 | Charleroi | 14 | C3 | Ch'engtu = | | |
| Cavendish | 62 | C3 | Chagos Arch. | 27 | K11 | Charles, C. | 73 | F8 | Chengdu | 35 | C5 |
| Caviana, I. | 92 | B3 | Chāh Bahār | 45 | E5 | Charleston, S.C., | | | Cheo Reo | 36 | B3 |
| Cavite | 38 | B2 | Chāh Gay Hills | 45 | D6 | U.S.A. | 75 | C8 | Cheom Ksan | 36 | B2 |
| Cawndilla L. | 62 | B3 | Chahar Burjak | 42 | D3 | Charleston, | | | Chepén | 91 | E3 |
| Cawnpore = | | | Chaibasa | 40 | F5 | W. Va., U.S.A. | 72 | E5 | Chepes | 94 | C3 |
| Kanpur | 40 | D3 | Chakhānsūr | 42 | D3 | Charlesville | 56 | F4 | Cher ➤ | 12 | C4 |
| Caxias | 92 | C5 | Chakradharpur | 40 | F5 | Charleville | 63 | A4 | Cherbourg | 12 | B3 |
| Caxias do Sul | 94 | B6 | Chakwal | 42 | C8 | Charleville- | | | Cherchell | 54 | A5 |
| Caxito | 56 | F2 | Chala | 91 | G4 | Mézières | 13 | B6 | Cherdyn | 28 | C6 |
| Cayambe | 90 | C3 | Chalcis = | | | Charlotte | 75 | B7 | Cherepanovo | 29 | D9 |
| Cayenne | 92 | A3 | Khalkís | 23 | E4 | Charlotte Amalie | 87 | C7 | Cherepovets | 24 | B4 |
| Cayman Is. ■ | 67 | H11 | Chalhuanca | 91 | F4 | Charlottesville | 73 | E6 | Chergui, Chott | | |
| Cazombo | 58 | A4 | Chalisgaon | 43 | J9 | Charlottetown | 69 | D4 | ech | 54 | B5 |
| Ceadâr-Lunga | 17 | E9 | Chalky Inlet | 65 | G2 | Charlton | 62 | C3 | Cherikov = | | |
| Ceanannus Mor | 11 | E3 | Challapata | 91 | G5 | Charolles | 13 | C6 | Cherykaw | 17 | B10 |
| Ceará = | | | Chalon-sur- | | | Charouine | 54 | C4 | Cherkasy | 24 | D3 |
| Fortaleza | 92 | C6 | Saône | 13 | C6 | Charters Towers | 61 | E8 | Cherlak | 29 | D8 |
| Ceará □ | 92 | D6 | Châlons-en- | | | Chartres | 12 | B4 | Chernaya | 30 | B6 |
| Ceará Mirim | 92 | D6 | Champagne | 13 | B6 | Chascomús | 94 | D5 | Chernigov = | | |
| Cebollar | 94 | B3 | Chaman | 42 | D5 | Châteaubriant | 12 | C3 | Chernihiv | 24 | C3 |
| Cebu | 38 | B2 | Chamba, India | 42 | C10 | Châteaulin | 12 | B1 | Chernihiv | 24 | C3 |
| Cecil Plains | 63 | A5 | Chamba, | | | Châteauroux | 12 | C4 | Chernivtsi | 17 | D7 |
| Cedar L. | 71 | C10 | Tanzania | 59 | A7 | Châtellerault | 12 | C4 | Chernobyl = | | |
| Cedar Rapids | 77 | E9 | Chambal ➤ | 42 | F11 | Chatham, N.B., | | | Chornobyl | 17 | C10 |
| Cedro | 92 | D6 | Chambéry | 13 | D6 | Canada | 69 | D4 | Chernovtsy = | | |
| Ceduna | 62 | B1 | Chamical | 94 | C3 | Chatham, Ont., | | | Chernivtsi | 17 | D7 |
| Cefalù | 21 | E5 | Chamonix-Mont | | | Canada | 69 | D2 | Chernyakhovsk | 28 | D3 |
| Cegléd | 16 | E4 | Blanc | 13 | D7 | Chatham, U.K. | 11 | F7 | Cherquenco | 94 | D2 |
| Celaya | 84 | C4 | Champagne | 13 | B6 | Chatrapur | 40 | H5 | Cherrapunji | 41 | E8 |
| Celebes = | | | Champaign | 72 | D1 | Chattahoochee ➤ | | | Cherven | 17 | B9 |
| Sulawesi □ | 39 | E2 | Champlain, L. | 73 | B9 | | 74 | D5 | Chervonohrad | 17 | C7 |
| Celebes Sea | 39 | D2 | Chañaral | 94 | B2 | Chattanooga | 74 | B5 | Cherykaw | 17 | B10 |
| Celje | 20 | A5 | Chandigarh | 42 | D10 | Chauk | 41 | G10 | Chesapeake | 73 | F7 |
| Celle | 14 | B6 | Chandler | 62 | A1 | Chaukan La | 41 | D11 | Chesapeake B. | 73 | E7 |
| Celtic Sea | 11 | F2 | Chandmani | 34 | B4 | Chaumont | 13 | B6 | Cheshskaya | | |
| Central, | | | Chandpur | 41 | F8 | Chaves, Brazil | 92 | C4 | Guba | 28 | C5 |
| Cordillera | 90 | C3 | Chandrapur | 43 | K11 | Chaves, Portugal | 18 | B2 | Chester, U.K. | 11 | E5 |
| Central African | | | Chang Jiang ➤ | 35 | C7 | Chavuma | 58 | A4 | Chester, U.S.A. | 73 | E8 |
| Rep. ■ | 56 | C4 | Changanacheri | 43 | Q10 | Cheb | 16 | C1 | Chesterfield | 11 | E6 |
| Central Makran | | | Changane ➤ | 59 | C6 | Cheboksary | 24 | B6 | Chesterfield, Is. | 64 | L10 |
| Range | 42 | F4 | Changchiak'ou | | | Chech, Erg | 54 | D4 | Chesterfield Inlet | 70 | B10 |
| Cephalonia = | | | = Zhangjiakou | 35 | B6 | Chechenia □ | 25 | E6 | Chesterton Ra. | 63 | A4 |
| Kefallinía | 23 | E3 | Ch'angchou = | | | Checheno- | | | Cheviot Hills | 10 | D5 |
| Ceram = Seram | 39 | E3 | Changzhou | 35 | C6 | Ingush | | | Chew Bahir | 53 | H6 |
| Ceram Sea = | | | Changchun | 35 | B7 | Republic = | | | Cheyenne | 76 | E2 |
| Seram Sea | 39 | E3 | Changde | 35 | D6 | Chechenia □ | 25 | E6 | Cheyenne ➤ | 76 | C4 |
| Ceres, Argentina | 94 | B4 | Changhai = | | | Chechnya = | | | Chhapra | 40 | E5 |
| Ceres, S. Africa | 58 | E3 | Shanghai | 35 | C7 | Chechenia □ | 25 | E6 | Chhatarpur | 43 | G11 |
| Cerignola | 20 | D5 | Changjiang | 35 | E5 | Cheduba I. | 41 | H9 | Chhindwara | 43 | H11 |
| Cerigo = Kíthira | 23 | F4 | Changsha | 35 | D6 | Cheepie | 63 | A4 | Chhlong | 36 | B3 |
| Çerkeş | 46 | B3 | Changting | 35 | D6 | Chegga | 54 | C3 | Chi ➤ | 36 | A2 |
| Çerkeşköy | 22 | D6 | Changzhi | 35 | C6 | Chegutu | 59 | B6 | Chiamussu = | | |
| Cervera | 19 | B6 | Changzhou | 35 | C6 | Chehalis | 80 | B2 | Jiamusi | 35 | B8 |
| Cesena | 20 | B4 | Channapatna | 43 | N10 | Cheju Do | 35 | C7 | Chiange | 58 | B2 |

| | | | | | | |
|---|---|---|---|---|---|---|
| Chiapa → .... | 85 | D6 | Chinsali ...... | 57 | G6 |
| Chiávari ...... | 20 | B2 | Chióggia ..... | 20 | B4 |
| Chiavenna ... | 20 | A2 | Chíos = Khíos . | 23 | E6 |
| Chiba ........ | 32 | B7 | Chipata ...... | 59 | A6 |
| Chibemba .... | 58 | B2 | Chiquián ..... | 91 | F3 |
| Chibia ........ | 58 | B2 | Chiquinquira .. | 90 | B4 |
| Chibougamau . | 69 | D3 | Chirchiq ..... | 29 | E7 |
| Chibuk ....... | 53 | F1 | Chirmiri ...... | 40 | F4 |

Churchill, C. ... 70 C10 — Clifden ....... 65 G2

Chiapa → .... 85 D6
Chiávari ...... 20 B2
Chiavenna ... 20 A2
Chiba ........ 32 B7
Chibemba .... 58 B2
Chibia ........ 58 B2
Chibougamau . 69 D3
Chibuk ....... 53 F1
Chicacole =
  Srikakulam .. 40 H4
Chicago ...... 72 D2
Chichagof I. ... 71 C6
Chichibu ..... 32 A6
Ch'ich'ihaerh =
  Qiqihar ..... 35 B7
Chickasha ... 78 B5
Chiclana de la
  Frontera .... 18 D2
Chiclayo ...... 91 E3
Chico ........ 80 F3
Chico →,
  Chubut,
  Argentina ... 95 E3
Chico →,
  Santa Cruz,
  Argentina ... 95 F3
Chicoutimi .... 69 D3
Chidambaram . 43 P11
Chidley, C. ... 68 B4
Chiemsee .... 15 E7
Chiengi ....... 57 F5
Chiese → ... 20 B3
Chieti ........ 20 C5
Chiguana .... 91 H5
Chihli, G. of =
  Bo Hai ..... 35 C6
Chihuahua .... 84 B3
Chiili ........ 29 E7
Chik Bollapur . 43 N10
Chikmagalur .. 43 N9
Chilapa ....... 84 D5
Chilas ....... 42 B9
Chilaw ....... 43 R11
Childers ..... 63 A5
Chile ■ ...... 94 D2
Chilete ....... 91 E3
Chililabombwe 59 A5
Chilin = Jilin .. 35 B7
Chilka L. ..... 40 H5
Chillán ....... 94 D2
Chiloé, I. de ... 95 E2
Chilpancingo .. 84 D5
Chiluage ...... 56 F4
Chilwa, L. .... 59 B7
Chimbay ..... 29 E6
Chimborazo ... 90 D3
Chimbote ..... 91 E3
Chimkent =
  Shymkent ... 29 E7
Chimoio ...... 59 B6
Chin □ ...... 41 F9
China ■ ...... 35 C5
Chinan = Jinan 35 C6
Chinandega .. 85 E7
Chincha Alta . 91 F3
Chinchilla .... 63 A5
Chinchou =
  Jinzhou .... 35 B7
Chinde ....... 59 B7
Chindwin → .. 41 G10
Chingola ..... 59 A5
Ch'ingtao =
  Qingdao ... 35 C7
Chinguetti ... 54 D2
Chinhoyi ..... 59 B6
Chiniot ....... 42 D8
Chinju ....... 35 C7
Chinnampo ... 35 C7
Chinon ....... 12 C4

Chinsali ...... 57 G6
Chióggia ..... 20 B4
Chíos = Khíos . 23 E6
Chipata ...... 59 A6
Chiquián ..... 91 F3
Chiquinquira .. 90 B4
Chirchiq ..... 29 E7
Chirmiri ...... 40 F4
Chiromo ..... 59 B7
Chisamba .... 59 A5
Chisapani Garhi 40 D5
Chişinău ..... 17 E9
Chistopol .... 24 B7
Chita ........ 30 D9
Chitado ...... 58 B2
Chitembo .... 58 A3
Chitral ....... 42 B7
Chitré ........ 86 E3
Chittagong ... 41 F8
Chittagong □ . 41 E8
Chittaurgarh .. 43 G9
Chittoor ...... 43 N11
Chiusi ........ 20 C3
Chivasso ..... 20 B1
Chivilcoy ..... 94 B4
Chkalov =
  Orenburg ... 29 D6
Choele Choel .. 95 D3
Chojnice ..... 16 B3
Cholet ....... 12 C3
Choluteca .... 85 E7
Choma ....... 59 B5
Chomutov .... 16 C1
Chon Buri ... 36 B2
Chone ....... 90 D3
Chŏngjin .... 35 B7
Chŏngju .... 35 C7
Chongqing ... 35 D5
Chŏnju .... 35 C7
Chonos, Arch.
  de los ..... 95 F2
Chop ........ 17 D6
Chornobyl .... 17 C10
Chortkiv ..... 17 D7
Chorzów ..... 16 C4
Chos-Malal ... 94 D2
Chōshi ....... 32 B7
Choszczno ... 16 B2
Chotila ....... 43 H7
Choybalsan ... 35 B6
Christchurch .. 65 E5
Christiana ... 59 D5
Christmas I. =
  Kiritimati ... 65 J15
Chu = Shu ... 29 E8
Ch'uanchou =
  Quanzhou ... 35 D6
Chubut → .. 95 E3
Chudskoye, Oz. 24 B2
Chūgoku-Sanchi 32 B3
Chula Vista ... 82 D4
Chulucanas ... 90 E2
Chulym → .. 29 D9
Chumbicha .. 94 B3
Chumphon ... 36 B1
Chuna → .. 30 D7
Chunchŏn ... 35 C7
Chungking =
  Chongqing .. 35 D5
Chunya ...... 57 F6
Chuquibamba . 91 G4
Chuquicamata . 94 A3
Chur ........ 13 C8
Churachandpur 41 E9
Churchill ..... 70 C10
Churchill →,
  Man., Canada 70 C10
Churchill →,
  Nfld., Canada 69 C4

Churchill, C. ... 70 C10
Churchill Falls . 69 C4
Churchill L. ... 71 C9
Churu ....... 42 E9
Chushal ...... 42 C11
Chusovoy ..... 28 D6
Chuvash
  Republic □ =
  Chuvashia □ . 24 B6
Chuvashia □ .. 24 B6
Cicero ........ 72 D2
Ciechanów ... 16 B5
Ciego de Avila . 86 B4
Ciénaga ...... 90 A4
Cienfuegos ... 86 B3
Cieszyn ...... 16 D4
Cieza ........ 19 C5
Cijara, Pantano
  de ......... 18 C3
Cilician Gates P. 46 C3
Cill Chainnigh =
  Kilkenny ... 11 E3
Cimişlia ...... 17 E9
Cimone, Mte. .. 20 B3
Cîmpina ...... 17 F7
Cîmpulung ... 17 F7
Cinca → .. 19 B6
Cincar ....... 20 C6
Cincinnati .... 72 E3
Çine ........ 23 F7
Cinto, Mte. .. 13 E8
Circle ........ 71 B5
Cirebon ...... 37 F3
Citlaltépetl ... 84 D5
Città di Castello 20 C4
Ciudad Bolívar 90 B6
Ciudad
  Chetumal ... 85 D7
Ciudad del
  Carmen ..... 85 D6
Ciudad Delicias
  = Delicias ... 84 B3
Ciudad Guayana 90 B6
Ciudad Juárez . 84 A3
Ciudad Madero 84 C5
Ciudad Mante . 84 C5
Ciudad Obregón 84 B3
Ciudad Real .. 18 C4
Ciudad Rodrigo 18 B2
Ciudad Trujillo
  = Santo
  Domingo ... 87 C6
Ciudad Victoria 84 C5
Civitanova
  Marche ..... 20 C4
Civitavécchia .. 20 C3
Cizre ........ 46 C5
Clanwilliam ... 58 E3
Clare ........ 62 B2
Clarence →,
  Australia ... 63 A5
Clarence →,
  N.Z. ........ 65 E5
Clarence, I. ... 95 G2
Clarence I. ... 96 A4
Clarie Coast .. 96 A13
Clarke I. ..... 62 D4
Clarksdale ... 79 B8
Clarksville ... 74 A4
Claveria ..... 38 A2
Clear, C. ..... 11 F2
Clearwater ... 75 F6
Clearwater Mts. 81 B6
Clermont-
  Ferrand ..... 13 D5
Cleveland,
  Australia, ... 63 A5
Cleveland,
  U.S.A. ...... 72 D5

Clifden ....... 65 G2
Clifton ....... 63 A5
Clifton Hills .. 62 A2
Clinton, Canada 71 C7
Clinton, N.Z. .. 65 G3
Clinton, U.S.A. 77 E9
Clinton Colden
  L. ......... 70 B9
Clones ...... 11 D3
Clonmel ..... 11 E3
Clovis ....... 78 B2
Cluj-Napoca .. 17 E6
Clunes ...... 62 C3
Clutha → .. 65 G3
Clyde ....... 65 F3
Clyde → .. 10 D4
Clyde, Firth of . 10 D4
Clyde River ... 68 A4
Coari ....... 90 D6
Coast Mts. ... 70 C7
Coast Ranges . 80 F2
Coats I. ..... 68 B2
Coats Land ... 96 B5
Coatzacoalcos . 85 D6
Cobalt ....... 69 D3
Cobar ....... 63 B4
Cóbh ....... 11 F2
Cobham ..... 62 B3
Cobija ....... 91 F5
Cobourg ..... 69 D3
Cobram ..... 63 C4
Cóbué ....... 59 A6
Coburg ...... 15 C6
Cocanada =
  Kakinada ... 40 J4
Cochabamba . 91 G5
Cochin ....... 43 Q10
Cochin China =
  Nam-Phan .. 36 B3
Cochrane .... 69 D2
Cochrane, L. .. 95 F2
Cockburn .... 62 B3
Cockburn, Canal 95 G2
Coco → .. 86 D3
Cocobeach ... 56 D1
Cod, C. ..... 73 C10
Codajás ..... 90 D6
Codó ........ 92 C5
Cœur d'Alene . 80 B5
Coffeyville .... 79 A6
Coffin B. ..... 62 B2
Coffin Bay
  Peninsula ... 62 B2
Coffs Harbour . 63 B5
Cognac ...... 12 D3
Cohuna ...... 63 C3
Coiba, I. ..... 86 E3
Coig → .. 95 G3
Coihaique .... 95 F2
Coimbatore ... 43 P10
Coimbra, Brazil 91 G7
Coimbra,
  Portugal ... 18 B1
Coín ........ 18 D3
Cojimies ..... 90 C3
Colac ........ 62 C3
Colatina ..... 93 F5
Colbeck, C. ... 96 B17
Colbinabbin ... 63 C3
Colchester ... 11 F7
Colebrook ... 62 D4
Coleman .... 71 D8
Coleraine,
  Australia .... 62 C3
Coleraine, U.K. 11 D3
Coleridge, L. .. 65 E4
Colesberg .... 59 E5
Colhué Huapi, L. 95 F3
Colima ....... 84 D4

# Colinas

Colinas ....... 92 D5
Coll .......... 10 C3
Collaguasi .... 91 H5
Collarenebri ... 63 A4
Collingwood .. 64 D5
Colmar ....... 13 B7
Colo ⟶ ...... 63 B5
Cologne = Köln 14 C4
Colomb-Béchar
  = Béchar .. 54 B4
Colômbia ..... 93 G4
Colombia ■ ... 90 C4
Colombo ...... 43 R11
Colón, Cuba ... 86 B3
Colón, Panama 85 F9
Colonia ...... 94 C5
Colonia Dora .. 94 B4
Colonsay ..... 10 C3
Colorado □ ... 83 A10
Colorado ⟶,
  Argentina ... 95 D4
Colorado ⟶,
  N. Amer. .... 82 E5
Colorado
  Plateau ..... 83 B7
Colorado
  Springs ..... 76 F2
Columbia, Mo.,
  U.S.A. ...... 77 F8
Columbia, S.C.,
  U.S.A. ...... 75 B7
Columbia,
  Tenn., U.S.A. 74 B4
Columbia ⟶ .. 80 B1
Columbia,
  District of □ . 73 E7
Columbia Basin 80 B4
Columbretes, Is. 19 C6
Columbus, Ga.,
  U.S.A. ...... 74 C5
Columbus,
  Miss., U.S.A. 74 C3
Columbus, Ohio,
  U.S.A. ...... 72 E4
Colville ⟶ ... 71 A4
Colville, C. .... 64 B6
Colwyn Bay ... 11 E5
Comácchio .... 20 B4
Comallo ...... 95 E2
Comilla ...... 41 F8
Comino, C. .... 21 D2
Committee B. . 68 B2
Commonwealth
  B. ........ 96 A14
Commoron
  Cr. ⟶ ...... 63 A5
Communism Pk.
  =
  Kommunizma,
  Pik ........ 29 F8
Como ........ 20 B2
Como, L. di ... 20 B2
Comodoro
  Rivadavia .. 95 F3
Comorin, C. ... 43 Q10
Comoro Is. =
Comoros ■ . 51 H8
Comoros ■ ... 51 H8
Comox ....... 71 D7
Compiègne ... 13 B5
Compton Downs 63 B4
Comrat ....... 17 E9
Conakry ...... 55 G2
Conara Junction 62 D4
Concarneau ... 12 C2
Conceição da
  Barra ...... 93 F6
Concepción,
  Bolivia ..... 91 G6

Concepción,
  Chile ....... 94 D2
Concepción,
  Paraguay ... 94 A5
Concepción, L. 91 G6
Concepción del
  Oro ........ 84 C4
Concepción del
  Uruguay ... 94 C5
Conchos ⟶ .. 84 B3
Concord, N.C.,
  U.S.A. ...... 75 B7
Concord, N.H.,
  U.S.A. ...... 73 C10
Concordia,
  Argentina ... 94 C5
Concórdia, Brazil 90 D5
Condamine ... 63 A5
Condeúba .... 93 E5
Condobolin ... 63 B4
Conegliano ... 20 B4
Confuso ⟶ .. 94 B5
Congo =
  Zaïre ⟶ ... 56 F2
Congo
  (Kinshasa) =
  Zaïre ■ ..... 56 E4
Congo ■ ..... 56 E3
Conjeeveram =
  Kanchipuram 43 N11
Conlea ....... 63 B3
Conn, L. ...... 11 D2
Connacht □ ... 11 E2
Connecticut □ . 73 D9
Connecticut ⟶ 73 D9
Connemara ... 11 E2
Conoble ...... 63 B3
Cononaco ⟶ . 90 D3
Conran, C. .... 63 C4
Conselheiro
  Lafaiete .... 93 G5
Constance =
  Konstanz ... 14 E5
Constance, L. =
  Bodensee .. 13 C8
Constanţa .... 22 B7
Constantine .. 54 A6
Constitución .. 94 D2
Contai ....... 40 G6
Contamana ... 91 E4
Contas ⟶ ... 93 E6
Conway, L. ... 62 A2
Coober Pedy .. 62 A1
Cooch Behar =
  Koch Bihar . 41 D7
Cook, B. ...... 95 H2
Cook, Mt. ..... 65 E4
Cook Inlet .... 71 C4
Cook Is. ...... 65 L14
Cook Strait ... 65 D6
Cooktown .... 61 D8
Coolabah .... 63 B4
Cooladdi ..... 63 A4
Coolah ....... 63 B4
Coolamon .... 63 B4
Coolangatta .. 63 A5
Cooma ....... 63 C4
Coonabarabran 63 B4
Coonamble ... 63 B4
Coondapoor .. 43 N9
Coongie ...... 62 A3
Coongoola .... 63 A4
Cooninie, L. .. 62 A2
Cooper Cr. ⟶,
  N. Terr.,
  Australia ... 60 C5
Cooper Cr. ⟶,
  S. Austral.,
  Australia .... 62 A2

Cooroy ....... 63 A5
Cootamundra . 63 B4
Cooyar ....... 63 A5
Copenhagen =
  København .. 9 G10
Copiapó ...... 94 B2
Copiapó ⟶ .. 94 B2
Copley ....... 62 B2
Copper Center . 71 B5
Copper Cliff .. 69 D2
Coppermine ... 70 B8
Coppermine ⟶ 70 B8
Coquimbo .... 94 C2
Corabia ...... 22 C5
Coracora ..... 91 G4
Coral Harbour . 68 B2
Coral Sea .... 64 L10
Corato ....... 21 D6
Corby ........ 11 E6
Corcaigh = Cork 11 F2
Corcubión .... 18 A1
Córdoba,
  Argentina ... 94 C4
Córdoba, Spain 18 D3
Córdoba, Sierra
  de ......... 94 C4
Cordon ....... 38 A2
Cordova ...... 71 B5
Corfu = Kérkira 23 E2
Coria ........ 18 C2
Corigliano
  Cálabro .... 21 E6
Corinna ...... 62 D4
Corinth =
  Kórinthos .. 23 F4
Corinth, G. of =
  Korinthiakós
  Kólpos .... 23 E4
Corinto ...... 93 F5
Cork ......... 11 F2
Çorlu ........ 22 D6
Corner Brook . 69 D5
Corneşti ..... 17 E9
Cornwall ..... 69 D3
Corny Pt. ..... 62 B2
Coro ......... 90 A5
Coroatá ...... 92 C5
Corocoro ..... 91 G5
Coroico ...... 91 G5
Coromandel ... 64 B6
Corona ....... 62 B3
Coronation Gulf 70 B8
Coronation I. .. 96 A4
Coronel Dorrego 94 D4
Coronel Suárez 94 D4
Corowa ....... 63 C4
Corpus Christi . 78 F5
Corque ....... 91 G5
Corrib, L. ..... 11 E2
Corrientes .... 94 B5
Corrientes ⟶ . 90 D4
Corrientes, C.,
  Colombia ... 90 B3
Corrientes, C.,
  Mexico ..... 84 C3
Corse ........ 13 E8
Corse, C. ..... 13 E8
Corsica = Corse 13 E8
Corsicana .... 79 C5
Corte ........ 13 E8
Çorum ....... 46 B3
Corumbá ..... 91 G7
Corumbá de
  Goiás ...... 93 F4
Corunna = La
  Coruña .... 18 A1
Corvallis ..... 80 C2
Cosenza ...... 21 E6

Costa Blanca .. 19 C5
Costa Brava ... 19 B7
Costa del Sol .. 18 D3
Costa Dorada . 19 B6
Costa Rica ■ .. 86 E3
Cotabato ..... 38 C2
Cotagaita ..... 91 H5
Côte d'Azur .. 13 E7
Côte-d'Ivoire ■
  = Ivory
  Coast ■ .... 55 G3
Cotentin ...... 12 B3
Cotonou ...... 55 G5
Cotopaxi ..... 90 D3
Cotswold Hills . 11 F5
Cottbus ...... 15 C8
Couedic, C. du . 62 C2
Coulman I. .... 96 B15
Council ....... 71 B3
Council Bluffs .. 77 E7
Courantyne ⟶ 90 B7
Courtrai =
  Kortrijk .... 14 C2
Coventry ..... 11 E6
Covilhã ...... 18 B2
Covington .... 72 E3
Cowal, L. .... 63 B4
Cowangie .... 62 C3
Cowarie ...... 62 A2
Cowell ....... 62 B2
Cowra ....... 63 B4
Coxim ....... 93 F3
Cox's Bazar .. 41 G8
Cozumel, I. de . 85 C7
Craboon ...... 63 B4
Cracow =
  Kraków .... 16 C4
Cracow ...... 63 A5
Cradock ...... 59 E5
Craigavon .... 11 D3
Crailsheim ... 14 D6
Craiova ...... 22 B4
Cranbrook,
  Australia ... 62 D4
Cranbrook,
  Canada ..... 71 D8
Crateús ...... 92 D5
Crato ........ 92 D6
Crawley ...... 11 F6
Crazy Mts. ... 81 B8
Crema ....... 20 B2
Cremona ..... 20 B3
Cres ........ 20 B5
Cressy ....... 62 C3
Crete = Kríti .. 23 G5
Créteil ....... 12 B5
Creus, C. de .. 19 A7
Creuse ⟶ ... 12 C4
Crewe ....... 11 E5
Criciúma ..... 94 B7
Crimean Pen. =
  Krymskyy
  Pivostriv ... 25 D3
Crişul Alb ⟶ . 16 E5
Crişul Negru ⟶ 16 E5
Crna Gora =
  Montenegro □ 22 C2
Crna Gora .... 22 C3
Crna Reka ⟶ . 22 D3
Croatia ■ ..... 20 B6
Crocker,
  Banjaran .... 36 C5
Croker, C. .... 60 C5
Cromer ...... 11 E7
Cromwell ..... 65 F3
Cronulla ..... 63 B5
Crookston .... 63 B4
Cross Sound .. 71 C6
Crotone ...... 21 E6

Crows Nest ... 63 A5
Crowsnest Pass 71 D8
Cruz Alta .... 94 B6
Cruz del Eje ... 94 C4
Cruzeiro ...... 93 G5
Cruzeiro do Sul 91 E4
Crystal Brook . 62 B2
Csongrád ..... 16 E5
Cuamba ...... 59 A7
Cuando → .... 58 B4
Cuarto → ... 94 C4
Cuba ■ ...... 86 B4
Cubango → ... 58 B4
Cuchi ........ 58 A3
Cúcuta ....... 90 B4
Cuddalore ... 43 P11
Cuddapah ... 43 M11
Cudgewa ..... 63 C4
Cuenca, Ecuador 90 D3
Cuenca, Spain . 19 B4
Cuenca,
    Serranía de . 19 C5
Cuernavaca ... 84 D5
Cuevas del
    Almanzora .. 19 D5
Cuevo ....... 91 H6
Cuiabá ....... 93 F2
Cuiabá → .... 93 F2
Cuima ....... 58 A3
Cuito → ..... 58 B4
Cukai ........ 36 D2
Culcairn ..... 63 C4
Culgoa → ... 63 A4
Culiacán ..... 84 C3
Culion ....... 38 B2
Cullarin Ra. ... 63 B4
Cullera ...... 19 C5
Culuene → ... 93 E3
Culverden ... 65 E5
Cumaná ..... 90 A6
Cumberland,
    Canada .... 71 D7
Cumberland,
    U.S.A. .... 73 E6
Cumberland
    Pen. ....... 68 B4
Cumberland
    Plateau .... 72 F3
Cumberland Sd. 68 B4
Cumborah ... 63 A4
Cumbum .... 43 M11
Cummins ..... 62 B2
Cumnock .... 63 B4
Cunene → ... 58 B2
Cúneo ....... 20 B1
Cunnamulla ... 63 A4
Cupica, G. de .. 90 B3
Curaçao ..... 87 D6
Curaray → ... 90 D4
Curiapo ..... 90 B6
Curicó ...... 94 C2
Curitiba ..... 94 B7
Currabubula .. 63 B5
Currais Novos . 92 D6
Curralinho .... 92 C4
Curraweena ... 63 B4
Currie ...... 62 C3
Curtea de Argeş 17 F7
Curtis Group .. 62 C4
Curuápanema →
............. 92 C2
Curuçá ....... 92 C4
Curup ....... 37 E2
Cururupu ..... 92 C5
Curuzú Cuatiá . 94 B5
Cuttaburra → . 63 A4
Cuttack ..... 40 G5
Cuvier I. ..... 64 B6
Cuxhaven ..... 14 B5

Cuyo ........ 38 B2
Cuzco, Bolivia . 91 H5
Cuzco, Peru ... 91 F4
Cwmbran ..... 11 F5
Cyclades =
    Kikládhes ... 23 F5
Cygnet ....... 62 D4
Cyprus ■ ..... 46 D3
Cyrenaica ... 52 C3
Cyrene =
    Shaḥḥāt .... 52 B3
Czech Rep. ■ .. 16 D2
Częstochowa .. 16 C4

D

Da Hinggan Ling 35 B7
Da Lat ........ 36 B3
Da Nang ..... 36 A3
Da Qaidam ... 34 C4
Da Yunhe → .. 35 C7
Daba Shan ... 35 C5
Dabakala ... 55 G4
Dabo ........ 37 E2
Dabola ...... 55 F2
Daboya ..... 55 G4
Dacca = Dhaka 41 F8
Dacca =
    Dhaka □ ... 41 E8
Dachau ....... 15 D6
Dadanawa ... 90 C7
Dadra and
    Nagar
    Haveli □ .... 43 J8
Dadu ........ 42 F5
Daet ........ 38 B2
Dagana ...... 55 E1
Dagestan □ ... 25 E6
Daghestan
    Republic =
    Dagestan □ . 25 E6
Dagö = Hiiumaa 24 B1
Dagupan ..... 38 A2
Dahlak Kebir .. 49 D3
Dahod ....... 43 H9
Dahomey =
    Benin ■ .... 55 G5
Dahra ....... 55 E1
Daiö-Misaki ... 32 B5
Dairût ....... 52 C5
Dakar ....... 55 F1
Dakhla ...... 54 D1
Dakhla, El
    Wâhât el- ... 52 C4
Dakhovskaya .. 25 E5
Đakovica ..... 22 C3
Dalandzadgad . 35 B5
Dālbandīn ... 42 E4
Dalby ....... 63 A5
Dalhousie .... 69 D4
Dali ........ 34 D5
Dalian ...... 35 C7
Daliang Shan .. 34 D5
Dallarnil .... 63 A5
Dallas ...... 79 C5
Dalmacija ..... 20 C6
Dalmatia =
    Dalmacija ... 20 C6
Daloa ....... 55 G3
Dalton ...... 74 B5
Dalton Iceberg
    Tongue .... 96 A13
Daly Waters .. 60 D5
Daman ....... 43 J8
Damanhûr ... 52 B5

Damar ....... 39 F3
Damaraland ... 58 C3
Damascus =
    Dimashq ... 46 D4
Damävand .... 44 C3
Damävand,
    Qolleh-ye ... 44 C3
Damba ...... 56 F3
Dāmghān .... 44 B3
Damiel ...... 18 C4
Damietta =
    Dumyât .... 52 B5
Dammam = Ad
    Dammām ... 47 F7
Damoh ...... 43 H11
Dampier ..... 60 E2
Dampier, Selat 39 E4
Danbury ..... 73 D9
Dandeldhura .. 40 C3
Dandeli ...... 43 M9
Dandenong ... 63 C4
Dandong ..... 35 B7
Danger Is. =
    Pukapuka ... 65 L14
Danger Pt. ... 58 E3
Dangora ..... 55 F6
Danilov ...... 24 B5
Dankhar Gompa 42 C11
Dannemora ... 9 F11
Dannevirke ... 64 D7
Dante ....... 49 E5
Danube =
    Dunărea → . 17 F9
Danville ..... 75 A8
Danzig =
    Gdańsk ..... 16 A4
Dao ........ 38 B2
Daoud = Aïn
    Beïda .... 54 A6
Dar el Beida =
    Casablanca . 54 B3
Dar es Salaam . 57 F7
Dārāb ....... 44 D3
Daraj ....... 54 B7
Darband .... 42 B8
Darbhanga ... 40 D5
Dardanelles =
    Çanakkale
    Boğazı ..... 23 D6
Dârfûr ...... 53 F3
Dargai ...... 42 B7
Dargan Ata ... 29 E7
Dargaville .... 64 A5
Darıca ...... 22 D7
Darién, G. del . 90 B3
Darjeeling =
    Darjiling ... 40 D7
Darjiling .... 40 D7
Darling → .... 62 B3
Darling Downs 63 A5
Darling Ra. ... 60 G2
Darlington ... 11 D6
Darłowo ..... 16 A3
Darmstadt ... 14 D5
Darnah ...... 52 B3
Darnley, C. ... 96 A10
Darnley B. ... 70 B7
Dart, C. ..... 96 B18
Dartmoor ... 11 F5
Dartmouth ... 69 D4
Dartmouth, L. . 63 A4
Darvaza ..... 29 E6
Darvel, Teluk . 37 D5
Darwha ..... 43 J10
Darwin ..... 60 C5
Daryoi Amu =
    Amudarya → 29 E6
Dās ......... 44 E3
Dashhowuz ... 29 E6

Dasht → ..... 42 G2
Dasht-e Kavīr .. 44 C3
Dasht-e Mārgow 42 D3
Datça ....... 23 F6
Datia ....... 43 G11
Datong ...... 35 B6
Datu, Tanjung . 37 D3
Datu Piang .... 38 C2
Daugava → .. 24 B1
Daugavpils ... 24 B2
Daulpur ...... 42 F10
Dauphin ..... 71 C9
Dauphiné ... 13 D6
Davangere .... 43 M9
Davao ....... 38 C3
Davao, G. of .. 38 C3
Dāvar Panāh .. 45 E5
Davenport ... 77 E9
David ....... 86 E3
David Gorodok
    = Davyd
    Haradok ... 17 B8
Davis Sea ... 96 A11
Davis Str. ... 68 B5
Davos ....... 13 C8
Davyd Haradok 17 B8
Dawson ..... 70 B6
Dawson, I. ... 95 G2
Dax ......... 12 E3
Daxian ...... 35 C5
Daxue Shan .. 34 C5
Daylesford ... 62 C3
Dayr az Zawr . 46 D5
Dayton ..... 72 E3
Daytona Beach 75 E7
Dead Sea .... 47 E3
Deakin ...... 60 G4
Deal I. ...... 62 C4
Deán Funes .. 94 C4
Death Valley . 82 B4
Deba Habe ... 55 F7
Debar ....... 22 D3
Dębica ...... 16 C5
Debre Markos . 53 F6
Debre Tabor .. 53 F6
Debrecen ... 16 E5
Decatur, Ala.,
    U.S.A. .... 74 B4
Decatur, Ill.,
    U.S.A. .... 77 F10
Deccan ..... 43 L11
Děčín ....... 16 C2
Dedéagach =
    Alexandroúpolis
    ........... 22 D5
Dédougou ... 55 F4
Dee → ...... 10 C5
Deepwater ... 63 A5
Degeh Bur ... 49 F3
Deggendorf .. 15 D7
Deh Bīd ..... 44 D3
Dehi Titan ... 42 C3
Dehibat ..... 54 B7
Dehkareqan .. 46 C6
Dehra Dun ... 42 D11
Dej ......... 17 E6
Dekese ..... 56 E4
Delano ...... 82 C3
Delaware □ ... 73 E8
Delaware → .. 73 E8
Delegate .... 63 C4
Delgado, C. ... 57 G8
Delgo ....... 53 D5
Delhi ....... 42 E10
Delice → .... 46 C3
Delicias ..... 84 B3
Delmenhorst . 14 B5
Delmiro Gouveia 93 D6
Deloraine ..... 62 D4

Delungra . . . . . 63 A5
Delvinë . . . . . . . 23 E3
Demanda, Sierra
  de la . . . . . . . 18 A4
Demavand =
  Damāvand . . 44 C3
Demba . . . . . . 56 F4
Dembecha . . . . 53 F6
Dembidolo . . . 53 G5
Demini → . . . . 90 D6
Demirci . . . . . 23 E7
Demirköy . . . . . 22 D6
Dempo . . . . . . . 37 E2
Den Haag = 's-
  Gravenhage . 14 B3
Den Helder . . . 14 B3
Denau . . . . . . . 29 F7
Dendang . . . . . 37 E3
Denia . . . . . . . 19 C6
Denial B. . . . . . 62 B1
Deniliquin . . . . 63 C3
Denman Glacier 96 A11
Denmark ■ . . . 9 G9
Denmark Str. . . 66 C17
Denpasar . . . . . 37 F5
Denton . . . . . . 78 C5
D'Entrecasteaux
  Is. . . . . . . . . 61 B9
Denver . . . . . . . 76 F2
Deoghar . . . . . . 40 E6
Deolali . . . . . . . 43 K8
Deoria . . . . . . . 40 D4
Deosai Mts. . . . 42 B9
Dêqên . . . . . . . . 34 D4
Dera Ghazi Khan 42 D7
Dera Ismail
  Khan . . . . . . 42 D7
Derbent . . . . . . 25 E6
Derby, Australia 60 D3
Derby, U.K. . . . 11 E6
Derg, L. . . . . . . 11 E2
Dergaon . . . . . . 41 D9
Derry =
  Londonderry 11 D3
Derudub . . . . . 53 E6
Des Moines . . . 77 E8
Des Moines → 77 E9
Desaguadero → 91 G5
Dese . . . . . . . . 49 E2
Desna → . . . . . 17 C10
Desolación, I. . . 95 G2
Despeñaperros,
  Paso . . . . . . 18 C4
Dessau . . . . . . 15 C7
Dessye = Dese 49 E2
D'Estrees B. . . . 62 C2
Detmold . . . . . . 14 C5
Detroit . . . . . . 72 C4
Deutsche Bucht 14 A5
Deva . . . . . . . . 17 F6
Devakottai . . . . 43 Q11
Deventer . . . . . 14 B4
Devonport,
  Australia . . . 62 D4
Devonport, N.Z. 64 B6
Dewas . . . . . . . 43 H10
Deyhük . . . . . . 44 C4
Deyyer . . . . . . . 44 E2
Dezfūl . . . . . . . 47 D7
Dezhneva, Mys 31 C16
Dhafra . . . . . . . 44 F3
Dhahira . . . . . . 44 F4
Dhahran = Az̧
  Z̧ahrān . . . . 47 F7
Dhaka . . . . . . . 41 F8
Dhaka □ . . . . . . 41 E8
Dhamar . . . . . . 49 E3
Dhamtari . . . . . 40 G3
Dhanbad . . . . . 40 F6

Dhangarhi . . . . 40 C3
Dhankuta . . . . . 40 D6
Dhar . . . . . . . . 43 H9
Dharmapuri . . . 43 N11
Dharwad . . . . . 43 M9
Dhaulagiri . . . . 40 C4
Dhenkanal . . . . 40 G5
Dhíkti Óros . . . 23 G5
Dhírfis . . . . . . . 23 E4
Dhodhekánisos 23 F6
Dhrol . . . . . . . . 43 H7
Dhubaibah . . . . 44 F3
Dhuburi . . . . . . 41 D7
Dhule . . . . . . . . 43 J9
Dhut → . . . . . . 49 E5
Diafarabé . . . . . 55 F4
Diamantina . . . 93 F5
Diamantina → 62 A2
Diamantino . . . 93 E2
Diamond
  Harbour . . . . 40 F7
Diapaga . . . . . . 55 F5
Dībā . . . . . . . . . 44 E4
Dibaya . . . . . . . 56 F4
Dibaya-Lubue . 56 E3
Dibbi . . . . . . . . 49 G3
Dibrugarh . . . . 41 D10
Dickson . . . . . . 28 B9
Didiéni . . . . . . . 55 F3
Diébougou . . . . 55 F4
Diefenbaker L. . 71 C9
Dieppe . . . . . . . 12 B4
Digby . . . . . . . . 69 D4
Digges Is. . . . . . 68 B3
Dighinala . . . . . 41 F9
Digne-les-Bains 13 D7
Digos . . . . . . . . 38 C3
Digul → . . . . . . 39 F5
Dihang → . . . . 41 D10
Dijlah, Nahr → 47 E6
Dijon . . . . . . . . 13 C6
Dikimdya . . . . . 31 D10
Dikson =
  Dickson . . . . 28 B9
Dikwa . . . . . . . 53 F1
Dili . . . . . . . . . . 39 F3
Dilling . . . . . . . 53 F4
Dillingham . . . . 71 C4
Dilolo . . . . . . . . 56 G4
Dilston . . . . . . . 62 D4
Dimashq . . . . . 46 D4
Dimbokro . . . . . 55 G4
Dimboola . . . . . 62 C3
Dîmbovița → . 22 B6
Dimitrovgrad,
  Bulgaria . . . . 22 C5
Dimitrovgrad,
  Russia . . . . . 24 C6
Dimitrovo =
  Pernik . . . . . 22 C4
Dinagat . . . . . . 38 B3
Dinajpur . . . . . . 41 E7
Dinan . . . . . . . . 12 B2
Dinant . . . . . . . 14 C3
Dinar . . . . . . . . 46 C2
Dīnār, Kūh-e . . 44 D2
Dinara Planina . 20 B6
Dinard . . . . . . . 12 B2
Dinaric Alps =
  Dinara Planina 20 B6
Dindigul . . . . . . 43 P11
Dingle . . . . . . . 11 E1
Dinguiraye . . . . 55 F2
Dingwall . . . . . . 10 C4
Dinosaur
  National
  Monument . . 81 E9
Diourbel . . . . . . 55 F1
Dipolog . . . . . . 38 C2

Dir . . . . . . . . . . 42 B7
Diré . . . . . . . . . 55 E4
Dire Dawa . . . . 49 F3
Dirico . . . . . . . . 58 B4
Dirranbandi . . . 63 A4
Disa . . . . . . . . . 43 G8
Disappointment,
  L. . . . . . . . . . 60 E3
Disaster B. . . . . 63 C4
Discovery B. . . . 62 C3
Disteghil Sar . . 42 A9
Distrito
  Federal □ . . . 93 F4
Diu . . . . . . . . . . 43 J7
Divinópolis . . . 93 G5
Divnoye . . . . . . 25 D5
Diwāl Kol . . . . . 42 B5
Diyarbakır . . . . 46 C5
Diz Chah . . . . . 44 C3
Djado . . . . . . . . 52 D1
Djakarta =
  Jakarta . . . . . 37 F3
Djambala . . . . . 56 E2
Djanet . . . . . . . 54 D6
Djawa = Jawa . 37 F3
Djelfa . . . . . . . . 54 B5
Djema . . . . . . . 57 C5
Djenné . . . . . . . 55 F4
Djerba, I. de . . 52 B1
Djerid, Chott . . 54 B6
Djibo . . . . . . . . 55 F4
Djibouti . . . . . . 49 E3
Djibouti ■ . . . 49 E3
Djolu . . . . . . . . 56 D4
Djougou . . . . . . 55 G5
Djoum . . . . . . . 56 D2
Djourab . . . . . . 53 E2
Djugu . . . . . . . . 57 D6
Dmitriya
  Lapteva, Proliv 31 B12
Dnepr → =
  Dnipro → . . 25 D3
Dneprodzerzhinsk
  =
  Dniprodzerzhynsk
  . . . . . . . . . . 25 D3
Dnepropetrovsk
  =
  Dnipropetrovsk
  . . . . . . . . . . 25 D4
Dnestr → =
  Dnister → . . 17 E10
Dnestrovski =
  Belgorod . . . 24 C4
Dnieper =
  Dnipro → . . 25 D3
Dniester =
  Dnister → . . 17 E10
Dnipro → . . . . 25 D3
Dniprodzerzhynsk
  . . . . . . . . . . 25 D3
Dnipropetrovsk 25 D4
Dnister → . . . . 17 E10
Dnistrovskyy
  Lyman . . . . . 17 E10
Dnyapro =
  Dnipro → . . 25 D3
Doba . . . . . . . . 53 G2
Doberai, Jazirah 39 E4
Doblas . . . . . . . 94 D4
Dobo . . . . . . . . 39 F4
Doboj . . . . . . . . 20 B7
Dobreta-Turnu-
  Severin . . . . 22 B4
Dobrich . . . . . . 22 C6
Dobruja . . . . . . 22 B7
Dobrush . . . . . . 17 B10
Dodecanese =
  Dhodhekánisos
  . . . . . . . . . . 23 F6

Dodge City . . . . 78 A3
Dodoma . . . . . . 57 F7
Dogi . . . . . . . . . 42 C3
Doha = Ad
  Dawhah . . . . 44 E2
Dohazari . . . . . 41 F9
Doi . . . . . . . . . . 39 D3
Dois Irmãos, Sa. 93 D5
Dolbeau . . . . . . 69 D3
Dole . . . . . . . . . 13 C6
Dolomites =
  Dolomiti . . . . 20 A3
Dolomiti . . . . . . 20 A3
Dolores . . . . . . 94 D5
Dolphin, C. . . . . 95 G5
Dolphin and
  Union Str. . . 70 B8
Dombarovskiy . 29 D6
Dominica ■ . . 87 C7
Dominican
  Rep. ■ . . . . . 87 C5
Domo . . . . . . . . 49 F4
Domodóssola . 20 A2
Domville, Mt. . . 63 A5
Don →, Russia 25 D4
Don →, U.K. . . 10 C5
Don Benito . . . 18 C3
Donald . . . . . . . 62 C3
Donau =
  Dunărea → . 17 F9
Donauwörth . . 14 D6
Doncaster . . . . 11 E6
Dondo, Angola 56 F2
Dondo, Mozam. 59 B6
Dondo, Teluk . 39 D2
Donegal . . . . . . 11 D2
Donets → . . . . 25 D5
Donetsk . . . . . . 25 D4
Donggala . . . . . 39 E1
Dongola . . . . . . 53 E5
Dongou . . . . . . 56 D3
Dongting Hu . . 35 D6
Dongxing . . . . . 35 D5
Donington, C. . 62 B2
Donnelly's
  Crossing . . . . 64 A5
Donostia = San
  Sebastián . . . 19 A5
Dora Báltea → 20 B2
Dorchester, C. . 68 B3
Dordogne → . 12 D3
Dordrecht . . . . 14 C3
Dori . . . . . . . . . 55 F4
Dornbirn . . . . . 14 E5
Dorohoi . . . . . . 17 E8
Döröö Nuur . . . 34 B4
Dorrigo . . . . . . 63 B5
Dortmund . . . . 14 C4
Doruma . . . . . . 57 D5
Dos Bahías, C. . 95 E3
Dos Hermanas 18 D3
Dosso . . . . . . . 55 F5
Dothan . . . . . . . 74 D5
Douai . . . . . . . . 13 A5
Douala . . . . . . . 56 D1
Douarnenez . . . 12 B1
Double Island
  Pt. . . . . . . . . 63 A5
Doubs → . . . . 13 C6
Doubtful Sd. . . 65 F2
Doubtless B. . . 64 A5
Douentza . . . . . 55 F4
Douglas, U.K. . 11 D4
Douglas, U.S.A. 83 E8
Doumé . . . . . . . 56 D2
Dourados . . . . . 94 A6
Douro → . . . . . 18 B1
Dover, Australia 62 D4
Dover, U.K. . . . 11 F7

Dover, Str. of .. 11 F7
Dovrefjell ...... 8 F9
Dowlat Yār ... 45 C6
Dowlatābād ... 44 D4
Dowshī ....... 45 C7
Draa, Oued → 54 C2
Drăgăşani ... 22 B5
Dragichyn .... 17 B7
Dragoman,
    Prokhod .. 22 C4
Draguignan ... 13 E7
Drake ....... 63 A5
Drakensberg .. 59 E5
Dráma ....... 22 D5
Drammen ..... 9 G10
Drau =
    Drava → ... 20 B7
Drava → ..... 20 B7
Dresden ..... 15 C7
Dreux ........ 12 B4
Drina → ..... 20 B7
Drini → ...... 22 C2
Drochia ...... 17 D8
Drogheda .... 11 E3
Drogichin =
    Dragichyn .. 17 B7
Drogobych =
    Drohobych .. 17 D6
Drohobych ... 17 D6
Droichead Atha
    = Drogheda . 11 E3
Dromedary, C. . 63 C5
Drumheller ... 71 C8
Drummond Pt. . 62 B2
Drut → ....... 17 B10
Drygalski I. .... 96 A11
Dschang ...... 55 G7
Dubā ........ 47 F3
Dubai = Dubayy 44 E3
Dubăsari ..... 17 E9
Dubăsari Vdkhr. . 17 E9
Dubawnt → ... 70 B9
Dubawnt, L. ... 70 B9
Dubayy ....... 44 E3
Dubbo ....... 63 B4
Dublin, Ireland . 11 E3
Dublin, U.S.A. . 75 C6
Dubno ....... 17 C7
Dubossary =
    Dubăsari .... 17 E9
Dubossary
    Vdkhr. =
    Dubăsari
    Vdkhr. ..... 17 E9
Dubovka ..... 24 D5
Dubréka ...... 55 G2
Dubrovitsa =
    Dubrovytsya 17 C8
Dubrovnik .... 20 C7
Dubrovytsya .. 17 C8
Dudhi ....... 40 E4
Dudinka ...... 30 C6
Duero =
    Douro → ... 18 B1
Dugi Otok .... 20 B5
Duisburg ..... 14 C4
Dukelský
    Průsmyk .... 16 D5
Dukhān ...... 44 E2
Duki ........ 42 D6
Duku ........ 55 F7
Dulce → ..... 94 C4
Dulit, Banjaran 37 D4
Duluth ....... 77 B8
Dum Duma ... 41 D10
Dum Hadjer .. 53 F2
Dumaguete ... 38 C2
Dumai ....... 37 D2
Dumaran ..... 38 B1

Dumfries ..... 11 D5
Dumyât ...... 52 B5
Dún Dealgan =
    Dundalk ... 11 D3
Dun Laoghaire 11 E3
Duna =
    Dunărea → . 17 F9
Dunaj =
    Dunărea → . 17 F9
Dunakeszi .... 16 E4
Dunărea → ... 17 F9
Dunaújváros .. 16 E4
Dunav =
    Dunărea → . 17 F9
Dunback ..... 65 F4
Dunbar ...... 10 D5
Duncan ...... 78 B5
Dundalk ..... 11 D3
Dundee,
    S. Africa .... 59 D6
Dundee, U.K. .. 10 C5
Dundoo ...... 63 A3
Dunedin ..... 65 F4
Dunfermline .. 10 C5
Dungarvan ... 11 E3
Dungog ...... 63 B5
Dungu ....... 57 D5
Dunhuang .... 34 B4
Dunkerque .. 12 A5
Dunkirk =
    Dunkerque .. 12 A5
Dunkwa ..... 55 G4
Dúnleary = Dun
    Laoghaire .. 11 E3
Dunolly ...... 62 C3
Dunqul ...... 52 D5
Dunstan Mts. .. 65 F3
Durance → ... 13 E6
Durango =
    Victoria de
    Durango .... 84 C4
Durango ..... 19 A4
Durazno ...... 94 C5
Durazzo =
    Durrësi .... 22 D2
Durban ...... 59 D6
Düren ....... 14 C4
Durg ........ 40 G3
Durgapur ..... 40 F6
Durham, U.K. .. 11 D6
Durham, U.S.A. 75 B8
Durham Downs 63 A4
Durmitor .... 22 C2
Durrësi ...... 22 D2
Dursunbey ... 23 E7
D'Urville,
    Tanjung ... 39 E5
D'Urville I. .... 65 D5
Dusa Mareb ... 49 F4
Dushak ...... 29 F7
Dushanbe .... 29 F7
Dusky Sd. .... 65 F2
Düsseldorf ... 14 C4
Dutch Harbor .. 71 C3
Duwādimi .... 47 F6
Duyun ....... 35 D5
Düzce ....... 46 B2
Duzdab =
    Zāhedān ... 45 D5
Dvina,
    Severnaya → 28 C5
Dvinsk =
    Daugavpils .. 24 B2
Dwarka ...... 43 H6
Dyatlovo =
    Dzyatlava ... 17 B7
Dyer, C. ...... 68 B4
Dyer Plateau .. 96 B3
Dyersburg .... 79 A9

Dymer ....... 17 C10
Dynevor Downs 63 A3
Dzamin Üüd .. 35 B6
Dzerzhinsk ... 24 B5
Dzhambul =
    Zhambyl ... 29 E8
Dzhankoy .... 25 D3
Dzhardzhan ... 30 C10
Dzhezkazgan =
    Zhezqazghan 29 E7
Dzhizak =
    Jizzakh .... 29 E7
Działdowa ... 16 B5
Dzierzoniów ... 16 C3
Dzungaria =
    Junggar Pendi 34 B3
Dzungarian Gate
    = Alataw
    Shankou ... 34 B3
Dzuumod ..... 35 B5
Dzyarzhynsk .. 17 B8
Dzyatlava ..... 17 B7

E

Earnslaw, Mt. . 65 F3
East Bengal ... 41 E7
East Beskids =
    Vychodné
    Beskydy .... 17 D5
East C. ...... 64 B8
East China Sea 35 C7
East Falkland .. 95 G5
East Kilbride .. 10 D4
East London .. 59 E5
East Main =
    Eastmain ... 69 C3
East Orange .. 73 D8
East St. Louis . 77 F9
East Toorale .. 63 B4
Eastbourne, N.Z. 65 D6
Eastbourne, U.K. 11 F7
Eastern Ghats . 43 N11
Eastmain ... 69 C3
Eastmain → .. 69 C3
Eau Claire .... 77 C9
Eberswalde-
    Finow ..... 15 B7
Ebolowa ...... 56 D2
Ebro → ..... 19 B6
Eceabat ..... 23 D6
Ech Cheliff ... 54 A5
Echo Bay ..... 70 B8
Echuca ....... 63 C3
Ecija ........ 18 D3
Ecuador ■ .... 90 D3
Ed Dâmer .... 53 E5
Ed Debba .... 53 E5
Ed Dueim .... 53 F5
Edd ........ 49 E3
Eddystone Pt. . 62 D4
Édea ........ 56 D2
Eden → ..... 14 C5
Édhessa ..... 23 D4
Edievale ..... 65 F3
Edinburg ..... 78 F4
Edinburgh ... 10 D5
Edinița ...... 17 D8
Edirne ....... 22 D6
Edithburgh ... 62 C2
Edmonton ... 71 C8
Edmundston .. 69 D4
Edremit ..... 23 E6
Edremit Körfezi 23 E6
Edson ........ 71 C8

Edward → ... 62 C3
Edward, L. ... 57 E5
Edward VII Land 96 C17
Edwards Plateau 78 D3
Égadi, Ísole ... 21 F4
Eger = Cheb .. 16 C1
Eger ......... 16 E5
Egersund .... 9 G9
Egmont, C. ... 64 C5
Egmont, Mt. .. 64 C6
Eğridir ....... 46 C2
Eğridir Gölü ... 46 C2
Egypt ■ ...... 52 C5
Eibar ........ 19 A4
Eidsvold ..... 63 A5
Eifel ........ 14 C4
Eigg ........ 10 C3
Eil ........... 49 F4
Eildon, L. ..... 63 C4
Eindhoven .... 14 C3
Eire = Ireland ■ 11 E3
Eirunepé ..... 91 E5
Eisenach .... 14 C6
Eisenerz ...... 15 E8
Eivissa = Ibiza . 19 C6
Eketahuna ... 64 D6
Ekibastuz ... 29 D8
El Aaiún ..... 54 C2
El Alamein ... 52 B4
El Aricha .... 54 B4
El 'Arîsh ..... 52 B5
El Asnam = Ech
    Cheliff ...... 54 A5
El Bawiti ..... 52 C4
El Bayadh .... 54 B5
El Callao .... 90 B6
El Centro .... 82 D5
El Cerro ..... 91 G6
El Cuy ....... 95 D3
El Cuyo ...... 85 C7
El Dere ...... 49 G4
El Diviso ..... 90 C3
El Djouf ..... 55 D3
El Dorado, Ark.,
    U.S.A. ..... 79 C7
El Dorado,
    Kans., U.S.A. 78 A5
El Dorado,
    Venezuela ... 90 B6
El Escorial ... 18 B3
El Faiyûm .... 52 C5
El Fâsher .... 53 F4
El Ferrol ..... 18 A1
El Fuerte .... 84 B3
El Gal ....... 49 E5
El Geneina = Al
    Junaynah ... 53 F3
El Geteina .... 53 F5
El Gîza ...... 52 C5
El Iskandarîya . 52 B4
El Jadida .... 54 B3
El Jebelein ... 53 F5
El Kab ....... 53 E5
El Kala ....... 54 A6
El Kamlin .... 53 E5
El Kef ....... 54 A6
El Khandaq ... 53 E5
El Khârga .... 52 C5
El Khartûm ... 53 E5
El Khartûm
    Bahrî ...... 53 E5
El Laqâwa .... 53 F4
El Mafâza .... 53 F5
El Mahalla el
    Kubra ...... 52 B5
El Mansûra ... 52 B5
El Minyâ .... 52 C5
El Obeid ..... 53 F5
El Odaiya .... 53 F4

El Oued . . . . . . 54 B6
El Paso . . . . . . . 83 E9
El Prat de
  Llobregat . . . 19 B7
El Puerto de
  Santa María . 18 D2
El Qâhira . . 52 B5
El Qantara . . . . 52 B5
El Qasr . . . . . . . 52 C4
El Reno . . . . . . 78 B5
El Salvador ■ . 85 E7
El Shallal . . . . . 52 D5
El Suweis . . . . . 52 C5
El Tigre . . . . . . 90 B6
El Tocuyo . . . . 90 B5
El Turbio . . . . 95 G2
El Uqsur . . . . . . 52 C5
El Vigía . . . . . . 90 B4
El Wak . . . . . . 57 D8
El Wuz . . . . . . 53 E5
Elat . . . . . . . . . 47 E3
Elâzığ . . . . . . . 46 C4
Elba . . . . . . . . 20 C3
Elbasani . . . . . . 22 D3
Elbe → . . . . . 14 B5
Elbert, Mt. . . 83 A9
Elbeuf . . . . . . . 12 B4
Elbidtan . . . . 46 C4
Elbing = Elbląg 16 A4
Elbląg . . . . . . 16 A4
Elbrus . . . . . 25 E5
Elburz Mts. =
  Alborz,
  Reshteh-ye
  Kühhä-ye . . 44 B3
Elche . . . . . . . 19 C5
Elda . . . . . . . . 19 C5
Elde → . . . . 15 B6
Eldoret . . . . . . 57 D7
Elektrostal . . . . 24 B4
Elephant I. . . . 96 A4
Eleuthera . . . . 86 A4
Elgin, U.K. . . 10 C5
Elgin, U.S.A. . . 72 C1
Elgon, Mt. . . 57 D6
Eliase . . . . . . . 39 F4
Elisabethville =
  Lubumbashi . 59 A5
Elista . . . . . . . 25 D5
Elizabeth,
  Australia . . . 62 B2
Elizabeth, U.S.A. 73 D8
Elizabeth City . 75 A9
Elizabethton . . 75 A6
Elk . . . . . . . . 16 B6
Elkhart . . . . . . 72 D3
Elkhovo . . . . . 22 C6
Elko . . . . . . . 80 E6
Ellery, Mt. . . . . 63 C4
Ellesmere, L. . . 65 G5
Ellice Is. =
  Tuvalu ■ . . 64 K12
Elliston . . . . . 62 B1
Ellore = Eluru . 40 J3
Ellsworth Land 96 B2
Ellsworth Mts. . 96 B2
Elmore . . . . . 63 C3
Elmshorn . . . . . 14 B5
Eltham . . . . . . 64 C6
Eluru . . . . . . . 40 J3
Elvas . . . . . . . 18 C2
Elx = Elche . . . 19 C5
Ely . . . . . . . 11 E7
Emämrüd . . . . 44 B3
Emba = Embi . 29 E6
Emba → =
  Embi → . . . 29 E6
Embarcación . . 94 A4
Embi . . . . . . . 29 E6

Embi → . . . . . 29 E6
Embrun . . . . . 13 D7
Embu . . . . . . 57 E7
Emden . . . . . 14 B4
Emerson . . . . 71 D10
Emet . . . . . . . 23 E7
Emi Koussi . . 53 E2
Emine, Nos . . . 22 C6
Emmen . . . . . . 14 B4
Empalme . . . . 84 B2
Empangeni . . . 59 D6
Empedrado . . 94 B5
Empty Quarter
  = Rub' al
  Khali . . . . 48 D4
Ems → . . . . . 14 B4
En Nahud . . . . 53 F4
Enaratoli . . . . 39 E5
Enare =
  Inarijärvi . . . . 8 E13
Encanto, C. . . . 38 A2
Encarnación . . 94 B5
Encounter B. . . 62 C2
Ende . . . . . . . 39 F2
Enderby Land . 96 A9
Enewetak Atoll 64 H11
Enez . . . . . . . 23 D6
Engadin . . . . 13 C9
Engaño, C. . . . 38 A2
Engels . . . . . . 24 C6
Enggano . . . . 37 F2
Engkilili . . . . 37 D4
England □ . . . 11 E6
Englewood . . . 76 F2
English Bazar =
  Ingraj Bazar . 40 E7
English Channel 11 F5
Enid . . . . . . . 78 A5
Enna . . . . . . . 21 F5
Ennedi . . . . . 53 E3
Enngonia . . . 63 A4
Ennis . . . . . . 11 E2
Enniskillen . . . 11 D3
Enns → . . . . 15 D8
Enschede . . . . 14 B4
Ensenada . . . . 84 A1
Entebbe . . . . . 57 D6
Entroncamento 18 C1
Enugu . . . . . . 55 G6
Enugu Ezike . . 55 G6
Eólie, Ís. . . . . 21 E5
Épernay . . . . 13 B5
Ephesus . . . . 23 F6
Épinal . . . . . 13 B7
Epukiro . . . . . 58 C3
Equatorial
  Guinea ■ . . 56 D1
Er Rahad . . . . 53 F5
Er Rif . . . . . . 54 A4
Er Roseires . . 53 F5
Erāwadī Myit =
  Irrawaddy → 41 K10
Erbil = Arbīl . 46 C6
Erciyaş Dağı . . 46 C3
Érd . . . . . . . 16 E4
Erdek . . . . . . 23 D6
Erebus, Mt. . . 96 B15
Erechim . . . . 94 B6
Ereğli, Konya,
  Turkey . . . . 46 C3
Ereğli,
  Zonguldak,
  Turkey . . . . 46 B2
Eresma → . . 18 B3
Erewadi
  Myitwanya . . 41 K10
Erfurt . . . . . . 15 C6
Ergani . . . . . . 46 C4
Érice . . . . . . . 21 E4

Erie . . . . . . . . 73 C5
Erie, L. . . . . . 72 C5
Erigavo . . . . . 49 E4
Erímanthos . . . 23 F3
Erimo-misaki . . 32 F12
Eritrea ■ . . . . 49 E2
Erlangen . . . . 15 D6
Ermenak . . . . 46 C3
Ermoúpolis =
  Síros . . . . . 23 F5
Ernakulam =
  Cochin . . . 43 Q10
Erne, Lower L. . 11 D3
Erode . . . . . . 43 P10
Eromanga . . 63 A3
Erramala Hills . 43 M11
Ertis → =
  Irtysh → . . 28 C7
Erzgebirge . . . 15 C7
Erzincan . . . . 46 C4
Erzurum . . . . 46 C5
Es Sahrâ' Esh
  Sharqîya . . . 52 C5
Es Sîna' . . . . . 52 C5
Esch-sur-Alzette 13 B6
Escuinapa . . . 84 C3
Eşfahān . . . . 44 C2
Esh Sham =
  Dimashq . . . 46 D4
Esil → =
  Ishim → . . . 29 D8
Eskilstuna . . . . 9 G11
Eskimo Pt. . . . 70 B10
Eskişehir . . . . 46 C2
Esla → . . . . . 18 B2
Eslāmābād-e
  Gharb . . . . 46 D6
Eşme . . . . . . 23 E7
Esmeraldas . . . 90 C3
Esperance . . . 60 G3
Esperanza . . . 94 C4
Espichel, C. . . . 18 C1
Espinazo, Sierra
  del =
  Espinhaço,
  Serra do . . . 93 F5
Espinhaço, Serra
  do . . . . . . . 93 F5
Espírito Santo □ 93 G5
Esquel . . . . . 95 E2
Esquina . . . . . 94 C5
Essaouira . . . 54 B3
Essen . . . . . 14 C4
Essequibo → . 90 B7
Esslingen . . . 14 D5
Estados, I. de
  Los . . . . . 95 G4
Estância . . . . 93 E6
Estevan . . . . . 71 D9
Estonia ■ . . . 24 B2
Estrêla, Serra da 18 B2
Estremoz . . . 18 C2
Estrondo, Serra
  do . . . . . . . 92 D4
Esztergom . . . 16 E4
Etadunna . . . 62 A2
Étampes . . . . 12 B5
Etawah . . . . 42 F11
Ethiopia ■ . . . 49 F2
Etna . . . . . . 21 F5
Etosha Pan . . 58 B3
Euboea =
  Évvoia . . . 23 E5
Eucumbene, L. 63 C4
Eufaula . . . . 74 D5
Eugene . . . . 80 C2
Eugowra . . . . 63 B4

Eulo . . . . . . . 63 A4
Euphrates =
  Furât, Nahr
  al → . . . . 47 E6
Eureka . . . . . 80 E1
Euroa . . . . . . 63 C4
Europa, I. . . . . 59 J8
Europa, Picos de 18 A3
Europa, Pta. de 18 D3
Europa Pt. =
  Europa, Pta.
  de . . . . . . 18 D3
Evans Head . . . 63 A5
Evanston . . . . 72 C2
Evansville . . . . 72 F2
Everard, L. . . . 62 B1
Everest, Mt. . . . 40 C6
Everett . . . . . 80 B2
Everglades
  National Park 75 G7
Evinayong . . . 56 D2
Évora . . . . . . 18 C2
Évreux . . . . . 12 B4
Évros → . . . 22 D6
Evry . . . . . . 12 B5
Évvoia . . . . . 23 E5
Ewo . . . . . . 56 E2
Exaltación . . . 91 F5
Exeter . . . . . 11 F5
Exmoor . . . . 11 F5
Exmouth . . . . 11 F5
Extremadura □ 18 C2
Eyasi, L. . . . . 57 E6
Eyre (North), L. 62 A2
Eyre (South), L. 62 A2
Eyre, L. . . . . 60 F6
Eyre Cr. → . . 62 A2
Eyre Mts. . . . 65 F3
Eyre Pen. . . . 62 B2
Ezine . . . . . . 23 E6

# F

F.Y.R.O.M. =
  Macedonia ■ 22 D3
Fabriano . . . . 20 C4
Facatativá . . . 90 C4
Fachi . . . . . . 55 E7
Fada . . . . . . 53 E3
Fada-n-Gourma 55 F5
Faddeyevskiy,
  Ostrov . . . 31 B12
Fāḍilī . . . . . . 47 F7
Faenza . . . . . 20 B3
Færoe Is. =
  Føroyar . . . . 6 C4
Făgăras . . . . 17 F7
Fagnano, L. . . 95 G3
Fahraj . . . . . 45 D4
Fahüd . . . . . 44 F4
Fair Isle . . . . 10 B6
Fairbanks . . . 71 B5
Fairfield, Ala.,
  U.S.A. . . . . 74 C4
Fairfield, Calif.,
  U.S.A. . . . . 80 F2
Fairlie . . . . . . 65 F4
Fairweather, Mt. 71 C6
Faisalabad . . . 42 D8
Faizabad . . . 40 D4
Fakfak . . . . . 39 E4
Falaise . . . . . 12 B3
Falam . . . . . 41 F9
Falconara
  Maríttima . . 20 C4
Falcone, C. . . 20 D2

Faleshty =
  Fălești ...... 17 E8
Fălești ...... 17 E8
Falkland Is. □ . 95 G5
Falkland Sd. ... 95 G5
Fall River .. 73 D10
Falmouth ..... 11 F4
False B. ...... 58 E3
Fălticeni ...... 17 E8
Falun ...... 9 F11
Famagusta .... 46 D3
Fandriana ..... 59 J9
Fano ........ 20 C4
Fao = Al Fāw . 47 E7
Faradje ....... 57 D5
Farafangana .. 59 J9
Farāh ....... 42 C3
Farāh □ ...... 42 C3
Faranah ...... 55 F2
Farasān, Jazā'ir 49 D3
Farasan Is. =
  Farasān,
  Jazā'ir ...... 49 D3
Fareham ...... 11 F6
Farewell, C. ... 64 D5
Farewell C. =
  Farvel, Kap .. 68 C6
Farghona ..... 29 E8
Fargo ........ 76 B6
Farim ........ 55 F1
Farīmān ...... 45 C4
Farina ....... 62 B2
Faro, *Brazil* ... 92 C2
Faro, *Portugal* . 18 D2
Farrāshband .. 44 D3
Farrell Flat ... 62 B2
Farrukhabad-
  cum-
  Fatehgarh ... 42 F11
Fārs □ ....... 44 D3
Fársala ....... 23 E4
Fartak, Râs .... 47 E3
Farvel, Kap .. 68 C6
Fāryāb □ ..... 45 B6
Fasā ......... 44 D3
Fasano ....... 21 D6
Fastiv ........ 17 C9
Fastov = Fastiv 17 C9
Fatagar, Tanjung 39 E4
Fatehgarh .... 42 F11
Fatehpur, *Raj.,*
  *India* ...... 42 F9
Fatehpur, *Ut. P.,*
  *India* ....... 40 E3
Favara ....... 21 F4
Favignana .... 21 F4
Faya-Largeau .. 53 E2
Fayd ........ 47 F5
Fayetteville,
  *Ark., U.S.A.* . 79 A6
Fayetteville,
  *N.C., U.S.A.* . 75 B8
Fazilka ....... 42 D9
Fdérik ....... 54 D2
Feather → .. 80 F3
Featherston ... 65 D6
Fécamp ...... 12 B4
Fehmarn ..... 15 A6
Feilding ...... 64 D6
Feira de Santana 93 E6
Feldkirch .... 14 E5
Felipe Carrillo
  Puerto ..... 85 D7
Felixstowe .... 11 F7
Fengjie ....... 35 C5
Fenyang ...... 35 C6
Feodosiya .... 25 D4
Ferdows ..... 44 C4
Ferfer ....... 49 F4

Fergana =
  Farghona ... 29 E8
Fermo ....... 20 C4
Fernando de
  Noronha .... 92 C7
Fernando Póo =
  Bioko ...... 56 D1
Ferozepore =
  Firozpur .... 42 D9
Ferrara ...... 20 B3
Ferreñafe ..... 91 E3
Ferret, C. ..... 12 D3
Ferrol = El
  Ferrol ...... 18 A1
Fès ......... 54 B4
Feshi ........ 56 F3
Feteşti ....... 22 B6
Fetlar ........ 10 A6
Feuilles → ... 68 C3
Fezzan ....... 52 C2
Fianarantsoa .. 59 J9
Fianga ....... 53 G2
Ficksburg .... 59 D5
Fieri ......... 23 D2
Figeac ....... 12 D5
Figueira da Foz 18 B1
Figueras ..... 19 A7
Figuig ....... 54 B4
Fiji ■ ...... 64 L12
Filiatrá ...... 23 F3
Filyos → ..... 46 B3
Fíngöe ....... 59 A6
Finike ....... 46 C2
Finisterre, C. .. 18 A1
Finke → ..... 62 A2
Finland ■ ... 8 F13
Finland, G. of . 9 G13
Finlay → ..... 70 C2
Finley ....... 63 C4
Finniss, C. .... 62 B1
Fiora → ..... 20 C3
Firat = Furāt,
  Nahr al → . 47 E6
Firenze ...... 20 C3
Firozabad .. 42 F11
Firozpur .... 42 D9
Firūzābād .. 44 D3
Firūzkūh .... 44 C3
Fish → ..... 58 D3
Fishguard ..... 11 E4
Fitri, L. ...... 53 F2
Fitz Roy ..... 95 F3
Fiume = Rijeka 20 B5
Fizi ......... 57 E5
Flagstaff .... 83 C7
Flaming Gorge
  Reservoir ... 81 E9
Flamingo, Teluk 39 F5
Flandre ...... 14 C2
Flathead L. .... 81 B6
Flattery, C. .... 80 A1
Flensburg ... 14 A5
Flers ........ 12 B3
Flesko, Tanjung 39 D2
Flin Flon .... 71 C9
Flinders → ... 61 D7
Flinders I. .... 62 C4
Flinders Ras. .. 62 B2
Flint ........ 72 C4
Flint I. ...... 65 L15
Flinton ...... 63 A4
Florence =
  Firenze ..... 20 C3
Florence, *Ala.,*
  *U.S.A.* .... 74 B4
Florence, *S.C.,*
  *U.S.A.* .... 75 B8
Florence, L. .. 62 A2
Flores ....... 39 F2

Flores Sea .... 39 F2
Floreşti ...... 17 E9
Floriano ..... 92 D5
Florianópolis .. 94 B7
Florida ....... 94 C5
Florida □ .... 75 F6
Florida, Straits
  of .......... 86 B3
Flórina ...... 23 D3
Florø ........ 8 F9
Fluk ......... 39 E3
Flushing =
  Vlissingen .. 14 C2
Fly → ...... 61 B7
Flying Fish, C. . 96 B1
Foça ........ 23 E6
Focşani ...... 17 F8
Fóggia ....... 20 D5
Föhr ......... 14 A5
Foix ......... 12 E4
Foligno ...... 20 C4
Folkestone ... 11 F7
Fond du Lac .. 77 D10
Fondi ........ 20 D4
Fonsagrada ... 18 A2
Fonseca, G. de 85 E7
Fontainebleau . 13 B5
Fonte Boa ... 90 D5
Fontenay-le-
  Comte ..... 12 C3
Foochow =
  Fuzhou .... 35 D6
Forbes ....... 63 B4
Ford's Bridge .. 63 A4
Forécariah .... 55 G2
Forestier Pen. . 62 D4
Forfar ....... 10 C5
Forlì ........ 20 B4
Formentera ... 19 C6
Formentor, C. de 19 C7
Former
  Yugoslav
  Republic of
  Macedonia =
  Macedonia ■ 22 D3
Fórmia ...... 20 D4
Formosa =
  Taiwan ■ .. 35 D7
Formosa ..... 94 B5
Formosa, Serra 93 E3
Formosa Bay .. 57 E8
Føroyar =
  Føroyar ..... 6 C4
Føroyar ...... 6 C4
Forrest ....... 62 C3
Forsayth ..... 61 D7
Forst ........ 15 C8
Forster ...... 63 B5
Fort Albany .. 69 C2
Fort Collins .. 76 E2
Fort-de-France . 87 D7
Fort de Possel =
  Possel ...... 56 C3
Fort Dodge ... 77 D7
Fort Franklin .. 70 B7
Fort Good-Hope 70 B7
Fort Hertz =
  Putao ..... 41 D11
Fort Lauderdale 75 F7
Fort Liard ... 70 B7
Fort Macleod .. 71 D8
Fort MacMahon 54 C5
Fort McPherson 70 B6
Fort Miribel .. 54 C5
Fort Myers ... 75 F7
Fort Norman . 70 B7
Fort Peck L. .. 81 B10
Fort Pierce ... 75 F7
Fort Portal ... 57 D6

Fort Providence 70 B8
Fort Resolution 70 B8
Fort Rosebery =
  Mansa ..... 57 G5
Fort Rupert =
  Waskaganish 69 C3
Fort Sandeman 42 D6
Fort Scott ..... 79 A6
Fort Severn ... 69 C2
Fort Shevchenko 29 E6
Fort Simpson . 70 B7
Fort Smith,
  *Canada* ..... 70 B8
Fort Smith,
  *U.S.A.* ...... 79 B6
Fort Trinquet =
  Bir Mogrein . 54 C2
Fort Walton
  Beach ..... 74 D4
Fort Wayne .. 72 D3
Fort William ... 10 C4
Fort Worth ... 78 C5
Fort Yukon ... 71 B5
Fortaleza ..... 92 C6
Forūr ........ 44 E3
Foshan ...... 35 D6
Fossano ..... 20 B1
Fougamou ... 56 E2
Fougères .... 12 B3
Foula ........ 10 A5
Foumban .... 55 G7
Foúrnoi ...... 23 F6
Fouta Djalon .. 55 F2
Foveaux Str. .. 65 G3
Foxe Basin ... 68 B3
Foxe Chan. ... 68 B2
Foxe Pen. .... 68 B3
Foxton ....... 64 D6
Foz do Gregório 91 E4
Foz do Iguaçu . 94 B6
Franca ....... 93 G4
Francavilla
  Fontana .... 21 D6
France ■ ... 13 C5
Frances ...... 62 C3
Franceville .... 56 E2
Franche-Comté 13 C6
Francistown .. 59 C5
Frankfurt,
  *Brandenburg,*
  *Germany* ... 15 B8
Frankfurt,
  *Hessen,*
  *Germany* ... 14 C5
Fränkische Alb 15 D6
Franklin B. ... 70 B7
Franklin I. .... 96 B15
Franklin Mts. .. 70 B7
Franklin Str. .. 70 A10
Frankston .... 63 C4
Frantsa Iosifa,
  Zemlya .... 28 A6
Franz ........ 69 D2
Franz Josef
  Land =
  Frantsa Iosifa,
  Zemlya ..... 28 A6
Fraser → .... 71 D7
Fraser I. ..... 63 A5
Fraserburgh .. 10 C5
Fray Bentos ... 94 C5
Fredericksburg 73 E7
Fredericton .. 69 D4
Fredrikstad .... 9 G10
Freeport,
  *Bahamas* ... 86 A4
Freeport, *U.S.A.* 77 D10
Freetown ... 55 G2
Fregenal de la
  Sierra ...... 18 C2

Freibourg =
Fribourg .... 13 C7
Freiburg ...... 14 E4
Freire ........ 95 D2
Freising ...... 15 D6
Freistadt ...... 15 D8
Fréjus ........ 13 E7
Fremont ...... 82 B2
French
Guiana ■ ... 92 B3
French
Polynesia ■ . 65 M16
Fresco → .... 92 D3
Freshfield, C. .. 96 A14
Fresnillo ...... 84 C4
Fresno ....... 82 B3
Freycinet Pen. . 62 D4
Fria, C. ....... 58 B2
Frías ......... 94 B3
Fribourg ...... 13 C7
Friedrichshafen 14 E5
Friendly Is. =
Tonga ■ .... 65 L13
Frobisher B. .. 68 B4
Frobisher Bay =
Iqaluit ...... 68 B4
Frome, L. ..... 62 B2
Frome Downs . 62 B2
Front Range ... 81 E11
Frosinone ..... 20 D4
Frunze =
Bishkek ..... 29 E8
Frutal ........ 93 F4
Frýdek-Místek . 16 D4
Fuchou =
Fuzhou ..... 35 D6
Fuengirola .... 18 D3
Fuentes de
Oñoro ...... 18 B2
Fuerte → .... 84 B3
Fuerte Olimpo . 91 H7
Fuerteventura . 54 C2
Fuhai ........ 34 B3
Fuji-San ...... 32 B6
Fujian □ ..... 35 D6
Fujinomiya .... 32 B6
Fujisawa ...... 32 B6
Fukien =
Fujian □ .... 35 D6
Fukuchiyama .. 32 B4
Fukui ........ 32 A5
Fukuoka ...... 32 C2
Fukushima .... 33 G12
Fukuyama .... 32 B3
Fulda ........ 14 C5
Fulda → ..... 14 C5
Fullerton ..... 82 D4
Funabashi .... 32 B7
Funchal ...... 54 B1
Fundación .... 90 A4
Fundão ...... 18 B2
Fundy, B. of .. 69 D4
Funtua ...... 55 F6
Furāt, Nahr
al → ...... 47 E6
Furneaux Group 62 D4
Fürstenwalde .. 15 B8
Fürth ........ 14 D6
Fury and Hecla
Str. ........ 68 B2
Fusagasuga ... 90 C4
Fushun ...... 35 B7
Futuna ....... 64 L12
Fuxin ........ 35 B7
Fuyuan ...... 35 B8
Fuzhou ...... 35 D6
Fyn .......... 9 G10

# G

Gabela ....... 56 G2
Gabès ....... 54 B7
Gabès, G. de .. 52 B1
Gabon ■ ..... 56 E2
Gaborone ..... 59 C5
Gabrovo ...... 22 C5
Gachsārān ... 44 D2
Gadag ....... 43 M9
Gadarwara ... 43 H11
Gadhada .... 43 J7
Gadsden ..... 74 B4
Gadwal ...... 43 L10
Gafsa ....... 54 B6
Gagnoa ...... 55 G3
Gagnon ...... 69 C4
Gaillimh =
Galway ..... 11 E2
Gainesville, Fla.,
U.S.A. ...... 75 E6
Gainesville, Ga.,
U.S.A. ...... 75 B6
Gainesville,
Tex., U.S.A. . 78 C5
Gairdner, L. ... 62 B2
Galangue ..... 58 A3
Galashiels .... 10 D5
Galați ........ 17 F9
Galatina ...... 21 D7
Galcaio ...... 49 F4
Galdhøpiggen . 8 F9
Galela ....... 39 D3
Galesburg .... 77 E9
Galich ....... 24 B5
Galicia □ ..... 18 A2
Galilee, Sea of
= Yam
Kinneret .... 46 D3
Gallabat ...... 53 F6
Gállego → .. 19 B5
Gallegos → .. 95 G3
Gallinas, Pta. .. 90 A4
Gallipoli =
Gelibolu .... 23 D6
Gallípoli ...... 21 D6
Gällivare ..... 8 E12
Galloway, Mull
of .......... 11 D4
Galong ....... 63 B4
Galveston .... 79 E6
Gálvez ....... 94 C4
Galway ...... 11 E2
Galway B. .... 11 E2
Gambaga .... 55 F4
Gambela ..... 53 G5
Gambia ■ .... 55 F1
Gambia → ... 55 F1
Gambier Is. .. 62 C2
Gamboma .... 56 E3
Gan Jiang → . 35 D6
Ganāveh ..... 44 D2
Gäncä ....... 25 E6
Gand = Gent .. 14 C2
Ganda ....... 58 A2
Gandak → ... 40 E5
Gandava ..... 42 E5
Gander ...... 69 D5
Gandhi Sagar . 43 G9
Gandi ....... 55 F6
Gandía ...... 19 C5
Ganedidalem =
Gani ....... 39 E3
Ganga → .... 41 F8
Ganganagar .. 42 E8
Gangara ..... 55 F6
Gangaw ..... 41 F10
Gangdisê Shan 40 B3

Ganges =
Ganga → .. 41 F8
Gangtok ...... 41 D7
Gani ......... 39 E3
Gansu □ ..... 34 C5
Ganta ....... 55 G3
Gantheaume, C. 62 C2
Gantsevichi =
Hantsavichy . 17 B8
Ganyem ...... 39 E6
Ganzhou ..... 35 D6
Gaoua ....... 55 F4
Gaoual ...... 55 F2
Gaoxiong .... 35 D7
Gap ......... 13 D7
Gar ......... 34 C2
Garabogazköl
Aylagy ..... 29 E6
Garanhuns ... 92 D6
Garawe ...... 55 H3
Gard ........ 49 F4
Garda, L. di ... 20 B3
Garden City .. 78 A3
Garden Grove . 82 D4
Gardēz ...... 42 C6
Gargano, Mte. . 20 D5
Garigliano → . 20 D4
Garland ...... 81 E7
Garm ....... 29 F8
Garmisch-
Partenkirchen 14 E6
Garmsār ..... 44 C3
Garoe ....... 49 F4
Garonne → .. 12 D3
Garoua ...... 53 G1
Garrison Res. =
Sakakawea, L. 76 B4
Garry, L. ..... 70 B9
Garsen ...... 57 E8
Garvie Mts. .. 65 F3
Garwa =
Garoua ..... 53 G1
Gary ........ 72 D2
Garzê ....... 34 C5
Garzón ...... 90 C3
Gasan Kuli =
Hasan Kuli .. 29 F6
Gascogne ... 12 E4
Gascogne, G. de 12 D2
Gascony =
Gascogne ... 12 E4
Gashaka ..... 55 G7
Gashua ...... 55 F1
Gaspé ....... 69 D4
Gaspé, C. de . 69 D4
Gaspé, Pén. de 69 D4
Gasteiz = Vitoria 19 A4
Gastonia ..... 75 B7
Gastre ....... 95 E3
Gata, C. de ... 19 D4
Gata, Sierra de 18 B2
Gateshead ... 11 D6
Gauhati ...... 41 D8
Gavāter ...... 45 E5
Gávdhos ..... 23 G5
Gawilgarh Hills 43 J10
Gawler ...... 62 B2
Gaxun Nur ... 34 B5
Gaya, India ... 40 E5
Gaya, Niger .. 55 F5
Gayndah .... 63 A5
Gaysin =
Haysyn ..... 17 D9
Gayvoron =
Hayvoron ... 17 D9
Gaza ........ 47 E3
Gaziantep ... 46 C4
Gazli ........ 29 E7
Gdańsk ...... 16 A4

Gdańska, Zatoka 16 A4
Gdov ........ 24 B2
Gdynia ...... 16 A4
Gebe ........ 39 D3
Gebeit Mine ... 52 D6
Gebze ....... 22 D7
Gedaref ..... 53 F6
Gede, Tanjung 37 F3
Gediz → ..... 23 E6
Gedser ...... 9 H10
Geelong ..... 63 C3
Geesthacht ... 14 B6
Geidam ...... 53 F1
Geili ........ 53 E5
Geita ........ 57 E6
Gejiu ........ 34 D5
Gela ......... 21 F5
Geladi ....... 49 F4
Gelehun ..... 55 G2
Gelibolu ..... 23 D6
Gelsenkirchen . 14 C4
Gemas ....... 37 D2
Gemena ..... 56 D3
Gemerek ..... 46 C4
Gemlik ...... 23 D7
General Acha . 94 D4
General Alvear,
Buenos Aires,
Argentina ... 94 D5
General Alvear,
Mendoza,
Argentina ... 94 D3
General Artigas 94 B5
General
Belgrano .. 94 D5
General Guido . 94 D5
General Juan
Madariaga . 94 D5
General La
Madrid ..... 94 D4
General
MacArthur .. 38 B3
General Martin
Miguel de
Güemes ... 94 A4
General Paz ... 94 B5
General Pico .. 94 D4
General Pinedo 94 B4
General Santos 38 C3
General Villegas 94 D4
Geneva =
Genève ..... 13 C7
Geneva, L. =
Léman, L. ... 13 C7
Genève ...... 13 C7
Genil → ..... 18 D3
Gennargentu,
Mti. del ..... 21 D2
Genoa =
Génova ..... 20 B2
Genoa ....... 63 C4
Génova ...... 20 B2
Génova, G. di . 20 C2
Gent ........ 14 C2
Georga, Zemlya 28 A5
George ...... 58 E4
George → .... 68 C4
George, L.,
N.S.W.,
Australia .... 63 C4
George, L.,
S. Austral.,
Australia .... 62 C3
George, L.,
Uganda ..... 57 D6
George River =
Kangiqsualujjuaq
............ 68 C4
George Sound . 65 F2

| Name | Page | Grid |
|---|---|---|
| George Town | 36 | C2 |
| George V Land | 96 | A14 |
| George VI Sound | 96 | B3 |
| Georgetown, *Gambia* | 55 | F2 |
| Georgetown, *Guyana* | 90 | B7 |
| Georgia □ | 75 | C6 |
| Georgia ■ | 25 | E5 |
| Georgian B. | 69 | D2 |
| Georgiu-Dezh = Liski | 24 | C4 |
| Georgiyevsk | 25 | E5 |
| Gera | 15 | C7 |
| Geral de Goiás, Serra | 93 | E4 |
| Geraldton | 60 | F1 |
| Gerede | 46 | B3 |
| Gereshk | 42 | D4 |
| Gerlogubi | 49 | F4 |
| Germany ■ | 14 | C6 |
| Germiston | 59 | D5 |
| Gerona | 19 | B7 |
| Geser | 39 | E4 |
| Getafe | 18 | B4 |
| Gettysburg | 73 | E7 |
| Getz Ice Shelf | 96 | B18 |
| Ghaghara → | 40 | E5 |
| Ghana ■ | 55 | G4 |
| Ghanzi | 58 | C4 |
| Ghardaïa | 54 | B5 |
| Gharyān | 52 | B1 |
| Ghat | 54 | D7 |
| Ghawdex = Gozo | 21 | F5 |
| Ghayl | 47 | G6 |
| Ghazal, Bahr el →, *Chad* | 53 | F2 |
| Ghazâl, Bahr el →, *Sudan* | 57 | C6 |
| Ghazaouet | 54 | A4 |
| Ghaziabad | 42 | E10 |
| Ghazipur | 40 | E4 |
| Ghaznī | 42 | C6 |
| Ghaznī □ | 42 | C6 |
| Ghèlinsor | 49 | F4 |
| Ghent = Gent | 14 | C2 |
| Ghizao | 42 | C4 |
| Ghowr □ | 42 | C4 |
| Ghugus | 43 | K11 |
| Ghūriān | 42 | B2 |
| Gia Lai = Pleiku | 36 | B3 |
| Gian | 38 | C3 |
| Giarabub = Al Jaghbūb | 52 | C3 |
| Giarre | 21 | F5 |
| Gibraltar ■ | 18 | D3 |
| Gibraltar, Str. of | 18 | E3 |
| Gibson Desert | 60 | E4 |
| Gidole | 53 | G6 |
| Giessen | 14 | C5 |
| Gifu | 32 | B5 |
| Giglio | 20 | C3 |
| Gijón | 18 | A3 |
| Gila → | 82 | D5 |
| Gīlān □ | 46 | C7 |
| Gilbert Is. | 64 | J12 |
| Gilgandra | 63 | B4 |
| Gilgit | 42 | B9 |
| Gilles, L. | 62 | B2 |
| Gilmore | 63 | C4 |
| Gimbi | 53 | G6 |
| Gin Gin | 63 | A5 |
| Ginir | 49 | F3 |
| Giohar | 49 | G4 |
| Gióna, Óros | 23 | E4 |
| Girardot | 90 | C4 |
| Giresun | 46 | B4 |
| Girga | 52 | C5 |
| Giridih | 40 | E6 |
| Girilambone | 63 | B4 |
| Girne = Kyrenia | 46 | D3 |
| Girona = Gerona | 19 | B7 |
| Gironde → | 12 | D3 |
| Girvan | 10 | D4 |
| Gisborne | 64 | C8 |
| Gisenyi | 57 | E5 |
| Gitega | 57 | E5 |
| Giuba → | 49 | G3 |
| Giurgiu | 22 | C5 |
| Giza = El Gîza | 52 | C5 |
| Giżycko | 16 | A5 |
| Gjirokastra | 23 | D3 |
| Gjoa Haven | 70 | B10 |
| Glace Bay | 69 | D5 |
| Gladstone, *Queens., Australia* | 61 | E9 |
| Gladstone, *S. Austral., Australia* | 62 | B2 |
| Glåma = Glomma → | 9 | G10 |
| Glasgow | 10 | D4 |
| Glazov | 28 | D6 |
| Gleiwitz = Gliwice | 16 | C4 |
| Glen Canyon National Recreation Area | 83 | B7 |
| Glen Innes | 63 | A5 |
| Glendale | 82 | C3 |
| Glenelg | 62 | B2 |
| Glenelg → | 62 | C3 |
| Glenmorgan | 63 | A4 |
| Glenorchy | 62 | D4 |
| Glenreagh | 63 | B5 |
| Glenrothes | 10 | C5 |
| Glens Falls | 73 | C9 |
| Gliwice | 16 | C4 |
| Głogów | 16 | C3 |
| Glomma → | 9 | G10 |
| Glorieuses, Is. | 59 | G9 |
| Gloucester, *Australia* | 63 | B5 |
| Gloucester, *U.K.* | 11 | F5 |
| Glusk | 17 | B9 |
| Gmünd | 15 | D8 |
| Gmunden | 15 | E7 |
| Gniezno | 16 | B3 |
| Go Cong | 36 | B3 |
| Goa | 43 | M8 |
| Goa □ | 43 | M8 |
| Goalen Hd. | 63 | C5 |
| Goalpara | 41 | D8 |
| Goba, *Ethiopia* | 49 | F2 |
| Goba, *Mozam.* | 59 | D6 |
| Gobabis | 58 | C3 |
| Gobi | 35 | B6 |
| Gochas | 58 | C3 |
| Godavari → | 40 | J4 |
| Godavari Point | 40 | J4 |
| Gods → | 71 | C10 |
| Gods L. | 71 | C10 |
| Godthåb | 68 | B5 |
| Godwin Austen = K2 | 42 | B10 |
| Goeie Hoop, Kaap die = Good Hope, C. of | 58 | E3 |
| Gogra = Ghaghara → | 40 | E5 |
| Goiânia | 93 | F4 |
| Goiás | 93 | F3 |
| Goiás □ | 93 | E4 |
| Goio-Ere | 94 | A6 |
| Gojra | 42 | D8 |
| Gökçeada | 23 | D5 |
| Gokteik | 41 | F11 |
| Gold Coast | 63 | A5 |
| Golden Gate | 80 | G2 |
| Goldsboro | 75 | B9 |
| Gołeniów | 16 | B2 |
| Golfo Aranci | 20 | D2 |
| Golspie | 10 | C5 |
| Goma | 57 | E5 |
| Gomel = Homyel | 17 | B10 |
| Gomera | 54 | C1 |
| Gómez Palacio | 84 | B4 |
| Gomogomo | 39 | F4 |
| Gomoh | 40 | F6 |
| Gompa = Ganta | 55 | G3 |
| Gonābād | 44 | C4 |
| Gonaïves | 87 | C5 |
| Gonbab-e Kāvūs | 44 | B3 |
| Gonda | 40 | D3 |
| Gonder | 53 | F6 |
| Gönen | 23 | D6 |
| Gonghe | 34 | C5 |
| Gongolgon | 63 | B4 |
| Goniri | 53 | F1 |
| Good Hope, C. of | 58 | E3 |
| Goodooga | 63 | A4 |
| Goolgowi | 63 | B4 |
| Goombalie | 63 | A4 |
| Goondiwindi | 63 | A5 |
| Gooray | 63 | A5 |
| Gop | 43 | H6 |
| Göppingen | 14 | D5 |
| Gorakhpur | 40 | D4 |
| Goražde | 20 | C7 |
| Gordon → | 62 | D4 |
| Gore, *Australia* | 63 | A5 |
| Goré, *Chad* | 53 | G2 |
| Gore, *Ethiopia* | 53 | G6 |
| Gore, *N.Z.* | 65 | G3 |
| Gorgān | 44 | B3 |
| Gorgona, I. | 90 | C3 |
| Gorízia | 20 | B4 |
| Gorki = Nizhniy Novgorod | 24 | B5 |
| Gorkiy = Nizhniy Novgorod | 24 | B5 |
| Gorkovskoye Vdkhr. | 24 | B5 |
| Görlitz | 15 | C8 |
| Gorlovka = Horlivka | 25 | D4 |
| Gorna Dzhumayo = Blagoevgrad | 22 | C4 |
| Gorna Oryakhovitsa | 22 | C5 |
| Gorno-Altay □ | 29 | D9 |
| Gorno-Altaysk | 29 | D9 |
| Gorno Slinkino = Gornopravdinsk | 29 | C8 |
| Gornopravdinsk | 29 | C8 |
| Gorodenka = Horodenka | 17 | D7 |
| Gorodok = Horodok | 17 | D6 |
| Gorokhov = Horokhiv | 17 | C7 |
| Gorontalo | 39 | D2 |
| Gorzów Wielkopolski | 16 | B2 |
| Gosford | 63 | B5 |
| Goslar | 14 | C6 |
| Gospič | 20 | B5 |
| Göta kanal | 9 | G11 |
| Göteborg | 9 | G10 |
| Gotha | 14 | C6 |
| Gothenburg = Göteborg | 9 | G10 |
| Gotland | 9 | G11 |
| Göttingen | 14 | C5 |
| Gottwaldov = Zlin | 16 | D3 |
| Gouda | 14 | B3 |
| Gouin, Rés. | 69 | D3 |
| Goulburn | 63 | B4 |
| Gounou-Gaya | 53 | G2 |
| Gouri | 53 | E2 |
| Gourma Rharous | 55 | E4 |
| Gourock Ra. | 63 | C4 |
| Governador Valadares | 93 | F5 |
| Gowd-e Zirreh | 42 | E3 |
| Goya | 94 | B5 |
| Goyder Lagoon | 62 | A2 |
| Goyllarisquisga | 91 | F3 |
| Goz Beîda | 53 | F3 |
| Gozo | 21 | F5 |
| Graaff-Reinet | 58 | E4 |
| Gračac | 20 | B5 |
| Gracias a Dios, C. | 86 | D3 |
| Grado | 18 | A2 |
| Gradule | 63 | A4 |
| Grafton | 63 | A5 |
| Graham Bell, Os. | 28 | A7 |
| Graham Land | 96 | A3 |
| Grahamstown | 59 | E5 |
| Grajaú | 92 | D4 |
| Grajaú → | 92 | C5 |
| Grampian Highlands = Grampian Mts. | 10 | C4 |
| Grampian Mts. | 10 | C4 |
| Gran Canaria | 54 | C1 |
| Gran Chaco | 94 | B4 |
| Gran Paradiso | 20 | B1 |
| Gran Sasso d'Italia | 20 | C4 |
| Granada, *Nic.* | 85 | E7 |
| Granada, *Spain* | 18 | D4 |
| Granby | 69 | D3 |
| Grand Bahama | 86 | A4 |
| Grand Bassam | 55 | G4 |
| Grand Canyon | 83 | B6 |
| Grand Cayman | 86 | C3 |
| Grand Coulee Dam | 80 | B4 |
| Grand Forks, *Canada* | 71 | D8 |
| Grand Forks, *U.S.A.* | 76 | B6 |
| Grand Island | 76 | E5 |
| Grand Lahou | 55 | G3 |
| Grand Rapids, *Canada* | 71 | C10 |
| Grand Rapids, *U.S.A.* | 72 | C3 |
| Grand St.-Bernard, Col du | 13 | D7 |
| Grand Teton | 81 | D8 |
| Grande →, *Argentina* | 94 | A3 |
| Grande →, *Bolivia* | 91 | G6 |
| Grande →, *Bahia, Brazil* | 93 | E5 |

Grande →,
Minas Gerais,
Brazil ...... 93 G3
Grande, B. .... 95 G3
Grande, Rio → . 79 F5
Grande Baleine,
R. de la → . . 69 C3
Grande de
Santiago → . 84 C3
Granite City ... 77 F9
Granity ....... 65 D4
Granja ....... 92 C5
Granollers .... 19 B7
Grantham .... 11 E6
Granville .... 12 B3
Gras, L. de .. 70 B8
Grasse ....... 13 E7
Grassmere ... 62 B3
Graulhet .... 12 E4
's-Gravenhage . 14 B3
Gravesend ... 63 A5
Graz ....... 15 E8
Great Abaco I. . 86 A4
Great Australian
Bight ...... 60 G4
Great Barrier I. 64 B6
Great Barrier
Reef ....... 61 D8
Great Basin ... 80 F5
Great Bear → . 70 B7
Great Bear L. . 70 B7
Great Belt =
Store Bælt .. 9 G10
Great Dividing
Ra. ....... 61 E8
Great Falls .... 81 B8
Great Inagua I. 86 B5
Great Indian
Desert = Thar
Desert .... 42 F7
Great Karoo ... 58 E4
Great Lake .... 62 D4
Great Ouse → 11 E7
Great Ruaha → 57 F7
Great Saint
Bernard P. =
Grand St.-
Bernard, Col
du ....... 13 D7
Great Salt L. .. 81 E7
Great Salt Lake
Desert ...... 81 E7
Great Sandy
Desert .... 60 E3
Great Sangi =
Sangihe, P. .. 39 D3
Great Slave L. . 70 B8
Great Smoky
Mts. Nat. Pk. 75 B6
Great Victoria
Desert ...... 60 F4
Great Wall ... 35 C5
Great Yarmouth 11 E7
Greater Antilles 86 C5
Greater Sunda
Is. ......... 37 F4
Gredos, Sierra
de ....... 18 B3
Greece ■ ..... 23 E4
Greeley ...... 76 E2
Green → .... 83 A8
Green Bay .... 72 B2
Green C. ...... 63 C5
Greenland ■ .. 66 C9
Greenock .... 10 D4
Greensboro ... 75 A8
Greenville,
Liberia .... 55 G3
Greenville, Ala.,
U.S.A. ...... 74 D4

Greenville,
Miss., U.S.A. 79 C8
Greenville, N.C.,
U.S.A. ...... 75 B9
Greenville, S.C.,
U.S.A. ...... 75 B6
Greenwood,
Miss., U.S.A. 79 C8
Greenwood,
S.C., U.S.A. . 75 B6
Gregory, L. ... 62 A2
Greifswald .... 15 A7
Greiz ....... 15 C7
Gremikha ..... 28 C4
Grenada ■ .. 87 D7
Grenfell .... 63 B4
Grenoble ..... 13 D6
Grey → ..... 65 E4
Grey Ra. .... 63 A3
Greymouth ... 65 E4
Greytown, N.Z. 65 D6
Greytown,
S. Africa .... 59 D6
Griffin ....... 75 C5
Griffith ....... 63 B4
Grimari ..... 56 C4
Grimaylov =
Hrymayliv ... 17 D8
Grimsby .... 11 E6
Gris-Nez, C. ... 12 A4
Grodno =
Hrodna ..... 17 B6
Grodzyanka =
Hrodzyanka . 17 B9
Grójec ....... 16 C5
Groningen .... 14 B4
Grootfontein .. 58 B3
Gross Glockner 15 E7
Grosser Arber . 15 D7
Grosseto ..... 20 C3
Groznyy ..... 25 E6
Grudziądz .... 16 B4
Gryazi ........ 24 C4
Gryazovets .... 28 D5
Gua ....... 40 F5
Guadalajara,
Mexico ..... 84 C4
Guadalajara,
Spain ...... 18 B4
Guadalcanal . 64 K11
Guadalete → . 18 D2
Guadalquivir → 18 D2
Guadalupe =
Guadalupe ■ 87 C7
Guadalupe,
Sierra de ... 18 C3
Guadarrama,
Sierra de .. 18 B4
Guadeloupe ■ . 87 C7
Guadiana → .. 18 D2
Guadix .... 18 D4
Guafo, Boca del 95 E2
Guaíra ..... 94 A6
Guaitecas, Is. .. 95 E2
Guajará-Mirim . 91 F5
Guajira, Pen. de
la ........ 90 A4
Gualeguay .... 94 C5
Gualeguaychú . 94 C5
Guam ■ .... 64 H9
Guamúchil ... 84 B3
Guan Xian .... 34 C5
Guanahani =
San Salvador 86 B5
Guanajuato ... 84 C4
Guanacol .... 94 B3
Guane ...... 86 B3
Guangdong □ . 35 D6
Guanghua .... 35 C6

Guangxi
Zhuangzu
Zizhiqu □ ... 35 D5
Guangzhou ... 35 D6
Guanipa → ... 90 B6
Guantánamo .. 86 B4
Guaporé → .. 91 F5
Guaqui ...... 91 G5
Guarapuava ... 94 B6
Guarda ....... 18 B2
Guardafui, C. =
Asir, Ras ... 49 E5
Guasdualito .. 90 B4
Guasipati .... 90 B6
Guatemala ... 85 E6
Guatemala ■ .. 85 D6
Guatire ....... 90 A5
Guaviare □ ... 90 C4
Guaviare → .. 90 C5
Guaxupé ..... 93 G4
Guayama .... 87 C6
Guayaquil .... 90 D3
Guayaquil, G. de 90 D2
Guaymas ..... 84 B2
Guddu Barrage 42 E3
Gudivada .... 40 J3
Gudur ....... 43 M11
Guecho ..... 19 A4
Guékédou ... 55 G2
Guelma .... 54 A6
Guelph ...... 69 D2
Guéréda .... 53 F3
Guéret ...... 12 C4
Guernica ..... 19 A4
Guernsey .... 11 G5
Guidónia-
Montecélio .. 20 C4
Guiglo ..... 55 G3
Guildford .... 11 F6
Guilin ....... 35 D6
Guimarães,
Brazil .... 92 C5
Guimarães,
Portugal .... 18 B1
Guimaras ..... 38 B2
Guinea ■ ..... 55 F2
Guinea, Gulf of 51 F3
Guinea-Bissau ■ 55 F1
Guingamp ... 12 B2
Guiping .... 35 D6
Güiria ........ 90 A6
Guiuan ....... 38 B3
Guiyang .... 35 D5
Guizhou □ ... 35 D5
Gujarat □ .... 43 H7
Gujranwala .. 42 C9
Gujrat ..... 42 C9
Gulbarga ... 43 L10
Gulf, The ..... 44 E2
Gulgong .... 63 B4
Güllük ....... 23 F6
Gulshad ... 29 E8
Gulu ....... 57 D6
Gum Lake ... 62 B3
Gummi ..... 55 F6
Gümüşhane .. 46 B4
Gumzai ..... 39 F4
Guna ....... 43 G10
Gundagai ... 63 C4
Gundih .... 37 F4
Gungu ..... 56 F3
Gunnedah ... 63 B5
Gunningbar
Cr. ...... 63 B4
Guntakal ... 43 M10
Guntur ...... 40 J3
Gununga pi .. 39 F3
Gunungsitoli .. 37 D1
Gunza ..... 56 G2
Gupis ........ 42 A8

Gürchän ...... 46 D7
Gurdaspur .... 42 C9
Gurgaon ...... 42 E10
Gurkha .... 40 C5
Gurley ...... 63 A4
Gurupá ..... 92 C3
Gurupá, I.
Grande de . 92 C3
Gurupi → ... 92 C4
Guryev =
Atyraū ...... 29 E6
Gusau ...... 55 F6
Güstrow ..... 15 B7
Gütersloh ..... 14 C5
Guthrie ...... 78 B5
Guyana ■ .... 90 B7
Guyane
française ■ =
French
Guiana ■ ... 92 B3
Guyenne .... 12 D4
Guyra ...... 63 B5
Gwa ....... 41 J10
Gwaai ...... 59 B5
Gwabegar ... 63 B4
Gwädar .... 42 G3
Gwalior .... 42 F11
Gwanda .... 59 C5
Gweru ...... 59 B5
Gwydir → .... 63 A4
Gyandzha =
Gäncä .... 25 E6
Gyaring Hu ... 34 C4
Gydanskiy P-ov. 28 B8
Gympie ..... 63 A5
Gyöngyös .... 16 E4
Györ ....... 16 E3
Gypsumville .. 71 C10
Gyula ....... 16 E5
Gyumri ....... 25 E5
Gyzylarbat .... 29 F6

# H

Ha 'Arava → . 47 E3
Haarlem ...... 14 B3
Haast → ..... 65 E3
Habaswein .. 57 D7
Hachinohe .... 33 F12
Hadarba, Ras .. 52 D6
Hadd, R'as al .. 45 F4
Hadejia ...... 55 F7
Haden ....... 63 A5
Hadera ..... 46 D3
Hadhramaut =
Ḥaḍramawt .. 49 D4
Ḥaḍramawt ... 49 D4
Haeju ...... 35 C7
Haerhpin =
Harbin ..... 35 B7
Hafar al Bāṭin . 47 E6
Hafizabad ... 42 C8
Haflong ..... 41 E9
Haft Gel .... 47 E7
Hafun, Ras ... 49 E5
Hagen ....... 14 C4
Hagerstown .. 73 E7
Hagi ....... 32 B2
Hagondange-
Briey ...... 13 B7
Hague, C. de la 12 B3
Hague, The = 's-
Gravenhage . 14 B3
Haguenau .... 13 B7
Hai'an ........ 35 C7
Haifa = Ḥefa .. 46 D3

Haikou ....... 35 D6
Ḥāʾil ......... 47 F5
Hailar ....... 35 B6
Haileybury .... 69 D3
Hailun ....... 35 B7
Hainan □ ..... 35 E5
Haiphong .... 35 D5
Haiti ■ ....... 87 C5
Haiya Junction 53 E6
Hajar Bangar .. 53 F3
Hajdúböszörmény
.......... 16 E5
Hajnówka .... 17 B6
Hakken-Zan ... 32 B4
Hakodate ..... 32 F12
Hala ........ 42 G6
Ḥalab ........ 46 C4
Ḥalabjah ...... 46 D6
Halaib ....... 52 D6
Halberstadt ... 15 C6
Halcombe .... 64 D6
Halcon, Mt. ... 38 B2
Halden ....... 9 G10
Haldia ....... 40 F7
Haldwani ..... 42 E11
Halifax, Canada 69 D4
Halifax, U.K. .. 11 E6
Halīl ⇢ ...... 44 E4
Hall Beach .... 68 B2
Halle ........ 15 C6
Hallett ....... 62 B2
Halmahera ... 39 D3
Halmstad ..... 9 G10
Halq el Oued .. 52 A1
Hälsingborg =
Helsingborg . 9 G10
Halul ........ 44 E3
Hamada ...... 32 B3
Hamadān .... 46 D7
Hamadān □ ... 46 D7
Hamāh ...... 46 D4
Hamamatsu .. 32 B5
Hamar ...... 8 F10
Hamburg .... 14 B5
Hameln ..... 14 B5
Hamersley Ra. . 60 E2
Hamhung ..... 35 C7
Hami ....... 34 B4
Hamilton,
Australia .... 62 C3
Hamilton,
Canada ..... 69 D3
Hamilton, N.Z. 64 B6
Hamilton, U.K. . 10 D4
Hamley Bridge 62 B2
Hamlin =
Hameln ..... 14 B5
Hamm ...... 14 C4
Hammerfest ... 8 D12
Hammond .... 72 D2
Hampden .... 65 F4
Hampton ..... 73 F7
Hamrat esh
Sheykh ..... 53 F4
Han Pijesak ... 20 B7
Hanamaki .... 33 G12
Hanau ...... 14 C5
Hancock ...... 77 C7
Handa ....... 49 E5
Handan ..... 35 C6
Handeni ...... 57 F7
Hangayn Nuruu 34 B4
Hangchou =
Hangzhou ... 35 C7
Hangu ...... 35 C6
Hangzhou .... 35 C7
Hangzhou Wan 35 C7
Ḥanīsh ...... 49 E3
Hanle ....... 42 C11

Hanmer Springs 65 E5
Hanna ........ 71 C8
Hannibal ..... 77 F9
Hannover ..... 14 B5
Hanoi ........ 35 D5
Hanover =
Hannover ... 14 B5
Hanover, I. .... 95 G2
Hansi ........ 42 E9
Hanson, L. .... 62 B2
Hantsavichy ... 17 B8
Hanzhong .... 35 C5
Haora ........ 40 F7
Haparanda .... 8 E12
Happy Valley-
Goose Bay .. 69 C4
Hapur ........ 42 E10
Ḥaql ......... 47 E3
Har .......... 39 F4
Har Hu ....... 34 C4
Har Us Nuur .. 34 B4
Ḥaraḍ ....... 47 F7
Haraisan Plateau
= Hurayṣān . 47 G6
Harardera .... 49 G4
Harare ....... 59 B6
Harazé ....... 53 F2
Harbin ....... 35 B7
Harbour Grace 69 D5
Hardangerfjorden
.......... 8 F9
Hardap Dam .. 58 C3
Hardwar =
Haridwar ... 42 E11
Hardy, Pen. ... 95 H3
Harer ........ 49 F3
Hargeisa ..... 49 F3
Hari ⇢ ....... 37 E2
Haridwar ..... 42 E11
Haringhata ⇢ 41 G7
Harīrūd ..... 45 C5
Harīrūd ⇢ .... 42 A2
Harlingen ..... 78 F5
Harlow ....... 11 F7
Harney Basin . 80 D4
Härnösand .... 8 F11
Harrat al
ʿUwairidh ... 47 F4
Harris ........ 10 C3
Harris L. ..... 62 B2
Harrisburg .... 73 D7
Harrison, C. ... 68 C5
Harrison Bay .. 71 A4
Harrogate ..... 11 D6
Hart, L. ...... 62 B2
Hartford ...... 73 D9
Hartlepool .... 11 D6
Harvey ....... 72 D2
Harwich ...... 11 F7
Haryana □ ... 42 E10
Haryn ⇢ ..... 17 B8
Harz ......... 14 C6
Hasa ......... 47 F7
Hasan Kuli .... 29 F6
Hassi Inifel .... 54 C5
Hassi Messaoud 54 B6
Hastings, N.Z. . 64 C7
Hastings, U.K. . 11 F7
Hastings, U.S.A. 76 E5
Hastings Ra. .. 63 B5
Hatay = Antalya 46 C2
Hatfield P.O. .. 62 B3
Hatgal ....... 34 A5
Hathras ...... 42 F11
Hatia ........ 41 F8
Hattah ....... 62 B3
Hatteras, C. ... 75 B10
Hattiesburg ... 79 D9

Hatvan ....... 16 E4
Hau Bon = Cheo
Reo ....... 36 B3
Haugesund ... 9 G9
Hauraki G. .... 64 B6
Haut Atlas .... 54 B3
Hautah, Wāḥat
al .......... 47 G6
Hauts Plateaux 54 B4
Havana = La
Habana ..... 86 B3
Havant ....... 11 F6
Havel ⇢ ...... 15 B7
Havelock ..... 65 D5
Haverfordwest . 11 F4
Havre ........ 81 A9
Havza ........ 46 B3
Hawaii □ ..... 82 J12
Hawaiian Is. ... 82 H12
Hawea, L. ..... 65 F3
Hawera ....... 64 C6
Hawick ....... 10 D5
Hawke B. ..... 64 C7
Hawker ....... 62 B2
Hawkwood .... 63 A5
Hay .......... 63 B3
Hay River ..... 70 B8
Haya ......... 39 E3
Hayes ⇢ ..... 71 C10
Hayrabolu .... 22 D6
Haysyn ....... 17 D9
Hayvoron ..... 17 D9
Hazaribag .... 40 F5
Healesville .... 63 C4
Hearst ....... 69 D2
Hebei □ ...... 35 C6
Hebel ........ 63 A4
Hebron = Al
Khalīl ...... 47 E3
Hebron ....... 68 C4
Hechi ........ 35 D5
Hechuan ..... 35 C5
Heerlen ...... 13 A6
Ḥefa ......... 46 D3
Hefei ........ 35 C6
Hegang ....... 35 B8
Heidelberg ... 14 D5
Heilbron ...... 59 D5
Heilbronn ..... 14 D5
Heilongjiang □ 35 B7
Heilunkiang =
Heilongjiang □
.......... 35 B7
Heinze Is. ..... 41 K11
Hejaz = Al Ḥijāz 47 F4
Hekimhan ..... 46 C4
Hekou ........ 34 D5
Helena, Ark.,
U.S.A. ..... 79 B8
Helena, Mont.,
U.S.A. ..... 81 B7
Helensville .... 64 B6
Helgoland ..... 14 A4
Heligoland =
Helgoland ... 14 A4
Heligoland B. =
Deutsche
Bucht ...... 14 A5
Hellín ........ 19 C5
Helmand □ ... 42 D3
Helmand ⇢ .. 42 D2
Helmand,
Hamun ..... 45 D5
Helmsdale .... 10 B5
Helsingborg ... 9 G10
Helsingfors =
Helsinki ..... 9 F13
Helsinki ...... 9 F13

Helwân ....... 52 C5
Hemel
Hempstead .. 11 F6
Henan □ ..... 35 C6
Henares ⇢ ... 18 B4
Henderson .... 75 A8
Hendon ...... 63 A5
Hengyang .... 35 D6
Henrietta Maria,
C. .......... 69 C2
Hentiyn Nuruu 35 B5
Henty ........ 63 C4
Henzada ..... 41 J10
Herāt ........ 42 B3
Herāt □ ...... 42 B3
Hercegnovi ... 22 C2
Hereford ..... 11 E5
Herford ...... 14 B5
Hermidale .... 63 B4
Hermitage .... 65 E4
Hermite, I. .... 95 H3
Hermon, Mt. =
Ash Shaykh,
J. .......... 46 D3
Hermosillo .... 84 B2
Hernád ⇢ ... 16 E5
Hernandarias .. 94 B6
Heroica Nogales
= Nogales .. 84 A2
Heron Bay .... 69 D2
Herrick ....... 62 D4
ʼs-
Hertogenbosch
.......... 14 C3
Hesse =
Hessen □ ... 14 C5
Hessen □ .... 14 C5
Hewett, C. .... 68 A4
Hexham ..... 11 D5
Heyfield ...... 63 C4
Heywood ..... 62 C3
Hibbing ...... 77 B8
Hibbs B. ..... 62 D4
Hickory ...... 75 B7
Hicks, Pt. .... 63 C4
Hida-Sammyaku 32 A5
Hidalgo del
Parral ..... 84 B3
Higashiōsaka .. 32 B4
High Atlas =
Haut Atlas .. 54 B3
High Point .... 75 B8
High River .... 71 C8
High Tatra =
Tatry ...... 16 D4
High Wycombe 11 F6
Hiiumaa ...... 24 B1
Ḥijārah, Ṣaḥrā'
al .......... 47 E6
Ḥijāz □ ...... 48 C2
Hijo = Tagum . 38 C3
Hikone ....... 32 B5
Hikurangi ..... 64 A6
Hikurangi, Mt. . 64 C7
Hildesheim .. 14 B5
Hillston ...... 63 B4
Hilo ......... 82 J13
Hilversum .... 14 B3
Himachal
Pradesh □ .. 42 D10
Himalaya .... 40 C5
Himatnagar .. 43 H8
Himeji ....... 32 B4
Himi ......... 32 A5
Ḥimṣ ........ 46 D4
Hindmarsh, L. . 62 C3
Hindu Kush .. 42 B7
Hindubagh .. 42 D5
Hindupur .... 43 N10

Hinganghat ... 43 J11
Hingoli ...... 43 K10
Hinna = Imi .. 49 F3
Hinojosa del
  Duque ...... 18 C3
Hirakud Dam .. 40 G4
Hiratsuka ..... 32 B6
Hirosaki ...... 33 F12
Hiroshima .. 32 B3
Hisar ......... 42 E9
Hispaniola .... 87 C5
Hita ......... 32 C2
Hitachi ....... 32 A7
Hjälmaren .... 9 G11
Hlyboka ...... 17 D7
Ho ......... 55 G5
Ho Chi Minh
  City = Phanh
  Bho Ho Chi
  Minh ....... 36 B3
Hoai Nhon ... 36 B3
Hoare B. ...... 68 B4
Hobart ....... 62 D4
Hobbs Coast .. 96 B18
Hodgson ... 71 C10
Hódmezővásárhely
  .......... 16 E5
Hodna, Chott el 54 A5
Hodonín ..... 16 D3
Hoek van
  Holland ..... 14 B3
Hof ......... 15 C6
Höfu ......... 32 B2
Hogan Group . 62 C4
Hoggar =
  Ahaggar .... 54 D6
Hoh Xil Shan . 34 C3
Hohe Rhön ... 14 C5
Hohhot ....... 35 B6
Hoi An ....... 36 A3
Hokianga
  Harbour .... 64 A5
Hokitika ...... 65 E4
Hokkaidō □ .. 32 F12
Holbrook .... 63 C4
Holguín ..... 86 B4
Hollandia =
  Jayapura ... 39 E6
Holman Island . 70 A8
Holy Cross .... 71 B4
Holyhead .... 11 E4
Homalin ..... 41 E10
Hombori ..... 55 E4
Home B. ..... 68 B4
Homer ....... 71 C4
Homs = Ḥimş . 46 D4
Homyel ...... 17 B10
Hon Chong .. 36 B2
Honan =
  Henan □ .... 35 C6
Honda ....... 90 B4
Hondeklipbaai . 58 E3
Honduras ■ .. 85 E7
Honduras, G. de 85 D7
Honfleur ..... 12 B4
Hong Kong ■ .. 35 D6
Hongjiang ... 35 D5
Hongshui He → 35 D5
Hongze Hu ... 35 C6
Honiara ..... 64 K10
Honolulu .... 82 H12
Honshū ..... 32 G11
Hood, Mt. ... 80 C3
Hooghly → =
  Hughli → .. 40 G7
Hook of Holland
  = Hoek van
  Holland ..... 14 B3
Hoorn ....... 14 B3

Hoover Dam .. 82 B5
Hope, L. ...... 62 A2
Hope, Pt. ..... 71 B3
Hopedale ..... 68 C4
Hopei =
  Hebei □ .... 35 C6
Hopetoun ..... 62 C3
Hopetown .... 58 D4
Hoquiam .... 80 B2
Horlick Mts. .. 96 C1
Horlivka ...... 25 D4
Hormoz ..... 44 E3
Hormoz, Jaz. ye 44 E4
Hormozgān □ . 44 E3
Hormuz, Str. of 44 E4
Horn ......... 15 D8
Horn, Cape =
  Hornos, C. de 95 H3
Hornavan ..... 8 E11
Hornos, C. de . 95 H3
Hornsby ...... 63 B5
Horodenka .... 17 D7
Horodok,
  Khmelnytskyy,
  Ukraine ..... 17 D8
Horodok, Lviv,
  Ukraine ..... 17 D6
Horokhiv ..... 17 C7
Horqin Youyi
  Qianqi ...... 35 B7
Horqueta ..... 94 A5
Horsham ..... 62 C3
Horton → .... 70 B7
Hose, Gunung-
  Gunung ... 37 D4
Hoshangabad . 43 H10
Hoshiarpur ... 42 D9
Hospet ..... 43 M10
Hospitalet de
  Llobregat ... 19 B7
Hoste, I. ...... 95 H3
Hot Springs ... 79 B7
Hotan ........ 34 C2
Houhora Heads 64 A5
Houlton ..... 73 A12
Houma ...... 79 E8
Houston ..... 79 E6
Hovd ....... 34 B4
Hövsgöl Nuur . 34 A5
Howard ..... 63 A5
Howe, C. ..... 63 C5
Howitt, L. .... 62 A2
Howrah = Haora 40 F7
Höxter ...... 14 C5
Hoy ......... 10 B5
Høyanger ..... 8 F9
Hoyerswerda .. 15 C8
Hpungan Pass . 41 D11
Hradec Králové 16 C2
Hrodna ....... 17 B6
Hrodzyanka .. 17 B9
Hron → ..... 16 E4
Hrvatska =
  Croatia ■ ... 20 B6
Hrymayliv .... 17 D8
Hsenwi ....... 41 F11
Hsiamen =
  Xiamen ..... 35 D6
Hsian = Xi'an . 35 C5
Hsinhailien =
  Lianyungang 35 C6
Hsisha Chuntao 36 A4
Hsüchou =
  Xuzhou .... 35 C6
Hua Hin ...... 36 B1
Huacho ...... 91 F3
Huachón ..... 91 F3
Huai He → .. 35 C6
Huainan ..... 35 C6

Huallaga → .. 90 E3
Huambo ..... 58 A3
Huancabamba . 91 E3
Huancane ..... 91 G5
Huancapi ..... 91 F4
Huancavelica .. 91 F3
Huancayo ... 91 F3
Huang Hai =
  Yellow Sea .. 35 C7
Huang He → . 35 C6
Huangliu ..... 35 E5
Huangshi .... 35 C6
Huánuco .... 91 E3
Huaraz ....... 91 E3
Huarmey ..... 91 F3
Huascarán ... 91 E3
Huasco ....... 94 B2
Huatabampo .. 84 B3
Huayllay ..... 91 F3
Hubei □ ..... 35 C6
Hubli-Dharwad
  = Dharwad . 43 M9
Huddersfield .. 11 E6
Hudiksvall ... 8 F11
Hudson → .. 73 D8
Hudson Bay ... 68 B2
Hudson Mts. .. 96 B2
Hudson Str. ... 68 B4
Hue .......... 36 A3
Huelva ...... 18 D2
Huesca ...... 19 A5
Hughenden ... 61 E7
Hughli → ... 40 G7
Huila, Nevado
  del ...... 90 C3
Huinca Renancó 94 C4
Huize ....... 34 D5
Hukawng Valley 41 D11
Hulan ....... 35 B7
Ḥulayfā' ..... 47 F5
Huld ........ 35 B5
Hull = Kingston
  upon Hull ... 11 E6
Hull ....... 69 D3
Hulun Nur ... 35 B6
Humahuaca ... 94 A3
Humaitá, Brazil 91 E6
Humaitá,
  Paraguay .. 94 B5
Humber → .. 11 E6
Humboldt ..... 71 C9
Humboldt → . 80 F4
Hume, L. ..... 63 C4
Humenné ... 16 D5
Hūn ........ 52 C2
Hunan □ .... 35 D6
Hunedoara .... 17 F6
Hungary ■ ... 16 E4
Hungerford ... 63 A3
Hŭngnam ... 35 C7
Hunsrück .... 14 D4
Hunter I. ..... 62 D3
Hunter Ra. ... 63 B5
Hunterville ... 64 C6
Huntingdon .. 72 E4
Huntington
  Beach ..... 82 D3
Huntly, N.Z. .. 64 B6
Huntly, U.K. .. 10 C5
Huntsville ... 74 B4
Huonville ... 62 D4
Hupeh =
  Hubei □ .... 35 C6
Hurayṣān .... 47 G6
Huron, L. .... 72 B4
Hurunui → .. 65 E5
Huşi ........ 17 E9
Hutchinson .. 78 A5
Hutton, Mt. ... 63 A4
Hvar ....... 20 C6

Hwang Ho =
  Huang He → 35 C6
Hwange ..... 59 B5
Hyargas Nuur . 34 B4
Hyderabad,
  India .... 43 L11
Hyderabad,
  Pakistan .... 42 G6
Hyères ...... 13 E7
Hyères, Is. d' . 13 E7

# I

I-n-Gall ....... 55 E6
Iaco → ...... 91 E5
Ialomiţa → .. 22 B6
Iaşi ......... 17 E8
Iba ......... 38 A2
Ibadan ..... 55 G5
Ibagué ..... 90 C3
Ibar → ..... 22 C3
Ibarra ..... 90 C3
Ibi ......... 55 G6
Ibiá ......... 93 F4
Ibicuy ..... 94 C5
Ibioapaba, Sa.
  da ....... 92 C5
Ibiza ..... 19 C6
Ibonma ..... 39 E4
Ibotirama ... 93 E5
Ibu ......... 39 D3
Icá ......... 91 F3
Iça → ..... 90 D5
Içana ..... 90 C5
İçel = Mersin .. 46 C3
Iceland ■ ... 8 B4
Ich'ang =
  Yichang .... 35 C6
Ichchapuram .. 40 H5
Ichihara ..... 32 B7
Ichikawa ..... 32 B6
Ichilo → ..... 91 G6
Ichinomiya ... 32 B5
Idaho □ ..... 81 C6
Idaho Falls .... 81 D7
Idar-Oberstein . 14 D4
Idd el Ghanam 53 F3
Iddan ........ 49 F4
Idehan ..... 52 C1
Idehan Marzūq 52 D1
Idelès ..... 54 D6
Idfû ........ 52 D5
Ídhi Óros .... 23 G5
Ídhra ..... 23 F4
Idi ......... 36 C1
Idiofa ..... 56 E3
Idlip ..... 46 D4
Ierápetra .... 23 G5
Iesi ......... 20 C4
Ifanadiana ... 59 J9
Ife ......... 55 G5
Ifni ......... 54 C2
Iforas, Adrar des 54 D5
Igarapava ... 93 G4
Igarapé Açu .. 92 C4
Igarka ..... 28 C9
Igbetti ..... 55 G5
Iglésias ..... 21 E2
Igli ......... 54 B4
Igloolik ..... 68 B2
İğneada Burnu 22 D7
Igoumenítsa .. 23 E3
Iguaçu → .... 94 B6
Iguaçu, Cat. del 94 B6
Iguaçu Falls =
  Iguaçu, Cat.
  del ......... 94 B6

Iguala . . . . . . . . 84 D5
Igualada . . . . . . 19 B6
Iguassu =
  Iguaçu ➤ . . 94 B6
Iguatu . . . . . . . . 92 D6
Iguéla . . . . . . . . 56 E1
Ihosy . . . . . . 59 J9
Iida . . . . . . . . . . 32 B5
Iisalmi . . . . . . 8 F13
Iizuka . . . . . . . . 32 C2
Ijebu-Ode . . . . . 55 G5
IJsselmeer . . . . 14 B3
Ikaría . . . . . . . . 23 F6
Ikela . . . . . . . . 56 E4
Iki . . . . . . . . . . 32 C1
Ilagan . . . . . . . . 38 A2
Īlām . . . . . . . . 46 D6
Ilawa . . . . . . . . 16 B4
Île-de-France . . 12 B5
Ilebo . . . . . . . . 56 E4
Ilhéus . . . . . . . . 93 E6
Ili ➤ . . . . . . . . 29 E8
Ilich . . . . . . . . 29 E7
Iligan . . . . . . . . 38 C2
Illampu =
  Ancohuma,
  Nevada . . . . 91 G5
Illana B. . . . . . . 38 C2
Illapel . . . . . . . . 94 C2
Iller ➤ . . . . . . . 14 D5
Illimani . . . . . . 91 G5
Illium = Troy . . 23 E6
Ilmen, Ozero . . 24 B3
Ilo . . . . . . . . . . 91 G4
Iloilo . . . . . . . . 38 B2
Ilorin . . . . . . . . 55 G5
Ilwaki . . . . . . . . 39 F3
Imabari . . . . . . 32 B3
Imandra, Ozero 28 C4
Imari . . . . . . . . 32 C1
imeni 26
  Bakinskikh
  Komissarov =
  Neftçala . . . . 46 C7
Imeri, Serra . . . 90 C5
Imi . . . . . . . . . . 49 F3
Imola . . . . . . . . 20 B3
Imperatriz . . . . 92 D4
Impéria . . . . . . 20 C2
Imperial Dam . . 82 D5
Impfondo . . . . . 56 D3
Imphal . . . . . . . 41 E9
İmroz =
  Gökçeada . . 23 D5
Imuruan B. . . . . 38 B1
In Belbel . . . . . . 54 C5
In Salah . . . . . . 54 C5
Ina . . . . . . . . . . 32 B5
Inangahua
  Junction . . . 65 D4
Inanwatan . . . . 39 E4
Iñapari . . . . . . . 91 F5
Inarijärvi . . . . . 8 E13
Inca . . . . . . . . . . 19 C7
İnce-Burnu . . . . 46 B3
Inchon . . . . . . . 35 C7
İncirliova . . . . . 23 F6
Incomáti ➤ . . 59 D6
Indalsälven ➤ . 8 F11
Indaw . . . . . . . . 41 E11
Independence,
  Kans., U.S.A. 79 A6
Independence,
  Mo., U.S.A. . 77 F7
India ■ . . . . . . . 43 J10
Indian ➤ . . . . . 75 F7
Indian Harbour 68 C5
Indian Head . . . 71 C9
Indiana □ . . . . . 72 D3

Indianapolis . . . 72 E2
Indiga . . . . . . . . 28 C5
Indigirka ➤ . . 31 B12
Indonesia ■ . . . 37 E4
Indore . . . . . . . . 43 H9
Indravati ➤ . . 40 H3
Indre ➤ . . . . . 12 C4
Indus ➤ . . . . . 43 G5
İnebolu . . . . . . 46 B3
Ingende . . . . . . 56 E3
Inglewood,
  Queens.,
  Australia . . . . 63 A5
Inglewood, Vic.,
  Australia . . . . 62 C3
Inglewood, N.Z. 64 C6
Ingolstadt . . . . 15 D6
Ingraj Bazar . . . 40 E7
Ingrid
  Christensen
  Coast . . . . . . 96 A10
Ingulec =
  Inhulec . . . . . 25 D3
Inhambane . . . . 59 C7
Inhaminga . . . . 59 B7
Inharrime . . . . . 59 C7
Inhulec . . . . . . . 25 D3
Ining = Yining . 34 B3
Inírida ➤ . . . . 90 C5
Injune . . . . . . . . 63 A4
Inle L. . . . . . . . 41 G11
Inn ➤ . . . . . . . 15 D7
Innamincka . . . 62 A3
Inner Hebrides 10 C3
Inner Mongolia
  = Nei
  Monggol
  Zizhiqu □ . . 35 B6
Innisfail . . . . . . 71 C8
Innsbruck . . . . . 15 E6
Inongo . . . . . . . 56 E3
Inoucdjouac =
  Inukjuak . . . . 68 C3
Inowrocław . . . 16 B4
Inquisivi . . . . . . 91 G5
Insein . . . . . . . . 41 J11
Interlaken . . . . 13 C7
International
  Falls . . . . . . . 77 A8
Intiyaco . . . . . . 94 B4
Inukjuak . . . . . . 68 C3
Inútil, B. . . . . . . 95 G2
Inuvik . . . . . . . . 70 B6
Invercargill . . . . 65 G3
Inverell . . . . . . . 63 A5
Invergordon . . . 10 C4
Inverness . . . . . 10 C4
Inverurie . . . . . . 10 C5
Investigator
  Group . . . . . 62 B1
Investigator Str. 62 C2
Inya . . . . . . . . . . 29 D9
Inza . . . . . . . . . . 24 C6
Ioánnina . . . . . . 23 E3
Ionian Is. =
  Iónioi Nísoi . 23 E3
Ionian Sea . . . . 21 F6
Iónioi Nísoi . . . 23 E3
Íos . . . . . . . . . . 23 F5
Iowa □ . . . . . . . 77 D8
Iowa City . . . . . 77 E9
Ipameri . . . . . . . 93 F4
Ipatinga . . . . . . 93 F5
Ipiales . . . . . . . 90 C3
Ipin = Yibin . . . 35 D5
Ipixuna . . . . . . 91 E4
Ipoh . . . . . . . . . 36 D2
Ippy . . . . . . . . . 56 C4
İpsala . . . . . . . . 22 D6

Ipswich,
  Australia . . . . 63 A5
Ipswich, U.K. . . 11 E7
Ipu . . . . . . . . . . 92 C5
Iqaluit . . . . . . . 68 B4
Iquique . . . . . . 91 H4
Iquitos . . . . . . . 90 D4
Iracoubo . . . . . 92 A3
Iráklion . . . . . . 23 G5
Iran ■ . . . . . . . 44 C3
Iran, Gunung-
  Gunung . . . 37 D4
Iran Ra. = Iran,
  Gunung-
  Gunung . . . . 37 D4
Īrānshahr . . . . . 45 E5
Irapuato . . . . . . 84 C4
Iraq ■ . . . . . . . 46 D5
Irbid . . . . . . . . 46 D3
Irebu . . . . . . . . 56 E3
Ireland ■ . . . . . 11 E3
Irian Jaya □ . . . 39 E5
Iringa . . . . . . . . 57 F7
Iriri ➤ . . . . . . 92 C3
Irish Sea . . . . . . 11 E4
Irkineyeva . . . . 30 D7
Irkutsk . . . . . . . 30 D8
Iron Baron . . . . 62 B2
Iron Gate =
  Portile de Fier 22 B4
Iron Knob . . . . . 62 B2
Ironwood . . . . . 77 B9
Irpin . . . . . . . . 17 C10
Irrara Cr. ➤ . . 63 A4
Irrawaddy □ . . 41 J10
Irrawaddy ➤ . 41 K10
Irtysh ➤ . . . . . 28 C7
Irumu . . . . . . . . 57 D5
Irún . . . . . . . . . 19 A5
Irunea =
  Pamplona . . 19 A5
Irvine . . . . . . . . 10 D4
Irymple . . . . . . 62 B3
Isabella . . . . . . 38 C2
Isangi . . . . . . . . 56 D4
Isar ➤ . . . . . . 15 D7
Íschia . . . . . . . . 21 D4
Ise . . . . . . . . . . 32 B5
Ise-Wan . . . . . . 32 B5
Isère ➤ . . . . . 13 D6
Isérnia . . . . . . . 20 D5
Ishikari-Wan . . 32 F12
Ishim ➤ . . . . . 29 D8
Ishinomaki . . . 33 G12
Ishkuman . . . . 42 A8
Isil Kul . . . . . . . 29 D8
Isiolo . . . . . . . . 57 D7
Isiro . . . . . . . . . 57 D5
İskenderun . . . . 46 C4
İskŭr ➤ . . . . . 22 C5
Islamabad . . . . 42 C8
Island L. . . . . . 71 C10
Island Lagoon . 62 B2
Islay . . . . . . . . 10 D3
Isle ➤ . . . . . . 12 D3
Isle of Wight □ 11 F6
Ismail = Izmayil 17 F9
Ismâ'ilîya . . . . 47 E3
Isna . . . . . . . . . 52 C5
İsparta . . . . . . . 46 C2
Íspica . . . . . . . . 21 F5
Israel ■ . . . . . . 46 E3
Issoire . . . . . . . 13 D5
Issyk-Kul, Ozero
  = Ysyk-Köl,
  Ozero . . . . . 29 E8
İstanbul . . . . . . 22 D7
Istiaía . . . . . . . 23 E4
Istra . . . . . . . . 20 B4

İstranca Dağları 22 D6
Istres . . . . . . . . 13 E6
Istria = Istra . . 20 B4
Itabaiana . . . . . 92 D6
Itaberaba . . . . . 93 E5
Itabira . . . . . . . 93 F5
Itabuna . . . . . . 93 E6
Itaipú, Reprêsa
  de . . . . . . . . 94 B6
Itaituba . . . . . . 92 C2
Itajaí . . . . . . . . 94 B7
Italy ■ . . . . . . . 20 C4
Itapecuru-Mirim 92 C5
Itaperuna . . . . . 93 G5
Itapicuru ➤,
  Bahia, Brazil . 93 E6
Itapicuru ➤,
  Maranhão,
  Brazil . . . . . . 92 C5
Itapipoca . . . . . 92 C6
Itaquatiara . . . . 90 D7
Itaquí . . . . . . . . 94 B5
Itatuba . . . . . . . 91 E6
Ithaca = Itháki 23 E3
Itháki . . . . . . . . 23 E3
Ito . . . . . . . . . . 32 B6
Itonamas ➤ . . 91 F6
Ituaçu . . . . . . . 93 E5
Ituiutaba . . . . . 93 F4
Itumbiara . . . . . 93 F4
Iturbe . . . . . . . . 94 A3
Itzehoe . . . . . . 14 B5
Ivanava . . . . . . 17 B7
Ivanhoe . . . . . . 63 B3
Ivano-Frankivsk 17 D7
Ivano-Frankovsk
  = Ivano-
  Frankivsk . . . 17 D7
Ivanovo =
  Ivanava . . . . 17 B7
Ivanovo . . . . . . 24 B5
Ivatsevichy . . . . 17 B7
Ivory Coast ■ . . 55 G3
Ivrea . . . . . . . . 20 B1
Ivujivik . . . . . . 68 B3
Iwahig . . . . . . . 36 C5
Iwaki . . . . . . . . 33 G12
Iwakuni . . . . . . 32 B3
Iwata . . . . . . . . 33 H11
Iwate-San . . . . 33 G12
Iwo . . . . . . . . . 55 G5
Ixiamas . . . . . . 91 F5
Izhevsk . . . . . . 28 D6
Izmayil . . . . . . 17 F9
İzmir . . . . . . . . 23 E6
İzmit . . . . . . . . 25 E2
İznik Gölü . . . . 23 D7
Izumi-sano . . . . 32 B4
Izumo . . . . . . . . 32 B3
Izyaslav . . . . . . 17 C8

**J**

Jabalpur . . . . . . 43 H11
Jablah . . . . . . . 46 D4
Jablanica . . . . . 22 D3
Jablonec . . . . . 16 C2
Jaboatão . . . . . 92 D6
Jaca . . . . . . . . . 19 A5
Jacareí . . . . . . . 94 A7
Jacarèzinho . . . 94 A7
Jackson,
  Australia . . . . 63 A4
Jackson, Mich.,
  U.S.A. . . . . . 72 C3
Jackson, Miss.,
  U.S.A. . . . . . 79 C8

| | | |
|---|---|---|
| Jackson, *Tenn.,* | | |
| *U.S.A.* | 74 | B3 |
| Jackson B. | 65 | E3 |
| Jacksons | 65 | E4 |
| Jacksonville, | | |
| *Fla., U.S.A.* | 75 | D7 |
| Jacksonville, *Ill.,* | | |
| *U.S.A.* | 77 | F9 |
| Jacksonville, | | |
| *N.C., U.S.A.* | 75 | B9 |
| Jacmel | 87 | C5 |
| Jacobabad | 42 | E6 |
| Jacobina | 93 | E5 |
| Jacundá → | 92 | C3 |
| Jadotville = | | |
| Likasi | 57 | G5 |
| Jādū | 52 | B1 |
| Jaén, *Peru* | 91 | E3 |
| Jaén, *Spain* | 18 | D4 |
| Jaffa = Tel Aviv- | | |
| Yafo | 46 | D3 |
| Jaffa, C. | 62 | C2 |
| Jaffna | 43 | Q12 |
| Jagadhri | 42 | D10 |
| Jagdalpur | 40 | H3 |
| Jagraon | 42 | D9 |
| Jagtial | 43 | K11 |
| Jaguariaíva | 94 | A7 |
| Jaguaribe → | 92 | C6 |
| Jahrom | 44 | D3 |
| Jailolo | 39 | D3 |
| Jailolo, Selat | 39 | D3 |
| Jaipur | 42 | F9 |
| Jakarta | 37 | F3 |
| Jalalabad | 42 | B7 |
| Jalapa Enríquez | 84 | D5 |
| Jalas, Jabal al | 47 | F4 |
| Jalgaon, | | |
| *Maharashtra,* | | |
| *India* | 43 | J10 |
| Jalgaon, | | |
| *Maharashtra,* | | |
| *India* | 43 | J9 |
| Jalna | 43 | K9 |
| Jalón → | 19 | B5 |
| Jalpaiguri | 41 | D7 |
| Jalq | 45 | E5 |
| Jaluit I. | 64 | J11 |
| Jamaica ■ | 86 | C4 |
| Jamalpur, | | |
| *Bangla.* | 41 | E7 |
| Jamalpur, *India* | 40 | E6 |
| Jamanxim → | 92 | C2 |
| Jambe | 39 | E4 |
| Jambi | 37 | E2 |
| Jambi □ | 37 | E2 |
| James → | 76 | D6 |
| James B. | 69 | C2 |
| James Ross I. | 96 | A4 |
| Jamestown, | | |
| *Australia* | 62 | B2 |
| Jamestown, | | |
| *N. Dak., U.S.A.* | 76 | B5 |
| Jamestown, | | |
| *N.Y., U.S.A.* | 73 | C6 |
| Jamkhandi | 43 | L9 |
| Jammu | 42 | C9 |
| Jammu & | | |
| Kashmir □ | 42 | B10 |
| Jamnagar | 43 | H7 |
| Jamrud | 42 | C7 |
| Jamshedpur | 40 | F6 |
| Jand | 42 | C8 |
| Jandaq | 44 | C3 |
| Jandowae | 63 | A5 |
| Janesville | 77 | D10 |
| Januária | 93 | F5 |
| Jaora | 43 | H9 |
| Japan ■ | 33 | G11 |
| Japan, Sea of | 33 | G11 |
| Japen = Yapen | 39 | E5 |
| Japurá → | 90 | D5 |
| Jaque | 90 | B3 |
| Jarama → | 18 | B4 |
| Jargalant = | | |
| Hovd | 34 | B4 |
| Jarosław | 17 | C6 |
| Jarso | 53 | G6 |
| Jarvis I. | 65 | K15 |
| Jarwa | 40 | D4 |
| Jäsk | 44 | E4 |
| Jasło | 16 | D5 |
| Jasper | 74 | C4 |
| Jászberény | 16 | E4 |
| Jataí | 93 | F3 |
| Játiva | 19 | C5 |
| Jaú | 93 | G4 |
| Jauja | 91 | F3 |
| Jaunpur | 40 | E4 |
| Java = Jawa | 37 | F3 |
| Java Sea | 37 | E3 |
| Javhlant = | | |
| Ulyasutay | 34 | B4 |
| Jawa | 37 | F3 |
| Jaya, Puncak | 39 | E5 |
| Jayanti | 41 | D7 |
| Jayapura | 39 | E6 |
| Jayawijaya, | | |
| Pegunungan | 39 | E5 |
| Jaynagar | 40 | D6 |
| Jean Marie | | |
| River | 70 | B7 |
| Jebba | 55 | G5 |
| Jebel, Bahr | | |
| el → | 53 | G5 |
| Jedburgh | 10 | D5 |
| Jedda = Jiddah | 47 | G4 |
| Jędrzejów | 16 | C5 |
| Jefferson City | 77 | F8 |
| Jega | 55 | F5 |
| Jelenia Góra | 16 | C2 |
| Jelgava | 24 | B1 |
| Jemaja | 37 | D3 |
| Jembongan | 36 | C5 |
| Jena | 15 | C6 |
| Jeparit | 62 | C3 |
| Jequié | 93 | E5 |
| Jequitinhonha | 93 | F5 |
| Jequitinhonha → | | |
| | 93 | F6 |
| Jerada | 54 | B4 |
| Jerantut | 37 | D2 |
| Jérémie | 86 | C5 |
| Jerez de la | | |
| Frontera | 18 | D2 |
| Jerez de los | | |
| Caballeros | 18 | C2 |
| Jerilderie | 63 | C4 |
| Jersey | 11 | G5 |
| Jersey City | 73 | D8 |
| Jerusalem | 47 | E3 |
| Jervis B. | 63 | C5 |
| Jesselton = | | |
| Kota Kinabalu | 36 | C5 |
| Jessore | 41 | F7 |
| Jeypore | 40 | H4 |
| Jhal Jhao | 42 | F4 |
| Jhalawar | 43 | G10 |
| Jhang Maghiana | 42 | D8 |
| Jhansi | 43 | G11 |
| Jharsaguda | 40 | G5 |
| Jhelum | 42 | C8 |
| Jhelum → | 42 | D8 |
| Jhunjhunu | 42 | E9 |
| Jiamusi | 35 | B8 |
| Ji'an | 35 | D6 |
| Jianchuan | 34 | D4 |
| Jiangling | 35 | C6 |
| Jiangmen | 35 | D6 |
| Jiangsu □ | 35 | C6 |
| Jiangxi □ | 35 | D6 |
| Jian'ou | 35 | D6 |
| Jianshui | 34 | D5 |
| Jiao Xian | 35 | C7 |
| Jiaozuo | 35 | C6 |
| Jiaxing | 35 | C7 |
| Jiayi | 35 | D7 |
| Jibuti = | | |
| Djibouti ■ | 49 | E3 |
| Jiddah | 47 | G4 |
| Jido | 41 | C10 |
| Jihlava | 16 | D2 |
| Jihlava → | 16 | D3 |
| Jijel | 54 | A6 |
| Jijiga | 49 | F3 |
| Jilin | 35 | B7 |
| Jilong | 35 | D7 |
| Jima | 53 | G6 |
| Jiménez | 84 | B4 |
| Jinan | 35 | C6 |
| Jindabyne | 63 | C4 |
| Jindrichuv | | |
| Hradeç | 16 | D2 |
| Jingdezhen | 35 | D6 |
| Jinggu | 34 | D5 |
| Jingxi | 35 | D5 |
| Jinhua | 35 | D6 |
| Jining, | | |
| *Nei Mongol Zizhiqu,* | | |
| *China* | 35 | B6 |
| Jining, | | |
| *Shandong,* | | |
| *China* | 35 | C6 |
| Jinja | 57 | D6 |
| Jinnah Barrage | 42 | C7 |
| Jinotega | 85 | E7 |
| Jinshi | 35 | D6 |
| Jinzhou | 35 | B7 |
| Jiparaná → | 91 | E6 |
| Jipijapa | 90 | D2 |
| Jisr ash | | |
| Shughūr | 46 | D4 |
| Jiu → | 22 | C4 |
| Jiujiang | 35 | D6 |
| Jiuquan | 34 | C4 |
| Jixi | 35 | B8 |
| Jizzakh | 29 | E7 |
| Joaçaba | 94 | B6 |
| João Pessoa | 92 | D7 |
| Joaquín V. | | |
| González | 94 | B4 |
| Jofane | 59 | C6 |
| Jogjakarta = | | |
| Yogyakarta | 37 | F4 |
| Johannesburg | 59 | D5 |
| Johnson City | 75 | A6 |
| Johnston Falls | | |
| = Mambilima | | |
| Falls | 57 | G5 |
| Johnstown | 73 | D6 |
| Johor Baharu | 37 | D2 |
| Joinvile | 94 | B7 |
| Joinville I. | 96 | A4 |
| Joliet | 72 | D1 |
| Joliette | 69 | D3 |
| Jolo | 38 | C2 |
| Jome | 39 | E3 |
| Jonesboro | 79 | B8 |
| Jönköping | 9 | G10 |
| Jonquière | 69 | D3 |
| Joplin | 79 | A6 |
| Jordan ■ | 47 | E4 |
| Jorhat | 41 | D10 |
| Jorong | 37 | E4 |
| Jos | 55 | G6 |
| Jowzjān □ | 45 | B6 |
| Juan de Fuca | | |
| Str. | 80 | A1 |
| Juan de Nova | 59 | H8 |
| Juan Fernández, | | |
| Arch. de | 89 | G3 |
| Juárez | 94 | D5 |
| Juàzeiro | 93 | D5 |
| Juàzeiro do | | |
| Norte | 92 | D6 |
| Jubbulpore = | | |
| Jabalpur | 43 | H11 |
| Juby, C. | 54 | C2 |
| Júcar → | 19 | C5 |
| Juchitán | 85 | D5 |
| Jugoslavia = | | |
| Yugoslavia ■ | 22 | B3 |
| Juiz de Fora | 93 | G5 |
| Juli | 91 | G5 |
| Juliaca | 91 | G4 |
| Jullundur | 42 | D9 |
| Jumilla | 19 | C5 |
| Jumla | 40 | C4 |
| Jumna = | | |
| Yamuna → | 40 | E3 |
| Junagadh | 43 | J7 |
| Jundiaí | 94 | A7 |
| Juneau | 71 | C6 |
| Junee | 63 | B4 |
| Jungfrau | 13 | C7 |
| Junggar Pendi | 34 | B3 |
| Junín | 94 | C4 |
| Junín de los | | |
| Andes | 95 | D2 |
| Jūniyah | 46 | D3 |
| Jur, Nahr el → | 53 | G4 |
| Jura = Jura, | | |
| Mts. du | 13 | C7 |
| Jura = | | |
| Schwäbische | | |
| Alb | 14 | D5 |
| Jura | 10 | D4 |
| Jura, Mts. du | 13 | C7 |
| Jurado | 90 | B3 |
| Juruá → | 90 | D5 |
| Juruena → | 91 | E7 |
| Juruti | 92 | C2 |
| Justo Daract | 94 | C3 |
| Jutland = | | |
| Jylland | 9 | G9 |
| Juventud, I. de | | |
| la | 86 | B3 |
| Juwain | 42 | D2 |
| Jylland | 9 | G9 |
| Jyväskylä | 8 | F13 |

## K

| | | |
|---|---|---|
| K2 | 42 | B10 |
| Kaapkruis | 58 | C2 |
| Kaapstad = | | |
| Cape Town | 58 | E3 |
| Kabaena | 39 | F2 |
| Kabala | 55 | G2 |
| Kabale | 57 | E6 |
| Kabalo | 57 | F5 |
| Kabambare | 57 | E5 |
| Kabanjahe | 37 | D1 |
| Kabara | 55 | E4 |
| Kabardino- | | |
| Balkar | | |
| Republic = | | |
| Kabardino | | |
| Balkaria □ | 25 | E5 |
| Kabardino | | |
| Balkaria □ | 25 | E5 |
| Kabare | 39 | E4 |

| | | |
|---|---|---|
| Kabarega Falls | 57 | D6 |
| Kabasalan | 38 | C2 |
| Kabba | 55 | G6 |
| Kabīr, Zab al → | 46 | C5 |
| Kabīr Kūh | 47 | D6 |
| Kabkabīyah | 53 | F3 |
| Kabompo → | 58 | A4 |
| Kabongo | 57 | F5 |
| Kabūd Gonbad | 44 | B4 |
| Kābul | 42 | B6 |
| Kābul □ | 42 | B6 |
| Kabul → | 42 | C8 |
| Kaburuang | 39 | D3 |
| Kabwe | 59 | A5 |
| Kachchh, Gulf of | 43 | H6 |
| Kachchh, Rann of | 43 | G6 |
| Kachin □ | 41 | D11 |
| Kachiry | 29 | D8 |
| Kaçkar | 46 | B5 |
| Kadan Kyun | 36 | B1 |
| Kadina | 62 | B2 |
| Kadirli | 46 | C4 |
| Kadiyevka = Stakhanov | 25 | D4 |
| Kadoma | 59 | B5 |
| Kâdugli | 53 | F4 |
| Kaduna | 55 | F6 |
| Kaédi | 55 | E2 |
| Kaelé | 53 | F1 |
| Kaesŏng | 35 | C7 |
| Kāf | 47 | E4 |
| Kafakumba | 56 | F4 |
| Kafan = Kapan | 25 | F6 |
| Kafanchan | 55 | G6 |
| Kaffrine | 55 | F1 |
| Kafia Kingi | 53 | G3 |
| Kafirévs, Ákra | 23 | E5 |
| Kafue → | 59 | B5 |
| Kafulwe | 57 | F5 |
| Kaga Bandoro | 56 | C3 |
| Kagan | 29 | F7 |
| Kağizman | 46 | B5 |
| Kagoshima | 33 | D2 |
| Kagoshima-Wan | 33 | D2 |
| Kagul = Cahul | 17 | F9 |
| Kahama | 57 | E6 |
| Kahayan → | 37 | E4 |
| Kahemba | 56 | F3 |
| Kahnūj | 44 | E4 |
| Kahoolawe | 82 | H12 |
| Kahramanmaraş | 46 | C4 |
| Kai, Kepulauan | 39 | F4 |
| Kai Besar | 39 | F4 |
| Kai Is. = Kai, Kepulauan | 39 | F4 |
| Kai Kecil | 39 | F4 |
| Kaiama | 55 | G5 |
| Kaiapoi | 65 | E5 |
| Kaieteur Falls | 90 | B7 |
| Kaifeng | 35 | C6 |
| Kaikohe | 64 | A5 |
| Kaikoura | 65 | E5 |
| Kaikoura Ra. | 65 | D5 |
| Kaimana | 39 | E4 |
| Kaimanawa Mts. | 64 | C6 |
| Kaingaroa Forest | 64 | C7 |
| Kainji Res. | 55 | F5 |
| Kaipara Harbour | 64 | B6 |
| Kaironi | 39 | E4 |
| Kairouan | 54 | A7 |
| Kaiserslautern | 14 | D4 |
| Kaitaia | 64 | A5 |
| Kaitangata | 65 | G3 |
| Kajaani | 8 | F13 |
| Kajabbi | 61 | D6 |
| Kajana = Kajaani | 8 | F13 |
| Kajo Kaji | 53 | H5 |
| Kaka | 53 | F5 |
| Kakamas | 58 | D4 |
| Kakamega | 57 | D6 |
| Kakanui Mts. | 65 | F4 |
| Kakhovka | 25 | D3 |
| Kakhovske Vdskh. | 25 | D3 |
| Kakinada | 40 | J4 |
| Kalabagh | 42 | C7 |
| Kalabahi | 39 | F2 |
| Kalabo | 58 | A4 |
| Kalach | 24 | C5 |
| Kaladan → | 41 | G9 |
| Kalahari | 58 | C4 |
| Kalakan | 31 | D9 |
| Kalámai | 23 | F4 |
| Kalamata = Kalámai | 23 | F4 |
| Kalamazoo | 72 | C3 |
| Kalan | 46 | C4 |
| Kalao | 39 | F2 |
| Kalaotoa | 39 | F2 |
| Kalat | 42 | E5 |
| Kalce | 20 | B5 |
| Kale | 23 | F7 |
| Kalegauk Kyun | 41 | K11 |
| Kalemie | 57 | F5 |
| Kalewa | 41 | F10 |
| Kalgan = Zhangjiakou | 35 | B6 |
| Kalgoorlie-Boulder | 60 | G3 |
| Kaliakra, Nos | 22 | C7 |
| Kalianda | 37 | F3 |
| Kalibo | 38 | B2 |
| Kalima | 57 | E5 |
| Kalimantan | 37 | E4 |
| Kalimantan Barat □ | 37 | D4 |
| Kalimantan Selatan □ | 37 | E5 |
| Kalimantan Tengah □ | 37 | E4 |
| Kalimantan Timur □ | 37 | D5 |
| Kálimnos | 23 | F6 |
| Kalinin = Tver | 24 | B4 |
| Kaliningrad, Kaliningd., Russia | 24 | C1 |
| Kaliningrad, Moskva, Russia | 24 | B4 |
| Kalinkavichy | 17 | B9 |
| Kalinkovichi = Kalinkavichy | 17 | B9 |
| Kalispell | 81 | A6 |
| Kalisz | 16 | C4 |
| Kaliua | 57 | F6 |
| Kalkrand | 58 | C3 |
| Kalmar | 9 | G11 |
| Kalmyk Republic = Kalmykia □ | 25 | D6 |
| Kalmykia □ | 25 | D6 |
| Kalocsa | 16 | E4 |
| Kalomo | 59 | B5 |
| Kaluga | 24 | C4 |
| Kalush | 17 | D7 |
| Kalutara | 43 | R11 |
| Kama → | 29 | D6 |
| Kamaishi | 33 | G12 |
| Kamaran | 49 | D3 |
| Kamchatka, P-ov. | 31 | D13 |
| Kamchatka Pen. = Kamchatka, P-ov. | 31 | D13 |
| Kamchiya → | 22 | C6 |
| Kamen | 29 | D9 |
| Kamenjak, Rt. | 20 | B4 |
| Kamenka Bugskaya = Kamyanka-Buzka | 17 | C7 |
| Kamensk Uralskiy | 29 | D7 |
| Kamin-Kashyrskyy | 17 | C7 |
| Kamina | 57 | F5 |
| Kamloops | 71 | C7 |
| Kampala | 57 | D6 |
| Kampar → | 37 | D2 |
| Kampen | 14 | B3 |
| Kampot | 36 | B2 |
| Kampuchea = Cambodia ■ | 36 | B3 |
| Kampung → | 39 | F5 |
| Kampungbaru = Tolitoli | 39 | D2 |
| Kamrau, Teluk | 39 | E4 |
| Kamsack | 71 | C9 |
| Kamyanets-Podilskyy | 17 | D8 |
| Kamyanka-Buzka | 17 | C7 |
| Kamyshin | 24 | C6 |
| Kanaaupscow | 69 | C3 |
| Kananga | 56 | F4 |
| Kanash | 24 | B6 |
| Kanastraíon, Ákra = Palioúrion, Ákra | 23 | E4 |
| Kanazawa | 32 | A5 |
| Kanchanaburi | 36 | B1 |
| Kanchenjunga | 40 | D7 |
| Kanchipuram | 43 | N11 |
| Kanda Kanda | 56 | F4 |
| Kandahar = Qandahār | 42 | D4 |
| Kandalaksha | 28 | C4 |
| Kandalu | 42 | E3 |
| Kandangan | 37 | E5 |
| Kandi | 55 | F5 |
| Kandla | 43 | H7 |
| Kandos | 63 | B4 |
| Kandy | 43 | R12 |
| Kangaroo I. | 62 | C2 |
| Kangāvar | 46 | D7 |
| Kangean, Kepulauan | 37 | F5 |
| Kangean Is. = Kangean, Kepulauan | 37 | F5 |
| Kangiqsualujjuaq | 68 | C4 |
| Kangiqsujuaq | 68 | B3 |
| Kangirsuk | 68 | C4 |
| Kangnŭng | 35 | C7 |
| Kango | 56 | D2 |
| Kangto | 41 | D9 |
| Kaniapiskau → | 68 | C4 |
| Kaniapiskau L. | 69 | C4 |
| Kanin, Poluostrov | 28 | C5 |
| Kanin Nos, Mys | 28 | C5 |
| Kanin Pen. = Kanin, Poluostrov | 28 | C5 |
| Kaniva | 62 | C3 |
| Kankakee | 72 | D2 |
| Kankan | 55 | F3 |
| Kankendy = Xankändi | 25 | F6 |
| Kanker | 40 | G3 |
| Kannapolis | 75 | B7 |
| Kannauj | 42 | F11 |
| Kannod | 43 | H10 |
| Kano | 55 | F6 |
| Kanowit | 37 | D4 |
| Kanoya | 33 | D2 |
| Kanpetlet | 41 | G9 |
| Kanpur | 40 | D3 |
| Kansas □ | 76 | F5 |
| Kansas City, Kans., U.S.A. | 77 | F7 |
| Kansas City, Mo., U.S.A. | 77 | F7 |
| Kansk | 30 | D7 |
| Kansu = Gansu □ | 34 | C5 |
| Kantang | 36 | C1 |
| Kanuma | 32 | A6 |
| Kanye | 59 | C5 |
| Kaohsiung = Gaoxiong | 35 | D7 |
| Kaokoveld | 58 | B2 |
| Kaolack | 55 | F1 |
| Kapan | 25 | F6 |
| Kapanga | 56 | F4 |
| Kapchagai = Qapshaghay | 29 | E8 |
| Kapfenberg | 15 | E8 |
| Kapiri Mposhi | 59 | A5 |
| Kāpīsā □ | 45 | C7 |
| Kapit | 37 | D4 |
| Kapoeta | 53 | H5 |
| Kaposvár | 16 | E3 |
| Kapuas → | 37 | E3 |
| Kapuas Hulu, Pegunungan | 37 | D4 |
| Kapuas Hulu Ra. = Kapuas Hulu, Pegunungan | 37 | D4 |
| Kapunda | 62 | B2 |
| Kapuni | 64 | C6 |
| Kaputar | 63 | B5 |
| Kara | 28 | C7 |
| Kara Bogaz Gol, Zaliv = Garabogazköl Aylagy | 29 | E6 |
| Kara Kalpak Republic □ = Karakalpakstan □ | 29 | E6 |
| Kara Kum | 29 | F6 |
| Kara Sea | 28 | B8 |
| Karabiğa | 23 | D6 |
| Karabük | 46 | B3 |
| Karaburun | 23 | E6 |
| Karabutak = Qarabutaq | 29 | E7 |
| Karacabey | 23 | D7 |
| Karacasu | 23 | F7 |
| Karachi | 43 | G5 |
| Karad | 43 | L9 |
| Karadeniz Boğazı | 22 | D7 |
| Karaganda = Qaraghandy | 29 | E8 |
| Karagayly | 29 | E8 |
| Karaikal | 43 | P11 |
| Karaikkudi | 43 | P11 |
| Karaj | 44 | C2 |
| Karakalpakstan □ | 29 | E6 |
| Karakas | 29 | E9 |
| Karakelong | 38 | D3 |
| Karakitang | 39 | D3 |
| Karaklis = Vanadzor | 25 | E5 |
| Karakoram Pass | 42 | B10 |
| Karakoram Ra. | 42 | B10 |
| Karalon | 30 | D9 |
| Karaman | 46 | C3 |

# Karamay

| | | | |
|---|---|---|---|
| Karamay ..... 34 B3 | Kāshān ....... 44 C2 | Keewatin □ ... 70 B10 | Ketapang ..... 37 E4 |
| Karambu ..... 37 E5 | Kashi ........ 34 C2 | Kefallinía ..... 23 E3 | Ketchikan ... 71 C6 |
| Karamea Bight 65 D4 | Kashk-e Kohneh 42 B3 | Kefamenanu .. 39 F2 | Kętrzyn ...... 16 A5 |
| Karasburg .... 58 D3 | Kāshmar ..... 44 C4 | Keffi ........ 55 G6 | Keweenaw B. . 69 D2 |
| Karasino ...... 28 C9 | Kashun Noerh = | Keighley ..... 11 E6 | Key West ..... 86 B3 |
| Karasuk ...... 29 D8 | Gaxun Nur .. 34 B5 | Keith ........ 62 C3 | Khabarovo .... 28 C7 |
| Karatau = | Kasimov ...... 24 C5 | Keith Arm .... 70 B7 | Khabarovsk .. 31 E11 |
| Qarataū .... 29 E8 | Kasiruta ...... 39 E3 | Kekri ........ 42 G9 | Khābūr ─► .... 46 D5 |
| Karatau, Khrebet 29 E7 | Kasongo ...... 57 E5 | Kël ........ 30 C10 | Khairpur ..... 42 F6 |
| Karawanken .. 20 A5 | Kasongo Lunda 56 F3 | Kelang ....... 37 D2 | Khakassia □ .. 30 D6 |
| Karazhal ...... 29 E8 | Kásos ........ 23 G6 | Kelibia ....... 52 A1 | Khakhea ...... 58 C4 |
| Karbalā ....... 47 D6 | Kassalâ ....... 53 E6 | Kellé ........ 56 E2 | Khalkhāl ..... 46 C7 |
| Karcag ....... 16 E5 | Kassel ....... 14 C5 | Kells = | Khalkís ...... 23 E4 |
| Kardhítsa ..... 23 E3 | Kassue ....... 39 F5 | Ceanannus | Khalmer-Sede = |
| Karelia □ ..... 28 C4 | Kastamonu ... 46 B3 | Mor ........ 11 E3 | Tazovskiy ... 28 C8 |
| Karelian | Kasulu ....... 57 E6 | Kélo ........ 53 G2 | Khalmer Yu .. 28 C7 |
| Republic □ = | Kasur ........ 42 D9 | Kelowna ..... 71 D8 | Khalturin ..... 24 B6 |
| Karelia □ ... 28 C4 | Katako Kombe . 56 E4 | Kelso ........ 65 F3 | Khalūf ...... 48 C6 |
| Kargānrūd .... 46 C7 | Katamatite ... 63 C4 | Keluang ...... 37 D2 | Khambat, G. of 43 J8 |
| Kargasok ..... 29 D9 | Katanga = | Kem ........ 28 C4 | Khambhat .... 43 H8 |
| Kargat ....... 29 D9 | Shaba □ .... 57 F4 | Kema ........ 39 D3 | Khamir ...... 49 D3 |
| Kargil ....... 42 B10 | Katangi ...... 43 J11 | Kemah ...... 46 C4 | Khānābād .... 45 B7 |
| Kariba, L. .... 59 B5 | Kateríni ...... 23 D4 | Kemerovo .... 29 D9 | Khānaqin .... 46 D6 |
| Kariba Dam ... 59 B5 | Katha ....... 41 E11 | Kemi ........ 8 E12 | Khandwa .... 43 J10 |
| Kariba Gorge . 59 B5 | Kathiawar .... 43 H7 | Kemi älv = | Khanewal .... 42 D7 |
| Karibib ...... 58 C3 | Katihar ....... 40 E6 | Kemijoki ─► .. 8 E12 | Khaniá ...... 23 G5 |
| Karimata, | Katima Mulilo . 58 B4 | Kemijoki ─► .. 8 E12 | Khanion, Kólpos 23 G4 |
| Kepulauan .. 37 E3 | Katingan = | Kemp Land ... 96 A9 | Khankendy = |
| Karimata, Selat 37 E3 | Mendawai ─► 37 E4 | Kempsey ..... 63 B5 | Xankändi ... 25 F6 |
| Karimata Is. = | Katiola ....... 55 G3 | Kempten ..... 14 E6 | Khanty- |
| Karimata, | Katmandu .... 40 D5 | Kendal ....... 37 F4 | Mansiysk ... 29 C7 |
| Kepulauan .. 37 E3 | Katoomba .... 63 B5 | Kendall ....... 63 B5 | Khapcheranga . 30 E9 |
| Karimnagar ... 43 K11 | Katowice ..... 16 C4 | Kendari ...... 39 E2 | Kharagpur .... 40 F6 |
| Karimunjawa, | Katsina ...... 55 F6 | Kendawangan . 37 E4 | Kharan Kalat . 42 E4 |
| Kepulauan .. 37 F4 | Kattegat ...... 9 G10 | Kende ....... 55 F5 | Khārānaq ..... 44 C3 |
| Karin ........ 49 E4 | Kauai ....... 82 G11 | Kendrapara ... 40 G6 | Kharda ...... 43 K9 |
| Karkaralinsk = | Kaunas ...... 24 C1 | Kenema ...... 55 G2 | Khârga, El |
| Qarqaraly ... 29 E8 | Kaura Namoda 55 F6 | Keng Tawng .. 41 G12 | Wâhât el ... 52 C5 |
| Karkinitska | Kaválla ...... 22 D5 | Keng Tung ... 41 G12 | Khargon ..... 43 J9 |
| Zatoka ...... 25 D3 | Kaw ........ 92 B3 | Kenge ....... 56 E3 | Khārk, Jazireh . 47 E7 |
| Karkinitskiy Zaliv | Kawagoe ..... 32 B6 | Kenhardt .... 58 D4 | Kharkiv ...... 24 D4 |
| = Karkinitska | Kawaguchi ... 32 B6 | Kenitra ...... 54 B3 | Kharkov = |
| Zatoka ...... 25 D3 | Kawambwa ... 57 F5 | Kennedy | Kharkiv ..... 24 D4 |
| Karl-Marx-Stadt | Kawardha .... 40 G3 | Taungdeik .. 41 F9 | Kharovsk .... 24 B5 |
| = Chemnitz . 15 C7 | Kawasaki .... 32 B6 | Kennewick ... 80 B4 | Kharsānīya ... 47 F7 |
| Karlovac ...... 20 B5 | Kawerau ..... 64 C7 | Kenogami ─► . 69 C2 | Kharta ...... 22 D7 |
| Karlovo ...... 22 C5 | Kawhia Harbour 64 C6 | Kenosha ..... 72 C2 | Khartoum = El |
| Karlovy Vary . 16 C1 | Kawio, | Kent Group ... 62 C4 | Khartûm .... 53 E5 |
| Karlsbad = | Kepulauan .. 38 D3 | Kent Pen. ..... 70 B9 | Khāsh ....... 42 E2 |
| Karlovy Vary 16 C1 | Kawnro ...... 41 F12 | Kentau ...... 29 E7 | Khashm el Girba 53 F6 |
| Karlskrona .. 9 G11 | Kawthoolei = | Kentucky □ ... 72 F3 | Khaskovo .... 22 D5 |
| Karlsruhe ..... 14 D5 | Kawthule □ .. 41 H11 | Kentville ..... 69 D4 | Khatanga .... 30 B8 |
| Karlstad ..... 9 G10 | Kawthule □ ... 41 H11 | Kenya ■ ...... 57 D7 | Khatanga ─► .. 30 B8 |
| Karnal ...... 42 E10 | Kaya ........ 55 F4 | Kenya, Mt. ... 57 E7 | Khaybar, Harrat 47 F5 |
| Karnali ─► .... 40 C3 | Kayah □ ..... 41 H11 | Kepi ........ 39 F5 | Khed Brahma . 43 G8 |
| Karnaphuli Res. 41 F9 | Kayan ─► ..... 37 D5 | Kerala □ ..... 43 P10 | Khemmarat ... 36 A3 |
| Karnataka □ .. 43 N10 | Kayeli ....... 39 E3 | Kerang ...... 62 C3 | Khenchela ... 54 A6 |
| Karnische Alpen 20 A4 | Kayes ....... 55 F2 | Kerch ....... 25 D4 | Khenifra .... 54 B3 |
| Kärnten □ .... 15 E7 | Kayoa ....... 39 D3 | Kerchoual ... 55 E5 | Kherson .... 25 D3 |
| Karonga ..... 57 F6 | Kayrunnera ... 62 B3 | Keren ....... 53 E6 | Kheta ─► .... 30 B8 |
| Karoonda .... 62 C2 | Kayseri ...... 46 C3 | Kericho ...... 57 E7 | Khilok ...... 30 D9 |
| Karora ...... 53 E6 | Kayuagung ... 37 E2 | Kerinci ...... 37 E2 | Khíos ....... 23 E6 |
| Kárpathos ... 23 G6 | Kazachye .... 31 B11 | Kerki ....... 29 F7 | Khiuma = |
| Kars ........ 46 B5 | Kazakstan ■ .. 29 E7 | Kérkira ...... 23 E2 | Hiiumaa .... 24 B1 |
| Karsakpay .... 29 E7 | Kazan ....... 24 B6 | Kermadec Is. .. 64 M13 | Khiva ...... 29 E7 |
| Karshi = Qarshi 29 F7 | Kazanlŭk ..... 22 C5 | Kermadec | Khīyāv ...... 46 C6 |
| Karsun ....... 24 C6 | Kazatin = | Trench ...... 65 N13 | Khmelnik .... 17 D8 |
| Karufa ....... 39 E4 | Kozyatyn ... 17 D9 | Kermān ...... 44 D4 | Khmelnitskiy = |
| Karungu ..... 57 E6 | Kāzerūn ..... 44 D2 | Kermān □ .... 44 D4 | Khmelnytskyy 17 D8 |
| Karviná ...... 16 D4 | Kazumba ..... 56 F4 | Kermānshāh = | Khmelnytskyy . 17 D8 |
| Karwar ...... 43 M9 | Kazym ─► .... 28 C7 | Bākhtarān .. 46 D6 | Khmer Rep. = |
| Kasai ─► ..... 56 E3 | Ké-Macina ... 55 F3 | Kerme Körfezi . 23 F6 | Cambodia ■ . 36 B3 |
| Kasama ...... 57 G6 | Kéa ........ 23 F5 | Kerrobert ... 71 C9 | Khodoriv .... 17 D7 |
| Kasanga ..... 57 F6 | Kebnekaise .. 8 E11 | Kerulen ─► ... 35 B6 | Khodzent = |
| Kasangulu .... 56 E3 | Kebri Dehar .. 49 F3 | Kerzaz ....... 54 C4 | Khudzhand .. 29 E7 |
| Kasaragod ... 43 N9 | Kecskemét ... 16 E4 | Keşan ....... 22 D6 | Khojak P. .... 42 D5 |
| Kasba L. ..... 70 B9 | Kediri ....... 37 F4 | Kestenga .... 28 C4 | Kholm, Afghan. 45 B6 |
| Kasempa ..... 59 A5 | Kédougou ... 55 F2 | Ket ─► ....... 29 D9 | Kholm, Russia . 24 B3 |
| Kasenga ..... 57 G5 | Keetmanshoop 58 D3 | Keta ........ 55 G5 | Khomeyn ..... 44 C2 |

| | | | | | | | | | | |
|---|---|---|---|---|---|---|---|---|---|---|
| Khon Kaen | .... | 36 | A2 | Kimberley | .... | 58 | D4 | Kirsanov | ...... | 24 | C5 | Kobarid | ...... | 20 | A4 |

Khon Kaen .... 36 A2
Khoper → .... 29 E5
Khóra Sfakíon . 23 G5
Khorat =
 Nakhon
 Ratchasima . 36 B2
Khorramābād . 46 D7
Khorrämshahr . 47 E7
Khotyn ....... 17 D8
Khouribga .... 54 B3
Khowai ....... 41 E8
Khoyniki ...... 17 C9
Khu Khan .... 36 B2
Khudzhand ... 29 E7
Khūgīānī ..... 42 D4
Khulna ....... 41 F7
Khulna □ ..... 41 F7
Khūr ......... 44 C4
Khurayş ...... 47 F7
Khūrīyā Mūrīyā,
 Jazā 'ir ..... 48 D6
Khush ........ 42 C3
Khushab ...... 42 C8
Khust ........ 17 D6
Khuzdar ...... 42 F5
Khvor ........ 44 C3
Khvormūj ..... 44 D2
Khvoy ........ 46 C6
Khyber Pass . 42 B7
Kiama ........ 63 B5
Kiamba ....... 38 C2
Kiangsi =
 Jiangxi □ ... 35 D6
Kiangsu =
 Jiangsu □ .. 35 C6
Kibangou ..... 56 E2
Kibombo ..... 57 E5
Kibondo ..... 57 E6
Kibwesa ..... 57 F5
Kibwezi ...... 57 E7
Kicking Horse
 Pass ...... 71 C8
Kidal ........ 55 E5
Kidnappers, C. . 64 C7
Kiel ......... 14 A6
Kiel Canal =
 Nord-Ostsee-
 Kanal → ... 14 A5
Kielce ....... 16 C5
Kieler Bucht ... 14 A6
Kiev = Kyyiv .. 17 C10
Kiffa ........ 55 E2
Kifrī ......... 46 D6
Kigali ........ 57 E6
Kigoma-Ujiji .. 57 E5
Kihee ........ 62 A3
Kii-Suidō ..... 32 C4
Kikinda ...... 22 B3
Kikládhes .... 23 F5
Kikwit ....... 56 E3
Kilcoy ....... 63 A5
Kilimanjaro .. 57 E7
Kilindini ..... 57 E7
Kilis ........ 46 C4
Kiliya ....... 17 F9
Kilkenny ..... 11 E3
Kilkís ....... 23 D4
Killarney,
 Australia .... 63 A5
Killarney, Ireland 11 E2
Killeen ...... 78 D5
Killíni ....... 23 F4
Kilmarnock .⸴. 10 D4
Kilmore ...... 63 C3
Kilosa ....... 57 F7
Kilrush ...... 11 E2
Kilwa Kivinje . 57 F7
Kimaam ..... 39 F5
Kimba ....... 62 B2

Kimberley .... 58 D4
Kimberley
 Plateau ..... 60 D4
Kimry ........ 24 B4
Kinabalu,
 Gunong .... 36 C5
Kindia ........ 55 G2
Kindu ........ 57 E5
Kineshma .... 24 B5
King George B. . 95 G4
King George I. . 96 A4
King George Is. 69 C2
King I. = Kadan
 Kyun ....... 36 B1
King I. ........ 62 C3
King William I. 70 B10
King William's
 Town ...... 59 E5
Kingaroy ..... 63 A5
Kingoonya ... 62 B2
Kings Canyon
 National Park 82 B3
King's Lynn .. 11 E7
Kingscote ..... 62 C2
Kingsport ..... 75 A6
Kingston,
 Canada ..... 69 D3
Kingston,
 Jamaica .... 86 C4
Kingston, N.Z. . 65 F3
Kingston South
 East ....... 62 C2
Kingston upon
 Hull ....... 11 E6
Kingstown ... 87 D7
Kingsville .... 78 F5
Kınık ........ 23 E6
Kinkala ...... 56 E2
Kinleith ..... 64 C6
Kinsale ...... 11 F2
Kinshasa .... 56 E3
Kinston ..... 75 B9
Kintampo ... 55 G4
Kintap ....... 37 E5
Kiparissía ... 23 F3
Kiparissiakós
 Kólpos ..... 23 F3
Kipembawe ... 57 F6
Kipili ....... 57 F6
Kipushi ...... 59 A5
Kirghizia ■ =
 Kyrgyzstan ■ 29 E8
Kirghizstan =
 Kyrgyzstan ■ 29 E8
Kiri ......... 56 E3
Kiribati ■ ..... 64 K12
Kırıkkale .... 46 C3
Kirillov ...... 24 B4
Kirin = Jilin .. 35 B7
Kiritimati .... 65 J15
Kirkcaldy .... 10 C5
Kirkcudbright . 11 D4
Kirkee ....... 43 K8
Kirkenes ..... 8 E14
Kirkland Lake . 69 D2
Kırklareli ..... 22 D6
Kirkūk ....... 46 D6
Kirkwall ..... 10 B5
Kirov ........ 28 D5
Kirovabad =
 Gäncä ..... 25 E6
Kirovakan =
 Vanadzor ... 25 E5
Kirovograd =
 Kirovohrad .. 25 D3
Kirovohrad ... 25 D3
Kirovsk =
 Babadayhan . 29 F7
Kirovsk ...... 28 C4

Kirsanov ...... 24 C5
Kırşehir ....... 46 C3
Kirteh ....... 45 C5
Kirthar Range . 42 F5
Kiruna ....... 8 E12
Kirundu ...... 57 E5
Kiryū ........ 32 A6
Kisangani .... 57 D5
Kisar ........ 39 F3
Kiselevsk .... 29 D9
Kishanganj ... 40 D7
Kishangarh .. 42 F7
Kishinev =
 Chişinău .... 17 E9
Kishiwada ... 32 B4
Kishtwar ..... 42 C9
Kisii ........ 57 E6
Kisiju ....... 57 F7
Kiska I. ...... 71 C1
Kisköros ..... 16 E4
Kiskunfélegyháza
 .......... 16 E4
Kiskunhalas ... 16 E4
Kislovodsk .... 25 E5
Kiso-Sammyaku 32 B5
Kissidougou .. 55 G2
Kisumu ....... 57 E6
Kita ......... 55 F3
Kitab ........ 29 F7
Kitakami-
 Gawa → .. 33 G12
Kitakyūshū .. 32 C2
Kitale ....... 57 D7
Kitchener .... 69 D2
Kitega = Gitega 57 E5
Kitgum ...... 57 D6
Kíthira ...... 23 F4
Kíthnos ...... 23 F5
Kitimkeot □ ... 70 B9
Kittakittaooloo,
 L. .......... 62 A2
Kitui ........ 57 E7
Kitwe ....... 59 A5
Kivertsi ...... 17 C7
Kivu, L. ..... 57 E5
Kiyev = Kyyiv . 17 C10
Kiyevskoye
 Vdkhr. =
 Kyyivske
 Vdskh. ..... 17 C10
Kızıl Irmak → . 25 E4
Kizlyar ...... 25 E6
Kizyl-Arvat =
 Gyzylarbat .. 29 F6
Kladno ...... 16 C2
Klagenfurt ... 15 E8
Klaipeda ..... 24 B1
Klamath Falls . 80 D3
Klamath Mts. .. 80 E2
Klarälven → . 9 G10
Klatovy ..... 16 D1
Klawer ...... 58 E3
Klerksdorp .. 59 D5
Kletsk = Klyetsk 17 B8
Klin ......... 28 D4
Kłodzko ..... 16 C3
Klondike .... 70 B6
Klouto ...... 55 G5
Kluane L. .... 70 B6
Kluczbork ... 16 C4
Klyetsk ..... 17 B8
Knossós ..... 23 G5
Knox Coast .. 96 A12
Knoxville .... 75 B6
Koartac =
 Quaqtaq .... 68 B4
Koba, Aru,
 Indonesia .. 39 F4
Koba, Bangka,
 Indonesia ... 37 E3

Kobarid ...... 20 A4
Kobdo = Hovd 34 B4
Kōbe ........ 32 B4
København ... 9 G10
Koblenz .... 14 C4
Kobroor,
 Kepulauan .. 39 F4
Kobryn ...... 17 B7
Kocaeli = İzmit 25 E2
Kočani ...... 22 D4
Koch Bihar ... 41 D7
Kōchi ........ 32 C3
Kochiu = Gejiu 34 D5
Kodiak ...... 71 C4
Kodiak I. ..... 71 C4
Koes ........ 58 D3
Kofiau ...... 39 E3
Koforidua .... 55 G4
Kōfu ........ 32 B6
Kogan ....... 63 A5
Koh-i-Bābā ... 42 B5
Kohat ....... 42 C7
Kohima ..... 41 E10
Kohkīlūyeh va
 Būyer
 Aḥmadi □ ... 44 D2
Kohler Ra. ... 96 B1
Kokand =
 Qŭqon ..... 29 E8
Kokas ...... 39 E4
Kokchetav =
 Kökshetaū .. 29 D7
Koko Kyunzu . 41 K9
Kokomo .... 72 D2
Kokonau .... 39 E5
Kökshetaū .. 29 D7
Koksoak → ... 68 C4
Kokstad ..... 59 E5
Kola, Indonesia 39 F4
Kola, Russia ... 28 C4
Kola Pen. =
 Kolskiy
 Poluostrov .. 28 C4
Kolaka ....... 39 E2
Kolar ........ 43 N11
Kolar Gold
 Fields ...... 43 N11
Kolayat ...... 42 F8
Kolchugino =
 Leninsk-
 Kuznetskiy .. 29 D9
Kolda ....... 55 F2
Kole ........ 56 E4
Kolepom = Yos
 Sudarso,
 Pulau ...... 39 F5
Kolguyev,
 Ostrov ..... 28 C5
Kolhapur .... 43 L9
Kolín ........ 16 C2
Köln ........ 14 C4
Koło ........ 16 B4
Kołobrzeg .... 16 A2
Kolokani ..... 55 F3
Kolomna ..... 24 B4
Kolomyya .... 17 D7
Kolondale .... 39 E2
Kolosib ...... 41 E9
Kolpashevo .. 29 D9
Kolpino ..... 24 B3
Kolskiy
 Poluostrov .. 28 C4
Kolwezi ...... 57 G5
Kolyma → .. 31 C13
Komárno .... 16 E4
Komatsu .... 32 A5
Komi □ ...... 28 C6
Kommunarsk =
 Alchevsk .... 25 D4

| | | |
|---|---|---|
| Kommunizma, | | |
| Pik | 29 | F8 |
| Komodo | 39 | F1 |
| Komono | 56 | E2 |
| Komoran, Pulau | 39 | F5 |
| Komotini | 22 | D5 |
| Kompong Cham | 36 | B3 |
| Kompong | | |
| Chhnang | 36 | B2 |
| Kompong Som | 36 | B2 |
| Komrat = | | |
| Comrat | 17 | E9 |
| Komsomolets, | | |
| Ostrov | 30 | A7 |
| Konarhá □ | 42 | B7 |
| Konch | 42 | G11 |
| Kondoa | 57 | E7 |
| Konduga | 53 | F1 |
| Köneürgench | 29 | E6 |
| Kong | 55 | G4 |
| Kong, Koh | 36 | B2 |
| Konglu | 41 | D11 |
| Kongolo | 57 | F5 |
| Kongor | 53 | G5 |
| Königsberg = | | |
| Kaliningrad | 24 | C1 |
| Konin | 16 | B4 |
| Konjic | 20 | C6 |
| Konosha | 28 | C5 |
| Konotop | 24 | C3 |
| Konqi He → | 34 | B4 |
| Końskie | 16 | C5 |
| Konstanz | 14 | E5 |
| Kontagora | 55 | F6 |
| Kontum | 36 | B3 |
| Konya | 46 | C3 |
| Konya Ovası | 46 | C3 |
| Konza | 57 | E7 |
| Kooloonong | 62 | B3 |
| Koondrook | 63 | C3 |
| Koonibba | 62 | B1 |
| Koorawatha | 63 | B4 |
| Kootenay L. | 71 | D8 |
| Kopaonik | 22 | C3 |
| Koper | 20 | B4 |
| Kopeysk | 29 | D7 |
| Kopi | 62 | B2 |
| Koprivnica | 20 | A6 |
| Kopychyntsi | 17 | D7 |
| Korab | 22 | D3 |
| Korça | 23 | D3 |
| Korce = Korça | 23 | D3 |
| Korčula | 20 | C6 |
| Kordestan □ | 46 | D5 |
| Kordestän □ | 46 | D6 |
| Kordofân | 53 | F4 |
| Korea, North ■ | 35 | C7 |
| Korea, South ■ | 35 | C7 |
| Korea Bay | 35 | C7 |
| Korea Strait | 35 | C7 |
| Korets | 17 | C8 |
| Korhogo | 55 | G3 |
| Korim | 39 | E5 |
| Korinthiakós | | |
| Kólpos | 23 | E4 |
| Kórinthos | 23 | F4 |
| Kōriyama | 33 | G12 |
| Korneshty = | | |
| Cornești | 17 | E9 |
| Koro, *Ivory C.* | 55 | G3 |
| Koro, *Mali* | 55 | F4 |
| Korogwe | 57 | F7 |
| Koroit | 62 | C3 |
| Koror | 38 | C4 |
| Körös → | 16 | E5 |
| Korosten | 17 | C9 |
| Korostyshev | 17 | C9 |
| Korti | 53 | E5 |
| Kortrijk | 14 | C2 |

| | | |
|---|---|---|
| Kos | 23 | F6 |
| Kościan | 16 | B3 |
| Kosciusko, Mt. | 63 | C4 |
| Kosha | 52 | D5 |
| K'oshih = Kashi | 34 | C2 |
| Košice | 16 | D5 |
| Kosovo □ | 22 | C3 |
| Kosovska-Mitrovica = | | |
| Titova-Mitrovica | 22 | C3 |
| Kôstî | 53 | F5 |
| Kostopil | 17 | C8 |
| Kostroma | 24 | B5 |
| Kostrzyn | 16 | B2 |
| Koszalin | 16 | A3 |
| Kota | 43 | G9 |
| Kota Baharu | 36 | C2 |
| Kota Belud | 36 | C5 |
| Kota Kinabalu | 36 | C5 |
| Kota Tinggi | 37 | D2 |
| Kotaagung | 37 | F2 |
| Kotabaru | 37 | E5 |
| Kotabumi | 37 | E2 |
| Kotamobagu | 39 | D2 |
| Kotawaringin | 37 | E4 |
| Kotelnich | 24 | B6 |
| Kotelnyy, Ostrov | 31 | B11 |
| Kotka | 9 | F13 |
| Kotlas | 28 | C5 |
| Kotli | 42 | C8 |
| Kotor | 22 | C2 |
| Kotovsk | 17 | E9 |
| Kotri | 42 | G6 |
| Kottayam | 43 | Q10 |
| Kotturu | 43 | M10 |
| Kotuy → | 30 | B8 |
| Kotzebue | 71 | B3 |
| Kouango | 56 | D4 |
| Koudougou | 55 | F4 |
| Kouilou → | 56 | E2 |
| Kouki | 56 | C3 |
| Koula Moutou | 56 | E2 |
| Koulen | 36 | B2 |
| Koulikoro | 55 | F3 |
| Koumra | 53 | G2 |
| Kounradskiy | 29 | E8 |
| Kouroussa | 55 | F3 |
| Kousseri | 53 | F1 |
| Koutiala | 55 | F3 |
| Kovel | 17 | C7 |
| Kovrov | 24 | B5 |
| Kowloon | 35 | D6 |
| Köyceğiz | 23 | F7 |
| Koyuk | 71 | B3 |
| Koyukuk → | 71 | B4 |
| Kozan | 46 | C3 |
| Kozáni | 23 | D3 |
| Kozhikode = | | |
| Calicut | 43 | P9 |
| Kozyatyn | 17 | D9 |
| Kpalimé | 55 | G5 |
| Kra, Isthmus of = Kra, Kho | | |
| Khot | 36 | B1 |
| Kra, Kho Khot | 36 | B1 |
| Kragujevac | 22 | B3 |
| Krajina | 20 | B6 |
| Krakatau = | | |
| Rakata, Pulau | 37 | F3 |
| Kraków | 16 | C4 |
| Kraljevo | 22 | C3 |
| Kramatorsk | 25 | D4 |
| Kranj | 20 | A5 |
| Kraśnik | 16 | C6 |
| Krasnoarmeysk | 29 | D5 |
| Krasnodar | 25 | D4 |
| Krasnoperekopsk | 25 | D3 |

| | | |
|---|---|---|
| Krasnoselkupsk | 28 | C9 |
| Krasnoturinsk | 28 | D7 |
| Krasnoufimsk | 29 | D6 |
| Krasnouralsk | 29 | D7 |
| Krasnovodsk = | | |
| Krasnowodsk | 29 | E6 |
| Krasnowodsk | 29 | E6 |
| Krasnoyarsk | 30 | D7 |
| Krasnyy Luch | 25 | D4 |
| Krasnyy Yar | 25 | D6 |
| Kratie | 36 | B3 |
| Krau | 39 | E6 |
| Krefeld | 14 | C4 |
| Kremen | 20 | B5 |
| Kremenchug = | | |
| Kremenchuk | 24 | D3 |
| Kremenchuk | 24 | D3 |
| Kremenchuksk | | |
| Vdskh. | 24 | D3 |
| Kremenets | 17 | C7 |
| Krems | 15 | D8 |
| Kribi | 56 | D1 |
| Krichev = | | |
| Krychaw | 17 | B10 |
| Krishna → | 40 | K3 |
| Krishnanagar | 41 | F7 |
| Kristiansand | 9 | G9 |
| Kristiansund | 8 | F9 |
| Kríti | 23 | G5 |
| Krivoy Rog = | | |
| Kryvyy Rih | 25 | D3 |
| Krk | 20 | B5 |
| Kronprins Olav | | |
| Kyst | 96 | A9 |
| Kronshtadt | 24 | B2 |
| Kroonstad | 59 | D5 |
| Kropotkin, | | |
| *Irkutsk, Russia* | 30 | D9 |
| Kropotkin, | | |
| *Krasnodar,* | | |
| *Russia* | 25 | D5 |
| Krosno | 16 | D5 |
| Krotoszyn | 16 | C3 |
| Krugersdorp | 59 | D5 |
| Krung Thep = | | |
| Bangkok | 36 | B2 |
| Krupki | 17 | A9 |
| Kruševac | 22 | C3 |
| Krychaw | 17 | B10 |
| Krymskiy | | |
| Poluostrov = | | |
| Krymskyy | | |
| Pivostriv | 25 | D3 |
| Krymskyy | | |
| Pivostriv | 25 | D3 |
| Kryvyy Rih | 25 | D3 |
| Ksar el Boukhari | 54 | A5 |
| Ksar el Kebir | 54 | B3 |
| Ksar es Souk = | | |
| Ar Rachidiya | 54 | B4 |
| Kuala | 37 | D3 |
| Kuala Kubu | | |
| Baharu | 37 | D2 |
| Kuala Lipis | 37 | D2 |
| Kuala Lumpur | 37 | D2 |
| Kuala | | |
| Terengganu | 36 | C2 |
| Kualajelai | 37 | E4 |
| Kualakapuas | 37 | E4 |
| Kualakurun | 37 | E4 |
| Kualapembuang | 37 | E4 |
| Kualasimpang | 37 | D1 |
| Kuandang | 39 | D2 |
| Kuangchou = | | |
| Guangzhou | 35 | D6 |
| Kuantan | 37 | D2 |
| Kuba = Quba | 25 | E6 |
| Kuban → | 25 | D4 |
| Kucing | 37 | D4 |

| | | |
|---|---|---|
| Kuda | 43 | H7 |
| Kudat | 36 | C5 |
| Kudymkar | 28 | D6 |
| Kueiyang = | | |
| Guiyang | 35 | D5 |
| Kufra Oasis = Al | | |
| Kufrah | 52 | D3 |
| Kufstein | 15 | E7 |
| Küh-e 'Alijūq | 44 | D2 |
| Küh-e-Hazārām | 44 | D4 |
| Küh-e Sorkh | 44 | C4 |
| Küh-e Taftän | 45 | D5 |
| Kühak | 42 | F3 |
| Kühhä-ye-Bashäkerd | 45 | E4 |
| Kühpäyeh | 44 | C3 |
| Kuito | 58 | A3 |
| Kujū-San | 32 | C2 |
| Kukawa | 53 | F1 |
| Kukësi | 22 | C3 |
| Kula | 23 | E7 |
| Kulasekarappattinam | 43 | Q11 |
| Kuldja = Yining | 34 | B3 |
| Kŭlob | 29 | F7 |
| Kulsary | 29 | E6 |
| Kulunda | 29 | D8 |
| Kulwin | 62 | C3 |
| Kulyab = Kŭlob | 29 | F7 |
| Kum Tekei | 29 | E8 |
| Kuma → | 25 | E6 |
| Kumagaya | 32 | A6 |
| Kumai | 37 | E4 |
| Kumamba, | | |
| Kepulauan | 39 | E5 |
| Kumamoto | 32 | C2 |
| Kumanovo | 22 | C3 |
| Kumara | 65 | E4 |
| Kumasi | 55 | G4 |
| Kumayri = | | |
| Gyumri | 25 | E5 |
| Kumba | 56 | D1 |
| Kumbakonam | 43 | P11 |
| Kumbarilla | 63 | A5 |
| Kumo | 55 | F7 |
| Kumon Bum | 41 | D11 |
| Kunama | 63 | C4 |
| Kungala | 63 | A5 |
| Kungrad = | | |
| Qŭnghirot | 29 | E6 |
| Kungur | 29 | D6 |
| Kunlong | 41 | F12 |
| Kunlun Shan | 34 | C3 |
| Kunming | 35 | D5 |
| Kunsan | 35 | C7 |
| Kunya-Urgench = | | |
| Köneürgench | 29 | E6 |
| Kuopio | 8 | F13 |
| Kupa → | 20 | B6 |
| Kupyansk | 28 | E4 |
| Kuqa | 34 | B3 |
| Kura → | 25 | E6 |
| Kura = Kür → | 25 | E6 |
| Kurashiki | 32 | B3 |
| Kurayoshi | 32 | B3 |
| Kŭrdzhali | 22 | D5 |
| Kure | 32 | B3 |
| Kurgaldzhinskiy | 29 | D8 |
| Kurgan | 29 | D7 |
| Kuria Maria Is. = Khūrīyā | | |
| Mūrīyā, Jazā | | |
| 'ir | 48 | D6 |
| Kurigram | 41 | E7 |
| Kuril Is. = | | |
| Kurilskiye | | |
| Ostrova | 31 | E12 |
| Kurilskiye | | |
| Ostrova | 31 | E12 |

Kurmuk ...... 53 F5
Kurnool ...... 43 L11
Kurow ....... 65 F4
Kurrajong .... 63 B5
Kurri Kurri .... 63 B5
Kursk ........ 24 C4
Kuruktag ..... 34 B3
Kuruman ..... 58 D4
Kurume ...... 32 C2
Kus Gölü ..... 23 D6
Kuşadası ..... 23 F6
Kushiro ...... 32 F12
Kushtia ...... 41 F7
Kuskokwim → 71 B3
Kuskokwim B. . 71 C3
Kustanay =
  Qostanay ... 29 D7
Kütahya ...... 46 C2
Kutaisi ...... 25 E5
Kutaraja =
  Banda Aceh . 36 C1
Kutch, Gulf of =
  Kachchh, Gulf
  of .......... 43 H6
Kutch, Rann of
  = Kachchh,
  Rann of ..... 43 G6
Kutno ........ 16 B4
Kutu ......... 56 E3
Kutum ........ 53 F3
Kuujjuaq ..... 68 C4
Kuwait = Al
  Kuwayt ..... 47 E7
Kuwait ■ ..... 47 E6
Kuwana ...... 32 B5
Kuybyshev =
  Samara ..... 24 C7
Kuybyshev ... 29 D8
Kuybyshevskoye
  Vdkhr. ...... 24 B6
Küysanjaq .... 46 C6
Kuyumba ..... 30 C7
Kuzey Anadolu
  Dağları ..... 46 B3
Kuznetsk ..... 24 C6
Kvarner ...... 20 B5
Kvarnerič ..... 20 B5
Kwakoegron .. 92 A2
Kwamouth .... 56 E3
Kwando → ... 58 B4
Kwangju ..... 35 C7
Kwangsi-Chuang
  = Guangxi
  Zhuangzu
  Zizhiqu □ ... 35 D5
Kwangtung =
  Guangdong □ 35 D6
Kwatisore .... 39 E4
Kweichow =
  Guizhou □ .. 35 D5
Kwekwe ...... 59 B5
Kwidzyn ...... 16 B4
Kwoka ....... 39 E4
Kyabé ........ 53 G2
Kyabra Cr. → . 63 A3
Kyabram ..... 63 C4
Kyancutta .... 62 B2
Kyangin ...... 41 H10
Kyaukpadaung 41 G10
Kyaukpyu .... 41 H9
Kyaukse ...... 41 G11
Kyle Dam ..... 59 C6
Kyneton ...... 63 C3
Kyō-ga-Saki .. 32 B4
Kyoga, L. .... 57 D6
Kyogle ....... 63 A5
Kyongpyaw ... 41 J10
Kyōto ........ 32 B4
Kyrenia ...... 46 D3

Kyrgyzstan ■ .. 29 E8
Kystatyam .... 30 C10
Kytal Ktakh .. 31 C10
Kyunhla ...... 41 F10
Kyūshū ....... 32 C2
Kyūshū-Sanchi 32 C2
Kyustendil ... 22 C4
Kyusyur ...... 30 B10
Kywong ...... 63 B4
Kyyiv ........ 17 C10
Kyyivske Vdskh. 17 C10
Kyzyl Kum .... 29 E7
Kyzyl-Kyya ... 29 E8
Kzyl-Orda =
  Qyzylorda ... 29 E7

L

La Albufera ... 19 C5
La Alcarria ... 19 B4
La Asunción .. 90 A6
La Banda ..... 94 B4
La Calera ..... 94 C2
La Carlota .... 94 C4
La Ceiba ...... 85 D7
La Chaux de
  Fonds ...... 13 C7
La Cocha ..... 94 B3
La Coruña .... 18 A1
La Crosse .... 77 D9
La Dorada .... 90 B4
La Estrada ... 18 A1
La Grange .... 74 C5
La Guaira .... 90 A5
La Güera ..... 54 D1
La Habana .... 86 B3
La Línea de la
  Concepción . 18 D3
La Mancha .... 19 C4
La Palma,
  Canary Is. ... 54 C1
La Palma,
  Panama .... 86 E4
La Palma del
  Condado ... 18 D2
La Paragua .. 90 B6
La Paz,
  Entre Ríos,
  Argentina ... 94 C5
La Paz, San Luis,
  Argentina ... 94 C3
La Paz, Bolivia . 91 G5
La Paz, Mexico . 84 C2
La Pedrera ... 90 D5
La Plata ...... 94 D5
La Quiaca ..... 94 A3
La Rioja ...... 94 B3
La Rioja □ ... 19 A4
La Robla ..... 18 A3
La Roche-sur-
  Yon ....... 12 C3
La Rochelle ... 12 C3
La Roda ...... 19 C4
La Romana ... 87 C6
La Serena .... 94 B2
La Seyne-sur-
  Mer ....... 13 E6
La Spézia .... 20 B2
La Tortuga .... 87 D6
La Tuque ..... 69 D3
La Unión ..... 95 E2
La Urbana .... 90 B5
La Vega ...... 87 C5
Labe = Elbe → 16 B5
Labé ......... 55 F2
Labis ........ 37 D2

Laboulaye .... 94 C4
Labrador, Coast
  of □ ....... 69 C4
Lábrea ....... 91 E6
Labuan, Pulau . 36 C5
Labuha ....... 39 E3
Labuhanbajo .. 39 F2
Labuk, Telok .. 36 C5
Labyrinth, L. .. 62 B2
Labytnangi ... 28 C7
Lac La Biche .. 71 C8
Lac la Martre .. 70 B8
Lacanau ..... 12 D3
Laccadive Is. =
  Lakshadweep
  Is. ......... 26 H11
Lacepede B. ... 62 C2
Lachine ...... 69 D3
Lachlan → ... 63 B3
Lackawanna .. 73 C6
Lacombe ..... 71 C8
Ladakh Ra. ... 42 B10
Lādīz ........ 45 D5
Ladoga, L. =
  Ladozhskoye
  Ozero ..... 28 C4
Ladozhskoye
  Ozero ..... 28 C4
Ladysmith,
  Canada .... 71 D7
Ladysmith,
  S. Africa .... 59 D5
Lae .......... 61 B8
Lafayette ..... 79 D7
Lafia ........ 55 G6
Laghmān □ ... 45 C7
Laghouat ..... 54 B5
Lagonoy Gulf . 38 B2
Lagos, Nigeria . 55 G5
Lagos, Portugal . 18 D1
Laguna ...... 94 B7
Lagunas, Chile . 91 H5
Lagunas, Peru . 90 E3
Lahad Datu ... 38 C1
Lahat ........ 37 E2
Lahewa ...... 37 D1
Lāhījān ...... 46 C7
Lahn → ...... 14 C4
Lahore ....... 42 D9
Lahti ........ 8 F13
Lahtis = Lahti . 8 F13
Laï .......... 53 G2
Laibin ....... 35 D5
Laidley ...... 63 A5
Laila = Laylá . 47 G6
Lairg ........ 10 B4
Lajere ....... 55 F7
Lajes ........ 94 B6
Lake Cargelligo 63 B4
Lake Charles .. 79 D7
Lake City .... 75 D6
Lake Harbour .. 68 B4
Lake Worth ... 75 F7
Lakeland ..... 75 E7
Lakes Entrance 63 C4
Lakewood .... 72 D5
Lakonikós
  Kólpos .... 23 F4
Lakor ........ 39 F3
Lakota ....... 76 D3
Lakshadweep Is. 26 H11
Lala Ghat .... 41 E9
Lalibela ...... 53 F6
Lalín ........ 18 A1
Lalitapur =
  Patan ..... 40 D5
Lamaing ..... 41 K11
Lamas ....... 91 E3
Lambaréné ... 56 E2

Lambert Glacier 96 B10
Lame ........ 55 F6
Lamego ...... 18 B2
Lameroo ..... 62 C3
Lamía ........ 23 E4
Lamon Bay ... 38 B2
Lampa ....... 91 G4
Lampedusa ... 21 G4
Lampione .... 21 G4
Lampung □ ... 37 F2
Lamu ........ 57 E8
Lanai I. ...... 82 H12
Lanak La ..... 42 B11
Lanak'o
  Shank'ou =
  Lanak La ... 42 B11
Lanao, L. .... 38 C2
Lancaster, U.K. 11 D5
Lancaster,
  U.S.A. ..... 73 D7
Lancaster Sd. . 68 A2
Lanchow =
  Lanzhou ... 35 C5
Lanciano .... 20 C5
Landeck ..... 14 E6
Landes ...... 12 D3
Landi Kotal ... 42 B7
Land's End ... 11 F4
Landshut .... 15 D7
La'nga Co .... 40 B3
Langkawi, P. .. 36 C1
Langkon ..... 36 C5
Langres ...... 13 C6
Langres, Plateau
  de ........ 13 C6
Langsa ...... 36 D1
Languedoc .... 13 E5
Langzhong ... 35 C5
Lannion ...... 12 B2
Lansdowne ... 63 B5
Lansing ...... 72 C3
Lanusei ...... 21 E2
Lanzarote .... 54 C2
Lanzhou ..... 35 C5
Laoag ....... 38 A2
Laoang ...... 38 B3
Laon ......... 13 B5
Laos ■ ...... 36 A3
Lapa ........ 94 B7
Laparan ..... 38 C1
Lapland =
  Lappland ... 8 E12
Lappland ..... 8 E12
Lapseki ...... 23 D6
Laptev Sea ... 30 B10
L'Aquila ..... 20 C4
Lär .......... 44 E3
Larache ...... 54 A3
Laramie ...... 76 E2
Larantuka .... 39 F2
Larap ........ 38 B2
Larat ........ 39 F4
Laredo ....... 78 F4
Lariang ...... 39 E1
Lárisa ....... 23 E4
Larnaca ...... 46 D3
Larne ........ 11 D4
Larrimah ..... 60 D5
Larsen Ice Shelf 96 A3
Larvik ........ 9 G9
Laryak ....... 29 C8
Las Anod ..... 49 F4
Las Cruces ... 83 D9
Las Flores .... 94 D5
Las Khoreh ... 49 E4
Las Lajas .... 94 D2
Las Lomitas .. 94 A4
Las Palmas ... 54 C1
Las Pipinas ... 94 D5

| | | |
|---|---|---|
| Las Plumas ... | 95 | E3 |
| Las Rosas .... | 94 | C4 |
| Las Varillas ... | 94 | C4 |
| Las Vegas .. | 82 | B5 |
| Lashio ....... | 41 | F11 |
| Lassen Pk. .... | 80 | E3 |
| Lastoursville .. | 56 | E2 |
| Lastovo ...... | 20 | C6 |
| Latacunga ... | 90 | D3 |
| Latakia = Al | | |
| Lādhiqīyah .. | 46 | D3 |
| Latina ........ | 20 | D4 |
| Latium = | | |
| Lazio □ ..... | 20 | C4 |
| Latrobe ....... | 62 | D4 |
| Latvia ■ ..... | 24 | B1 |
| Lauchhammer . | 15 | C7 |
| Launceston ... | 62 | D4 |
| Laurel ........ | 79 | D9 |
| Lauria ....... | 21 | D5 |
| Laurium ...... | 69 | D2 |
| Lausanne ..... | 13 | C7 |
| Laut ......... | 36 | D3 |
| Laut Kecil, | | |
| Kepulauan .. | 37 | E5 |
| Laval ........ | 12 | B3 |
| Lávrion ....... | 23 | F5 |
| Lawas ........ | 36 | D5 |
| Lawele ....... | 39 | F2 |
| Lawng Pit ..... | 41 | E11 |
| Lawrence, N.Z. | 65 | F3 |
| Lawrence, | | |
| U.S.A. ...... | 77 | F7 |
| Lawton ....... | 78 | B4 |
| Laylá ......... | 47 | G6 |
| Lazio □ ...... | 20 | C4 |
| Le Creusot .... | 13 | C6 |
| Le Havre ..... | 12 | B4 |
| Le Mans ..... | 12 | C4 |
| Le Mont-St.- | | |
| Michel ...... | 12 | B3 |
| Le Moule ..... | 87 | C7 |
| Le Puy-en-Velay | 13 | D5 |
| Le Touquet- | | |
| Paris-Plage .. | 12 | A4 |
| Le Tréport .... | 12 | A4 |
| Le Verdon-sur- | | |
| Mer ....... | 12 | D3 |
| Leamington Spa | | |
| = Royal | | |
| Leamington | | |
| Spa ........ | 11 | E6 |
| Leandro Norte | | |
| Alem ....... | 94 | B5 |
| Leavenworth .. | 77 | F7 |
| Lebak ........ | 38 | C2 |
| Lebanon ■ .... | 46 | D3 |
| Lębork ....... | 16 | A3 |
| Lebrija ....... | 18 | D2 |
| Lebu ......... | 94 | D2 |
| Lecce ........ | 23 | D2 |
| Lecco ........ | 20 | B2 |
| Lech → ..... | 14 | D6 |
| Łęczyca ...... | 16 | B6 |
| Leduc ........ | 71 | C8 |
| Leeds ........ | 11 | E6 |
| Leer ......... | 14 | B4 |
| Leeton ....... | 63 | B4 |
| Leeuwarden ... | 14 | B3 |
| Leeuwin, C. ... | 60 | G2 |
| Leeward Is. ... | 87 | C7 |
| Leganés ...... | 18 | B4 |
| Legazpi ...... | 38 | B2 |
| Leghorn = | | |
| Livorno ..... | 20 | C3 |
| Legionowo .... | 16 | B5 |
| Legnago ...... | 20 | B3 |
| Legnica ...... | 16 | C3 |
| Legume ...... | 63 | A5 |
| Leh .......... | 42 | B10 |
| Leicester ..... | 11 | E6 |
| Leiden ....... | 14 | B3 |
| Leie → ....... | 14 | C2 |
| Leine → ..... | 14 | B5 |
| Leinster □ .... | 11 | E3 |
| Leipzig ....... | 15 | C7 |
| Leiria ........ | 18 | C1 |
| Leitrim ....... | 11 | D2 |
| Leizhou Bandao | 35 | D6 |
| Leksula ....... | 39 | E3 |
| Lékva Ori ..... | 23 | G5 |
| Leleque ...... | 95 | E2 |
| Léman, L. ..... | 13 | C7 |
| Lemhi Ra. .... | 81 | C7 |
| Lena → ..... | 30 | B10 |
| Leninabad = | | |
| Khudzhand .. | 29 | E7 |
| Leninakan = | | |
| Gyumri ..... | 25 | E5 |
| Leningrad = | | |
| Sankt- | | |
| Peterburg ... | 24 | B3 |
| Leninogorsk = | | |
| Ridder ...... | 29 | D9 |
| Leninsk ...... | 25 | D6 |
| Leninsk- | | |
| Kuznetskiy .. | 29 | D9 |
| Lenmalu ...... | 39 | E4 |
| Lens ........ | 13 | A5 |
| Lentini ....... | 21 | F5 |
| Leoben ....... | 15 | E8 |
| Leodhas = | | |
| Lewis ...... | 10 | B3 |
| León, Mexico .. | 84 | C4 |
| León, Nic. .... | 85 | E7 |
| León, Spain ... | 18 | A3 |
| León, Montañas | | |
| de ......... | 18 | A2 |
| Leongatha .... | 63 | C4 |
| Léopold II, Lac | | |
| = Mai- | | |
| Ndombe, L. . | 56 | E3 |
| Léopoldville = | | |
| Kinshasa ... | 56 | E3 |
| Leova ........ | 17 | E9 |
| Lepel = Lyepyel | 24 | C2 |
| Lepikha ...... | 31 | C10 |
| Léré ......... | 53 | G1 |
| Lérida ........ | 19 | B6 |
| Lerwick ...... | 10 | A6 |
| Les Cayes .... | 86 | C5 |
| Les Sables- | | |
| d'Olonne ... | 12 | C3 |
| Lesbos = | | |
| Lésvos ..... | 23 | E6 |
| Leskovac ..... | 22 | C3 |
| Lesotho ■ .... | 59 | D5 |
| Lesser Antilles . | 87 | D7 |
| Lesser Sunda Is. | 39 | F2 |
| Lésvos ....... | 23 | E6 |
| Leszno ....... | 16 | C3 |
| Lethbridge ... | 71 | D8 |
| Leti, Kepulauan | 39 | F3 |
| Leti Is. = Leti, | | |
| Kepulauan .. | 39 | F3 |
| Leticia ....... | 90 | D4 |
| Letpadan ..... | 41 | J10 |
| Letpan ....... | 41 | H10 |
| Letterkenny ... | 11 | D3 |
| Leuser, G. .... | 37 | D1 |
| Leuven ....... | 14 | C3 |
| Levádhia ..... | 23 | E4 |
| Levice ....... | 16 | D4 |
| Levin ........ | 64 | D6 |
| Lévis ........ | 69 | D3 |
| Levkás ....... | 23 | E3 |
| Levkôsia = | | |
| Nicosia ..... | 46 | D3 |
| Levskigrad = | | |
| Karlovo ..... | 22 | C5 |
| Lewis ....... | 10 | B3 |
| Lewisporte .... | 69 | D5 |
| Lewiston, Idaho, | | |
| U.S.A. ...... | 80 | B5 |
| Lewiston, | | |
| Maine, U.S.A. | 73 | B10 |
| Lexington, Ky., | | |
| U.S.A. ...... | 72 | E3 |
| Lexington, N.C., | | |
| U.S.A. ...... | 75 | B7 |
| Leyte ........ | 38 | B2 |
| Lezha ........ | 22 | D2 |
| Lhasa ........ | 34 | D4 |
| Lhazê ........ | 34 | D3 |
| Lhokkruet ..... | 36 | D1 |
| Lhokseumawe . | 36 | C1 |
| Lhuntsi Dzong . | 41 | D8 |
| Lianga ....... | 38 | C3 |
| Lianyungang .. | 35 | C6 |
| Liaoning □ .... | 35 | B7 |
| Liaoyuan ..... | 35 | B7 |
| Liard → ...... | 70 | B7 |
| Libau = Liepāja | 24 | B1 |
| Libenge ...... | 56 | D3 |
| Liberal ....... | 78 | A3 |
| Liberec ...... | 16 | C2 |
| Liberia ■ ..... | 55 | G3 |
| Lîbîya, Sahrâ' . | 52 | C4 |
| Libobo, Tanjung | 39 | E3 |
| Libonda ...... | 58 | A4 |
| Libourne ..... | 12 | D3 |
| Libreville ..... | 56 | D1 |
| Libya ■ ...... | 52 | C2 |
| Libyan Desert = | | |
| Lîbîya, Sahrâ' | 52 | C4 |
| Licantén ..... | 94 | D2 |
| Licata ....... | 21 | F4 |
| Lichinga ...... | 59 | A7 |
| Lichtenburg .. | 59 | D5 |
| Lida ........ | 17 | B7 |
| Liechtenstein ■ | 14 | E5 |
| Liège ........ | 14 | C3 |
| Liegnitz = | | |
| Legnica ..... | 16 | C3 |
| Lienyünchiangshih | | |
| = | | |
| Lianyungang | 35 | C6 |
| Lienz ........ | 15 | E7 |
| Liepāja ....... | 24 | B1 |
| Liffey → ..... | 11 | E3 |
| Lifford ....... | 11 | D3 |
| Lightning Ridge | 63 | A4 |
| Liguria □ ..... | 20 | B2 |
| Ligurian Sea .. | 20 | C2 |
| Lijiang ....... | 34 | D5 |
| Likasi ....... | 57 | G5 |
| Lille ......... | 13 | A5 |
| Lillehammer .. | 8 | F10 |
| Lilongwe ..... | 59 | A6 |
| Liloy ........ | 38 | C2 |
| Lim → ....... | 20 | C7 |
| Lima, Indonesia | 39 | E3 |
| Lima, Peru ... | 91 | F3 |
| Lima, U.S.A. .. | 72 | D3 |
| Lima → ...... | 18 | B1 |
| Limassol ..... | 46 | D3 |
| Limay Mahuida | 94 | D3 |
| Limbang ..... | 36 | D5 |
| Limbe ....... | 56 | D1 |
| Limbri ....... | 63 | B5 |
| Limburg ..... | 14 | C5 |
| Limeira ...... | 94 | A7 |
| Limerick ..... | 11 | E2 |
| Limfjorden ... | 9 | G9 |
| Limia = | | |
| Lima → .... | 18 | B1 |
| Límnos ....... | 23 | E5 |
| Limoeiro do | | |
| Norte ...... | 92 | D6 |
| Limoges ...... | 12 | D4 |
| Limón ........ | 86 | E3 |
| Limousin ..... | 12 | D4 |
| Limoux ...... | 12 | E5 |
| Limpopo → .. | 59 | D6 |
| Limuru ....... | 57 | E7 |
| Linares, Chile . | 94 | D2 |
| Linares, Mexico | 84 | C5 |
| Linares, Spain . | 18 | C4 |
| Linchuan ..... | 35 | D6 |
| Lincoln, | | |
| Argentina .. | 94 | C4 |
| Lincoln, N.Z. .. | 65 | E5 |
| Lincoln, U.K. .. | 11 | E6 |
| Lincoln, U.S.A. | 77 | E6 |
| Linden ....... | 90 | B7 |
| Líndhos ...... | 23 | F7 |
| Lindi ........ | 57 | F7 |
| Lingayen ..... | 38 | A2 |
| Lingayen G. .. | 38 | A2 |
| Lingen ....... | 14 | B4 |
| Lingga ....... | 37 | E2 |
| Lingga, | | |
| Kepulauan .. | 37 | E2 |
| Lingga Arch. = | | |
| Lingga, | | |
| Kepulauan .. | 37 | E2 |
| Linguéré ...... | 55 | E1 |
| Lingyun ...... | 35 | D5 |
| Linhai ........ | 35 | D7 |
| Linhares ...... | 93 | F5 |
| Linköping ..... | 9 | G11 |
| Linosa, I. ..... | 21 | G4 |
| Lins ......... | 94 | A7 |
| Linville ...... | 63 | A5 |
| Linxia ....... | 34 | C5 |
| Linz ......... | 15 | D8 |
| Lion, G. du .. | 13 | E6 |
| Lions, G. of = | | |
| Lion, G. du .. | 13 | E6 |
| Lipa ......... | 38 | B2 |
| Lípari ........ | 21 | E5 |
| Lípari, Is. = | | |
| Eólie, Ís. .. | 21 | E5 |
| Lipcani ...... | 17 | D8 |
| Lipetsk ...... | 24 | C4 |
| Lipkany = | | |
| Lipcani ..... | 17 | D8 |
| Lipovets ..... | 17 | D9 |
| Lippe → ..... | 14 | C4 |
| Liptrap C. .... | 63 | C4 |
| Lira ......... | 57 | D6 |
| Liria ........ | 19 | C5 |
| Lisala ....... | 56 | D4 |
| Lisboa ....... | 18 | C1 |
| Lisbon = Lisboa | 18 | C1 |
| Lisburn ...... | 11 | D3 |
| Lisburne, C. .. | 71 | B3 |
| Lishui ....... | 35 | D6 |
| Lisichansk = | | |
| Lysychansk . | 25 | D4 |
| Lisieux ....... | 12 | B4 |
| Liski ........ | 24 | C4 |
| Lismore ...... | 63 | A5 |
| Lister, Mt. .... | 96 | B15 |
| Liston ....... | 63 | A5 |
| Listowel ..... | 11 | E2 |
| Litang ....... | 38 | C1 |
| Litani → ..... | 46 | D3 |
| Lithgow ...... | 63 | B5 |
| Líthinon, Ákra . | 23 | G5 |
| Lithuania ■ ... | 24 | B1 |
| Litoměřice .... | 16 | C2 |
| Little Barrier I. . | 64 | B6 |
| Little Laut Is. = | | |
| Laut Kecil, | | |
| Kepulauan .. | 37 | E5 |

Little
  Missouri → . 76 B3
Little River .... 65 E5
Little Rock ... 79 B7
Liukang
  Tenggaja ... 39 F1
Liuwa Plain ... 58 A4
Liuzhou ...... 35 D5
Liverpool,
  Australia .... 63 B5
Liverpool,
  Canada ..... 69 D4
Liverpool, U.K. 11 E5
Liverpool Plains 63 B5
Liverpool Ra. .. 63 B5
Livingstone ... 59 B5
Livingstonia .. 57 G6
Livny ........ 24 C4
Livorno ....... 20 C3
Livramento .. 94 C5
Liwale ....... 57 F7
Ljubljana ..... 20 A5
Ljungan → ... 8 F11
Ljusnan → ... 8 F11
Llancanelo,
  Salina .... 94 D3
Llanelli ....... 11 F4
Llanes ........ 18 A3
Llano Estacado 78 C2
Llanos ....... 90 C4
Lleida = Lérida 19 B6
Llobregat → .. 19 B7
Lloret de Mar . 19 B7
Lluchmayor ... 19 C7
Llullaillaco,
  Volcán .... 94 A3
Loa → ....... 94 A2
Lobatse ...... 59 D5
Lobería ...... 94 D5
Lobito ........ 58 A2
Locarno ...... 13 C8
Loch Garman =
  Wexford .... 11 E3
Loches ....... 12 C4
Lock ......... 62 B2
Lodhran ...... 42 E7
Lodi, Italy .... 20 B2
Lodi, U.S.A. .. 80 F3
Lodja ........ 56 E4
Lodwar ....... 57 D7
Łódź ......... 16 C4
Lofoten ...... 8 E10
Logan ........ 81 E8
Logan, Mt. ... 70 B5
Logone → ... 53 F2
Logroño ...... 19 A4
Lohardaga ... 40 F5
Loi-kaw ...... 41 H11
Loir → ....... 12 C3
Loire → ...... 12 C2
Loja, Ecuador . 90 D3
Loja, Spain ... 18 D3
Loji ......... 39 E3
Lokandu ...... 57 E5
Lokitaung .... 57 D7
Lokoja ....... 55 G6
Lokolama .... 56 E3
Loliondo ..... 57 E7
Lom ......... 22 C4
Lomami → ... 56 D4
Lombárdia □ .. 20 B2
Lombardy =
  Lombárdia □ 20 B2
Lomblen ..... 39 F2
Lombok ...... 37 F5
Lomé ........ 55 G5
Lomela ....... 56 E4
Lomela → ... 56 E4
Lomié ........ 56 D2

Lomond, L. ... 10 C4
Lompobatang . 39 F1
Łomza ....... 16 B6
Loncoche .... 95 D2
Londa ........ 43 M9
London ....... 11 F6
Londonderry .. 11 D3
Londonderry, C. 60 C4
Londonderry, I. 95 H2
Londrina ..... 94 A6
Long Beach ... 82 D3
Long I.,
  Bahamas ... 86 B4
Long I., U.S.A. 73 D9
Long Xuyen ... 36 B3
Longford,
  Australia .... 62 D4
Longford,
  Ireland .... 11 E3
Longiram ..... 37 E5
Longlac ...... 69 D2
Longnawan ... 37 D4
Longreach .... 61 E7
Longview, Tex.,
  U.S.A. ...... 79 C6
Longview,
  Wash., U.S.A. 80 B2
Lons-le-Saunier 13 C6
Lop Nor = Lop
  Nur ....... 34 B4
Lop Nur ...... 34 B4
Lopez, C. .... 56 E1
Lora → ....... 42 D4
Lora, Hamun-i- 42 E4
Lora Cr. → ... 62 A2
Lora del Río .. 18 D3
Lorain ....... 72 D4
Loralai ...... 42 D6
Lorca ........ 19 D5
Lorestān □ .... 46 D6
Loreto ....... 92 D4
Lorient ...... 12 C2
Lorne ........ 62 C3
Lorraine ..... 13 B7
Los Alamos ... 83 C9
Los Andes .... 94 C2
Los Angeles,
  Chile ...... 94 D2
Los Angeles,
  U.S.A. ...... 82 C3
Los Blancos .. 94 A4
Los Hermanos . 90 A6
Los Mochis ... 84 B3
Los Roques ... 90 A5
Los Testigos .. 90 A6
Los Vilos ..... 94 C2
Lošinj ........ 20 B5
Lot → ........ 12 D4
Lota ......... 94 D2
Loubomo ..... 56 E2
Louga ........ 55 E1
Louis Trichardt 59 C5
Louis XIV, Pte. . 69 C3
Louisiade Arch. 61 C9
Louisiana □ ... 79 D8
Louisville ..... 72 E3
Loulé ........ 18 D1
Lourdes ...... 12 E3
Louth, Australia 63 B4
Louth, U.K. ... 11 E6
Louvain =
  Leuven ..... 14 C3
Lovech ....... 22 C5
Low Tatra =
  Nízké Tatry .. 16 D4
Lowell ....... 73 C10
Lower California
  = Baja
  California ... 84 A1

Lower Hutt .... 65 D6
Lower Saxony =
  Niedersachsen □
  .......... 14 B5
Lower Tunguska
  = Tunguska,
  Nizhnyaya → 30 C6
Lowestoft ..... 11 E7
Łowicz ....... 16 B4
Lowyar □ ..... 45 C7
Loxton ....... 62 B3
Loyalty Is. =
  Loyauté, Is. . 64 M11
Loyang =
  Luoyang .... 35 C6
Loyauté, Is. ... 64 M11
Loyev = Loyew 17 C10
Loyew ....... 17 C10
Luachimo .... 56 F4
Luacono ..... 56 G4
Lualaba → ... 57 D5
Luanda ...... 56 F2
Luangwa ..... 59 B6
Luangwa → .. 59 A6
Luanshya .... 59 A5
Luapula → ... 57 F5
Luarca ....... 18 A2
Luashi ....... 56 G4
Luau ........ 56 G4
Lubalo ....... 56 F3
Lubang Is. ... 38 B2
Lubbock ..... 78 C3
Lübeck ....... 15 B6
Lubefu ....... 56 E4
Lubero = Luofu 57 E5
Lubin ........ 16 C3
Lublin ....... 17 C6
Lubuagan .... 38 A2
Lubuk Antu ... 37 D4
Lubuklinggau . 37 E2
Lubuksikaping . 37 D2
Lubumbashi .. 59 A5
Lubutu ....... 57 E5
Lucca ........ 20 C3
Lucena, Phil. .. 38 B2
Lucena, Spain . 18 D3
Lučenec ..... 16 D4
Lucerne =
  Luzern ..... 13 C8
Lucira ....... 58 A2
Luckenwalde .. 15 B7
Lucknow ..... 40 D3
Lüda = Dalian . 35 C7
Lüderitz ...... 58 D3
Ludhiana .... 42 D9
Ludwigsburg . 14 D5
Ludwigshafen . 14 D5
Luebo ....... 56 F4
Lufira → ..... 57 F5
Lufkin ....... 79 D6
Luga ........ 24 B2
Lugano ...... 13 C8
Lugansk =
  Luhansk .... 25 D4
Lugh Ganana .. 49 G3
Lugo, Italy ... 20 B3
Lugo, Spain .. 18 A2
Lugoj ....... 17 F5
Lugovoy ..... 29 E8
Luhansk ..... 25 D4
Luiana ....... 58 B4
Luimneach =
  Limerick .... 11 E2
Luís Correia .. 92 C5
Luitpold Coast . 96 B5
Luiza ....... 56 F4
Luján ........ 94 C5
Lukanga Swamp 59 A5
Lukenie → ... 56 E3

Lukolela ...... 56 E3
Łuków ....... 17 C6
Lule älv → ... 8 E12
  .......... 8 E12
Luleå ........ 8 E12
Lüleburgaz ... 22 D6
Lulonga → ... 56 D3
Lulua → ..... 56 E4
Luluabourg =
  Kananga .... 56 F4
Lumai ....... 58 A4
Lumbala
  N'guimbo ... 58 A4
Lumsden ..... 65 F3
Lumut, Tg. ... 37 E3
Lundazi ...... 59 A6
Lundu ....... 37 D3
Lüneburg .... 14 B6
Lüneburg Heath
  = Lüneburger
  Heide ...... 14 B6
Lüneburger
  Heide ...... 14 B6
Lunéville .... 13 B7
Lunglei ...... 41 F9
Luni ......... 42 G8
Luni → ...... 43 G7
Luninets =
  Luninyets ... 17 B8
Luninyets .... 17 B8
Luofu ....... 57 E5
Luoyang ..... 35 C6
Luozi ....... 56 E2
Luremo ...... 56 F3
Lurgan ...... 11 D3
Lusaka ...... 59 B5
Lusambo .... 56 E4
Lushnja ...... 23 D2
Lushoto ..... 57 E7
Luta = Dalian . 35 C7
Luton ....... 11 F6
Lutong ...... 36 D4
Lutsk ....... 17 C7
Lützow
  Holmbukta .. 96 A8
Luwuk ....... 39 E2
Luxembourg .. 14 D4
Luxembourg ■ 14 D4
Luxor = El
  Uqsur ..... 52 C5
Luza ........ 24 A6
Luzern ...... 13 C8
Luzhou ...... 35 D5
Luziânia ..... 93 F4
Luzon ....... 38 A2
Lviv ......... 17 D7
Lvov = Lviv ... 17 D7
Lyakhavichy ... 17 B8
Lyakhovskiye,
  Ostrova ... 31 B12
Lyallpur =
  Faisalabad .. 42 D8
Lydenburg ... 59 D6
Lydia ....... 23 E7
Lyell ........ 65 D5
Lyepyel ...... 24 C2
Łyna → ...... 16 A5
Lynchburg ... 73 F6
Lynd Ra. ..... 63 A4
Lyndhurst .... 62 B2
Lynn Lake .... 71 C9
Lyon ........ 13 D6
Lyonnais .... 13 D6
Lyons = Lyon . 13 D6
Lys = Leie → . 14 C2
Lysychansk ... 25 D4
Lyttelton .... 65 E5
Lyubertsy .... 24 B4
Lyuboml ..... 17 C7

# Ma'alah

## M

Ma'alah ...... 47 F6
Ma'ān ........ 47 E3
Ma'anshan ... 35 C6
Ma'arrat an
  Nu'mān .... 46 D4
Maas → .... 14 C3
Maastricht .... 13 A6
Mabrouk ..... 55 E4
Macaé ....... 93 G5
McAllen ...... 78 F4
Macao =
  Macau ■ ... 35 D6
Macapá ...... 92 B3
Macau ....... 92 D6
Macau ■ ..... 35 D6
M'Clintock Chan. 70 A9
McComb ..... 79 D8
Macdonnell Ras. 60 E5
McDouall Peak 62 A1
Macdougall L. . 70 B10
Macedonia =
  Makedhonía □ 23 D4
Macedonia ■ .. 22 D3
Maceió ....... 93 D6
Macenta ..... 55 G3
Macerata ..... 20 C4
Macfarlane, L. . 62 B2
Macgillycuddy's
  Reeks ...... 11 F2
McGregor Ra. . 62 A3
Mach ........ 42 E5
Machado =
  Jiparaná → . 91 E6
Machakos .... 57 E7
Machala ..... 90 D3
Machilipatnam 40 J3
Machiques .... 90 A4
Machupicchu .. 91 F4
Macintyre → . 63 A5
Mackay ....... 61 E8
Mackay, L. ... 60 E4
Mackenzie → . 70 B6
Mackenzie City
  = Linden .. 90 B7
Mackenzie Mts. 70 B6
McKinley, Mt. . 71 B4
McKinney ..... 79 C5
Macksville .... 63 B5
Maclean ...... 63 A5
Maclear ...... 59 E5
Macleay → ... 63 B5
McMurdo Sd. . 96 B15
Mâcon, France 13 C6
Macon, U.S.A. . 75 C6
Macondo ..... 58 A4
McPherson Ra. 63 A5
Macquarie
  Harbour .... 62 D4
MacRobertson
  Land ....... 96 B10
Madagali ..... 53 F1
Madagascar ■ . 59 J9
Madā'in Sālih . 47 F4
Madama ..... 52 D1
Madang ...... 61 B8
Madaoua ..... 55 F6
Madaripur .... 41 F8
Madauk ...... 41 J11
Madaya ...... 41 F11
Maddalena ... 20 D2
Madeira ..... 54 B1
Madeira → ... 90 D7
Madha ....... 43 L9
Madhya
  Pradesh □ .. 43 H10
Madikeri ...... 43 N9

Madimba ..... 56 E3
Madīnat ash
  Sha'b ...... 49 E3
Madingou .... 56 E2
Madison ...... 77 D10
Madiun ...... 37 F4
Madras = Tamil
  Nadu □ .... 43 P10
Madras ...... 43 N12
Madre, Laguna 78 F5
Madre, Sierra . 38 A2
Madre de
  Dios → .... 91 F5
Madre de Dios,
  I. ......... 95 G1
Madre
  Occidental,
  Sierra ...... 84 B3
Madrid ...... 18 B4
Madurai ...... 43 Q11
Madurantakam 43 N11
Mae Sot ..... 36 A1
Maebashi .... 32 A6
Maestrazgo,
  Mts. del .... 19 B5
Maevatanana . 59 H9
Mafeking =
  Mafikeng .. 59 D5
Maffra ...... 63 C4
Mafia I. ...... 57 F7
Mafikeng .... 59 D5
Mafra, Brazil . 94 B7
Mafra, Portugal 18 C1
Magadan ..... 31 D13
Magadi ...... 57 E7
Magallanes,
  Estrecho de . 95 G2
Magangué ... 90 B4
Magburaka ... 55 G2
Magdalena,
  Argentina ... 94 D5
Magdalena,
  Bolivia ..... 91 F6
Magdalena,
  Malaysia .... 36 D5
Magdalena → 90 A4
Magdeburg ... 15 B6
Magelang .... 37 F4
Magellan's Str.
  = Magallanes,
  Estrecho de . 95 G2
Maggiore, L. .. 20 B2
Magnetic Pole
  (South) =
  South
  Magnetic Pole 96 A13
Magnitogorsk . 29 D6
Magosa =
  Famagusta .. 46 D3
Maguarinho, C. 92 C4
Mağusa =
  Famagusta .. 46 D3
Magwe ...... 41 G10
Mahābād ..... 46 C6
Mahabo ...... 59 J8
Mahagi ...... 57 D6
Mahajanga ... 59 H9
Mahakam → . 37 E5
Mahalapye ... 59 C5
Mahallāt ..... 44 C2
Mahanadi → . 40 G6
Mahanoro .... 59 H9
Maharashtra □ 43 J9
Mahbubnagar . 43 L10
Mahdia ...... 52 A1
Mahenge ..... 57 F7
Mahesana ... 43 H8
Mahia Pen. ... 64 C7

Mahilyow ..... 17 B10
Mahón ....... 19 C8
Mai-Ndombe, L. 56 E3
Maicurú → ... 92 C3
Maidstone .... 11 F7
Maiduguri .... 53 F1
Maijdi ....... 41 F8
Maikala Ra. ... 40 G3
Main → ..... 14 D5
Maine ....... 12 C3
Maingkwan ... 41 D11
Mainit, L. ..... 38 C3
Mainland,
  Orkney, U.K. 10 B5
Mainland, Shet.,
  U.K. ....... 10 A6
Maintirano .... 59 H8
Mainz ...... 14 C5
Maipú ...... 94 D5
Maiquetía .... 90 A5
Mairabari ..... 41 D9
Maitland,
  N.S.W.,
  Australia .... 63 B5
Maitland,
  S. Austral.,
  Australia .... 62 B2
Maizuru ..... 32 B4
Majene ...... 39 E1
Maji ........ 53 G6
Majorca =
  Mallorca ... 19 C7
Maka ........ 55 F2
Makale ...... 39 E1
Makari ...... 56 B2
Makarikari =
  Makgadikgadi
  Salt Pans .. 59 C5
Makasar =
  Ujung
  Pandang .... 39 F1
Makasar, Selat 39 E1
Makasar, Str. of
  = Makasar,
  Selat ...... 39 E1
Makat ....... 29 E6
Makedhonía □ 23 D4
Makedonija =
  Macedonia ■ 22 D3
Makeni ...... 55 G2
Makeyevka =
  Makiyivka .. 25 D4
Makgadikgadi
  Salt Pans .. 59 C5
Makhachkala . 25 E6
Makian ...... 39 D3
Makindu ..... 57 E7
Makinsk ..... 29 D8
Makiyivka .... 25 D4
Makkah ...... 47 G4
Makó ........ 16 E5
Makokou .... 56 D2
Makoua ..... 56 E3
Makrai ...... 43 H10
Makran ...... 45 E5
Makran Coast
  Range ..... 42 G4
Maksimkin Yar 29 D9
Mākū ...... 46 C6
Makumbi .... 56 F4
Makurazaki ... 33 D2
Makurdi ..... 55 G6
Malabang .... 38 C2
Malabar Coast 43 P9
Malabo = Rey
  Malabo .... 56 D1
Malacca, Str. of 36 D1
Maladzyechna . 17 A8
Málaga ....... 18 D3

Malakâl ...... 53 G5
Malakand .... 42 B7
Malang ...... 37 F4
Malanje ..... 56 F3
Mälaren ..... 9 G11
Malargüe .... 94 D3
Malaryta ..... 17 C7
Malatya ..... 46 C4
Malawi ■ .... 59 A6
Malawi, L. .... 59 A6
Malaybalay ... 38 C3
Malāyer ..... 46 D7
Malaysia ■ ... 36 D4
Malazgirt .... 46 C5
Malbooma ... 62 B1
Malbork ..... 16 A4
Malden I. ..... 65 K15
Maldives ■ ... 26 J11
Maldonado ... 94 C6
Malé Karpaty .. 16 D3
Maléa, Ákra .. 23 F4
Malegaon .... 43 J9
Malema ..... 59 A7
Malha ....... 53 E4
Mali ■ ...... 55 E4
Mali → ...... 41 E11
Malik ....... 39 E2
Malili ....... 39 E2
Malin Hd. .... 10 D3
Malindi ...... 57 E8
Malines =
  Mechelen ... 14 C3
Malino ...... 39 D2
Malita ....... 38 C3
Malkara ..... 22 D6
Mallacoota ... 63 C4
Mallacoota Inlet 63 C4
Mallaig ...... 10 C4
Mallawi ...... 52 C5
Mallorca ..... 19 C7
Mallow ...... 11 E2
Malmö ...... 9 G10
Malolos ..... 38 B2
Malpelo ..... 90 C2
Malta ■ ..... 21 G5
Maltahöhe ... 58 C3
Maluku ...... 39 E3
Maluku □ .... 39 E3
Maluku Sea =
  Molucca Sea 39 E2
Malvan ...... 43 L8
Malvinas, Is. =
  Falkland Is. □ 95 G5
Malyn ....... 17 C9
Malyy
  Lyakhovskiy,
  Ostrov ...... 31 B12
Mamahatun .. 46 C5
Mamanguape . 92 D6
Mamasa ..... 39 E1
Mamberamo → 39 E5
Mambilima Falls 57 G5
Mamburao ... 38 B2
Mamfe ...... 55 G6
Mamoré → ... 91 F5
Mamou ...... 55 F2
Mamuju ..... 39 E1
Man ........ 55 G3
Man, I. of .... 11 D4
Man Na ...... 41 F11
Mana ....... 92 A3
Manaar, G. of =
  Mannar, G. of 43 Q11
Manacapuru .. 90 D6
Manacor ..... 19 C7
Manado ..... 39 D2
Managua .... 85 E7
Manakara ... 59 J9
Manama = Al
  Manāmah ... 44 E2

| | | | |
|---|---|---|---|
| Mananara .... 59 H9 | Mannahill ..... 62 B3 | Maranhão □ .. 92 D4 | Marrakech .... 54 B3 |
| Mananjary .... 59 J9 | Mannar ...... 43 Q11 | Maranoa → .. 63 A4 | Marrawah .... 62 D3 |
| Manaos = | Mannar, G. of . 43 Q11 | Marañón → .. 90 D4 | Marree ....... 62 A2 |
| Manaus .... 90 D7 | Mannar I. ..... 43 Q11 | Marão ...... 59 C6 | Marromeu .... 59 B7 |
| Manapouri .... 65 F2 | Mannheim .... 14 D5 | Maraş = | Marrowie Cr. → 63 B4 |
| Manapouri, L. . 65 F2 | Mannum ..... 62 B2 | Kahramanmaraş | Marrupa ..... 59 A7 |
| Manas .... 34 B3 | Mano ........ 55 G2 | ............ 46 C4 | Marsá Matrûh . 52 B4 |
| Manas → .... 41 D8 | Manokwari .... 39 E4 | Maratua ...... 39 D1 | Marsá Susah .. 52 B3 |
| Manasir .... 44 E2 | Manombo ..... 59 J8 | Marbella ..... 18 D3 | Marsabit ..... 57 D7 |
| Manaung .... 41 H9 | Manono ...... 57 F5 | Marburg ..... 14 C5 | Marsala ...... 21 F4 |
| Manaus ...... 90 D7 | Manosque .... 13 E6 | Marche ...... 12 C4 | Marsden ..... 63 B4 |
| Manay ....... 38 C3 | Manresa ..... 19 B6 | Marchena .... 18 D3 | Marseille .... 13 E6 |
| Manchester, | Mansa ...... 57 G5 | Mardan ..... 42 B8 | Marseilles = |
| U.K. ........ 11 E5 | Mansel I. ..... 68 B2 | Mardin ...... 46 C5 | Marseille ... 13 E6 |
| Manchester, | Mansfield, | Marek = Stanke | Marshall, Liberia 55 G2 |
| U.S.A. ..... 73 C10 | Australia .... 63 C4 | Dimitrov .... 22 C4 | Marshall, U.S.A. 79 C6 |
| Mand → ..... 44 D3 | Mansfield, U.K. 11 E6 | Marek ...... 39 E2 | Marshall Is. ■ . 64 J12 |
| Manda ...... 57 G6 | Mansfield, | Margarita, I. de 90 A6 | Marshalltown . 77 D8 |
| Mandal .. 9 G9 | U.S.A. ..... 72 D4 | Margate ...... 11 F7 | Martaban ..... 41 J11 |
| Mandalay ..... 41 F11 | Manta ........ 90 D2 | Margelan = | Martaban, G. of 41 J11 |
| Mandale = | Mantalingajan, | Marghilon .. 29 E8 | Martapura, |
| Mandalay .. 41 F11 | Mt. ........ 36 C5 | Marghilon .. 29 E8 | Kalimantan, |
| Mandalī ...... 46 D6 | Mantes-la-Jolie 12 B4 | Mari El □ .... 24 B6 | Indonesia ... 37 E4 |
| Mandar, Teluk . 39 E1 | Manthani ..... 43 K11 | Mari Republic □ | Martapura, |
| Mandaue ..... 38 B2 | Mantiqueira, | = Mari El □ . 24 B6 | Sumatera, |
| Mandi ...... 42 D10 | Serra da . 93 G5 | Maria I. ...... 62 D4 | Indonesia ... 37 E2 |
| Mandimba .... 59 A7 | Mántova ...... 20 B3 | Maria van | Marte ........ 53 F1 |
| Mandioli ..... 39 E3 | Mantua = | Diemen, C. . 64 A5 | Martigny .... 13 C7 |
| Mandla ..... 40 F3 | Mántova .... 20 B3 | Mariana Trench 64 H9 | Martigues .... 13 E6 |
| Mandritsara ... 59 H9 | Manu ........ 91 F4 | Marianao .... 86 B3 | Martin ...... 16 D4 |
| Mandsaur .... 43 G9 | Manuae ..... 65 L15 | Ma'rib ...... 49 D4 | Martina Franca 21 D6 |
| Mandvi ...... 43 H6 | Manuel | Maribor ...... 20 A5 | Martinborough 65 D6 |
| Mandya ...... 43 N10 | Alves → .. 93 E4 | Marîdî ........ 53 H4 | Martinique ■ .. 87 D7 |
| Manfalût ..... 52 C5 | Manui ........ 39 E2 | Marie Byrd Land 96 B18 | Martinique |
| Manfred ...... 63 B3 | Manyara, L. .. 57 E7 | Marie-Galante . 87 C7 | Passage .... 87 C7 |
| Manfredónia .. 20 D5 | Manych-Gudilo, | Mariecourt = | Martinsville ... 75 A8 |
| Mangalia ..... 22 C7 | Ozero ...... 25 D5 | Kangiqsujuaq 68 B3 | Marton ...... 64 D6 |
| Mangalore .... 43 N9 | Manyoni ...... 57 F6 | Mariental .... 58 C3 | Martos ...... 18 D4 |
| Mangaweka ... 64 C6 | Manzai ...... 42 C7 | Mariinsk ..... 29 D9 | Marudi ...... 37 D4 |
| Manggar ..... 37 E3 | Manzanares .. 18 C4 | Marília ...... 93 G3 | Ma'ruf ...... 42 D5 |
| Manggawitu .. 39 E4 | Manzanillo, | Marín ...... 18 A1 | Marugame .... 32 B3 |
| Mangkalihat, | Cuba ...... 86 B4 | Marinduque .. 38 B2 | Marulan ..... 63 B5 |
| Tanjung .... 39 D1 | Manzanillo, | Maringá ..... 94 A6 | Marwar ..... 42 G8 |
| Mangla Dam .. 42 C8 | Mexico .... 84 D4 | Marion ...... 79 A9 | Mary ...... 29 F7 |
| Mangnai ..... 34 C4 | Manzhouli .... 35 B6 | Mariscal | Maryborough = |
| Mango ....... 55 F5 | Mao ........ 53 F2 | Estigarribia .. 91 H6 | Port Laoise .. 11 E3 |
| Mangoche .... 59 A7 | Maoke, | Maritime Alps = | Maryborough, |
| Mangole ..... 39 E3 | Pegunungan 39 E5 | Maritimes, | Queens., |
| Mangonui .... 64 A5 | Maoming .... 35 D6 | Alpes ...... 13 D7 | Australia .... 63 A5 |
| Mangueigne .. 53 F3 | Mapam Yumco 40 B3 | Maritimes, Alpes 13 D7 | Maryborough, |
| Mangueira, L. da 94 C6 | Mapia, | Maritsa = | Vic., Australia 62 C3 |
| Mangyshlak | Kepulauan . 39 D4 | Évros → ... 22 D6 | Maryland □ ... 73 E7 |
| Poluostrov .. 29 E6 | Mapuera → .. 90 D7 | Mariupol .... 25 D4 | Maryvale .... 63 A5 |
| Manhuaçu .... 93 G5 | Maputo ...... 59 D6 | Marīvān ..... 46 D6 | Marzūq ...... 52 C1 |
| Manica ...... 59 B6 | Maqnā ...... 47 E3 | Markazī □ .... 44 C2 | Masaka ..... 57 E6 |
| Manicoré ..... 91 E6 | Maquela do | Markham, Mt. . 96 C15 | Masalembo, |
| Manicouagan → | Zombo .... 56 F3 | Marks ...... 24 C6 | Kepulauan .. 37 F4 |
| ............ 69 D4 | Maquinchao .. 95 E3 | Marla ...... 62 A1 | Masalima, |
| Manifah ...... 47 F7 | Mar, Serra do . 94 B7 | Marmagao .... 43 M8 | Kepulauan .. 37 F5 |
| Manihiki ..... 65 L14 | Mar Chiquita, L. 94 C4 | Marmara ..... 23 D6 | Masamba .... 39 E2 |
| Manila ...... 38 B2 | Mar del Plata . 94 D5 | Marmara, Sea of | Masan ...... 35 C7 |
| Manila B. ..... 38 B2 | Mar Menor .. 19 D5 | = Marmara | Masandam, Ras 44 E4 |
| Manilla ...... 63 B5 | Maraã ....... 90 D5 | Denizi ...... 22 D7 | Masasi ...... 57 G7 |
| Manipur □ .... 41 E9 | Marabá ...... 92 D4 | Marmara Denizi 22 D7 | Masaya ..... 85 E7 |
| Manipur → ... 41 F10 | Maracá, I. de . 92 B3 | Marmaris .... 23 F7 | Masbate ..... 38 B2 |
| Manisa ...... 23 E6 | Maracaibo .... 90 A4 | Marmolada, | Mascara ..... 54 A5 |
| Manitoba □ .. 71 C10 | Maracaibo, L. de 90 B4 | Mte. ...... 20 A3 | Masela ...... 39 F3 |
| Manitoba, L. .. 71 C10 | Maracay ..... 90 A5 | Marne → .... 12 B5 | Maseru ...... 59 D5 |
| Manitowoc .... 72 B2 | Marādah ..... 52 C2 | Maroantsetra . 59 H9 | Mashābih .... 47 F4 |
| Manizales .... 90 B3 | Maradi ...... 55 F6 | Marondera .... 59 B6 | Mashhad .... 44 B4 |
| Manja ...... 59 J8 | Marágheh .... 46 C6 | Maroni → .... 92 A3 | Mashike ..... 32 F12 |
| Manjacaze .... 59 C6 | Marāh ...... 47 F6 | Maroochydore . 63 A5 | Mashkel, |
| Manjhand .... 42 G6 | Marajó, I. de .. 92 C4 | Maroona ..... 62 C3 | Hamun-i- .. 42 E3 |
| Manjil ...... 46 C7 | Maralal ...... 57 D7 | Maroua ...... 53 F1 | Mashki Chāh .. 42 E3 |
| Manjra → .... 43 K10 | Marama ..... 62 C3 | Marovoay .... 59 H9 | Masi Manimba 56 E3 |
| Mankono .... 55 G3 | Marampa .... 55 G2 | Marquesas Is. = | Masindi ...... 57 D6 |
| Manly ...... 63 B5 | Marand ..... 46 C6 | Marquises, Is. 65 K17 | Masisea ..... 91 E4 |
| Manmad .... 43 J9 | Maranguape .. 92 C6 | Marquette .... 69 D2 | Masjed |
| Manna ....... 37 E2 | Maranhão = | Marquises, Is. . 65 K17 | Soleyman ... 47 E7 |
| | São Luís .... 92 C5 | | |

# Mask, L.

| | | | | | | | | | | | |
|---|---|---|---|---|---|---|---|---|---|---|---|
| Mask, L. | 11 | E2 | Maui | 82 | H12 | Medgidia | 22 | B7 | Menindee L. | 62 | B3 |
| Masohi | 39 | E3 | Maulamyaing = | | | Mediaş | 17 | E7 | Meningie | 62 | C2 |
| Mason City | 77 | D8 | Moulmein | 41 | J11 | Medicine Bow | | | Menominee | 72 | B2 |
| Masqat | 45 | F4 | Maumere | 39 | F2 | Ra. | 81 | E10 | Menongue | 58 | A3 |
| Massa | 20 | B3 | Maun | 58 | B4 | Medicine Hat | 71 | C8 | Menorca | 19 | C7 |
| Massachusetts □ | | | Maungmagan | | | Medina = Al | | | Mentawai, | | |
| | 73 | C9 | Kyunzu | 41 | K11 | Madīnah | 47 | F4 | Kepulauan | 37 | E1 |
| Massaguet | 53 | F2 | Mauritania ■ | 55 | D2 | Medina del | | | Menton | 13 | E7 |
| Massakory | 53 | F2 | Mauritius ■ | 51 | H9 | Campo | 18 | B3 | Meppel | 14 | B4 |
| Massangena | 59 | C6 | Mavinga | 58 | B4 | Medina-Sidonia | 18 | D3 | Merabéllou, | | |
| Massawa = | | | Mawk Mai | 41 | G11 | Medinipur | 40 | F6 | Kólpos | 23 | G5 |
| Mitsiwa | 53 | E6 | Mawlaik | 41 | F10 | Mediterranean | | | Meran = | | |
| Massena | 73 | B8 | Mawson Coast | 96 | A10 | Sea | 50 | C5 | Merano | 20 | A3 |
| Massénya | 53 | F2 | Maxixe | 59 | C7 | Médoc | 12 | D3 | Merano | 20 | A3 |
| Massif Central | 13 | D5 | Mayaguana | 87 | B5 | Medveditsa ➙ | 24 | D5 | Merauke | 39 | F6 |
| Massinga | 59 | C7 | Mayagüez | 87 | C6 | Medvezhyegorsk | 28 | C4 | Merbein | 62 | B3 |
| Masson I. | 96 | A11 | Maydena | 62 | D4 | Meekatharra | 60 | F2 | Merca | 49 | G3 |
| Mastanli = | | | Mayenne ➙ | 12 | C3 | Meerut | 42 | E10 | Merced | 82 | B2 |
| Momchilgrad | 22 | D5 | Maykop | 25 | E5 | Mega | 53 | H6 | Mercedes, | | |
| Masterton | 65 | D6 | Mayo | 70 | B6 | Mégara | 23 | F4 | Buenos Aires, | | |
| Mastuj | 42 | A8 | Mayo L. | 70 | B6 | Meghalaya □ | 41 | E8 | Argentina | 94 | C5 |
| Mastung | 42 | E5 | Mayon Volcano | 38 | B2 | Mei Xian | 35 | D6 | Mercedes, | | |
| Masty | 17 | B7 | Mayor I. | 64 | B7 | Meiganga | 56 | C2 | Corrientes, | | |
| Masuda | 32 | B2 | Mayu | 39 | D3 | Meiktila | 41 | G10 | Argentina | 94 | B5 |
| Masvingo | 59 | C6 | Mazabuka | 59 | B5 | Meissen | 15 | C7 | Mercedes, | | |
| Mataboor | 39 | E5 | Mazagán = El | | | Mejillones | 94 | A2 | San Luis, | | |
| Matad | 35 | B6 | Jadida | 54 | B3 | Mékambo | 56 | D2 | Argentina | 94 | C3 |
| Matadi | 56 | F2 | Mazagão | 92 | C3 | Mekdela | 53 | F6 | Mercedes, | | |
| Matagalpa | 85 | E7 | Mazán | 90 | D4 | Mekhtar | 42 | D6 | Uruguay | 94 | C5 |
| Matagami, L. | 69 | D3 | Māzandarān □ | 44 | B3 | Meknès | 54 | B3 | Merceditas | 94 | B2 |
| Matak, P. | 37 | D3 | Mazar-e Sharīf | 45 | B6 | Mekong ➙ | 36 | C3 | Mercer | 64 | B6 |
| Matakana | 63 | B4 | Mazara del Vallo | 21 | F4 | Mekongga | 39 | E2 | Mercy C. | 68 | B4 |
| Matam | 55 | E2 | Mazarredo | 95 | F3 | Mekvari = | | | Meredith, C. | 95 | G4 |
| Matamoros, | | | Mazarrón | 19 | D5 | Kür ➙ | 25 | E6 | Merga = | | |
| Coahuila, | | | Mazaruni ➙ | 90 | B7 | Melagiri Hills | 43 | N10 | Nukheila | 53 | E4 |
| Mexico | 84 | B4 | Mazatlán | 84 | C3 | Melaka | 37 | D2 | Mergui Arch. = | | |
| Matamoros, | | | Māzhān | 44 | C4 | Melalap | 36 | C5 | Myeik Kyunzu | 36 | B1 |
| Tamaulipas, | | | Mazīnān | 44 | B4 | Melanesia | 64 | K10 | Mérida, Mexico | 85 | C7 |
| Mexico | 84 | B5 | Mazoe ➙ | 59 | B6 | Melbourne, | | | Mérida, Spain | 18 | C2 |
| Ma'ṭan as Sarra | 52 | D3 | Mazurian Lakes | | | Australia | 63 | C3 | Mérida, | | |
| Matane | 69 | D4 | = Mazurski, | | | Melbourne, | | | Venezuela | 90 | B4 |
| Matanzas | 86 | B3 | Pojezierze | 16 | B5 | U.S.A. | 75 | E7 | Mérida, Cord. de | 87 | E5 |
| Matapan, C. = | | | Mazurski, | | | Mélèzes ➙ | 68 | C3 | Meridian | 74 | C3 |
| Taínaron, Ákra | 23 | F4 | Pojezierze | 16 | B5 | Melfi | 21 | D5 | Meriruma | 92 | B3 |
| Mataram | 37 | F5 | Mazyr | 17 | C9 | Melfort | 71 | C9 | Merowe | 53 | E5 |
| Matarani | 91 | G4 | Mbabane | 59 | D6 | Melilla | 19 | E4 | Merriwa | 63 | B5 |
| Mataró | 19 | B7 | Mbaïki | 56 | D3 | Melitopol | 25 | D4 | Merriwagga | 63 | B4 |
| Mataura | 65 | G3 | Mbala | 57 | F6 | Melk | 15 | D8 | Merrygoen | 63 | B4 |
| Matehuala | 84 | C4 | Mbale | 57 | D6 | Melo | 94 | C6 | Mersa Fatma | 49 | E3 |
| Matera | 21 | D6 | Mbalmayo | 56 | D2 | Melolo | 39 | F2 | Merseburg | 15 | C6 |
| Mathura | 42 | F10 | Mbamba Bay | 57 | G6 | Melrose | 63 | B4 | Mersin | 46 | C3 |
| Mati | 38 | C3 | Mbandaka | 56 | D3 | Melun | 13 | B5 | Mersing | 37 | D2 |
| Matiri Ra. | 65 | D5 | Mbanza Congo | 56 | F2 | Melut | 53 | F5 | Merthyr Tydfil | 11 | F5 |
| Matmata | 54 | B6 | Mbanza Ngungu | 56 | F2 | Melville | 71 | C9 | Mértola | 18 | D2 |
| Mato Grosso □ | 93 | E3 | Mbarara | 57 | E6 | Melville I. | 60 | C5 | Meru | 57 | D7 |
| Mato Grosso, | | | Mbeya | 57 | F6 | Melville Pen. | 68 | B2 | Mesa | 83 | D7 |
| Planalto do | 93 | F3 | Mbini □ | 56 | D2 | Memba | 59 | G8 | Meshed = | | |
| Mato Grosso do | | | Mbour | 55 | F1 | Memboro | 39 | F1 | Mashhad | 44 | B4 |
| Sul □ | 93 | F3 | Mbout | 55 | E2 | Memel = | | | Meshra er Req | 53 | G4 |
| Matochkin Shar | 28 | B6 | Mbuji-Mayi | 56 | F4 | Klaipéda | 24 | B1 | Mesolóngion | 23 | E3 |
| Matosinhos | 18 | B1 | Mbulu | 57 | E7 | Memmingen | 14 | E6 | Mesopotamia = | | |
| Matrah | 45 | F4 | Mchinji | 59 | A6 | Mempawah | 37 | D3 | Al Jazirah | 46 | D5 |
| Matsue | 32 | B3 | Mead, L. | 82 | B5 | Memphis, Tenn., | | | Messina, Italy | 21 | E5 |
| Matsumoto | 32 | A6 | Mearim ➙ | 92 | C5 | U.S.A. | 74 | B3 | Messina, | | |
| Matsusaka | 32 | B5 | Meaux | 13 | B5 | Memphis, Tex., | | | S. Africa | 59 | C6 |
| Matsuyama | 32 | C3 | Mecca = | | | U.S.A. | 78 | B3 | Messina, Str. di | 21 | E5 |
| Mattagami ➙ | 69 | C2 | Makkah | 47 | G4 | Ménaka | 55 | E5 | Messíni | 23 | F4 |
| Mattancheri | 43 | Q10 | Mechelen | 14 | C3 | Menan = Chao | | | Messiniakós | | |
| Matterhorn | 13 | D7 | Mecheria | 54 | B4 | Phraya ➙ | 36 | B2 | Kólpos | 23 | F4 |
| Matthew's Ridge | 90 | B6 | Mecklenburg | 15 | B6 | Menate | 37 | E4 | Mesta ➙ | 22 | D5 |
| Matucana | 91 | F3 | Mecklenburger | | | Mendawai ➙ | 37 | E4 | Meta ➙ | 90 | B5 |
| Matun | 42 | C6 | Bucht | 15 | A6 | Mende | 13 | D5 | Metairie | 79 | E8 |
| Maturín | 90 | B6 | Meconta | 59 | A7 | Mendocino, C. | 80 | E1 | Metán | 94 | B4 |
| Mau Ranipur | 43 | G11 | Medan | 37 | D1 | Mendoza | 94 | C3 | Metangula | 59 | A6 |
| Maubeuge | 13 | A5 | Medanosa, Pta. | 95 | F3 | Mene Grande | 90 | B4 | Metema | 53 | F6 |
| Maude | 63 | B3 | Medéa | 54 | A5 | Menemen | 23 | E6 | Methven | 65 | E4 |
| Maudin Sun | 41 | K10 | Medellín | 90 | B3 | Menggala | 37 | E3 | Metil | 59 | B7 |
| Maués | 90 | D7 | Mederdra | 55 | E1 | Mengzi | 34 | D5 | Metlakatla | 71 | C6 |
| Mauganj | 40 | E3 | Medford | 80 | D2 | Menindee | 62 | B3 | Mettur Dam | 43 | P10 |

Metz ......... 13 B7
Meulaboh .... 37 D1
Meureudu ... 36 C1
Meuse → .... 13 A6
Mexiana, I. .... 92 C4
Mexicali ..... 84 A1
México ....... 84 D5
México □ ..... 84 D5
Mexico ■ ..... 84 C4
Mexico, G. of .. 85 B7
Meymaneh ... 42 B4
Mezen ....... 28 C5
Mezen → .... 28 C5
Mézene ...... 13 D6
Mezökövesd .. 16 E5
Mezötúr ..... 16 E5
Mhow ....... 43 H9
Miami ....... 75 G7
Miami Beach .. 75 G7
Mīāndowāb .. 46 C6
Miandrivazo ... 59 H9
Mīāneh ...... 46 C6
Mianwali ..... 42 C7
Miaoli ....... 35 D7
Miarinarivo ... 59 H9
Miass ....... 29 D7
Michalovce ... 17 D5
Michigan □ ... 72 C3
Michigan, L. .. 72 C2
Michipicoten .. 69 D2
Michurin ..... 22 C6
Michurinsk .... 24 C5
Micronesia,
  Federated
  States of ■ .. 64 J10
Middelburg .. 58 E5
Middlesbrough 11 D6
Midi, Canal
  du → ...... 12 E4
Midland ...... 78 D3
Midyat ....... 46 C5
Midzôr ....... 22 C4
Międzychód ... 16 B2
Międzyrzec
  Podlaski .... 17 C6
Mielec ....... 16 C5
Miercurea Ciuc 17 E7
Mieres ....... 18 A3
Miguel Alves .. 92 C5
Mihara ....... 32 B3
Mikhaylovgrad 22 C4
Míkonos ..... 23 F5
Mikura-Jima .. 32 C6
Milagro ...... 90 D3
Milan = Milano 20 B2
Milang ....... 62 B2
Milano ....... 20 B2
Milâs ....... 23 F6
Milazzo ...... 21 E5
Mildura ...... 62 B3
Miles ....... 63 A5
Miletus ...... 23 F6
Milford Haven . 11 F4
Milford Sd. ... 65 F2
Milḥ, Baḥr al .. 47 D5
Miliana ...... 54 C5
Mill I. ....... 96 A12
Millau ....... 13 D5
Millicent ..... 62 C3
Millinocket .... 73 B11
Millmerran ... 63 A5
Milne Inlet .... 68 A2
Mílos ....... 23 F5
Milparinka P.O. 62 A3
Milton ....... 65 G3
Milton Keynes . 11 E6
Miltou ....... 53 F2
Milwaukee .... 72 C2
Min Chiang → 35 D6

Min Jiang → . 35 D5
Mina Pirquitas . 94 A3
Mīnā Su'ud ... 47 E7
Mīnā'al Aḥmadī 47 E7
Mīnāb ........ 44 E4
Minamata .... 32 C2
Minas ....... 94 C5
Minas Gerais □ 93 F4
Minbu ........ 41 G10
Mindanao .... 38 C2
Mindanao Sea =
  Bohol Sea .. 38 C2
Mindanao
  Trench ..... 38 B3
Minden ....... 14 B5
Mindiptana ... 39 F6
Mindoro ...... 38 B2
Mindoro Str. .. 38 B2
Mindouli ..... 56 E2
Mingäçevir Su
  Anbarı ...... 25 E6
Mingan ...... 69 C4
Mingechaurskoye
  Vdkhr. =
  Mingäçevir Su
  Anban ...... 25 E6
Mingin ....... 41 F10
Mingt'iehkaitafan
  = Mintaka
  Pass ....... 42 A9
Minho =
  Miño → .... 18 B1
Minho ....... 18 B1
Minna ....... 55 G6
Minneapolis ... 77 C8
Minnedosa ... 71 C10
Minnesota □ .. 77 B7
Minnipa ...... 62 B2
Miño → ...... 18 B1
Minorca =
  Menorca ... 19 C7
Minore ....... 63 B4
Minot ....... 76 A4
Minsk ....... 24 C2
Mińsk
  Mazowiecki . 16 B5
Mintaka Pass .. 42 A9
Minto ....... 71 B5
Minutang .... 41 C11
Minvoul ..... 56 D2
Mir ....... 53 F1
Mira ....... 20 B4
Miraj ....... 43 L9
Miram Shah .. 42 C7
Miranda ..... 93 G2
Miranda de Ebro 19 A4
Miranda do
  Douro ..... 18 B2
Miri ....... 36 D4
Mirim, L. .... 94 C6
Mirpur Khas .. 42 G6
Mirzapur ..... 40 E4
Mirzapur-cum-
  Vindhyachal =
  Mirzapur ... 40 E4
Mish'āb, Ra'as
  al ....... 47 E7
Mishan ...... 35 B8
Miskīn ...... 44 F4
Miskolc ...... 16 D5
Misool ...... 39 E4
Misrātah ..... 52 B2
Misriç ....... 46 C5
Missinaibi → . 69 C2
Mississippi □ . 79 C9
Mississippi → 79 E9
Mississippi River
  Delta ...... 79 E9
Missoula ..... 81 B6

Missouri □ .... 77 F8
Missouri → .. 77 F9
Mistassini L. .. 69 C3
Misurata =
  Misrātah .... 52 B2
Mitchell,
  Australia .... 63 A4
Mitchell, U.S.A. 76 D5
Mitchell → ... 61 D7
Mitilíni ...... 23 E6
Mito ....... 32 A7
Mitrovica =
  Titova-
  Mitrovica ... 22 C3
Mitsinjo ..... 59 H9
Mitsiwa ...... 53 E6
Mittagong .... 63 B5
Mitú ....... 90 C4
Mitumba,
  Chaîne des .. 57 F5
Mitumba Mts. =
  Mitumba,
  Chaîne des .. 57 F5
Mitwaba ..... 57 F5
Mitzic ....... 56 D2
Miyake-Jima .. 32 B6
Miyako ....... 33 G12
Miyakonojō ... 32 D2
Miyazaki ..... 32 D2
Miyet, Bahr el =
  Dead Sea ... 47 E3
Mizal ....... 47 G6
Mizdah ....... 52 B1
Mizoram □ ... 41 F9
Mjøsa ....... 8 F10
Mladá Boleslav 16 C2
Mława ....... 16 B5
Mljet ....... 20 C6
Mmabatho ... 59 D5
Moa ....... 39 F3
Moabi ....... 56 E2
Moalie Park .. 62 A3
Moba ....... 57 F5
Mobaye ...... 56 D4
Mobayi ...... 56 D4
Mobile ....... 74 D3
Mobutu Sese
  Seko, L. = 
  Albert L. .... 57 D6
Moçambique .. 59 H8
Moçâmedes =
  Namibe ..... 58 B2
Mochudi ...... 59 C5
Mocimboa da
  Praia ....... 57 G8
Mocoa ....... 90 C3
Mocuba ...... 59 B7
Modane ...... 13 D7
Módena ...... 20 B3
Modesto ..... 82 B2
Módica ....... 21 F5
Moe ....... 63 C4
Moengo ...... 92 A3
Mogadishu =
  Muqdisho ... 49 G4
Mogador =
  Essaouira ... 54 B3
Mogami → ... 33 G12
Mogaung ..... 41 E11
Mogi das Cruzes 94 A7
Mogi-Mirim ... 94 A7
Mogilev =
  Mahilyow ... 17 B10
Mogilev-
  Podolskiy =
  Mohyliv-
  Podilskyy ... 17 D8
Mogoi ....... 39 E4
Mogok ....... 41 F11

Mohács ...... 16 F4
Moḥammadābād
  ........... 44 B4
Mohoro ...... 57 F7
Mohyliv-
  Podilskyy ... 17 D8
Mointy ....... 29 E8
Moisie ....... 69 C4
Moisie → .... 69 C4
Moïssala ..... 53 G2
Mojave Desert . 82 C4
Mokai ....... 64 C6
Mokokchung .. 41 D10
Mokra Gora ... 22 C3
Molchanovo .. 29 D9
Moldavia ■ =
  Moldova ■ .. 17 E9
Molde ....... 8 F9
Moldova ■ ... 17 E9
Moldoveana .. 17 F7
Molepolole ... 59 C5
Molfetta ..... 20 D6
Moline ....... 77 E9
Moliro ....... 57 F6
Mollendo ..... 91 G4
Molodechno =
  Maladzyechna 17 A8
Molokai ...... 82 H12
Molong ...... 63 B4
Molopo → ... 58 D4
Molotov = Perm 29 D6
Moloundou ... 56 D3
Molu ....... 39 F4
Molucca Sea . 39 E2
Moluccas =
  Maluku ..... 39 E3
Moma ....... 59 B7
Mombasa ..... 57 E7
Momchilgrad .. 22 D5
Mompós ...... 90 B4
Mon → ...... 41 G10
Mona, Canal de
  la ....... 87 C6
Monaco ■ .... 13 E7
Monahans .... 78 D2
Monastir =
  Bitola ...... 22 D3
Monastir ..... 52 A1
Moncayo, Sierra
  del ....... 19 B5
Mönchengladbach
  ........... 14 C4
Monchique ... 18 D1
Monclova ..... 84 B4
Mondego → .. 18 B1
Mondeodo ... 39 E2
Mondoví ..... 20 B1
Monforte de
  Lemos ..... 18 A2
Mong Hsu ... 41 G12
Mong Kung ... 41 G11
Mong Nai ... 41 G11
Mong Pawk .. 41 F12
Mong Ton ... 41 G12
Mong Wa .... 41 G13
Mong Yai ... 41 F12
Mongalla ..... 53 G5
Monghyr =
  Munger .... 40 E6
Mongibello =
  Etna ....... 21 F5
Mongo ....... 53 F2
Mongolia ■ .. 35 B5
Mongororo ... 53 F3
Mongu ....... 58 B4
Monkoto ..... 56 E4
Monópoli ..... 21 D6
Monqoumba .. 56 D3

# Monroe

Monroe, La., U.S.A. ...... 79 C7
Monroe, N.C., U.S.A. ...... 75 B7
Monrovia ..... 55 G2
Mons ........ 14 C2
Monse ........ 39 E2
Mont-de-Marsan 12 E3
Mont-St.-Michel, Le = Le Mont-St.-Michel ... 12 B3
Montalbán .... 19 B5
Montana □ .... 81 B9
Montargis .... 13 C5
Montauban ... 12 D4
Montbéliard ... 13 C7
Montceau-les-Mines ...... 13 C6
Monte Alegre . 92 C3
Monte Azul . 93 F5
Monte-Carlo .. 20 C1
Monte Caseros 94 C5
Monte Comán . 94 C3
Monte Santu, C. di ......... 21 D2
Montecristi ... 90 D2
Montecristo ... 20 C3
Montego Bay .. 86 C4
Montélimar ... 13 D6
Montemorelos . 84 B5
Montenegro □ 22 C2
Montepuez .... 59 A7
Monterey .... 82 B2
Montería ..... 90 B3
Monterrey .... 84 B4
Montes Claros . 93 F5
Montesilvano Marina ..... 20 C5
Montevideo ... 94 C5
Montgomery = Sahiwal .... 42 D8
Montgomery .. 74 C4
Montijo ...... 18 C2
Montilla ...... 18 D3
Montluçon .... 13 C5
Montmorillon . 12 C4
Montoro ...... 18 C3
Montpellier ... 13 E5
Montréal ..... 69 D3
Montreux ..... 13 C7
Montrose, U.K. 10 C5
Montrose, U.S.A. ...... 83 A9
Montserrat ■ .. 87 C7
Monveda ..... 56 D4
Monywa ..... 41 F10
Monza ........ 20 B2
Monze ....... 59 B5
Monze, C. ..... 43 G5
Monzón ...... 19 B6
Moolawatana . 62 A2
Moomin Cr. → 63 A4
Moonie ....... 63 A5
Moonie → .... 63 A4
Moonta ...... 62 B2
Mooroopna ... 63 C4
Moose Jaw .. 71 C9
Moosomin ... 71 C9
Moosonee .... 69 C2
Mopeia Velha . 59 B7
Mopti ....... 55 F4
Moquegua .... 91 G4
Mora ......... 8 F10
Moradabad .. 42 E11
Morafenobe ... 59 H8
Moramanga .. 59 H9
Moratuwa .. 43 R11
Morava →, Serbia, Yug. . 22 B3

Morava →, Slovak Rep. . 16 D3
Moravian Hts. = Ceskomoravská Vrchovina ... 16 D2
Morawhanna .. 90 B7
Moray Firth .. 10 C5
Morden ...... 71 D10
Mordovian Republic □ = Mordvinia □ 24 C5
Mordvinia □ .. 24 C5
Morea ........ 62 C3
Moree ........ 63 A4
Morelia ....... 84 D4
Morella ...... 19 B5
Morena, Sierra 18 C3
Moreton I. .... 63 A5
Morgan ....... 62 B2
Morgan City . 79 E8
Morioka ...... 33 G12
Morlaix ...... 12 B2
Mornington .. 63 C4
Mornington, I. . 95 F1
Moro G. ...... 38 C2
Morocco ■ ... 54 B3
Morococha .. 91 F3
Morogoro ... 57 F7
Morombe .... 59 J8
Morón ....... 86 B4
Mörön → .... 35 B6
Morón de la Frontera ... 18 D3
Morondava ... 59 J8
Morotai ...... 39 D3
Moroto ...... 57 D6
Morphou ..... 46 D3
Morrinhos ... 93 F4
Morrinsville . 64 B6
Morristown ... 75 A6
Morrumbene .. 59 C7
Morshansk ... 24 C5
Morteros ..... 94 C4
Mortes, R. das → ...... 93 E3
Mortlake ..... 62 C3
Morundah .... 63 B4
Moruya ...... 63 C5
Morvan ...... 13 C6
Morven ...... 63 A4
Morwell ..... 63 C4
Moscos Is. .. 41 L11
Moscow = Moskva ..... 24 B4
Moscow .... 80 B5
Mosel → ..... 13 A7
Moselle = Mosel → ... 13 A7
Mosgiel ...... 65 F4
Moshi ........ 57 E7
Moskva ...... 24 B4
Moskva → ... 24 B4
Moson-magyaróvár . 16 E3
Mosquera .... 90 C3
Moss Vale ... 63 B5
Mossaka ..... 56 E3
Mossburn ... 65 F3
Mosselbaai .. 58 E4
Mossendjo ... 56 E2
Mossgiel .... 63 B3
Mossoró ...... 92 D6
Mossuril .... 59 G8
Most ......... 16 C1
Mostaganem .. 54 A5
Mostar ....... 20 C6
Mostardas ... 94 C6
Mostiska = Mostyska ... 17 D6

Mosty = Masty 17 B7
Mostyska ..... 17 D6
Mosul = Al Mawşil ... 46 C5
Motihari ...... 40 D5
Motril ........ 18 D4
Motueka ..... 65 D5
Motueka → .. 65 D5
Mouanda ..... 56 E2
Moúdhros ... 23 E5
Moudjeria .... 55 E2
Mouila ....... 56 E2
Moulamein .. 63 C3
Moulins ...... 13 C5
Moulmein .... 41 J11
Moundou .... 53 G2
Mount Barker . 62 C2
Mount Darwin . 59 B6
Mount Eba ... 62 B2
Mount Gambier 62 C3
Mount Hope, N.S.W., Australia .... 63 B4
Mount Hope, S. Austral., Australia ... 62 B2
Mount Howitt . 62 A3
Mount Isa .... 61 E6
Mount Lofty Ra. 62 B2
Mount McKinley National Park 71 B4
Mount Margaret 63 A3
Mount Maunganui .. 64 B7
Mount Olympus = Uludağ .. 23 D7
Mount Perry .. 63 A5
Mount Vernon . 73 D9
Mountain View 82 B1
Moura, Brazil .. 90 D6
Moura, Portugal 18 C2
Mourdi, Dépression du 53 E3
Mourdiah ..... 55 F3
Moussoro ... 53 F2
Moutohara ... 64 C7
Moutong ..... 39 D2
Moyale ....... 57 D7
Moyamba .... 55 G2
Moyen Atlas . 54 B3
Moyo ........ 37 F5
Moyyero → .. 30 C8
Mozambique = Moçambique 59 H8
Mozambique ■ 59 B7
Mozambique Chan. ..... 59 H8
Mozdok ...... 25 E5
Mozyr = Mazyr 17 C9
Mpanda ..... 57 F6
Mpika ....... 59 A6
Mpwapwa ... 57 F7
Msaken ..... 52 A1
Msoro ....... 59 A6
Mu Us Shamo . 35 C5
Muaná ....... 92 C4
Muar ........ 37 D2
Muarabungo .. 37 E2
Muaraenim ... 37 E2
Muarajuloi ... 37 E4
Muarakaman .. 37 E5
Muaratebo ... 37 E2
Muaratembesi . 37 E2
Muaratewe ... 37 E4
Mubarraz = Al Mubarraz ... 47 F7
Mubende .... 57 D6
Mubi ........ 53 F1
Muckadilla ... 63 A4

Muconda ..... 56 G4
Mucuri ....... 93 F6
Mudanjiang ... 35 B7
Mudanya .... 23 D7
Mudgee ..... 63 B4
Mufulira ..... 59 A5
Muğla ....... 23 F7
Mugu ....... 40 C4
Muhammad Qol 52 D6
Mühlhausen .. 14 C6
Mühlig Hofmann fjell ........ 96 B7
Mukacheve .. 17 D6
Mukachevo = Mukacheve .. 17 D6
Mukah ....... 37 D4
Mukden = Shenyang ... 35 B7
Mukomuko ... 37 E2
Muktsar ..... 42 D9
Mukur ....... 42 C5
Mula ........ 19 C5
Mulchén .... 94 D2
Mulde → .... 15 C7
Mulgathing ... 62 B1
Mulgrave .... 69 D4
Mulhacén ... 18 D4
Mulhouse .... 13 C7
Mull ........ 10 C4
Mullengudgery 63 B4
Muller, Pegunungan 37 D4
Mullingar ... 11 E3
Mullumbimby . 63 A5
Multan ....... 42 D7
Mulwala .... 63 C4
Mumbai = Bombay .... 43 K8
Mumbwa .... 59 A5
Muna ....... 39 F2
München .... 15 D6
Munchen-Gladbach = Mönchengladbach .......... 14 C4
Muncie ...... 72 D3
Mundala ..... 39 E6
Münden ..... 14 C5
Mundo Novo . 93 E5
Mungallala ... 63 A4
Mungallala Cr. → ..... 63 A4
Mungbere ... 57 D5
Munger ..... 40 E6
Mungindi .... 63 A4
Munhango ... 58 A3
Munich = München ... 15 D6
Muñoz Gamero, Pen. ...... 95 G2
Münster ..... 14 C4
Munster □ ... 11 E2
Muntok ..... 37 E3
Mupa ....... 58 B3
Muqdisho ... 49 G4
Murallón, Cuerro ... 95 F2
Murang'a ..... 57 E7
Murashi .... 24 B6
Muratlı ...... 22 D6
Murchison → . 60 F1
Murchison, Mt. 96 B15
Murchison Falls = Kabarega Falls ...... 57 D6
Murcia ...... 19 C5
Murcia □ .... 19 D5
Mureş → .... 16 E5

Mureşul =
Mureş → ... 16 E5
Murfreesboro . 74 B4
Murgab =
Murghob ... 29 F8
Murghob .... 29 F8
Murgon .... 63 A5
Müritz-see .... 15 B7
Murmansk ... 28 C4
Murom ...... 24 B5
Muroran ...... 32 F12
Muroto-Misaki . 32 C4
Murray → .... 62 C2
Murray Bridge . 62 C2
Murree ....... 42 C8
Murrumbidgee →
........ 62 B3
Murrumburrah 63 B4
Murrurundi .. 63 B5
Murtoa ...... 62 C3
Murwara ..... 40 F3
Murwillumbah . 63 A5
Mürzzuschlag . 15 E8
Muş ...... 46 C5
Mûsa, G. .... 47 E3
Musa Khel .. 42 D6
Mūsá Qal'eh . 42 C4
Musaffargarh . 42 D7
Musala, Bulgaria 22 C4
Musala,
Indonesia ... 37 D1
Musay'īd ...... 44 E2
Muscat =
Masqat ..... 45 F4
Muscat & Oman
= Oman ■ .. 48 C6
Muscatine .... 77 E9
Musgrave Ras. 60 F5
Mushie ...... 56 E3
Musi → ...... 37 E2
Muskogee .... 79 B6
Musmar ...... 53 E6
Musoma ...... 57 E6
Mussoorie .. 42 D11
Mustafakemalpaşa
.......... 23 D7
Mustang .... 40 C4
Musters, L. ... 95 F3
Muswellbrook . 63 B5
Mût, Egypt .... 52 C4
Mut, Turkey .. 46 C3
Mutare ...... 59 B6
Muting ....... 39 F6
Mutoray .... 30 C8
Muxima ...... 56 F2
Muynak ...... 29 E6
Muzaffarabad . 42 B8
Muzaffarnagar . 42 E10
Muzaffarpur ... 40 D5
Muzhi ....... 28 C7
Muztag ...... 34 C3
Mvuma ....... 59 B6
Mwanza,
Tanzania .... 57 E6
Mwanza, Zaïre . 57 F5
Mweka ....... 56 E4
Mwenezi .... 59 C6
Mwenga ..... 57 E5
Mweru, L. .... 57 F5
Mwinilunga .. 58 A4
My Tho ...... 36 B3
Myanaung .... 41 H10
Myanmar =
Burma ■ .. 41 G11
Myaungmya .. 41 J10
Mycenæ .... 23 F4
Myeik Kyunzu . 36 B1
Myingyan ..... 41 G10
Myitkyina ..... 41 E11

Mykolayiv .... 25 D3
Mymensingh .. 41 E8
Mysia ....... 23 E6
Mysore =
Karnataka □ . 43 N10
Mysore ...... 43 N10
Myszków .... 16 C4
Mytishchi ..... 24 B4

## N

Na Hearadh =
Harris ..... 10 C3
Naab → ..... 15 D7
Naberezhnyye
Chelny ..... 29 D6
Nabeul ...... 52 A1
Nabire ....... 39 E5
Nablus =
Nābulus ... 46 D3
Nābulus ...... 46 D3
Nachingwea .. 57 G7
Nackara ..... 62 B2
Nacogdoches . 79 D6
Nacozari ..... 84 A3
Nadiad ...... 43 H8
Nadūshan .... 44 C3
Nadvirna ..... 17 D7
Nadvornaya =
Nadvirna ... 17 D7
Nadym ...... 28 C8
Nadym → .... 28 C8
Nafada ...... 55 F7
Nafūd ad Dahy 47 G6
Nafud Desert =
An Nafūd ... 47 E5
Naga ....... 38 B2
Nagaland □ .. 41 E10
Nagano ..... 32 A6
Nagaoka ...... 33 G11
Nagappattinam 43 P11
Nagar Parkar . 43 G7
Nagasaki .... 32 C1
Nagaur ...... 42 F8
Nagercoil .... 43 Q10
Nagīneh ..... 44 C4
Nagoya ..... 32 B5
Nagpur ...... 43 J11
Nagykanizsa . 16 E3
Nagykörös .... 16 E4
Nahanni Butte . 70 B7
Nahāvand .... 46 D7
Nā'ifah ....... 48 D5
Nain, Canada .. 68 C4
Nā'īn, Iran .... 44 C3
Nairn ....... 10 C5
Nairobi ...... 57 E7
Naivasha .... 57 E7
Najafābād .... 44 C2
Najd ....... 47 F5
Najibabad .... 42 E11
Nakamura .... 32 C3
Nakfa ....... 53 E6
Nakhichevan =
Naxçıvan ... 25 F6
Nakhichevan
Republic □ =
Naxçıvan □ . 25 F6
Nakhodka .... 31 E11
Nakhon Phanom 36 A2
Nakhon
Ratchasima . 36 B2
Nakhon Sawan 36 A2
Nakhon Si
Thammarat . 36 C2
Nakina ....... 69 C2

Nakuru ....... 57 E7
Nal → ...... 42 G4
Nalchik ...... 25 E5
Nalgonda ..... 43 L11
Nallamalai Hills 43 M11
Nālūt ....... 52 B1
Nam Co ...... 34 C4
Nam-Phan ... 36 B3
Namacurra ... 59 B7
Namak,
Daryācheh-ye 44 C3
Namak, Kavir-e 44 C4
Namaland ... 58 C3
Namangan .... 29 E8
Namapa ..... 59 A7
Namber ...... 39 E4
Nambour ..... 63 A5
Nambucca
Heads ... 63 B5
Nameh ....... 37 D5
Namib Desert =
Namibwoestyn
........ 58 C2
Namibe ..... 58 B2
Namibia ■ .. 58 C3
Namibwoestyn 58 C2
Namlea ...... 39 E3
Namoi → .... 63 B4
Nampa ...... 80 D5
Nampula ..... 59 B7
Namrole ...... 39 E3
Namse Shankou 40 C4
Namtu ....... 41 F11
Namur ...... 14 C3
Namutoni .... 58 B3
Namwala ..... 59 B5
Nanaimo .... 71 D7
Nanango ..... 63 A5
Nanao ...... 32 A5
Nanchang .... 35 D6
Nanching =
Nanjing .... 35 C6
Nanchong .... 35 C5
Nancy ...... 13 B7
Nanda Devi .. 42 D11
Nanded ...... 43 K10
Nandewar Ra. . 63 B5
Nandurbar ... 43 J9
Nandyal ..... 43 M11
Nanga-Eboko . 56 D2
Nanga Parbat . 42 B9
Nangapinoh .. 37 E4
Nangarhár □ . 42 B7
Nangatayap .. 37 E4
Nanjing ..... 35 C6
Nanking =
Nanjing .... 35 C6
Nanning ..... 35 D5
Nanping ..... 35 D6
Nansei-Shotō =
Ryūkyū-rettō 35 D7
Nantes ...... 12 C3
Nanuque .... 93 F5
Nanusa,
Kepulauan .. 38 D3
Nanyang .... 35 C6
Nanyuki ..... 57 D7
Nao, C. de la .. 19 C6
Naoetsu ...... 32 A6
Napa ....... 80 F2
Napier ...... 64 C7
Naples = Nápoli 21 D5
Naples ...... 75 F7
Napo → ..... 90 D4
Nápoli ...... 21 D5
Nappa Merrie . 62 A3
Nara, Japan ... 32 B4
Nara, Mali ... 55 E3
Naracoorte ... 62 C3

Naradhan ..... 63 B4
Narasapur .... 40 J3
Narathiwat ... 36 C2
Narayanganj .. 41 F8
Narayanpet .. 43 L10
Narbonne .... 13 E5
Nardò ...... 23 D2
Narew → .... 16 B5
Narin ....... 42 A6
Narmada → .. 43 J8
Narooma .... 63 C5
Narrabri ..... 63 B4
Narran → .... 63 A4
Narrandera ... 63 B4
Narromine ... 63 B4
Narsimhapur .. 43 H11
Narva ...... 24 B2
Narvik ...... 8 E11
Naryan-Mar .. 28 C6
Naryilco ..... 62 A3
Narym ...... 29 D9
Narymskoye .. 29 E9
Naryn ...... 29 E8
Nasarawa .... 55 G6
Naseby ...... 65 F4
Naser, Buheirat
en ......... 52 D5
Nashville .... 74 A4
Nasik ....... 43 K8
Nasirabad ... 42 F9
Nassau ...... 86 A4
Nassau, B. .... 95 H3
Nasser, L. =
Naser,
Buheirat en . 52 D5
Nat Kyizin .... 41 K11
Nata ....... 59 C5
Natagaima ... 90 C3
Natal, Brazil ... 92 D6
Natal, Indonesia 37 D1
Naţanz ...... 44 C2
Natashquan .. 69 C4
Natashquan → 69 C4
Natchez ...... 79 D8
Nathalia ..... 63 C4
Nathdwara ... 43 G8
Natitingou ... 55 F5
Natron, L. .... 57 E7
Natuna Besar,
Kepulauan .. 37 D3
Natuna Is. =
Natuna Besar,
Kepulauan .. 37 D3
Natuna Selatan,
Kepulauan .. 37 D3
Naturaliste, C. . 62 D4
Naumburg ... 15 C6
Nauru ■ ...... 64 K11
Naushahra =
Nowshera .. 42 B8
Nauta ...... 90 D4
Nautanwa ... 40 D4
Navahrudak ... 17 B7
Navalmoral de
la Mata .... 18 C3
Navarino, I. .. 95 H3
Navarra □ .... 19 A5
Năvodari .... 22 B7
Navoi = Nawoiy 29 E7
Navojoa ..... 84 B3
Návpaktos ... 23 E3
Návplion .... 23 F4
Navsari ...... 43 J8
Nawabshah .. 42 F6
Nawakot .... 40 D5
Nawalgarh ... 42 F9
Nawāsif, Harrat 47 G5
Nawoiy ...... 29 E7
Naxçıvan .... 25 F6

# Naxçıvan

| | | |
|---|---|---|
| Naxçıvan □ ... | 25 | F6 |
| Náxos ........ | 23 | F5 |
| Nāy Band ..... | 44 | E3 |
| Nazas → ..... | 84 | B4 |
| Nazilli ........ | 23 | F7 |
| Nazir Hat ..... | 41 | F8 |
| Ncheu ........ | 59 | A6 |
| Ndalatando ... | 56 | F2 |
| Ndélé ........ | 56 | C4 |
| Ndendé ...... | 56 | E2 |
| Ndjamena .... | 53 | F1 |
| Ndjolé ....... | 56 | E2 |
| Ndola ........ | 59 | A5 |
| Neagh, Lough . | 11 | D3 |
| Near Is. ...... | 71 | C1 |
| Neath ........ | 11 | F5 |
| Nebine Cr. → . | 63 | A4 |
| Nebitdag ..... | 29 | F6 |
| Nebraska □ ... | 76 | E5 |
| Nébrodi, Monti | 21 | F5 |
| Neckar → .... | 14 | D5 |
| Necochea ..... | 94 | D5 |
| Neemuch = | | |
| Nimach ..... | 43 | G9 |
| Neepawa ..... | 71 | C10 |
| Nefta ........ | 54 | B6 |
| Neftçala ...... | 46 | C7 |
| Negapatam = | | |
| Nagappattinam | | |
| ........... | 43 | P11 |
| Negele ....... | 49 | F2 |
| Negombo ..... | 43 | R11 |
| Negotin ...... | 22 | B4 |
| Negra Pt. ..... | 38 | A2 |
| Negrais, C. = | | |
| Maudin Sun . | 41 | K10 |
| Negro →, | | |
| Argentina ... | 95 | E4 |
| Negro →, Brazil | 90 | D6 |
| Negro →, | | |
| Uruguay .... | 94 | C5 |
| Negros ....... | 38 | C2 |
| Nehbandān ... | 45 | D5 |
| Nei Monggol | | |
| Zizhiqu □ ... | 35 | B6 |
| Neijiang ...... | 35 | D5 |
| Neiva ........ | 90 | C3 |
| Nejd = Najd .. | 47 | F5 |
| Nekemte ..... | 53 | G6 |
| Nellore ....... | 43 | M11 |
| Nelson, Canada | 71 | D8 |
| Nelson, N.Z. .. | 65 | D5 |
| Nelson → .... | 71 | C10 |
| Nelson, C. .... | 62 | C3 |
| Nelson, Estrecho | 95 | G2 |
| Nelspruit ..... | 59 | D6 |
| Néma ........ | 55 | E3 |
| Neman → .... | 24 | B1 |
| Nemunas = | | |
| Neman → .. | 24 | B1 |
| Nemuro ...... | 32 | F13 |
| Nemuro-Kaikyō | 32 | F13 |
| Nenagh ...... | 11 | E2 |
| Nenana ...... | 71 | B5 |
| Nenjiang ..... | 35 | B7 |
| Nepal ■ ..... | 40 | D5 |
| Nepalganj .... | 40 | C3 |
| Neretva → ... | 20 | C6 |
| Ness, L. ...... | 10 | C4 |
| Nesterov ..... | 17 | C6 |
| Nesvizh = | | |
| Nyasvizh .... | 17 | B8 |
| Netherlands ■ . | 14 | B3 |
| Netherlands | | |
| Antilles ■ ... | 87 | D6 |
| Nettilling L. .. | 68 | B3 |
| Neubrandenburg | | |
| ........... | 15 | B7 |
| Neuchâtel .... | 13 | C7 |
| Neuchâtel, Lac | | |
| de ........ | 13 | C7 |
| Neumünster .. | 14 | A5 |
| Neunkirchen .. | 14 | D4 |
| Neuquén ..... | 94 | D3 |
| Neuruppin .... | 15 | B7 |
| Neustrelitz .... | 15 | B7 |
| Neva → ..... | 24 | B3 |
| Nevada □ .... | 80 | F5 |
| Nevada, Sierra, | | |
| Spain ...... | 18 | D4 |
| Nevada, Sierra, | | |
| U.S.A. ...... | 80 | F3 |
| Nevers ....... | 13 | C5 |
| Nevertire ..... | 63 | B4 |
| Nevinnomyssk | 25 | E5 |
| Nevis ........ | 87 | C7 |
| Nevşehir ..... | 46 | C3 |
| New Amsterdam | 90 | B7 |
| New Angledool | 63 | A4 |
| New Bedford .. | 73 | D10 |
| New Bern .... | 75 | B9 |
| New Brighton . | 65 | E5 |
| New Britain, | | |
| Papua N. G. . | 64 | K10 |
| New Britain, | | |
| U.S.A. ...... | 73 | D9 |
| New | | |
| Brunswick □ | 69 | D4 |
| New | | |
| Caledonia ■ . | 64 | M11 |
| New Delhi .... | 42 | E10 |
| New England | | |
| Ra. ........ | 63 | B5 |
| New Glasgow . | 69 | D4 |
| New Guinea .. | 64 | K9 |
| New | | |
| Hampshire □ | 73 | C10 |
| New Haven ... | 73 | D9 |
| New Hebrides = | | |
| Vanuatu ■ .. | 64 | L11 |
| New Ireland .. | 64 | K10 |
| New Jersey □ . | 73 | E9 |
| New London .. | 73 | D9 |
| New Mexico □ | 83 | C9 |
| New Norfolk .. | 62 | D4 |
| New Orleans .. | 79 | E8 |
| New Plymouth | 64 | C6 |
| New Providence | 86 | A4 |
| New Siberian Is. | | |
| = | | |
| Novosibirskiye | | |
| Ostrova ..... | 31 | B12 |
| New South | | |
| Wales □ ..... | 63 | B4 |
| New | | |
| Westminster | 71 | D7 |
| New York □ ... | 73 | C8 |
| New York City . | 73 | D9 |
| New Zealand ■ | 64 | D7 |
| Newala ....... | 57 | G7 |
| Newark ....... | 73 | D8 |
| Newburgh .... | 73 | D8 |
| Newbury ..... | 11 | F6 |
| Newcastle, | | |
| Australia .... | 63 | B5 |
| Newcastle, | | |
| S. Africa .... | 59 | D5 |
| Newcastle-upon- | | |
| Tyne ....... | 11 | D6 |
| Newfoundland □ | | |
| ........... | 69 | C5 |
| Newman ..... | 60 | E2 |
| Newport, | | |
| I. of W., U.K. | 11 | F6 |
| Newport, Newp., | | |
| U.K. ....... | 11 | F5 |
| Newport, U.S.A. | 73 | D10 |
| Newport News | 73 | F7 |
| Newquay ..... | 11 | F4 |
| Newry ....... | 11 | D3 |
| Newton Boyd . | 63 | A5 |
| Neya ........ | 24 | B5 |
| Neyrīz ....... | 44 | D3 |
| Neyshābūr .... | 44 | B4 |
| Nezhin = Nizhyn | 24 | C3 |
| Ngabang ..... | 37 | D3 |
| Ngabordamlu, | | |
| Tanjung ... | 39 | F4 |
| Ngami | | |
| Depression .. | 58 | C4 |
| Nganglong | | |
| Kangri ...... | 40 | A3 |
| Ngaoundéré .. | 56 | C2 |
| Ngapara ...... | 65 | F4 |
| Ngoring Hu ... | 34 | C4 |
| Ngudu ....... | 57 | E6 |
| Nguigmi ..... | 53 | F1 |
| Nguru ........ | 55 | F7 |
| Nha Trang .... | 36 | B3 |
| Nhill ........ | 62 | C3 |
| Niafounké .... | 55 | E4 |
| Niagara Falls, | | |
| Canada .... | 69 | D3 |
| Niagara Falls, | | |
| U.S.A. ...... | 73 | C6 |
| Niah ........ | 37 | D4 |
| Niamey ...... | 55 | F5 |
| Niangara ..... | 57 | D5 |
| Nias ........ | 37 | D1 |
| Nicaragua ■ .. | 85 | E7 |
| Nicaragua, L. de | 85 | E7 |
| Nicastro ...... | 21 | E6 |
| Nice ........ | 13 | E7 |
| Nichinan ..... | 33 | D2 |
| Nicobar Is. ... | 27 | J13 |
| Nicosia ....... | 46 | D3 |
| Nicoya, Pen. de | 85 | F7 |
| Niedersachsen □ | | |
| ........... | 14 | B5 |
| Niemen = | | |
| Neman → .. | 24 | B1 |
| Nienburg .... | 14 | B5 |
| Nieuw | | |
| Amsterdam . | 92 | A2 |
| Nieuw Nickerie | 92 | A2 |
| Niğde ....... | 46 | C3 |
| Niger ■ ...... | 55 | E6 |
| Niger → ..... | 55 | G6 |
| Nigeria ■ ..... | 55 | G6 |
| Nightcaps .... | 65 | F3 |
| Nii-Jima ..... | 32 | B6 |
| Niigata ....... | 33 | G11 |
| Niihama ..... | 32 | C3 |
| Niihau ....... | 82 | H11 |
| Nijmegen .... | 14 | C3 |
| Nikiniki ...... | 39 | F2 |
| Nikki ........ | 55 | G5 |
| Nikolayev = | | |
| Mykolayiv .. | 25 | D3 |
| Nikolayevsk ... | 24 | C6 |
| Nikopol ...... | 25 | D3 |
| Nīkshahr ..... | 45 | E5 |
| Nikšić ....... | 22 | C2 |
| Nîl, Nahr en → | 52 | B5 |
| Nîl el Abyad → | 53 | E5 |
| Nîl el Azraq → | 53 | E5 |
| Nile = Nîl, Nahr | | |
| en → ...... | 52 | B5 |
| Nimach ...... | 43 | G9 |
| Nîmes ....... | 13 | E6 |
| Nimfaíon, Ákra | | |
| = Pínnes, | | |
| Ákra ....... | 23 | D5 |
| Nimmitabel .. | 63 | C4 |
| Nīmrūz □ ..... | 45 | D5 |
| Nimule ...... | 57 | D6 |
| Nīnawá ....... | 46 | C5 |
| Nindigully .... | 63 | A4 |
| Nineveh = | | |
| Nīnawá ..... | 46 | C5 |
| Ningbo ...... | 35 | D7 |
| Ningde ....... | 35 | D6 |
| Ningpo = | | |
| Ningbo ..... | 35 | D7 |
| Ningsia Hui A.R. | | |
| = Ningxia | | |
| Huizu | | |
| Zizhiqu □ ... | 35 | C5 |
| Ningxia Huizu | | |
| Zizhiqu □ ... | 35 | C5 |
| Niobrara → .. | 76 | D5 |
| Nioro du Sahel | 55 | E3 |
| Niort ........ | 12 | C3 |
| Nipawin ..... | 71 | C9 |
| Nipigon, L. .... | 69 | D2 |
| Niquelândia .. | 93 | E4 |
| Nirmal ....... | 43 | K11 |
| Nirmali ...... | 40 | D6 |
| Niš ........ | 22 | C3 |
| Nişāb, Si. Arabia | 47 | E6 |
| Nişāb, Yemen . | 49 | E4 |
| Nishinomiya .. | 32 | B4 |
| Nistru = | | |
| Dnister → .. | 17 | E10 |
| Niţă' ......... | 47 | F7 |
| Niterói ....... | 93 | G5 |
| Nitra ........ | 16 | D4 |
| Nitra → ..... | 16 | E4 |
| Niue ........ | 65 | L14 |
| Niut ........ | 37 | D4 |
| Nivernais ..... | 13 | C5 |
| Nizamabad .. | 43 | K11 |
| Nizamghat ... | 41 | C10 |
| Nizhne-Vartovsk | 29 | C8 |
| Nizhneyansk .. | 31 | B11 |
| Nizhniy | | |
| Novgorod ... | 24 | B5 |
| Nizhniy Tagil .. | 29 | D6 |
| Nizhyn ....... | 24 | C3 |
| Nizip ........ | 46 | C4 |
| Nízké Tatry ... | 16 | D4 |
| Njombe ...... | 57 | F6 |
| Nkambe ...... | 55 | G7 |
| Nkawkaw .... | 55 | G4 |
| Nkhata Bay ... | 57 | G6 |
| Nkhota Kota .. | 59 | A6 |
| Nkongsamba .. | 56 | D1 |
| Nmai → ..... | 41 | E11 |
| Noakhali = | | |
| Maijdi ..... | 41 | F8 |
| Noatak ....... | 71 | B3 |
| Nobeoka ..... | 32 | C2 |
| Nocera Inferiore | 21 | D5 |
| Nockatunga .. | 62 | A3 |
| Nogales, Mexico | 84 | A2 |
| Nogales, U.S.A. | 83 | E7 |
| Nōgata ....... | 32 | C2 |
| Noginsk ...... | 30 | C7 |
| Noire, Mts. ... | 12 | B2 |
| Noirmoutier, I. | | |
| de ........ | 12 | C2 |
| Nok Kundi .... | 42 | E3 |
| Nokhtuysk ... | 30 | C9 |
| Nokomis ..... | 71 | C9 |
| Nola ........ | 56 | D3 |
| Nome ........ | 71 | B3 |
| Nong Khai ... | 36 | A2 |
| Noondoo .... | 63 | A4 |
| Nóqui ....... | 56 | F2 |
| Noranda ..... | 69 | D3 |
| Nord-Ostsee- | | |
| Kanal → ... | 14 | A5 |
| Nordegg ..... | 71 | C8 |
| Norderney ... | 14 | B4 |
| Norderstedt ... | 14 | B5 |

Nordfriesische
Inseln ...... 14 A5
Nordhausen ... 14 C6
Nordkapp ..... 8 D13
Nordrhein-
Westfalen □ . 14 C4
Nordvik ...... 30 B9
Norfolk ....... 73 F7
Norfolk I. ..... 64 M11
Norilsk ...... 30 C6
Norley ....... 63 A3
Norman ...... 78 B5
Norman Wells . 70 B7
Normandie ... 12 B4
Normandy =
Normandie .. 12 B4
Normanton ... 61 D7
Norquinco .... 95 E2
Norrköping ... 9 G11
Norrland ..... 8 F11
Norseman .... 60 G3
North Battleford 71 C9
North Bay .... 69 D3
North Bend ... 80 D1
North C. ..... 64 A5
North Cape =
Nordkapp ... 8 D13
North
Carolina □ .. 75 B7
North Channel,
Canada ..... 69 D2
North Channel,
U.K. ....... 11 D4
North Dakota □ 76 B4
North Frisian Is.
=
Nordfriesische
Inseln ...... 14 A5
North I. ....... 64 B5
North Korea ■ . 35 C7
North
Lakhimpur .. 41 D10
North Minch .. 10 B4
North Ossetia □ 25 E5
North Pagai, I. =
Pagai Utara . 37 E2
North Platte ... 76 E4
North Platte → 76 E4
North Rhine
Westphalia □
= Nordrhein-
Westfalen □ . 14 C4
North
Saskatchewan →
........... 71 C8
North Sea .... 10 D8
North Sporades
= Voríai
Sporádhes . 23 E4
North Taranaki
Bight ....... 64 C6
North
Thompson → 71 C7
North Uist .... 10 C3
North West C. . 60 E1
North West
Frontier □ . 42 B8
North West
Highlands ... 10 C4
North West
River ....... 69 C4
North West
Territories □ . 70 B9
Northampton .. 11 E6
Northern Circars 40 J4
Northern
Ireland □ ... 11 D3
Northern
Marianas ■ . 64 H9

Northern
Territory □ .. 60 D5
Northland □ .. 64 A5
Northumberland,
C. .......... 62 C3
Northumberland
Str. ......... 69 D4
Norton Sd. .... 71 B3
Norway ■ .... 8 F10
Norway House 71 C10
Norwegian Sea 6 B5
Norwich ...... 11 E7
Nosok ....... 28 B9
Noşratābād ... 45 D4
Nossob → ... 58 D4
Nosy Bé ..... 59 G9
Nosy Boraha .. 59 H9
Nosy Mitsio ... 59 G9
Nosy Varika ... 59 J9
Noteć → ..... 16 B2
Noto-Hanto ... 33 G11
Notre Dame B. 69 D5
Notre Dame de
Koartac =
Quaqtaq .... 68 B4
Notre Dame
d'Ivugivic =
Ivujivik ..... 68 B3
Nottaway → .. 69 C3
Nottingham .. 11 E6
Nouâdhibou .. 54 D1
Nouâdhibou,
Ras ........ 54 D1
Nouakchott ... 55 E1
Nouméa ...... 64 M11
Noupoort ..... 58 E4
Nouveau
Comptoir =
Wemindji .. 69 C3
Nouvelle-
Calédonie =
New
Caledonia ■ . 64 M11
Nova Casa Nova 93 D5
Nova Cruz .... 92 D6
Nova Friburgo . 93 G5
Nova Gaia =
Cambundi-
Catembo .... 56 G3
Nova Iguaçu .. 93 G5
Nova Iorque .. 92 D5
Nova Lima .... 93 F5
Nova Mambone 59 C7
Nova Scotia □ . 69 D4
Nova Sofala .. 59 C6
Nova Venécia . 93 F5
Nova Zagora .. 22 C5
Novara ....... 20 B2
Novaya Ladoga 24 A3
Novaya Lyalya 29 D7
Novaya Zemlya 28 B6
Nové Zámky .. 16 D4
Novgorod .... 24 B3
Novgorod-
Severskiy =
Novhorod-
Siverskyy ... 24 C3
Novhorod-
Siverskyy ... 24 C3
Novi Lígure ... 20 B2
Novi Pazar ... 22 C3
Novi Sad ..... 22 B2
Novo Mesto .. 20 B5
Novo Remanso 93 D5
Novoataysk ... 29 D9
Novocherkassk 25 D5
Novogrudok =
Navahrudak . 17 B7

Novohrad-
Volynskyy ... 17 C8
Novokazalinsk =
Zhangaqazaly 29 E7
Novokuybyshevsk
........... 24 C6
Novokuznetsk . 29 D9
Novomoskovsk 24 C4
Novorossiysk . 25 E4
Novorybnoye . 30 B8
Novoselytsya .. 17 D8
Novoshakhtinsk 25 D4
Novosibirsk ... 29 D9
Novosibirskiye
Ostrova ... 31 B12
Novotroitsk ... 29 D6
Novouzensk .. 24 C6
Novovolynsk . 17 C7
Novska ...... 20 B6
Novvy Port ... 28 C8
Now Shahr ... 44 B2
Nowa Sól .... 16 C2
Nowgong .... 41 D9
Nowra ....... 63 B5
Nowshera .... 42 B8
Nowy Sącz ... 16 D5
Nowy Targ .... 16 D5
Nowy Tomyśl . 16 B3
Noyon ....... 13 B5
Nsanje ....... 59 B7
Nsawam ..... 55 G4
Nsukka ...... 55 G6
Nubian Desert =
Nûbîya, Es
Sahrâ En ... 52 D5
Nûbîya, Es
Sahrâ En ... 52 D5
Nuboai ...... 39 E5
Nueltin L. .... 70 B10
Nueva Imperial 94 D2
Nueva Rosita . 84 B4
Nuéve de Julio 94 D4
Nuevitas ..... 86 B4
Nuevo, G. .... 95 E4
Nuevo Laredo . 84 B5
Nugget Pt. .... 65 G3
Nuhaka ...... 64 C7
Nukey Bluff .. 62 B2
Nukheila .... 53 E4
Nukus ....... 29 E6
Nulato ....... 71 B4
Nullarbor Plain 60 G4
Numalla, L. ... 63 A3
Numan ...... 53 G1
Numazu ..... 32 B6
Numfoor ..... 39 E4
Numurkah ... 63 C4
Nuneaton .... 11 E6
Nunivak I. .... 71 B3
Nunkun ..... 42 C10
Núoro ....... 21 D2
Nuremberg =
Nürnberg ... 15 D6
Nuriootpa .... 62 B2
Nürnberg .... 15 D6
Nurran, L. =
Terewah, L. . 63 A4
Nusa Tenggara
Barat □ .... 37 F5
Nusa Tenggara
Timur □ ... 39 F2
Nushki ....... 42 E5
Nutak ....... 68 C4
Nuuk =
Godthåb .... 68 B5
Nuwakot .... 40 C4
Nuweveldberge 58 E4
Nuyts Arch. .. 62 B1
Nyah West .... 62 C3

Nyahanga .... 57 E6
Nyahururu .... 57 D7
Nyainqentanglha
Shan ... 34 C4
Nyâlâ ........ 53 F3
Nyasa, L. =
Malawi, L. .. 59 A6
Nyasvizh ..... 17 B8
Nyda ........ 28 C8
Nyeri ........ 57 E7
Nyíregyháza .. 17 E5
Nylstroom .... 59 C5
Nymagee .... 63 B4
Nyngan ...... 63 B4
Nyoman =
Neman → .. 24 B1
Nysa ........ 16 C3
Nysa → ..... 16 B2
Nyurbe ...... 30 C9
Nzega ....... 57 E6
N'Zérékoré ... 55 G3
Nzeto ....... 56 F2

O

Ō-Shima ...... 32 B6
Oahe, L. ...... 76 C4
Oahu ........ 82 H12
Oak Ridge ... 75 A5
Oakbank ..... 62 B3
Oakey ....... 63 A5
Oakland ..... 82 B1
Oamaru ...... 65 F4
Oates Land ... 96 A15
Oaxaca ...... 84 D5
Ob → ....... 28 C7
Oba ......... 69 D2
Oban ........ 10 C4
Obbia ....... 49 F4
Oberhausen .. 14 C4
Oberon ...... 63 B4
Obi, Kepulauan 39 E3
Obi Is. = Obi,
Kepulauan .. 39 E3
Óbidos ....... 92 C2
Obihiro ...... 32 F12
Obilatu ...... 39 E3
Obo ......... 57 C5
Obozerskaya =
Obozerskiy .. 28 C5
Obozerskiy ... 28 C5
Obskaya Guba . 28 C8
Obuasi ...... 55 G4
Ocala ....... 75 E6
Ocaña ....... 18 C4
Occidental,
Cordillera .. 90 C3
Ocean I. =
Banaba ..... 64 K11
Oceanside ... 82 D4
Ocniţa ...... 17 D8
Ocumare del
Tuy ........ 90 A5
Odate ....... 33 F12
Odawara ..... 32 B6
Oddur ....... 49 G3
Ödemiş ...... 23 E7
Odense ...... 9 G10
Oder → ...... 15 B8
Odesa ....... 25 D3
Odessa = Odesa 25 D3
Odessa ...... 78 D2
Odienné ..... 55 G3
Odintsovo ... 24 B4
Odorheiu
Secuiesc .... 17 E7

# Odra

Odra = Oder → 15 B8
Odra → 16 B2
Oeiras 92 D5
Ofanto → 20 D6
Offa 55 G5
Offenbach 14 C5
Offenburg 14 D4
Oga-Hantō 33 G11
Ōgaki 32 B5
Ogbomosho 55 G5
Ogden 81 E8
Ogdensburg 73 B8
Oglio → 20 B3
Ogooué → 56 E1
Ogowe =
  Ogooué → 56 E1
Ohai 65 F2
Ohakune 64 C6
Ohanet 54 C6
Ohau, L. 65 F3
Ohio □ 72 D4
Ohio → 72 F1
Ohre → 16 C2
Ohrid 22 D3
Ohridsko Jezero 23 D3
Oise → 12 B5
Ōita 32 C2
Oiticica 92 D5
Ojos del Salado,
  Cerro 94 B3
Oka → 28 D5
Okaba 39 F5
Okahandja 58 C3
Okahukura 64 C6
Okandja 56 E2
Okanogan → 80 A4
Okara 42 D8
Okarito 65 E4
Okaukuejo 58 B3
Okavango
  Swamps 58 B4
Okaya 32 A6
Okayama 32 B3
Okazaki 32 B5
Okeechobee, L. 75 F7
Okefenokee
  Swamp 75 D6
Okhotsk, Sea of 31 D12
Oki-Shotō 32 A3
Okiep 58 D3
Okinawa-Jima 35 D7
Oklahoma □ 78 B5
Oklahoma City 78 B5
Okmulgee 79 B6
Oknitsa =
  Ocniţa 17 D8
Okrika 55 H6
Oktabrsk =
  Oktyabrsk 29 E6
Oktyabrsk 29 E6
Oktyabrskiy =
  Aktsyabrski 17 B9
Oktyabrskoy
  Revolyutsii,
  Os. 30 B7
Oktyabrskoye 28 C7
Okuru 65 E3
Okushiri-Tō 32 F11
Öland 9 G11
Olary 62 B3
Olavarría 94 D4
Oława 16 C3
Ólbia 20 D2
Old Crow 70 B6
Oldenburg 14 B5
Oldham 11 E5
Olekma → 31 C10
Olekminsk 31 C10
Oleksandriya 17 C8

Olenek 30 C9
Olenek → 30 B10
Oléron, I. d' 12 D3
Oleśnica 16 C3
Olevsk 17 C8
Olhão 18 D2
Olifants → 59 C6
Ólimbos, Óros 23 D4
Olinda 92 D7
Oliveira 93 G5
Olivenza 18 C2
Ollagüe 91 H5
Olomouc 16 D3
Olongapo 38 B2
Olot 19 A7
Olsztyn 16 B5
Olt → 22 C5
Olteniţa 22 B6
Oltu 46 B5
Olympia, Greece 23 F3
Olympia, U.S.A. 80 B2
Olympic Mts. 80 B2
Olympus, Mt. =
  Ólimbos, Óros 23 D4
Om → 29 D8
Omagh 11 D3
Omaha 77 E7
Oman ■ 48 C6
Oman, G. of 45 E4
Omaruru 58 C3
Omate 91 G4
Ombai, Selat 39 F2
Omboué 56 E1
Ombrone → 20 C3
Omdurmân 53 E5
Ometepec 84 D5
Ōmiya 32 B6
Omo → 53 G6
Omsk 29 D8
Omul, Vf. 17 F7
Ōmura 32 C1
Omuramba
  Omatako → 58 B4
Ōmuta 32 C2
Onang 39 E1
Oncócua 58 B2
Onda 19 C5
Ondangua 58 B3
Ondo 55 G5
Öndörhaan 35 B6
Onega 28 C4
Onega → 8 F15
Onega, G. of =
  Onezhskaya
  Guba 28 C4
Onega, L. =
  Onezhskoye
  Ozero 28 C4
Onehunga 64 B6
Oneşti 17 E8
Onezhskaya
  Guba 28 C4
Onezhskoye
  Ozero 28 C4
Ongarue 64 C6
Onilahy → 59 J8
Onitsha 55 G6
Onoda 32 B2
Ontario □ 69 D2
Ontario, L. 73 C7
Oodnadatta 62 A2
Oostende 14 C2
Ootacamund 43 P10
Opala 56 E4
Opava 16 D3
Opole 16 C3
Oporto = Porto 18 B1
Opotiki 64 C7
Opua 64 A6

Opunake 64 C5
Oradea 17 E5
Orai 42 G11
Oral =
  Zhayyq → 29 E6
Oral 24 C7
Oran, Algeria 54 A4
Oran, Argentina 94 A4
Orange =
  Oranje → 58 D3
Orange,
  Australia 63 B4
Orange, France 13 D6
Orange, U.S.A. 79 D7
Orange, C. 92 B3
Orangeburg 75 C7
Oranienburg 15 B7
Oranje → 58 D3
Oranjemund 58 D3
Oras 38 B3
Oraşul Stalin =
  Braşov 17 F7
Orbetello 20 C3
Orbost 63 C4
Orchila, I. 90 A5
Ordos = Mu Us
  Shamo 35 C5
Ordu 46 B4
Ordzhonikidze =
  Vladikavkaz 25 E5
Ore Mts. =
  Erzgebirge 15 C7
Örebro 9 G11
Oregon □ 80 C3
Orekhovo-
  Zuyevo 24 B4
Orel 24 C4
Ören 23 F6
Orenburg 29 D6
Orense 18 A2
Orepuki 65 G2
Øresund 9 G10
Orgaz 18 C4
Orgeyev =
  Orhei 17 E9
Orgün 45 C7
Orhaneli 23 E7
Orhangazi 23 D7
Orhei 17 E9
Orhon Gol → 35 A5
Orient 62 A3
Oriental,
  Cordillera 90 B4
Orihuela 19 C5
Orinoco → 90 B6
Orissa □ 40 G5
Oristano 21 E2
Oristano, G. di 21 E2
Orizaba 84 D5
Orkney Is. 10 B5
Orlando 75 E7
Orléanais 12 C5
Orléans 12 C4
Ormara 42 G4
Ormoc 38 B2
Ormond 64 C7
Örnsköldsvik 8 F11
Orocué 90 C4
Orol Dengizi =
  Aral Sea 29 E6
Oroquieta 38 C2
Orós 92 D6
Orosháza 16 E5
Orroroo 62 B2
Orsha 24 C3
Orsk 29 D6
Orşova 22 B4
Ortaca 23 F7
Ortegal, C. 18 A2

Orthez 12 E3
Ortigueira 18 A2
Ortles 20 A3
Ortón → 91 F5
Orūmīyeh 46 C6
Orūmīyeh,
  Daryācheh-ye 46 C6
Oruro 91 G5
Oruzgān □ 42 C5
Orvieto 20 C4
Oryakhovo 22 C4
Ōsaka 32 B4
Ösel =
  Saaremaa 24 B1
Osh 29 E8
Oshawa 69 D3
Oshkosh 76 E3
Oshmyany =
  Ashmyany 17 A7
Oshogbo 55 G5
Oshwe 56 E3
Osijek 20 B7
Osipenko =
  Berdyansk 25 D4
Osipovichi =
  Asipovichy 17 B9
Oskarshamn 9 G11
Öskemen 29 E9
Oslo 9 G10
Oslob 38 C2
Oslofjorden 9 G10
Osmanabad 43 K10
Osmaniye 46 C4
Osnabrück 14 B5
Osorio 94 B6
Osorno 95 E2
Ossa, Mt. 62 D4
Óssa, Oros 23 E4
Ostend =
  Oostende 14 C2
Oster 17 C10
Österdalälven 8 F10
Östersund 8 F10
Ostfriesische
  Inseln 14 B4
Ostrava 16 D4
Ostróda 16 B4
Ostroh 17 C8
Ostrołęka 16 B5
Ostrów
  Mazowiecka 16 B5
Ostrów
  Wielkopolski 16 C3
Ostrowiec-
  Świętokrzyski 16 C5
Ostuni 21 D6
Ōsumi-Kaikyō 33 D2
Osuna 18 D3
Oswego 73 C7
Oświęcim 16 C4
Otago □ 65 F3
Otago Harbour 65 F4
Ōtake 32 B3
Otaki 64 D6
Otaru 32 F12
Otaru-Wan =
  Ishikari-Wan 32 F12
Otavalo 90 C3
Otavi 58 B3
Otira Gorge 65 E4
Otjiwarongo 58 C3
Otorohanga 64 C6
Otranto 23 D2
Otranto, C. d' 23 D2
Otranto, Str. of 23 D2
Ōtsu 32 B4
Ottawa 69 D3
Ottawa Is. 68 C2
Ottumwa 77 E8

| | | |
|---|---|---|
| Oturkpo | 55 | G6 |
| Otway, B. | 95 | G2 |
| Otway, C. | 62 | C3 |
| Otwock | 16 | B5 |
| Ouachita Mts. | 79 | B6 |
| Ouadâne | 54 | D2 |
| Ouadda | 56 | C4 |
| Ouagadougou | 55 | F4 |
| Ouahran = Oran | 54 | A4 |
| Ouallene | 54 | D5 |
| Ouanda Djallé | 56 | C4 |
| Ouango | 56 | D4 |
| Ouargla | 54 | B6 |
| Ouarzazate | 54 | B3 |
| Oubangi ⟶ | 56 | E3 |
| Oudtshoorn | 58 | E4 |
| Ouessant, I. d' | 12 | B1 |
| Ouesso | 56 | D3 |
| Ouezzane | 54 | B3 |
| Ouidah | 55 | G5 |
| Oujda | 54 | B4 |
| Oujeft | 55 | D2 |
| Ouled Djellal | 54 | B6 |
| Oulu | 8 | E13 |
| Oulujärvi | 8 | F13 |
| Oulujoki ⟶ | 8 | E13 |
| Oum Chalouba | 53 | E3 |
| Ounianga-Kébir | 53 | E3 |
| Ounianga Sérir | 53 | E3 |
| Ourense = | | |
| Orense | 18 | A2 |
| Ouricuri | 92 | D5 |
| Ouro Prêto | 93 | G5 |
| Ouse | 62 | D4 |
| Outer Hebrides | 10 | C3 |
| Outjo | 58 | C3 |
| Ouyen | 62 | C3 |
| Ovalle | 94 | C2 |
| Ovamboland | 58 | B3 |
| Oviedo | 18 | A3 |
| Ovruch | 17 | C9 |
| Owaka | 65 | G3 |
| Owambo = | | |
| Ovamboland | 58 | B3 |
| Owase | 32 | B5 |
| Owbeh | 42 | B3 |
| Owen Sound | 69 | D2 |
| Owen Stanley | | |
| Ra. | 61 | B8 |
| Owendo | 56 | D1 |
| Owo | 55 | G6 |
| Owyhee ⟶ | 80 | D5 |
| Oxford, N.Z. | 65 | E5 |
| Oxford, U.K. | 11 | F6 |
| Oxley | 63 | B3 |
| Oxnard | 82 | C3 |
| Oxus = | | |
| Amudarya ⟶ | 29 | E6 |
| Oya | 37 | D4 |
| Oyama | 32 | A6 |
| Oyem | 56 | D2 |
| Oyo | 55 | G5 |
| Ozamiz | 38 | C2 |
| Ozark Plateau | 79 | A8 |
| Ózd | 16 | D5 |

**P**

| | | |
|---|---|---|
| Pa-an | 41 | J11 |
| Paarl | 58 | E3 |
| Pab Hills | 42 | F5 |
| Pabianice | 16 | C4 |
| Pabna | 41 | E7 |
| Pacaja ⟶ | 92 | C3 |
| Pacaraima, | | |
| Sierra | 90 | C6 |

| | | |
|---|---|---|
| Pacasmayo | 91 | E3 |
| Pachpadra | 42 | G8 |
| Pachuca | 84 | C5 |
| Padaido, | | |
| Kepulauan | 39 | E5 |
| Padang | 37 | E2 |
| Padangpanjang | 37 | E2 |
| Padangsidempuan | | |
| | 37 | D1 |
| Paderborn | 14 | C5 |
| Padloping Island | 68 | B4 |
| Pádova | 20 | B3 |
| Padua = Pádova | 20 | B3 |
| Paducah | 72 | F1 |
| Paeroa | 64 | B6 |
| Pafúri | 59 | C6 |
| Pag | 20 | B5 |
| Pagadian | 38 | C2 |
| Pagai Selatan, P. | 37 | E2 |
| Pagai Utara | 37 | E2 |
| Pagalu = | | |
| Annobón | 51 | G4 |
| Pagastikós | | |
| Kólpos | 23 | E4 |
| Pagatan | 37 | E5 |
| Pahiatua | 64 | D6 |
| Painan | 37 | E2 |
| Paint Hills = | | |
| Wemindji | 69 | C3 |
| Painted Desert | 83 | C7 |
| País Vasco □ | 19 | A4 |
| Paisley | 10 | D4 |
| Paita | 90 | E2 |
| Pajares, Puerto | | |
| de | 18 | A3 |
| Pakaraima Mts. | 90 | B6 |
| Pakistan ■ | 42 | E7 |
| Pakokku | 41 | G10 |
| Pakse | 36 | A3 |
| Paktiā □ | 42 | C6 |
| Pala | 53 | G2 |
| Palagruža | 20 | C6 |
| Palam | 43 | K10 |
| Palampur | 42 | C10 |
| Palana | 62 | C4 |
| Palanan | 38 | A2 |
| Palanan Pt. | 38 | A2 |
| Palangkaraya | 37 | E4 |
| Palani Hills | 43 | P10 |
| Palanpur | 43 | G8 |
| Palanro | 39 | E1 |
| Palapye | 59 | C5 |
| Palau ■ | 38 | C4 |
| Palawan | 36 | C5 |
| Palayankottai | 43 | Q10 |
| Paleleh | 39 | D2 |
| Palembang | 37 | E2 |
| Palencia | 18 | A3 |
| Palermo | 21 | E4 |
| Palestine | 79 | D6 |
| Paletwa | 41 | G9 |
| Palghat | 43 | P10 |
| Pali | 42 | G8 |
| Palioúrion, Ákra | 23 | E4 |
| Palitana | 43 | J7 |
| Palk Bay | 43 | Q11 |
| Palk Strait | 43 | Q11 |
| Pallanza = | | |
| Verbánia | 20 | B2 |
| Palm Springs | 82 | D4 |
| Palma | 57 | G8 |
| Palma ⟶ | 93 | E4 |
| Palma, B. de | 19 | C7 |
| Palma de | | |
| Mallorca | 19 | C7 |
| Palmares | 92 | D6 |
| Palmas, C. | 55 | H3 |
| Pálmas, G. di | 21 | E2 |

| | | |
|---|---|---|
| Palmeira dos | | |
| Índios | 93 | D6 |
| Palmeirinhas, | | |
| Pta. das | 56 | F2 |
| Palmer | 71 | B5 |
| Palmer Arch. | 96 | A3 |
| Palmer Land | 96 | B3 |
| Palmerston | 65 | F4 |
| Palmerston | | |
| North | 64 | D6 |
| Palmi | 21 | E5 |
| Palmira | 90 | C3 |
| Palmyra = | | |
| Tudmur | 46 | D4 |
| Palopo | 39 | E2 |
| Palos, C. de | 19 | D5 |
| Palu, Indonesia | 39 | E1 |
| Palu, Turkey | 46 | C5 |
| Paluan | 38 | B2 |
| Pama | 55 | F5 |
| Pamiers | 12 | E4 |
| Pamirs | 29 | F8 |
| Pámlico Sd. | 75 | B10 |
| Pampa | 78 | B3 |
| Pampa de las | | |
| Salinas | 94 | C3 |
| Pampanua | 39 | E2 |
| Pampas, | | |
| Argentina | 94 | D4 |
| Pampas, Peru | 91 | F4 |
| Pamplona, | | |
| Colombia | 90 | B4 |
| Pamplona, | | |
| Spain | 19 | A5 |
| Panaji | 43 | M8 |
| Panamá | 85 | F9 |
| Panama ■ | 86 | E4 |
| Panamá, G. de | 86 | E4 |
| Panama City | 74 | D5 |
| Panão | 91 | E3 |
| Panay | 38 | B2 |
| Panay, G. | 38 | B2 |
| Pančevo | 22 | B3 |
| Pandan | 38 | B2 |
| Pandharpur | 43 | L9 |
| Pando | 94 | C5 |
| Pando, L. = | | |
| Hope, L. | 62 | A2 |
| Panevežys | 24 | B1 |
| Panfilov | 29 | E8 |
| Pang-Long | 41 | F12 |
| Pang-Yang | 41 | F12 |
| Pangani | 57 | F7 |
| Pangfou = | | |
| Bengbu | 35 | C6 |
| Pangkajene | 39 | E1 |
| Pangkalanbrandan | | |
| | 37 | D1 |
| Pangkalanbuun | 37 | E4 |
| Pangkalansusu | 37 | D1 |
| Pangkalpinang | 37 | E3 |
| Pangkoh | 37 | E4 |
| Pangnirtung | 68 | B4 |
| Pangutaran | | |
| Group | 38 | C2 |
| Panjgur | 42 | F4 |
| Panjim = Panaji | 43 | M8 |
| Panjinad | | |
| Barrage | 42 | E7 |
| Panorama | 94 | A6 |
| Pantar | 39 | F2 |
| Pante Macassar | 39 | F2 |
| Pantelleria | 21 | F3 |
| Pánuco | 84 | C5 |
| Panyam | 55 | G6 |
| Paoting = | | |
| Baoding | 35 | C6 |
| Paot'ou = | | |
| Baotou | 35 | B6 |

| | | |
|---|---|---|
| Paoua | 56 | C3 |
| Pápa | 16 | E3 |
| Papakura | 64 | B6 |
| Papantla | 84 | C5 |
| Papar | 36 | C5 |
| Papua New | | |
| Guinea ■ | 61 | B8 |
| Papudo | 94 | C2 |
| Papun | 41 | H11 |
| Pará = Belém | 92 | C4 |
| Pará □ | 92 | C3 |
| Paracatu | 93 | F4 |
| Paracel Is. = | | |
| Hsisha | | |
| Chuntao | 36 | A4 |
| Parachilna | 62 | B2 |
| Parachinar | 42 | C7 |
| Paradip | 40 | G6 |
| Parado | 39 | F1 |
| Paragua ⟶ | 90 | B6 |
| Paraguaçu ⟶ | 93 | E6 |
| Paraguaná, Pen. | | |
| de | 90 | A4 |
| Paraguarí | 94 | B5 |
| Paraguay ■ | 94 | A5 |
| Paraguay ⟶ | 94 | B5 |
| Paraíba = João | | |
| Pessoa | 92 | D7 |
| Paraíba □ | 92 | D6 |
| Paraíba do | | |
| Sul ⟶ | 93 | G5 |
| Parakou | 55 | G5 |
| Paramaribo | 92 | A2 |
| Paraná, | | |
| Argentina | 94 | C4 |
| Paranã, Brazil | 93 | E4 |
| Paraná □ | 94 | A6 |
| Paraná ⟶ | 94 | C5 |
| Paranaguá | 94 | B7 |
| Paranaíba ⟶ | 93 | G3 |
| Paranapanema ⟶ | | |
| | 94 | A6 |
| Paranapiacaba, | | |
| Serra do | 94 | A7 |
| Parang, Jolo, | | |
| Phil. | 38 | C2 |
| Parang, | | |
| Mindanao, | | |
| Phil. | 38 | C2 |
| Paratinga | 93 | E5 |
| Paratoo | 62 | B2 |
| Parattah | 62 | D4 |
| Parbhani | 43 | K10 |
| Parchim | 15 | B6 |
| Pardo ⟶, | | |
| Bahia, Brazil | 93 | F6 |
| Pardo ⟶, | | |
| Mato Grosso, | | |
| Brazil | 93 | G3 |
| Pardo ⟶, | | |
| São Paulo, | | |
| Brazil | 93 | G4 |
| Pardubice | 16 | C2 |
| Parecis, Serra | | |
| dos | 91 | F7 |
| Parepare | 39 | E1 |
| Párga | 23 | E3 |
| Pariaguán | 90 | B6 |
| Pariaman | 37 | E2 |
| Parigi | 39 | E2 |
| Parika | 90 | B7 |
| Parima, Serra | 90 | C6 |
| Parinari | 90 | D4 |
| Parîngul Mare | 17 | F6 |
| Parintins | 92 | C2 |
| Pariparit Kyun | 41 | K9 |
| Paris, France | 12 | B5 |
| Paris, U.S.A. | 79 | C6 |
| Park Range | 81 | F10 |

| | | | | | | | | | | |
|---|---|---|---|---|---|---|---|---|---|---|
| Parkersburg | ... | 72 | E5 | Pawtucket | .... | 73 | D10 | Penas, G. de | .. | 95 | F2 |

Parkersburg ... 72 E5
Parkes ....... 63 B4
Parla ......... 18 B4
Parma ........ 20 B3
Parnaguá ..... 93 E5
Parnaíba, *Piauí,*
  *Brazil* ....... 92 C5
Parnaíba,
  *São Paulo,*
  *Brazil* ...... 93 F3
Parnaíba → . 92 C5
Parnassós .... 23 E4
Parnu ........ 24 B1
Paroo → ..... 63 B3
Páros ........ 23 F5
Parral ....... 94 D2
Parramatta ... 63 B5
Parry Sound .. 69 D3
Partinico ...... 21 E4
Paru → ....... 92 C3
Paruro □ ..... 91 F4
Parvân □ ..... 42 B6
Parvatipuram .. 40 H4
Pasadena, *Calif.,*
  *U.S.A.* ..... 82 C3
Pasadena, *Tex.,*
  *U.S.A.* ..... 79 E6
Pasaje ....... 90 D3
Pascagoula ... 79 D9
Paşcani ...... 17 E8
Pasco ........ 80 B4
Pasco, Cerro de 91 F3
Pashmakli =
  Smolyan .... 22 D5
Pašman ...... 20 C5
Pasni ........ 42 G3
Paso de Indios 95 E3
Passau ....... 15 D7
Passero, C. .... 21 F5
Passo Fundo .. 94 B6
Passos ....... 93 G4
Pastaza → ... 90 D3
Pasto ........ 90 C3
Patagonia ..... 95 F3
Patan, *India* .. 43 H8
Patan, *Nepal* .. 40 D5
Patani ........ 39 D3
Patchewollock . 62 C3
Patea ........ 64 C6
Pategi ........ 55 G6
Paternò ...... 21 F5
Paterson ..... 73 D8
Pathankot ..... 42 C9
Patiala ....... 42 D10
Patkai Bum ... 41 D10
Pátmos ...... 23 F6
Patna ........ 40 E5
Patos, I. dos .. 94 C6
Patos de Minas 93 F4
Patquía ...... 94 C3
Pátrai ....... 23 E3
Pátraïkós Kólpos 23 E3
Patras = Pátrai 23 E3
Patrocínio ... 93 F4
Pattani ....... 36 C2
Patuakhali .... 41 F8
Pau .......... 12 E3
Pauini → ..... 90 D6
Pauk ......... 41 G10
Paulis = Isiro . 57 D5
Paulistana ... 92 D5
Paulo Afonso .. 93 D6
Pavia ........ 20 B2
Pavlodar ..... 29 D8
Pavlograd =
  Pavlohrad ... 25 D4
Pavlohrad .... 25 D4
Pavlovo ...... 24 B5
Pavlovsk ...... 24 C5

Pawtucket .... 73 D10
Paxoí ........ 23 E3
Payakumbuh .. 37 E2
Payne Bay =
  Kangirsuk ... 68 C4
Paysandú ..... 94 C5
Paz, B. la .... 84 C2
Pazar ........ 46 B5
Pazardzhik .... 22 C5
Peace → .... 70 C8
Peak Hill ..... 63 B4
Peake ........ 62 C2
Peake Cr. → .. 62 A2
Pebane ....... 59 B7
Pebas ........ 90 D4
Peć .......... 22 C3
Pechenga ..... 28 C4
Pechenizhyn .. 17 D7
Pechora → ... 28 C6
Pechorskaya
  Guba ....... 28 C6
Pecos → ..... 78 E3
Pécs ......... 16 E4
Pedder, L. .... 62 D4
Pedirka ...... 62 A2
Pedra Azul ... 93 F5
Pedreiras ..... 92 C5
Pedro Afonso . 93 D4
Pedro Juan
  Caballero ... 94 A5
Peebinga ..... 62 B3
Peel → ,
  *Australia* .... 63 B5
Peel → , *Canada* 70 B6
Peera Peera
  Poolanna L. . 62 A2
Pegasus Bay .. 65 E5
Pegu ......... 41 J11
Pegu Yoma ... 41 H10
Pehuajó ...... 94 D4
Peine ........ 14 B6
Peip'ing =
  Beijing .... 35 C6
Peipus, L. =
  Chudskoye,
  Oz. ........ 24 B2
Peixe ........ 93 E4
Pekalongan ... 37 F3
Pekanbaru .... 37 D2
Pekin ........ 77 E10
Peking = Beijing 35 C6
Pelagie, Is. .... 21 G4
Pelaihari ..... 37 E4
Peleaga, Vf. .. 17 F6
Peleng ....... 39 E2
Pelješac ...... 20 C6
Pelly → ..... 70 B6
Pelly Bay ..... 68 B2
Pelly L. ....... 70 B9
Peloponnese =
  Pelopónnisos □
         ........ 23 F4
Pelopónnisos □ 23 F4
Peloro, C. .... 21 E5
Pelorus Sd. .. 65 D5
Pelotas ...... 94 C6
Pelvoux, Massif
  du ......... 13 D7
Pematangsiantar 37 D1
Pemba I. ...... 57 F7
Pembroke,
  *Canada* ..... 69 D3
Pembroke, *U.K.* 11 F4
Penang =
  Pinang ..... 36 C2
Penápolis ..... 94 A6
Peñarroya-
  Pueblonuevo 18 C3
Peñas, C. de .. 18 A3

Penas, G. de .. 95 F2
Pench'i = Benxi 35 B7
Pend Oreille L. 80 A5
Pendembu .... 55 G2
Pendleton .... 80 C4
Penedo ....... 93 E6
Penguin ...... 62 D4
Peniche ...... 18 C1
Penida ....... 37 F5
Peninsular
  Malaysia □ .. 37 D2
Penmarch, Pte.
  de ......... 12 C1
Pennines ..... 11 D5
Pennsylvania □ 73 D7
Penola ....... 62 C3
Penong ....... 60 G5
Penrith ....... 63 B5
Pensacola .... 74 D4
Pensacola Mts. 96 C4
Penshurst ..... 62 C3
Penticton .... 71 D8
Pentland Firth . 10 B5
Penza ........ 24 C6
Penzance ..... 11 F4
Peoria ....... 77 E10
Perabumulih .. 37 E2
Perche, Collines
  du ......... 12 B4
Perdido, Mte. .. 19 A6
Perdu, Mt. =
  Perdido, Mte. 19 A6
Pereira ....... 90 C3
Perekerten .... 62 B3
Pereyaslav-
  Khmelnytskyy 24 C3
Pergamino .... 94 C4
Péribonca → .. 69 D3
Perico ........ 94 A3
Périgueux .... 12 D4
Perijá, Sierra de 90 B4
Perlas, Arch. de
  las ......... 86 E4
Perm ......... 29 D6
Pernambuco =
  Recife ...... 92 D7
Pernatty Lagoon 62 B2
Pernik ....... 22 C4
Perpendicular
  Pt. ......... 63 B5
Perpignan .... 13 E5
Persepolis .... 44 D3
Pershotravensk 17 C8
Persian Gulf =
  Gulf, The ... 44 E2
Perth, *Australia* 60 G2
Perth, *U.K.* .... 10 C5
Perth Amboy .. 73 D8
Peru ■ ...... 90 C3
Perúgia ...... 20 C4
Pervomaysk ... 25 D3
Pervouralsk ... 29 D6
Pésaro ....... 20 C4
Pescara ...... 20 C5
Peshawar .... 42 B7
Peshkopi ..... 22 D3
Pesqueira .... 92 D6
Petah Tiqwa .. 46 D3
Petauke ...... 59 A6
Peter I.s Øy .. 96 A2
Peterborough,
  *Australia* .... 62 B2
Peterborough,
  *Canada* ..... 69 D3
Peterborough,
  *U.K.* ........ 11 E6
Peterhead .... 10 C6
Petersburg,
  *Alaska, U.S.A.* 71 C6

Petersburg, *Va.,*
  *U.S.A.* ...... 73 F7
Petitsikapau, L. 69 C4
Petlad ....... 43 H8
Peto ......... 85 C7
Petone ....... 65 D6
Petrich ...... 22 D4
Petrikov =
  Pyetrikaw ... 17 B9
Petrograd =
  Sankt-
  Peterburg ... 24 B3
Petrolândia .. 93 D6
Petrolina .... 93 D5
Petropavl ..... 29 D7
Petropavlovsk =
  Petropavl ... 29 D7
Petropavlovsk-
  Kamchatskiy 31 D13
Petrópolis ... 93 G5
Petroşani .... 17 F6
Petrovaradin .. 22 B2
Petrovsk ..... 24 C6
Petrozavodsk .. 28 C4
Peureulak .... 36 D1
Pforzheim ... 14 D5
Phagwara .... 42 D9
Phalodi ...... 42 F8
Phan Rang ... 36 B3
Phangan, Ko .. 36 C2
Phangnga .... 36 C1
Phanh Bho Ho
  Chi Minh ... 36 B3
Phatthalung .. 36 C2
Phetchabun ... 36 A2
Philadelphia .. 73 E8
Philippines ■ .. 38 B2
Philippopolis =
  Plovdiv .... 22 C5
Phillip I. ...... 63 C4
Phillott ...... 63 A4
Phitsanulok .. 36 A2
Phnom Dangrek 36 B2
Phnom Penh .. 36 B2
Phoenix ...... 83 D6
Phra Nakhon Si
  Ayutthaya ... 36 B2
Phuket ....... 36 C1
Phumiphon,
  Khuan .... 36 A1
Piacenza ..... 20 B2
Pialba ....... 63 A5
Pian Cr. → .. 63 B4
Pianosa ...... 20 C3
Piatra Neamţ .. 17 E8
Piauí □ ....... 92 D5
Piave → ..... 20 B4
Pibor Post ... 53 G5
Pica ......... 91 H5
Picardie ...... 13 B5
Picardy =
  Picardie ... 13 B5
Pichilemu ..... 94 C2
Pico Truncado . 95 F3
Picton, *Australia* 63 B5
Picton, *N.Z.* ... 65 D6
Pictou ....... 69 D4
Picún Leufú .. 95 D3
Piedmont =
  Piemonte □ . 20 B1
Piedras, R. de
  las → ...... 91 F5
Piedras Negras 84 B4
Piemonte □ ... 20 B1
Piet Retief ... 59 D6
Pietermaritzburg 59 D6
Pietersburg .. 59 C5
Pietrosul,
  *Romania* .... 17 E7

Pietrosul,
Romania .... 17 E7
Pigüe ........ 94 D4
Piketberg ...... 58 E3
Piła .......... 16 B3
Pilar, Brazil .. 93 D6
Pilar, Paraguay 94 B5
Pilas Group ... 38 C2
Pilcomayo → . 94 B5
Pilibhit ...... 42 E11
Pilica → ..... 16 C5
Pílos ......... 23 F3
Pilsen = Plzeň . 16 D1
Pimba ........ 62 B2
Pimenta Bueno 91 F6
Pimentel .... 91 E3
Pinang ....... 36 C2
Pinar del Río .. 86 B3
Pınarhisar ... 22 D6
Pińczów ...... 16 C5
Pindiga ....... 55 G7
Pindos Óros ... 23 E3
Pindus Mts. =
Pindos Óros . 23 E3
Pine Bluff ... 79 B7
Pine Point .... 70 B8
Pinega → ... 28 C5
Pinerolo ...... 20 B1
Pinetown ..... 59 D6
Ping → ...... 36 A2
Pingdong .... 35 D7
Pingliang .... 35 C5
Pingwu ...... 35 C5
Pingxiang .... 35 D5
Pinhel ........ 18 B2
Pini ......... 37 D1
Piniós → ..... 23 E4
Pinnaroo ..... 62 C3
Pínnes, Ákra .. 23 D5
Pinrang ...... 39 E1
Pinsk ......... 17 B8
Pintados ...... 91 H5
Pinyug ....... 24 A6
Piombino ..... 20 C3
Pioner, Os. ... 30 B7
Piorini, L. ..... 90 D6
Piotrków
Trybunalski . 16 C4
Pĩp .......... 45 E5
Piquiri → .... 94 A6
Piracicaba ... 94 A7
Piracuruca ... 92 C5
Piræus =
Piraiévs ... 23 F4
Piraiévs ...... 23 F4
Pirané ........ 94 B5
Pirapora ...... 93 F5
Pírgos ....... 23 F3
Pirin Planina .. 22 D4
Piripiri ....... 92 C5
Pirmasens ... 14 D4
Pirot ........ 22 C4
Piru ......... 39 E3
Pisa .......... 20 C3
Pisagua ...... 91 G4
Pisciotta ..... 21 D5
Pisco ........ 91 F3
Písek ........ 16 D2
Pishan ....... 34 C2
Pising ........ 39 F2
Pistóia ...... 20 C3
Pisuerga → .. 18 B3
Pitarpunga, L. . 62 B3
Pitcairn I. .... 65 M17
Piteå ........ 8 E12
Piteşti ....... 22 B5
Pithapuram ... 40 J4
Pittsburg ..... 79 A6
Pittsburgh .... 73 D5

Pittsworth .... 63 A5
Piura ......... 90 E2
Placentia ..... 69 D5
Placentia B. ... 69 D5
Plainview ..... 78 B3
Pláka, Ákra ... 23 G6
Plakhino ...... 28 C9
Plasencia ..... 18 B2
Plata, Río de la 94 C5
Platani → ... 21 F4
Plato ......... 90 B4
Platte → ..... 77 F7
Plauen ....... 15 C7
Pleiku ........ 36 B3
Plenty, B. of .. 64 B7
Pleven ....... 22 C5
Plevlja ....... 22 C2
Płock ........ 16 B4
Plöckenstein .. 15 D7
Ploieşti ...... 22 B6
Plovdiv ....... 22 C5
Plumtree ..... 59 C5
Plymouth .... 11 F4
Plzeň ........ 16 D1
Po → ........ 20 B4
Po Hai = Bo Hai 35 C6
Pobedy Pik .... 29 E8
Pocatello ..... 81 D7
Poços de Caldas 93 G4
Podgorica .... 22 C2
Podilska
Vysochyna .. 17 D8
Podkamennaya
Tunguska → 30 C7
Podolsk ...... 24 B4
Podor ........ 55 E1
Pofadder ..... 58 D3
Poh .......... 39 E2
Pohnpei ...... 64 J10
Poinsett, C. .. 96 A12
Pointe-à-Pitre .. 87 C7
Pointe Noire .. 56 E2
Poitiers ...... 12 C4
Poitou ....... 12 C3
Pokaran ...... 42 F7
Pokataroo .... 63 A4
Pokrovsk =
Engels ...... 24 C6
Pola = Pula ... 20 B4
Polan ........ 45 E5
Poland ■ .... 16 B5
Polatsk ....... 24 B2
Polcura ....... 94 D2
Polesye = Pripet
Marshes .... 17 B9
Poli .......... 56 C2
Police ........ 16 B2
Polillo Is. .... 38 B2
Políyiros ...... 23 D4
Pollachi ...... 43 P10
Polnovat ..... 28 C7
Polonne ...... 17 C8
Polonnoye =
Polonne .... 17 C8
Poltava ....... 24 D3
Polunochnoye .. 28 C7
Polynesia ..... 65 L15
Polynésie
française =
French
Polynesia ■ . 65 M16
Pombal, Brazil . 92 D6
Pombal,
Portugal .... 18 C1
Pomézia ...... 20 D4
Pomorski,
Pojezierze ... 16 B3
Ponape =
Pohnpei .... 64 J10

Ponca City .... 78 A5
Ponce ........ 87 C6
Pond Inlet .... 68 A3
Pondicherry ... 43 P11
Ponferrada .... 18 A2
Ponnani ...... 43 P9
Ponnyadaung . 41 F10
Ponoy → .... 28 C5
Ponta Grossa .. 94 B6
Ponta Pora ... 94 A5
Pontarlier ..... 13 C7
Pontchartrain L. 79 D8
Ponte Nova ... 93 G5
Pontevedra ... 18 A1
Pontiac ....... 72 C4
Pontianak .... 37 E3
Pontine Is. =
Ponziane,
Ísole ...... 21 D4
Pontine Mts. =
Kuzey
Anadolu
Dağları .... 46 B3
Pontivy ...... 12 B2
Pontoise ...... 12 B5
Ponziane, Ísole 21 D4
Poochera ..... 62 B1
Poole ........ 11 F6
Poona = Pune . 43 K8
Pooncarie .... 62 B3
Poopelloe L. .. 63 B3
Poopó, L. de . 91 G5
Popayán ...... 90 C3
Popigay ...... 30 B9
Popilta, L. .... 62 B3
Popio L. ...... 62 B3
Poplar Bluff ... 79 A8
Popocatépetl,
Volcán .... 84 D5
Popokabaka ... 56 F3
Poprád ....... 16 D5
Porbandar .... 43 J6
Porcupine → . 71 B5
Pordenone ... 20 B4
Pori ......... 8 F12
Porkkala ..... 9 G12
Porlamar ..... 90 A6
Poroshiri-Dake . 32 F12
Porpoise B. ... 96 A13
Porretta, Passo
di ........ 20 B3
Port Adelaide . 62 B2
Port Alberni ... 71 D7
Port Alfred ... 59 E5
Port Angeles .. 80 A2
Port Antonio .. 86 C4
Port Arthur,
Australia ... 62 D4
Port Arthur,
U.S.A. ..... 79 E7
Port-au-Prince . 87 C5
Port Augusta . 62 B2
Port Augusta
West ...... 62 B2
Port Bergé
Vaovao ..... 59 H9
Port Bou ..... 19 A7
Port Broughton 62 B2
Port-Cartier ... 69 C4
Port Chalmers . 65 F4
Port Darwin .. 95 G5
Port Davey .... 62 D4
Port Dickson .. 37 D2
Port Elizabeth . 59 E5
Port Fairy .... 62 C3
Port-Gentil ... 56 E1
Port Harcourt .. 55 H6
Port Harrison =
Inukjuak .... 68 C3

Port
Hawkesbury . 69 D4
Port Hedland .. 60 E2
Port Huron .... 72 C4
Port Kembla .. 63 B5
Port Kenny ... 62 B1
Port Lairge =
Waterford ... 11 E3
Port Laoise ... 11 E3
Port Lincoln .. 62 B2
Port Loko ..... 55 G2
Port MacDonnell 62 C3
Port Macquarie 63 B5
Port Moresby . 61 B8
Port Nelson ... 71 C10
Port Nolloth .. 58 D3
Port Nouveau-
Québec =
Kangiqsualujjuaq
.......... 68 C4
Port of Spain .. 87 D7
Port Pegasus . 65 G2
Port Phillip B. . 63 C3
Port Pirie ..... 62 B2
Port Safaga =
Bûr Safâga .. 52 C5
Port Said = Bûr
Sa'îd ....... 52 B5
Port Shepstone 59 E6
Port Stanley =
Stanley ..... 95 G5
Port Sudan =
Bûr Sûdân .. 53 E6
Port Talbot .... 11 F5
Port-Vendres .. 13 E5
Port Wakefield . 62 B2
Port Weld ..... 36 D2
Porta Orientalis 22 B4
Portachuelo .. 91 G6
Portadown .... 11 D3
Portage La
Prairie ..... 71 D10
Portalegre .... 18 C2
Portile de Fier . 22 B4
Portimão ..... 18 D1
Portland,
N.S.W.,
Australia ... 63 B4
Portland, Vic.,
Australia .... 62 C3
Portland, Maine,
U.S.A. ..... 73 C10
Portland, Oreg.,
U.S.A. ..... 80 C2
Portland B. ... 62 C3
Portland Prom. 68 C3
Porto ........ 18 B1
Pôrto Alegre .. 94 C6
Porto Amboim
= Gunza ... 56 G2
Pôrto de Móz . 92 C3
Porto
Empédocle .. 21 F4
Pôrto Esperança 91 G7
Pôrto Franco . 92 D4
Porto Mendes . 94 A6
Pôrto Murtinho 91 H7
Pôrto Nacional 93 E4
Porto Novo ... 55 G5
Pôrto Santo .. 54 B1
Pôrto Seguro . 93 F6
Pôrto Tórres .. 20 D2
Pôrto Velho ... 91 E6
Pôrto Válter .. 91 E4
Porto-Vecchio . 13 F8
Pôrto Velho ... 91 E6
Portoferráio .. 20 C3
Portoscuso ... 21 E2
Portovíejo .... 90 D2

Portree ....... 10 C3
Portsmouth,
  U.K. ...... 11 F6
Portsmouth,
  U.S.A. ...... 73 F7
Porttipahtan
  tekojärvi .... 8 E13
Portugal ■ .... 18 C1
Porvenir ...... 95 G2
Posadas ...... 94 B5
Poshan =
  Boshan ..... 35 C6
Poso ........ 39 E2
Posse ........ 93 E4
Possel ........ 56 C3
Possession I. .. 96 B15
Poste Maurice
  Cortier ..... 54 D5
Postojna ...... 20 B5
Potchefstroom . 59 D5
Potenza ...... 21 D5
Poteriteri, L. .. 65 G2
Potgietersrus .. 59 C5
Poti ......... 25 E5
Potiskum ..... 55 F7
Potomac → .. 73 E7
Potosí ....... 91 G5
Pototan ...... 38 B2
Potrerillos .... 94 B3
Potsdam ..... 15 B7
Poughkeepsie . 73 D9
Pouso Alegre .. 93 E2
Považská
  Bystrica .... 16 D4
Povenets ..... 28 C4
Poverty B. .... 64 C8
Póvoa de Varzim 18 B1
Powder → ... 76 B2
Powell L. ..... 83 B7
Poyang Hu ... 35 D6
Požarevac .... 22 B3
Poznań ...... 16 B3
Pozo Almonte . 91 H5
Pozoblanco ... 18 C3
Pozzuoli ..... 21 D5
Prachuap Khiri
  Khan ...... 36 B1
Prado ........ 93 F6
Prague = Praha 16 C2
Praha ........ 16 C2
Prainha,
  Amazonas,
  Brazil ...... 91 E6
Prainha, Pará,
  Brazil ....... 92 C3
Prairies ...... 71 C9
Prapat ........ 37 D1
Prata ........ 93 F4
Prato ........ 20 C3
Pravia ....... 18 A2
Praya ........ 37 F5
Preparis North
  Channel .... 41 K9
Preparis South
  Channel .... 41 K9
Přerov ....... 16 D3
Preservation
  Inlet ........ 65 G2
Presidencia
  Roque Saenz
  Peña ....... 94 B4
Presidente
  Epitácio .... 93 G3
Presidente
  Hermes ..... 91 F6
Presidente
  Prudente .... 93 G3
Prešov ....... 16 D5

Prespa, L. =
  Prespansko
  Jezero ...... 23 D3
Prespansko
  Jezero ...... 23 D3
Presque Isle ... 73 A11
Preston ...... 11 E5
Pretoria ..... 59 D5
Préveza ..... 23 E3
Příbram ..... 16 D2
Prichard ..... 74 D3
Prieska ..... 58 D4
Prievidza .... 16 D4
Prilep ....... 22 D3
Priluki = Pryluky 24 C3
Prime Seal I. .. 62 D4
Prince Albert . 71 C9
Prince Albert
  Mts. ....... 96 B15
Prince Albert
  Pen. ....... 70 A8
Prince Albert Sd. 70 A8
Prince Charles I. 68 B3
Prince Charles
  Mts. ....... 96 B10
Prince Edward
  I. □ ........ 69 D4
Prince of Wales
  I., Canada .. 70 A10
Prince of Wales
  I., U.S.A. .... 71 C6
Principe da
  Beira ...... 91 F6
Prins Harald
  Kyst ........ 96 B8
Prinsesse Astrid
  Kyst ........ 96 B7
Prinsesse
  Ragnhild Kyst 96 B8
Pripet → =
  Prypyat → .. 17 C10
Pripet Marshes 17 B9
Pripyat Marshes
  = Pripet
  Marshes .... 17 B9
Pripyats =
  Prypyat → .. 17 C10
Priština ....... 22 C3
Privas ....... 13 D6
Privolzhskaya
  Vozvyshennost
  ........... 24 C6
Prizren ....... 22 C3
Proddatur ..... 43 M11
Progreso ..... 85 C7
Prokopyevsk .. 29 D9
Prokuplje .... 22 C3
Prome = Pyè . 41 H10
Propriá ....... 93 E6
Prostějov .... 16 D3
Proston ...... 63 A5
Provence ..... 13 E6
Providence .. 73 D10
Providencia, I.
  de ......... 86 D3
Provins ....... 13 B5
Provo ........ 81 E8
Prozna → .... 16 B3
Pruszków .... 16 B5
Prut → ....... 17 F9
Pruzhany .... 17 B7
Prydz B. ..... 96 A10
Pryluky ....... 24 C3
Prypyat → ... 17 C10
Przemyśl .... 17 D6
Przhevalsk ... 29 E8
Psará ........ 23 E5
Pskov ....... 24 B2

Ptich =
  Ptsich → ... 17 B9
Ptsich → ..... 17 B9
Puán ......... 94 D4
Pucallpa ..... 91 E4
Pudukkottai .. 43 P11
Puebla ....... 84 D5
Pueblo ....... 76 F2
Pueblo Hundido 94 B2
Puelches ..... 94 D3
Puente Alto ... 94 C2
Puente-Genil .. 18 D3
Puerto Aisén .. 95 F2
Puerto
  Ayacucho ... 90 B5
Puerto Barrios . 85 D7
Puerto Bermejo 94 B5
Puerto
  Bermúdez .. 91 F4
Puerto Bolívar . 90 D3
Puerto Cabello 90 A5
Puerto Cabezas 86 D3
Puerto Carreño 90 B5
Puerto Chicama 91 E3
Puerto Coig ... 95 G3
Puerto Cortés . 85 D7
Puerto
  Cumarebo .. 90 A5
Puerto del
  Rosario ..... 54 C2
Puerto Deseado 95 F3
Puerto Heath .. 91 F5
Puerto La Cruz 90 A6
Puerto
  Leguízamo .. 90 D4
Puerto Lobos .. 95 E3
Puerto Madryn 95 E3
Puerto
  Maldonado .. 91 F5
Puerto Montt .. 95 E2
Puerto Morelos 85 C7
Puerto Natales 95 G2
Puerto Páez .. 90 B5
Puerto Pinasco 94 A5
Puerto
  Pirámides ... 95 E4
Puerto Plata .. 87 C5
Puerto Princesa 38 C1
Puerto Quellón 95 E2
Puerto Rico ■ . 87 C6
Puerto Sastre . 91 H7
Puerto Suárez . 91 G7
Puerto Wilches 90 B4
Puertollano ... 18 C3
Pueyrredón, L. . 95 F2
Pugachev ..... 24 C6
Puget Sound .. 80 B2
Puigcerdá .... 19 A6
Pukaki L. ..... 65 F4
Pukapuka .... 65 L14
Pukekohe .... 64 B6
Pula ......... 20 B4
Puławy ....... 16 C5
Pullman ..... 80 B5
Pulog ........ 38 A2
Pułtusk ...... 16 B5
Puna ......... 91 G5
Puná, I. ...... 90 D2
Punakha ..... 41 D7
Punata ....... 91 G5
Punch ....... 42 C9
Pune ......... 43 K8
Punjab □, India 42 D9
Punjab □,
  Pakistan .... 42 D8
Puno ......... 91 G4
Punta Alta ... 94 D4
Punta Arenas .. 95 G2
Punta de Díaz . 94 B2

Puntabie ...... 62 B1
Puntarenas .. 86 E3
Punto Fijo .... 90 A4
Puquio ....... 91 F4
Pur → ....... 28 C8
Purace, Vol. ... 90 C3
Puralia =
  Puruliya .... 40 F6
Puri ......... 40 H5
Purnia ....... 40 E6
Purukcahu ... 37 E4
Puruliya ..... 40 F6
Purus → ..... 90 D6
Pusan ........ 35 C7
Pushkino .... 24 C6
Putao ........ 41 D11
Putaruru ...... 64 C6
Puthein Myit → 41 K10
Putignano .... 21 D6
Puting, Tanjung 37 E4
Putorana, Gory 30 C7
Puttalam ..... 43 Q11
Puttgarden ... 15 A6
Putumayo → . 90 D5
Putussibau ... 37 D4
Puy-de-Dôme . 13 D5
Pweto ........ 57 F5
Pwllheli ...... 11 E4
Pyapon ...... 41 J10
Pyasina → ... 30 B6
Pyatigorsk ... 25 E5
Pyè ......... 41 H10
Pyetrikaw .... 17 B9
Pyinmana ..... 41 H11
P'yŏngyang .. 35 C7
Pyrénées .... 19 A6
Pyu ......... 41 H11

## Q

Qādib ........ 49 E5
Qā'emshahr ... 44 B3
Qahremānshahr
  = Bākhtarān . 46 D6
Qaidam Pendi . 34 C4
Qalāt ........ 45 C6
Qal'at al Akhḍar 47 E4
Qal'eh Shaharak 42 B4
Qal'eh-ye Now 45 C5
Qamar, Ghubbat
  al ......... 49 D5
Qamruddin
  Karez ....... 42 D6
Qandahār .... 42 D4
Qandahār □ .. 42 D4
Qapshaghay . 29 E8
Qâra ........ 52 C4
Qarabutaq ... 29 E7
Qarachuk .... 46 C5
Qaraghandy .. 29 E8
Qārah ....... 47 E5
Qarataū ..... 29 E8
Qarqan ...... 34 C3
Qarqan He → . 34 C3
Qarqaraly ... 29 E8
Qarshi ....... 29 F7
Qaşr-e Qand .. 45 E5
Qasr Farâfra .. 52 C4
Qatar ■ ...... 44 E2
Qattâra,
  Munkhafed el 52 C4
Qattâra
  Depression =
  Qattâra,
  Munkhafed el 52 C4
Qâyen ........ 44 C4

Qazaqstan =
Kazakstan ■ . 29 E7
Qazvin ....... 46 C7
Qena ........ 52 C5
Qeshm ....... 44 E4
Qila Safed .... 42 E2
Qila Saifullāh .. 42 D6
Qilian Shan ... 34 C4
Qingdao ...... 35 C7
Qinghai □ .... 34 C4
Qinghai Hu ... 34 C5
Qinhuangdao . 35 C6
Qinzhou ...... 35 D5
Qiqihar ....... 35 B7
Qitai ........ 34 B3
Qom ........ 44 C2
Qomsheh ..... 44 C2
Qondūz ...... 45 B7
Qondūz □ .... 45 B7
Qostanay ..... 29 D7
Qu Xian,
  Sichuan,
  China ...... 35 C5
Qu Xian,
  Zhejiang,
  China ...... 35 D6
Quambatook .. 62 C3
Quambone ... 63 B4
Quan Long ... 36 C3
Quandialla .... 63 B4
Quang Ngai ... 36 A3
Quanzhou .... 35 D6
Quaqtaq ..... 68 B4
Quaraí ....... 94 C5
Quartu
  Sant'Elena .. 21 E2
Quatsino ..... 71 C7
Quba ........ 25 E6
Qūchān ...... 44 B4
Queanbeyan .. 63 C4
Québec ...... 69 D3
Québec □ .... 69 D3
Queen
  Alexandra Ra. 96 C15
Queen Charlotte
  Is. ......... 70 C6
Queen Charlotte
  Str. ........ 71 C7
Queen Elizabeth
  Is. ......... 66 B9
Queen Mary
  Land ...... 96 B11
Queen Maud G. 70 B9
Queen Maud
  Land ...... 96 B7
Queen Maud
  Mts. ...... 96 C16
Queenscliff ... 63 C3
Queensland □ . 61 E7
Queenstown,
  Australia .... 62 D4
Queenstown,
  N.Z. ...... 65 F3
Queenstown,
  S. Africa .... 59 E5
Queimadas .. 93 E6
Quela ....... 56 F3
Quelimane .... 59 B7
Quelpart =
  Cheju Do ... 35 C7
Quequén ..... 94 D5
Querétaro .... 84 C4
Quetta ...... 42 D5
Quezon City .. 38 B2
Qui Nhon .... 36 B3
Quibaxe ..... 56 F2
Quibdo ...... 90 B3
Quiberon .... 12 C2
Quilán, C. .... 95 E2

Quilengues ... 58 A2
Quillabamba .. 91 F4
Quillagua .... 91 H5
Quillota ...... 94 C2
Quilon ...... 43 Q10
Quilpie ...... 63 A3
Quimilí ...... 94 B4
Quimper ..... 12 B1
Quimperlé ... 12 C2
Quincy ...... 77 F9
Quines ...... 94 C3
Quinga ...... 59 H8
Quintanar de la
  Orden .... 18 C4
Quintero ..... 94 C2
Quinyambie ... 62 B3
Quipungo .... 58 A2
Quirindi ..... 63 B5
Quissanga ... 59 G8
Quitilipi ...... 94 B4
Quito ....... 90 D3
Quixadá ..... 92 C6
Qŭnghirot ... 29 E6
Quondong ... 62 B3
Quorn ....... 62 B2
Qŭqon ...... 29 E8
Qûs ........ 52 C5
Quseir ...... 52 C5
Qyzylorda .... 29 E7

# R

Raahe ....... 8 F12
Raba ........ 39 F1
Rába → ..... 16 E3
Rabat, Malta .. 21 G5
Rabat, Morocco 54 B3
Rabaul ..... 64 K10
Rābigh ...... 47 G4
Race, C. ..... 69 D5
Rach Gia ... 36 B3
Racibórz .... 16 C4
Racine ...... 72 C2
Rădăuți .... 17 E7
Radekhiv ... 17 C7
Radekhov =
  Radekhiv ... 17 C7
Radhwa, Jabal 47 F4
Radom ...... 16 C5
Radomsko ... 16 C4
Radomyshl ... 17 C9
Radstock, C. ... 62 B1
Rae ........ 70 B8
Rae Bareli ... 40 D3
Rae Isthmus .. 68 B2
Raetihi ...... 64 C6
Rafaela ..... 94 C4
Rafai ....... 56 D4
Rafḥā ...... 47 E5
Rafsanjān ... 44 D4
Ragachow ... 17 B10
Ragama ..... 43 R11
Raglan ...... 64 B6
Ragusa ...... 21 F5
Raha ........ 39 E2
Rahad al Bardī 53 F3
Rahaeng = Tak 36 A1
Rahimyar Khan 42 E7
Raichur ..... 43 L10
Raigarh ..... 40 G4
Railton ...... 62 D4
Rainier, Mt. .. 80 B3
Raipur ...... 40 G3
Ra'is ....... 47 G4
Raj Nandgaon . 40 G3
Raja, Ujung ... 37 D1

Raja Ampat,
  Kepulauan .. 39 E3
Rajahmundry .. 40 J3
Rajang → .... 37 D4
Rajapalaiyam .. 43 Q10
Rajasthan □ .. 42 F8
Rajasthan Canal 42 F8
Rajgarh ...... 43 G10
Rajkot ...... 43 H7
Rajpipla ..... 43 J8
Rajshahi ..... 41 E7
Rakaia ...... 65 E5
Rakaia → .... 65 E5
Rakan, Ra's ... 44 E2
Rakaposhi ... 42 A9
Rakata, Pulau . 37 F3
Rakhiv ..... 17 D7
Raleigh ...... 75 B8
Ram Hd. .... 63 C4
Ramanathapuram
  ........... 43 Q11
Ramechhap ... 40 D6
Ramelau ..... 39 F3
Ramgarh, Bihar,
  India .... 40 F5
Ramgarh, Raj.,
  India .... 42 F7
Rāmhormoz ... 47 E7
Ramnad =
  Ramanathapuram
  ........... 43 Q11
Rampur ..... 42 E11
Rampur Hat ... 40 E6
Ramree I. =
  Ramree Kyun 41 H9
Ramree Kyun . 41 H9
Ramtek ...... 43 J11
Ranaghat ... 41 F7
Ranau ...... 36 C5
Rancagua .... 94 C2
Ranchi ...... 40 F5
Randers ..... 9 G10
Rangaunu B. .. 64 A5
Rangia ...... 41 D8
Rangiora .... 65 E5
Rangitaiki → . 64 B7
Rangitata → .. 65 E4
Rangon → ... 41 J11
Rangoon .... 41 J11
Rangpur ..... 41 E7
Ranibennur ... 43 M9
Raniganj ..... 40 F6
Raniwara .... 43 G8
Rankin Inlet ... 70 B10
Rankins Springs 63 B4
Ranong ...... 36 C1
Ransiki ...... 39 E4
Rantau ...... 37 E5
Rantauprapat .. 37 D1
Rantemario ... 39 E1
Rapa ....... 65 M16
Rapallo ..... 20 B2
Rāpch ...... 45 E4
Rapid City ... 76 C3
Rarotonga ... 65 M14
Ra's al Khaymah 44 E4
Ra's al-Unuf .. 52 B2
Ras Bânâs ... 52 D6
Ras Dashen ... 57 B7
Râs Timirist .. 55 E1
Rasa, Punta .. 95 E4
Rashad ..... 53 F5
Rashîd ..... 52 B5
Rasht ...... 46 C7
Rat Islands .. 71 C1
Ratangarh ... 42 E9
Rathenow ... 15 B7
Ratibor =
  Racibórz ... 16 C4

Ratlam ....... 43 H9
Ratnagiri ..... 43 L8
Raukumara Ra. 64 C7
Raurkela ..... 40 F5
Rava-Ruska ... 17 C6
Rava Russkaya
  = Rava-Ruska 17 C6
Rāvar ........ 44 D4
Ravenna ..... 20 B4
Ravensburg .. 14 E5
Ravi → ..... 42 D7
Rawalpindi ... 42 C8
Rawāndūz ... 46 C6
Rawene ..... 64 A5
Rawlins ..... 81 E10
Rawson ..... 95 E3
Ray, C. ...... 69 D5
Rayadurg ... 43 M10
Rayagada ... 40 H4
Raymond ..... 71 D8
Raz, Pte. du ... 12 B1
Razdel'naya =
  Rozdilna ... 17 E10
Razelm, Lacul . 22 B7
Razgrad ..... 22 C6
Ré, I. de .... 12 C3
Reading, U.K. . 11 F6
Reading, U.S.A. 73 D8
Realicó ..... 94 D4
Rebi ........ 39 F4
Rebiana .... 52 D3
Rebun-Tō ... 32 E12
Rechytsa ... 17 B10
Recife ...... 92 D7
Reconquista ... 94 B5
Recreo ..... 94 B3
Red →, La.,
  U.S.A. .... 79 D8
Red →, N. Dak.,
  U.S.A. .... 76 A6
Red Cliffs .... 62 B3
Red Deer .... 71 C8
Red Sea ..... 48 C2
Red Tower Pass
  = Turnu Roșu,
  P. ........ 17 F7
Redcar ..... 11 D6
Redcliffe ..... 63 A5
Redding ..... 80 E2
Redditch ..... 11 E6
Redon ...... 12 C2
Redondela ... 18 A1
Redwood City . 82 B1
Ree, L. ..... 11 E3
Reefton ..... 65 E4
Regensburg ... 15 D7
Réggio di
  Calábria .... 21 E5
Réggio
  nell'Emília .. 20 B3
Reghin ..... 17 E7
Regina ..... 71 C9
Rehoboth ... 58 C3
Rehovot ..... 46 E3
Rei-Bouba ... 53 G1
Reichenbach .. 15 C7
Reidsville ... 75 A8
Reigate ..... 11 F6
Reims ...... 13 B6
Reina Adelaida,
  Arch. ..... 95 G2
Reindeer L. ... 71 C9
Reinga, C. ... 64 A5
Reinosa ..... 18 A3
Reliance ..... 70 B9
Remarkable, Mt. 62 B2
Remeshk ... 45 E4
Rendsburg .... 14 A5
Rengat ...... 37 E2

| | | | | | | | | | |
|---|---|---|---|---|---|---|---|---|---|
| Reni | 17 | F9 | Ridder | 29 | D9 | Roanoke | 73 | F6 | Rosario, |
| Renk | 53 | F5 | Ried | 15 | D7 | Robbins I. | 62 | D4 | *Paraguay* ... 94 A5 |
| Renmark | 62 | B3 | Riesa | 15 | C7 | Robertson | 58 | E3 | Rosario de la |
| Rennes | 12 | B3 | Rieti | 20 | C4 | Robertson I. | 96 | A4 | Frontera ... 94 B3 |
| Reno | 80 | F4 | Rig Rig | 53 | F1 | Robertsport | 55 | G2 | Rosário do Sul 94 C6 |
| Reno ⇢ | 20 | B4 | Rīga | 24 | B1 | Robertstown | 62 | B2 | Rosas, G. de .. 19 A7 |
| Rentería | 19 | A5 | Riga, G. of | 24 | B1 | Robinvale | 62 | B3 | Roscommon .. 11 E2 |
| Republican ⇢ | 76 | F6 | Rīgas Jūras Līcis | | | Roboré | 91 | G7 | Roseau, *Domin.* 87 C7 |
| Repulse Bay | 68 | B2 | = Riga, G. of | 24 | B1 | Robson, Mt. ... | 71 | C8 | Roseau, *U.S.A.* 77 A7 |
| Requena, *Peru* . | 90 | E4 | Rīgestān □ .... | 42 | D4 | Roca, C. da ... | 18 | C1 | Rosebery ..... 62 D4 |
| Requena, *Spain* | 19 | C5 | Rigolet | 68 | C5 | Rocas, I. | 92 | C7 | Roseburg ..... 80 D2 |
| Resadiye = | | | Riiser-Larsen- | | | Rocha | 94 | C6 | Rosenheim ... 15 E7 |
| Datça | 23 | F6 | halvøya ... | 96 | A8 | Rochefort ..... | 12 | D3 | Rosetown ..... 71 C9 |
| Resht = Rasht . | 46 | C7 | Rijeka | 20 | B5 | Rochester, | | | Rosetta = |
| Resistencia ... | 94 | B5 | Rimah, Wadi | | | *Minn., U.S.A.* | 77 | C8 | Rashîd ..... 52 B5 |
| Reşiţa | 17 | F5 | ar ⇢ | 47 | F5 | Rochester, *N.Y.,* | | | Roseville ..... 80 F3 |
| Resolution I., | | | Rímini | 20 | B4 | *U.S.A.* | 73 | C7 | Rosewood .... 63 A5 |
| *Canada* ..... | 68 | B4 | Rîmnicu Sărat . | 17 | F8 | Rock Hill ...... | 75 | B7 | Rosignano |
| Resolution I., | | | Rîmnicu Vîlcea | 17 | F7 | Rock Island ... | 77 | E9 | Maríttimo ... 20 C3 |
| *N.Z.* | 65 | F2 | Rimouski | 69 | D4 | Rock Springs .. | 81 | E9 | Rosignol ..... 90 B7 |
| Réthímnon .... | 23 | G5 | Rinca | 39 | F1 | Rockefeller | | | Roşiori-de-Vede 22 B5 |
| Réunion ■ .... | 51 | J9 | Rinconada .... | 94 | A3 | Plateau ... | 96 | C18 | Roslavl ..... 24 C3 |
| Reus | 19 | B6 | Rinjani | 37 | F5 | Rockford ..... | 77 | D10 | Roslyn ..... 63 B4 |
| Reutlingen .... | 14 | D5 | Rio Branco, | | | Rockhampton . | 61 | E9 | Ross, *Australia* 62 D4 |
| Reval = Tallinn | 24 | B1 | *Brazil* ...... | 91 | E5 | Rocky Mount . | 75 | B9 | Ross, *N.Z.* .... 65 E4 |
| Revelstoke .... | 71 | C8 | Río Branco, | | | Rocky Mts. .... | 70 | C7 | Ross I. ..... 96 B15 |
| Rewa | 40 | E3 | *Uruguay* .... | 94 | C6 | Rod | 42 | E3 | Ross Ice Shelf . 96 C16 |
| Rewari | 42 | E10 | Río Cuarto .... | 94 | C4 | Rodez | 13 | D5 | Ross Sea ..... 96 B15 |
| Rey Malabo ... | 56 | D1 | Rio de Janeiro . | 93 | G5 | Ródhos ....... | 23 | F7 | Rossano Cálabro 21 E6 |
| Reykjavík ..... | 8 | B2 | Rio de | | | Rodney, C. .... | 64 | B6 | Rossland ..... 71 D8 |
| Reynosa ...... | 84 | B5 | Janeiro □ ... | 93 | G5 | Roes Welcome | | | Rosslare ..... 11 E3 |
| Rhein ⇢ | 14 | C4 | Rio do Sul .... | 94 | B7 | Sd. ...... | 68 | B2 | Rosso ........ 55 E1 |
| Rhein-Main- | | | Río Gallegos . | 95 | G3 | Rogachev = | | | Rossosh ..... 24 C4 |
| Donau- | | | Río Grande, | | | Ragachow .. | 17 | B10 | Rosthern ..... 71 C9 |
| Kanal ⇢ ... | 15 | D6 | *Argentina* ... | 95 | G3 | Rogagua, L. ... | 91 | F5 | Rostock ..... 15 A7 |
| Rheine | 14 | B4 | Rio Grande, | | | Rogatyn ...... | 17 | D7 | Rostov, *Don,* |
| Rheinland- | | | *Brazil* ...... | 94 | C6 | Rogoaguado, L. | 91 | F5 | *Russia* ...... 25 D4 |
| Pfalz □ ..... | 14 | C4 | Rio Grande ⇢ | 78 | E3 | Rohri ........ | 42 | F6 | Rostov, *Yarosl.,* |
| Rhin = | | | Rio Grande do | | | Rohtak ...... | 42 | E10 | *Russia* ...... 24 B4 |
| Rhein ⇢ ... | 14 | C4 | Norte □ .... | 92 | D6 | Roi Et ........ | 36 | A2 | Roswell ..... 78 C1 |
| Rhine = | | | Rio Grande do | | | Rojas ........ | 94 | C4 | Rotherham ... 11 E6 |
| Rhein ⇢ ... | 14 | C4 | Sul □ ...... | 94 | B6 | Rojo, C. ...... | 84 | C5 | Roto ........ 63 B4 |
| Rhineland- | | | Rio Largo ..... | 93 | D6 | Rokan ⇢ ..... | 37 | D2 | Rotondo Mte. . 13 E8 |
| Palatinate □ = | | | Río Mulatos .. | 91 | G5 | Rolândia ..... | 94 | A6 | Rotorua ...... 64 C7 |
| Rheinland- | | | Río Muni = | | | Roma, *Australia* | 63 | A4 | Rotorua, L. ... 64 C7 |
| Pfalz □ ..... | 14 | C4 | Mbini □ ..... | 56 | D2 | Roma, *Italy* ... | 20 | D4 | Rotterdam ... 14 C3 |
| Rhode Island □ | 73 | D10 | Rio Negro .... | 94 | B7 | Roman ...... | 17 | E8 | Rottweil ..... 14 D5 |
| Rhodes = | | | Rio Verde .... | 93 | F3 | Romang ...... | 39 | F3 | Rotuma ...... 64 L12 |
| Ródhos ..... | 23 | F7 | Ríobamba .... | 90 | D3 | Romania ■ ... | 22 | B5 | Roubaix ..... 13 A5 |
| Rhodope Mts. = | | | Ríohacha ..... | 90 | A4 | Romanovka = | | | Rouen ........ 12 B4 |
| Rhodopi | | | Ríosucio, | | | Basarabeasca | 17 | E9 | Round Mt. ... 63 B5 |
| Planina ..... | 22 | D5 | *Caldas,* | | | Romans-sur- | | | Roussillon ... 13 E5 |
| Rhodopi Planina | 22 | D5 | *Colombia* ... | 90 | B3 | Isère ....... | 13 | D6 | Rouyn ...... 69 D3 |
| Rhön = Hohe | | | Ríosucio, *Choco,* | | | Romblon .... | 38 | B2 | Rovaniemi .... 8 E13 |
| Rhön ..... | 14 | C5 | *Colombia* ... | 90 | B3 | Rome = Roma | 20 | D4 | Rovereto ..... 20 B3 |
| Rhondda ..... | 11 | F5 | Rishiri-Tō ..... | 32 | E12 | Rome ........ | 74 | B5 | Rovigo ..... 20 B3 |
| Rhône ⇢ ..... | 13 | E6 | Riva del Garda | 20 | B3 | Romorantin- | | | Rovinj ..... 20 B4 |
| Rhum ........ | 10 | C3 | Rivadavia .... | 94 | B2 | Lanthenay .. | 12 | C4 | Rovno = Rivne 17 C8 |
| Riachão ...... | 92 | D4 | Rivera ........ | 94 | C5 | Roncador, Serra | | | Rovuma ⇢ .... 57 G8 |
| Riasi ........ | 42 | C9 | Riversdale .... | 58 | E4 | do ........ | 93 | E3 | Rowena ..... 63 A4 |
| Riau □ ...... | 37 | E2 | Riverside ..... | 82 | D4 | Ronda ...... | 18 | D3 | Roxas ........ 38 B2 |
| Riau, Kepulauan | 37 | D2 | Riverton, | | | Rondônia □ ... | 91 | F6 | Roxburgh ..... 65 F3 |
| Riau Arch. = | | | *Australia* .... | 62 | B2 | Rondonópolis . | 93 | F3 | Royal |
| Riau, | | | Riverton, | | | Ronge, L. la ... | 71 | C9 | Leamington |
| Kepulauan .. | 37 | D2 | *Canada* ..... | 71 | C10 | Ronne Ice Shelf | 96 | B3 | Spa ....... 11 E6 |
| Ribadeo ...... | 18 | A2 | Riverton, *N.Z.* . | 65 | G2 | Roodepoort ... | 59 | D5 | Royan ........ 12 D3 |
| Ribeirão Prêto . | 93 | G4 | Riviera di | | | Roorkee ...... | 42 | E10 | Rozdilna ..... 17 E10 |
| Riberalta ..... | 91 | F5 | Levante .... | 20 | B2 | Roosevelt ⇢ .. | 91 | E6 | Rozhyshche ... 17 C7 |
| Rîbniţa ....... | 17 | E9 | Riviera di | | | Roosevelt I. ... | 96 | B16 | Rtishchevo .... 24 C5 |
| Riccarton ..... | 65 | E5 | Ponente .... | 20 | B2 | Roquetas de | | | Ruahine Ra. ... 64 C7 |
| Richland ..... | 80 | B4 | Rivière-du-Loup | 69 | D4 | Mar ...... | 19 | D4 | Ruapehu ...... 64 C6 |
| Richmond, | | | Rivne ........ | 17 | C8 | Roraima □ .... | 90 | C6 | Ruapuke I. .... 65 G3 |
| *Australia* .... | 63 | B5 | Rívoli ........ | 20 | B1 | Roraima, Mt. .. | 90 | B6 | Rub' al Khali .. 48 D4 |
| Richmond, *N.Z.* | 65 | D5 | Rivoli B. ...... | 62 | C3 | Rosa ........ | 57 | F6 | Rubio ........ 90 B4 |
| Richmond, | | | Riyadh = Ar | | | Rosa, Monte .. | 13 | D7 | Rubtsovsk .... 29 D9 |
| *Calif., U.S.A.* | 80 | G2 | Riyāḍ ...... | 47 | F6 | Rosario, | | | Rudall ........ 62 B2 |
| Richmond, *Va.,* | | | Rize ........ | 46 | B5 | *Argentina* ... | 94 | C4 | Rudolf, Ostrov . 28 A6 |
| *U.S.A.* | 73 | F7 | Rizzuto, C. .... | 21 | E6 | Rosário, *Brazil* . | 92 | C5 | Rufa'a ........ 53 F5 |
| Richmond Ra. . | 63 | A5 | Roanne ...... | 13 | C6 | Rosario, *Mexico* | 84 | C3 | Rufiji ⇢ ..... 57 F7 |

Rufino ...... 94 C4
Rufisque ...... 55 F1
Rugby ........ 11 E6
Rügen ........ 15 A7
Ruhr → ...... 14 C4
Rukwa L. ..... 57 F6
Rum = Rhum . 10 C3
Rumāḥ ....... 47 F6
Rumania =
  Romania ■ .. 22 B5
Rumbêk ...... 53 G4
Rumia ....... 16 A4
Rumoi ....... 32 F12
Runanga ..... 65 E4
Runaway, C. .. 64 B7
Rungwa ...... 57 F6
Ruoqiang .... 34 C3
Rupa ........ 41 D9
Rupat ....... 37 D2
Rupert → .... 69 C3
Rupert House =
  Waskaganish 69 C3
Rurrenabaque . 91 F5
Rusape ....... 59 B6
Ruschuk = Ruse 22 C5
Ruse ........ 22 C5
Rushworth .... 63 C4
Russas ....... 92 C6
Russellkonda .. 40 H5
Russkaya
  Polyana .... 29 D8
Rustavi ...... 25 E6
Rustenburg ... 59 D5
Ruteng ....... 39 F2
Rutshuru .... 57 E5
Ruwenzori ... 57 D5
Ružomberok .. 16 D4
Rwanda ■ .. 57 E6
Ryazan ...... 24 C4
Ryazhsk ..... 24 C5
Rybache =
  Rybachye .. 29 E9
Rybachye ..... 29 E9
Rybinsk ..... 24 B4
Rybinskoye
  Vdkhr. ..... 24 B4
Rybnitsa =
  Rîbnița ... 17 E9
Rylstone ..... 63 B4
Rypin ........ 16 B4
Ryūkyū Is. =
  Ryūkyū-rettō 35 D7
Ryūkyū-rettō .. 35 D7
Rzeszów ...... 16 C5
Rzhev ....... 24 B3

# S

Sa Dec ....... 36 B3
Sa'ādatābād .. 44 D3
Saale → ..... 15 C6
Saalfeld ..... 15 C6
Saar → ...... 13 B7
Saarbrücken .. 14 D4
Saaremaa ... 24 B1
Šabac ........ 22 B2
Sabadell ..... 19 B7
Sabah □ ... 36 C5
Şabāḥ, Wadi → 47 G7
Sabalān, Kūhhā-
  ye ....... 46 C6
Sábanalarga .. 90 A4
Sabang ...... 36 C1
Sabará ...... 93 F5
Saberania ... 39 E5
Sabhah ...... 52 C1

Sabinas ...... 84 B4
Sabinas Hidalgo 84 B4
Sablayan ..... 38 B2
Sable, C.,
  Canada ..... 69 D4
Sable, C., U.S.A. 86 A3
Sable I. ...... 69 D5
Sabrina Coast . 96 A12
Sabulubek ... 37 E1
Sabzevār .... 44 B4
Sabzvārān .... 44 D4
Săcele ....... 17 F7
Sachsen □ .... 15 C7
Sachsen-
  Anhalt □ .... 15 C7
Sacramento → 80 F3
Sacramento → 80 F3
Sacramento
  Mts. ........ 83 D10
Sadani ....... 57 F7
Sadd el Aali ... 52 D5
Sado ........ 33 G11
Sadon ....... 41 E11
Safi ......... 54 B3
Safid Kūh .... 42 B3
Saga, Indonesia 39 E4
Saga, Japan .. 32 C2
Sagala ....... 55 F3
Sagar ........ 43 M9
Sagil ........ 34 A4
Saginaw ..... 72 C4
Şagīr, Zāb aş → 46 D5
Saglouc =
  Salluit ...... 68 B3
Sagua la Grande 86 B3
Saguenay → . 69 D3
Sagunto ...... 19 C5
Sahagún ..... 18 A3
Sahand, Kūh-e 46 C6
Sahara ....... 54 D6
Saharan Atlas =
  Saharien,
  Atlas ....... 54 B5
Saharanpur ... 42 E10
Saharien, Atlas 54 B5
Sahiwal ...... 42 D8
Sa'id Bundas .. 53 G3
Saïda ........ 54 B5
Sa'īdābād .... 44 D3
Sa'īdīyeh ..... 46 C7
Saidpur ...... 41 E7
Saidu ........ 42 B8
Saigon = Phanh
  Bho Ho Chi
  Minh ...... 36 B3
Saijō ........ 32 C3
Saikhoa Ghat .. 41 D10
Saiki ........ 32 C2
Sailolof ...... 39 E4
St. Andrews .. 10 C5
St. Arnaud ... 62 C3
St-Augustin-
  Saguenay ... 69 C5
St. Augustine . 75 E7
St. Austell ... 11 F4
St. Boniface ... 71 D10
St.-Brieuc ... 12 B2
St. Catharines . 69 D3
St.-Chamond .. 13 D6
St. Christopher-
  Nevis ■ = St.
  Kitts & Nevis 87 C7
St. Cloud .... 77 C7
St. Croix .... 87 C7
St.-Denis .... 12 B5
St.-Dizier .... 13 B6
St. Elias, Mt. .. 70 B5
St.-Étienne .. 13 D6
St.-Flour .... 13 D5

St. Francis, C. . 58 E4
St. Gallen =
  Sankt Gallen 13 C8
St.-Gaudens ... 12 E4
St. George .... 63 A4
St.-Georges,
  Fr. Guiana .. 92 B3
St. George's,
  Grenada .... 87 D7
St. George's
  Channel .... 11 F3
St. Georges Hd. 63 C5
St. Gotthard P.
  = San
  Gottardo, P.
  del ........ 13 C8
St. Helena ■ .. 51 H3
St. Helena B. .. 58 E3
St. Helens .... 62 D4
St. Helier .... 11 G5
St-Hyacinthe .. 69 D3
St. John ..... 69 D4
St. John's,
  Antigua ..... 87 C7
St. John's,
  Canada ..... 69 D5
St. Johns → .. 75 D7
St. Joseph ... 77 F7
St. Joseph, L. . 69 C1
St. Kilda, N.Z. . 65 F4
St. Kilda, U.K. . 10 C2
St. Kitts & Nevis ■ 87 C7
St.-Laurent .. 92 A3
St. Lawrence → 69 D4
St. Lawrence,
  Gulf of ..... 69 D4
St. Lawrence I. 71 B2
St. Leonard ... 69 D4
St.-Lô ....... 12 B3
St-Louis ..... 55 E1
St. Louis ..... 77 F9
St. Lucia ■ .. 87 D7
St. Lucia, L. ... 59 D6
St. Maarten .. 87 C7
St.-Malo ..... 12 B2
St-Marc ..... 87 C5
St. Mary Pk. ... 62 B2
St. Marys .... 62 D4
St.-Mathieu, Pte. 12 B1
St. Matthews, I.
  = Zadetkyi
  Kyun ...... 36 C1
St.-Nazaire .... 12 C2
St.-Omer .... 12 A5
St. Paul ..... 77 C8
St. Peter Port .. 11 G5
St. Petersburg =
  Sankt-
  Peterburg ... 24 B3
St. Petersburg . 75 F6
St.-Pierre et
  Miquelon □ . 69 D5
St.-Quentin .. 13 B5
St. Thomas I. .. 87 C7
St.-Tropez ... 13 E7
St. Vincent, G. . 62 C2
St. Vincent &
  the
  Grenadines ■ 87 D7
Saintes ...... 12 D3
Saintonge ... 12 D3
Saipan ...... 64 H9
Sairang ...... 41 F9
Sairecábur,
  Cerro ....... 94 A3
Sajama ...... 91 G5
Sajó ........ 16 D5
Sakai ....... 32 B4
Sakākah ..... 47 E5

Sakakawea, L. . 76 B4
Sakarya =
  Adapazarı ... 46 B2
Sakarya → .. 25 E3
Sakata ...... 33 G11
Sakhalin ..... 31 D12
Sakon Nakhon . 36 A2
Sala ....... 9 G11
Sala Consilina . 21 D5
Saladillo .... 94 D5
Salado →,
  Buenos Aires,
  Argentina ... 94 D5
Salado →,
  La Pampa,
  Argentina ... 94 D3
Salado →,
  Santa Fe,
  Argentina ... 94 C4
Salaga ...... 55 G4
Salālah ...... 49 D5
Salamanca,
  Chile ....... 94 C2
Salamanca,
  Spain ...... 18 B3
Salamís ..... 23 F4
Salar de
  Atacama ... 94 A3
Salar de Uyuni 91 H5
Salaverry .... 91 E3
Salawati ..... 39 E4
Salayar ...... 39 F2
Saldanha .... 58 E3
Sale, Australia . 63 C4
Salé, Morocco . 54 B3
Salekhard ... 28 C7
Salem, India .. 43 P11
Salem, U.S.A. . 80 C2
Salerno ...... 21 D5
Salgótarján ... 16 D4
Salihli ...... 23 E7
Salihorsk ... 17 B8
Salima ...... 59 A6
Salina, Italy ... 21 E5
Salina, U.S.A. . 76 F6
Salina Cruz ... 85 D5
Salinas, Brazil . 93 F5
Salinas, Ecuador 90 D2
Salinas, U.S.A. 82 B2
Salinas Grandes 94 C3
Salinópolis .... 92 C4
Salisbury,
  Australia .... 62 B2
Salisbury, U.K. . 11 F6
Salisbury, U.S.A. 75 B7
Salluit ...... 68 B3
Salmās ...... 46 C6
Salmon → ... 80 C5
Salmon River
  Mts. ........ 81 C6
Salon-de-
  Provence ... 13 E6
Salonica =
  Thessaloníki . 23 D4
Salonta ...... 16 E5
Salsk ....... 25 D5
Salso → ..... 21 F4
Salt Creek ... 62 C2
Salt Lake City . 81 E8
Salta ....... 94 A3
Saltillo ..... 84 B4
Salto → ..... 94 C5
Salto → ..... 20 C4
Salton Sea .. 82 D5
Saltpond .... 55 G4
Salûm ...... 52 B4
Salûm, Khâlig el 52 B4
Salur ....... 40 H4
Salvador .... 93 E6

| | | |
|---|---|---|
| Salwa | 44 | E2 |
| Salween → | 41 | J11 |
| Salyan | 25 | F6 |
| Salzach → | 15 | D7 |
| Salzburg | 15 | E7 |
| Salzgitter | 14 | B6 |
| Salzwedel | 15 | B6 |
| Sama | 28 | C7 |
| Sama de Langreo | 18 | A3 |
| Samales Group | 38 | C2 |
| Samangán □ | 45 | B7 |
| Samar | 38 | B3 |
| Samara | 24 | C7 |
| Samarinda | 37 | E5 |
| Samarkand = Samarqand | 29 | F7 |
| Samarqand | 29 | F7 |
| Sāmarrā | 46 | D5 |
| Sambalpur | 40 | G5 |
| Sambar, Tanjung | 37 | E4 |
| Sambas | 37 | D3 |
| Sambava | 59 | G10 |
| Sambhal | 42 | E11 |
| Sambhar | 42 | F9 |
| Sambiase | 21 | E6 |
| Sambir | 17 | D6 |
| Same | 57 | E7 |
| Samokov | 22 | C4 |
| Sámos | 23 | F6 |
| Samothráki, Évros, Greece | 23 | D5 |
| Samothráki, Kérkira, Greece | 23 | E2 |
| Sampacho | 94 | C4 |
| Sampit | 37 | E4 |
| Sampit, Teluk | 37 | E4 |
| Samra | 47 | F5 |
| Samsun | 46 | B4 |
| Samui, Ko | 36 | C2 |
| Samut Prakan | 36 | B2 |
| Samut Songkhram → | 36 | B2 |
| San | 55 | F4 |
| San → | 16 | C5 |
| San Agustin, C. | 38 | C3 |
| San Andrés, I. de | 86 | D3 |
| San Andrés Tuxtla | 85 | D5 |
| San Angelo | 78 | D3 |
| San Antonio, Chile | 94 | C2 |
| San Antonio, Spain | 19 | C6 |
| San Antonio, U.S.A. | 78 | E4 |
| San Antonio, C., Argentina | 94 | D5 |
| San Antonio, C., Cuba | 85 | C8 |
| San Antonio Oeste | 95 | E4 |
| San Benedetto del Tronto | 20 | C4 |
| San Bernardino | 82 | C4 |
| San Bernardino Str. | 38 | B2 |
| San Bernardo | 94 | C2 |
| San Bernardo, I. de | 90 | B3 |
| San Borja | 91 | F5 |
| San Carlos, Argentina | 94 | C3 |
| San Carlos, Chile | 94 | D2 |
| San Carlos, Phil. | 38 | B2 |
| San Carlos, Amazonas, Venezuela | 90 | C5 |
| San Carlos, Cojedes, Venezuela | 90 | B5 |
| San Carlos de Bariloche | 95 | E2 |
| San Carlos del Zulia | 90 | B4 |
| San Cristóbal, Argentina | 94 | C4 |
| San Cristóbal, Mexico | 85 | D6 |
| San Cristóbal, Venezuela | 90 | B4 |
| San Diego | 82 | D4 |
| San Diego, C. | 95 | G3 |
| San Felipe, Chile | 94 | C2 |
| San Felipe, Venezuela | 90 | A5 |
| San Felíu de Guíxols | 19 | B7 |
| San Fernando, Chile | 94 | C2 |
| San Fernando, La Union, Phil. | 38 | A2 |
| San Fernando, Pampanga, Phil. | 38 | A2 |
| San Fernando, Spain | 18 | D2 |
| San Fernando, Trin. & Tob. | 87 | D7 |
| San Fernando, U.S.A. | 82 | C3 |
| San Fernando de Apure | 90 | B5 |
| San Fernando de Atabapo | 90 | C5 |
| San Francisco, Argentina | 94 | C4 |
| San Francisco, U.S.A. | 82 | B1 |
| San Francisco de Macorîs | 87 | C5 |
| San Francisco del Monte de Oro | 94 | C3 |
| San Gil | 90 | B4 |
| San Gottardo, P. del | 13 | C8 |
| San Ignacio, Bolivia | 91 | G6 |
| San Ignacio, Paraguay | 94 | B5 |
| San Ildefonso, C. | 38 | A2 |
| San Javier, Argentina | 94 | C5 |
| San Javier, Bolivia | 91 | G6 |
| San Joaquin → | 82 | A2 |
| San Jorge, B. de | 84 | A2 |
| San Jorge, G. | 95 | F3 |
| San Jorge, G. de | 19 | B6 |
| San José, Bolivia | 91 | G6 |
| San José, Costa Rica | 86 | E3 |
| San José, Guatemala | 85 | E6 |
| San Jose, Phil. | 38 | A2 |
| San Jose, U.S.A. | 82 | B2 |
| San Jose de Buenovista | 38 | B2 |
| San José de Jáchal | 94 | C3 |
| San José de Mayo | 94 | C5 |
| San José de Ocune | 90 | C4 |
| San José del Guaviare | 90 | C4 |
| San Juan, Argentina | 94 | C3 |
| San Juan, Phil. | 38 | C3 |
| San Juan, Puerto Rico | 87 | C6 |
| San Juan → | 86 | D3 |
| San Juan, C. | 56 | D1 |
| San Juan de los Morros | 90 | B5 |
| San Juan Mts. | 83 | B9 |
| San Julián | 95 | F3 |
| San Justo | 94 | C4 |
| San Leandro | 82 | B1 |
| San Lorenzo | 90 | C3 |
| San Lorenzo, I. | 91 | F3 |
| San Lorenzo, Mt. | 95 | F2 |
| San Lucas | 91 | H5 |
| San Lucas, C. | 84 | C2 |
| San Luis | 94 | C3 |
| San Luis Obispo | 82 | C2 |
| San Luis Potosí | 84 | C4 |
| San Marino | 20 | C4 |
| San Marino ■ | 20 | C4 |
| San Martín, L. | 95 | F2 |
| San Matías | 91 | G7 |
| San Matías, G. | 95 | E4 |
| San Miguel | 85 | E7 |
| San Miguel → | 91 | F6 |
| San Miguel de Tucumán | 94 | B3 |
| San Narciso | 38 | A2 |
| San Nicolás de los Arroyas | 94 | C4 |
| San-Pédro | 55 | H3 |
| San Pedro de las Colonias | 84 | B4 |
| San Pedro de Lloc | 91 | E3 |
| San Pedro de Macorís | 87 | C6 |
| San Pedro del Paraná | 94 | B5 |
| San Pedro Sula | 85 | D7 |
| San Pieto | 21 | E2 |
| San Rafael, Argentina | 94 | C3 |
| San Rafael, U.S.A. | 80 | G2 |
| San Ramón de la Nueva Orán | 94 | A4 |
| San Remo | 20 | C1 |
| San Roque, Argentina | 94 | B5 |
| San Roque, Spain | 18 | D3 |
| San Rosendo | 94 | D2 |
| San Salvador, Bahamas | 86 | B5 |
| San Salvador, El Salv. | 85 | E7 |
| San Salvador de Jujuy | 94 | A4 |
| San Sebastián, Argentina | 95 | G3 |
| San Sebastián, Spain | 19 | A5 |
| San Severo | 20 | D5 |
| San Valentin, Mte. | 95 | F2 |
| San Vicente de la Barquera | 18 | A3 |
| Sana' | 49 | D3 |
| Sana → | 20 | B6 |
| Sanaga → | 56 | D1 |
| Sanana | 39 | E3 |
| Sanandaj | 46 | D6 |
| Sanco Pt. | 38 | C3 |
| Sancti-Spíritus | 86 | B4 |
| Sancy, Puy de | 13 | D5 |
| Sandakan | 36 | C5 |
| Sandanski | 22 | D4 |
| Sanday | 10 | B5 |
| Sandgate | 63 | A5 |
| Sandía | 91 | F5 |
| Sandıklı | 46 | C2 |
| Sandoa | 56 | F4 |
| Sandomierz | 16 | C5 |
| Sandoway | 41 | H10 |
| Sandusky | 72 | D4 |
| Sandwip Chan. | 41 | F8 |
| Sandy C. | 62 | D3 |
| Sandy L. | 71 | C10 |
| Sanford, Fla., U.S.A. | 75 | E7 |
| Sanford, N.C., U.S.A. | 75 | B8 |
| Sanford, Mt. | 71 | B5 |
| Sanga → | 56 | E3 |
| Sangamner | 43 | K9 |
| Sangar | 31 | C10 |
| Sangasangadalam | 37 | E5 |
| Sangeang | 39 | F1 |
| Sangerhausen | 15 | C6 |
| Sanggau | 37 | D4 |
| Sangihe, P. | 39 | D3 |
| Sangkapura | 37 | F4 |
| Sangli | 43 | L9 |
| Sangmélina | 56 | D2 |
| Sangre de Cristo Mts. | 78 | A1 |
| Sankt Gallen | 13 | C8 |
| Sankt Moritz | 13 | C8 |
| Sankt-Peterburg | 24 | B3 |
| Sankt Pölten | 15 | D8 |
| Sankuru → | 56 | E4 |
| Sanliurfa | 46 | C4 |
| Sanlúcar de Barrameda | 18 | D2 |
| Sannicandro Gargánico | 20 | D5 |
| Sanok | 17 | D6 |
| Sanshui | 35 | D6 |
| Santa Ana, Bolivia | 91 | F5 |
| Santa Ana, Ecuador | 90 | D2 |
| Santa Ana, El Salv. | 85 | E7 |
| Santa Ana, U.S.A. | 82 | D4 |
| Santa Barbara | 82 | C3 |
| Santa Catalina I. | 82 | D3 |
| Santa Catarina □ | 94 | B7 |
| Santa Clara | 86 | B4 |
| Santa Clotilde | 90 | D4 |
| Santa Coloma de Gramanet | 19 | B7 |
| Santa Cruz, Argentina | 95 | G3 |
| Santa Cruz, Bolivia | 91 | G6 |
| Santa Cruz, Phil. | 38 | B2 |
| Santa Cruz, U.S.A. | 82 | B1 |
| Santa Cruz → | 95 | G3 |
| Santa Cruz de Tenerife | 54 | C1 |

Santa Cruz do Sul ........ 94 B6
Santa Cruz I. .. 64 L11
Santa Elena ... 90 D2
Santa Eugenia, Pta. ........ 84 B1
Santa Fe, Argentina ... 94 C4
Santa Fe, U.S.A. 83 C10
Santa Filomena 93 D4
Santa Inés, I. .. 95 G2
Santa Isabel = Rey Malabo . 56 D1
Santa Isabel, Argentina ... 94 D3
Santa Isabel, Brazil ....... 93 E3
Santa Lucia Range ...... 82 C2
Santa Maria, Brazil ....... 94 B6
Santa Maria, U.S.A. ...... 82 C2
Santa María → 84 A3
Santa Maria da Vitória ..... 93 E5
Santa Maria di Leuca, C. ... 23 E2
Santa Marta ... 90 A4
Santa Marta, Sierra Nevada de ......... 90 A4
Santa Maura = Levkás ..... 23 E3
Santa Rosa, La Pampa, Argentina ... 94 D4
Santa Rosa, San Luis, Argentina ... 94 C3
Santa Rosa, Bolivia ..... 91 F5
Santa Rosa, Brazil ....... 94 B6
Santa Rosa, U.S.A. ...... 80 F2
Santa Rosa de Copán ...... 85 E7
Santa Vitória do Palmar ..... 94 C6
Santai ........ 35 C5
Santana, Coxilha de ........... 94 C5
Santana do Livramento .. 94 C5
Santander .... 18 A4
Sant'Antíoco .. 21 E2
Santarém, Brazil 92 C3
Santarém, Portugal .... 18 C1
Santiago, Brazil 94 B6
Santiago, Chile 94 C2
Santiago → .. 90 D3
Santiago de Compostela . 18 A1
Santiago de Cuba ....... 86 C4
Santiago de los Cabelleros .. 87 C5
Santiago del Estero ...... 94 B4
Santo Amaro . 93 E6
Santo Ângelo . 94 B6
Santo Antonio . 93 F2
Santo Corazón 91 G7
Santo Domingo 87 C6
Santo Tomás .. 91 F4
Santo Tomé ... 94 B5

Santo Tomé de Guayana = Ciudad Guayana .... 90 B6
Santoña ...... 18 A4
Santoríni = Thíra ...... 23 F5
Santos ....... 94 A7
Santos Dumont 94 A8
Sanza Pombo . 56 F3
São Anastácio . 94 A6
São Bernado de Campo ..... 93 G4
São Borja ..... 94 B5
São Carlos .... 94 A7
São Cristóvão . 93 E6
São Domingos 93 E4
São Francisco . 93 F5
São Francisco → 93 E6
São Francisco do Sul ..... 94 B7
São Gabriel .. 94 C6
São João da Madeira .. 18 B1
São João del Rei ......... 93 G5
São João do Araguaia .. 92 D4
São João do Piauí ....... 92 D5
São José do Rio Prêto ..... 94 A7
São Leopoldo . 94 B6
São Lourenço . 93 G4
São Lourenço → 93 F2
São Luís ...... 92 C5
São Marcos → 93 F4
São Marcos, B. de ........ 92 C5
São Mateus .. 93 F6
São Paulo .... 94 A7
São Paulo □ .. 94 A7
São Roque, C. de ........ 92 D6
São Sebastião, I. de ........ 94 A7
São Tomé & Principe ■ . 51 F4
São Vicente, C. de ......... 18 D1
Saône → .... 13 D6
Saonek ...... 39 E4
Saparua ...... 39 E3
Sapele ....... 55 G6
Saposoa ...... 91 E3
Sapporo ..... 32 F12
Sapulpa ...... 79 B5
Saqqez ....... 46 C6
Sar-e Pol .... 45 B6
Sar-e Pol □ .. 45 B6
Sar Planina ... 22 C3
Sarāb ........ 46 C6
Sarada → .... 40 D3
Saragossa = Zaragoza ... 19 B5
Saraguro ..... 90 D3
Sarajevo ..... 20 C7
Saran, G. .... 37 E4
Sarandí del Yi . 94 C5
Sarangani B. .. 38 C3
Sarangani Is. .. 38 C3
Sarangarh .... 40 G4
Saransk ...... 24 C6
Sarapul ...... 29 D6
Sarasota ..... 75 F6
Saratov ...... 24 C6
Saravane ..... 36 A3

Sarawak □ .... 37 D4
Saray ........ 22 D6
Sarayköy ..... 23 F7
Sarbāz ....... 45 E5
Sarbīsheh .... 45 C4
Sarda → = Sarada → .. 40 D3
Sardalas ..... 54 C7
Sardarshahr ... 42 E9
Sardegna □ ... 21 D2
Sardinia = Sardegna □ . 21 D2
Sardis ........ 23 E7
Sargodha ..... 42 C8
Sarh ......... 53 G2
Sārī ......... 44 B3
Saṅgöl ....... 23 E7
Sarikamiş .... 46 B5
Sarikei ....... 37 D4
Sark ......... 11 G5
Şarköy ....... 23 D6
Sarlat-la-Canéda 12 D4
Sarmi ........ 39 E5
Sarmiento .... 95 F3
Sarnia ....... 69 D2
Sarny ........ 24 C2
Sarolangun ... 37 E2
Saronikós Kólpos ... 23 F4
Sarre = Saar → 13 B7
Sarreguemines 13 B7
Sarro ........ 55 F3
Sarthe → .... 12 C3
Sartynya ..... 28 C7
Sarvestān .... 44 D3
Sary-Tash .... 29 F8
Saryshagan ... 29 E8
Sasabeneh ... 49 F3
Sasaram ..... 40 E5
Sasebo ....... 32 C1
Saser ........ 43 B10
Saskatchewan □ 71 C9
Saskatchewan → 71 C9
Saskatoon .... 71 C9
Saskylakh .... 30 B9
Sasovo ....... 24 C5
Sassandra .... 55 H3
Sassandra → . 55 H3
Sássari ....... 21 D2
Sassnitz ..... 15 A7
Sassuolo ..... 20 B3
Sasyk, Ozero .. 17 F9
Sata-Misaki ... 33 D2
Satadougou .. 55 F2
Satara ........ 43 L8
Satmala Hills .. 43 J9
Satna ........ 40 E3
Sátoraljaújhely 16 D5
Satpura Ra. ... 43 J10
Satu Mare .... 17 E6
Satui ........ 37 E5
Saturnina → .. 91 F7
Saudi Arabia ■ 47 F6
Sauerland .... 14 C4
Sault Ste. Marie, Canada ..... 69 D2
Sault Ste. Marie, U.S.A. ...... 72 A3
Saumlaki .... 39 F4
Saumur ...... 12 C3
Saunders C. ... 65 F4
Sauri ........ 55 F6
Saurimo ..... 56 F4
Sava → ...... 22 B3
Savage I. = Niue ...... 65 L14
Savalou ...... 55 G5
Savanna la Mar 86 C4

Savannah ..... 75 C7
Savannah → . 75 C7
Savannakhet .. 36 A2
Savanur ..... 43 M9
Savé ........ 55 G5
Save → ...... 59 C6
Sāveh ....... 46 D7
Savelugu ..... 55 G4
Savoie □ ..... 13 D7
Savona ...... 20 B2
Sawahlunto ... 37 E2
Sawai ........ 39 E3
Sawai Madhopur .. 42 F10
Sawara ...... 32 B7
Sawatch Mts. . 83 A9
Sawmills ..... 59 B5
Sawu ........ 39 F2
Sawu Sea ... 39 F2
Saxony, Lower = Niedersachsen □ ......... 14 B5
Say .......... 55 F5
Sayán ........ 91 F3
Sayan, Zapadnyy ... 30 D7
Saydā ........ 46 D3
Sayghān ..... 45 C6
Sayḥut ....... 49 D5
Saynshand ... 35 B6
Sazanit ...... 23 D2
Sázava → .... 16 D2
Sazin ........ 42 B8
Scandicci .... 20 C3
Scandinavia ... 8 F10
Scarborough .. 11 D6
Scebeli, Wabi → .... 49 G3
Schaffhausen . 13 C8
Schefferville .. 69 C4
Schelde → ... 14 C3
Schenectady .. 73 C9
Schiermonnikoog ....... 14 B4
Schio ........ 20 B3
Schleswig .... 14 A5
Schleswig-Holstein □ .. 14 A5
Schouten I. ... 62 D4
Schouten Is. = Supiori ..... 39 E5
Schwäbische Alb ...... 14 D5
Schwaner, Pegunungan 37 E4
Schwarzwald .. 14 D5
Schwedt ..... 15 B8
Schweinfurt ... 14 C6
Schwenningen = Villingen-Schwenningen 14 D5
Schwerin .... 15 B6
Schwyz ...... 13 C8
Sciacca ...... 21 F4
Scilla ........ 21 E5
Scilly, Isles of . 11 G3
Scone ....... 63 B5
Scotland □ ... 10 C4
Scott Glacier . 96 A12
Scott Inlet ... 68 A3
Scottsbluff .... 76 E3
Scottsdale ... 62 D4
Scranton ..... 73 D8
Scunthorpe ... 11 E6
Scusciuban .. 49 E5
Scutari = Üsküdar .... 25 E2
Seaspray ..... 63 C4

Seattle . . . . . . . 80 B2
Sebastopol =
  Sevastopol . . 25 E3
Sebha =
  Sabhah . . . . . 52 C1
Şebinkarahisar 46 B4
Sebta = Ceuta . 18 E3
Sebuku . . . . . . . 37 E5
Sebuku, Teluk . 37 D5
Secretary I. . . . 65 F2
Secunderabad . 43 L11
Sedalia . . . . . . . 77 F8
Sedan, Australia 62 B2
Sedan, France . 13 B6
Seddon . . . . . . 65 D6
Seddonville . . . 65 D5
Sedhiou . . . . . . 55 F1
Sedova, Pik . . . 28 B6
Seeheim . . . . . . 58 D3
Seferihisar . . . 23 E6
Segamat . . . . . 37 D2
Segesta . . . . . . 21 F4
Seget . . . . . . . . 39 E4
Ségou . . . . . . . . 55 F3
Segovia =
  Coco . → . . . 86 D3
Segovia . . . . . . 18 B3
Segre . → . . . . . 19 B6
Séguéla . . . . . . 55 G3
Segura . → . . . . 19 C5
Sehitwa . . . . . . 58 C4
Sehore . . . . . . . 43 H10
Seine . → . . . . . 12 B4
Seistan . . . . . . . 45 D5
Seistan,
  Daryācheh-ye 45 D5
Sekayu . . . . . . . 37 E2
Sekondi-
  Takoradi . . . 55 H4
Selaru . . . . . . . . 39 F4
Selçuk . . . . . . . 23 F6
Sele . → . . . . . . 21 D5
Selenga =
  Selenge
  Mörön . → . . 35 A5
Selenge
  Mörön . → . . 35 A5
Seletan, Tg. . . . 37 E4
Sélibabi . . . . . . 55 E2
Selîma, El
  Wâhât el . . . 52 D4
Selkirk . . . . . . . 71 C10
Selkirk Mts. . . . 71 C8
Selma . . . . . . . . 75 B8
Selpele . . . . . . . 39 E4
Selu . . . . . . . . . 39 F4
Selva . . . . . . . . 94 B4
Selvas . . . . . . . 91 E5
Semani . → . . . . 23 D2
Semarang . . . . 37 F4
Semey . . . . . . . 29 D9
Semiozernoye . 29 D7
Semipalatinsk =
  Semey . . . . . 29 D9
Semirara Is. . . . 38 B2
Semisopochnoi
  I. . . . . . . . . . . 71 C1
Semitau . . . . . . 37 D4
Semiyarka . . . . 29 D8
Semiyarskoye =
  Semiyarka . . 29 D8
Semmering P. . 15 E8
Semnān . . . . . . 44 C3
Semnān □ . . . . 44 C3
Semporna . . . . 38 D1
Semuda . . . . . . 37 E4
Sena Madureira 91 E5
Senador
  Pompeu . . . . 92 D6

Senaja . . . . . . . 36 C5
Senanga . . . . . . 58 B4
Sendai,
  Kagoshima,
  Japan . . . . . . 32 D2
Sendai, Miyagi,
  Japan . . . . . . 33 G12
Senegal ■ . . . . 55 F2
Senegal . → . . . 55 E1
Senge Khambab
  = Indus . → . 43 G5
Sengkang . . . . 39 E2
Senhor-do-
  Bonfim . . . . . 93 E5
Senigállia . . . . 20 C4
Senj . . . . . . . . . 20 B5
Senja . . . . . . . . 8 E11
Senlis . . . . . . . . 13 B5
Senmonorom . 36 B3
Sennâr . . . . . . . 53 F5
Senneterre . . . . 69 D3
Sens . . . . . . . . . 13 B5
Senta . . . . . . . . 22 B3
Sentani . . . . . . . 39 E6
Seo de Urgel . . 19 A6
Seoul = Sŏul . 35 C7
Sepīdān . . . . . . 44 D3
Sept-Îles . . . . . 69 C4
Sequoia
  National Park 82 B3
Seram . . . . . . . 39 E3
Seram Laut,
  Kepulauan . . 39 E4
Seram Sea . . . . 39 E3
Serasan . . . . . . 37 D3
Serbia □ . . . . . 22 C3
Serdobsk . . . . . 24 C5
Seremban . . . . 37 D2
Serenje . . . . . . . 59 A6
Sereth =
  Siret . → . . . 17 F9
Sergino . . . . . . 28 C7
Sergipe □ . . . . 93 E6
Sergiyev Posad 24 B4
Seria . . . . . . . . . 36 D4
Serian . . . . . . . . 37 D4
Seribu,
  Kepulauan . . 37 F3
Sérifos . . . . . . . 23 F5
Sermata . . . . . . 39 F3
Serny Zavod . . 29 F6
Serov . . . . . . . . 28 D7
Serowe . . . . . . . 59 C5
Serpukhov . . . . 24 C4
Sérrai . . . . . . . . 22 D4
Serrezuela . . . . 94 C3
Serrinha . . . . . . 93 E6
Sertânia . . . . . . 92 D6
Serua . . . . . . . . 39 F4
Serui . . . . . . . . . 39 E5
Serule . . . . . . . . 59 C5
Sesepe . . . . . . . 39 E3
Sesfontein . . . . 58 B2
Sesheke . . . . . . 58 B4
Sète . . . . . . . . . 13 E5
Sete Lagôas . . 93 F5
Sétif . . . . . . . . . 54 A6
Seto . . . . . . . . . 32 B5
Settat . . . . . . . . 54 B3
Setté-Cama . . . 56 E1
Setúbal . . . . . . 18 C1
Setúbal, B. de . 18 C1
Seulimeum . . . 36 C1
Sevan, Ozero =
  Sevana Lich . 25 E6
Sevana Lich . . 25 E6
Sevastopol . . . 25 E3
Severn . →,
  Canada . . . . . 69 C2

Severn . →, U.K. 11 F5
Severnaya
  Zemlya . . . . . 30 B7
Severnyye Uvaly 24 B6
Severo-
  Yeniseyskiy . 30 C7
Severodvinsk . . 28 C4
Sevilla . . . . . . . 18 D2
Seville = Sevilla 18 D2
Sevlievo . . . . . . 22 C5
Seward . . . . . . . 71 B5
Seward Pen. . . 71 B3
Sewer . . . . . . . . 39 F4
Seychelles ■ . . 26 K9
Seymour . . . . . 63 C4
Sfax . . . . . . . . . 52 B1
Sfîntu Gheorghe 17 F7
Shaanxi □ . . . . 35 C5
Shaba □ . . . . . . 57 F4
Shabunda . . . . 57 E5
Shache . . . . . . . 34 C2
Shackleton Ice
  Shelf . . . . . . . 96 A11
Shackleton Inlet 96 C15
Shadrinsk . . . . 29 D7
Shāhābād . . . . 44 B4
Shahdād . . . . . 44 D4
Shahdād,
  Namakzār-e . 44 D4
Shahdadkot . . . 42 F5
Shahgarh . . . . . 42 F6
Shaḥḥāt . . . . . . 52 B3
Shahjahanpur . 42 F11
Shahr Kord . . . 44 C2
Shahrig . . . . . . 42 D5
Shaikhabad . . . 42 B6
Shajapur . . . . . 43 H10
Shakhty . . . . . . 25 D5
Shakhunya . . . . 24 B6
Shaki . . . . . . . . 55 G5
Shala, L. . . . . . 53 G6
Shalqar . . . . . . 29 E6
Sham, J. ash . . 44 F4
Shamil . . . . . . . 44 E4
Shammar, Jabal 47 F5
Shamo = Gobi 35 B6
Shamo, L. . . . . 53 G6
Shamva . . . . . . 59 B6
Shan □ . . . . . . 41 G12
Shandong □ . . 35 C6
Shanghai . . . . . 35 C7
Shangqiu . . . . . 35 C6
Shangrao . . . . . 35 D6
Shangshui . . . . 35 C6
Shannon . . . . . 64 D6
Shannon . → . . 11 E2
Shansi =
  Shanxi □ . . . 35 C6
Shantou . . . . . . 35 D6
Shantung =
  Shandong □ 35 C6
Shanxi □ . . . . . 35 C6
Shaoguan . . . . 35 D6
Shaowu . . . . . . 35 D6
Shaoxing . . . . . 35 C7
Shaoyang . . . . 35 D6
Shaqra',
  Si. Arabia . . . 47 F6
Shaqrā', Yemen 49 E4
Sharjah = Ash
  Shāriqah . . . 44 E3
Sharon . . . . . . . 72 D5
Sharya . . . . . . . 24 B6
Shashi,
  Botswana . . . 59 C5
Shashi, China . 35 C6
Shasta, Mt. . . . 80 E2
Shatt al'Arab . → 47 E7
Shaunavon . . . 71 D9

Shawan . . . . . . 34 B3
Shawinigan . . . 69 D3
Shcherbakov =
  Rybinsk . . . . . 24 B4
Shchuchinsk . . 29 D8
Shebele =
  Scebeli,
  Wabi . → . . . . 49 G3
Sheboygan . . . 72 C2
Sheffield . . . . . 11 E6
Shekhupura . . . 42 D8
Shelburne . . . . 69 D4
Shelby . . . . . . . 75 B7
Shelbyville . . . . 74 B4
Shellharbour . . 63 B5
Shenandoah . → 73 E7
Shendam . . . . . 55 G6
Shendî . . . . . . . 53 E5
Shensi =
  Shaanxi □ . . 35 C5
Shenyang . . . . 35 B7
Sheopur Kalan 42 G10
Shepetivka . . . 17 C8
Shepetovka =
  Shepetivka . . 17 C8
Shepparton . . . 63 C4
Sherbro I. . . . . 55 G2
Sherbrooke . . . 69 D3
Sheridan . . . . . 81 C10
Sherman . . . . . 79 C5
Sherridon . . . . 71 C9
Shetland Is. . . . 10 A6
Shibām . . . . . . 49 D4
Shigaib . . . . . . 53 E3
Shihchiachuangi
  =
  Shijiazhuang 35 C6
Shijiazhuang . . 35 C6
Shikarpur . . . . . 42 F6
Shikoku . . . . . . 32 C3
Shikoku □ . . . . 33 H10
Shikoku-Sanchi 32 C3
Shilabo . . . . . . 49 F3
Shiliguri . . . . . . 40 D7
Shillong . . . . . . 41 E8
Shilong . . . . . . 35 D6
Shimada . . . . . 32 B6
Shimizu . . . . . . 32 B6
Shimoga . . . . . 43 N9
Shimonoseki . . 32 C2
Shinano . → . . . 32 A6
Shindand . . . . . 42 C3
Shingū . . . . . . . 32 C4
Shinyanga . . . . 57 E6
Shipehenski
  Prokhod . . . . 22 C5
Shipki La . . . . . 42 D11
Shīr Kūh . . . . . 44 D3
Shirane-San . . 32 A6
Shīrāz . . . . . . . 44 D3
Shire . → . . . . . 59 B7
Shiretoko-Misaki 32 F13
Shiriya-Zaki . . . 32 F12
Shīrvān . . . . . . 44 B4
Shirwa, L. =
  Chilwa, L. . . . 59 B7
Shivpuri . . . . . . 43 G10
Shizuoka . . . . . 32 B6
Shklov =
  Shklow . . . . . 17 A10
Shklow . . . . . . . 17 A10
Shkoder =
  Shkodra . . . . 22 C2
Shkodra . . . . . . 22 C2
Shkumbini . → . 23 D2
Shmidta, O. . . . 30 A7
Sholapur =
  Solapur . . . . . 43 L9
Shoshone Mts. 80 F5

Shoshong .... 59 C5
Shreveport .... 79 C7
Shrewsbury ... 11 E5
Shrirampur ... 40 F7
Shu .......... 29 E8
Shuangyashan 35 B8
Shule ........ 34 C2
Shumagin Is. .. 71 C4
Shungnak .... 71 B4
Shūr → ..... 44 D3
Shurugwi .... 59 B5
Shūsf ........ 45 D5
Shūshtar .... 47 D7
Shwebo ...... 41 F10
Shwegu ...... 41 E11
Shweli → .... 41 F11
Shymkent .... 29 E7
Shyok ........ 42 B11
Shyok → ..... 42 B9
Si Kiang = Xi
  Jiang → ... 35 D6
Si-ngan = Xi'an 35 C5
Si Racha ...... 36 B2
Siah .......... 47 G6
Siahan Range . 42 F4
Siaksriindrapura 37 D2
Sialkot ....... 42 C9
Siantan, P. .... 37 D3
Šiāreh ........ 45 D5
Siargao ...... 38 C3
Siasi ......... 38 C2
Siau .......... 39 D3
Šiauliai ....... 24 B1
Šibenik ...... 20 C5
Siberut ....... 37 E1
Sibi .......... 42 E5
Sibil ......... 39 E6
Sibiti ........ 56 E2
Sibiu ......... 17 F7
Sibolga ....... 37 D1
Sibsagar ..... 41 D10
Sibu ......... 37 D4
Sibuco ....... 38 C2
Sibuguey B. .. 38 C2
Sibut ........ 56 C3
Sibutu ....... 38 D1
Sibutu Passage 38 D1
Sibuyan ...... 38 B2
Sibuyan Sea .. 38 B2
Sichuan □ ... 34 C5
Sicilia ........ 21 F5
Sicily = Sicilia . 21 F5
Sicuani ...... 91 F4
Siddipet ...... 43 K11
Sidéradougou . 55 F4
Sîdi Barrâni .. 52 B4
Sidi-bel-Abbès . 54 A4
Sidley, Mt. .... 96 B18
Sidon = Saydā 46 D3
Sidra, G. of =
  Surt, Khalīj .. 52 B2
Siedlce ....... 17 B6
Sieg → ...... 14 C4
Siegen ....... 14 C5
Siem Reap ... 36 B2
Siena ........ 20 C3
Sieradz ...... 16 C4
Sierra Colorada 95 E3
Sierra Gorda . 94 A3
Sierra Leone ■ 55 G2
Sífnos ........ 23 F5
Sighetu-
  Marmatiei ... 17 E6
Sighişoara .... 17 E7
Sigli ......... 36 C1
Sigsig ........ 90 D3
Sigüenza ...... 19 B4
Siguiri ....... 55 F3

Sihanoukville =
  Kompong
  Som ....... 36 B2
Siirt ......... 46 C5
Sikar ......... 42 F9
Sikasso ...... 55 F3
Sikhote Alin,
  Khrebet ..... 31 E11
Sikhote Alin Ra.
  = Sikhote
  Alin, Khrebet 31 E11
Síkinos ....... 23 F5
Sikkim □ ..... 40 D7
Sil → ....... 18 A2
Silchar ....... 41 E9
Silesia = Śląsk 16 C3
Silgarhi Doti .. 40 C3
Silghat ....... 41 D9
Silifke ....... 46 C3
Siliguri =
  Shiliguri .... 40 D7
Siling Co ..... 34 C3
Silistra ...... 22 B6
Silivri ........ 22 D7
Sillajhuay,
  Cordillera .. 91 G5
Silva Porto =
  Kuito ....... 58 A3
Simanggang .. 37 D4
Simav ........ 23 E7
Simbirsk ..... 24 C6
Simeria ...... 17 F6
Simeulue ..... 37 D1
Simferopol ... 25 E3
Sími ......... 23 F6
Simikot ...... 40 C3
Simla ........ 42 D10
Simplon P. ... 13 C8
Simpson Desert 60 F6
Simunjan ..... 37 D4
Sinabang ..... 37 D1
Sinadogo ..... 49 F4
Sinai = Es Sînâ' 52 C5
Sinai, Mt. =
  Mûsa, G. .... 47 E3
Sinaloa de
  Leyva ...... 84 B3
Sīnāwan ..... 54 B7
Sincelejo ..... 90 B3
Sincorá, Serra
  do ........ 93 E5
Sind □ ...... 42 F6
Sind Sagar
  Doab ...... 42 D7
Sindangan ... 38 C2
Sines ........ 18 D1
Sines, C. de .. 18 D1
Singa ........ 53 F5
Singapore ■ .. 37 D2
Singaraja ..... 37 F5
Singida ...... 57 E6
Singitikós
  Kólpos .... 23 D5
Singkaling
  Hkamti .... 41 E10
Singkawang ... 37 D3
Singleton ..... 63 B5
Singora =
  Songkhla ... 36 C2
Sinjai ........ 39 F2
Sinjār ........ 46 C5
Sinkat ....... 53 E6
Sinkiang Uighur
  = Xinjiang
  Uygur
  Zizhiqu □ ... 34 B3
Sinni → ..... 21 D6
Sinnuris ..... 52 C5
Sinop ........ 46 B3

Sintang ...... 37 D4
Sintra ........ 18 C1
Sinŭiju ....... 35 B7
Siocon ....... 38 C2
Siófok ....... 16 E4
Sioma ........ 58 B4
Sion ......... 13 C7
Sioux City ... 77 D6
Sioux Falls ... 76 D6
Sioux Lookout . 71 C10
Siping ....... 35 B7
Sipura ....... 37 E1
Siquijor ...... 38 C2
Siracusa ...... 21 F5
Sirajganj ..... 41 E7
Sirdaryo =
  Syrdarya → 29 E7
Siret → ...... 17 F9
Sirohi ........ 43 G8
Sironj ........ 43 G10
Síros ........ 23 F5
Sirsa ......... 42 E9
Sisak ........ 20 B6
Sisaket ...... 36 A2
Sisophon ..... 36 B2
Sīstān va
  Balūchestān □ 45 E5
Sitapur ...... 40 D3
Sitges ........ 19 B6
Sitía ......... 23 G6
Sitka ......... 71 C6
Sittang Myit → 41 J11
Sittwe ....... 41 G9
Siuri ......... 40 F6
Sīvand ....... 44 D3
Sivas ........ 46 C4
Siverek ...... 46 C4
Sivrihisar .... 46 C2
Sîwa ......... 52 C4
Siwalik Range . 40 D4
Siwan ........ 40 D5
Sjælland ...... 9 G10
Sjumen =
  Šumen ..... 22 C6
Skadarsko
  Jezero ..... 22 C2
Skagerrak ..... 9 G9
Skagway ..... 71 C6
Skala-Podilska . 17 D8
Skala
  Podolskaya =
  Skala-Podilska 17 D8
Skalat ....... 17 D7
Skardu ....... 42 B9
Skarzysko-
  Kamienna ... 16 C5
Skeena → ... 70 C6
Skegness ..... 11 E7
Skeldon ...... 90 B7
Skellefte älv → 8 F12
Skellefteå .... 8 F12
Skíathos ..... 23 E4
Skien ........ 9 G9
Skierniewice .. 16 C5
Skikda ....... 54 A6
Skipton ...... 62 C3
Skíros ........ 23 E5
Skole ........ 17 D6
Skópelos ..... 23 E4
Skopje ....... 22 C3
Skvyra ....... 17 D9
Skye ......... 10 C3
Skyros = Skíros 23 E5
Slamet ....... 37 F3
Śląsk ........ 16 C3
Slatina ....... 22 B5
Slave → ..... 70 B8
Slavgorod .... 29 D8
Slavonski Brod 20 B7

Slavuta ....... 17 C8
Slavyansk =
  Slovyansk ... 25 D4
Slawharad ... 17 B10
Sleaford B. .... 62 B2
Sleeper Is. .... 68 C2
Sligeach = Sligo 11 D2
Sligo ......... 11 D2
Sliven ........ 22 C6
Slobodskoy ... 24 B7
Slobozia ...... 22 B6
Slonim ....... 17 B7
Slough ....... 11 F6
Slovak Rep. ■ . 16 D5
Slovakia =
  Slovak Rep. ■ 16 D5
Slovakian Ore
  Mts. =
  Slovenské
  Rudohorie .. 16 D4
Slovenia ■ .... 20 B5
Slovenija =
  Slovenia ■ .. 20 B5
Slovenská
  Republika =
  Slovak Rep. ■ 16 D5
Slovenské
  Rudohorie .. 16 D4
Slovyansk .... 25 D4
Sluch → ..... 17 C8
Słupsk ....... 16 A3
Slutsk ....... 17 B8
Smara ........ 54 B3
Smarhon ..... 17 A8
Smederevo ... 22 B3
Smith Arm ... 70 B7
Smithton ..... 62 D4
Smithtown ... 63 B5
Smoky Bay ... 62 B1
Smolensk .... 24 C3
Smolikas, Óros 23 D3
Smolyan ..... 22 D5
Smorgon =
  Smarhon ... 17 A8
Smyrna = İzmir 23 E6
Snake → ..... 80 B4
Snake I. ...... 63 C4
Snake River
  Plain ...... 81 D7
Sneek ........ 14 B3
Snĕžka ....... 16 C2
Snøhetta ..... 8 F9
Snowdon ..... 11 E4
Snowdrift .... 70 B8
Snowtown .... 62 B2
Snowy → .... 63 C4
Snowy Mts. .. 63 C4
Snyatyn ..... 17 D7
Snyder ....... 78 C3
Soalala ....... 59 H9
Sobat, Nahr → 53 G5
Sobral ....... 92 C5
Soc Trang .... 36 C3
Soch'e =
  Shache .... 34 C2
Sochi ........ 25 E5
Société, Is. de la 65 L15
Society Is. =
  Société, Is. de
  la ......... 65 L15
Socompa,
  Portezuelo de 94 A3
Socorro ...... 90 B4
Socotra ...... 49 E5
Soda Plains .. 42 B11
Söderhamn .. 8 F11
Sodiri ....... 53 F4
Sodo ........ 53 G6

# Sofia

Sofia = Sofiya . 22 C4
Sofia → . . . . . 59 H9
Sofiya . . . . . . . . 22 C4
Sogamoso . . . . 90 B4
Sognefjorden . 8 F9
Sohâg . . . . . . . . 52 C5
Soissons . . . . . 13 B5
Sokal . . . . . . . 17 C7
Söke . . . . . . . . . 23 F6
Sokhumi . . . . . 25 E5
Sokodé . . . . . . . 55 G5
Sokol . . . . . . . . 24 B5
Sokółka . . . . . . 17 B6
Sokolo . . . . . . . 55 F3
Sokolów
  Podlaski . . . . 17 B6
Sokoto . . . . . . . 55 F6
Solano . . . . . . . 38 A2
Solapur . . . . . . 43 L9
Soledad . . . . . . 90 B6
Soligalich . . . . 24 B5
Soligorsk =
  Salihorsk . . . 17 B8
Solikamsk . . . 28 D6
Solimões =
  Amazonas → 92 C3
Solingen . . . . . 14 C4
Sóller . . . . . . . . 19 C7
Sologne . . . . . . 12 C4
Solok . . . . . . . . 37 E2
Solomon Is. ■ . 64 K10
Solomon Sea . 61 B9
Solon . . . . . . . . 35 B7
Solor . . . . . . . . 39 F2
Solothurn . . . . . 13 C7
Šolta . . . . . . . . . 20 C6
Solţānābād . . 44 B4
Solunska Glava 22 D3
Solwezi . . . . . . 59 A5
Soma . . . . . . . . 23 E6
Somali Rep. ■ . 49 F4
Somalia =
  Somali Rep. ■ 49 F4
Sombor . . . . . . 22 B2
Sombrerete . . 84 C4
Sombrero . . . . 87 C7
Somerset East . 59 E5
Somerset I. . . . 70 A10
Someş → . . . 17 E6
Sommariva . . . 63 A4
Somme → . . . 12 A4
Somosierra,
  Puerto de . . . 18 B4
Somport, Puerto
  de . . . . . . . . . 12 E3
Søndre
  Strømfjord . . 68 B5
Sóndrio . . . . . . 20 A2
Sonepur . . . . . . 40 G4
Song Cau . . . . . 36 B3
Songea . . . . . . 57 G7
Songhua
  Jiang → . . . 35 B8
Songkhla . . . . . 36 C2
Songpan . . . . 34 C5
Sonipat . . . . . 42 E10
Sonmiani . . . . . 42 G5
Sono → . . . . . 93 D4
Sonora → . . . . 84 B2
Sonsonate . . . . 85 E7
Soochow =
  Suzhou . . . . . 35 C7
Sopi . . . . . . . . . 39 D3
Sopot . . . . . . . . 16 A4
Sopron . . . . . . 16 E3
Sør-Rondane . 96 B8
Sorata . . . . . . . 91 G5

Sorel . . . . . . . . . 69 D3
Sorgono . . . . . . 21 D2
Soria . . . . . . . . . 19 B4
Sorkh, Kuh-e . . 44 C4
Soroca . . . . . . . 17 D9
Sorocaba . . . . . 94 A7
Soroki = Soroca 17 D9
Sorong . . . . . . . 39 E4
Soroti . . . . . . . . 57 D6
Sørøya . . . . . . . 8 D12
Sorrento . . . . . . 63 C3
Sorsogon . . . . . 38 B2
Sosnowiec . . . . 16 C4
Souanké . . . . . 56 D2
Soúdhas, Kólpos 23 G5
Sŏul . . . . . . . . . 35 C7
Sound, The =
  Øresund . . . . 9 G10
Sources, Mt. aux 59 D5
Soure . . . . . . . . 92 C4
Souris . . . . . . . 71 D9
Souris → . . . 71 D10
Sousa . . . . . . . . 92 D6
Sousel . . . . . . . 92 C3
Sousse . . . . . . . 52 A1
South Africa ■ . 58 E4
South
  Australia □ . . 62 B2
South Bend . . . 72 D2
South
  Carolina □ . . 75 C7
South China Sea 36 C4
South Dakota □ 76 C4
South East C. . 62 D4
South Horr . . . . 57 D7
South I. . . . . . . 65 E3
South
  Invercargill . . 65 G3
South Korea ■ . 35 C7
South Magnetic
  Pole . . . . . . . . 96 A13
South
  Nahanni → . 70 B7
South Natuna Is.
  = Natuna
  Selatan,
  Kepulauan . . 37 D3
South Orkney Is. 96 A4
South Pagai, I.
  = Pagai
  Selatan, P. . . 37 E2
South Platte → 76 E4
South Pole . . . . 96 C
South
  Ronaldsay . . 10 B5
South
  Saskatchewan →
  . . . . . . . . . . . . 71 C9
South Shetland
  Is. . . . . . . . . . 96 A4
South Shields . 11 D6
South Taranaki
  Bight . . . . . . . 64 C6
South Uist . . . . 10 C3
South West C. . 62 D4
Southampton . 11 F6
Southampton I. 68 B2
Southbridge . . 65 E5
Southend-on-
  Sea . . . . . . . . 11 F7
Southern Alps . 65 E4
Southern Indian
  L. . . . . . . . . . . 71 C10
Southern Ocean 96 A9
Southern
  Uplands . . . . 10 D5
Southport . . . . 63 A5

Southwest C. . . 65 G2
Soutpansberg . 59 C5
Sovetsk,
  Kaliningd.,
  Russia . . . . . . 24 B1
Sovetsk, Kirov,
  Russia . . . . . . 24 B6
Sōya-Misaki . . . 32 E12
Soyo . . . . . . . . . 56 F2
Sozh → . . . . . . 17 C10
Spain ■ . . . . . . 18 C4
Spalding . . . . . 62 B2
Spanish Town . 86 C4
Sparta = Spárti 23 F4
Spartanburg . . 75 B7
Spárti . . . . . . . . 23 F4
Spartivento, C.,
  Calabria, Italy 21 F6
Spartivento, C.,
  Sard., Italy . . 21 E2
Spátha, Ákra . . 23 G4
Spence Bay . . . 70 B10
Spencer, C. . . . 62 C2
Spencer G. . . . . 62 B2
Spenser Mts. . . 65 E5
Spey → . . . . . . 10 C5
Speyer . . . . . . . 14 D5
Split . . . . . . . . . 20 C6
Spokane . . . . . . 80 B5
Spoleto . . . . . . 20 C4
Sporyy Navolok,
  Mys . . . . . . . . 28 B7
Spratly I. . . . . . 36 C4
Spree → . . . . . 15 B7
Springbok . . . . 58 D3
Springfield, N.Z. 65 E4
Springfield, Ill.,
  U.S.A. . . . . . . 77 F10
Springfield,
  Mass., U.S.A. 73 C9
Springfield, Mo.,
  U.S.A. . . . . . . 79 A7
Springfield,
  Ohio, U.S.A. . 72 E4
Springfield,
  Oreg., U.S.A. 80 C2
Springfontein . 59 E5
Springhill . . . . . 69 D4
Springhurst . . . 63 C4
Springs . . . . . . 59 D5
Squamish . . . . 71 D7
Srbija =
  Serbia □ . . . . 22 C3
Sre Umbell . . . 36 B2
Srebrnica . . . . . 20 B7
Sredinny Ra. =
  Sredinnyy
  Khrebet . . . . . 31 D14
Sredinnyy
  Khrebet . . . . . 31 D14
Srednevilyuysk 31 C10
Šrem . . . . . . . . 16 B3
Sremska
  Mitrovica . . . 22 B2
Srikakulam . . . 40 H4
Srinagar . . . . . . 42 B9
Stade . . . . . . . . 14 B5
Stadlandet . . . 8 F9
Stafford . . . . . . 11 E5
Stakhanov . . . . 25 D4
Stalingrad =
  Volgograd . . 25 D5
Staliniri =
  Tskhinvali . . . 25 E5
Stalino =
  Donetsk . . . . 25 D4

Stalinogorsk =
  Novomoskovsk
  . . . . . . . . . . . 24 C4
Stalowa Wola . 17 C6
Stamford . . . . . 73 D9
Stanislav =
  Ivano-
  Frankivsk . . . 17 D7
Stanke Dimitrov 22 C4
Stanley,
  Australia . . . . 62 D4
Stanley, Canada 71 C9
Stanley, Falk. Is. 95 G5
Stanovoy
  Khrebet . . . . . 31 D10
Stanovoy Ra. =
  Stanovoy
  Khrebet . . . . . 31 D10
Stanthorpe . . . . 63 A5
Stara Planina . 22 C4
Stara Zagora . . 22 C5
Starachowice . . 16 C5
Staraya Russa . 24 B3
Starbuck I. . . . . 65 K15
Stargard
  Szczeciński . . 16 B2
Staritsa . . . . . . 24 B3
Starogard
  Gdański . . . . 16 B4
Starokonstantinov
  =
  Starokonstyantyniv
  . . . . . . . . . . . 17 D8
Starokonstyantyniv
  . . . . . . . . . . . 17 D8
Staryy
  Chartoriysk . . 17 C7
Staryy Oskol . . 24 C4
State College . . 73 D7
Staten, I. =
  Estados, I. de
  Los . . . . . . . . 95 G4
Statesville . . . . 75 B7
Stavanger . . . . 9 G9
Staveley . . . . . . 65 E4
Stavropol . . . . . 25 D5
Stawell . . . . . . . 62 C3
Steenkool =
  Bintuni . . . . . 39 E4
Stefanie L. =
  Chew Bahir . 53 H6
Stefansson Bay 96 A9
Steiermark □ . . 15 E8
Steinkjer . . . . . . 8 F10
Stellenbosch . . 58 E3
Stendal . . . . . . 15 B6
Steornabhaigh
  = Stornoway 10 B3
Stepanakert =
  Xankändi . . . 25 F6
Stephens Creek 62 B3
Stepnoi = Elista 25 D5
Stepnyak . . . . . 29 D8
Sterlitamak . . . 29 D6
Stettin =
  Szczecin . . . . 16 B2
Stettiner Haff . . 15 B8
Stettler . . . . . . 71 C8
Steubenville . . 72 D5
Stevenage . . . . 11 F6
Stewart . . . . . . 70 B6
Stewart, I. . . . . 95 G2
Stewart I. . . . . . 65 G2
Steyr . . . . . . . . 15 D8
Stillwater, N.Z. 65 E4
Stillwater,
  U.S.A. . . . . . . 78 A5

Štip . . . . . . . . . 22 D4
Stirling . . . . . . 10 C5
Stockerau . . . . . 15 D9
Stockholm . . . . 9 G11
Stockport . . . . . 11 E5
Stockton . . . . . . 82 B2
Stockton-on-
Tees . . . . . . . 11 D6
Stoke on Trent 11 E5
Stokes Pt. . . . . 62 D3
Stolac . . . . . . . . 20 C6
Stolbovoy,
Ostrov . . . . . . 30 B11
Stolbtsy =
Stowbtsy . . . 17 B8
Stolin . . . . . . . 17 C8
Stonehaven . . 10 C5
Stonewall . . . . . 71 C10
Stony Tunguska
=
Podkamennaya
Tunguska → 30 C7
Stora Lulevatten 8 E11
Storavan . . . . . 8 E11
Store Bælt . . . . 9 G10
Store Creek . . . 63 B4
Storm B. . . . . . 62 D4
Stormberge . . . 59 E5
Stornoway . . . . 10 B3
Storozhinets =
Storozhynets 17 D7
Storozhynets . . 17 D7
Storsjön . . . . . . 8 F10
Storuman . . . . . 8 E11
Stowbtsy . . . . . 17 B8
Strahan . . . . . . 62 D4
Stralsund . . . . 15 A7
Strand . . . . . . . 58 E3
Stranraer . . . . . 11 D4
Strasbourg . . . . 13 B7
Stratford,
Canada . . . . . 69 D2
Stratford, N.Z. . 64 C6
Strathalbyn . . . 62 C2
Straubing . . . . 15 D7
Streaky B. . . . . 62 B1
Streaky Bay . . . 62 B1
Strelka . . . . . . . 30 D7
Strezhevoy . . . . 29 C8
Strimón → . . . . 23 D4
Strimonikós
Kólpos . . . . . 23 D5
Strómboli . . . . . 21 E5
Stronsay . . . . . 10 B5
Stroud Road . . 63 B5
Strumica . . . . . 22 D4
Stryy . . . . . . . . 17 D6
Strzelecki Cr. → 62 A2
Stuart Ra. . . . . . 62 A1
Stung Treng . . 36 B3
Stutterheim . . 59 E5
Stuttgart . . . . . 14 D5
Styria =
Steiermark □ 15 E8
Suakin . . . . . . . 53 E6
Subansiri → . . 41 D9
Subi . . . . . . . . . 37 D3
Subotica . . . . . . 16 E4
Suceava . . . . . 17 E8
Suchou =
Suzhou . . . . . 35 C7
Süchow =
Xuzhou . . . . . 35 C6
Sucre . . . . . . . . 91 G5
Sudair . . . . . . . 47 F6
Sudan ■ . . . . . 53 E4
Sudbury . . . . . . 69 D2

Sûdd . . . . . . . . . 53 G4
Sudeten Mts. =
Sudety . . . . . 16 C3
Sudety . . . . . . . 16 C3
Sudirman,
Pegunungan 39 E5
Sueca . . . . . . . . 19 C5
Suez = El
Suweis . . . . . 52 C5
Suez, G. of =
Suweis, Khalîg
el . . . . . . . . . . 52 C5
Sugluk = Salluit 68 B3
Suhâr . . . . . . . . 44 E4
Suhbaatar . . . . 35 A5
Suhl . . . . . . . . . 14 C6
Suihua . . . . . . . 35 B7
Sukadana,
Kalimantan,
Indonesia . . . 37 E3
Sukadana,
Sumatera,
Indonesia . . . 37 F3
Sukaraja . . . . . . 37 E4
Sukarnapura =
Jayapura . . . . 39 E6
Sukhona → . . . 28 C5
Sukhumi =
Sokhumi . . . . 25 E5
Sukkur . . . . . . . 42 F6
Sukkur Barrage 42 F6
Sula, Kepulauan 39 E3
Sulaiman Range 42 D6
Sulawesi □ . . . 39 E2
Sulawesi Sea =
Celebes Sea . 39 D2
Sulima . . . . . . . 55 G2
Sulina . . . . . . . 17 F9
Sulitjelma . . . . 8 E11
Sullana . . . . . . . 90 D2
Sultanpur . . . . 40 D4
Sulu Arch. . . . . 38 C2
Sulu Sea . . . . . 38 C2
Suluq . . . . . . . . 52 B3
Sulzberger Ice
Shelf . . . . . . . 96 B17
Sumalata . . . . . 39 D2
Sumatera □ . . . 37 D2
Sumatra =
Sumatera □ . 37 D2
Sumba . . . . . . . 39 F1
Sumba, Selat . . 39 F1
Sumbawa . . . . . 37 F5
Sumbawa Besar 37 F5
Sumbe . . . . . . . 56 G2
Šumen . . . . . . . 22 C6
Sumgait =
Sumqayıt . . . 25 E6
Summerside . . 69 D4
Sumperk . . . . . 16 D3
Sumqayıt . . . . . 25 E6
Sumter . . . . . . . 75 C7
Sumy . . . . . . . . 24 C3
Sunbury . . . . . . 63 C3
Sunda, Selat . . 37 F3
Sunda Str. =
Sunda, Selat 37 F3
Sundarbans,
The . . . . . . . . 41 G7
Sundargarh . . . 40 F5
Sunderland . . . 11 D6
Sundsvall . . . . . 8 F11
Sungaigerong . 37 E2
Sungailiat . . . . 37 E3
Sungaipakning 37 D2
Sungaipenuh . . 37 E2
Sungaitiram . . . 37 E5

Sungari =
Songhua
Jiang → . . . 35 B8
Sungguminasa 39 F1
Sunghua Chiang
= Songhua
Jiang → . . . 35 B8
Sungurlu . . . . . 46 B3
Sunnyvale . . . . 82 B1
Suntar . . . . . . . 30 C9
Supaul . . . . . . . 40 D6
Superior . . . . . . 77 B8
Superior, L. . . . 69 D2
Suphan Dağı . . 46 C5
Supiori . . . . . . . 39 E5
Sûr, Lebanon . . 46 D3
Sûr, Oman . . . . 45 F4
Sura → . . . . . . 24 B6
Surabaja =
Surabaya . . . 37 F4
Surabaya . . . . . 37 F4
Surakarta . . . . . 37 F4
Surat, Australia 63 A4
Surat, India . . . 43 J8
Surat Thani . . . 36 C1
Suratgarh . . . . . 42 E8
Surgut . . . . . . . 29 C8
Suriapet . . . . . . 43 L11
Surigao . . . . . . 38 C3
Surinam ■ . . . 92 B2
Suriname ■ =
Surinam ■ . . 92 B2
Suriname → . . 92 A2
Surt . . . . . . . . . 52 B2
Surt, Khalîj . . . . 52 B2
Suruga-Wan . 32 B6
Süsangerd . . . . 47 E7
Susanville . . . . 80 E3
Susquehanna →
. . . . . . . . . . . . 73 E7
Susques . . . . . . 94 A3
Susunu . . . . . . . 39 E4
Susurluk . . . . . . 23 E7
Sutherland Falls 65 F2
Sutlej → . . . . . 42 E7
Suva . . . . . . . . . 64 L12
Suva Planina . . 22 C4
Suvorov Is. =
Suwarrow Is. 65 L14
Suwałki . . . . . . 17 A6
Suwarrow Is. . . 65 L14
Suweis, Khalîg
el . . . . . . . . . . 52 C5
Suzdal . . . . . . . 24 B5
Suzhou . . . . . . 35 C7
Suzu-Misaki . . . 32 A5
Svealand □ . . . 9 G10
Sverdlovsk =
Yekaterinburg 29 D7
Svetlogorsk =
Svyetlahorsk 17 B9
Svetozarevo . . 22 B3
Svishtov . . . . . . 22 C5
Svislach . . . . . . 17 B7
Svyetlahorsk . . 17 B9
Swabian Alps =
Schwäbische
Alb . . . . . . . . 14 D5
Swakopmund . 58 C2
Swan Hill . . . . . 62 C3
Swansea,
Australia . . . . 63 B5
Swansea, U.K. . 11 F5
Swatow =
Shantou . . . . 35 D6
Swaziland ■ . . 59 D6
Sweden ■ . . . . 9 G10

Sweetwater . . . 78 C3
Swellendam . . 58 E4
Świdnica . . . . . 16 C3
Świdnik . . . . . . 17 C6
Świebodzin . . . 16 B2
Świecie . . . . . . 16 B4
Swift Current . . 71 C9
Swindon . . . . . 11 F6
Swinemünde =
Świnoujście . 16 B2
Świnoujście . . . 16 B2
Switzerland ■ . 13 C8
Sydney,
Australia . . . . 63 B5
Sydney, Canada 69 D4
Sydra, G. of =
Surt, Khalîj . . 52 B2
Syktyvkar . . . . . 28 C6
Sylhet . . . . . . . 41 E8
Sylt . . . . . . . . . 14 A5
Sym . . . . . . . . . 29 C9
Syracuse . . . . . 73 C7
Syrdarya → . . 29 E7
Syria ■ . . . . . . 46 D4
Syrian Desert =
Ash Shâm,
Bâdiyat . . . . . 47 D4
Syzran . . . . . . . 24 C6
Szczecin . . . . . 16 B2
Szczecinek . . . 16 B3
Szczytno . . . . . 16 B5
Szechwan =
Sichuan □ . . 34 C5
Szeged . . . . . . 16 E5
Székesfehérvár 16 E4
Szekszárd . . . . 16 E4
Szentes . . . . . . 16 E5
Szolnok . . . . . . 16 E5
Szombathely . . 16 E3

T

Tabacal . . . . . . 94 A4
Tabaco . . . . . . . 38 B2
Ţābah . . . . . . . 47 F5
Tabarka . . . . . . 54 A6
Ţabas,
Khorāsān, Iran 44 C4
Ţabas,
Khorāsān, Iran 45 C5
Tabatinga, Serra
da . . . . . . . . . 93 E5
Tablas . . . . . . . 38 B2
Table B. =
Tafelbaai . . . . 58 E3
Table Mt. . . . . . 58 E3
Tábor . . . . . . . . 16 D2
Tabora . . . . . . . 57 F6
Tabou . . . . . . . 55 H3
Tabrīz . . . . . . . 46 C6
Tabuk . . . . . . . 47 E4
Tacheng . . . . . 34 B3
Tacloban . . . . . 38 B2
Tacna . . . . . . . . 91 G4
Tacoma . . . . . . 80 B2
Tacuarembó . . 94 C5
Tademaït,
Plateau du . . 54 C5
Tadjoura . . . . . 49 E3
Tadmor . . . . . . 65 D5
Tadoussac . . . . 69 D4
Tadzhikistan =
Tajikistan ■ . 29 F8
Taegu . . . . . . . 35 C7

| | | |
|---|---|---|
| Taejŏn | 35 | C7 |
| Tafalla | 19 | A5 |
| Tafelbaai | 58 | E3 |
| Tafermaar | 39 | F4 |
| Taft | 38 | B3 |
| Taga Dzong | 41 | D7 |
| Taganrog | 25 | D4 |
| Tagbilaran | 38 | C2 |
| Tagish | 70 | B6 |
| Tagish L. | 70 | B6 |
| Tagliamento → | 20 | B4 |
| Taguatinga | 93 | E5 |
| Tagum | 38 | C3 |
| Tagus = Tejo → | 18 | C1 |
| Tahakopa | 65 | G3 |
| Tahan, Gunong | 36 | D2 |
| Tahat | 54 | D6 |
| Tâherī | 44 | E3 |
| Tahiti | 65 | L16 |
| Tahoe, L. | 80 | F3 |
| Tahoua | 55 | F6 |
| Tahta | 52 | C5 |
| Tahulandang | 39 | D3 |
| Tahuna | 39 | D3 |
| Taï | 55 | G3 |
| Tai Hu | 35 | C7 |
| Taibei | 35 | D7 |
| T'aichung = Taizhong | 35 | D7 |
| Taidong | 35 | D7 |
| Taieri → | 65 | G4 |
| Taihape | 64 | C6 |
| Tailem Bend | 62 | C2 |
| Taimyr Peninsula = Taymyr, Poluostrov | 30 | B7 |
| Tain | 10 | C4 |
| Tainan | 35 | D7 |
| Taínaron, Ákra | 23 | F4 |
| T'aipei = Taibei | 35 | D7 |
| Taiping | 36 | D2 |
| Taitao, Pen. de | 95 | F1 |
| Taiwan ■ | 35 | D7 |
| Taïyetos Óros | 23 | F4 |
| Taiyuan | 35 | C6 |
| Taizhong | 35 | D7 |
| Ta'izz | 49 | E3 |
| Tajikistan ■ | 29 | F8 |
| Tajo = Tejo → | 18 | C1 |
| Tājūrā | 52 | B1 |
| Tak | 36 | A1 |
| Takada | 32 | A6 |
| Takaka | 65 | D5 |
| Takamatsu | 32 | B4 |
| Takaoka | 32 | A5 |
| Takapuna | 64 | B6 |
| Takasaki | 32 | A6 |
| Takatsuki | 32 | B4 |
| Takaungu | 57 | E7 |
| Takayama | 32 | A5 |
| Takefu | 32 | B5 |
| Takengon | 36 | D1 |
| Takeo | 36 | B2 |
| Tākestān | 46 | D7 |
| Takhār □ | 45 | B7 |
| Takum | 55 | G6 |
| Talara | 90 | D2 |
| Talas | 29 | E8 |
| Talaud, Kepulauan | 38 | D3 |
| Talaud Is. = Talaud, Kepulauan | 38 | D3 |
| Talavera de la Reina | 18 | C3 |
| Talayan | 38 | C2 |
| Talbragar → | 63 | B4 |
| Talca | 94 | D2 |
| Talcahuano | 94 | D2 |
| Talcher | 40 | G5 |
| Taldy Kurgan = Taldyqorghan | 29 | E8 |
| Taldyqorghan | 29 | E8 |
| Ţalesh, Kūhhā-ye | 46 | C7 |
| Tali Post | 53 | G5 |
| Talibon | 38 | B2 |
| Taliwang | 37 | F5 |
| Tall 'Afar | 46 | C5 |
| Talladega | 74 | C4 |
| Tallahassee | 75 | D5 |
| Tallangatta | 63 | C4 |
| Tallarook | 63 | C4 |
| Tallinn | 24 | B1 |
| Talodi | 53 | F5 |
| Taltal | 94 | B2 |
| Talwood | 63 | A4 |
| Talyawalka Cr. → | 62 | B3 |
| Tamale | 55 | G4 |
| Tamanrasset | 54 | D6 |
| Tamarang | 63 | B5 |
| Tamaské | 55 | F6 |
| Tambacounda | 55 | F2 |
| Tambelan, Kepulauan | 37 | D3 |
| Tambo de Mora | 91 | F3 |
| Tambora | 37 | F5 |
| Tambov | 24 | C5 |
| Tamburâ | 53 | G4 |
| Tâmchekket | 55 | E2 |
| Tamega → | 18 | B1 |
| Tamenglong | 41 | E9 |
| Tamgak, Mts. | 55 | E6 |
| Tamil Nadu □ | 43 | P10 |
| Tammerfors = Tampere | 8 | F12 |
| Tamo Abu, Pegunungan | 37 | D5 |
| Tampa | 75 | F6 |
| Tampere | 8 | F12 |
| Tampico | 84 | C5 |
| Tamrida = Qādib | 49 | E5 |
| Tamsagbulag | 35 | B6 |
| Tamu | 41 | E10 |
| Tamworth | 63 | B5 |
| Tana → , Kenya | 57 | E8 |
| Tana → , Norway | 8 | D13 |
| Tana, L. | 53 | F6 |
| Tanahbala | 37 | E1 |
| Tanahgrogot | 37 | E5 |
| Tanahjampea | 39 | F2 |
| Tanahmasa | 37 | E1 |
| Tanahmerah | 39 | F6 |
| Tanami Desert | 60 | D5 |
| Tanana | 71 | B4 |
| Tanana → | 71 | B4 |
| Tananarive = Antananarivo | 59 | H9 |
| Tánaro → | 20 | B2 |
| Tandag | 38 | C3 |
| Tandil | 94 | D5 |
| Tandil, Sa. del | 94 | D5 |
| Tando Adam | 42 | G6 |
| Tandou L. | 62 | B3 |
| Tane-ga-Shima | 33 | D2 |
| Taneatua | 64 | C7 |
| Tanen Tong Dan | 41 | J12 |
| Tanezrouft | 54 | D5 |
| Tanga | 57 | F7 |
| Tanganyika, L. | 57 | F5 |
| Tanger = Tangier | 54 | A3 |
| Tanggula Shan | 34 | C4 |
| Tangier | 54 | A3 |
| Tangshan | 35 | C6 |
| Tanimbar, Kepulauan | 39 | F4 |
| Tanimbar Is. = Tanimbar, Kepulauan | 39 | F4 |
| Tanjay | 38 | C2 |
| Tanjore = Thanjavur | 43 | P11 |
| Tanjung | 37 | E5 |
| Tanjungbalai | 37 | D1 |
| Tanjungbatu | 37 | D5 |
| Tanjungkarang Telukbetung | 37 | F3 |
| Tanjungpandan | 37 | E3 |
| Tanjungpinang | 37 | D2 |
| Tanjungredeb | 37 | D5 |
| Tanjungselor | 37 | D5 |
| Tanout | 55 | F6 |
| Tanta | 52 | B5 |
| Tantung = Dandong | 35 | B7 |
| Tanunda | 62 | B2 |
| Tanzania ■ | 57 | F6 |
| Taolanaro | 59 | K9 |
| Taoudenni | 54 | D4 |
| Taourirt | 54 | B4 |
| Tapa Shan = Daba Shan | 35 | C5 |
| Tapah | 37 | D2 |
| Tapajós → | 92 | C3 |
| Tapaktuan | 37 | D1 |
| Tapanui | 65 | F3 |
| Tapauá → | 91 | E6 |
| Tapeta | 55 | G3 |
| Tapi → | 43 | J8 |
| Tapirapecó, Serra | 90 | C6 |
| Tapuaenuku, Mt. | 65 | D5 |
| Tapul Group | 38 | C2 |
| Taquari → | 91 | G7 |
| Tara, Australia | 63 | A5 |
| Tara, Russia | 29 | D8 |
| Tara → , Montenegro, Yug. | 22 | C2 |
| Tara → , Russia | 29 | D8 |
| Tarabagatay, Khrebet | 29 | E9 |
| Tarābulus, Lebanon | 46 | D3 |
| Tarābulus, Libya | 52 | B1 |
| Tarakan | 37 | D5 |
| Taralga | 63 | B4 |
| Taranaki □ | 64 | C6 |
| Tarancón | 19 | B4 |
| Taranga Hill | 43 | H8 |
| Táranto | 21 | D6 |
| Táranto, G. di | 21 | D6 |
| Tarapacá | 90 | D5 |
| Tararua Ra. | 64 | D6 |
| Tarashcha | 17 | D10 |
| Tarauacá | 91 | E4 |
| Tarauacá → | 91 | E5 |
| Tarawera | 64 | C7 |
| Tarawera L. | 64 | C7 |
| Tarazona | 19 | B5 |
| Tarbela Dam | 42 | B8 |
| Tarbes | 12 | E4 |
| Tarcoola | 62 | B1 |
| Tarcoon | 63 | B4 |
| Taree | 63 | B5 |
| Tarfaya | 54 | C2 |
| Tarifa | 18 | D3 |
| Tarija | 94 | A4 |
| Tariku → | 39 | E5 |
| Tarim Basin = Tarim Pendi | 34 | C3 |
| Tarim He → | 34 | C3 |
| Tarim Pendi | 34 | C3 |
| Taritatu → | 39 | E5 |
| Tarkhankut, Mys | 25 | D3 |
| Tarko Sale | 28 | C8 |
| Tarkwa | 55 | G4 |
| Tarlac | 38 | A2 |
| Tarma | 91 | F3 |
| Tarn → | 12 | D4 |
| Tarnobrzeg | 16 | C5 |
| Tarnów | 16 | C5 |
| Tarnowskie Góry | 16 | C4 |
| Taroom | 63 | A4 |
| Taroudannt | 54 | B3 |
| Tarragona | 19 | B6 |
| Tarrasa | 19 | B7 |
| Tarso Emissi | 52 | D2 |
| Tarsus | 46 | C3 |
| Tartagal | 94 | A4 |
| Tartu | 24 | B2 |
| Tartūs | 46 | D3 |
| Tarutung | 37 | D1 |
| Tasāwah | 52 | C1 |
| Taschereau | 69 | D3 |
| Tash-Kömür | 29 | E8 |
| Tash-Kumyr = Tash-Kömür | 29 | E8 |
| Tashauz = Dashhowuz | 29 | E6 |
| Tashi Chho Dzong = Thimphu | 41 | D7 |
| Tashkent = Toshkent | 29 | E7 |
| Tashtagol | 29 | D9 |
| Tasman B. | 65 | D5 |
| Tasman Mts. | 65 | D5 |
| Tasman Pen. | 62 | D4 |
| Tasmania □ | 62 | D4 |
| Tatabánya | 16 | E4 |
| Tatar Republic □ = Tatarstan □ | 29 | D6 |
| Tatarbunary | 17 | F9 |
| Tatarsk | 29 | D8 |
| Tatarstan □ | 29 | D6 |
| Tateyama | 32 | B6 |
| Tathra | 63 | C4 |
| Tatra = Tatry | 16 | D4 |
| Tatry | 16 | D4 |
| Tatta | 43 | G5 |
| Tatuī | 94 | A7 |
| Tat'ung = Datong | 35 | B6 |
| Tatvan | 46 | C5 |
| Taubaté | 94 | A7 |
| Tauern | 15 | E7 |
| Taumarunui | 64 | C6 |
| Taumaturgo | 91 | E4 |
| Taungdwingyi | 41 | G10 |
| Taunggyi | 41 | G11 |
| Taungup | 41 | H10 |
| Taungup Pass | 41 | H10 |
| Taungup Taunggya | 41 | H9 |
| Taunton | 11 | F5 |
| Taunus | 14 | C5 |
| Taupo | 64 | C7 |
| Taupo, L. | 64 | C6 |
| Tauranga | 64 | B7 |
| Tauranga Harb. | 64 | B7 |

| | | |
|---|---|---|
| Taurianova ... | 21 | E6 |
| Taurus Mts. = | | |
| Toros Dağları | 46 | C3 |
| Tavda ........ | 29 | D7 |
| Tavda ➜ ..... | 29 | D7 |
| Taveta ....... | 57 | E7 |
| Tavira ........ | 18 | D2 |
| Tavoy ........ | 36 | B1 |
| Tawau ........ | 36 | D5 |
| Tawitawi ..... | 38 | C2 |
| Tay ➜ ....... | 10 | C5 |
| Tayabamba .. | 91 | E3 |
| Taylakova .... | 29 | D8 |
| Taylakovy = | | |
| Taylakova ... | 29 | D8 |
| Taymā ....... | 47 | F4 |
| Taymyr, Oz. ... | 30 | B8 |
| Taymyr, | | |
| Poluostrov .. | 30 | B7 |
| Taytay ....... | 38 | B1 |
| Taz ➜ ....... | 28 | C8 |
| Taza ......... | 54 | B4 |
| Tazovskiy ..... | 28 | C8 |
| Tbilisi ........ | 25 | E5 |
| Tchad = Chad ■ | 53 | F1 |
| Tchad, L. ..... | 53 | F1 |
| Tch'eng-tou = | | |
| Chengdu .... | 35 | C5 |
| Tchibanga .... | 56 | E2 |
| Tch'ong-k'ing = | | |
| Chongqing .. | 35 | D5 |
| Tczew ........ | 16 | A4 |
| Te Anau, L. ... | 65 | F2 |
| Te Aroha ..... | 64 | B6 |
| Te Awamutu .. | 64 | C6 |
| Te Kuiti ...... | 64 | C6 |
| Te Puke ..... | 64 | B7 |
| Te Waewae B. . | 65 | G2 |
| Tebakang .... | 37 | D4 |
| Tébessa ...... | 54 | A6 |
| Tebicuary ➜ | 94 | B5 |
| Tebingtinggi .. | 37 | D1 |
| Tecuci ....... | 22 | B6 |
| Tedzhen = | | |
| Tejen ....... | 29 | F7 |
| Tefé ......... | 90 | D6 |
| Tegal ........ | 37 | F3 |
| Tegina ....... | 55 | F6 |
| Tegucigalpa .. | 85 | E7 |
| Tehachapi .... | 82 | C3 |
| Tehrān ....... | 44 | C2 |
| Tehuantepec .. | 85 | D5 |
| Tehuantepec, G. | | |
| de ......... | 85 | D5 |
| Tehuantepec, | | |
| Istmo de .... | 85 | D6 |
| Tejen ........ | 29 | F7 |
| Tejo ➜ ...... | 18 | C1 |
| Tekapo, L. ... | 65 | E4 |
| Tekeli ....... | 29 | E8 |
| Tekirdağ ..... | 22 | D6 |
| Tekkali ....... | 40 | H5 |
| Tel Aviv-Yafo .. | 46 | D3 |
| Tela ......... | 85 | D7 |
| Telanaipura = | | |
| Jambi ...... | 37 | E2 |
| Telavi ........ | 25 | E6 |
| Telekhany = | | |
| Tsyelyakhany | 17 | B7 |
| Teles Pires ➜ | 91 | E7 |
| Telford ....... | 11 | E5 |
| Télimélé ..... | 55 | F2 |
| Tellicherry .... | 43 | P9 |
| Telsen ....... | 95 | E3 |
| Teluk Anson . | 37 | D2 |
| Teluk Betung = | | |
| Tanjungkarang | | |
| Telukbetung . | 37 | F3 |

| | | |
|---|---|---|
| Teluk Intan = | | |
| Teluk Anson . | 37 | D2 |
| Telukbutun ... | 37 | D3 |
| Telukdalem ... | 37 | D1 |
| Tema ........ | 55 | G4 |
| Temax ....... | 85 | C7 |
| Temerloh ..... | 37 | D2 |
| Temir ........ | 29 | E6 |
| Temirtau, | | |
| Kazakstan ... | 29 | D8 |
| Temirtau, Russia | 29 | D9 |
| Temma ....... | 62 | D3 |
| Temora ....... | 63 | B4 |
| Tempe ....... | 83 | D7 |
| Temple ....... | 78 | D5 |
| Temuco ...... | 94 | D2 |
| Temuka ...... | 65 | F4 |
| Tenali ........ | 40 | J3 |
| Tenasserim ... | 36 | B1 |
| Tenda, Col di .. | 20 | B1 |
| Tendaho ...... | 49 | E3 |
| Tenerife ...... | 54 | C1 |
| Teng Xian .... | 35 | C6 |
| Tengah □ ..... | 39 | E2 |
| Tengah | | |
| Kepulauan .. | 37 | F5 |
| Tengchong .... | 34 | D4 |
| Tenggara □ ... | 39 | E2 |
| Tenggarong ... | 37 | E5 |
| Tengiz, Ozero . | 29 | D7 |
| Tenkasi ....... | 43 | Q10 |
| Tenke ........ | 57 | G5 |
| Tenkodogo ... | 55 | F4 |
| Tennessee □ .. | 74 | B4 |
| Tennessee ➜ . | 72 | F1 |
| Tenom ....... | 36 | C5 |
| Tenryū- | | |
| Gawa ➜ ... | 32 | B5 |
| Tenterfield ... | 63 | A5 |
| Teófilo Otoni .. | 93 | F5 |
| Tepa ......... | 39 | F3 |
| Tepic ........ | 84 | C4 |
| Teplice ....... | 16 | C1 |
| Ter ➜ ....... | 19 | A7 |
| Téra ......... | 55 | F5 |
| Téramo ...... | 20 | C4 |
| Terang ....... | 62 | C3 |
| Terebovlya .... | 17 | D7 |
| Terek ➜ ..... | 25 | E6 |
| Teresina ..... | 92 | D5 |
| Terewah, L. .. | 63 | A4 |
| Terhazza ..... | 54 | D3 |
| Teridgerie | | |
| Cr. ➜ ...... | 63 | B4 |
| Termez = | | |
| Termiz ...... | 29 | F7 |
| Términi Imerese | 21 | F4 |
| Termiz ....... | 29 | F7 |
| Térmoli ...... | 20 | C5 |
| Ternate ...... | 39 | D3 |
| Terni ......... | 20 | C4 |
| Ternopil ...... | 17 | D7 |
| Ternopol = | | |
| Ternopil ..... | 17 | D7 |
| Terowie, N.S.W., | | |
| Australia .... | 63 | B4 |
| Terowie, | | |
| S. Austral., | | |
| Australia .... | 62 | B2 |
| Terracina ..... | 20 | D4 |
| Terralba ...... | 21 | E2 |
| Terranova = | | |
| Ólbia ....... | 20 | D2 |
| Terrassa = | | |
| Tarrasa ..... | 19 | B7 |
| Terre Haute .. | 72 | E2 |
| Terschelling ... | 14 | B3 |

| | | |
|---|---|---|
| Teruel ........ | 19 | B5 |
| Teryaweyna L. . | 62 | B3 |
| Teshio-Gawa ➜ | 32 | F12 |
| Tesiyn Gol ➜ . | 34 | A4 |
| Teslin ........ | 70 | B6 |
| Tessalit ...... | 54 | D5 |
| Tessaoua ..... | 55 | F6 |
| Tetas, Pta. .... | 94 | A2 |
| Tete ......... | 59 | B6 |
| Teterev ➜ ... | 17 | C10 |
| Teteven ...... | 22 | C5 |
| Tetiyev ....... | 17 | D9 |
| Tétouan ...... | 54 | A3 |
| Tetovo ....... | 22 | C3 |
| Teuco ➜ ..... | 94 | B4 |
| Teun ......... | 39 | F3 |
| Teutoburger | | |
| Wald ....... | 14 | B5 |
| Tévere ➜ .... | 20 | D4 |
| Tewantin ..... | 63 | A5 |
| Texarkana ... | 79 | C6 |
| Texas ....... | 63 | A5 |
| Texas □ ...... | 78 | D4 |
| Texas City .... | 79 | E6 |
| Texel ........ | 14 | B3 |
| Teyvareh ..... | 45 | C6 |
| Tezpur ....... | 41 | D9 |
| Thabana | | |
| Ntlenyana ... | 59 | D5 |
| Thabazimbi .. | 59 | C5 |
| Thailand ■ ... | 36 | A2 |
| Thailand, G. of | 36 | B2 |
| Thakhek ...... | 36 | A2 |
| Thal ......... | 42 | C7 |
| Thala La ..... | 41 | C11 |
| Thallon ....... | 63 | A4 |
| Thames ...... | 64 | B6 |
| Thames ➜ ... | 11 | F7 |
| Thane ........ | 43 | K8 |
| Thanh Pho Ho | | |
| Chi Minh = | | |
| Phanh Bho Ho | | |
| Chi Minh .. | 36 | B3 |
| Thanjavur .... | 43 | P11 |
| Thar Desert ... | 42 | F7 |
| Tharad ....... | 43 | G7 |
| Thargomindah | 63 | A3 |
| Tharrawaddy .. | 41 | J10 |
| Thásos ....... | 23 | D5 |
| Thaton ....... | 41 | J11 |
| Thaungdut ... | 41 | E10 |
| Thayetmyo ... | 41 | H10 |
| Thazi ........ | 41 | G11 |
| The Alberga ➜ | 62 | A2 |
| The Coorong .. | 62 | C2 |
| The Frome ➜ . | 62 | A2 |
| The Grampians | 62 | C3 |
| The Great Divide | | |
| = Great | | |
| Dividing Ra. . | 61 | E8 |
| The Hague = 's- | | |
| Gravenhage . | 14 | B3 |
| The | | |
| Hamilton ➜ | 62 | A2 |
| The | | |
| Macumba ➜ | 62 | A2 |
| The Neales ➜ | 62 | A2 |
| The Pas ...... | 71 | C9 |
| The Rock ..... | 63 | C4 |
| The Salt L. ... | 62 | B3 |
| The | | |
| Stevenson ➜ | 62 | A2 |
| The | | |
| Warburton ➜ | 62 | A2 |
| Thebes = Thívai | 23 | E4 |
| Theebine ..... | 63 | A5 |
| Thermaïkós | | |
| Kólpos ..... | 23 | D4 |
| Thermopylae P. | 23 | E4 |

| | | |
|---|---|---|
| Thessaloníki .. | 23 | D4 |
| Thessaloniki, | | |
| Gulf of = | | |
| Thermaïkós | | |
| Kólpos ..... | 23 | D4 |
| Thetford ..... | 11 | E7 |
| Thetford Mines | 69 | D3 |
| Thevenard ... | 62 | B1 |
| Thiel Mts. ..... | 96 | C2 |
| Thiers ........ | 13 | D5 |
| Thies ........ | 55 | F1 |
| Thika ........ | 57 | E7 |
| Thimphu ..... | 41 | D7 |
| Thionville ..... | 13 | B7 |
| Thíra ........ | 23 | F5 |
| Thistle I. ...... | 62 | C2 |
| Thívai ........ | 23 | E4 |
| Thomas, L. ... | 62 | A2 |
| Thomasville, | | |
| Ga., U.S.A. .. | 75 | D6 |
| Thomasville, | | |
| N.C., U.S.A. . | 75 | B7 |
| Thompson .... | 71 | C10 |
| Thomson's Falls | | |
| = Nyahururu | 57 | D7 |
| Thrace ....... | 22 | D6 |
| Three Hummock | | |
| I. .......... | 62 | D3 |
| Three Points, C. | 55 | H4 |
| Thun ........ | 13 | C7 |
| Thunder Bay .. | 69 | D2 |
| Thung Song .. | 36 | C1 |
| Thunkar ...... | 41 | D8 |
| Thüringer Wald | 14 | C6 |
| Thurles ...... | 11 | E3 |
| Thurloo Downs | 63 | A3 |
| Thurso ....... | 10 | B5 |
| Thurston I. .... | 96 | B2 |
| Thylungra .... | 63 | A3 |
| Tia .......... | 63 | B5 |
| Tian Shan .... | 34 | B3 |
| Tianjin ....... | 35 | C6 |
| Tianshui ...... | 35 | C5 |
| Tiaret ........ | 54 | A5 |
| Tiassalé ...... | 55 | G4 |
| Tibati ........ | 53 | G1 |
| Tiber = | | |
| Tévere ➜ .. | 20 | D4 |
| Tiberias, L. = | | |
| Yam Kinneret | 46 | D3 |
| Tibesti ....... | 52 | D2 |
| Tibet = | | |
| Xizang □ ... | 34 | C3 |
| Tibooburra ... | 62 | A3 |
| Tiburón ...... | 84 | B2 |
| Tîchît ........ | 55 | E3 |
| Ticino ➜ ..... | 20 | B2 |
| Tiddim ....... | 41 | F9 |
| Tidjikja ....... | 55 | E2 |
| Tidore ........ | 39 | D3 |
| Tiel ......... | 55 | F1 |
| Tierra de | | |
| Campos .... | 18 | A3 |
| Tierra del | | |
| Fuego, I. Gr. | | |
| de ......... | 95 | G3 |
| Tiétar ➜ ..... | 18 | C2 |
| Tieyon ....... | 62 | A1 |
| Tiflis = Tbilisi . | 25 | E5 |
| Tifu ......... | 39 | E3 |
| Tighina ....... | 17 | E9 |
| Tignish ....... | 69 | D4 |
| Tigre ➜ ...... | 90 | D4 |
| Tigris = Dijlah, | | |
| Nahr ➜ .... | 47 | E6 |
| Tigyaing ...... | 41 | F11 |
| Tih, Gebel el . | 52 | C5 |
| Tijuana ...... | 84 | A1 |
| Tikamgarh .... | 43 | G11 |

# Tikhoretsk

| Name | Page | Grid |
|---|---|---|
| Tikhoretsk | 25 | D5 |
| Tikrīt | 46 | D5 |
| Tiksi | 30 | B10 |
| Tilamuta | 39 | D2 |
| Tilburg | 14 | C3 |
| Tillabéri | 55 | F5 |
| Tilos | 23 | F6 |
| Tilpa | 63 | B3 |
| Tilsit = Sovetsk | 24 | B1 |
| Timaru | 65 | F4 |
| Timbedgha | 55 | E3 |
| Timboon | 62 | C3 |
| Timbuktu = Tombouctou | 55 | E4 |
| Timimoun | 54 | C5 |
| Timișoara | 16 | F5 |
| Timmins | 69 | D2 |
| Timok → | 22 | B4 |
| Timon | 92 | D5 |
| Timor | 39 | F2 |
| Tinaca Pt. | 38 | C3 |
| Tindouf | 54 | C3 |
| Tingo Maria | 91 | E3 |
| Tinjoub | 54 | C3 |
| Tinnevelly = Tirunelveli | 43 | Q10 |
| Tinogasta | 94 | B3 |
| Tinos | 23 | F5 |
| Tintinara | 62 | C3 |
| Tioman, Pulau | 37 | D2 |
| Tipongpani | 41 | D10 |
| Tipperary | 11 | E2 |
| Tīrān | 44 | C2 |
| Tirana | 22 | D2 |
| Tiranë = Tirana | 22 | D2 |
| Tiraspol | 17 | E9 |
| Tire | 23 | E6 |
| Tirebolu | 46 | B4 |
| Tiree | 10 | C3 |
| Tîrgoviște | 22 | B5 |
| Tîrgu-Jiu | 17 | F6 |
| Tîrgu Mureș | 17 | E7 |
| Tirich Mir | 42 | A7 |
| Tîrnăveni | 17 | E7 |
| Tîrnavos | 23 | E4 |
| Tirodi | 43 | J11 |
| Tirol □ | 14 | E6 |
| Tirso → | 21 | E2 |
| Tiruchchirappalli | 43 | P11 |
| Tirunelveli | 43 | Q10 |
| Tirupati | 43 | N11 |
| Tiruppur | 43 | P10 |
| Tiruvannamalai | 43 | N11 |
| Tisa → | 22 | B3 |
| Tisdale | 71 | C9 |
| Tisza = Tisa → | 22 | B3 |
| Tit-Ary | 30 | B10 |
| Titicaca, L. | 91 | G5 |
| Titograd = Podgorica | 22 | C2 |
| Titov Veles | 22 | D3 |
| Titova-Mitrovica | 22 | C3 |
| Titovo Užice | 22 | C2 |
| Titule | 57 | D5 |
| Tivaouane | 55 | F1 |
| Tívoli | 20 | D4 |
| Tiwī | 45 | F4 |
| Tizi-Ouzou | 54 | A5 |
| Tiznit | 54 | C3 |
| Tjirebon = Cirebon | 37 | F3 |
| Tlaxcala | 84 | D5 |
| Tlaxiaco | 84 | D5 |
| Tlemcen | 54 | B4 |
| Tmassah | 52 | C2 |
| Toamasina | 59 | H9 |
| Toay | 94 | D4 |
| Toba | 32 | B5 |
| Toba Kakar | 42 | D6 |
| Tobago | 87 | D7 |
| Tobelo | 39 | D3 |
| Tobermory | 10 | C3 |
| Toboali | 37 | E3 |
| Tobol → | 29 | D7 |
| Toboli | 39 | E2 |
| Tobolsk | 29 | D7 |
| Tobruk = Tubruq | 52 | B3 |
| Tobyl = Tobol → | 29 | D7 |
| Tocantinópolis | 92 | D4 |
| Tocantins □ | 93 | E4 |
| Tocantins → | 92 | C4 |
| Tochigi | 32 | A6 |
| Tocopilla | 94 | A2 |
| Tocumwal | 63 | C4 |
| Tocuyo → | 90 | A5 |
| Todeli | 39 | E2 |
| Todenyang | 57 | D7 |
| Todos os Santos, B. de | 93 | E6 |
| Togba | 55 | E2 |
| Togian, Kepulauan | 39 | E2 |
| Togliatti | 24 | C6 |
| Togo ■ | 55 | G5 |
| Toinya | 53 | G4 |
| Tojikiston = Tajikistan ■ | 29 | F8 |
| Tojo | 39 | E2 |
| Tokala | 39 | E2 |
| Tōkamachi | 32 | A6 |
| Tokanui | 65 | G3 |
| Tokar | 53 | E6 |
| Tokarahi | 65 | F4 |
| Tokat | 46 | B4 |
| Tokelau Is. | 65 | K13 |
| Tokmak | 29 | E8 |
| Tokushima | 32 | B4 |
| Tokuyama | 32 | B2 |
| Tōkyō | 32 | B6 |
| Tolaga Bay | 64 | C8 |
| Tolbukhin = Dobrich | 22 | C6 |
| Toledo, Spain | 18 | C3 |
| Toledo, U.S.A. | 72 | D4 |
| Toledo, Montes de | 18 | C3 |
| Tolga | 54 | B6 |
| Toliara | 59 | J8 |
| Tolima | 90 | C3 |
| Tolitoli | 39 | D2 |
| Tolo | 56 | E3 |
| Tolo, Teluk | 39 | E2 |
| Toluca | 84 | D5 |
| Tomakomai | 32 | F12 |
| Tomar | 18 | C1 |
| Tomaszów Mazowiecki | 16 | C4 |
| Tombé | 53 | G5 |
| Tombouctou | 55 | E4 |
| Tombua | 58 | B2 |
| Tomelloso | 18 | C4 |
| Tomingley | 63 | B4 |
| Tomini | 39 | D2 |
| Tomini, Teluk | 39 | E2 |
| Tomorit | 23 | D3 |
| Tomsk | 29 | D9 |
| Tonantins | 90 | D5 |
| Tonawanda | 73 | C6 |
| Tondano | 39 | D2 |
| Tonekābon | 44 | B2 |
| Tong Xian | 35 | C6 |
| Tonga ■ | 65 | L13 |
| Tonga Trench | 65 | L13 |
| Tongareva | 65 | K15 |
| Tongchuan | 35 | C5 |
| Tonghua | 35 | B7 |
| Tongjiang | 35 | B8 |
| Tongking, G. of = Tonkin, G. of | 35 | D5 |
| Tongoy | 94 | C2 |
| Tongren | 35 | D5 |
| Tongsa Dzong | 41 | D8 |
| Tongue → | 76 | B2 |
| Tonk | 42 | F9 |
| Tonkin, G. of | 35 | D5 |
| Tonlé Sap | 36 | B2 |
| Toompine | 63 | A3 |
| Toora | 63 | C4 |
| Toowoomba | 63 | A5 |
| Topeka | 77 | F7 |
| Topki | 29 | D9 |
| Topol'čany | 16 | D4 |
| Topolobampo | 84 | B3 |
| Torata | 91 | G4 |
| Torbalı | 23 | E6 |
| Torbat-e Heydārīyeh | 44 | C4 |
| Torbat-e Jām | 45 | C5 |
| Torbay | 11 | F5 |
| Tordesillas | 18 | B3 |
| Torgau | 15 | C7 |
| Torino | 20 | B1 |
| Torit | 53 | H5 |
| Tormes → | 18 | B2 |
| Torne älv → | 8 | E12 |
| Torneå = Tornio | 8 | E12 |
| Torneträsk | 8 | E11 |
| Tornio | 8 | E12 |
| Tornquist | 94 | D4 |
| Toro, Cerro del | 94 | B3 |
| Toroníios Kólpos | 23 | D4 |
| Toronto, Australia | 63 | B5 |
| Toronto, Canada | 69 | D3 |
| Toropets | 24 | B3 |
| Tororo | 57 | D6 |
| Toros Dağları | 46 | C3 |
| Tôrre de Moncorvo | 18 | B2 |
| Torre del Greco | 21 | D5 |
| Torrejón de Ardoz | 18 | B4 |
| Torrelavega | 18 | A3 |
| Torremolinos | 18 | D3 |
| Torrens, L. | 62 | B2 |
| Torrente | 19 | C5 |
| Torreón | 84 | B4 |
| Torres | 84 | B2 |
| Torres Vedras | 18 | C1 |
| Torrevieja | 19 | D5 |
| Tortosa | 19 | B6 |
| Tortosa, C. de | 19 | B6 |
| Ţorūd | 44 | C3 |
| Toruń | 16 | B4 |
| Tosa-Wan | 32 | C3 |
| Toscana □ | 20 | C3 |
| Toshkent | 29 | E7 |
| Tostado | 94 | B4 |
| Tosya | 46 | B3 |
| Toteng | 58 | C4 |
| Totma | 24 | A5 |
| Totten Glacier | 96 | A12 |
| Tottenham | 63 | B4 |
| Tottori | 32 | B4 |
| Touba | 55 | G3 |
| Toubkal, Djebel | 54 | B3 |
| Tougan | 55 | F4 |
| Touggourt | 54 | B6 |
| Tougué | 55 | F2 |
| Toul | 13 | B6 |
| Toulepleu | 55 | G3 |
| Toulon | 13 | E6 |
| Toulouse | 12 | E4 |
| Toummo | 52 | D1 |
| Toungoo | 41 | H11 |
| Touraine | 12 | C4 |
| Tourane = Da Nang | 36 | A3 |
| Tourcoing | 13 | A5 |
| Touriñán, C. | 18 | A1 |
| Tournai | 14 | C2 |
| Tournon | 13 | D6 |
| Tours | 12 | C4 |
| Towamba | 63 | C4 |
| Towang | 41 | D8 |
| Townsville | 61 | D8 |
| Toyama | 32 | A5 |
| Toyohashi | 32 | B5 |
| Toyonaka | 32 | B4 |
| Toyooka | 32 | B4 |
| Toyota | 32 | B5 |
| Tozeur | 54 | B6 |
| Trá Li = Tralee | 11 | E2 |
| Trabzon | 46 | B4 |
| Trafalgar, C. | 18 | D2 |
| Trail | 71 | D8 |
| Tralee | 11 | E2 |
| Trancas | 94 | B3 |
| Trang | 36 | C1 |
| Trangan | 39 | F4 |
| Trangie | 63 | B4 |
| Trani | 20 | D6 |
| Transantarctic Mts. | 96 | C3 |
| Transilvania | 17 | F7 |
| Transilvanian Alps = Carpații Meridionali | 17 | F7 |
| Transylvania = Transilvania | 17 | F7 |
| Trápani | 21 | E4 |
| Traralgon | 63 | C4 |
| Trasimeno, L. | 20 | C4 |
| Traun | 15 | D8 |
| Travemünde | 15 | B6 |
| Travers, Mt. | 65 | E5 |
| Travnik | 20 | B6 |
| Trébbia → | 20 | B2 |
| Třebíč | 16 | D2 |
| Trebinje | 20 | C7 |
| Treinta y Tres | 94 | C6 |
| Trelew | 95 | E3 |
| Tremp | 19 | A6 |
| Trenčín | 16 | D4 |
| Trenque Lauquen | 94 | D4 |
| Trent → | 11 | E6 |
| Trento | 20 | A3 |
| Trenton | 73 | D8 |
| Trepassey | 69 | D5 |
| Tres Arroyos | 94 | D4 |
| Três Corações | 93 | G4 |
| Três Lagoas | 93 | G3 |
| Tres Montes, C. | 95 | F1 |
| Tres Puentes | 94 | B2 |
| Tres Puntas, C. | 95 | F3 |
| Três Rios | 93 | G5 |
| Treviso | 20 | B4 |
| Triabunna | 62 | D4 |
| Trichinopoly = Tiruchchirappalli | 43 | P11 |
| Trichur | 43 | P10 |
| Trida | 63 | B4 |
| Trier | 14 | D4 |
| Trieste | 20 | B4 |
| Triglav | 20 | A4 |
| Tríkkala | 23 | E3 |
| Trikora, Puncak | 39 | E5 |
| Trinidad, Bolivia | 91 | F6 |
| Trinidad, Colombia | 90 | B4 |

Trinidad, *Cuba* 86 B3
Trinidad,
　*Uruguay* .... 94 C5
Trinidad, *U.S.A.* 78 A1
Trinidad, I. .... 95 D4
Trinidad &
　Tobago ■ ... 87 D7
Trinity → .... 79 E6
Trinity B. ..... 69 D5
Trinity Range .. 80 E4
Trinkitat ...... 53 E6
Tripoli =
　Tarābulus,
　*Lebanon* .... 46 D3
Tripoli =
　Tarābulus,
　*Libya* ....... 52 B1
Trípolis ....... 23 F4
Tripura □ ..... 41 F8
Trivandrum ... 43 Q10
Trnava ....... 16 D3
Troglav ....... 20 C6
Trois-Rivières . 69 D3
Troitsko
　Pechorsk .... 28 C6
Trollhättan .... 9 G10
Tronador ..... 95 E2
Trondheim .. 8 F10
Trondheimsfjorden
　.......... 8 F10
Trout L. ..... 70 B7
Trouville-sur-
　Mer ........ 12 B4
Troy, *Turkey* .. 23 E6
Troy, *Ala.,*
　*U.S.A.* ...... 74 D5
Troy, *N.Y.,*
　*U.S.A.* ...... 73 C9
Troyes ....... 13 B6
Trucial States =
　United Arab
　Emirates ■ .. 44 F3
Trujillo,
　*Honduras* ... 85 D7
Trujillo, *Peru* .. 91 E3
Trujillo, *Spain* . 18 C3
Trujillo,
　*Venezuela* ... 90 B4
Truk ......... 64 J10
Trundle ...... 63 B4
Truro, *Canada* . 69 D4
Truro, *U.K.* .... 11 F4
Truskavets .... 17 D6
Trutnov ...... 16 C2
Tsaratanana .. 59 H9
Tsarevo =
　Michurin .... 22 C6
Tsau ......... 58 C4
Tselinograd =
　Aqmola ..... 29 D8
Tsetserleg .... 34 B5
Tshabong .... 58 D4
Tshane ....... 58 C4
Tshela ....... 56 E2
Tshikapa ..... 56 F4
Tshofa ....... 57 F5
Tshwane ..... 58 C4
Tsihombe ..... 59 K9
Tsimlyansk Res.
　=
Tsimlyanskoye
　Vdkhr. ...... 25 D5
Tsimlyanskoye
　Vdkhr. ...... 25 D5
Tsinan = Jinan 35 C6
Tsinghai =
　Qinghai □ .. 34 C4
Tsingtao =
　Qingdao .... 35 C7

Tskhinvali .... 25 E5
Tsna → ...... 24 C5
Tsu ......... 32 B5
Tsuchiura .... 32 A7
Tsugaru-Kaikyō 32 F12
Tsumeb ...... 58 B3
Tsumis ....... 58 C3
Tsuruga ..... 32 B5
Tsurugi-San .. 32 C4
Tsuruoka .... 33 G11
Tsyelyakhany . 17 B7
Tual ......... 39 F4
Tuamotu Arch.
　= Tuamotu Is. 65 L16
Tuamotu Is. ... 65 L16
Tuamotu Ridge 65 M17
Tuao ......... 38 A2
Tuapse ...... 25 E4
Tuatapere .... 65 G2
Tubarão ..... 94 B7
Tubau ....... 37 D4
Tübingen .... 14 D5
Tubruq ...... 52 B3
Tubuai Is. .... 65 M16
Tucacas ..... 90 A5
Tucson ...... 83 D7
Tucumcari ... 78 B2
Tucupita ..... 90 B6
Tucuruí ...... 92 C4
Tucuruí, Reprêsa
　de ......... 92 C4
Tudela ....... 19 A5
Tudmur ...... 46 D4
Tuen ......... 63 A4
Tuguegarao ... 38 A2
Tukangbesi,
　Kepulauan .. 39 F2
Tükrah ...... 52 B3
Tuktoyaktuk .. 70 B6
Tukuyu ...... 57 F6
Tula, *Mexico* .. 84 C5
Tula, *Russia* .. 24 C4
Tulak ....... 45 C5
Tulancingo ... 84 C5
Tulare ....... 82 B3
Tulcán ...... 90 C3
Tulcea ....... 17 F9
Tulchyn ...... 17 D9
Tuli, *Indonesia* 39 E2
Tuli, *Zimbabwe* 59 C5
Tullamore,
　*Australia* .... 63 B4
Tullamore,
　*Ireland* ..... 11 E3
Tulle ......... 12 D4
Tullibigeal .... 63 B4
Tulmaythah ... 52 B3
Tulsa ........ 79 A6
Tulua ........ 90 C3
Tulungagung .. 37 F4
Tum ......... 39 E4
Tumaco ...... 90 C3
Tumatumari .. 90 B7
Tumba, L. .... 56 E3
Tumbarumba . 63 C4
Túmbes ...... 90 D2
Tumby Bay ... 62 B2
Tumeremo ... 90 B6
Tumkur ...... 43 N10
Tump ........ 42 F3
Tumpat ...... 36 C2
Tumu ........ 55 F4
Tumucumaque,
　Serra ...... 92 B3
Tumut ....... 63 C4
Tuncurry ..... 63 B5
Tunduru ..... 57 G7
Tundzha → ... 22 D6
Tunga Pass .. 41 C10

Tungabhadra →
　.......... 43 M11
Tungaru ..... 53 F5
Tunguska,
　Nizhnyaya → 30 C6
Tunis ........ 54 A7
Tunisia ■ .... 54 B6
Tunja ........ 90 B4
Tunuyán → .. 94 C3
Tunxi ........ 35 D6
Tupelo ....... 74 B3
Tupinambaranas 90 D7
Tupiza ....... 94 A3
Tupungato,
　Cerro ...... 94 C3
Túquerres .... 90 C3
Tura ......... 30 C8
Turabah ..... 47 E5
Tūrān ....... 44 C4
Turayf ....... 47 E4
Turda ........ 17 E6
Turek ........ 16 B4
Turfan = Turpan 34 B3
Turfan
　Depression =
　Turpan Hami 34 B3
Tŭrgovishte ... 22 C6
Turgutlu ..... 23 E6
Turhal ....... 46 B4
Turia → ..... 19 C5
Turiaçu ...... 92 C4
Turiaçu → ... 92 C4
Turin = Torino 20 B1
Turkana, L. ... 57 D7
Turkestan =
　Türkistan ... 29 E7
Turkey ■ ..... 46 C3
Türkistan .... 29 E7
Turkmenistan ■ 29 F6
Turks & Caicos
　Is. ■ ....... 87 B5
Turku ........ 9 F12
Turnagain, C. .. 64 D7
Turneffe Is. ... 85 D7
Turnhout .... 14 C3
Tŭrnovo =
　Veliko
　Tŭrnovo .... 22 C5
Turnu Măgurele 22 C5
Turnu Roşu, P. 17 F7
Turpan ...... 34 B3
Turpan Hami .. 34 B3
Turukhansk .. 30 C6
Tuscaloosa ... 74 C4
Tuscany =
　Toscana □ .. 20 C3
Tuticorin .... 43 Q11
Tutóia ....... 92 C5
Tutong ....... 36 D4
Tutrakan ..... 22 B6
Tuttlingen .... 14 E5
Tutuala ...... 39 F3
Tutuila ...... 65 L13
Tuvalu ■ ..... 64 K12
Tuxpan ...... 84 C5
Tuxtla Gutiérrez 85 D6
Tuy ......... 18 A1
Tuz Gölü .... 46 C3
Ṭūz Khurmātū . 46 D6
Tuzla ........ 20 B7
Tver ......... 24 B4
Tweed Heads . 63 A5
Twillingate ... 69 D5
Twin Falls ... 81 D6
Twofold B. .... 63 C4
Tyachiv ...... 17 D6
Tychy ........ 16 C4
Tyler ........ 79 C6
Tyre = Sür .... 46 D3

Tyrol = Tirol □ 14 E6
Tyrrell → .... 62 C3
Tyrrell, L. .... 62 C3
Tyrrhenian Sea 21 E4
Tyumen ...... 29 D7
Tzaneen ..... 59 C6
Tzukong =
　Zigong ..... 35 D5

# U

U.S.A. = United
　States of
　America ■ .. 67 F10
Uarsciek ..... 49 G4
Uato-Udo .... 39 F3
Uatumã → ... 90 D7
Uaupés ...... 90 D5
Uaupés → ... 90 C5
Ubá ......... 93 G5
Ubaitaba ..... 93 E6
Ubangi =
　Oubangi → . 56 E3
Ubauro ...... 42 E6
Ube ......... 32 C2
Ubeda ....... 18 C4
Uberaba ..... 93 F4
Uberlândia .. 93 F4
Ubon
　Ratchathani . 36 A2
Ubort → ..... 17 B9
Ubundu ...... 57 E5
Ucayali → ... 90 D4
Uchiura-Wan .. 32 F12
Udaipur ..... 43 G8
Udaipur Garhi . 40 D6
Udgir ........ 43 K10
Udhampur ... 42 C9
Udi ......... 55 G6
Údine ........ 20 A4
Udmurtia □ .. 28 D6
Udon Thani .. 36 A2
Udupi ....... 43 N9
Ueda ........ 32 A6
Uele → ...... 57 D4
Uelzen ...... 14 B6
Ufa ......... 29 D6
Ugab → ..... 58 C2
Ugalla → ..... 57 F6
Uganda ■ ... 57 D6
Ugljane ...... 20 B5
Ugolyak ..... 30 C10
Uibhist a Deas
　= South Uist 10 C3
Uibhist a Tuath
　= North Uist 10 C3
Uíge ........ 56 F2
Uinta Mts. .... 81 E8
Uitenhage .... 59 E5
Ujjain ....... 43 H9
Ujung Pandang 39 F1
Ukerewe I. ... 57 E6
Ukhrul ...... 41 E10
Ukhta ....... 28 C6
Ukraine ■ .... 25 D3
Ulaanbaatar .. 35 B5
Ulan Bator =
　Ulaanbaatar . 35 B5
Ulan Ude .... 30 D8
Ulcinj ....... 22 D2
Ulhasnagar ... 43 K8
Ulladulla ..... 63 C5
Ullapool ..... 10 C4
Ulm ......... 14 D5
Ulmarra ...... 63 A5

| | | |
|---|---|---|
| Ulonguè | 59 | A6 |
| Ulster □ | 11 | D3 |
| Ulubat Gölü | 23 | D7 |
| Uludağ | 23 | D7 |
| Ulungur He ⇢ | 34 | B3 |
| Uluru = Ayers | | |
| Rock | 60 | F5 |
| Ulutau | 29 | E7 |
| Ulverstone | 62 | D4 |
| Ulyanovsk = | | |
| Simbirsk | 24 | C6 |
| Ulyasutay | 34 | B4 |
| Umala | 91 | G5 |
| Uman | 17 | D10 |
| Umaria | 40 | F3 |
| Umarkot | 43 | G6 |
| Umba | 28 | C4 |
| Umbrella Mts. | 65 | F3 |
| Ume älv ⇢ | 8 | F12 |
| Umeå | 8 | F12 |
| Umera | 39 | E3 |
| Umm al | | |
| Qaywayn | 44 | E3 |
| Umm Bel | 53 | F4 |
| Umm Lajj | 47 | F4 |
| Umm Ruwaba | 53 | F5 |
| Umnak I. | 71 | C3 |
| Umniati ⇢ | 59 | B5 |
| Umtata | 59 | E5 |
| Umuarama | 93 | G3 |
| Una ⇢ | 20 | B6 |
| Unalaska | 71 | C3 |
| Uncía | 91 | G5 |
| Underbool | 62 | C3 |
| Ungarie | 63 | B4 |
| Ungarra | 62 | B2 |
| Ungava B. | 68 | C4 |
| Ungava Pen. | 68 | B3 |
| Ungeny = | | |
| Ungheni | 17 | E8 |
| Ungheni | 17 | E8 |
| União da Vitória | 94 | B6 |
| Unimak I. | 71 | C3 |
| United Arab | | |
| Emirates ■ | 44 | F3 |
| United | | |
| Kingdom ■ | 11 | E5 |
| United States of | | |
| America ■ | 67 | F10 |
| Unnao | 40 | D3 |
| Unst | 10 | A6 |
| Ünye | 46 | B4 |
| Upata | 90 | B6 |
| Upemba, L. | 57 | F5 |
| Upington | 58 | D4 |
| Upper Hutt | 65 | D6 |
| Upper Volta = | | |
| Burkina | | |
| Faso ■ | 55 | F4 |
| Uppsala | 9 | G11 |
| Ur | 47 | E6 |
| Uracara | 90 | D7 |
| Ural = | | |
| Zhayyq ⇢ | 29 | E6 |
| Ural | 63 | B4 |
| Ural Mts. = | | |
| Uralskie Gory | 28 | D6 |
| Uralla | 63 | B5 |
| Uralsk = Oral | 24 | C7 |
| Uralskie Gory | 28 | D6 |
| Uranquinty | 63 | C4 |
| Urawa | 32 | B6 |
| Uray | 29 | C7 |
| Urbana | 72 | D1 |
| Urbino | 20 | C4 |
| Urbión, Picos de | 19 | A4 |
| Urcos | 91 | F4 |
| Urda | 25 | D6 |
| Urdzhar | 29 | E9 |
| Ures | 84 | B2 |
| Urfa = Sanliurfa | 46 | C4 |
| Urganch | 29 | E7 |
| Urgench = | | |
| Urganch | 29 | E7 |
| Uribia | 90 | A4 |
| Urla | 23 | E6 |
| Urmia = | | |
| Orūmīyeh | 46 | C6 |
| Urmia, L. = | | |
| Orūmīyeh, | | |
| Daryācheh-ye | 46 | C6 |
| Uroševac | 22 | C3 |
| Uruana | 93 | F4 |
| Urubamba | 91 | F4 |
| Urubamba ⇢ | 91 | F4 |
| Uruçuí | 92 | D5 |
| Uruguai ⇢ | 94 | B6 |
| Uruguaiana | 94 | B5 |
| Uruguay ■ | 94 | C5 |
| Uruguay ⇢ | 94 | C5 |
| Urumchi = | | |
| Ürümqi | 34 | B3 |
| Ürümqi | 34 | B3 |
| Usakos | 58 | C3 |
| Usedom | 15 | B8 |
| Ush-Tobe | 29 | E8 |
| Ushant = | | |
| Ouessant, I. d' | 12 | B1 |
| Ushuaia | 95 | G3 |
| Üsküdar | 25 | E2 |
| Usman | 24 | C4 |
| Usoke | 57 | F6 |
| Uspallata, P. de | 94 | C3 |
| Uspenskiy | 29 | E8 |
| Ussuriysk | 31 | E11 |
| Ust-Aldan = | | |
| Batamay | 31 | C10 |
| Ust Ilimpeya = | | |
| Yukti | 30 | C8 |
| Ust Ishim | 29 | D8 |
| Ust- | | |
| Kamenogorsk | | |
| = Öskemen | 29 | E9 |
| Ust-Karenga | 31 | D9 |
| Ust Kuyga | 31 | B11 |
| Ust Muya | 30 | D9 |
| Ust Olenek | 30 | B10 |
| Ust Port | 28 | C9 |
| Ust Tsilma | 28 | C6 |
| Ust Urt = | | |
| Ustyurt, | | |
| Plateau | 29 | E6 |
| Ust Vorkuta | 28 | C7 |
| Ústí nad Labem | 16 | C2 |
| Ustica | 21 | E4 |
| Ustinov = | | |
| Izhevsk | 28 | D6 |
| Ustye | 30 | D7 |
| Ustyurt, Plateau | 29 | E6 |
| Usu | 34 | B3 |
| Usuki | 32 | C2 |
| Usumacinta ⇢ | 85 | D6 |
| Usumbura = | | |
| Bujumbura | 57 | E5 |
| Uta | 39 | E5 |
| Utah □ | 81 | F8 |
| Utete | 57 | F7 |
| Utiariti | 91 | F7 |
| Utica | 73 | C8 |
| Utrecht | 14 | B3 |
| Utrera | 18 | D3 |
| Utsunomiya | 32 | A6 |
| Uttar Pradesh □ | 42 | F11 |
| Uttaradit | 36 | A2 |
| Uummannarsuaq | | |
| = Farvel, Kap | 68 | C6 |
| Uusikaupunki | 8 | F12 |
| Uvat | 29 | D7 |
| Uvinza | 57 | F6 |
| Uvira | 57 | E5 |
| Uvs Nuur | 34 | A4 |
| Uwajima | 32 | C3 |
| Uyuni | 91 | H5 |
| Uzbekistan ■ | 29 | E7 |
| Uzerche | 12 | D4 |
| Uzh ⇢ | 17 | C10 |
| Uzhgorod = | | |
| Uzhhorod | 17 | D6 |
| Uzhhorod | 17 | D6 |
| Uzunköprü | 22 | D6 |

**V**

| | | |
|---|---|---|
| Vaal ⇢ | 58 | D4 |
| Vaasa | 8 | F12 |
| Vác | 16 | E4 |
| Vach ⇢ = | | |
| Vakh ⇢ | 29 | C8 |
| Vadodara | 43 | H8 |
| Vadsø | 8 | D13 |
| Vaduz | 13 | C8 |
| Váh ⇢ | 16 | E4 |
| Vahsel B. | 96 | B5 |
| Vaigach | 28 | B6 |
| Vakh ⇢ | 29 | C8 |
| Val d'Or | 69 | D3 |
| Valahia | 22 | B5 |
| Valandovo | 22 | D4 |
| Valcheta | 95 | E3 |
| Valdayskaya | | |
| Vozvyshennost | | |
| | 24 | B3 |
| Valdepeñas | 18 | C4 |
| Valdés, Pen. | 95 | E4 |
| Valdez | 71 | B5 |
| Valdivia | 95 | D2 |
| Valdosta | 75 | D6 |
| Valença | 93 | E6 |
| Valença do Piauí | 92 | D5 |
| Valence | 13 | D6 |
| Valencia, Spain | 19 | C5 |
| Valencia, | | |
| Venezuela | 90 | A5 |
| Valencia □ | 19 | C5 |
| Valencia, G. de | 19 | C6 |
| Valencia de | | |
| Alcántara | 18 | C2 |
| Valencia I. | 11 | F1 |
| Valenciennes | 13 | A5 |
| Valentim, Sa. do | 92 | D5 |
| Valera | 90 | B4 |
| Valjevo | 22 | B2 |
| Vall de Uxó | 19 | C5 |
| Valladolid, | | |
| Mexico | 85 | C7 |
| Valladolid, Spain | 18 | B3 |
| Valle de la | | |
| Pascua | 90 | B5 |
| Valledupar | 90 | A4 |
| Vallejo | 80 | F2 |
| Vallenar | 94 | B2 |
| Valletta | 21 | G5 |
| Valls | 19 | B6 |
| Valognes | 12 | B3 |
| Valona = Vlóra | 23 | D7 |
| Valozhyn | 17 | A8 |
| Valparaíso | 94 | C2 |
| Vals, Tanjung | 39 | F5 |
| Valsad | 43 | J8 |
| Valverde del | | |
| Camino | 18 | D2 |
| Van | 46 | C5 |
| Van, L. = Van | | |
| Gölü | 46 | C5 |
| Van Gölü | 46 | C5 |
| Van Rees, | | |
| Pegunungan | 39 | E5 |
| Vanadzor | 25 | E5 |
| Vancouver, | | |
| Canada | 71 | D7 |
| Vancouver, | | |
| U.S.A. | 80 | C2 |
| Vancouver I. | 71 | D7 |
| Vänern | 9 | G10 |
| Vanga | 57 | E7 |
| Vangaindrano | 59 | J9 |
| Vännäs | 8 | F11 |
| Vannes | 12 | C2 |
| Vanrhynsdorp | 58 | E3 |
| Vanua Levu | 64 | L12 |
| Vanuatu ■ | 64 | L11 |
| Vapnyarka | 17 | D9 |
| Varanasi | 40 | E4 |
| Varangerfjorden | 8 | D13 |
| Varaždin | 20 | A6 |
| Varberg | 9 | G10 |
| Vardak □ | 45 | C7 |
| Vardar = | | |
| Axiós ⇢ | 23 | D4 |
| Varese | 20 | B2 |
| Varna | 22 | C6 |
| Varzaneh | 44 | C3 |
| Vasa Barris ⇢ | 93 | E6 |
| Vascongadas = | | |
| País Vasco □ | 19 | A4 |
| Vasht = Khāsh | 42 | E2 |
| Vasilevichi | 17 | B9 |
| Vasilkov = | | |
| Vasylkiv | 17 | C10 |
| Vaslui | 17 | E8 |
| Västerås | 9 | G11 |
| Västervik | 9 | G11 |
| Vasto | 20 | C5 |
| Vasylkiv | 17 | C10 |
| Vatican City ■ | 20 | D4 |
| Vatomandry | 59 | H9 |
| Vatra-Dornei | 17 | E7 |
| Vättern | 9 | G10 |
| Vaupés = | | |
| Uaupés ⇢ | 90 | C5 |
| Vawkavysk | 17 | B7 |
| Vaygach, Ostrov | 28 | C6 |
| Vedea ⇢ | 22 | C5 |
| Vega | 8 | E10 |
| Vegreville | 71 | C8 |
| Vejer de la | | |
| Frontera | 18 | D3 |
| Velebit Planina | 20 | B5 |
| Vélez | 90 | B4 |
| Vélez Málaga | 18 | D3 |
| Vélez Rubio | 19 | D4 |
| Velhas ⇢ | 93 | F5 |
| Velika Kapela | 20 | B5 |
| Velikaya ⇢ | 24 | B2 |
| Veliki Ustyug | 24 | A6 |
| Velikiye Luki | 24 | B3 |
| Veliko Tŭrnovo | 22 | C5 |
| Velikonda Range | 43 | M11 |
| Velletri | 20 | D4 |
| Vellore | 43 | N11 |
| Venado Tuerto | 94 | C4 |
| Vendée □ | 12 | C3 |
| Vendôme | 12 | C4 |
| Venézia | 20 | B4 |
| Venézia, G. di | 20 | B4 |
| Venezuela ■ | 90 | B5 |
| Venezuela, G. de | 90 | A4 |
| Vengurla | 43 | M8 |
| Venice = | | |
| Venézia | 20 | B4 |
| Venkatapuram | 40 | H3 |
| Ventotene | 21 | D4 |
| Ventoux, Mt. | 13 | D6 |

| | | |
|---|---|---|
| Ventspils | 24 | B1 |
| Ventuarí ⟶ | 90 | C5 |
| Ventura | 82 | C3 |
| Venus B. | 63 | C4 |
| Vera, *Argentina* | 94 | B4 |
| Vera, *Spain* | 19 | D5 |
| Veracruz | 84 | D5 |
| Veraval | 43 | J7 |
| Verbánia | 20 | B2 |
| Vercelli | 20 | B2 |
| Verde ⟶ | 95 | E3 |
| Verden | 14 | B5 |
| Verdun | 13 | B6 |
| Vereeniging | 59 | D5 |
| Verga, C. | 55 | F2 |
| Verín | 18 | B2 |
| Verkhnevilyuysk | 30 | C10 |
| Verkhniy Baskunchak | 25 | D6 |
| Verkhoyansk | 31 | C11 |
| Verkhoyansk Ra. = Verkhoyanskiy Khrebet | 31 | C10 |
| Verkhoyanskiy Khrebet | 31 | C10 |
| Vermilion | 71 | C8 |
| Vermont □ | 73 | C9 |
| Vernon, *Canada* | 71 | C8 |
| Vernon, *U.S.A.* | 78 | B4 |
| Véroia | 23 | D4 |
| Verona | 20 | B3 |
| Versailles | 12 | B5 |
| Vert, C. | 55 | F1 |
| Verviers | 14 | C3 |
| Veselovskoye Vdkhr. | 25 | D5 |
| Vesoul | 13 | C7 |
| Vesterålen | 8 | E11 |
| Vestfjorden | 8 | E10 |
| Vesuvio | 21 | D5 |
| Vesuvius, Mt. = Vesuvio | 21 | D5 |
| Veszprém | 16 | E3 |
| Vetlugu ⟶ | 28 | D5 |
| Vettore, Mte. | 20 | C4 |
| Veys | 47 | E7 |
| Vezhen | 22 | C5 |
| Viacha | 91 | G5 |
| Viamão | 94 | C6 |
| Viana | 92 | C5 |
| Viana do Alentejo | 18 | C2 |
| Viana do Castelo | 18 | B1 |
| Vianópolis | 93 | F4 |
| Viaréggio | 20 | C3 |
| Vibo Valéntia | 21 | E6 |
| Vicenza | 20 | B3 |
| Vich | 19 | B7 |
| Vichy | 13 | C5 |
| Vicksburg | 79 | C8 |
| Viçosa | 93 | D6 |
| Victor | 43 | J7 |
| Victor Harbor | 62 | C2 |
| Victoria, *Canada* | 71 | D7 |
| Victoria, *Chile* | 94 | D2 |
| Victoria, *Guinea* | 55 | F2 |
| Victoria, *Malaysia* | 36 | C5 |
| Victoria □ | 62 | C3 |
| Victoria, L., *Africa* | 57 | E6 |
| Victoria, L., *Australia* | 62 | B3 |
| Victoria Beach | 71 | C10 |
| Victoria de Durango | 84 | C4 |
| Victoria Falls | 59 | B5 |
| Victoria I. | 70 | A8 |
| Victoria Ld. | 96 | B14 |
| Victoria Taungdeik | 41 | G9 |
| Victoria West | 58 | E4 |
| Victorica | 94 | D3 |
| Vicuña | 94 | C2 |
| Vidin | 22 | C4 |
| Vidisha | 43 | H10 |
| Viedma | 95 | E4 |
| Viedma, L. | 95 | F2 |
| Vienna = Wien | 15 | D9 |
| Vienne | 13 | D6 |
| Vienne ⟶ | 12 | C4 |
| Vientiane | 36 | A2 |
| Vierzon | 12 | C5 |
| Vietnam ■ | 36 | A3 |
| Vigan | 38 | A2 |
| Vigévano | 20 | B2 |
| Vigia | 92 | C4 |
| Vigo | 18 | A1 |
| Vijayawada | 40 | J3 |
| Vikeke | 39 | F3 |
| Vikna | 8 | F10 |
| Vila da Maganja | 59 | B7 |
| Vila de João Belo = Xai-Xai | 59 | D6 |
| Vila do Bispo | 18 | D1 |
| Vila Franca de Xira | 18 | C1 |
| Vila Machado | 59 | B6 |
| Vila Nova de Gaia | 18 | B1 |
| Vila Real | 18 | B2 |
| Vila Real de Santo António | 18 | D2 |
| Vila Velha | 93 | G5 |
| Vilaine ⟶ | 12 | C2 |
| Vilanculos | 59 | C7 |
| Vileyka | 17 | A8 |
| Vilhelmina | 8 | F11 |
| Vilhena | 91 | F6 |
| Vilkitskogo, Proliv | 30 | B8 |
| Vilkovo = Vylkove | 17 | F9 |
| Villa Ahumada | 84 | A3 |
| Villa Ángela | 94 | B4 |
| Villa Bella | 91 | F5 |
| Villa Bens = Tarfaya | 54 | C2 |
| Villa Colón | 94 | C3 |
| Villa de María | 94 | B4 |
| Villa Dolores | 94 | C3 |
| Villa Hayes | 94 | B5 |
| Villa María | 94 | C4 |
| Villa Mazán | 94 | B3 |
| Villa Montes | 94 | A4 |
| Villa Ocampo | 94 | B5 |
| Villacarrillo | 18 | C4 |
| Villach | 15 | E7 |
| Villagarcía de Arosa | 18 | A1 |
| Villaguay | 94 | C5 |
| Villahermosa | 85 | D6 |
| Villajoyosa | 19 | C5 |
| Villalba | 18 | A2 |
| Villanueva de la Serena | 18 | C3 |
| Villanueva y Geltrú | 19 | B6 |
| Villarreal | 19 | C5 |
| Villarrica, *Chile* | 95 | D2 |
| Villarrica, *Paraguay* | 94 | B5 |
| Villarrobledo | 19 | C4 |
| Villavicencio | 90 | C4 |
| Villaviciosa | 18 | A3 |
| Villazón | 94 | A3 |
| Villena | 19 | C5 |
| Villeneuve-d'Ascq | 13 | A5 |
| Villeneuve-sur-Lot | 12 | D4 |
| Villingen-Schwenningen | 14 | D5 |
| Vilnius | 24 | C2 |
| Vilyuy ⟶ | 31 | C10 |
| Vilyuysk | 31 | C10 |
| Viña del Mar | 94 | C2 |
| Vinaroz | 19 | B6 |
| Vindhya Ra. | 43 | H10 |
| Vineland | 73 | E8 |
| Vinkovci | 20 | B7 |
| Vinnitsa = Vinnytsya | 17 | D9 |
| Vinnytsya | 17 | D9 |
| Virac | 38 | B2 |
| Viramgam | 43 | H8 |
| Viranşehir | 46 | C4 |
| Virden | 71 | D9 |
| Vire | 12 | B3 |
| Vírgenes, C. | 95 | G3 |
| Virgin Is. (British) ■ | 87 | C7 |
| Virginia □ | 73 | F6 |
| Virginia Beach | 73 | F8 |
| Virovitica | 20 | B6 |
| Virudunagar | 43 | Q10 |
| Vis | 20 | C6 |
| Visalia | 82 | B3 |
| Visayan Sea | 38 | B2 |
| Visby | 9 | G11 |
| Višegrad | 20 | C7 |
| Viseu, *Brazil* | 92 | C4 |
| Viseu, *Portugal* | 18 | B2 |
| Vishakhapatnam | 40 | J4 |
| Viso, Mte. | 20 | B1 |
| Vistula = Wisła ⟶ | 16 | A4 |
| Vitebsk = Vitsyebsk | 24 | B3 |
| Viterbo | 20 | C4 |
| Viti Levu | 64 | L12 |
| Vitigudino | 18 | B2 |
| Vitória, *Brazil* | 93 | G5 |
| Vitoria, *Spain* | 19 | A4 |
| Vitória da Conquista | 93 | E5 |
| Vitsyebsk | 24 | B3 |
| Vittória | 21 | F5 |
| Vittório Véneto | 20 | B4 |
| Vivero | 18 | A2 |
| Vize | 22 | D6 |
| Vizianagaram | 40 | H4 |
| Vjosa ⟶ | 23 | D2 |
| Vladikavkaz | 25 | E5 |
| Vladimir | 24 | B5 |
| Vladimir Volynskiy = Volodymyr-Volynskyy | 17 | C7 |
| Vladivostok | 31 | E11 |
| Vlissingen | 14 | C2 |
| Vlóra | 23 | D2 |
| Vltava ⟶ | 16 | C2 |
| Vogelsberg | 14 | C5 |
| Voghera | 20 | B2 |
| Vohibinany | 59 | H9 |
| Vohimarina | 59 | G10 |
| Vohimena, Tanjon' i | 59 | K9 |
| Vohipeno | 59 | J9 |
| Voi | 57 | E7 |
| Voiron | 13 | D6 |
| Vojvodina □ | 22 | B2 |
| Volga ⟶ | 25 | D6 |
| Volga Hts. = Privolzhskaya Vozvyshennost | 24 | C6 |
| Volgodonsk | 25 | D5 |
| Volgograd | 25 | D5 |
| Volgogradskoye Vdkhr. | 24 | C6 |
| Volkhov ⟶ | 24 | A3 |
| Volkovysk = Vawkavysk | 17 | B7 |
| Volochanka | 30 | B7 |
| Volodymyr-Volynskyy | 17 | C7 |
| Vologda | 24 | B4 |
| Vólos | 23 | E4 |
| Volovets | 17 | D6 |
| Volozhin = Valozhyn | 17 | A8 |
| Volsk | 24 | C6 |
| Volta ⟶ | 55 | G5 |
| Volta, L. | 55 | G5 |
| Volta Redonda | 93 | G5 |
| Volterra | 20 | C3 |
| Volturno ⟶ | 20 | D4 |
| Volzhskiy | 25 | D5 |
| Voríai Sporádhes | 23 | E4 |
| Vorkuta | 28 | C7 |
| Voronezh | 24 | C4 |
| Voroshilovgrad = Luhansk | 25 | D4 |
| Voroshilovsk = Alchevsk | 25 | D4 |
| Vosges | 13 | B7 |
| Vostok I. | 65 | L15 |
| Vouga ⟶ | 18 | B1 |
| Voznesensk | 25 | D3 |
| Voznesenye = | 28 | C4 |
| Vrangelya, Ostrov | 31 | B15 |
| Vranje | 22 | C3 |
| Vratsa | 22 | C4 |
| Vrbas ⟶ | 20 | B6 |
| Vrede | 59 | D5 |
| Vredenburg | 58 | E3 |
| Vršac | 22 | B3 |
| Vryburg | 58 | D4 |
| Vryheid | 59 | D6 |
| Vukovar | 20 | B7 |
| Vulcan | 17 | F6 |
| Vulcaneşti | 17 | F9 |
| Vulcano | 21 | E5 |
| Vulkaneshty = Vulcaneşti | 17 | F9 |
| Vung Tau | 36 | B3 |
| Vyatka = Kirov | 28 | D5 |
| Vyatskiye Polyany | 24 | B7 |
| Vyazma | 24 | B3 |
| Vyborg | 28 | C3 |
| Vychegda ⟶ | 28 | C5 |
| Vychodné Beskydy | 17 | D5 |
| Vylkove | 17 | F9 |
| Vynohradiv | 17 | D6 |
| Vyshniy Volochek | 24 | B3 |
| Vyškov | 16 | D3 |

**W**

| | | |
|---|---|---|
| Wa | 55 | F4 |
| Waal ⟶ | 14 | C3 |
| Wabash ⟶ | 72 | F1 |
| Waco | 78 | D5 |
| Wad Banda | 53 | F4 |
| Wad Hamid | 53 | E5 |
| Wâd Medanî | 53 | F5 |
| Waddington, Mt. | 71 | C7 |

Waddy Pt. .... 63 A5
Wadi Halfa .... 52 D5
Wafrah ....... 47 E6
Wager B. ..... 68 B2
Wager Bay .... 68 B1
Wagga Wagga 63 C4
Waghete ..... 39 E5
Wah ......... 42 C8
Wahai ....... 39 E3
Waiau ~→ .... 65 E5
Waibeem ..... 39 E4
Waigeo ....... 39 E4
Waihi ....... 64 B6
Waihou ~→ ... 64 B6
Waikabubak ... 39 F1
Waikari ...... 65 E5
Waikato ~→ .. 64 B6
Waikerie ..... 62 B2
Waikokopu ... 64 C7
Waikouaiti ... 65 F4
Waimakariri ~→ 65 E5
Waimate ..... 65 F4
Wainganga ~→ 43 K11
Waingapu ... 39 F2
Wainwright,
  Canada ..... 71 C8
Wainwright,
  U.S.A. ...... 71 A3
Waiouru ...... 64 C6
Waipara ..... 65 E5
Waipawa ..... 64 C7
Waipiro ...... 64 C8
Waipu ....... 64 A6
Waipukurau ... 64 D7
Wairakei ..... 64 C7
Wairarapa, L. .. 65 D6
Wairoa ...... 64 C7
Waitaki ~→ ... 65 F4
Waitara ..... 64 C6
Waiuku ..... 64 B6
Wajima ..... 32 A5
Wajir ....... 57 D8
Wakasa-Wan .. 32 B4
Wakatipu, L. .. 65 F3
Wakayama .... 32 B4
Wakefield .... 65 D5
Wakema ..... 41 J10
Wakkanai ..... 32 E12
Wakool ...... 63 C3
Wakool ~→ ... 62 C3
Wakre ....... 39 E4
Wałbrzych ... 16 C3
Walcha ...... 63 B5
Wałcz ....... 16 B3
Wales □ ...... 11 E4
Walgett ..... 63 A4
Walgreen Coast 96 B1
Walhalla ..... 63 C4
Walla Walla .. 80 B4
Wallachia =
  Valahia ..... 22 B5
Wallal ....... 63 A4
Wallaroo .... 62 B2
Wallerawang . 63 B5
Wallis & Futuna,
  Is. ....... 64 L13
Wallowa Mts. . 80 C5
Wallsend ..... 63 B5
Wallumbilla .. 63 A4
Walvisbaai ... 58 C2
Wamba ...... 57 D5
Wamena ..... 39 E5
Wamulan .... 39 E3
Wana ........ 42 C6
Wanaaring ... 63 A3
Wanaka ..... 65 F3
Wanaka L. .... 65 F3
Wanapiri ..... 39 E5

Wanbi ........ 62 B3
Wandoan ..... 63 A4
Wangal ...... 39 F4
Wanganella .. 63 C3
Wanganui .... 64 C6
Wangaratta ... 63 C4
Wangary ..... 62 B2
Wangerooge .. 14 B4
Wangiwangi .. 39 F2
Wanxian ..... 35 C5
Warangal ..... 43 L11
Waratah ..... 62 D4
Waratah B. .... 63 C4
Warburton ... 63 C4
Ward ~→ ..... 65 D6
Ward ~→ ..... 63 A4
Wardha ...... 43 J11
Wardha ~→ ... 43 K11
Warialda ..... 63 A5
Wariap ...... 39 E4
Warkopi ...... 39 E4
Warmbad,
  Namibia .... 58 D3
Warmbad,
  S. Africa .... 59 C5
Warner Mts. .. 80 E3
Warracknabeal 62 C3
Warragul .... 63 C4
Warrego ~→ .. 63 B4
Warren ...... 63 B4
Warrenton ... 58 D4
Warrenville ... 63 A4
Warri ....... 55 G6
Warrina ...... 62 A2
Warrington, U.K. 11 E5
Warrington,
  U.S.A. ..... 74 D4
Warrnambool . 62 C3
Warsa ....... 39 E5
Warsaw =
  Warszawa ... 16 B5
Warszawa ... 16 B5
Warta ~→ .... 16 B2
Warthe =
  Warta ~→ ... 16 B2
Waru ....... 39 E4
Warwick ..... 63 A5
Wasatch Ra. .. 81 E8
Wash, The ... 11 E7
Washim ...... 43 J10
Washington .. 73 E7
Washington □ . 80 B3
Washington, Mt. 73 B10
Wasian ...... 39 E4
Wasior ...... 39 E4
Waskaganish .. 69 C3
Wasserkuppe . 14 C5
Watangpone .. 39 E2
Waterbury ... 73 D9
Waterford ... 11 E3
Waterloo,
  S. Leone .... 55 G2
Waterloo, U.S.A. 77 D8
Waterton-Glacier
  International
  Peace Park .. 81 A6
Watertown ... 73 C8
Waterville ... 73 B11
Watford ..... 11 F6
Watling I. = San
  Salvador ... 86 B5
Watrous ..... 71 C9
Watsa ....... 57 D5
Watson Lake .. 70 B7
Watsonville ... 82 B2
Wattiwarriganna
  Cr. ~→ .... 62 A2
Watuata =
  Batuata .... 39 F2

Watubela,
  Kepulauan .. 39 E4
Watubela Is. =
  Watubela,
  Kepulauan .. 39 E4
Wauchope .... 63 B5
Waukegan ... 72 C2
Waukesha .... 72 C1
Wausau ..... 77 C10
Wauwatosa ... 72 C2
Waverley .... 64 C6
Wâw ........ 53 G4
Wāw al Kabīr .. 52 C2
Waxahachie .. 79 C5
Wayabula Rau . 39 D3
Wayatinah .... 62 D4
Waycross .... 75 D6
Wazirabad .... 42 C9
We ......... 36 C1
Weda ....... 39 D3
Weda, Teluk .. 39 D3
Weddell I. ... 95 G4
Weddell Sea .. 96 A4
Wedderburn .. 62 C3
Wee Waa ..... 63 B4
Weemelah .... 63 A4
Weiden ..... 15 D7
Weifang ..... 35 C6
Weimar ..... 15 C6
Weipa ...... 61 C7
Weir ~→ ..... 63 A4
Wejherowo ... 16 A4
Welbourn Hill . 62 A1
Welkom ..... 59 D5
Wellesley Is. .. 60 D6
Wellington,
  Australia .... 63 B4
Wellington, N.Z. 65 D6
Wellington, I. .. 95 F1
Wellington, L. . 63 C4
Wels ......... 15 D8
Welshpool ... 11 E5
Wemindji .... 69 C3
Wenatchee ... 80 B3
Wenchi ...... 55 G4
Wenchow =
  Wenzhou ... 35 D7
Wendesi ..... 39 E4
Wensu ...... 34 B3
Wentworth ... 62 B3
Wenut ...... 39 E4
Wenzhou .... 35 D7
Werda ...... 58 D4
Werder ..... 49 F4
Weri ....... 39 E4
Werra ~→ .... 14 C5
Werribee .... 63 C3
Werrimull .... 62 B3
Werris Creek . 63 B5
Wersar ...... 39 E4
Weser ~→ .... 14 B5
Wesiri ...... 39 F3
West Bengal □ . 40 F7
West Beskids =
  Západné
  Beskydy .... 16 D4
West Falkland . 95 G4
West Fjord =
  Vestfjorden .. 8 E10
West Ice Shelf . 96 A11
West Nicholson 59 C5
West Palm
  Beach ..... 75 F7
West Pt. ..... 62 C2
West Virginia □ 72 E5
West Wyalong . 63 B4
Westall Pt. .... 62 B1
Westbury .... 62 D4

Westerland ... 14 A5
Western
  Australia □ .. 60 F3
Western Dvina
  =
  Daugava ~→ . 24 B1
Western Ghats 43 N9
Western
  Sahara ■ ... 54 D2
Western
  Samoa ■ ... 65 L13
Westerwald .. 14 C4
Westland Bight 65 E4
Weston ...... 36 C5
Weston-super-
  Mare ....... 11 F5
Westport,
  Ireland ..... 11 E2
Westport, N.Z. . 65 D4
Westray ..... 10 B5
Wetar ....... 39 F3
Wetaskiwin .. 71 C8
Wetzlar ..... 14 C5
Wexford ..... 11 E3
Weyburn .... 71 D9
Weymouth ... 11 F5
Whakatane ... 64 B7
Whale ~→ .... 68 C4
Whale Cove .. 70 B10
Whales, B. of . 96 B16
Whangamomona
  ........... 64 C6
Whangarei ... 64 A6
Whangarei Harb. 64 A6
Wheeling .... 72 D5
White ~→, Ark.,
  U.S.A. ..... 79 C8
White ~→, Ind.,
  U.S.A. ..... 72 E2
White Cliffs .. 62 B3
White I. ..... 64 B7
White Nile = Nîl
  el Abyad ~→ . 53 E5
White Russia =
  Belarus ■ ... 24 C2
White Sea =
  Beloye More . 28 C4
Whitecliffs .... 65 E4
Whitehaven ... 11 D5
Whitehorse ... 70 B6
Whitemark ... 62 D4
Whitfield .... 63 C4
Whitianga ... 64 B6
Whitney, Mt. .. 82 B3
Whittlesea ... 63 C4
Wholdaia L. .. 70 B9
Whyalla ..... 62 B2
Whyjonta .... 62 A3
Wichita ..... 78 A5
Wichita Falls .. 78 C4
Wick ........ 10 B5
Wickham, C. .. 62 C3
Wicklow Mts. . 11 E3
Wieluń ...... 16 C4
Wien ........ 15 D9
Wiener Neustadt 15 E9
Wiesbaden ... 14 C5
Wilcannia .... 62 B3
Wildspitze ... 14 E6
Wilhelm, Mt. . 61 B8
Wilhelm II Coast 96 A11
Wilhelmshaven 14 B5
Wilkes-Barre .. 73 D8
Wilkie ...... 71 C9
Willandra
  Billabong
  Creek ~→ ... 63 B4
Willemstad ... 87 D6

William Creek . 62 A2
Williams Lake . 71 C7
Williamsburg .. 73 F7
Williamsport .. 73 D7
Williamstown . 63 C3
Williston ...... 76 A3
Willowmore ... 58 E4
Willunga ..... 62 C2
Wilmington,
Australia .... 62 B2
Wilmington,
Del., U.S.A. . 73 E8
Wilmington,
N.C., U.S.A. . 75 B9
Wilpena Cr. → 62 B2
Wilson ........ 75 B9
Wilson → .... 62 A3
Wilsons
Promontory . 63 C4
Wimmera → . 62 C3
Winchester ... 11 F6
Wind River
Range ...... 81 D9
Windau =
Ventspils .. 24 B1
Windhoek .... 58 C3
Windsor,
Australia .... 63 B5
Windsor, N.S.,
Canada .... 69 D4
Windsor, Ont.,
Canada ..... 69 D2
Windward Is. .. 87 D7
Wingen ...... 63 B5
Wingham ..... 63 B5
Winisk → .... 69 C2
Winneba ..... 55 G4
Winnipeg ..... 71 D10
Winnipeg, L. .. 71 C10
Winnipegosis L. 71 C9
Winona ...... 77 C9
Winston-Salem 75 A7
Winterthur .... 13 C8
Winton,
Australia .... 61 E7
Winton, N.Z. .. 65 G3
Wirrulla ..... 62 B1
Wisconsin □ .. 77 C10
Wisła → .... 16 A4
Wismar ..... 15 B6
Witbank ..... 59 D5
Wittenberg .. 15 C7
Wittenberge ... 15 B6
Wkra → .... 16 B5
Włocławek .... 16 B4
Włodawa .... 17 C6
Wodonga .... 63 C4
Wokam ....... 39 F4
Wolfsberg .. 15 E8
Wolfsburg ... 15 B6
Wolin ....... 16 B2
Wollaston, Is. . 95 H3
Wollaston Pen. 70 B8
Wollongong .. 63 B5
Wolseley ..... 62 C3
Wolverhampton 11 E5
Wondai ...... 63 A5
Wongalarroo L. 63 B3
Wŏnsan ...... 35 C7
Wonthaggi ... 63 C4
Woocalla .... 62 B2
Woodburn .... 63 A5
Woodenbong .. 63 A5
Woodend .... 63 C3
Woodland .... 80 F3
Woodroffe, Mt. 60 F5
Woods, L. of the 71 D10
Woodstock .... 69 D4

Woodville .... 64 D6
Woolamai, C. .. 63 C4
Woolgoolga ... 63 B5
Woombye .... 63 A5
Woomera ..... 62 B2
Worcester,
S. Africa .... 58 E3
Worcester, U.K. 11 E5
Worcester,
U.S.A. ...... 73 C10
Workington ... 11 D5
Worms ....... 14 D5
Worthing .... 11 F6
Wosi ......... 39 E3
Wou-han =
Wuhan .... 35 C6
Wour ........ 52 D2
Wousi = Wuxi . 35 C7
Wowoni ...... 39 E2
Woy Woy ... 63 B5
Wrangel I. =
Vrangelya,
Ostrov ...... 31 B15
Wrangell ..... 71 C6
Wrangell Mts. . 71 B5
Wrath, C. .... 10 B4
Wrexham .... 11 E5
Wright ....... 38 B3
Wrigley ...... 70 B7
Wrocław ..... 16 C3
Września ..... 16 B3
Wu Jiang → . 35 D5
Wuhan ....... 35 C6
Wuhsi = Wuxi . 35 C7
Wuhu ........ 35 C6
Wukari ....... 55 G6
Wuliaru ...... 39 F4
Wulumuchi =
Ürümqi .... 34 B3
Wum ......... 55 G7
Wuntho ...... 41 F10
Wuppertal ... 14 C4
Würzburg .... 14 D5
Wutongqiao ... 34 D5
Wuwei ....... 34 C5
Wuxi ......... 35 C7
Wuyi Shan ... 35 D6
Wuzhi Shan .. 35 E5
Wuzhong .... 35 C5
Wuzhou ..... 35 D6
Wyandotte .... 72 C4
Wyandra ..... 63 A4
Wyangala Res. 63 B4
Wyara, L. .... 63 A3
Wycheproof .. 62 C3
Wynbring .... 62 B1
Wyndham,
Australia .... 60 D4
Wyndham, N.Z. 65 G3
Wynnum ..... 63 A5
Wynyard ..... 62 D4
Wyoming □ .. 81 D10
Wyong ....... 63 B5

## X

Xai-Xai ....... 59 D6
Xainza ....... 34 C3
Xangongo ... 58 B3
Xankändi .... 25 F6
Xánthi ....... 22 D5
Xapuri ....... 91 F5
Xi Jiang → .. 35 D6
Xiaguan ..... 34 D5
Xiamen ...... 35 D6

Xi'an ......... 35 C5
Xiang Jiang → 35 D6
Xiangfan ..... 35 C6
Xiangtan ..... 35 D6
Xiao Hinggan
Ling ........ 35 B7
Xiapu ........ 35 D6
Xichang ...... 34 D5
Xigazê ....... 34 D3
Xinavane ..... 59 D6
Xing'an ...... 35 D6
Xingren ...... 35 D5
Xingtai ....... 35 C6
Xingu → ..... 92 C3
Xining ....... 34 C5
Xinjiang Uygur
Zizhiqu □ .. 34 B3
Xinjin ........ 35 C7
Xinxiang ..... 35 C6
Xinyang ..... 35 C6
Xinzhu ....... 35 D7
Xique-Xique .. 93 E5
Xisha Qundao =
Hsisha
Chuntao .... 36 A4
Xixabangma
Feng ....... 40 C5
Xizang □ ..... 34 C3
Xuanhua ..... 35 B6
Xuchang ..... 35 C6
Xuzhou ...... 35 C6

## Y

Ya'an ........ 34 D5
Yaapeet ...... 62 C3
Yabelo ....... 53 H6
Yablonovy Ra. =
Yablonovyy
Khrebet .... 30 D9
Yablonovyy
Khrebet ..... 30 D9
Yacuiba ...... 94 A4
Yadgir ....... 43 L10
Yagoua ...... 56 B3
Yahuma ..... 56 D4
Yakima ...... 80 B3
Yakutat ...... 71 C6
Yakutsk ..... 31 C10
Yala ......... 36 C2
Yalinga ...... 56 C4
Yalong Jiang → 34 D5
Yalova ....... 22 D7
Yalta ........ 25 E3
Yalutorovsk .. 29 D7
Yam Ha Melah
= Dead Sea . 47 E3
Yam Kinneret . 46 D3
Yamagata ... 33 G12
Yamaguchi ... 32 B2
Yamal,
Poluostrov .. 28 B8
Yamal Pen. =
Yamal,
Poluostrov .. 28 B8
Yamantau, Gora 29 D6
Yamba, N.S.W.,
Australia ... 63 A5
Yamba,
S. Austral.,
Australia ... 62 B3
Yâmbiô ...... 53 H4
Yambol ...... 22 C6
Yamdena ..... 39 F4
Yamethin ..... 41 G11

Yamma-Yamma,
L. .......... 62 A3
Yamoussoukro 55 G3
Yampil ....... 17 D9
Yampol =
Yampil ..... 17 D9
Yamuna → ... 40 E3
Yamzho Yumco 34 D4
Yana → ..... 31 B11
Yanac ....... 62 C3
Yanbu 'al Baḥr 47 F4
Yancannia .... 62 B3
Yanco Cr. → .. 63 C4
Yandoon ..... 41 J10
Yangambi .... 56 D4
Yangch'ü =
Taiyuan ... 35 C6
Yangchun ... 35 D6
Yangjiang ... 35 D6
Yangon =
Rangoon ... 41 J11
Yangquan ... 35 C6
Yanji ........ 35 B7
Yanna ....... 63 A4
Yanqi ....... 34 B3
Yantabulla ... 63 A4
Yantai ....... 35 C7
Yanykurgan ... 29 E7
Yao ......... 53 F2
Yaoundé .... 56 D2
Yapen ....... 39 E5
Yapen, Selat . 39 E5
Yaqui → .... 84 B2
Yar-Sale ..... 28 C8
Yaraka ...... 61 E7
Yaransk ..... 24 B6
Yardea P.O. .. 62 B2
Yaremcha ... 17 D7
Yarensk ..... 28 C5
Yarí → ...... 90 D4
Yarkand =
Shache ..... 34 C2
Yarkhun → ... 42 A8
Yaroslavl .... 24 B4
Yarram ...... 63 C4
Yarraman ... 63 A5
Yarranvale ... 63 A4
Yarras ...... 63 B5
Yartsevo .... 30 C7
Yaselda ..... 17 B8
Yasinya ..... 17 D7
Yass ........ 63 B4
Yatağan ..... 23 F7
Yathkyed L. ... 70 B10
Yatsushiro ... 32 C2
Yauyos ...... 91 F3
Yavari → .... 90 D4
Yavatmal .... 43 J11
Yavorov ..... 17 D6
Yavoriv =
Yavorov ..... 17 D6
Yawatahama . 32 C3
Yazd ........ 44 D3
Yazd □ ...... 44 C3
Yazdān ...... 45 C5
Yazoo → .... 79 C8
Ye Xian ..... 35 C6
Yebyu ....... 41 K12
Yecla ........ 19 C5
Yedintsy =
Edinița ..... 17 D8
Yeelanna .... 62 B2
Yegros ...... 94 B5
Yei ......... 53 H5
Yekaterinburg . 29 D7
Yekaterinodar =
Krasnodar .. 25 D4
Yelarbon ..... 63 A5

Yelets ........ 24 C4
Yelizavetgrad =
  Kirovohrad .. 25 D3
Yell .......... 10 A6
Yellow Sea ... 35 C7
Yellowhead Pass 71 C8
Yellowknife ... 70 B8
Yellowknife ➔ 70 B8
Yellowstone ➔ 76 B3
Yellowstone
  National Park 81 C8
Yelsk ......... 17 C9
Yemen ■ .... 49 E3
Yenangyaung . 41 G10
Yenbo = Yanbu
  'al Baḥr ..... 47 F4
Yenda ........ 63 B4
Yenice ....... 23 E6
Yenisey ➔ ... 28 B9
Yeniseysk .... 30 D7
Yeniseyskiy
  Zaliv ....... 28 B9
Yenyuka ...... 31 D10
Yeola ........ 43 J9
Yeovil ........ 11 F5
Yerbent ...... 29 F6
Yerevan ...... 25 E5
Yermak ....... 29 D8
Yershov ...... 24 C6
Yerushalayim =
  Jerusalem .. 47 E3
Yessey ....... 30 C8
Yeu, I. d' .... 12 C2
Yevpatoriya ... 25 D3
Yeysk ........ 25 D4
Yezd = Yazd .. 44 D3
Yiannitsa ..... 23 D4
Yibin ......... 35 D5
Yichang ...... 35 C6
Yichun ....... 35 B7
Yilan ......... 35 D7
Yinchuan ..... 35 C5
Yingkou ...... 35 B7
Yingtan ...... 35 D6
Yining ........ 34 B3
Yinmabin ..... 41 F10
Yishan ....... 35 D5
Yíthion ....... 23 F4
Yiyang ........ 35 D6
Yog Pt. ....... 38 B2
Yogyakarta ... 37 F4
Yokadouma ... 56 D2
Yokkaichi .... 32 B5
Yoko ......... 53 G1
Yokohama .... 32 B6
Yokosuka .... 32 B6
Yola ......... 53 G1
Yonago ...... 32 B3
Yongji ........ 35 C6
Yonibana ..... 55 G2
Yonkers ...... 73 D9
Yonne ➔ .... 13 B5
York, U.K. .... 11 E6
York, U.S.A. ... 73 E7
York, C. ...... 61 C7
Yorke Pen. ... 62 B2
Yorkton ...... 71 C9
Yos Sudarso,
  Pulau ...... 39 F5
Yosemite
  National Park 82 B3
Yoshkar Ola ... 24 B6
Youghal ...... 11 F3
Young ........ 63 B4
Younghusband,
  L. ......... 62 B2
Younghusband
  Pen. ....... 62 C2

Youngstown .. 72 D5
Yozgat ....... 46 C3
Ysyk-Köl, Ozero 29 E8
Yu Jiang ➔ .. 35 D6
Yu Shan ...... 35 D7
Yuan Jiang ➔ . 35 D6
Yuanling ..... 35 D6
Yuanyang .... 34 D5
Yuba City .... 80 F3
Yūbari ....... 32 F12
Yucatán □ .... 85 C7
Yucatán, Canal
  de ......... 85 C7
Yucatán,
  Península de 85 D7
Yucatan Str. =
  Yucatán,
  Canal de .... 85 C7
Yuci ......... 35 C6
Yugoslavia ■ . 22 B3
Yukon ➔ .... 71 B3
Yukon
  Territory □ .. 70 B6
Yukti ........ 30 C8
Yuma ........ 82 D5
Yumen ....... 34 C4
Yun Xian ..... 35 C6
Yungas ...... 91 G5
Yunnan □ .... 34 D5
Yunta ........ 62 B2
Yurgao ....... 29 D9
Yuribei ....... 28 B8
Yurimaguas ... 91 E3
Yuryung Kaya . 30 B9
Yushu ........ 34 C4
Yuzhno-
  Sakhalinsk .. 31 E12
Yvetot ........ 12 B4

## Z

Zabid ........ 49 E3
Zābol ........ 45 D5
Zābol □ ...... 45 D6
Zābolī ........ 45 E5
Zabrze ....... 16 C4
Zacapa ....... 85 E7
Zacatecas .... 84 C4
Zacoalco .... 84 C4
Zadar ........ 20 B5
Zadetkyi Kyun . 36 C1
Zafra ........ 18 C2
Żagań ........ 16 C2
Zagazig ...... 52 B5
Zagorsk =
  Sergiyev
  Posad ..... 24 B4
Zagreb ....... 20 B6
Zāgros, Kūhhā-
  ye ......... 44 C2
Zagros Mts. =
  Zāgros,
  Kūhhā-ye ... 44 C2
Zāhedān ..... 45 D5
Zahlah ....... 46 D3
Zaïre ■ ...... 56 E4
Zaïre ➔ ..... 56 F2
Zaječar ...... 22 C4
Zakhodnaya
  Dzvina =
  Daugava ➔ . 24 B1
Zākhū ........ 46 C5
Zákinthos .... 23 F3
Zakopane .... 16 D4
Zalaegerszeg .. 16 E3

Zalău ........ 17 E6
Zaleshchiki =
  Zalishchyky . 17 D7
Zalew Wiślany . 16 A4
Zalingei ...... 53 F3
Zalishchyky ... 17 D7
Zambeze ➔ . 59 B7
Zambezi =
  Zambeze ➔ 59 B7
Zambezi ..... 58 A4
Zambia ■ .... 59 B5
Zamboanga ... 38 C2
Zamora, Mexico 84 D4
Zamora, Spain 18 B3
Zamość ...... 17 C6
Zanaga ...... 56 E2
Zanesville .... 72 E4
Zanjān ....... 46 C7
Zanjān □ ..... 46 C7
Zante =
  Zákinthos ... 23 F3
Zanzibar ..... 57 F7
Zaouiet El-Kala
  = Bordj Omar
  Driss ...... 54 C6
Zaouiet Reggane 54 C5
Zap Suyu =
  Kabīr, Zab
  al ➔ ...... 46 C5
Zapadnaya
  Dvina ...... 28 D4
Zapadnaya
  Dvina ➔ =
  Daugava ➔ . 24 B1
Západné
  Beskydy ... 16 D4
Zaporizhzhya .. 25 D4
Zaporozhye =
  Zaporizhzhya 25 D4
Zara ......... 46 C4
Zaragoza ..... 19 B5
Zarand ....... 44 D4
Zaranj ....... 42 D2
Zaria ........ 55 F6
Zaruma ....... 90 D3
Żary ......... 16 C2
Zarzis ....... 52 B1
Zaskar Mts. .. 42 C10
Zavāreh ...... 44 C3
Zawiercie .... 16 C4
Zāyandeh ➔ . 44 C3
Zaysan ....... 29 E9
Zaysan, Oz. ... 29 E9
Zbarazh ...... 17 D7
Zdolbuniv .... 17 C8
Zduńska Wola . 16 C4
Zeebrugge ... 14 C2
Zeehan ....... 62 D4
Zeerust ...... 59 D5
Zeila ........ 49 E3
Zeitz ........ 15 C7
Zelenograd ... 24 B4
Zémio ........ 57 C5
Zemun ....... 22 B3
Zenica ....... 20 B6
Zepce ........ 20 B7
Zêzere ➔ .... 18 C1
Zgorzelec .... 16 C2
Zhabinka ..... 17 B7
Zhailma ...... 29 D7
Zhambyl ...... 29 E8
Zhangaqazaly . 29 E7
Zhanghua .... 35 D7
Zhangjiakou .. 35 B6
Zhangye ...... 34 C5
Zhangzhou ... 35 D6
Zhanjiang .... 35 D6
Zhanyi ....... 34 D5

Zhaotong ..... 34 D5
Zhashkiv ..... 17 D10
Zhayyq ➔ ... 29 E6
Zhdanov =
  Mariupol ... 25 D4
Zhejiang □ ... 35 D7
Zhengzhou ... 35 C6
Zhenjiang .... 35 C6
Zhenyuan .... 35 D5
Zhezqazghan .. 29 E7
Zhigansk ..... 30 C10
Zhijiang ...... 35 D5
Zhilinda ...... 30 B9
Zhitomir =
  Zhytomyr ... 17 C9
Zhlobin ...... 17 B10
Zhmerinka =
  Zhmerynka .. 17 D9
Zhmerynka ... 17 D9
Zhodino =
  Zhodzina ... 17 A9
Zhodzina ..... 17 A9
Zhongdian .... 34 D4
Zhumadian ... 35 C6
Zhuzhou ..... 35 D6
Zhytomyr ..... 17 C9
Zibo ......... 35 C6
Zielona Góra .. 16 C2
Zigey ........ 53 F2
Zigong ....... 35 D5
Zigui ........ 35 C6
Ziguinchor ... 55 F1
Zile ......... 46 B3
Žilina ........ 16 D4
Zillah ........ 52 C2
Zimbabwe ■ . 59 B5
Zimnicea ..... 22 C5
Zinder ....... 55 F6
Zion National
  Park ....... 83 B6
Zipaquirá .... 90 C4
Ziway, L. .... 53 G6
Zlatograd .... 22 D5
Zlatoust ..... 29 D6
Zlin ......... 16 D3
Żlitan ........ 52 B1
Zmeinogorsk .. 29 D9
Znojmo ...... 16 D3
Zolochev =
  Zolochiv ... 17 D7
Zolochiv ..... 17 D7
Zomba ....... 59 B7
Zongo ....... 56 D3
Zonguldak ... 46 B2
Zorritos ...... 90 D2
Zouar ........ 52 D2
Zouérate ..... 54 D2
Zrenjanin .... 22 B3
Zuetina = Az
  Zuwaytīnah . 52 B3
Zufar ........ 48 D5
Zug ......... 13 C8
Zugspitze .... 14 E6
Zula ......... 53 E6
Zumbo ....... 59 B6
Zungeru ...... 55 G6
Zunyi ........ 35 D5
Zürich ....... 13 C8
Zuwārah ..... 52 B1
Zvishavane ... 59 C6
Zvolen ....... 16 D4
Zwettl ....... 15 D8
Zwickau ..... 15 C7
Zwolle ....... 14 B4
Żyrardów .... 16 B5
Zyryan ....... 29 E9
Zyryanovsk =
  Zyryan ..... 29 E9
Żywiec ....... 16 D4

# THE WORLD

CANADA

Alaska (U.S.A.)

GREENLAND (Den.)

ICELAN

IRELAND

UNITED STATES

NORTH

PORT. S

ATLANTIC

MOROCCO

A

Tropic of Cancer

W. SAHARA

Hawaiian Is. (U.S.A.)

MEXICO

CUBA

OCEAN

MAURITANIA

HAITI/DOM. REP.

JAMAICA

BELIZE

HOND.

CAPE VERDE IS.

SEN.

GUATEMALA

EL SAL. NICARAGUA

COSTA RICA

PANAMA

VENEZUELA

GUY.

SUR.

F. GUIANA

G.B

GUINEA

SI.

IVOR

COAS

LIBERIA

N

COLOMBIA

ECUADOR

Equator

BRAZIL

PERU

FRENCH POLYNESIA

OCEAN

BOLIVIA

SOUTH

Tropic of Capricorn

PARAGUAY

ATLANTI

URUGUAY

CHILE

ARGENTINA

OCEAN

S

A n t a r

PACIFIC

OCEAN